KEY INDICATORS

FOR ASIA AND THE PACIFIC 2025

MEASURING SUSTAINABLE GLOBAL PRODUCTION

56TH EDITION

ASIAN DEVELOPMENT BANK

6 ADB Avenue, Mandaluyong City, 1550 Metro Manila, Philippines
Tel +63 2 8632 4444; Fax +63 2 8636 2444
www.adb.org

ISBN 978-92-9277-403-5 (print); 978-92-9277-404-2 (PDF); 978-92-9277-405-9 (e-book)
ISSN 0116-3000
Publication Stock No. FLS250326-3
DOI: http://dx.doi.org/10.22617/FLS250326-3

Notes:
In this publication, "$" refers to United States dollars.
ADB recognizes "China" as the People's Republic of China; "Hong Kong" as Hong Kong, China; "Korea" as the Republic of Korea; "Republic of Nauru" as Nauru; and "USA" as the United States.
All photos are from ADB unless otherwise indicated.

Cover design by Rowell Kristoffer Sotero.

Contents

Figures

Tables

Figures

Boxes

Figures

Boxes

Regional Trends and Tables

People

Economy and Output

Money, Finance, and Prices

Globalization

Transport and Communication

Foreword

Sustainable development in Asia and the Pacific—whether in food systems, health care, jobs, or energy—cannot be achieved without addressing environmental risks. Intensifying weather disruptions, rising heat stress, and growing pressures on land and water systems demand urgent action. These risks must be tackled not only where they emerge, but also where they are embedded in global production, consumption, and trade.

Effective responses require the right data: we need data that link environmental pressures to the locations of economic production to show us where environmental risks originate, how they move through global supply chains, and where interventions may be most effective. Last year's *Key Indicators for Asia and the Pacific* identified persistent data gaps in assessing these risks and emphasized the need for enhanced analytical frameworks and data sources. This 56th edition addresses these needs by measuring the sustainability of production across global value chains and includes data for new Asian Development Bank regional member Türkiye in the statistical tables.

Key Indicators for Asia and the Pacific 2025 introduces cutting-edge analysis using our environmentally extended multiregional input–output (EE-MRIO) tables—a framework that integrates emissions data with economic accounts across economies and sectors. This approach reveals the environmental cost of economic activity by tracing emissions through domestic and cross-border supply chains, capturing both direct and indirect impacts. This is especially relevant for Asia and the Pacific, which bears significant environmental costs due to the concentration of global production of manufactured goods—a relatively emissions-intensive activity—in the region, even though many of those goods end up being consumed elsewhere in the world. Further, it highlights where economies in the region have decoupled emissions from economic growth—achieving impressive development gains while slowing emissions increases—and identifies high-impact sectors, such as utilities, that require targeted action.

As the Asia and the Pacific region navigates growing uncertainty from shifting trade dynamics and environmental shocks, data that combine economic and environmental information are essential. Such analysis can guide coordinated action, protect the most vulnerable, build resilience, and align growth with long-term sustainability. With more accurate data facilitating deeper cross-border cooperation, the region can advance inclusive human development in a changing environment.

Through close collaboration with our members and international partners, we continue strengthening our collective capacity and rich regional insights to solve these complex challenges together with bold and decisive action. We remain steadfast in fostering these partnerships further, as we continue to fulfill our mandate to improve the lives of the poor and most vulnerable.

Masato Kanda
President
Asian Development Bank

Acknowledgments

Key Indicators for Asia and the Pacific 2025 was prepared by the Data Division (ERDD) within the Economic Research and Development Impact Department (ERDI) at the Asian Development Bank (ADB). The bank wishes to recognize the invaluable contributions of the many individuals and organizations who have made this 56th edition a success.

Publication Team: Elaine S. Tan (supervisor); John Arvin Bernabe, Nomundari Baatar, Nalwino Billones, Joseph Albert Nino Bulan, Madeline Dumaua-Cabauatan, Rose Anne Dumayas, Karen Firshan, Pamela Lapitan, Mahinthan Joseph Mariasingham, Arturo Martinez Jr, Melissa Pascua, Stefan Schipper, Shambhavi Sawhney, and Eric Suan.

Authors and Contributors: Mahinthan Joseph Mariasingham (team leader); John Arvin Bernabe, Nomundari Baatar, Yejee Chung, Loubill Dayne Aceron, Janine de Vera, Arushi Gupta, Dieu Huyen Nguyen, Angelo Jose Lumba, Ina Judith Calabio, Ed Kieran Reyes, Kenneth Reyes, Maria Loraine Satairapan, Mimika Mukherjee, Aparajita Pandharkar, Divya Sangaraju, Maegan Saroca, Shambhavi Sawhney, and Eric Suan.

Feedback and Guidance: Sabah Abdulla, Abdul Abiad, Madhusree Dasgupta, Carla Ferreira, Neil Foster-McGregor, Simon H. Olsen, Jairus Josol, Martino Pelli, Dave Pipon, and Joseph E. Zveglich Jr.

Data Provision and Compilation: ADB Japanese Representative Office, Pacific Liaison and Coordination Office, Philippines Country Office, and Pacific Subregional Office; ADB resident missions and/or support teams in Afghanistan, Armenia, Azerbaijan, Bangladesh, Bhutan, Cambodia, the People's Republic of China, Georgia, India, Indonesia, Kazakhstan, the Kyrgyz Republic, the Lao People's Democratic Republic, Mongolia, Maldives, Myanmar, Nepal, Pakistan, Papua New Guinea, the Philippines, Sri Lanka, Tajikistan, Thailand, Timor-Leste, Turkmenistan, Uzbekistan, and Viet Nam. Note: ADB also greatly appreciates the continuing cooperation of the governments of ADB member economies and other international agencies.

Statistical Tables (also available online via kidb.adb.org): Arturo Martinez (team leader); Mildred Addawe, Raymond Adofina, Maria Concordia Alfonso, Ma. Roselia Babalo, Remedios Baes-Espineda, Nalwino Billones, Joseph Albert Nino Bulan, Criselda De Dios, Dennis Dizon, Madeline Dumaua-Cabauatan, Rose Anne Dumayas, Anna Marie Fernando, Karen Firshan, Oshean Lee Garonita, Aileen Gatson, Aileen Guyos, Christian Leny Hernandez, Kaushal Joshi, Pamela Lapitan, Jayzon Mag-Atas, Mahinthan Joseph Mariasingham, Marymell Martillan, Melissa Pascua, Lea Rotairo, Stefan Schipper, Flora Mae Soco, Eric Suan, and Mar Andriel Umali.

Global Value Chain and Multiregional Input-Output Tables (available online via kidb.adb.org/globalization): Mahinthan Joseph Mariasingham (team leader); John Arvin Bernabe, Arushi Gupta, Dean Joseph Villanueva, Maegan Saroca, Sameeksha Jain, Grant Rene Mesa, Jenny Lou De Las Alas, Christian Marvin Zamora, Maria Loraine Satairapan, Ina Judith Calabio, Aparajita Pandharkar, Loubill Dayne Aceron, Shambhavi Shawney, Julieta Magallanes, Irene Talam, Stephanie Rose Moscoso, Mimika Mukherjee, Madeth Gayosa, Angelo Jose Lumba, Aishwarya Nahata, and Nomundari Baatar.

Database Management and Technology Support: ADB's Information Technology Department in coordination with Stefan Schipper (team leader), Joseph Garcia, Pamela Lapitan, and Le Kim Nguyen.

Design, Production, and Awareness: Paul Dent (editor); Rowell Kristoffer Sotero (graphic design); Mark Ganaban, Joseph Manglicmot, and Rommel Marilla (typesetting); Robert Alcala, Ramoncito Dela Cruz, Robert Hugh Davis, Mira Catherine Gloria, Kristel Marie Gonzales, Luca Lamorte, Terje Langeland, Duncan Mcleod, Patricia Anne Mendoza, Andrew Perrin, Lean Alfred Santos, Kae Sugawara, and Bernard Leigh Woods (production advice and awareness activities). The Logistics Management Unit of ADB's Corporate Services Department oversaw the timely and smooth production of the publication.

Albert Park
Chief Economist and Director General
Economic Research and Development Impact Department
Asian Development Bank

Statistical Partners

The preparation and publication of *Key Indicators for Asia and the Pacific 2025* would not have been possible without the support, assistance, and cooperation of statistical partners in Asian Development Bank member economies[1] throughout the Asia and Pacific region, along with the invaluable contributions of international, private, and nongovernment organizations. These partners—who share their data, knowledge, expertise, and other information—help provide the Asian Development Bank, policymakers, and other data users with a better understanding of the performance of economies across the region, encouraging the design, formulation, and monitoring of better policies to improve the quality of life for people in this part of the world.

REGIONAL MEMBERS

Armenia	Central Bank of Armenia (https://www.cba.am) Ministry of Finance of the Republic of Armenia (https://www.minfin.am) Statistical Committee of the Republic of Armenia (https://www.armstat.am)
Australia	Australian Bureau of Statistics (https://www.abs.gov.au) Department of Climate Change, Energy, the Environment and Water (https://www.dcceew.gov.au) Reserve Bank of Australia (https://www.rba.gov.au)
Azerbaijan	Central Bank of the Republic of Azerbaijan (https://www.cbar.az) Ministry of Finance (https://www.maliyye.gov.az) State Statistical Committee of the Republic of Azerbaijan (https://www.stat.gov.az)
Bangladesh	Bangladesh Bank (https://www.bb.org.bd) Bangladesh Bureau of Statistics (https://www.bbs.gov.bd) Ministry of Finance (https://mof.gov.bd)
Bhutan	Ministry of Finance (https://www.mof.gov.bt) Ministry of Industry, Commerce and Employment (https://www.moice.gov.bt/) National Statistics Bureau (https://www.nsb.gov.bt) Royal Monetary Authority of Bhutan (https://www.rma.org.bt)

1 ADB placed its regular assistance to Afghanistan on hold effective 15 August 2021. Effective 1 February 2021, ADB placed a temporary hold on sovereign project disbursements and new contracts in Myanmar. ADB did not conduct any consultations with either Afghanistan or Myanmar for the data in this publication.

Brunei Darussalam	Brunei Darussalam Central Bank (https://www.bdcb.gov.bn) Department of Economic Planning and Statistics (https://deps.mofe.gov.bn) Ministry of Finance and Economy (https://www.mofe.gov.bn)
Cambodia	Electricity Authority of Cambodia (https://eac.gov.kh) Ministry of Economy and Finance (https://mef.gov.kh) National Bank of Cambodia (https://www.nbc.org.kh) National Institute of Statistics (https://nis.gov.kh)
China, People's Republic of	National Bureau of Statistics of China (https://www.stats.gov.cn) The People's Bank of China (http://www.pbc.gov.cn/english/) State Administration of Foreign Exchange (https://www.safe.gov.cn)
Cook Islands	Cook Islands Statistics Office under Ministry of Finance and Economic Management (https://www.stats.gov.ck)
Fiji	Fiji Bureau of Statistics (https://www.statsfiji.gov.fj) Reserve Bank of Fiji (http://www.rbf.gov.fj)
Georgia	Ministry of Finance of Georgia (https://www.mof.ge) National Bank of Georgia (https://www.nbg.gov.ge) National Statistics Office of Georgia (https://www.geostat.ge)
Hong Kong, China	Census and Statistics Department (https://www.censtatd.gov.hk) Financial Services and the Treasury Bureau (https://www.fstb.gov.hk) The Treasury (https://www.try.gov.hk)
India	National Statistics Office under the Ministry of Statistics and Programme Implementation (https://www.mospi.gov.in) India Budget, Ministry of Finance (https://www.indiabudget.gov.in/) Reserve Bank of India (https://website.rbi.org.in/en/web/rbi)
Indonesia	Bank Indonesia (https://www.bi.go.id) Badan Pusat Statistik-Statistics Indonesia (https://www.bps.go.id) Ministry of Energy and Mineral Resources (https://www.esdm.go.id) Ministry of Finance (https://www.kemenkeu.go.id/home) Pertamina (https://www.pertamina.com)
Japan	Bank of Japan (https://www.boj.or.jp) Economic and Social Research Institute (https://www.esri.cao.go.jp) Japan Customs (https://www.customs.go.jp) Ministry of Economy, Trade and Industry (https://www.meti.go.jp) Ministry of Finance (https://www.mof.go.jp)

	Statistics Bureau of Japan (https://www.e-stat.go.jp) The Institute of Energy Economics, Japan (https://oil-info.ieej.or.jp)
Kazakhstan	Bureau of National Statistics, Agency for Strategic Planning and Reforms of the Republic of Kazakhstan (https://stat.gov.kz) Ministry of Finance of the Republic of Kazakhstan (https://www.gov.kz/memleket/entities/minfin?lang=en) National Bank of Kazakhstan (https://nationalbank.kz)
Kiribati	Kiribati National Statistics Office (https://nso.gov.ki/)
Korea, Republic of	Bank of Korea (https://bok.or.kr) Statistics Korea (https://kostat.go.kr)
Kyrgyz Republic	National Bank of the Kyrgyz Republic (https://www.nbkr.kg) National Statistical Committee of the Kyrgyz Republic (http://www.stat.kg)
Lao People's Democratic Republic	Bank of the Lao PDR (https://www.bol.gov.la) Lao Statistics Bureau (https://www.lsb.gov.la) Ministry of Finance (https://www.mof.gov.la)
Malaysia	Bank Negara Malaysia (https://www.bnm.gov.my) Department of Statistics Malaysia (https://www.dosm.gov.my) Ministry of Finance Malaysia (https://www.mof.gov.my)
Maldives	Maldives Bureau of Statistics (https://statisticsmaldives.gov.mv) Maldives Monetary Authority (https://www.mma.gov.mv) Ministry of Finance and Planning (https://www.finance.gov.mv)
Marshall Islands	Economic Policy, Planning and Statistics Office (https://www.rmieppso.org)
Micronesia, Federated States of	Division of Statistics (https://stats.gov.fm)
Mongolia	The Bank of Mongolia (https://www.mongolbank.mn/en/) The Ministry of Finance Mongolia (https://mof.gov.mn) National Statistics Office of Mongolia (https://en.nso.mn/)
Nauru	Nauru Bureau of Statistics (https://stats.gov.nr)
Nepal	National Statistics Office (https://nsonepal.gov.np) Financial Comptroller General Office, Ministry of Finance (https://www.fcgo.gov.np) Nepal Rastra Bank (https://www.nrb.org.np)

	Water and Energy Commission Secretariat (https://www.wecs.gov.np) Ministry of Energy, Water Resources and Irrigation (https://www.moewri.gov.np) Ministry of Industry, Commerce and Supplies (https://moics.gov.np) Ministry of Industry, Commerce and Supplies, Department of Mines and Geology (https://www.dmgnepal.gov.np)
New Zealand	Ministry of Business, Innovation and Employment (https://www.mbie.govt.nz) Reserve Bank of New Zealand (https://www.rbnz.govt.nz) Stats NZ Tatauranga Aotearoa (https://www.stats.govt.nz)
Niue	Niue Statistics Office (https://niuestatistics.nu/)
Pakistan	Ministry of Finance and Revenue (https://www.finance.gov.pk) Pakistan Bureau of Statistics (https://www.pbs.gov.pk) State Bank of Pakistan (https://www.sbp.org.pk)
Palau	Bureau of Budget and Planning, Ministry of Finance (https://www.palaugov.pw/mof)
Papua New Guinea	Bank of Papua New Guinea (https://www.bankpng.gov.pg) Department of Treasury (http://www.treasury.gov.pg) National Statistical Office (https://www.nso.gov.pg)
Philippines	Bangko Sentral ng Pilipinas (http://www.bsp.gov.ph) Bureau of Local Government Finance (https://blgf.gov.ph) Bureau of the Treasury (http://www.treasury.gov.ph) Department of Budget and Management (http://www.dbm.gov.ph) Department of Energy (https://www.doe.gov.ph) Philippine Statistics Authority (https://psa.gov.ph/)
Samoa	Samoa Bureau of Statistics (https://www.sbs.gov.ws) Central Bank of Samoa (https://www.cbs.gov.ws)
Singapore	Department of Statistics Singapore (https://www.tablebuilder.singstat.gov.sg) Enterprise Singapore (https://www.enterprisesg.gov.sg) Ministry of Finance (https://www.mof.gov.sg) Ministry of Manpower (https://www.mom.gov.sg) Ministry of Trade and Industry (https://www.mti.gov.sg) Monetary Authority of Singapore (https://www.mas.gov.sg)
Solomon Islands	Central Bank of Solomon Islands (https://www.cbsi.com.sb) Solomon Islands National Statistics Office (https://www.statistics.gov.sb)

Sri Lanka	Central Bank of Sri Lanka (https://www.cbsl.gov.lk) Department of Census and Statistics (https://www.statistics.gov.lk)
Taipei,China	Central bank of Taipei,China Directorate-General of Budget, Accounting and Statistics Ministry of Finance Ministry of the Interior
Tajikistan	National Bank of Tajikistan (https://www.nbt.tj) Agency on Statistics under the President of the Republic of Tajikistan (https://www.stat.tj)
Thailand	Bank of Thailand (https://www.bot.or.th) Ministry of Commerce (https://www.moc.go.th) Ministry of Finance (https://www.mof.go.th/) National Economic and Social Development Council (https://www.nesdc.go.th) National Statistical Office (https://www.nso.go.th) Ministry of Energy, Energy Policy and Planning Office (https://www.eppo.go.th)
Timor-Leste	Central Bank of Timor-Leste (https://www.bancocentral.tl) Ministry of Finance (https://www.mof.gov.tl) National Institute of Statistics Timor-Leste (https://inetl-ip.gov.tl/)
Tonga	Ministry of Finance (https://www.finance.gov.to) National Reserve Bank of Tonga (https://www.reservebank.to) Tonga Statistics Department (https://tongastats.gov.to)
Türkiye	Turkish Statistical Institute (https://www.tuik.gov.tr) Central Bank of the Republic of Türkiye (https://www.tcmb.gov.tr) Ministry of Treasury and Finance (https://en.hmb.gov.tr)
Turkmenistan	Central Bank of Turkmenistan (https://www.cbt.tm) Ministry of Finance and Economy of Turkmenistan (https://www.fineconomic.gov.tm) State Committee on Statistics of Turkmenistan (https://www.stat.gov.tm)
Tuvalu	Central Statistics Division (https://tuvalu.prism.spc.int)
Uzbekistan	The Central Bank of the Republic of Uzbekistan (https://www.cbu.uz) National Statistics Committee of the Republic of Uzbekistan (https://www.stat.uz) Ministry of Economy and Finance of the Republic of Uzbekistan (https://www.imv.uz)

Vanuatu	Department of Finance and Treasury (https://doft.gov.vu) Reserve Bank of Vanuatu (https://rbv.gov.vu) Vanuatu Bureau of Statistics (https://vbos.gov.vu)
Viet Nam	National Statistics Office (https://www.nso.gov.vn) Ministry of Finance (https://www.mof.gov.vn) State Bank of Viet Nam (https://www.sbv.gov.vn)

INTERNATIONAL, PRIVATE, AND NONGOVERNMENT ORGANIZATIONS

Association of Southeast Asian Nations
European Environment Agency
Food and Agriculture Organization of the United Nations
International Energy Agency
International Labour Organization
International Monetary Fund
International Telecommunication Union
Interstate Statistical Committee of the Commonwealth of Independent States
Joint United Nations Programme on HIV/AIDS
Organisation for Economic Co-operation and Development
Secretariat of the Pacific Community
Transparency International
United Nations Children's Fund (UNICEF)
United Nations Conference on Trade and Development
United Nations Department of Economic and Social Affairs
United Nations Development Programme
United Nations Economic Commission for Europe
United Nations Economic and Social Commission for Asia and the Pacific
United Nations Educational, Scientific and Cultural Organization (UNESCO) Institute for Statistics
United Nations Environment Programme
United Nations Human Settlements Programme
United Nations Office on Drugs and Crime
United Nations Population Division
United Nations Statistics Division
United Nations World Tourism Organization
WHO/UNICEF Joint Monitoring Programme for Water Supply, Sanitation and Hygiene
World Bank
World Health Organization
World Meteorological Organization
World Trade Organization

Guide for Users

Key Indicators for Asia and the Pacific 2025 begins with a Highlights section that presents key messages from various parts of the publication.

Part I centers on the use of related environmental and economic data to address statistical gaps in the assessment of environmentally sustainable global production. This analysis is necessary since the standard inventory reporting frameworks currently implemented under the United Nations Framework Convention on Climate Change do not reflect complexities such as the sources, locations, and/or intensities of global greenhouse gas (GHG) emissions. The report first focuses on the evolving relationship between economic activities and the environmental impacts of these emissions. It then explores how new statistical paradigms, drawing on more granular datasets, can be used to accurately identify the sources and drivers of emissions. This includes the ability of such datasets to measure emissions intensities and the decoupling trends of individual economies (whereby economic growth "decouples" from rises in emissions). An assessment of emissions production and responsibility along global value chains is integral to this discussion. This is followed by detailed sectoral analyses, with emissions facts, trends, and guidance for six broad sectoral groupings: (i) Agriculture, (ii) Industries, (iii) Utilities, (iv) Transport and Travel, (v) Services, and (vi) Waste. Part I is complemented by charts and graphics based primarily on data, unless highlighted otherwise, from the environmentally extended multiregional input-output tables (EE-MRIOTs) developed by the Asian Development Bank (ADB). The EE-MRIOTs express monetary values in current prices (ADB plans to make EE-MRIOTs in constant prices available in 2026). The report also includes a reference appendix, describing the compilation methodology and sources for the EE-MRIOT data and other relevant mappings.

Part II comprises data tables of selected indicators for the Sustainable Development Goals (SDGs) for which data were available. The indicators are presented according to the United Nations' SDG global indicator framework. In addition, Part II presents specific indicators on social, economic, and environmental developments in member economies of ADB located in Asia and the Pacific. The tables containing these indicators are grouped into eight themes: People; Economy and Output; Money, Finance, and Prices; Globalization; Transport and Communications; Energy and Electricity; Environment; and Government and Governance. The SDGs and regional tables presented in Part II cover 50 national economies across Asia and the Pacific, all of which are members of ADB.

The term "country," used interchangeably with "economy", is not intended to make any judgment as to the legal or other status of any territory or area. The 50 economies have been broadly grouped into developing ADB member economies and developed ADB member economies. The term "developing Asia" refers to the 47 developing member economies of ADB. The developed economies refer to the economies of Australia, Japan, and New Zealand. Based on ADB's geographic operations, the 47 developing ADB member economies are divided into five subregions within the Asia and Pacific region. These subregions are Central and West Asia, East Asia, South Asia, Southeast Asia, and the Pacific. Economies are listed alphabetically within each subregion. The term "regional members", often used interchangeably with "Asia and the Pacific", refers to all 50 ADB members, both developing and developed. Indicators are shown for the most recent year (usually

2024) or period for which data were available and, in most tables, for a starting year or period (usually 2010). Depending on available data, the starting point may be a year nearest to 2010, and the most recent year (usually the year nearest to 2024). There may, however, be some exceptions to these general principles. In the tables, aggregates for regions include economies with available data and are shown if the indicator is available for more than half of the economies and if more than two-thirds of the reference population is represented.

This publication is also available on ADB's website at adb.org/ki-2025, along with individual statistical tables for each of the 50 ADB regional members. The publication's vitally important data and time series are also accessible in digitized format via the Key Indicators Database (kidb.adb.org), which also presents longer data series (usually starting from 2000) for each indicator. Data for the SDG indicators, regional tables, and individual member tables were obtained mainly from two sources: (i) ADB's statistical partners linked to regional member economies, and (ii) international statistics agencies, particularly from the United Nations' SDG Global Database, a master set of data prepared by the Department of Economic and Social Affairs of the United Nations Secretariat. The term "economies' official sources", cited as a source in some tables, refers to data provided by the statistical partners linked to the ADB regional member economies. Online, the Key Indicators Database also contains selected indicators for depicting participation by economies of Asia and the Pacific in global value chains, and the sector-specific comparative advantage of each economy in terms of exports. Typical indicators of international trade, which mainly refer to the value of exports and imports of goods and services, can be traced back to the traditional trading of final goods across borders. For indicator on the people living below international poverty lines, the World Bank has released updated poverty estimates based on the 2021 purchasing power parities (PPP). These updated figures are reflected in the regional tables of this publication, specifically in Regional Table 2.1.6: Poverty and Inequality. However, the SDG tables continue to use poverty estimates based on the 2017 PPP, in alignment with the most recent data available in the official SDG global database at the time of publication.

The data presented for indicators in Part II were derived from either official economy sources, the SDG Global Database, or databases maintained by international agencies that, based on their areas of expertise, prepared one or more of the series of statistical indicators included in the SDG Global Database.

Data produced and disseminated by international agencies are generally based on data produced and disseminated by an individual economy (including data adjusted by the economy to meet international standards). However, it should be noted that national data may be compiled using national standards and practices and, as such, international agencies often adjust the data for international comparability. In such cases, data disseminated by the international agencies may differ from data available from national sources. In other cases, when data for a specific year, or set of years, are not available; or they are available from multiple national sources (surveys, administrative data sources, and other sources); or when there are data quality issues; the relevant international agency may estimate the data. Some indicators are regularly produced for the purpose of global monitoring by the designated agency, and there are no corresponding data at the national level (e.g., population living on less than $2.15 a day at 2017 PPP). In other cases, the differences between data from national and international agencies may be because the most recent and/or revised data available at the national level are not yet available with the relevant international agency. Some data gaps are filled by supplementing or deriving data collected through sample surveys financed and carried out by international agencies. For example, many of the health indicators are estimated using data from the Multiple Indicator Cluster Surveys and Demographic and Health Surveys. Data on money and interest rates, featured in several individual economy tables, are presented based on the International Monetary Fund's 2016 Monetary and Financial Statistics Manual and Compilation Guide, but there are a few economies that continue to present their data using the format applied in Key Indicators for Asia and the Pacific 2020 and prior editions. Key Indicators for Asia and the Pacific now also features additional transport and communications indicators from ADB's Asian Transportation Outlook Database.

ADB exercises due care and caution in collecting data before publication. Nevertheless, data from international sources presented in this publication may differ from those available within individual member economies. Thus, for a detailed description of how the indicators are compiled by the international agencies, readers may refer to the metadata available from databases of the individual international agencies, or to the SDG Global Database website for metadata of SDG indicators. Modeled estimates as presented in the SDG Global Database are also identified. Comparable and standardized national data gathered through a robust data-reporting mechanism of the international agencies serve as the basis for all data in the global monitoring databases.

Data obtained from ADB member economies are comparable to the extent that the ADB members follow standard statistical concepts, definitions, and estimation methods recommended by the United Nations and other applicable international agencies. Nevertheless, member economies invariably develop and use their own concepts, definitions, and estimation methodologies to suit their individual circumstances, and these may not necessarily comply with recommended international standards. Therefore, even though attempts are made to present the data in a comparable and uniform format, the data are subject to variations in the statistical methods used by individual economies, so full comparability may not be possible. These variations are reflected in the footnotes of the statistical tables or noted in the Data Issues and Comparability sections. Information about changes in compilation methodology is also provided in the footnotes. In addition, some indicators are expressed as functions of two or more indicators (e.g., indicators expressed as a proportion of gross domestic product). Hence, a change in the compilation methodology of one component indicator might affect other indicators based upon it. Hence, readers are encouraged to refer to the footnotes before making comparisons between economies and/or over time.

Moreover, the aggregates shown in some tables for the developing ADB member economies and ADB regional members are treated as approximations of the actual total or average, or growth rates, due to missing data from the primary source. For a description of the regional aggregation method, readers may refer to the footnotes presented in the tables and/or the metadata in the Key Indicators Database (kidb.adb.org). Footnotes also provide information for earlier years (earlier than 2000), which are relevant for the longer data series presented in the Key Indicators Database. Aggregates for the World were sourced from international agencies, and readers may refer to the metadata available from databases of the individual international agencies.

Pilot initiatives have been introduced to enhance this year's *Key Indicators for Asia and the Pacific*. One of these initiatives is the inclusion of subnational data on labor force, national accounts, and consumer price indexes for specific economies in the region. The subnational tables are also available in the Key Indicators Database (kidb.adb.org). As Türkiye is the newest regional member of ADB, it is now included in *Key Indicators for Asia and the Pacific*, with data sourced from publicly available government websites integrated into the economy table, regional tables, SDG tables, and application programming interface (API).

The inclusion of Türkiye enhances the comprehensiveness of the dataset and improves the analysis of regional development.

The data published by ADB do not constitute any form of advice or recommendation. For answers to any questions on the data, users of this publication are requested to seek advice from the relevant data source or organization.

Fiscal Year

There are 25 regional members of the Asian Development Bank with fiscal years that do not coincide with the calendar year. Whenever statistical series (for example, national accounts or government finance) are compiled on the basis of a fiscal year, these series are presented in the column for the single-year during which most of the fiscal year occurred. The 25 fiscal year definitions for 2025 are outlined below.

Regional Member	Fiscal Year	Year Caption
Afghanistan (fiscal year since 2021)	21 March 2023 to 20 March 2024	2024
Brunei Darussalam (fiscal year since 2002) Hong Kong, China India Japan New Zealand Singapore	1 April 2024 to 31 March 2025	2024
Fiji	1 August 2023 to 31 July 2024	2024
Australia Bangladesh Bhutan Cook Islands Kiribati Nauru Niue Pakistan Samoa Tonga	1 July 2023 to 30 June 2024	2024
Nepal	16 July 2023 to 15 July 2024	2024
Lao People's Democratic Republic Marshall Islands Micronesia, Federated States of Myanmar Palau Thailand	1 October 2023 to 30 September 2024	2024

Key Symbols

...	data not available
–	magnitude equals zero
(-/+) 0 or 0.0	magnitude is less than half of unit employed
*	provisional/preliminary/estimate/budget figure
|	marks break in series
>	greater than
<	less than
≥	greater than or equal to
≤	less than or equal to
n.a.	not applicable
%	percentage

Units of Measurement

GW	gigawatt
GWh	gigawatt-hour
$GgCO_2e$	gigagrams of carbon dioxide equivalent
$GtCO_2e$	gigatons of carbon dioxide equivalent
kg	kilogram
km	kilometer
km^2	square kilometer
kWh	kilowatt-hour
kt	kiloton
L	liter
m^3	cubic meter
$MtCO_2e$	megatons of carbon dioxide equivalent
t	metric ton
tCO_2e	tons of carbon dioxide equivalent
$\mu g/m^3$	micrograms per cubic meter

Abbreviations

ADB	Asian Development Bank
ADBI	Asian Development Bank Institute
AEA	Air Emission Accounts
AFOLU	Agriculture, Forestry, and Other Land Use
APAC	Asia and the Pacific
BUR	Biennial Update Report
PRC	People's Republic of China
CBE	consumption-based emissions
CO_2	carbon dioxide
COVID-19	Coronavirus Disease 2019
EDGAR	Emission Database for Global Atmospheric Research
EE-MRIOT	Environmentally-Extended Multiregional Input-Output table
ERDD	Data Division
EU	European Union
F-gases	fluorinated gases
FAO	Food and Agriculture Organization of the United Nations
GDP	gross domestic product
GHG	global greenhouse gas
GO	gross output
GVA	gross value-added
GVC	global value chain
HIV	human immunodeficiency virus
HS	Harmonised System
ICT	information and communication technology
IDA	International Development Association
IEA	International Energy Agency
ILO	International Labour Organization
IMF	International Monetary Fund
IOT	input-output table
IPCC	Intergovernmental Panel on Climate Change
IPPU	Industrial Processes and Product Use
ISIC	International Standard Industrial Classification
ITU	International Telecommunication Union
JRC	Joint Research Center
KIDB	Key Indicators Database
LFS	labor force survey
LULUCF	Land Use, Land-Use Change, and Forestry
MOF	Ministry of Finance
MRIOT	multiregional input-output table
NDC	nationally determined contribution
ND-GAIN	Notre Dame Global Application Initiative

NH_4	Methane
NIR	National Inventory Report
N_2O	nitrous oxide
NSO	national statistics office; national statistical office
NSS	national statistical system
ODA	official development assistance
OECD	Organisation for Economic Co-operation and Development
PBE	production-based emissions
PIP	Poverty and Inequality Platform
PLI	price level index
PPP	purchasing power parity
RoW	rest of the world
SDG	Sustainable Development Goal
SEEA	System of Environmental-Economic Accounting
SEEA-CF	SEEA Central Framework
SNA	System of National Accounts
UN	United Nations
UNAIDS	Joint United Nations Programme on HIV/AIDS
UNDESA	United Nations Department of Economic and Social Affairs
UNDP	United Nations Development Programme
UNECE	United Nations Economic Commission for Europe
UNESCAP	United Nations Economic and Social Commission for Asia and the Pacific
UNFCC	UN Framework Convention on Climate Change
UNICEF	United Nations Children's Fund
UNSD	United Nations Statistics Division
UNWTO	United Nations World Tourism Organization
US	United States
WEF	World Economic Forum
WHO	World Health Organization
WMO	World Meteorological Organization
WTO	World Trade Organization

Unless otherwise indicated, "$" refers to United States dollars.

Highlights

Key Indicators for Asia and the Pacific 2025 presents the Asian Development Bank's measurements of sustainability in global value chains, by region and economic sectors. By doing so, the report fosters a better understanding of the complex development challenges in Asia and the Pacific as well as their underlying drivers.

Advancing human development through strengthening sustainability and resilience is central to overcoming today's complex challenges. As temperatures rise across the globe, greater ecological degradation, disasters, and uncertain weather patterns cost lives, damage infrastructure, disrupt food production, aggravate water scarcity, and harm human health. Such losses have enduring impacts that strain public services, reduce economic productivity, and leave communities with fewer resources to recover. Crop failures affect the nutritional and economic security of millions each year. Droughts increase water stress experienced by vulnerable populations as well as hinder the effectiveness of hydropowered technologies. New and emerging climate-related vector-borne diseases further threaten progress made by global health initiatives in a post-pandemic world.

Sustainability and resilience are cross-border issues that require regional cooperation, supported by good data. As greenhouse gas emissions originating in one part of the world contribute to environmental consequences elsewhere, they need to be measured and addressed not only where they take place, but also where they are embedded in global production, consumption, and trade. Reducing emissions also is the key to reducing air pollution which can significantly improve health outcomes, given that Asia has many of the most polluted cities in the world. Achieving these objectives depends on long-term, data-centric strategies. Reliable and consistent data, including the development of targeted indicators, support interregional and intersectoral coordination of policy and monitoring of progress.

This report contributes to cooperative efforts by providing a data framework for measuring the sustainability of global value chains. The report releases new, consistent data on emissions in each sector in each economy. This makes it possible to account for direct and indirect emissions within an economy's production processes as well as for domestic and cross-border production chains, disaggregated at the sectoral level. These new data meet the growing demand within the global statistical community for aligned, comprehensive measures of sustainability in economic activities.

The new framework centers on the Asian Development Bank's environmentally extended multiregional input-output tables (EE-MRIOTs). The data within these tables connect and harmonize economic outputs of an economy with their associated emissions. Emissions data are further disaggregated into direct and indirect categories, depending on sectoral linkages, with the analysis extended across global production chains.

Main Findings

As a net exporter of goods and services, Asia and the Pacific has emissions from consumption that are less than those from production. Complex global value chains mean that production of goods and services, and the emissions generated, traverse many economies. This report compiles consumption-based emissions to attribute emissions to the final consumer, rather than the producer. It shows that Asia and the Pacific has significantly lower consumption-based emissions than production-based emissions. The reverse is true for advanced economies. This trend was consistent from 2017 to 2023.

With increasing global trade, sector-specific indirect emissions embedded in cross-border supply chains are rising. Through the compilation of emissions data throughout production processes and across economies, this report shows that certain sectoral groupings dominate direct and indirect emissions. Utilities and agriculture account for the majority of direct emissions. On the other hand, industries and services receive inputs from upstream sectors and are more reliant on emissions-intensive inputs such as buildings, electricity, logistics, and data infrastructure: these sectors are responsible for up to 77% of embedded indirect emissions.

Although agriculture is a major source of emissions, Asia and the Pacific has the lowest emissions intensity globally in this sectoral grouping. Farmers, fishers, and other agricultural enterprises in the region limited emissions growth to 3.2% from 2017 to 2023, against a 24% rise in output. Driven by technological innovation and efficiency improvements, major food producers, such as Cambodia, Nepal, and Viet Nam, have reduced the carbon emissions of their agriculture sectors.

Asia and the Pacific has a central role in shaping global industrial emissions. From 2017 to 2023, as the world's leading manufacturing base, the Asia and Pacific region was responsible for 58% of global industrial emissions. Nevertheless, in terms of emissions per dollar of production, 60% of the region's economies have been reducing their carbon emissions, with 20% of the economies cutting emissions as production rose.

The region's utilities have the world's highest emissions intensity and play a critical role in the transition to renewable energy. Utilities in Asia and the Pacific accounted for over 40% of sectoral emissions globally in 2023 due to fossil fuel dependence and old power grid infrastructure. This contribution can potentially be reduced by further adoption of renewable energy and infrastructure initiatives such as the Association of Southeast Asian Nations power grid.

PART I
Measuring Sustainable Global Production

SECTION 1

Accounting for the Environment in Global Value Chains

Sustainability and resilience are key to driving human development and addressing complex socioeconomic challenges. From 1970 to 2021, extreme weather events around the world led to 11,778 documented disasters, resulting in over 2 million fatalities and $4.3 trillion in economic losses. The Asia and Pacific region bore the brunt of these impacts, accounting for nearly half (47%) of the global fatalities even though it had less than a third (3,612) of the documented disasters. These disasters cost the region $1.4 trillion in economic losses (WMO 2023).

Such impacts fall disproportionately on poor and vulnerable populations. In 2025, an estimated 808 million people (approximately 10% of the global population) continued to live in extreme poverty on less than $3 per day (World Bank 2025). Over 1.1 billion people lack access to adequate sanitation; nearly 500 million lack safe and reliable drinking water; and many more face persistent inequalities in access to social protection, education, transportation, and essential infrastructure (ADB 2024). Environmental stressors, such as heatwaves, droughts, floods, and cyclones, are likely to deepen these vulnerabilities. Limited resources and adaptive capacity make low-income regions particularly sensitive to these shocks.

Responding to these challenges through the development of green economies could create an additional 1.5 million jobs in Asia and the Pacific by 2050 (ADB 2024), reduce agricultural losses, improve public health outcomes, and prevent nearly 346,000 deaths annually. Without action, however, modelled economic losses could reach up to 16.9% of global gross domestic product (GDP) by 2070 across the region (ADB 2024).

Solving these problems requires integrated and intersectoral data. Transboundary impacts also underscore the need to evaluate and address emissions not only where they are generated, but also where they are embedded across global systems of production, consumption, and trade.

Emissions continue to rise as the international economy expands, but new paradigms are emerging.

Global carbon emissions[1] continue to increase, primarily driven by economies in Asia and the Pacific (Figure 1.1). Since about 2013, this region, home to around 60% of the world's population, has been contributing over half the annual rises in global emissions. In 2024, as the world experienced its hottest year in recorded history, Asia and the Pacific warmed even faster (WMO 2025, Crippa et al. 2024).

Figure 1.1: Global Carbon Emissions by Region, 1970–2023

Asia and the Pacific generates half of all global carbon emissions.

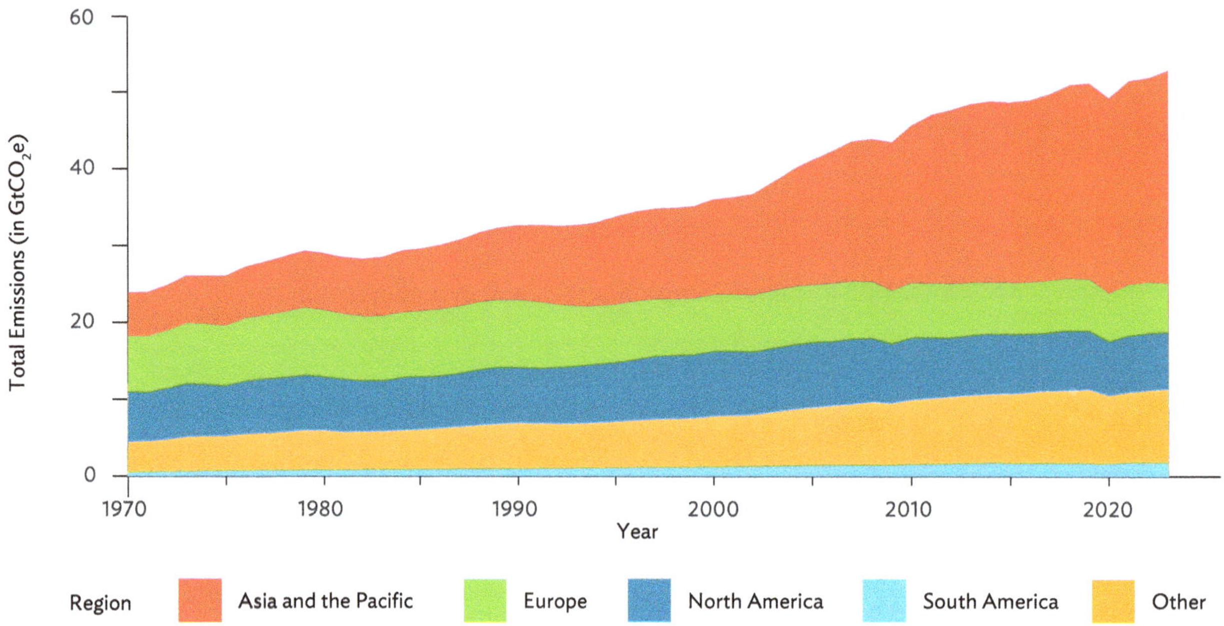

$GtCO_2e$ = gigatons of carbon dioxide equivalent.

Notes: Developed Asia and the Pacific consists of the following economies: Australia; Brunei Darussalam; Hong Kong, China; Japan; the Republic of Korea; New Zealand; Singapore; and Taipei,China.
Developing Asia and the Pacific consists of the following economies: Armenia, Bangladesh, Bhutan, Cambodia, Fiji, Georgia, Indonesia, Kazakhstan, the Kyrgyz Republic, the Lao People's Democratic Republic, Malaysia, Maldives, Mongolia, Nepal, Pakistan, the Philippines, Sri Lanka, Thailand, Türkiye, and Viet Nam.
Europe consists of the following economies: Austria, Belgium, Bulgaria, Croatia, Cyprus, Czech Republic, Denmark, Estonia, Finland, France, Germany, Greece, Hungary, Ireland, Italy, Latvia, Lithuania, Luxembourg, Malta, the Netherlands, Norway, Poland, Portugal, Romania, the Russian Federation, Slovakia, Slovenia, Spain, Sweden, Switzerland, and the United Kingdom.
South America consists of the following economies: Argentina, Brazil, Colombia, and Ecuador.
North America consists of the following economies: Canada, Mexico, and the United States.
Other consists of the following economies: Egypt, Kuwait, Saudi Arabia, the United Arab Emirates, and the Rest of the World.

Source: Asian Development Bank analysis using the European Commission's Emissions Database for Global Atmospheric Research at https://edgar.jrc.ec.europa.eu/ (accessed January 2025).

1 Carbon emissions cover greenhouse gases and, for brevity, will be referred to as "emissions" throughout this report.

Addressing environmental risks can be challenging due to perceived trade-offs between economic growth, which drives emissions, and the need for sustainability and resilience. National governments, global corporations, and international bodies have made considerable efforts to reduce emissions while preserving economic growth. Recent evidence shows that sustained GDP growth need not be coupled with ever-higher emissions. Advances in low-carbon technologies, stricter efficiency standards further enabled by digital solutions, and concerted policies focusing on climate resilient solutions have slowed emissions growth. In many economies, these factors have triggered a decline in absolute emissions even as output continues to grow.

Existing data underscore this trend of a "decoupling" between economic growth and accelerating emissions. In many advanced economies, continued growth in GDP has been accompanied by a decline in emissions. More notably, a growing number of high-emitting emerging economies, such as India and the People's Republic of China (PRC), are beginning to achieve sustainable economic growth alongside decelerating emissions. However, there are still economies in Asia and the Pacific, especially in Southeast Asia and South Asia, where GDP and emissions continue to expand in lockstep (IEA 2024). It should also be noted that the scenarios described here may be driven by factors such as dematerialization in advanced economies or offshoring of emissions-intensive production to developing economies.

Asia and the Pacific's emissions-intensive activities are not wholly benefiting the region's people.

Aggregate figures can obscure important nuances. On a per capita basis, consumption levels in many of Asia and the Pacific's developing economies remain well below those of advanced economies. This points to the fact that the main drivers of emissions are concentrated in export-oriented manufacturing and industrial bases rather than in household consumption. The distinction highlights the need to view emissions from two complementary angles: production-based emissions, which capture the emissions released within an economy's borders, and consumption-based emissions, which reallocate those emissions along value chains to the economies where final demand occurs.

Asia and the Pacific accounted for the largest share (59%) of the world's material footprint in 2022[2], and yet the region is also home to nearly two-thirds of the world's poor and undernourished people (UNESCAP, ADB, and UNDP 2025). This stark contrast suggests that the region's growing environmental burden is not translating into proportionate reductions in poverty and improvements in health and well-being for its people. In many cases, the environmental production costs are borne locally, while much of the value added and consumption benefits are realized elsewhere through

2 "material footprint" refers to the total amount of raw materials extracted to meet final consumption demands as described at https://unstats.un.org/sdgs/report/2019/goal-12/.

global production networks. As a result, the material footprint of economic growth across Asia and the Pacific has yet to deliver the inclusive benefits that can eradicate hunger and reduce poverty, raising questions about the sustainability of current growth patterns.

Granular data systems remain key to informing targeted policies on climate resilience.

The 2025 Asia-Pacific SDG Partnership Report (UNESCAP, ADB, and UNDP 2025) found that none of the Sustainable Development Goals (SDGs) are on track to be achieved in the region by 2030. Particularly concerning is the regression in progress on SDG 13 (Climate Action), which poses direct risks to achieving SDG 1 (No Poverty) and SDG 2 (Zero Hunger) as climate-related shocks increasingly threaten food security.

The *Key Indicators for Asia and the Pacific 2024* report highlighted that economy-specific emissions are rarely reported with the frequency, granularity, or economic linkages required for targeted action. It called for datasets that are comprehensive, geographically disaggregated, and aligned with national statistical systems to support economy-specific and sector-specific policy responses.

This 2025 edition of *Key Indicators for Asia and the Pacific* aims to demonstrate how statistical gaps can be filled by mapping the links between emissions and economic activity at the economy and sectoral levels. Such analyses are made possible using new environmentally extended multiregional input-output tables (EE-MRIOTs) created by the Asian Development Bank (ADB). A key insight from this report is that the decoupling of economic growth and emissions acceleration varies not only across economies but also across sectors. Sector- and source-level data reveal that, while some economic activities in Asia and the Pacific are reducing emissions per unit of output, others (particularly in energy-intensive sectors such as electricity and heat production) remain harder to decarbonize. These findings allow policymakers to tailor emissions reduction strategies to the realities of each sector, balancing economic growth with environmental goals.

The remainder of this section of the report highlights the need for, and the methodology behind, the EE-MRIOT framework, which links emissions data with production, trade, and consumption statistics across 72 economies and "the rest of the world". Section 2 describes the analytical application of the EE-MRIOT framework, focusing on key indicators across geographic regions and measuring emissions intensity, decoupling trends, and the distribution of direct and indirect emissions embedded in trade and global value chains. Section 3 provides a sectoral lens, illustrating how environmental strategies must be tailored to the unique characteristics of various forms of economic activity. The final section summarizes key findings and offers considerations for policymakers, emphasizing the importance of data-driven, economy-specific, and sector-sensitive approaches to climate resilience.

Data gaps inhibit the progress of time-sensitive environmental initiatives.

Improving data on emissions is essential for achieving the objectives of local and global environmental initiatives. Emissions datasets still face challenges related to granularity, integration with other variables, and fragmentation of reporting practices. Surveys of national statistics offices conducted by ADB (2024) and the Network for Greening the Financial System (2022) highlighted a significant lack of granularity in emissions data. Additionally, the inconsistent and delayed reporting of emissions across many economies leads to a lack of comprehensive global emissions accounting. This incompleteness can lead to inaccurate environmental policies, hinder global progress on emissions reduction, and erode international accountability.

At the economy level, studies have shown that policies built on robust data are more likely to achieve significant reductions in emissions, whereas those relying on incomplete or inaccurate data often fall short of their targets (Stechemesser et al. 2024). At the industry level, limited visibility into how value chains are exposed to climate-related risks (both physical risks and transition risks such as exposure to higher costs from carbon pricing), has left many sectors ill-prepared for unexpected ripple effects across their supply chains[3]. At the enterprise level, historical cases—such as the overallocation of allowances in early emission trading systems along with challenges in estimating the carbon content of imports for carbon border adjustments—highlight how insufficient data can skew market mechanisms and distort regulatory design (Ellerman and Joskow 2008; Bashmakov et al. 2022). Addressing these gaps presents a unique opportunity for data systems, particularly the national statistical systems (NSSs), to mobilize local and international cooperation, digital innovation, and private sector participation to effectively integrate statistics into environmental strategies.

Data gaps persist in economies where environment-related measures are urgently needed.

Assessing index scores under the Notre Dame Global Application Initiative (ND-GAIN), more environmentally vulnerable economies (those with lower ND-GAIN Index scores) face significant statistical challenges, including issues with availability, completeness, timeliness, and accessibility of environment-related data (Figure 1.2). Vulnerability to adverse environmental impacts is also negatively correlated with statistical

[3] For example, the disruption of quartz mining during Hurricane Helene in 2024 impacted chipmakers and electronics firms worldwide. Similarly, Hurricane Katrina in 2005 damaged oil and gas infrastructure, raising fuel prices and forcing airlines to impose surcharges that dampened passenger demand (Scott 2025). On the emissions side, the Carbon Disclosure Project (CDP 2021) finds that supply chain emissions are about 11 times higher than direct operational emissions. These emissions can translate to significant cost increases across manufacturing, food, and energy sectors, which are ultimately passed along the value chain to end consumers.

performance, since collecting environment-related information often competes with other priorities in the overburdened NSSs of developing economies (ADB 2024; World Bank 2021).

Figure 1.2: Climate Data Gaps and Challenges in Economies with Higher Environmental Vulnerability (ND-GAIN Index)

More vulnerable economies have poorer environment-related data.

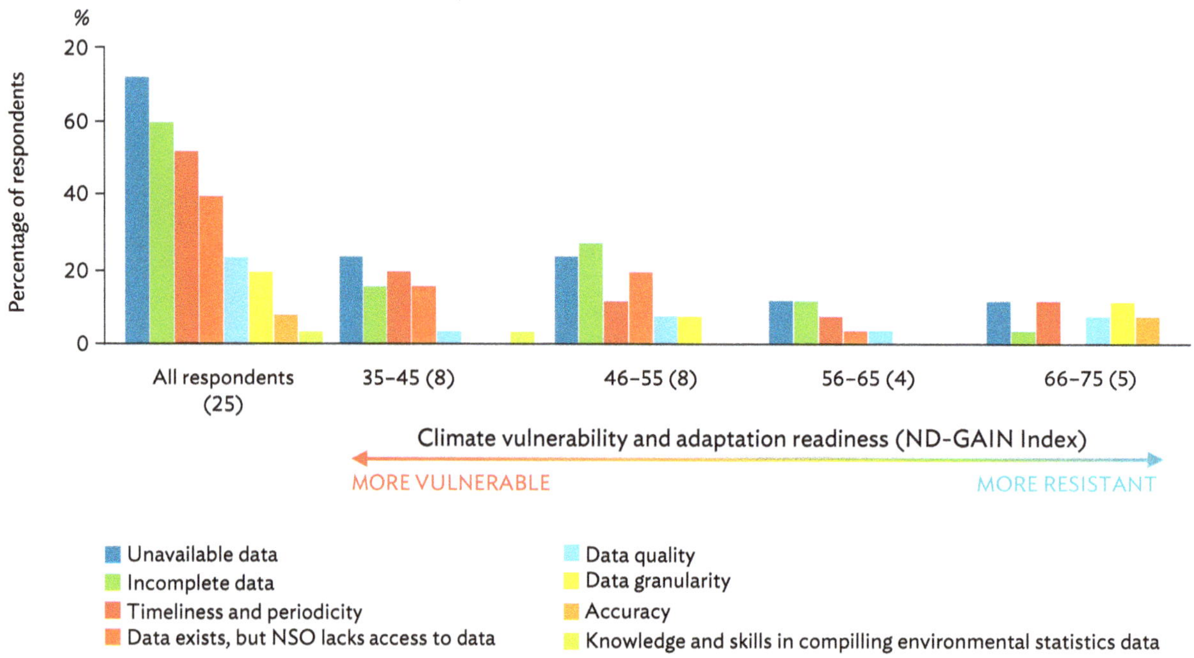

ND-GAIN = Notre Dame Global Application Initiative, NSO = national statistics office.

Sources: Asian Development Bank analysis using the Key Indicators 2024 Climate Change Data Granularity and Statistical Capacity Building Survey and the ND-GAIN economy index (accessed October 2024).

While many economies use improved technologies to measure emissions, several NSSs still lack the capability to collect and report relevant and necessary data (ADB 2024). Instead, national emissions in these economies are measured using guidelines developed in the 1990s.[4] These guidelines estimate emissions by combining activity data with the emissions expected from those activities. For instance, emissions from the cement industry can be estimated by determining the carbon dioxide (CO_2) emissions generated per unit of cement production and the total amount of cement produced. This methodology has, over time, become known as the process of compiling carbon emission inventories.

---

4 Most notable would be the Intergovernmental Panel on Climate Change (IPCC) Guidelines for National Greenhouse Gas Inventories, which were first accepted in 1994, published in 1995, and reaffirmed in 1997 in Kyoto. These guidelines were updated in 2006 and have since been the methodological basis for compiling emissions inventories.

Reporting national carbon emission inventories has become a standard practice under the United Nations Framework Convention on Climate Change (UNFCCC). These inventories—submitted as National Inventory Reports and National Communications, Biennial Reports, and Biennial Update Reports—remain essential for monitoring and reducing emissions in the absence of more advanced statistical analysis. They provide vital data to track progress by identifying major sources of emissions and guiding policy decisions. Beyond fulfilling compliance obligations, these inventories promote transparency, foster international accountability, and enable evidence-based environmental initiatives.

Established inventory protocols often fall short in terms of data reporting and availability.

Compiling emissions inventories can be technically demanding and resource-intensive (Umemiya and White 2023). To account for varying statistical capacities, the UNFCCC allows a flexible reporting schedule for developing economies (Non-Annex 1 parties) but requires annual submissions from industrialized economies and economies-in-transition[5] (Annex 1 parties). Consequently, emerging emitters have some of the most outdated inventories (Pearce 2024).

Despite accounting for about half of global emissions, Asia and the Pacific consistently struggled to produce timely and complete emissions inventory data. From 2014 to 2024, only 51% of ADB's regional member economies submitted at least one Biennial Update Report, and just 24% submitted at least one National Inventory Report. In most years, less than 20% of the world's emissions from the region were covered by available reports (Figure 1.3). While there have been occasional improvements, data availability remains low and uneven, underscoring persistent capacity gaps in emissions reporting.

Independent organizations help deliver timely and comparable emissions data.

A growing number of databases on global emissions inventories, published by independent organizations, are closing reporting gaps. Prominent examples include the Emissions Database for Global Atmospheric Research (Crippa et al. 2024), the Potsdam Real-time Integrated Model for Probabilistic Assessment of Emissions Paths (Gütschow et al. 2021), the Global Carbon Budget (Friedlingstein et al. 2024), and Climate Watch (2024) from the World Resources Institute. These databases offer the advantages of global coverage and better comparability across regions, using consistent methodologies for activity and energy data.

5 These economies include the industrialized economies that were members of the Organisation for Economic Co-operation and Development in 1992, plus regions with economies in transition, including the Russian Federation, the Baltic States, and several Central European and Eastern European states.

Figure 1.3: Share of Global Emissions and Level of Reporting in Asia and the Pacific, 2014–2023

Irregular emissions reporting affects the region's capacity to assess trends and progress in a timely manner.

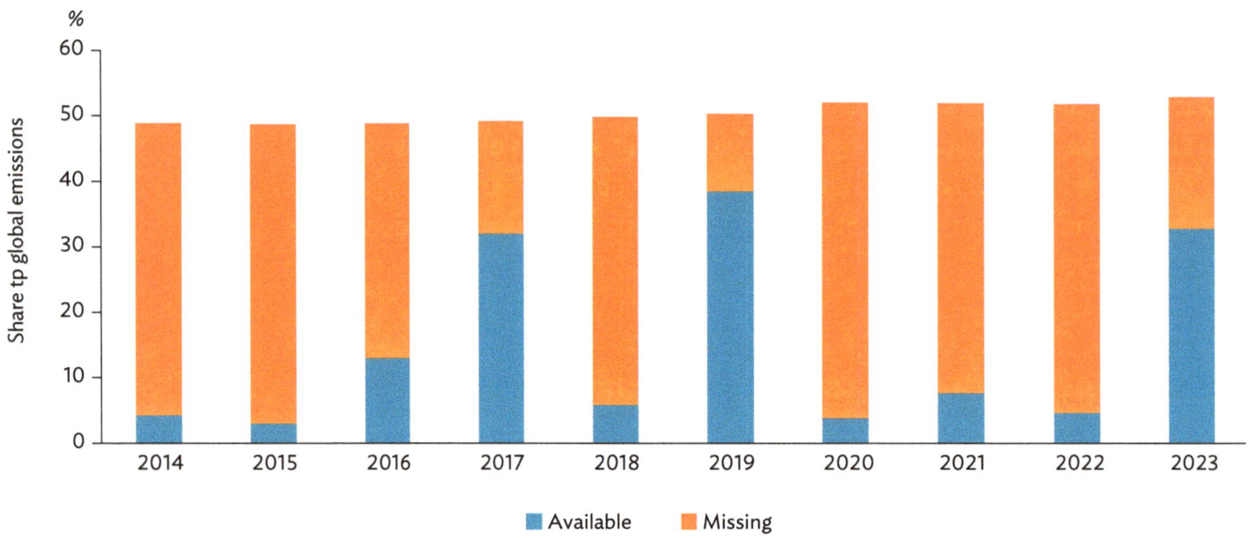

Notes: Reporting levels are based on National Inventory Reports and Biennial Update Reports submitted to the United Nations Framework Convention on Climate Change. Annex 1 parties required to submit annual emissions inventories include the industrialized economies that were members of the Organisation for Economic Co-operation and Development in 1992, plus economies in transition, including the Russian Federation, the Baltic states, and several central and eastern European states, while Non-Annex 1 parties required to submit periodically are mostly developing economies, including most of the Asian Development Bank's developing member economies. Emissions data are from the European Commission's Emissions Database for Global Atmospheric Research, up to 2023 only. Shares of emissions were used as weights.

Sources: Asian Development Bank analysis using data from the United Nations Climate Change Time Series at https://di.unfccc.int/time_series (accessed May 2025) and the European Commission's Emissions Database for Global Atmospheric Research at https://edgar.jrc.ec.europa.eu/ (accessed October 2024).

The Emissions Database for Global Atmospheric Research (EDGAR), a key data source used in this report, covers CO_2, methane, nitrous oxide, and fluorinated gases, expressed in their CO_2-equivalent values, across five broad emissions sectors and 37 major activities, capturing emissions from both market and nonmarket sources. The database's latest release shows that the bulk of emissions still stem from fossil fuel combustion for energy, transportation, and industrial processes and product use (IPPU), while noncombustion sources such as agriculture, forestry, and other land use (AFOLU), biomass burning, waste disposal, and fugitive emissions have become increasingly significant (Figure 1.4). However, although the database provides standardized global coverage of the sources of emissions, it says little about the economic forces that drive them and how those forces can be redirected to achieve meaningful reductions.

Figure 1.4: Carbon Emissions by Type and Source, 2023

Most carbon emissions stem from energy use.

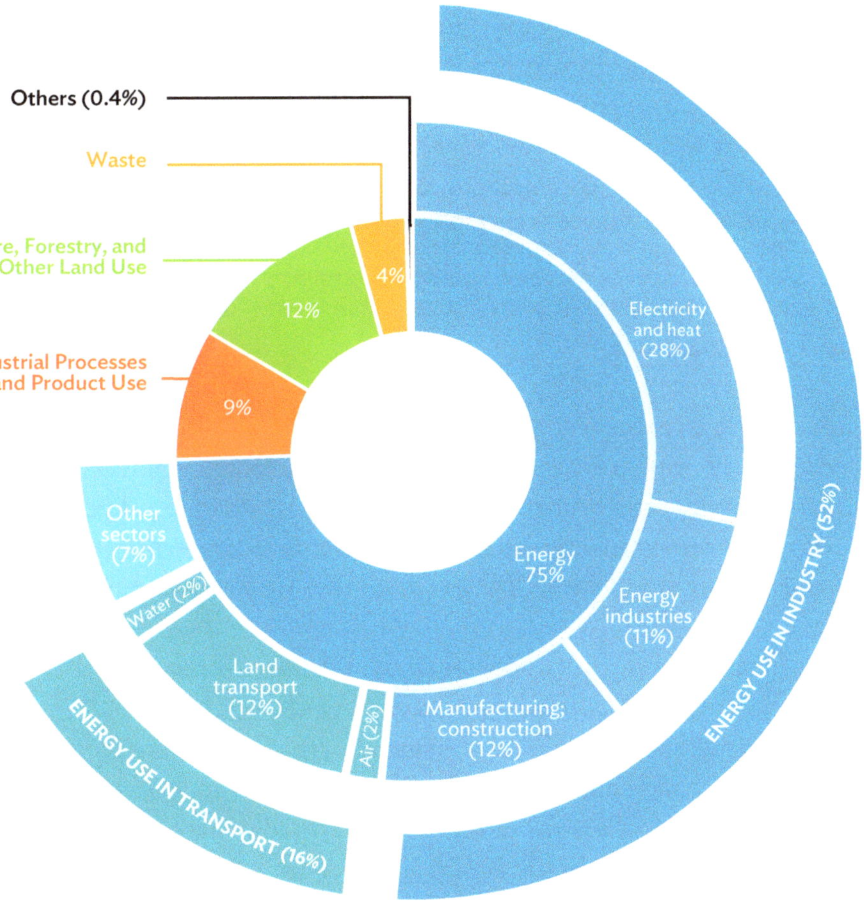

Sources: Asian Development Bank analysis using 2024 data from the European Commission, the Joint Research Centre, the International Energy Agency, and the Emissions Database for Global Atmospheric Research (EDGAR) https://edgar.jrc.ec.europa.eu/ (accessed October 2024).

Emissions inventories can be misaligned with other data used for decision-making.

Even when available, emissions inventories alone are insufficient for fully understanding the drivers of emissions and in designing effective environmental policies. This is primarily because the inventories are often disconnected from, and not coherent with, other key variables, especially the economic activities that generate the emissions. Without explicitly linking emissions to economic data, it becomes difficult to analyze trends at more granular levels, such as specific industries or economic sectors, or the degree to which emissions are changing in relation to economic production (Sakata et al. 2024). Several factors contribute to the incompatibility between environmental and economic data, but one major challenge is the difference in economic territories defined in emissions inventories and economic accounts.

National emissions inventories use a "territorial principle", recording emissions and removals within an economy's territorial borders, including offshore areas under its jurisdiction. This approach is less straightforward for services than for produced goods, as services are often mobile, transacted across borders, and sometimes delivered by digital means. Service activities that are provided from within a given territory can often be accessed by residents and nonresidents alike, but the associated emissions are attributed wholly to the host economy. For example, an international flight departing from an economy's territory, even if operated by a foreign carrier, is recorded in the host economy's emissions inventory under international aviation bunker fuels.[6] Although the jet fuel is burned by a foreign entity, the emissions are attributed to the host economy where the fuel was sold.

By contrast, the system of national accounts (SNA) follows the "residence principle". This principle attributes economic activity to the enterprise's place of residence, regardless of where the production or service activity physically occurs.[7] To continue the airline example, the foreign carrier operating an international flight from another territory records its revenues and profits in its home economy's GDP, not in the economy of departure.

If emissions are recorded using the territorial principle while output is recorded using the residence principle, this creates a misalignment between emissions and the corresponding economic activity. Applying the residence principle to emissions accounting ensures both output and emissions are attributed to the unit undertaking the economic activity, regardless of where these activities occur. Aligning emissions accounting with the residence principle would ensure consistency with concepts such as gross domestic product and better reflect who is responsible for the emissions.

Reporting and analysis should consider emissions along production and consumption chains.

Under the territorial principle, major exporting economies often bear the burden of emissions generated when producing goods intended for consumption in other regions. This may encourage economies to circumvent emissions responsibility by moving polluting activities abroad, while importing the finished goods for consumption. As a result, national emissions inventories may show a decrease in emissions, but global emissions could remain unchanged or even increase (Peters and Hertwich 2008; Zhou 2010). Such unilateral emissions reductions are ineffective if they simply shift emissions to other economies or regions.

---

6 International aviation bunker fuels are recorded separately as "memo item" under the Energy sector and excluded from national totals in inventories.

7 Residents are institutional units with a predominant economic interest within an economy's territory, typically engaging in economic activities within that territory for an extended period (practically defined as 1 year or more). Unlike geographic or administrative boundaries, an economy's territory encompasses its airspace, territorial waters, and any territorial enclaves located abroad (United Nations et al. 2009).

Moreover, with the fragmentation of production evident in modern trade and globalization, it is no longer necessary to relocate entire production processes overseas. Instead, specific stages such as mining, manufacturing, and assembly can be outsourced.[8] As a result, emissions associated with a given product may be generated at multiple points across different economies. This is where alternative perspectives, such as consumption-based emissions, prove particularly useful because they trace a product's emissions from their origin to their final consumption.

National inventories often lack classifications for economic sectors that drive emissions.

Another key challenge is that sector classifications differ between emission inventories and economic accounts. Emissions inventories typically use process-based recording, which tracks emissions based on the physical processes that generate them, rather than the sectors or entities responsible for them. For example, all emissions from vehicles burning fuel on roads are grouped under "road transport," regardless of whether the car is used by a family driving to a grocery store or a company delivering goods.

This approach is effective for understanding the direct sources of emissions and targeting specific processes for improving the environment, such as promoting electric vehicles to reduce emissions from transportation emissions. However, it does not differentiate between economic sectors, limiting its usefulness for policies aimed at identifying which sectors are responsible for emissions or analyzing emissions across supply chains.[9]

Environmental-economic accounting both complements and enhances emissions inventories.

Environmental-economic accounting serves as a valuable complement to traditional emissions inventories by bridging inconsistencies in geographic boundaries and sector classifications. Specifically, the System of Environmental-Economic Accounting (SEEA), adopted in 2012 by the United Nations Statistical Commission, provides a coherent and internationally recognized framework for integrating environmental and economic data. The framework is a response to the long-standing challenge that environmental statistics are often compiled using fragmented or ad hoc methods, unlike the structured systems used in macroeconomic statistics. The SEEA fully aligns with the principles of the SNA and this relationship is further reinforced in the 2025 update to the SNA. The revised SNA 2025 places greater emphasis on sustainability and

8 For example, a technology firm such as Apple, generates less than 1% of its CO_2 emissions directly within the United States. However, approximately 59% of its emissions stem from product manufacturing predominantly carried out in Asian economies such as the People's Republic of China, India, and Viet Nam (Apple 2024).

9 For more information, see Appendix 1.

provides clearer guidance on incorporating environmental data, such as emissions, into economic accounting frameworks. This, in part, reflects the growing demand within the global statistical community for aligned, comprehensive measures of sustainability in economic activities.

The SEEA Central Framework provides guidelines for compiling **Air Emission Accounts** (AEAs) to link emissions inventories with macroeconomic data from national accounts. A key compilation guideline is the application of residence adjustments to help reconcile the inconsistencies between inventory and national account boundaries. These adjustments reallocate emissions to the resident economy of the producing entity, rather than to the location where the emissions physically occur. The process effectively converts territory-based emissions into **production-based emissions**, ensuring closer alignment with the SNA.

For instance, under a production-based approach, international transport emissions, such as those from maritime activities, are allocated based on the residence of the vessel operators instead of being explicitly excluded in the territorial inventories. This alignment ensures that the output of maritime transport in national accounts is comparable with their respective emissions. Furthermore, the SEEA and AEAs address the issue of sector classifications by estimating or allocating emissions to sectors based on the International Standard Industrial Classification (ISIC). This approach enables AEAs to identify the contributions of specific sectors to total emissions relative to economic indicators such as value-added and employment.

By providing an integrated accounting structure, the SEEA enables emissions data to be coherently linked with economic data on production, income, and expenditure. As emphasized in the 2025 update to the SNA, this integration provides a strong foundation for developing coherent and policy-relevant information that reflects both the economic and environmental dimensions of well-being and sustainability.

Extended environmental-economic accounts reveal hidden emissions across value chains.

Despite their relevance and advantages, AEAs provide only a partial explanation of a sector's overall environmental impacts. By definition, production-based emissions in AEAs refer exclusively to emissions directly generated by a sector. For example, a bread maker may produce relatively low direct emissions during the baking process. However, substantial emissions may arise from earlier processes such as wheat cultivation, milling, transportation of inputs, and purchased electricity. These **indirect emissions**, which are not captured in production-based emissions accounting, can constitute a large portion of a sector's environmental footprint.

Emissions can be organized into different "scopes" based on where they occur along the supply chain. **Scope 1 emissions** refer to direct emissions from owned or controlled sources, such as fuel burned in factories and business operations. **Scope 2** covers indirect emissions from purchased energy not used directly in production processes,[10] such as electricity for heating and lighting. **Scope 3** includes all other indirect emissions from upstream activities in the value chain, i.e., the production arrangements in which different stages of production are undertaken in different territories, typically by different firms.[11] These indirect emissions include those from suppliers, raw material production and transportation, finished product transportation, and retail activities (Figure 1.5). Classifying emissions this way aligns data with the global standards of the GHG Protocol, enhancing its relevance to wider initiatives on sustainability reporting, disclosures standards, and investment frameworks.[12]

When combined with Scope 1 emissions, Scope 2 and Scope 3 emissions reveal that strong environmental safeguards at the sector level do not necessarily equate to a low overall environmental footprint for the sector or its products. As illustrated in the baker example, the final production stages typically produce fewer emissions compared to earlier stages of cultivation and processing (Copeland et al. 2021). By quantifying and incorporating Scope 2 and Scope 3 emissions, sectors achieve greater transparency and can better manage potential risks such as rising energy costs, fluctuating carbon prices, and evolving regulatory requirements (NGFS 2024).

10 In this report, Scope 2 emissions only refer to indirect emissions embodied in a sector's own purchases of electricity, steam, heating, or cooling. They do not include indirect emissions embodied in electricity purchased by a sector's suppliers because these are counted under Scope 3. For example, when a farmer uses electricity to run irrigation systems, those embodied emissions are the farmer's Scope 2. However, if the farmer buys fertilizer from a manufacturer, which in turn used electricity in making it, those emissions are the manufacturer's Scope 2, not the farmer's. From the farmer's perspective, emissions embodied in the electricity used to make the fertilizer are Scope 3 emissions, as part of purchased goods and services. This distinction ensures each entity reports only its own electricity use under Scope 2, avoiding double-counting.

11 For an overview of the concept, see Inomata (2017).

12 The GHG Protocol was developed by the GHG Protocol Initiative, a collaboration between the World Resources Institute and the World Business Council for Sustainable Development. It has become the most widely used standard for reporting emissions, adopted by companies globally and supported by organizations such as the International Sustainability Standards Board. While other standards exist, the GHG Protocol is broadly recognized as the global benchmark for emissions reporting (Shirai and Dang 2024).

Figure 1.5: Example of Emissions Accounting by Scope

Indirect emissions contribute to total carbon emissions.

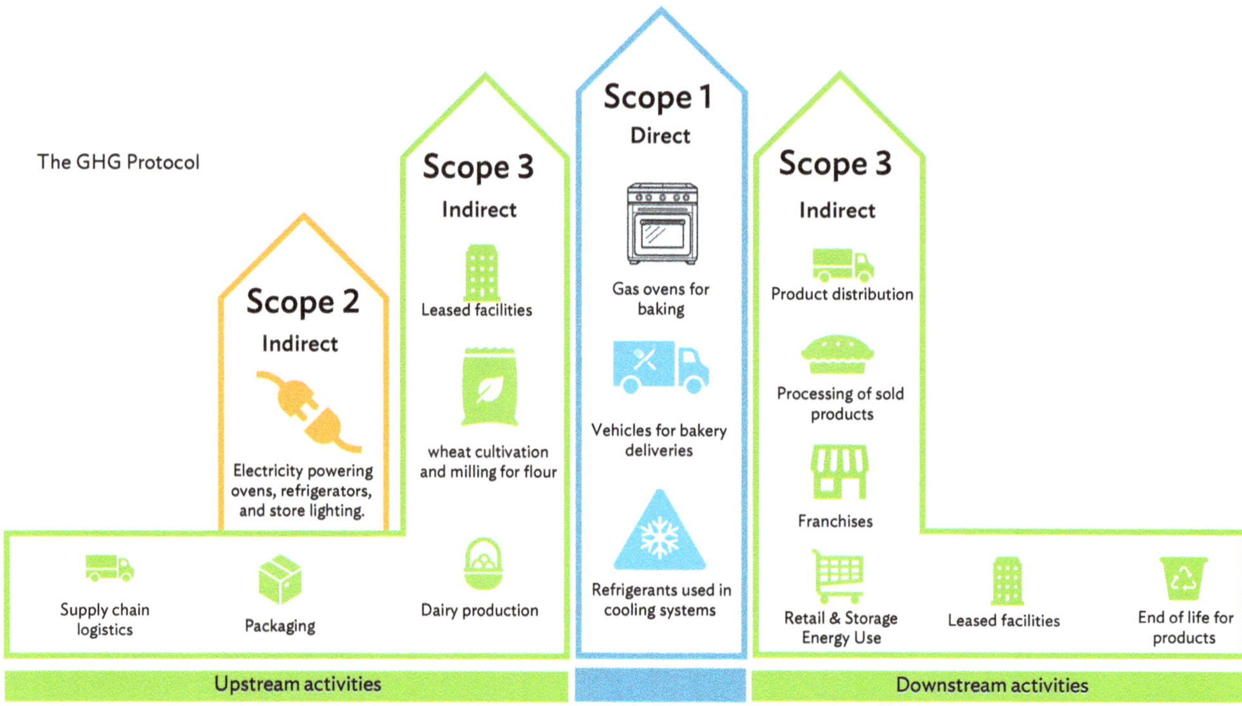

GHG = greenhouse gas.

Source: Asian Development Bank adaptation from the GHG Protocol at https://ghgprotocol.org/.

Accounting for indirect emissions allows sectors to reduce environmental impacts beyond direct operations.

Aside from enhancing transparency, accounting for indirect emissions recognizes that sectors can influence and reduce emissions beyond their immediate operations. Producers can control the full extent of emissions by making procurement decisions in favor of low-carbon providers or engaging with local suppliers to promote environment-friendly practices. For example, by understanding the carbon emissions associated with power purchases, the baker in the example may choose to shift from a high-emitting electricity supplier to renewable energy sources.

Scope 1 and Scope 2 emissions are relatively more straightforward to quantify since producers can directly monitor fuel consumption, electricity expenses, and records of emission-generating operations. By comparison, measuring Scope 3 emissions, which account for the highest proportion of total emissions, is more challenging as this process requires data from numerous parties, including from suppliers and their upstream supply chain partners (CDP 2022). This requirement to tap information from multiple sources highlights the urgent need for measurement frameworks that can trace emissions across the sectoral interdependencies required to meet final demand.

Input-output tables are a powerful tool for carbon emissions accounting.

Tracing the chain of transactions among producers is a key strength of input-output tables (IOTs). Such tables provide detailed information on how much a given sector purchases from others, accumulating emissions data to calculate carbon emissions across the supply chain.

For example, if a baker buys $1,000 worth of wheat flour and the miller generates 5 tons of CO_2 per dollar of flour, the baker is indirectly responsible for emitting 5,000 tons of CO_2 (1,000 x $1 x 5 tons). This example can be extended upstream to also account for the emissions associated with farming the flour. For example, if producing flour worth $1,000 requires $700 worth of wheat, and each dollar of wheat cultivation generates 10 tons of CO_2, the baker's flour purchase is now indirectly linked to a total of 12,000 tons of CO_2, i.e., the 5,000 tons from milling plus 7,000 tons from upstream wheat cultivation.

Using IOTs allows the link between the baker and the farmer (through the miller) to be traced with ease. This illustrates how IOTs can support emissions accounting by tracing the carbon embedded in the flows of goods and services across the economy (Figure 1.6). However, it is important to note that IOTs assume uniform carbon intensity across all firms within a sector. This can lead to overestimates of emissions for more carbon-efficient entities or underestimates of emissions from entities using inefficient technologies.

National input-output tables enhance environmental accounting, but there are limitations.

The ability to capture sectoral interdependencies makes IOTs particularly suitable for national carbon emissions accounting. By breaking down production into a series of transactions, IOTs can systematically trace emissions across the entire supply chains of an economy (Miller and Blair 2022; Mattila 2018). This provides a significant advantage over bottom-up **life-cycle analysis**, which can struggle with determining the boundaries for accounting, such as deciding whether to stop at the point of wheat cultivation or extend further upstream to include seed and fertilizer production. The integration of IOTs into environmental accounting frameworks can then facilitate more accessible and cumulative accounting of a nation's carbon emissions (Alfieri et al. 2024).

Figure 1.6: Stylized Accounting of a Baker's Carbon Emissions with Input-Output Tables

Input-output data traces emissions to every dollar spent by producers.

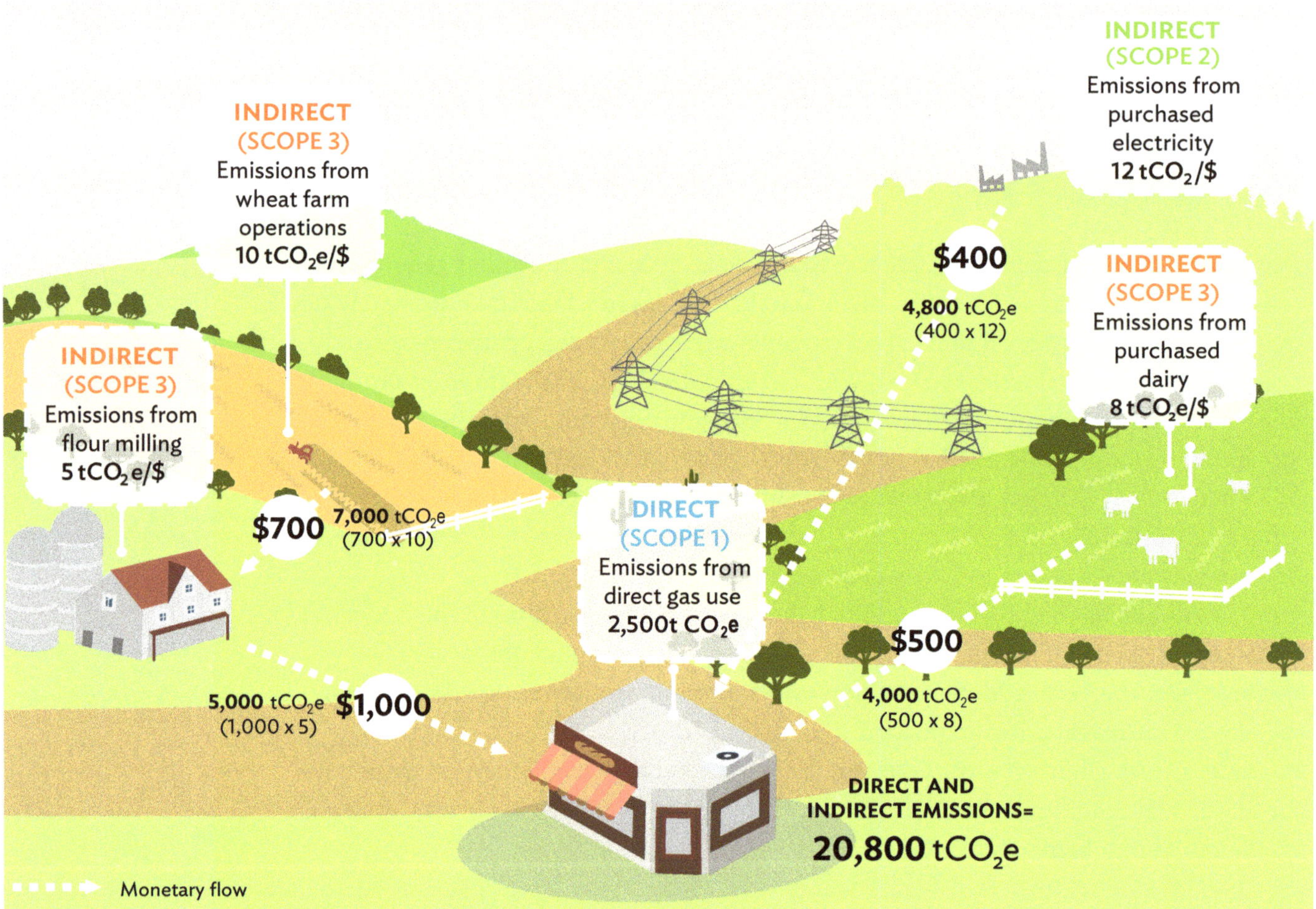

$ = United States dollars, tCO_2e = tons of carbon dioxide equivalent.

Notes: Values are for illustration purposes. Scope 1 refers to emissions directly produced by the sector's own activities. Scope 2 covers indirect emissions from the generation of purchased electricity, steam, heat, or cooling used by the sector. Scope 3 (upstream) includes all other indirect emissions embodied in the inputs used by the sector.

Source: Asian Development Bank compilation and visualization.

Multiregional input-output tables enhance precision with cross-border accounting.

For national carbon emissions accounting, the emissions from inputs can only be sourced from domestic producers. Consequently, the approach relies on the assumption that imports from any foreign producer contain the same emissions as domestically produced goods (UN 2017). Taking up the baking example, if the miller decided to import wheat instead of sourcing it locally, national IOT-based accounting would assume that the emissions per unit of imported wheat would be identical to those of locally grown wheat. While this assumption may be reasonable for simpler products, it becomes problematic for more complex goods. Differences in production processes, technologies, and productivity levels between domestic and foreign suppliers can lead to significant errors in estimating the carbon emissions of inputs (Figure 1.7).

Figure 1.7: Degree of Bias from Domestic Technology Assumption, 2023
(mean absolute percentage error as a percentage of consumption-based emissions)

Percentage errors reveal gaps from assuming domestic production methods for imported goods and services.

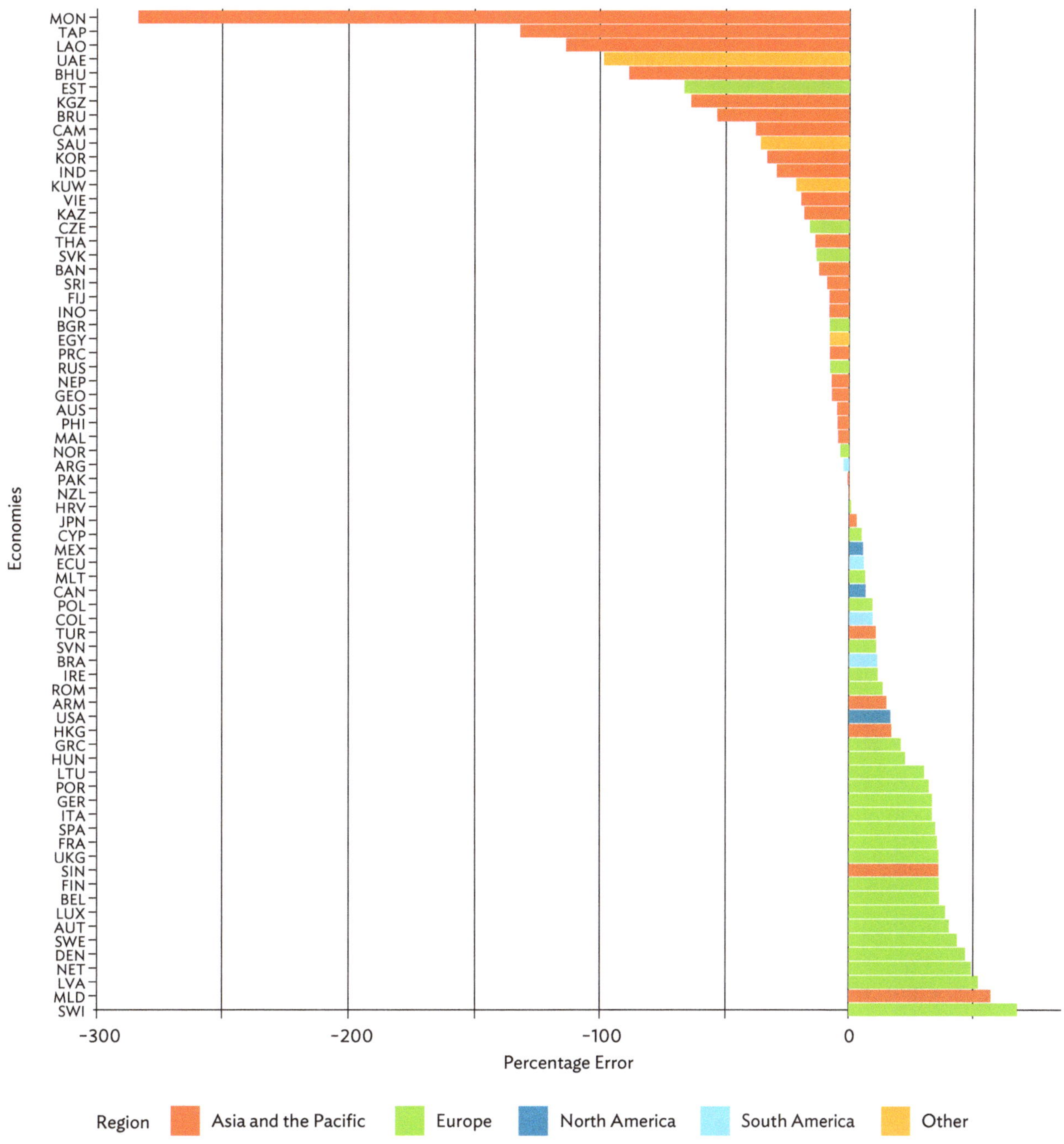

ARM = Armenia; AUS = Australia; AUT = Austria; BAN = Bangladesh; BEL = Belgium; BGR = Bulgaria; BHU = Bhutan; BRA = Brazil; BRU = Brunei Darussalam; CAM = Cambodia; CAN = Canada; PRC = People's Republic of China; COL = Colombia; CYP = Cyprus; CZE = Czech Republic; DEN = Denmark; ECU = Ecuador; EGY = Egypt; EST = Estonia; FIJ = Fiji; FIN = Finland; FRA = France; GEO = Georgia; GER = Germany; GRC = Greece; HKG = Hong Kong, China; HRV = Croatia; HUN = Hungary; IND = India; INO = Indonesia; IRE = Ireland; ITA = Italy; JPN = Japan; KAZ = Kazakhstan; KOR = Republic of Korea; KGZ = Kyrgyz Republic; KUW = Kuwait; LAO = Lao People's Democratic Republic; LTU = Lithuania; LUX = Luxembourg; LVA = Latvia; MAL = Malaysia; MEX = Mexico; MLD = Maldives; MLT = Malta; MON = Mongolia; NEP = Nepal; NET = Netherlands; NOR = Norway; NZL = New Zealand; PAK = Pakistan; PHI = Philippines; POL = Poland; POR = Portugal; ROM = Romania; RUS = Russian Federation; RoW = Rest of the World; SAU = Saudi Arabia; SIN = Singapore; SPA = Spain; SRI = Sri Lanka; SVK = Slovak Republic; SVN = Slovenia; SWE = Sweden; SWI = Switzerland; TAP = Taipei,China; THA = Thailand; TUR = Türkiye; UAE = United Arab Emirates; UKG = United Kingdom; USA = United States; VIE = Viet Nam.

Source: Asian Development Bank analysis using multiregional input-output tables at https://kidb.adb.org/globalization (accessed January 2025).

Multiregional analysis bolsters accuracy in tracing third-party emissions, but data gaps exist.

In today's globalized economy, two-thirds of goods traded internationally are imported for local production and such importing is especially prevalent in small and open economies. The rise of global value chains further complicates economic and environmental analyses, such that imported inputs from a trade partner may have gone through processing in third-party economies before reaching their destination. Such complexities underscore the importance of environmentally extended multiregional input-output tables (EE-MRIOTs) for accurate carbon emissions accounting. As these tables provide global coverage, they yield more robust estimates of emission intensity for direct exporters compared to exercises using national IOTs, while tracing emissions back to upstream economies within the same value chain.

Several factors influence the uptake of EE-MRIOTs, such as coverage, timeliness, accessibility, and transparency. Integrating individual input-output and emissions data into a standardized global dataset is resource-intensive. While some databases have established comprehensive integration, they often rely on historical benchmark assumptions (Table 1.1). A preferable option is to base estimates on official economic data, which are closer to sources of activity and emissions. However, as compiling agencies differ in capacities, source data tend to differ in levels of granularity, frequency, and quality. As such, institutions that compile EE-MRIOTs adopt a more regional focus, prioritizing higher-quality data, albeit from fewer economies.

As a result, there remains an unmet need to integrate underrepresented economies and regions into global carbon emissions databases. Asia and the Pacific, despite being a significant source of emissions and a major player in global value chains (Mariasingham et al. 2023), is one such region. It is one of the world's largest consumers and producers of energy, fueled by rapid industrialization (Dhakal et al. 2022), making it a critical area for driving the low-carbon transition. The exclusion of the region's emerging economies from global datasets not only creates a knowledge gap but also limits the ability to implement effective environmental solutions.

ADB's latest statistical platform aims to bridge gaps in emissions data for developing Asia and the Pacific.

In December 2024, to meet the increasing demand for granular analysis of global carbon emissions, ADB introduced EE-MRIOTs linking emissions to economic activities by sectors and households. The structure of the extended tables mirrors the classic MRIOTs, but the new dataset incorporates production-based emissions for each economy-sector pairing (Figure 1.8). This extension adjusts for place of residence, while the allocation of physical process-based emissions to individual industries is based on the ISIC categories.

Table 1.1: Databases of Multiregional Input-Output Tables with Air Emissions

ADB's publicly available database provides broader regional coverage and more recent data on emissions.

Database	Accounts	Economies	Sector	Years	Proponents/ Custodians	Freely Availability/ Regular Production	No. of ADB Regional Members Covered
ADB EE-MRIOT	**Greenhouse gases from five key IPCC categories**	**72, plus Rest of the World**	**35**	**2017-2023***	**ADB (forthcoming)**	**Yes/Yes**	**29**
GHG Footprint	Greenhouse gases	76 economies and regions and Rest of the World	45	1995-2020	Yamano et al. (OECD)	Yes/Yes	19
OECD-TECO$_2$	CO_2 from fuel combustion	65 economies	36	2005-2015	Yamano et al. (OECD)	Yes/Yes	19
GTAP-MRIOT	Greenhouse gas, material flows	140 economies	57	1995-2011	Chepeliev et al. (Purdue University)	No/No	26
FIGARO	Air Emission Accounts (greenhouse gases and air pollutants)	32 economies	64	2010-2022	Rueda-Cantuche et al. (Eurostat)	Yes/Yes	0
EXIOBASE 3	Energy, greenhouse gas, air pollution, land, water, materials, waste, labor	44 economies, plus 5 world regions	163	1995-2022	Stadler et al. (European Commission)	Yes/Yes	7
WIOD-EA	Energy, greenhouse gas, materials, land, water	43 economies, plus Rest of the World	56	2000-2016	Genty et al. (Groningen Growth Center)	Yes/No	7
Eora Global Supply Chain Database	Energy, greenhouse gas, local air pollution, land, water	190 economies	26	1990-2022	Lenzen et al. (University of Sydney)	No/Yes	38
GLORIA	Material, land, water, energy, air emissions	164 economies	97	1990-2021	Lenzen et al.	No/Yes	33

ADB = Asian Development Bank; CO_2 = carbon dioxide; EE-MRIOT = environmentally extended multiregional input-output table; FIGARO = Full International and Global Accounts for Research in Input-Output Analysis; GHG = greenhouse gas; GLORIA = Global Resource Input-Output Assessment; GTAP-MRIO = Global Trade Analysis Project Multiregional Input-Output; IPCC = Intergovernmental Panel on Climate Change; OECD = Organisation for Economic Co-operation and Development; TECO$_2$ = Trade in Embodied Carbon Dioxide; WIOD-EA = World Input-Output Database Environmental Accounts.

Source: Asian Development Bank analysis.

The adjustments and compilation strategy of the EE-MRIOTs in the Key Indicators Database (kidb.adb.org/globalization) rely on detailed emissions and activity data. The primary source for emissions data is the Emissions Database for Global Atmospheric Research (EDGAR), due to its comprehensive coverage and fit-for-purpose quality as outlined in Crippa et al. (2024). Activity data are drawn primarily from the International Energy Agency's (IEA) extended world energy balances, while fuel consumption is used for residence adjustments and sectoral emissions allocations by ISIC. Additionally, the tables assign emissions to specific sectors, providing two perspectives simultaneously: (i) identifying the types of gases emitted by individual sectors, and (ii) specifying the value chains driving those emissions.

Figure 1.8: Stylized Example of an ADB Environmentally Extended Multiregional Input-Output Table

ADB's EE-MRIOTs link emissions with economic activity across regions and sectors.

Core accounts

Economy (G = 72+1)	Industries (N = 35)	Intermediate demand ($\mathbf{Z}$)			Final demand ($\mathbf{Y}$)			Output ($\mathbf{x}$)
		A	B	RoW	A	B	RoW	
A	1...N	$\mathbf{Z}^{AA}$	$\mathbf{Z}^{AB}$	$\mathbf{Z}^{AR}$	$\mathbf{F}^{AA}$	$\mathbf{F}^{AB}$	$\mathbf{F}^{AR}$	$\mathbf{x}^{A}$
B	1...N	$\mathbf{Z}^{BA}$	$\mathbf{Z}^{BB}$	$\mathbf{Z}^{BR}$	$\mathbf{F}^{BA}$	$\mathbf{F}^{BB}$	$\mathbf{F}^{BR}$	$\mathbf{x}^{B}$
RoW	1...N	$\mathbf{Z}^{RA}$	$\mathbf{Z}^{RB}$	$\mathbf{Z}^{RR}$	$\mathbf{F}^{RA}$	$\mathbf{F}^{RB}$	$\mathbf{F}^{RR}$	$\mathbf{x}^{R}$
Value-added ($\mathbf{v}'$)		$(\mathbf{v}^{A})'$	$(\mathbf{v}^{B})'$	$(\mathbf{v}^{R})'$				
Output ($\mathbf{x}'$)		$(\mathbf{x}^{A})'$	$(\mathbf{x}^{B})'$	$(\mathbf{x}^{R})'$				

Satellite accounts

GHG Emissions ($\mathbf{e}'$)	$(\mathbf{e}_{U}^{A})'$	$(\mathbf{e}_{U}^{B})'$	$(\mathbf{e}_{U}^{R})'$	$(\mathbf{e}_{HH}^{A})'$	$(\mathbf{e}_{HH}^{B})'$	$(\mathbf{e}_{HH}^{R})'$

ADB = Asian Development Bank, EE-MRIOT = environmentally extended multiregional input-output table, GHG = greenhouse gas, RoW = rest of the world.

Source: Asian Development Bank compilation and visualization.

Technical details of the compilation methodology for the EE-MRIOTs, including data sources, are described in Appendix 1.

ADB's new dataset offers the most recent and extensive coverage of emissions in developing Asia and the Pacific.

ADB's EE-MRIOT dataset covers the years 2017 to 2023 and analyzes 35 economic sectors across 72 economies and "the rest of the world". It includes CO_2, methane, nitrous oxide, and fluorinated gases from five broad emissions source categories: (i) agriculture, forestry, and land use; (ii) industrial processes and product use; (iii) energy; (iv) waste; and (v) other sectors.

ADB aims to broaden the coverage of the dataset by incorporating more of the Bank's regional members, with near-term plans to integrate economies of Central and West Asia and the Pacific. The dataset will be annually updated to better capture recent trends in emissions, trade patterns, and technological development in the global economy.

Ultimately, the ADB EE-MRIOTs will enhance both economic and environmental policymaking by integrating emissions inventories with mainstream productivity variables and by facilitating carbon emissions accounting throughout global value chains (Figure 1.9). These tables represent a powerful tool for gaining enhanced insights into the economies of developing Asia.

Figure 1.9: Accounting Principles and Advantages of Using Environmentally Extended Multiregional Input-Output Tables

Harmonized environmental and economic accounting captures direct and indirect emissions across production and use.

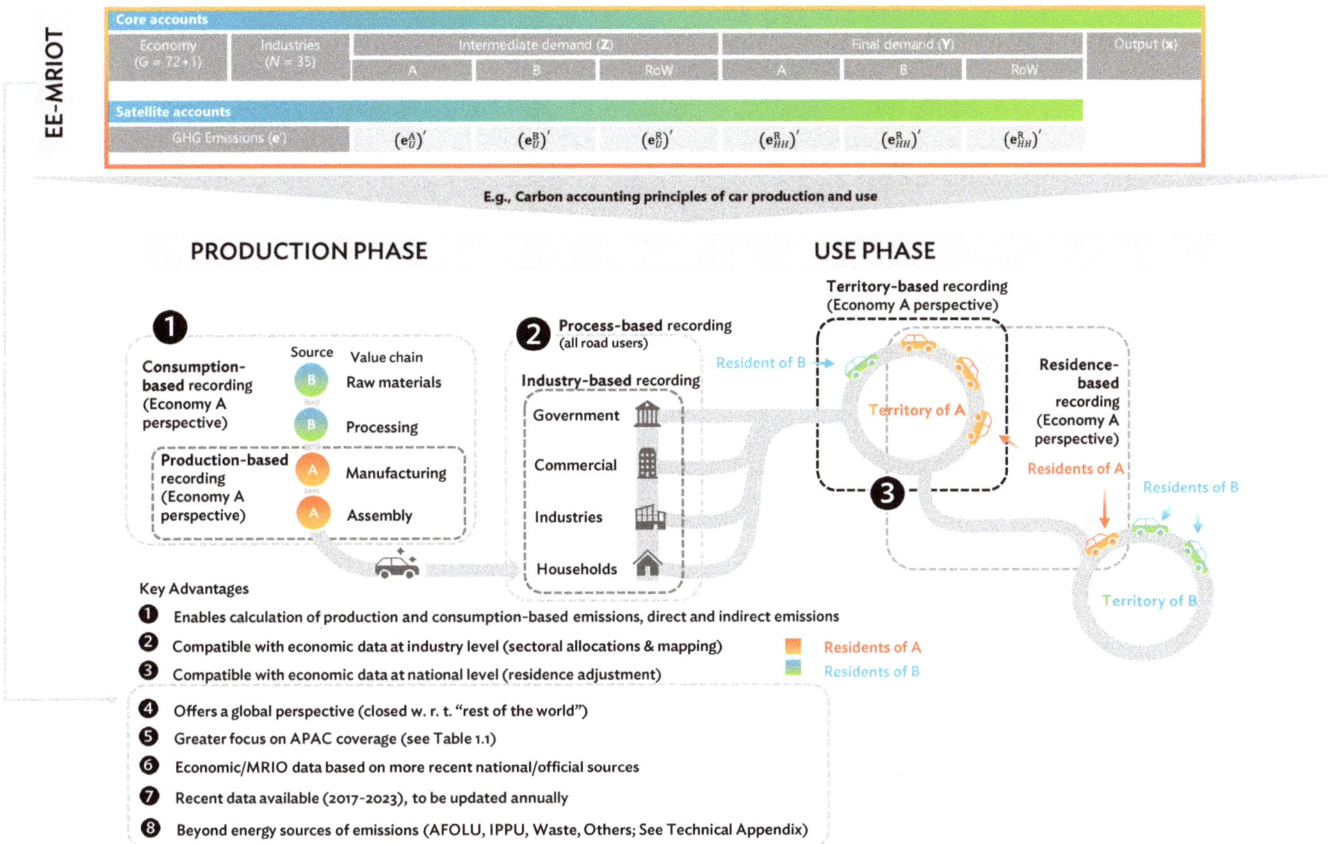

APAC = Asia and the Pacific; AFOLU = agriculture, forestry, and land use; EE-MRIOT = environmentally extended multiregional input-output table; GHG = greenhouse gas; IPPU = industrial processes and product use; RoW = rest of the world.

Source: Asian Development Bank compilation and visualization.

References

Alfieri, A., L. Holloway, U. V. Kalckreuth, S. Moll, C. Schmeider, B. Tissot. 2024. *Empowering Carbon Accounting: From Data to Action.* Irving Fischer Committee on Central Bank Statistics (IFC). Report No. 16. Bank of International Settlements. https://www.bis.org/ifc/publ/ifc_report_16.pdf

Apple, Inc. 2024. *Environmental Progress Report 2024.* https://www.apple.com/environment/pdf/Apple_Environmental_Progress_Report_2024.pdf

Asian Development Bank (ADB). 2024a. *Asia-Pacific Climate Report 2024: Catalyzing Finance and Policy Solutions.* https://dx.doi.org/10.22617/SGP240498-2 https://dx.doi.org/10.22617/SGP240498-2

ADB. 2024b. *Key Indicators for Asia and the Pacific 2024: Data for Climate Action.* http://dx.doi.org/10.22617/FLS240399-3http://dx.doi.org/10.22617/FLS240399-3

Bashmakov, I., L. J. Nilsson, A. Acquaye, C. Bataille, J. M. Cullen, S. de la Rue du Can, M. Fischedick, Y. Geng, K. Tanaka. 2022. Industry. In: P. R. Shukla, J. Skea, R. Slade, A. Al Khourdajie, R. van Diemen, D. McCollum, M. Pathak, et al., eds. *Climate Change 2022: Mitigation of Climate Change.* Contribution of Working Group III to the Sixth Assessment Report of the Intergovernmental Panel on Climate Change. doi: 10.1017/9781009157926.013

Carbon Disclosure Project (CDP). 2021. *Transparency to Transformation: A Chain Reaction.* https://www.cdp.net/en/press-releases/environmental-supply-chain-risks-to-cost-companies-120-billion-by-2026

CDP. 2022. *Technical note: Relevance of Scope 3 Categories by Sector* (Version 3.0). https://cdn.cdp.net/cdp-production/cms/guidance_docs/pdfs/000/003/504/original/CDP-technical-note-scope-3-relevance-by-sector.pdf

Copeland, B. R., J. S. Shapiro, and M. S. Taylor. 2021. Globalization and the Environment. *NBER Working Paper.* No. 28797. National Bureau of Economic Research. http://www.nber.org/papers/w28797

Crippa, M., D. Guizzardi, F. Pagani, M. Banja, M. Muntean, E. Schaaf, F. Monforti-Ferrario, et al. 2024. *GHG Emissions of All World Countries.* Publications Office of the European Union. https://publications.jrc.ec.europa.eu/repository/handle/JRC138862 (accessed October 2024).

Dhakal, S., J. C. Minx, F. L. Toth, A. Abdel-Aziz, M. J. Figueroa Meza, K. Hubacek, I. G. C. Jonckheere, et al. 2022. Emissions Trends and Drivers (Chapter 2). In A. R. Shukla et al., eds. *Climate Change 2022: Mitigation of Climate Change.* Intergovernmental Panel on Climate Change. Cambridge University Press. pp. 215–294. https://doi.org/10.1017/9781009157926.004

Ellerman, A. D. and P. Joskow. 2008. *The European Union's CO_2 Cap-and-Trade System in Perspective.* Pew Center on Global Climate Change Report. http://www.pewclimate.org/eu-ets

Friedlingstein, O., M. O'Sullivan, M. W. Jones, R. M. Andrew, J. Hauck, P. Landschützer, C. Le Quéré, et al. 2025. Global Carbon Budget 2024. *Earth System Science Data* 17 (3): 965–1039. https://doi.org/10.5194/essd-17-965-2025.

Gütschow, J., M. L. Jeffery, A. Günther, and M. Meinshausen. 2021. Country-Resolved Combined Emission and Socio-Economic Pathways Based on the Representative Concentration Pathway (RCP) and Shared Socio-Economic Pathway (SSP) Scenarios. *Earth System Science Data*. 13 (3). pp. 1005–1040. https://doi.org/10.5194/essd-13-1005-2021

Inomata, S. 2017. Analytical Frameworks for Global Value Chains: An Overview. *Global Value Chain Development Report 2017.* Institute of Developing Economies (IDE-JETRO). https://papers.ssrn.com/sol3/papers.cfm?abstract_id=3074988

International Energy Agency (IEA). 2024. *CO_2 Emissions in 2023.* https://www.iea.org/reports/co2-emissions-in-2023

Mariasingham, M. J., A. J. Lumba, and C. R. Jabagat. 2023. *Examining Global Value Chains in Times of International Shocks.* In: Global Value Chain Development Report 2023: Resilient and Sustainable GVCs in Turbulent Times. World Trade Organization; University of International Business and Economics; Asian Development Bank; and JETRO Institute of Developing Economies.

Mattila, T. J. 2013. *Input-Output Analysis of the Networks of Production, Consumption and Environmental Destruction in Finland.* Aalto University. https://aaltodoc.aalto.fi/items/c2573314-8221-4cfb-9403-e13bc0a55547

Miller, E. and P. Blair. 2022. *Input-Output Analysis: Foundations and Extensions.* 3rd ed. Cambridge University Press. https://doi.org/10.1017/9781108676212.

Network for Greening the Financial System (NGFS). *Final Report on Bridging Data Gaps.* https://www.ngfs.net/system/files/import/ngfs/medias/documents/final_report_on_bridging_data_gaps.pdf

NGFS. 2024. *Improving Greenhouse Gas Emissions Data.* https://www.ngfs.net/system/files/import/ngfs/medias/documents/ngfs_information_note_on_improving_ghg_emission_data.pdf

Pearce, F. 2024. *Nations are Undercounting Emissions, Putting UN Goals at Risk.* Yale Environment 360. https://e360.yale.edu/features/undercounted-emissions-un-climate-change

Peters, G. P. and E. G. Hertwich. 2008. CO_2 Embodied in International Trade with Implications for Global Climate Policy. *Environmental Science & Technology.* 42 (5). pp. 1401–1407. https://doi.org/10.1021/es072023k.

Sakata, S., A. A. Aklilu, and R. Pizarro. 2024. Greenhouse Gas Emissions Data: Concepts and Data Availability. *OECD Statistics Working Papers No. 2024/03.* Organisation for Economic Co-operation and Development. https://doi.org/10.1787/b3e6c074-en.

Scott, M. 2025. ESG Watch: Why Extreme Weather Events are Just the Tip of the Iceberg for Companies in a Riskier World. *Reuters.* 17 June. https://www.reuters.com/sustainability/sustainable-finance-reporting/esg-watch-why-extreme-weather-events-are-just-tip-iceberg-companies-riskier-2025-06-16/

Shirai, S. and L. N. Dang. 2024. Promoting Global Greenhouse Gas Accounting to Drive Corporate Climate Actions and Asian Practices. *ADBI Policy Brief No. 2024-10.* Asian Development Bank Institute. https://doi.org/10.56506/DMHO1958.

Stechemesser, A., N. Koch, E. Mark, E. Dilger, P. Klösel, L. Menicacci, D. Nachtigall, et al. 2024. Climate Policies That Achieved Major Emission Reductions: Global Evidence from Two Decades. *Science*. 385 (6711). pp. 884–892. https://doi.org/10.1126/science.adl6547.

Umemiya, C. and M. K. White. 2023. National GHG Inventory Capacity in Developing Countries – a Global Assessment of Progress. *Climate Policy*. 24 (2). pp. 164–76. doi:10.1080/14693062.2023.2167802.

United Nations Economic and Social Commission for Asia and the Pacific (UNESCAP), Asian Development Bank (ADB), and United Nations Development Programme (UNDP). 2025. *Delivering a Just Transition: Advancing Decent Work, Gender Equality, and Social Protection.* United Nations.

United Nations (UN), European Commission (EC), International Monetary Fund (IMF), Organisation for Economic Co-operation and Development (OECD), and World Bank. 2009. *System of National Accounts 2008.* United Nations. https://unstats.un.org/unsd/nationalaccount/sna2008.asp

United Nations (UN), European Commission (EC), Food and Agriculture Organization of the United Nations (FAO), International Monetary Fund (IMF), Organisation for Economic Co-operation and Development (OECD), and World Bank. 2017. *System of Environmental-Economic Accounting 2012: Applications and Extensions.* United Nations. https://seea.un.org/sites/seea.un.org/files/ae_final_en.pdf

World Meteorological Organization (WMO). 2023. *Economic Costs of Weather-Related Disasters Soars, but Early Warnings Save Lives.* https://wmo.int/news/media-centre/economic-costs-of-weather-related-disasters-soars-early-warnings-save-lives

WMO. 2025. *State of the Climate in Asia 2024.* https://library.wmo.int/idurl/4/69575https://library.wmo.int/idurl/4/69575

World Bank. 2021. World Development Report 2021: Data for Better Lives. https://wdr2021.worldbank.org/..https://wdr2021.worldbank.org/.

World Bank. 2025. *June 2025 Update to Global Poverty Lines.* https://www.worldbank.org/en/news/factsheet/2025/06/05/june-2025-update-to-global-poverty-lines

Zhou, X. 2010. Environmentally Extended Multi-Region Input-Output Model: Sharing Responsibility Across the Globe. In: J. Murray and R. Wood, eds. *The Sustainability Practitioner's Guide to Input-Output Analysis.* pp. 165-176. Common Ground Publishing.

SECTION 2

Analytical Perspectives on Reducing Carbon Emissions

Can economies grow without increasing their carbon emissions?

Historically, emissions rose in line with economic activity, as growth relied heavily on burning fossil fuels to generate electricity, sustain transportation, and expand industrial production. This relationship is, however, shifting. Since the first influential studies on the subject in the 1970s,[13] rapid advances in technology, production efficiency, global value chains, and cleaner energy have enabled some economies to produce more output with fewer emissions (Copeland et al. 2021). Yet the decoupling of economic growth from rising emissions is not always linear or permanent. Economies that make progress may revert to higher emissions due to changing industrial patterns or economic pressures (Dhakal et al. 2022). At the same time, some economies perceived to be locked into fossil-fuel-based systems are still progressing, albeit more slowly, toward their environmental objectives. Continuous monitoring of the evolving dynamics between economics and the environment is therefore essential.

New statistical frameworks are providing greater understanding of trends in emissions.

Progress has been made in weakening the link between economic expansion and accelerating emissions. In many economies, the slower pace of emissions has reflected shifts toward clean energy, more efficient technologies, and targeted climate adaptation policies, among other initiatives. These efforts have allowed the generation of more output with fewer emissions per dollar. However, total global emissions continue to rise yearly, largely due to the increasing scale of demand.

Understanding the drivers behind these trends—whether improvements in efficiency, changes in production technologies, or shifts in demand—requires emissions data that are fully aligned with economic output. The framework for environmentally extended multiregional input-output tables (EE-MRIOTs) enables such analyses. It does so by

13 Early influential studies on the relationship between economic growth and environmental impact include works such as Kenneth Boulding's *The Economics of the Coming Spaceship Earth* (1966) and The Club of Rome's *Limits to Growth* (Meadows et al. 1972). Wassily Leontief's *Environmental Repercussions and the Economic Structure* (1970) formalized quantitative links between economic activity and environmental impacts. These works shaped the discourse on environmental resilience and sustainable development and informed early frameworks for analyzing the economic dimensions of environmental issues.

linking emissions with output across sectors and regions, allowing for a more detailed assessment of decoupling. To support this, the framework offers four key analytical advantages, as outlined in this section.

Perspective 1: Decoupling Economic Growth from Rising Emissions

Policymakers can benefit greatly from more granular information on decoupling.

Decoupling is commonly assessed by comparing the growth rates of emissions and economic output. Tapio (2005) introduced a classification system that categorizes decoupling based on the relative growth rates of emissions and output.[14] **Absolute decoupling** occurs when total emissions decline while the economy grows. **Relative decoupling** happens when economic growth outpaces increases in emissions, indicating improved efficiency despite rising total emissions. **No decoupling** occurs when emissions and output increase at the same rate or when emissions grow faster than economic output.

One of the most significant applications of the EE-MRIOT framework in the Key Indicators Database (kidb.adb.org/globalization) is its ability to measure decoupling indicators on both an economy and sector level. By linking emissions data with economic output, the framework evaluates whether economic growth is achieved with reduced environmental impacts. This analysis is essential in understanding whether economies are moving towards absolute or relative decoupling.

While the current EE-MRIOT dataset from the Asian Development Bank (ADB) spans from 2017 to 2023, its annual expansion will allow policymakers to track whether early signals of decoupling are sustained or reversed over time, information that is crucial for setting timely and achievable targets.

There are varying degrees of decoupling observed across economies worldwide.

Decoupling of economic growth from emissions varies widely across economies.[15] From 2017 to 2023, most European economies and six economies in Asia and the Pacific achieved absolute decoupling (Figure 2.1). Over the same period, 19 economies

14 This report follows the method for calculating decoupling indexes in the IPCC Sixth Assessment Report Working Group II Chapter 2 (Dhakal et al. 2022). This is derived using equation $DI = \left(\frac{G1 - G0}{G0} - \frac{E1 - E0}{E0}\right) / \left(\frac{G1 - G0}{G0}\right)$, where DI refers to decoupling index; G1 refers to the GDP of reporting year while G0 refers to the base year; E1 refers to the emissions of the reporting year while E0 refers to emissions of the base year.

15 The results vary marginally based on whether current or constant prices were used. For the rationale and decision to use current prices in the report, see Box 2.1.

Figure 2.1: Decoupling of Emissions and Economic Growth by Economy, 2017–2023

Many economies produced more while emitting less from 2017 to 2023.

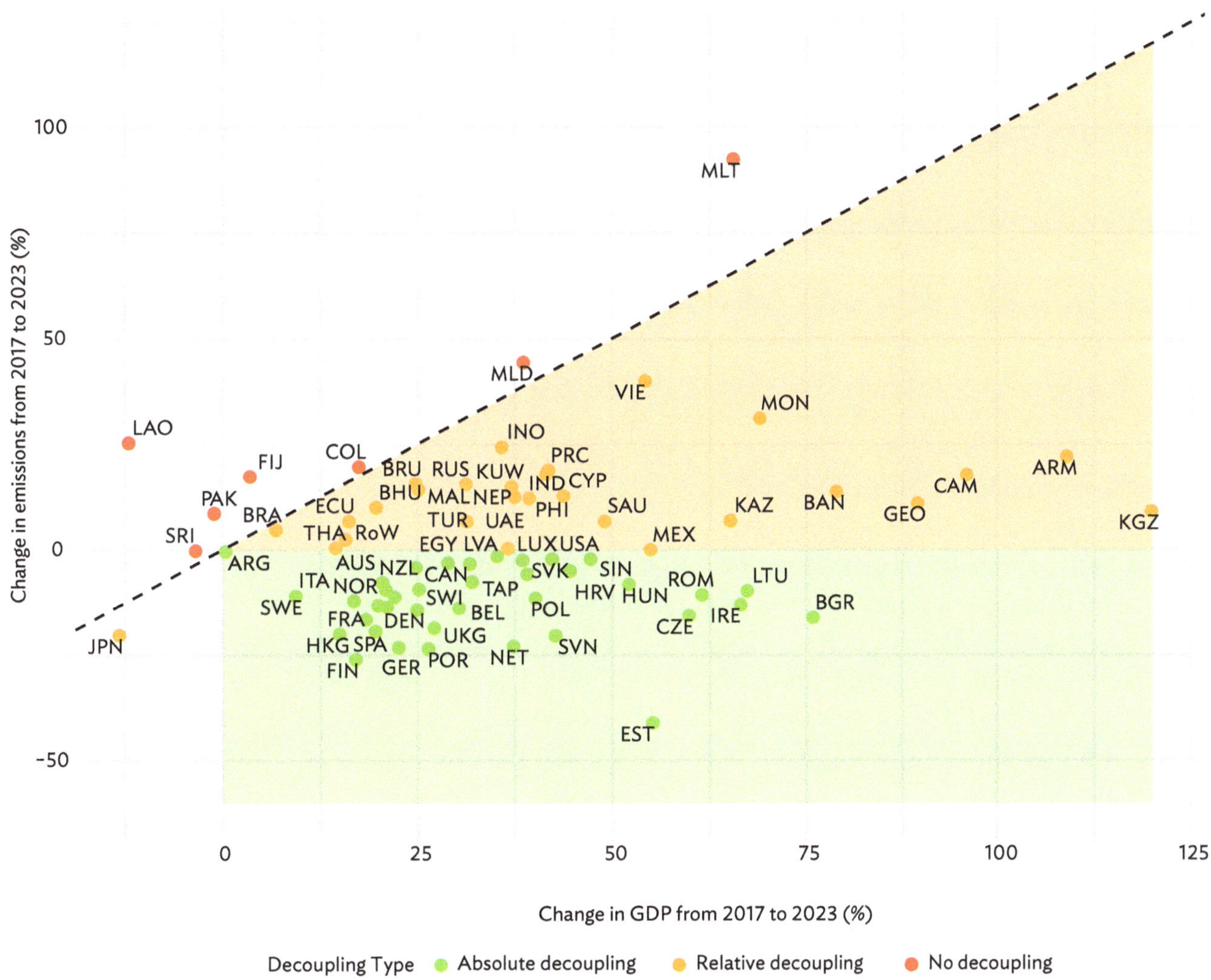

ARM = Armenia; AUS = Australia; AUT = Austria; BAN = Bangladesh; BEL = Belgium; BGR = Bulgaria; BHU = Bhutan; BRA = Brazil; BRU = Brunei Darussalam; CAM = Cambodia; CAN = Canada; PRC = People's Republic of China; COL = Colombia; CYP = Cyprus; CZE = Czech Republic; DEN = Denmark; ECU = Ecuador; EGY = Egypt; EST = Estonia; FIJ = Fiji; FIN = Finland; FRA = France; GDP = gross domestic product; GEO = Georgia; GER = Germany; GRC = Greece; HKG = Hong Kong, China; HRV = Croatia; HUN = Hungary; IND = India; INO = Indonesia; IRE = Ireland; ITA = Italy; JPN = Japan; KAZ = Kazakhstan; KOR = Republic of Korea; KGZ = Kyrgyz Republic; KUW = Kuwait; LAO = Lao People's Democratic Republic; LTU = Lithuania; LUX = Luxembourg; LVA = Latvia; MAL = Malaysia; MEX = Mexico; MLD = Maldives; MLT = Malta; MON = Mongolia; NEP = Nepal; NET = Netherlands; NOR = Norway; NZL = New Zealand; PAK = Pakistan; PHI = Philippines; POL = Poland; POR = Portugal; ROM = Romania; RUS = Russian Federation; RoW = Rest of the World; SAU = Saudi Arabia; SIN = Singapore; SPA = Spain; SRI = Sri Lanka; SVK = Slovak Republic; SVN = Slovenia; SWE = Sweden; SWI = Switzerland; TAP = Taipei,China; THA = Thailand; TUR = Türkiye; UAE = United Arab Emirates; UKG = United Kingdom; USA = United States; VIE = Viet Nam.

Note: GDP percentage changes should be interpreted with caution as they were calculated from current price figures, thus being confounded by price effects.

Source: Asian Development Bank analysis using multiregional input-output tables and environmentally extended multiregional input-output tables at https://kidb.adb.org/globalization (accessed January 2025).

in Asia and the Pacific experienced relative decoupling, indicating efficiency gains but not absolute reductions in emissions. Only six economies (four in Asia and the Pacific and one in South America) showed no decoupling, with emissions outpacing or matching economic growth. While these results reflect the interim use of nominal growth in gross domestic product (GDP),[16] sensitivity checks using constant prices suggest the direction of decoupling trends remains stable in nearly nine out of 10 cases (Box 2.1). These diverse outcomes highlight the need for tailored policies to hasten progress toward absolute decoupling, particularly in regions where economic growth is still heavily dependent on carbon-intensive activities.

Decoupling trends do not expose the underlying factors driving growth patterns.

The concept of "emissions intensity" offers a more precise metric of the relationship between economic growth and the pace of emissions. This measure explicitly links emissions and output, often calculated by dividing direct emissions by output. Emissions intensity has economic significance, revealing the level of emissions generated per unit of economic output. A decline in emissions intensity over time signals efficiency improvements driven by technological innovation, structural economic shifts, or stronger regulatory measures. From 2017 to 2023, a decline in emissions intensity was observed across all regions assessed (Figure 2.2). Asia and the Pacific's emissions intensity, one of the highest in the world, declined by 13% from 2017 to 2023. This indicates progress toward relative decoupling, though absolute decoupling (whereby total emissions decline) remains elusive.

Emissions intensity metrics are the most useful at an economy level.

Approximately 75% of global emissions originate from a handful of large emitters. These include high-income economies such as the United States, Japan, Germany, the Republic of Korea, Saudi Arabia, and Canada, alongside fast-growing economies such as the People's Republic of China (PRC), India, the Russian Federation, Indonesia, and Brazil. Therefore, rather than generalize with region-level information, more geographically granular data at the economy level allow for more targeted strategies to lower either absolute emissions or emissions intensities.

As shown in Figure 2.3, advanced economies generally exhibited lower emissions intensities than did emerging economies in both 2017 and 2023. Emissions in advanced economies such as the Republic of Korea and Japan slowed and even declined, as material demand also showed signs of desaturating. This is in line with studies demonstrating that the intensity of material use decelerates at higher stages of economic development, due to largely completed urbanization and infrastructure development and a shift towards a services-dominated economy (IEA 2019b; Wiedenhofer et al. 2019; Bashmakov 2021; Haberl et al. 2021; Cao et al. 2017).

16 Constant-price indicators for decoupling and related measures will be made available upon completion of the constant-price MRIOT database, which is under development at the time of writing.

Box 2.1: Interpretation of Decoupling Using Nominal and Real Growth Measures

Using constant-price or real gross domestic product (GDP) remains the standard for assessing whether economies are truly decoupling economic growth from emissions. It does so by removing the distortions of inflation and exchange rate fluctuations, enabling consistent comparisons of real changes in output over time. By contrast, using current-price or nominal GDP confounds quantity and price effects. This can lead to false positives, overstating decoupling during high inflation periods or commodity price hikes even if real output remains unchanged. It can also result in false negatives, understating progress during downturns or deflation despite stable or growing real output.

An examination of 72 economies from 2017 to 2023 suggests that in 87.5% of instances (63 of 72 economies) the directional outcome of decoupling—whether absolute, relative, or none—remained consistent, regardless of whether the decoupling index was derived from current-price or constant-price GDP growth rates. This consistency, calculated using production-based emissions, supports the use of nominal data for preliminary assessments. Nevertheless, the magnitude of decoupling may vary considerably, necessitating a detailed examination of the 12.5% of outlier cases as depicted in the figure below.

Comparison of Decoupling Using Nominal and Real Gross Domestic Product, 2017 and 2023

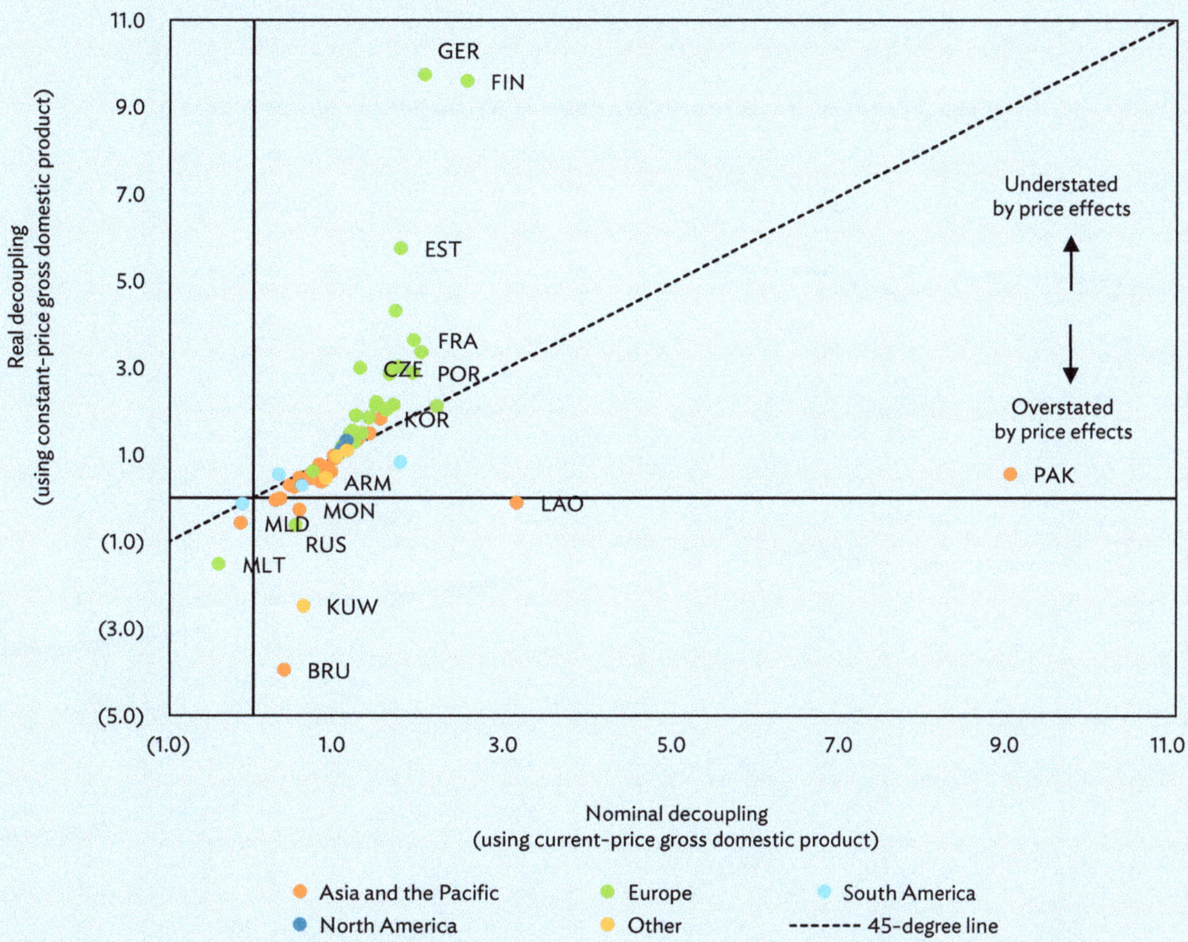

ARG = Argentina; BRA = Brazil; BRU = Brunei Darussalam; COL = Colombia; CZE = Czech Republic; EST = Estonia; FIJ = Fiji; GER = Germany; KOR = Republic of Korea; KUW = Kuwait; LAO = Lao People's Democratic Republic; MLD = Maldives; MON = Mongolia; PAK = Pakistan; RUS = Russian Federation; SAU = Saudi Arabia; SPA = Spain; SWE = Sweden.

Note: Decoupling index is measured as 1- (E2023/E2017)/(G2023/G2017), where E is emissions and G is gross domestic product (GDP). Real decoupling uses GDP in constant 2021 international dollars, adjusted using power purchasing parities. Nominal decoupling uses current-price GDP in US dollar, converted using market exchange rates.

Source: Asian Development Bank analysis using environmentally extended multiregional input-output tables at https://kidb.adb.org/globalization (accessed January 2025) and gross domestic product and purchasing power parity (constant 2021 international dollars) data from the World Bank's World Development Indicators at https://databank.worldbank.org/source/world-development-indicators/ (accessed July 2025).

continued on next page

In economies experiencing significant inflation or currency depreciation, a divergence between nominal and real GDP growth may be observed, potentially leading to a misrepresentation of decoupling progress. Pakistan serves as an example, where severe currency depreciation resulted in a substantial overstatement of decoupling progress. Conversely, in the case of Germany, the reliance on current-price data understates the true extent of decoupling, as its real-term performance is considerably stronger than nominal figures indicate. This highlights the application of current-price data for timely monitoring while underscoring the importance of constant-price data for a more accurate structural assessment.

The findings presented offer valuable policy guidance. Given that 87.5% of economies show consistent decoupling directions regardless of the GDP price basis used, current-price data can serve as a reliable early indicator for most economies. However, policymakers should be cautious when interpreting nominal data for economies with volatile exchange rates, high inflation, or heavy dependence on commodity exports. For such economies, which constitute 12.5% of outlier cases, nominal GDP indicators should be supplemented with real-time physical data (e.g., energy consumption, industrial output volumes) to distinguish genuine structural change from price effects. This targeted approach allows for timely policy assessment while reducing the risk of misinterpretation.

Source: Asian Development Bank analysis.

Figure 2.2: Emissions and Production-Based Emissions Intensity by Region, 2017–2023

The Asia and Pacific region decarbonized production from 2017 to 2023.

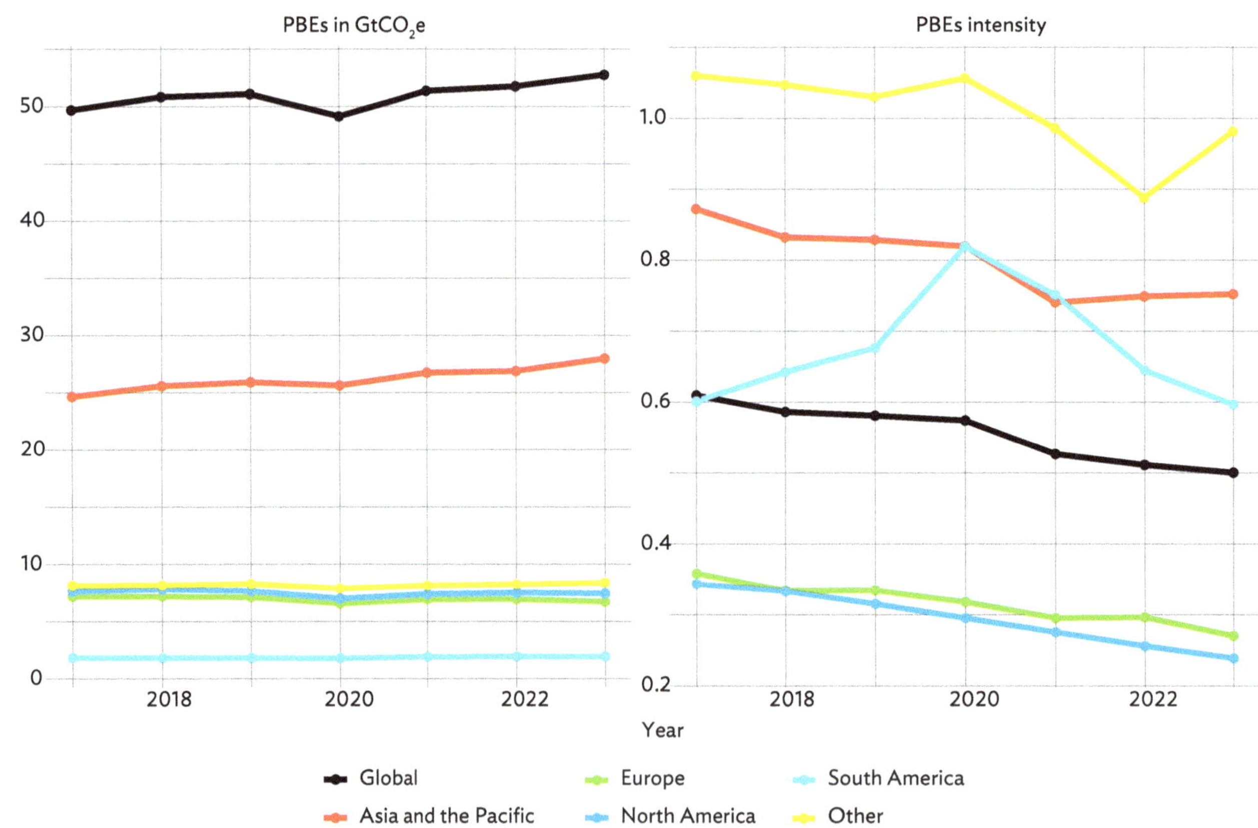

$GtCO_2e$ = gigatons of carbon dioxide equivalent, PBEs = production-based emissions.

Note: Emissions intensity is calculated by dividing those emissions that were recorded for a year with the corresponding estimate of gross domestic product in United States dollars.

Source: Asian Development Bank analysis using multiregional input-output tables and environmentally extended multiregional input-output tables at https://kidb.adb.org/globalization (accessed January 2025).

Figure 2.3: Absolute Emissions Versus Emissions Intensities by Economy, 2017 and 2023

Lower-income economies generally exhibit higher emissions intensities.

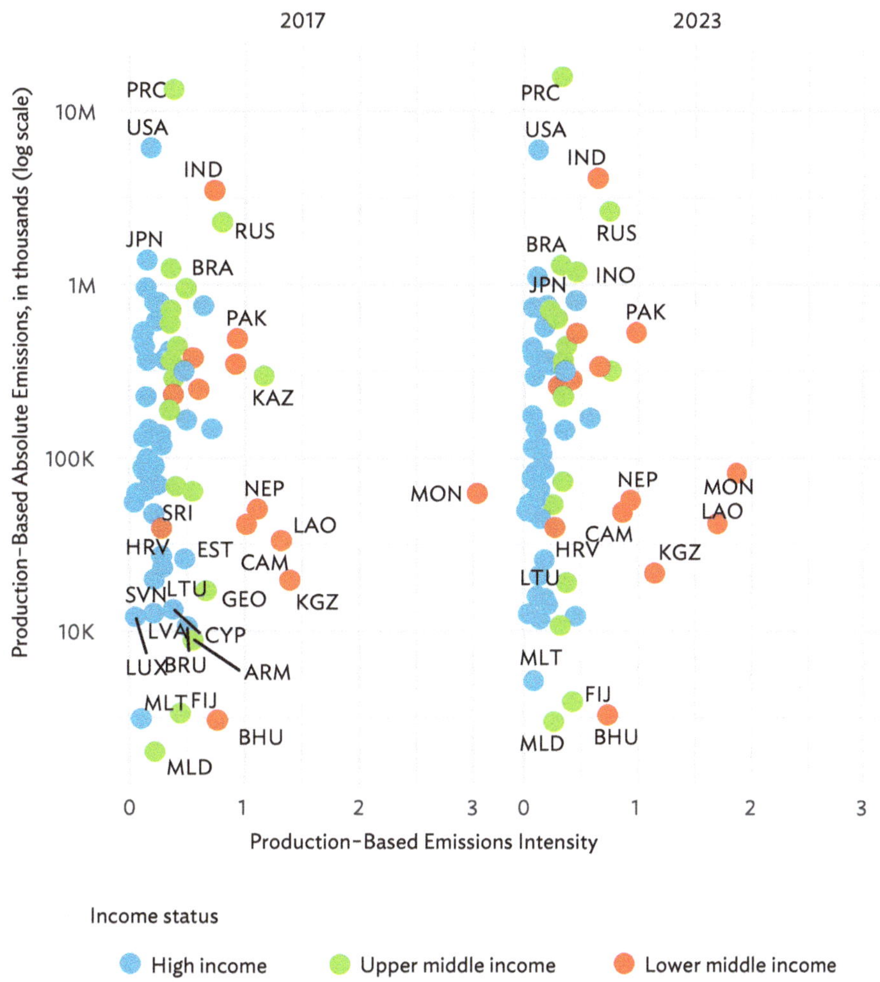

ARM = Armenia; AUS = Australia; AUT = Austria; BAN = Bangladesh; BEL = Belgium; BGR = Bulgaria; BHU = Bhutan; BRA = Brazil; BRU = Brunei Darussalam; CAM = Cambodia; CAN = Canada; PRC = People's Republic of China; COL = Colombia; CYP = Cyprus; CZE = Czech Republic; DEN = Denmark; ECU = Ecuador; EGY = Egypt; EST = Estonia; FIJ = Fiji; FIN = Finland; FRA = France; GEO = Georgia; GER = Germany; GRC = Greece; HKG = Hong Kong, China; HRV = Croatia; HUN = Hungary; IND = India; INO = Indonesia; IRE = Ireland; ITA = Italy; JPN = Japan; K = thousand; KAZ = Kazakhstan; KOR = Republic of Korea; KGZ = Kyrgyz Republic; KUW = Kuwait; LAO = Lao People's Democratic Republic; LTU = Lithuania; LUX = Luxembourg; LVA = Latvia; M = million; MAL = Malaysia; MEX = Mexico; MLD = Maldives; MLT = Malta; MON = Mongolia; NEP = Nepal; NET = Netherlands; NOR = Norway; NZL = New Zealand; PAK = Pakistan; PHI = Philippines; POL = Poland; POR = Portugal; ROM = Romania; RUS = Russian Federation; RoW = Rest of the World; SAU = Saudi Arabia; SIN = Singapore; SPA = Spain; SRI = Sri Lanka; SVK = Slovak Republic; SVN = Slovenia; SWE = Sweden; SWI = Switzerland; TAP = Taipei,China; THA = Thailand; TUR = Türkiye; UAE = United Arab Emirates; UKG = United Kingdom; USA = United States; VIE = Viet Nam.

Note: Emissions intensity is calculated by dividing production-based emissions that were recorded for a year with the corresponding estimate of gross output in millions of United States dollars.

Source: Asian Development Bank analysis using multiregional input-output tables and environmentally extended multiregional input-output tables at https://kidb.adb.org/globalization (accessed January 2025).

Conversely, from 2017 to 2023, large and intensive emitters such as the PRC, the Russian Federation, and India increased their combined contribution to total global emissions by 5%. This presents a dual challenge because the growing emissions in these economies stem from both high output levels and carbon-inefficient processes.

Some economies, such as Lao People's Democratic Republic and Fiji, contributed only marginally to global emissions but exhibited relatively high emissions intensities compared to other economies. Developing economies such as Mongolia, the Kyrgyz Republic, Kazakhstan, Nepal, and Cambodia (many of which are resource-dependent) steadily increased their emissions but reduced their emissions intensities from 2017 to 2023.

Targeted technologies can help in lowering both emissions intensities and total emissions.

Understanding differences in emissions intensities among similar industries presents opportunities to accelerate decarbonization. Because EE-MRIOTs use comparable measures of emissions and production across economies and industries, the data can support identification of key intervention points by highlighting relatively carbon-intensive activities across value chains.

Evidence shows that targeting underperforming industries can yield exceptional gains in clean technology deployment and spur low-carbon innovation (Baumert et al. 2005; Fei and Lin 2016; Valayden and Chabaud 2024; Meng et al. 2023). In one scenario, narrowing emissions intensity gaps between high- and low-performing producers could avoid emissions equivalent to a latent global demand value of about $1.4 trillion in green technology opportunities. Of this, about $782 billion lies untapped in Asia and the Pacific, equivalent to 2.1% of the region's GDP in 2023.[17] While factors, such as technological readiness, capital access, or policy environments may constrain how fully or quickly this value can be realized, the scenario illustrates the scale of the opportunity and the economic value at stake if emissions intensity gaps remain unaddressed.

The findings in Figure 2.3 suggest that some economies with high emissions intensities, while contributing less to total global emissions than other economies, pose a growing challenge due to their rapid industrial growth and carbon-intensive processes. Indeed, these economies have been growing faster than the global average, with their material demand fast increasing as well. Addressing global decarbonization thus requires not

17 This value reflects the market-equivalent of emissions that could be avoided if more carbon-intensive industries in the EE-MRIOT dataset matched the emissions efficiency of top-performing peers operating closer to the technological or operational frontier. For illustration, top performers were operationalized as those in the top 10 percentile in emissions intensity for a given group of industries. Potentially avoidable emissions can be converted into monetary terms using a price that ideally reflects the prevailing cost of cutting a ton of CO_2 through technologies (e.g., direct air capture, renewable technologies) or more-efficient production processes. The resulting value therefore indicates the latent demand for decarbonization. For this exercise, average explicit prices in carbon markets were used.

only continued efficiency gains among the big emitters, but also targeted technology and investment support to help smaller, high-intensity economies shift to cleaner production pathways.

Widespread adoption of cleaner technologies, energy efficient processes, and digital innovations can also contribute to emissions reductions. These outcomes echo wider literature that links falling emissions intensities to technology diffusion and structural change (UNEP 2024). In the utilities sector, for instance, satellite monitoring suggests that methane releases from oil and gas facilities are around 80% higher than reported by governments. However, about 70% of these emissions could be avoided by applying existing technologies, such as leak detection and repair campaigns, and through the installation of emissions control devices (IE 2025). Digital solutions offer another way to cut emissions, while energy efficiencies in buildings and process efficiencies in mining and upstream production could reduce sectoral emissions by as much as 20% by 2050 (WEF 2022). However, significant financial and capacity limitations generally impede adoption of these technologies in developing economies, underscoring the need for targeted support to implement cleaner solutions that can deliver emissions reductions without inhibiting economic growth.

The scale of economic output equally influences outcomes on emissions.

While emission intensity provides valuable insights into the efficiency of economic activities, it captures only part of the story. The scale of economic activity, or the sheer level of output, is an equally critical driver of emissions. As indicated in Figure 2.3, even if economies improve their emission intensities, growing economic demand and production can offset these gains, resulting in increasing total emissions.

In the EE-MRIOT framework, the total emissions of an economy (E) are determined by two key factors: the emissions intensity (e), which measures emissions per unit of output, and the total output (x). Simply stated, emissions are the product of volume of production and the level emitted per unit of production.

The Leontief model expands this framework by breaking down output (x) into two components: the level of final demand (y) and the interconnections among sectors captured by the Leontief inverse matrix (**B**). In this formulation, total emissions can be expressed as $\mathrm{E} = \mathrm{e} \cdot \mathrm{B} \cdot \mathrm{y}$, where y represents the final demand for goods and services, such as household consumption, government spending, and exports, and **B** captures the interconnectedness of sectors, showing how the output from one sector depends on inputs from others. This relationship demonstrates that as final demand (y) increases or sectors become more interconnected (**B**), the production scales up ($\mathbf{B} \cdot \mathbf{y}$), often leading to higher emissions.

This relationship underscores the importance of scale effects in understanding emissions levels. For instance, even if an economy reduces its emissions intensity by 10%, total emissions will rise if its total output doubles due to rising demand. Therefore, improvements in efficiency (reductions in $\mathbf{e}$) must outpace the output growth ($\mathbf{B} \cdot \mathbf{y}$) to achieve meaningful emissions reductions. Scale effects suggest that economic growth, if unchecked by sustainable practices, can offset gains from technological and efficiency improvements.

Analyzing recent trends of individual components indicates that scale effects have driven the global rise in emissions amid improvements in intensity. Results from structural decomposition analysis[18] suggest that, from 2017 to 2023, global emissions intensity declined by 9.2 gigatons of carbon dioxide equivalent ($GtCO_2e$) or 20.7% (Figure 2.4); However, global demand surged by 12.2 $GtCO_2e$ (27.5%) over the same time period. Therefore, the increase in global demand offset the reductions gained by emission intensity improvements by 3.0 $GtCO_2e$ (6.8%) in global production-based emissions.[19]

Analysis demonstrates the interconnected nature of factors driving emissions.

While the decline in global emissions intensity from 2017 to 2023 reflects technological progress and structural efficiency, the overwhelming growth in economic demand underscores the challenge of achieving absolute decoupling or reductions in total emissions. The relatively stable cross-sectoral linkages suggest that emissions-decreasing efficiencies in production structures are alone insufficient to counterbalance the scale effects driven by rising demand. Without coordinated efforts to curb growth in final demand or radically improve emissions efficiency, global emissions are likely to continue rising.

---

18 Structural decomposition analysis is an input-output-based method used to identify the key drivers behind changes in economic or environmental indicators over time. It distinguishes the roles played by factors such as emissions intensity, production structure or intermediate input composition, and final demand. For a technical explanation of the method, see Appendix 2.

19 Note that these results should be interpreted with caution since they were calculated from current price figures, thus being confounded by price effects.

Figure 2.4: Change in Production-Based Emissions Due to Specific Factors, 2017–2023 (%)

Emissions increased globally from 2017 to 2023, driven by the rise in global demand.

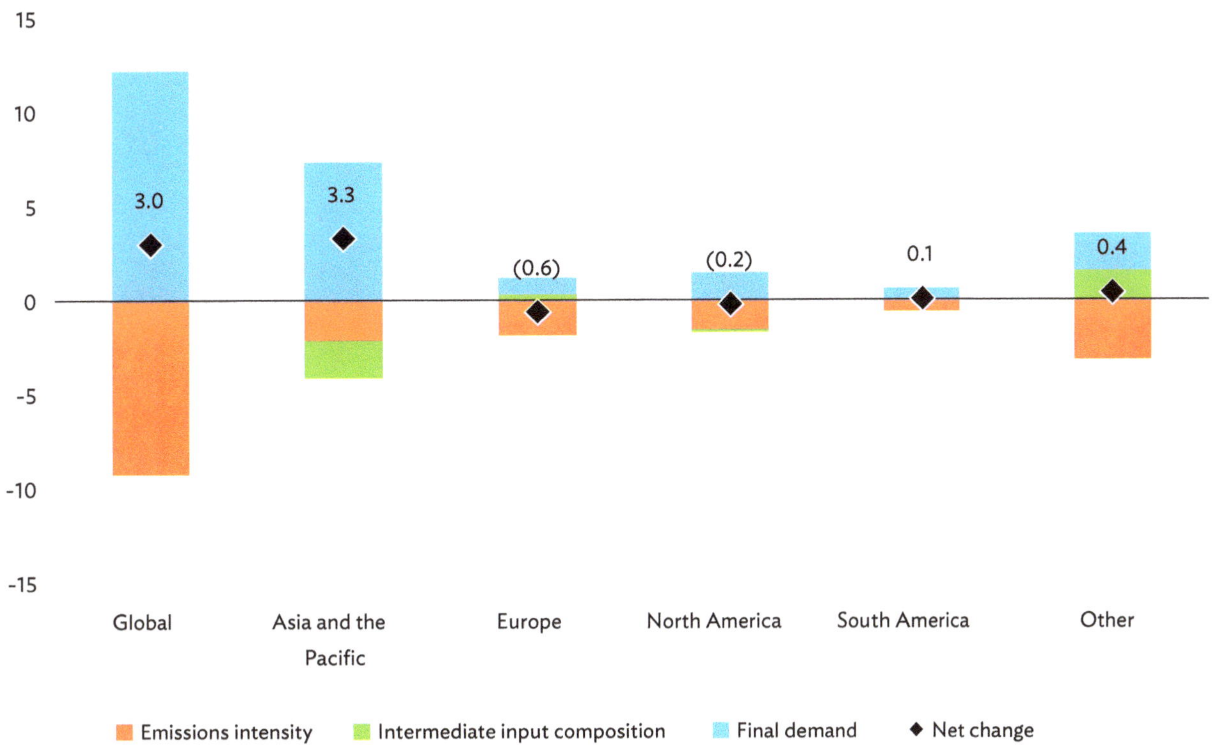

Source: Asian Development Bank analysis using multiregional input-output tables and environmentally extended multiregional input-output tables at https://kidb.adb.org/globalization (accessed January 2025).

Perspective 2: Identifying the Sources of Carbon Emissions in Supply Chains

Almost no economic sector operates independently.

When carbon accounting is applied to the ADB EE-MRIOTs, it reveals trends in global emissions distribution. In the real world, nearly every economic sector relies on inputs from another, meaning demand in one sector can trigger emissions in another. For example, when bakers increase their demand for flour, millers must scale up production, resulting in additional emissions. Although these emissions are physically generated in milling factories, they are inherently linked to the baker's demand for flour.

The interconnected structure of input-output tables allows the tracing of emissions throughout the supply chain. This reveals not only the direct emissions of each sector, but also the indirect emissions embedded in the inputs the sector consumes. For many sectors, Scope 3 emissions, that is indirect emissions other than those from energy providers, (e.g., emissions from suppliers, raw material production and transportation, finished product transportation, and retail activities) constitute up a significant portion of total emissions, highlighting the crucial role of upstream supply chain activities (Figure 2.5).

Figure 2.5: Emissions Shares by Scope per Broad Sector Category, 2017 and 2023

Scope 3 emissions are predominant in the services sectors

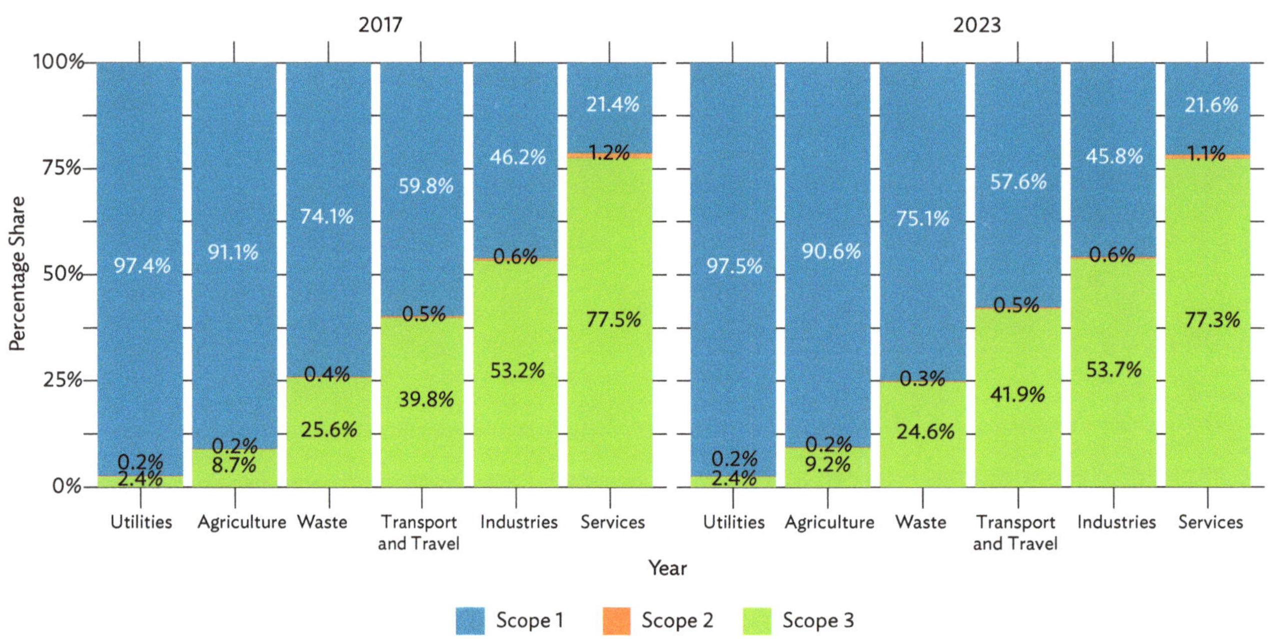

Note: Scope 1 refers to emissions directly produced by the sector's own activities. Scope 2 covers indirect emissions from the generation of purchased electricity, steam, heat, or cooling used by the sector. Scope 3 (upstream) includes all other indirect emissions embodied in the inputs used by the sector.

Source: Asian Development Bank analysis using multiregional input-output tables and environmentally extended multiregional input-output tables at https://kidb.adb.org/globalization (accessed January 2025).

Environmentally extended analysis can sharpen policy focus.

Beyond being used merely as an accounting tool, EE-MRIOT facilitates analysis that can produce findings that suggest ways for producers to act on environmental challenges. For example, identifying emissions scopes and their concentrations can help in setting more ambitious yet achievable decarbonization targets. This includes collaborating with suppliers to reduce emissions, improving energy efficiency in manufacturing, and embedding environmental criteria into supplier and purchasing agreements—measures already being taken in some industry groups.[20] While reporting

20 A notable example is the Fashion Industry Charter for Climate Action, launched under the United Nations Framework Convention on Climate Change. With most emissions concentrated in Scope 3, accounting for as much as 97%–99% of total emissions in some cases, the fashion industry's greatest opportunity to reduce its emissions footprint lies within its supply chain (Hohmann et al. 2023).

gaps persist, alternative frameworks such as the EE-MRIOTs provide a vital means of bridging these gaps and enabling more targeted and accurate environmental policies

Perspective 3: Linking Trade and Global Value Chains to Emissions Trajectories

Supply chains are increasingly dispersed across different regions and economies.

Today's global corporations source inputs from several suppliers worldwide, each using different energy sources, production processes, and technologies. For example, an electric vehicle's design may originate in Germany or the United States, while components such as batteries are manufactured in the Republic of Korea, using raw materials mined in Australia. These components may be finally assembled in the PRC or the European Union (EU) before the vehicles are marketed and sold globally. These intricate supply chains have revolutionized industries by optimizing efficiencies and reducing costs. However, they also complicate the assessment of the environmental impacts embedded across stages of production and consumption.

In the same way that official trade statistics have initially struggled to keep pace with the complexities of global value chains, national carbon emissions measures face challenges in accurately assigning sources of emissions from the supply side. For example, national accounting models often assume that imports are produced with the same emissions intensities as domestic goods,[21] ignoring significant differences in production processes, energy sources, and environmental standards between economies.

From a demand perspective, trade and global value chains also complicate the analysis of emissions drivers by extending their scope to include consumption in foreign markets. Emissions generated in exporting economies are often driven by global consumption patterns (Hubacek et al. 2014; Wiedmann and Lenzen 2018). This makes it necessary to understand why emissions occur and how consumption choices and associated supply chains contribute to total emissions. This perspective cannot be captured solely through production-based emissions (PBEs), much less territorial emissions.[22]

In light of global complexities, it is essential to account for emissions across the entire supply chain associated with final demand, regardless of their physical location. This alternative approach, known as **consumption-based emissions (CBEs)**, attributes emissions to the final consumer rather than the producer. CBEs capture all emissions generated throughout the supply chain, from raw material extraction to the final product.

---

21 A concept known as domestic technology assumption.

22 These two differ in that PBEs include emissions from international activities such as aviation, shipping, and nonresident activities, whereas territorial emissions exclude these (Karstensen et al. 2018).

For example, emissions from mining lithium and producing electricity to manufacture batteries for an electric vehicle are ultimately attributed to the consumer who purchases the vehicle.

CBEs provide a comprehensive understanding of the environmental impact of economic consumption, creating new policy levers by highlighting emissions embodied in trade, the impact of household consumption patterns on emissions footprints, and upstream supply chain choices by producers (Dhakal et al. 2022). Examples of such policies include border adjustment mechanisms that raise tariffs on imports with high carbon costs, as well as other taxation policies to encourage behavioral shifts among consumers towards low-carbon alternatives. The need for measuring CBEs reflects a shared understanding that a wider system beyond territorial emissions is critical to prevent pollution outsourcing and achieve meaningful decarbonization globally.

Statistical analysis confirms the relevance of consumption-based emissions accounting.

As economies increasingly participate in international trade, the emissions they produce do not necessarily align with the emissions they consume. This discrepancy arises from the emissions embedded in traded goods and services. In Asia and the Pacific, home to the world's largest production bases, PBEs exceeded CBEs from 2017 to 2023 (Figure 2.6). This surplus reflects the region's role as a net emissions exporter, driven by its emissions-intensive production of supply chain inputs and goods for export. Conversely, advanced economies from other regions exhibited the opposite pattern: as major importers of goods from Asia and the Pacific, their CBEs surpassed their PBEs, partly reflecting the emissions outsourced through global trade (Dhakal et al. 2022).

Production-based carbon pricing may have unintended consequences for controlling emissions.

Goods produced in Asia and the Pacific often reach markets that have some form of carbon pricing on their locally produced output. Carbon pricing is a mechanism that aims to capture the external costs of greenhouse gas emissions by placing a fee on emissions-producing activities and/or offering an incentive for reduced emissions (UNFCCC 2025). This is a means of stimulating changes in consumption, production, and investment patterns, aligning economic goals with environmental protection and climate resilience. In jurisdictions such as the EU, carbon pricing adjusts the cost of a locally produced good based on the producers' amount of direct emissions. By contrast, in 2024, there were only eight economies in Asia and the Pacific applying carbon pricing instruments, although momentum is growing[23] (ADB 2024).

23 Eight national initiatives have been implemented or are in development across Asia and the Pacific, including carbon taxes in Japan and Singapore and emissions trading systems in Australia, the PRC, Indonesia, Kazakhstan, the Republic of Korea, and New Zealand. Additionally, the Philippines, Thailand, and Viet Nam are considering the adoption of domestic emissions trading systems.

Carbon pricing may impose higher production costs for manufacturers relative to those in no-price jurisdictions. This disparity, if sufficiently strong, induces relocation of plants and firms to jurisdictions with lower carbon costs. This is also referred to as the "pollution haven hypothesis" or "pollution outsourcing" in cases when only portions of the value chains are relocated (Copeland and Taylor 2004; Cherniwchan 2017).

To illustrate the pollution haven hypothesis, if a producer in an EU economy faces high carbon taxes and therefore higher production costs, it may move operations to an economy with no carbon pricing or lower carbon costs, then export the finished product back to the home economy. In some cases, this relocation exacerbates emissions because the new host economy may allow outdated production processes, use less-efficient technologies, or rely on energy from coal rather than renewable sources. Additionally, emissions generated by shipping goods across long distances can further contribute to environmental impacts. These transport-related emissions are often overlooked, but they can significantly increase the carbon emissions of global value chains, particularly when goods are shipped by air or sea, which are high-emitting modes of transport.

Figure 2.6: Trends in Production-Based and Consumption-Based Emissions, 2017–2023

Asia and the Pacific's production-based emissions exceed the region's consumption-based emissions.

APAC = Asia and the Pacific, CBEs = consumption-based emissions, $GtCO_2e$ = gigatons of carbon dioxide equivalent, PBEs = production-based emissions.

Source: Asian Development Bank analysis using multiregional input-output tables and environmentally extended multiregional input-output tables at https://kidb.adb.org/globalization (accessed January 2025).

Reevaluating decoupling patterns through the lens of CBEs offers a more nuanced view of an economy's emissions responsibilities. When shifting from a production-based perspective to a consumption-based perspective, eight economies previously categorized as achieving absolute decoupling—such as Hong Kong,China, New Zealand, Bulgaria, and Luxembourg—now fall under relative decoupling (Figure 2.7). Conversely, in 19 economies across Asia and the Pacific, the growth rate of PBEs exceeded that of CBEs, indicating their role as net exporters of emissions-intensive goods.

Figure 2.7: Changes in Consumption-Based Emissions and Economic Output by Economy, 2017–2023

Assessing consumption-based emissions can alter decoupling trends in some economies.

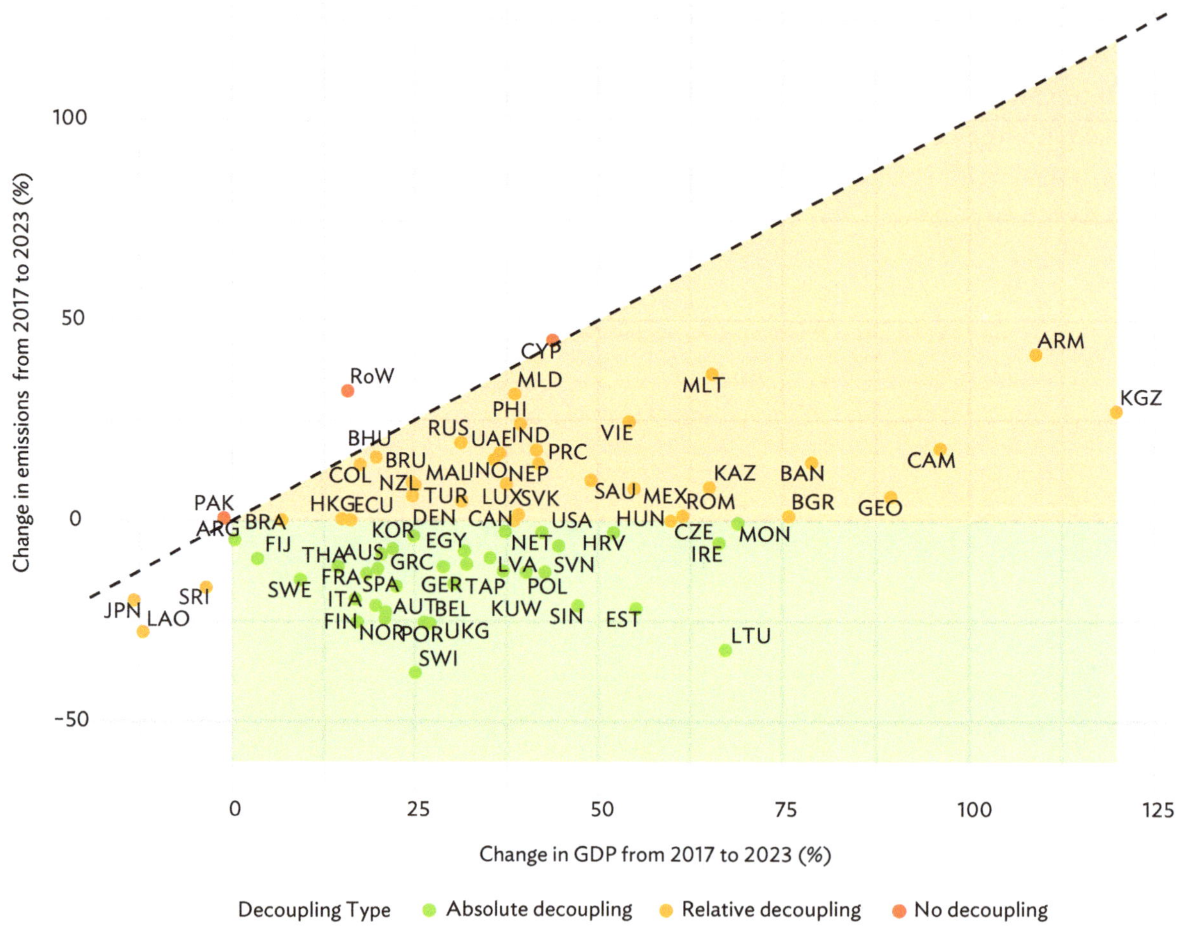

ARM = Armenia; AUS = Australia; AUT = Austria; BAN = Bangladesh; BEL = Belgium; BGR = Bulgaria; BHU = Bhutan; BRA = Brazil; BRU = Brunei Darussalam; CAM = Cambodia; CAN = Canada; PRC = People's Republic of China; COL = Colombia; CYP = Cyprus; CZE = Czech Republic; DEN = Denmark; ECU = Ecuador; EGY = Egypt; EST = Estonia; FIJ = Fiji; FIN = Finland; FRA = France; GDP = gross domestic product; GEO = Georgia; GER = Germany; GRC = Greece; HKG = Hong Kong, China; HRV = Croatia; HUN = Hungary; IND = India; INO = Indonesia; IRE = Ireland; ITA = Italy; JPN = Japan; KAZ = Kazakhstan; KOR = Republic of Korea; KGZ = Kyrgyz Republic; KUW = Kuwait; LAO = Lao People's Democratic Republic; LTU = Lithuania; LUX = Luxembourg; LVA = Latvia; MAL = Malaysia; MEX = Mexico; MLD = Maldives; MLT = Malta; MON = Mongolia; NEP = Nepal; NET = Netherlands; NOR = Norway; NZL = New Zealand; PAK = Pakistan; PHI = Philippines; POL = Poland; POR = Portugal; ROM = Romania; RUS = Russian Federation; RoW = Rest of the World; SAU = Saudi Arabia; SIN = Singapore; SPA = Spain; SRI = Sri Lanka; SVK = Slovak Republic; SVN = Slovenia; SWE = Sweden; SWI = Switzerland; TAP = Taipei,China; THA = Thailand; TUR = Türkiye; UAE = United Arab Emirates; UKG = United Kingdom; USA = United States; VIE = Viet Nam.

Note: GDP percentage changes should be interpreted with caution as they were calculated from current price figures, thus being confounded by price effects.

Source: Asian Development Bank analysis using multiregional input-output tables and environmentally extended multiregional input-output tables at https://kidb.adb.org/globalization (accessed January 2025).

The widening gap between CBEs and PBEs among advanced economies fuels ongoing concerns about the rise of "carbon leakage" (Arto and Dietzenbacher 2014). Similar in concept to pollution outsourcing, whereby production relocation is driven by environment-related policies such as carbon pricing and emissions regulations, carbon leakage can also occur due to economic factors such as lower labor costs, tax incentives, and trade policies that make relocation more attractive, even if environmental policies aren't the main driver.

Carbon leakage can have significant impacts on the attribution and reporting of emissions (Box 2.2). Notably, the emissions embedded in the net imports of advanced economies from developing economies are equal to, or even greater than, the size of their officially stated emissions reduction commitments (Bashmakov et al. 2022).

Consumption-based reporting should also be considered in a regional context.

Although CBEs are useful for revealing trends in economy-specific emissions, regional patterns remain broadly consistent. From 2017 to 2023, the Asia and Pacific region accounted for the largest share of global emissions in terms of both PBEs and CBEs (Figure 2.8). While the region's intensity of CBEs was slightly lower than for PBEs in 2023, this measure has largely plateaued since 2021. In comparison, Europe and North America experienced modest increases in total CBEs, but both regions maintained downward trends in emissions intensity. Notably, South America had a more pronounced reduction in emissions intensity under the CBEs framework, implying that a larger share of its emissions is embedded in goods supplied for its consumption through greener global value chains.

Furthermore, while distinguishing between CBEs and PBEs is important for understanding emissions responsibilities and developing pathways to emissions reduction, it is also necessary to recognize that PBEs have direct, localized impacts on environmental quality and human development, regardless of where the final demand originates.

Environmental objectives need to be balanced with the potential benefits of trade.

While global trade is associated with greater emissions, reducing its extent could result in significant economic losses, including major declines in GDP and employment. Considering a hypothetical scenario in which all cross-border trade is removed, carbon dioxide (CO_2) emissions could be reduced by around 38% (13.2 $GtCO_2e$) compared to baseline (2023) values. However, global GDP would also plummet by about 27.4% or \$22.05 trillion, bringing potential employment losses in the millions. Indeed, studies show that the economic benefits lost to both producers and consumers due to the absence of international trade would be about 100 times the environmental savings from reduced emissions (Shapiro 2016; WTO 2022).

Figure 2.8: Volume and Intensity of Production-Based and Consumption-Based Emissions by Region, 2017–2023

Emissions intensity trends hold under assessment of consumption-based emissions.

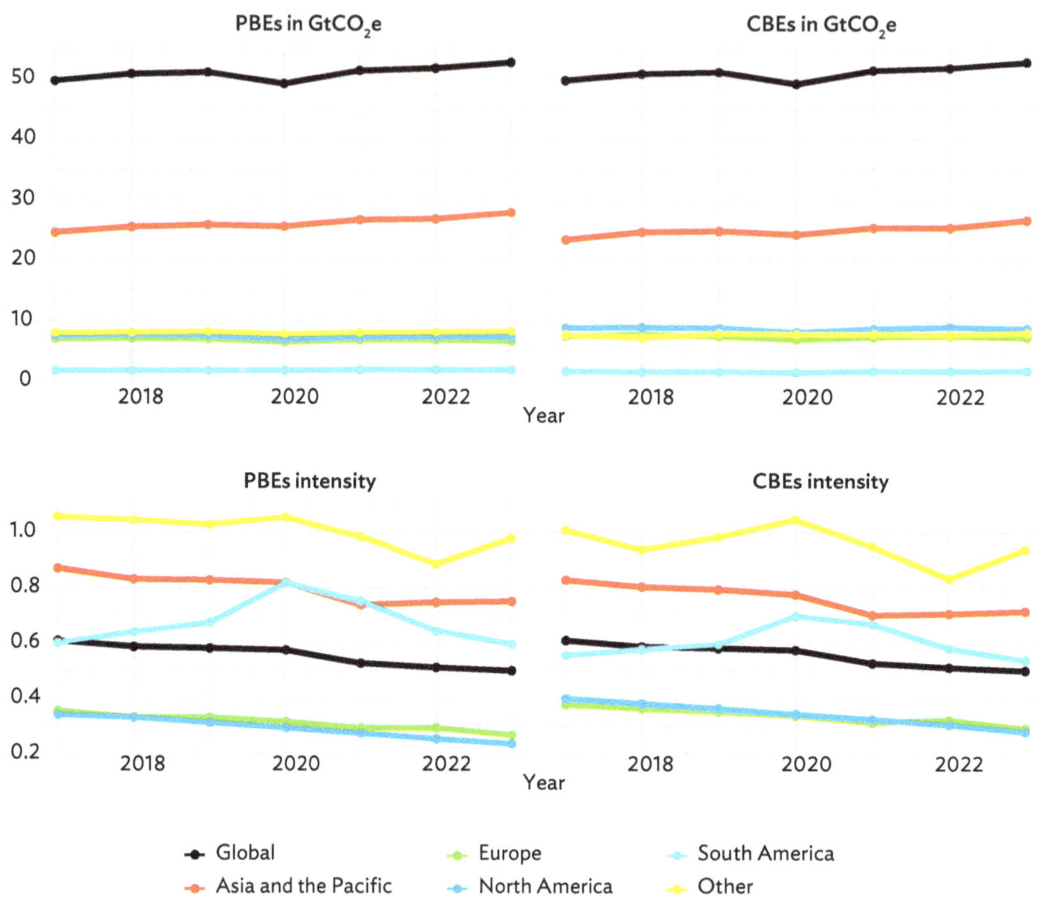

CBEs = consumption-based emissions, $GtCO_2e$ = gigatons of carbon dioxide equivalent, PBEs = production-based emissions.

Note: Emissions intensity is calculated by dividing those emissions that were recorded for a year with the corresponding estimate of gross domestic product in United States dollars.

Source: Asian Development Bank analysis using multiregional input-output tables and environmentally extended multiregional input-output tables at https://kidb.adb.org/globalization (accessed January 2025).

Although higher levels of trade can pose further challenges to global decarbonization through risks such as carbon leakage and scale effects, these challenges must be weighed against benefits such as faster productivity growth through access to foreign technology, know-how, and investment. More critically, trade serves as a conduit for advancing environmental goals by enabling the dispersion of green solutions and production processes through market access and technology transfer (WTO 2022). Instead of halting or reversing trade, the better path is to engage in more environmentally sustainable trade and foster greener global value chains across regions.

Box 2.2: Environmental Impacts of Relocating Production to Developing Economies

Comparing emissions intensities across trading partners helps reveal when environmental burdens are effectively being outsourced through global trade. If production shifts from a location with a lower emissions intensity to one with a higher relative measure, global emissions can rise, even as importing economies report lower production-based emissions.

The Asian Development Bank's environmentally extended multiregional input-output tables (EE-MRIOTs) allow for testing hypothetical scenarios to model the effects of shifting production and to analyze the implications for production-based versus consumption-based emissions responsibility.

To illustrate with one such hypothetical example, imagine Italy's textiles exports (excluding domestic production) are relocated to Bangladesh, an economy that has pursued an export-led industrialization strategy since its independence in 1971.

Bangladesh's textiles sector contributes over 80% of the economy's exports, provides 10% of gross domestic product (GDP), and employs around 4 million people (Sharpe, Retamal, and Martinez Fernandez 2022). This rapid expansion—from just a dozen factories in the early 1980s to several thousand in 2023—has made Bangladesh the world's second-largest garment exporter (Economics Observatory 2025). However, environmental pressures have also intensified. Untreated effluent from textiles factories is a major source of water pollution in the capital, Dhaka, where multiple rivers have been declared biologically "dead" (Sharpe, Retamal, and Martinez Fernandez 2022). Based on analysis of EE-MRIOTs, Bangladesh's emissions intensity for the textiles sector was about 0.12 gigagrams of carbon dioxide equivalent ($GgCO_2e$) per $1,000 output in 2023, down markedly from 0.35 $GgCO_2e$ in 2017, but still high relative to advanced economies.

Bangladesh has implemented environmental legislation, such as the Environmental Conservation Act (1995) and Environmental Courts (2000s), but enforcement challenges remain. While environmental considerations have entered national planning frameworks, they are often deprioritized (Sharpe, Retamal, and Martinez Fernandez 2022). Bangladeshi mills often rely on diesel generators, older dyeing machinery, and limited wastewater-energy recovery.

Italy, long a leader in high-value textiles manufacturing and fashion, has a comparatively high export value of textiles and apparel, but the sector made up only 6% of the economy's total exports in 2023. Italy's emissions intensity in textiles production was 0.04 $GgCO_2e$ per $1,000 output in 2023 and has remained stable since 2017, reflecting EU-driven cleaner energy inputs and stricter environmental regulations driven by the European Union.

Impacts of a Selective Hypothetical Relocation of the Textiles Sector from Italy to Bangladesh

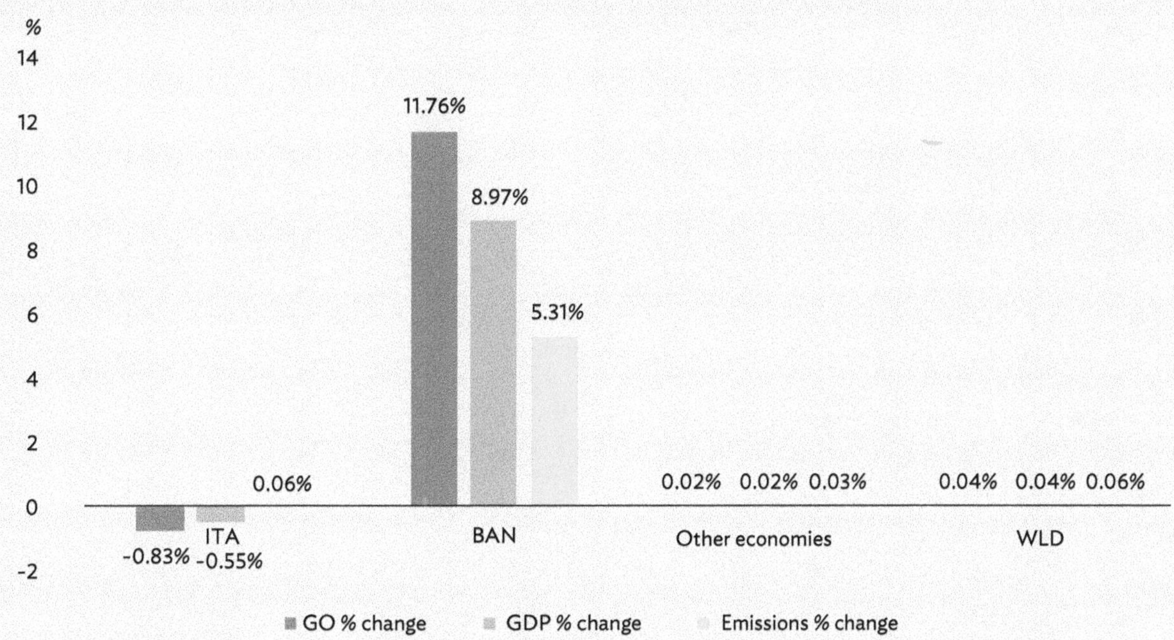

BAN = Bangladesh, GDP = Gross Domestic Product, GO = gross output, ITA = Italy, WLD = World

Source: Asian Development Bank analysis using multiregional input-output tables and environmentally extended multiregional input-output tables at https://kidb.adb.org/globalization (accessed January 2025).

continued on next page

Using the EE-MRIOTs, in a simulated reallocation where Italy's textiles exports are entirely replaced by production in Bangladesh (and imports from Bangladesh replace Italy's exports to third markets), the following impacts are observed:

Bangladesh experiences significant economic benefits, with its GDP increasing by 9% and gross output rising by 12%. However, these gains come at a climate cost, as national emissions rise by 5.3% or 14 megatons of carbon dioxide equivalent. Textiles sector emissions rise by 63%, reflecting the impacts of both larger scale production and the higher emissions intensity of Bangladesh.

In contrast, Italy's GDP decreases by 0.55%, but emissions remain similar as Italy retains textiles production for domestic consumption and corresponding upstream inputs.

At the global level, this reallocation would lead to a 0.06% rise in total emissions, as shown in the figure below, illustrating that shifting production from a more-efficient to a less-efficient location can undermine progress in curbing global emissions.

This simulated scenario shows that host economies could bear disproportionate environmental impacts relative to the economic value added. Moreover, many such host economies are already vulnerable to the impacts of a changing climate. Bangladesh, for instance, ranked ninth globally on the climate disaster risk index in 2024 (BEH and ILPAC 2024). Projections suggest the economy could lose 17% of its land area (IMF 2019) and 30% of its agricultural output by 2050 due to sea level rise, putting over 900,000 people at risk of climate-induced displacement (Huq et al. 2024). As the agricultural sector contributes 12.6% of total GDP and employs 40% of the labor force, environmental shocks significantly risk both the economy's food and labor security (ADB 2023).

Applying the same reallocation simulations across sectors can help policymakers and industry leaders assess whether shifting production to developing Asia reduces costs at the expense of higher global emissions, and whether joint investment in cleaner technology could deliver both climate and development gains.

References:

Asian Development Bank (ADB). 2023. *Bangladesh's Agriculture, Natural Resources, and Rural Development Sector Assessment and Strategy.* Country Sector and Thematic Assessments. https://www.adb.org/sites/default/files/institutional-document/864661/bangladesh-agriculture-sector-assessment-strategy.pdf.

Bündnis Entwicklung Hilft (BEH) and Institute for International Law of Peace and Armed Conflict (ILPAC). 2024. *World Risk Report 2024: Multiple Crises.* Bündnis Entwicklung Hilft and Ruhr University Bochum. https://weltrisikobericht.de/worldriskreport/

Huq, S., M. Khan, A. K. M. S. Islam, and A. Binte Mirza. 2024. *Climate Change Impacts in Bangladesh: What Climate Change Means for a Country and Its People.* International Centre for Climate Change and Development. https://www.icccad.net/wp-content/uploads/2024/02/Bangladesh_Final_Covers_26-Jan-2024_ONLINE_compressed.pdf

International Monetary Fund (IMF). 2019. Bangladesh: Selected Issues. *IMF Country Report.* No. 19/300. https://www.imf.org/en/Publications/CR/Issues/2019/09/17/Bangladesh-Selected-Issues-48683

Siddiqi, D. M. 2025. What's Happening in Bangladesh's Garment Industry? *Economics Observatory.* 26 March. https://www.economicsobservatory.com/whats-happening-in-bangladeshs-garment-industry.

Sharpe S., M. Retamal, and M. C. Martinez Fernandez. 2022. Assessing the Impact: Environmental Impact Assessment in the Textile and Garment Sector in Bangladesh, Cambodia, Indonesia and Viet Nam. *ILO Working Paper.* No 51. International Labour Organization. https://www.ilo.org/sites/default/files/wcmsp5/groups/public/@asia/@ro-bangkok/documents/publication/wcms_838007.pdf

Source: Asian Development Bank analysis.

Trade facilitation can support the uptake of green technologies in developing economies.

Developing economies, which need clean technologies the most urgently, ironically face the steepest trade barriers to importing them. In 2022, the average tariffs on a subset of green products were only 1.4% in high-income economies, but climbed to 7.3% in low-income economies (WTO 2022). Regional trade agreements focusing on the facilitation of these technologies, such as the revival of the Environmental Goods Agreement[24], and digital green technology marketplaces could further widen the channels through which these products move. Furthermore, embedding environmental outcomes in trade facilitation—such as expedited customs procedures for certified green products or concessional export finance—would greatly benefit technology transfer while systemically restricting carbon leakage.

Emissions from traditional trade add another dimension to environmental accounting.

Traditional trade, characterized by goods crossing international borders only once, differs from trade related to global value chains (GVCs) and involving multiple border crossings. In 2023, emissions related to both traditional trade and GVC trade, combined here as "trade-related emissions", contributed approximately 30% of total emissions globally. This is especially relevant for the Asia and Pacific region where emissions per dollar of traded goods and services are improving more slowly than the global average. From 2017 to 2023, the region's emissions intensity in global trade and value chains fell by 11%, compared to the global reduction of 20%. Closing this gap requires clearer visibility into where emissions are concentrated along supply chains, guiding climate action toward areas with the greatest potential for environmental and economic gains.

The contribution of trade and GVC emissions vary significantly by world regions. In 2023, trade-related emissions constituted about 22% of total PBEs in Asia and the Pacific, whereas this figure was 38% in Europe (Figure 2.9).[25] The relatively high proportion of trade-related emissions in Europe suggests significant opportunities for emissions reduction within Asia and the Pacific and indirectly among its trading partners through GVCs. Additionally, trade-related emissions remained remarkably stable across regions from 2017 to 2023, indicating that trade and domestic consumption patterns were closely aligned and resilient to the impacts of the coronavirus disease (COVID-19) pandemic.

24 In July 2014, a group of World Trade Organization members launched plurilateral negotiations for the establishment of the Environmental Goods Agreement, seeking to promote trade in key environmental products, such as wind turbines and solar panels. However, due to the lack of participation from developing economies and disputes over the definition of "environmental goods", the initiative remains dormant as of 2025.

25 Calculated using a decomposition approach of Wang et al. (2017), replacing value-added coefficients with total greenhouse gas emissions per unit of output (ADB 2024).

Figure 2.9: Decomposition of Production-Based Emissions by Activity and Region, 2017–2023

Trade and GVC emissions remained a significant share of regional emissions footprints despite pandemic restrictions.

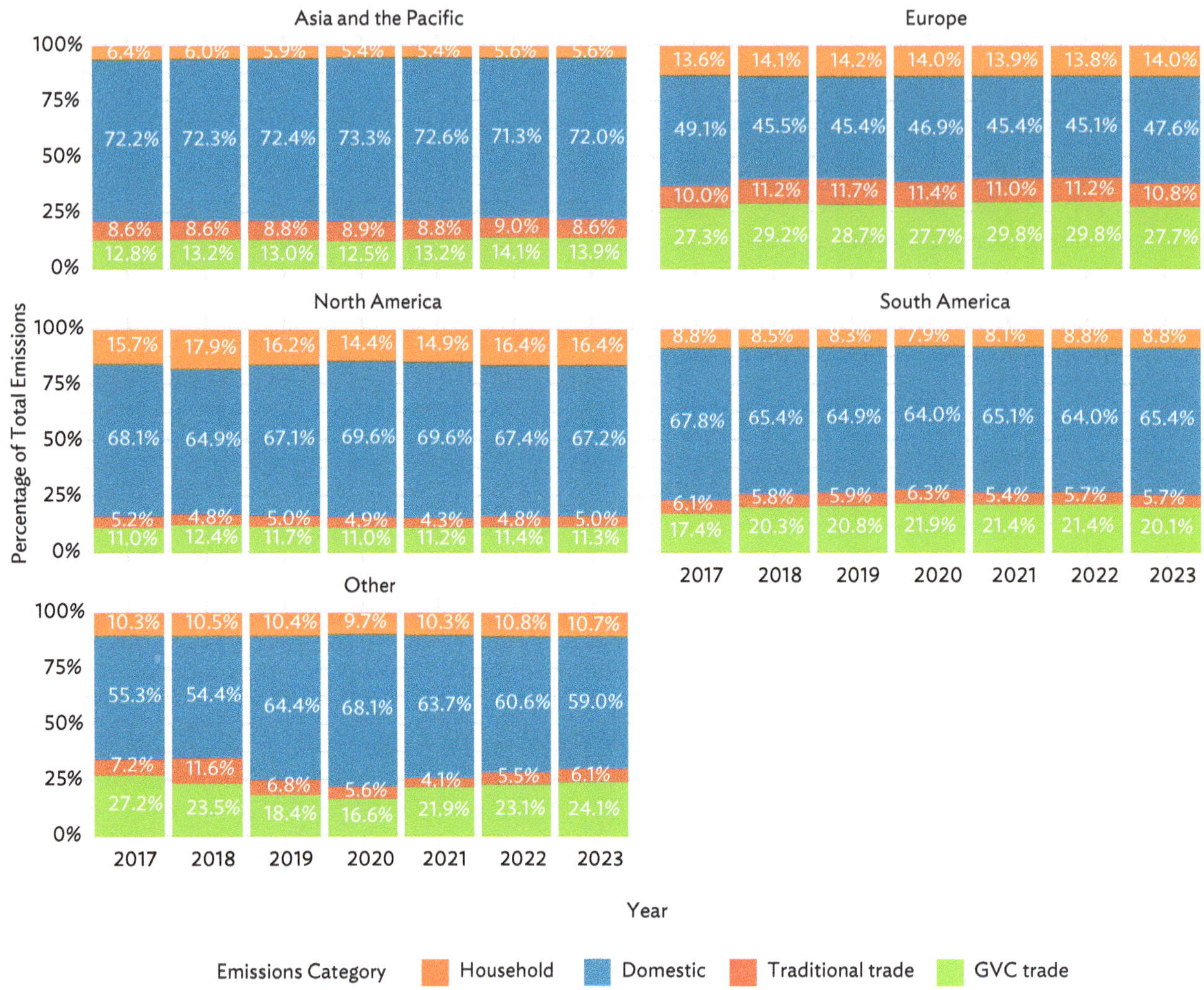

GVC = global value chains.

Source: Asian Development Bank analysis using multiregional input-output tables and environmentally extended multiregional input-output tables at https://kidb.adb.org/globalization (accessed January 2025).

From 2017 to 2023, economies worldwide exhibited varying trends in emissions from traditional trade compared to GVC trade (Figure 2.10). Although most economies experienced an increase in the pace of emissions from both types of trade, the acceleration was uneven, reflecting their different economic structures and levels of integration into global trade networks. Resource-intensive economies such as the Russian Federation, Brunei Darussalam, Armenia, the Lao People's Republic, and Kazakhstan continued to depend heavily on traditional trade, resulting in the related emissions rising at more than twice the rate of their GVC-related emissions.

Some economies managed to slow emissions in one trade category but increased the pace of emissions in the other, reflecting their economic dynamics and policy interventions.

Additionally, several high-income economies, such as Japan, Estonia, and Finland, successfully decelerated emissions from both traditional and GVC-related trade while maintaining trade growth for 2017–2023, indicating effective decarbonization strategies and efficiency improvements across their broader trade activities.

Figure 2.10: Change in Production-Based Emissions from Traditional Trade and Global Value Chains, 2017–2023 (%)

More economies in Asia and the Pacific saw stronger growth in GVC-related emissions than in traditional trade.

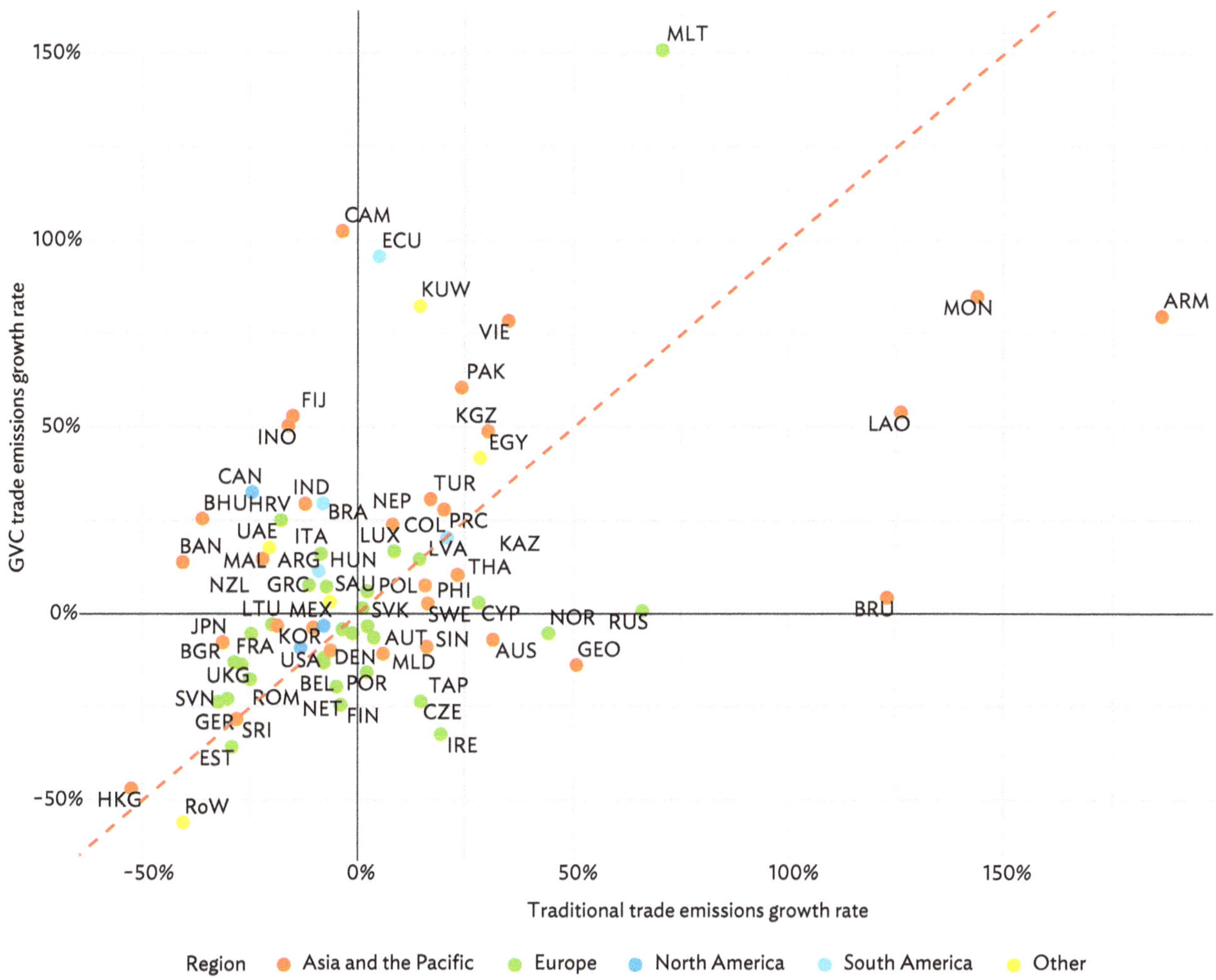

ARM = Armenia; AUS = Australia; AUT = Austria; BAN = Bangladesh; BEL = Belgium; BGR = Bulgaria; BHU = Bhutan; BRA = Brazil; BRU = Brunei Darussalam; CAM = Cambodia; CAN = Canada; PRC = People's Republic of China; COL = Colombia; CYP = Cyprus; CZE = Czech Republic; DEN = Denmark; ECU = Ecuador; EGY = Egypt; EST = Estonia; FIJ = Fiji; FIN = Finland; FRA = France; GEO = Georgia; GER = Germany; GRC = Greece; GVC = global value chain; HKG = Hong Kong, China; HRV = Croatia; HUN = Hungary; IND = India; INO = Indonesia; IRE = Ireland; ITA = Italy; JPN = Japan; KAZ = Kazakhstan; KOR = Republic of Korea; KGZ = Kyrgyz Republic; KUW = Kuwait; LAO = Lao People's Democratic Republic; LTU = Lithuania; LUX = Luxembourg; LVA = Latvia; MAL = Malaysia; MEX = Mexico; MLD = Maldives; MLT = Malta; MON = Mongolia; NEP = Nepal; NET = Netherlands; NOR = Norway; NZL = New Zealand; PAK = Pakistan; PHI = Philippines; POL = Poland; POR = Portugal; ROM = Romania; RoW = Rest of the World; RUS = Russian Federation; SAU = Saudi Arabia; SIN = Singapore; SPA = Spain; SRI = Sri Lanka; SVK = Slovak Republic; SVN = Slovenia; SWE = Sweden; SWI = Switzerland; TAP = Taipei,China; THA = Thailand; TUR = Türkiye; UAE = United Arab Emirates; UKG = United Kingdom; USA = United States; VIE = Viet Nam.

Source: Asian Development Bank analysis using multiregional input-output tables and environmentally extended multiregional input-output tables at https://kidb.adb.org/globalization (accessed January 2025).

Perspective 4: Applying Sector-Specific Characteristics to Emissions Reduction Strategies

Composite emissions totals do little to inform targeted initiatives.

Different gases vary significantly in their global warming potential and atmospheric lifetimes. Similarly, different economic sectors may be responsible for the majority of emissions of certain types of gases. This matrix of cause and effect requires a sophisticated data platform to deliver tailored insights that can inform sector-specific strategies for emissions reduction.

ADB's EE-MRIOT framework provides detailed sectoral insights enriched by two additional dimensions: (i) differentiating the type of gases emitted, and (ii) identifying the sources or physical processes responsible for emissions. These dimensions allow for targeted initiatives such as reducing reliance on high-emitting processes in energy generation, industrial production, and waste management.

EE-MRIOT analysis reveals that CO_2 made up 74% of global emissions in 2023, primarily released through fossil fuel combustion and energy use across all sectors (Figure 2.11). Methane, which is 34 times more potent than CO_2 in its ability to trap heat in the atmosphere over 100 years, followed at 19% and was primarily emitted from the agriculture and waste sectors. Although far more effective at trapping heat, methane remains in the atmosphere for a much shorter duration (about 12 years) compared to CO_2. Nitrous oxide, 298 times more powerful than CO_2 in its atmospheric warming effect and produced by agricultural practices such as the use of nitrate fertilizers, contributed an additional 5% to overall emissions. Other gases, such as hydrofluorocarbons, perfluorocarbons, sulfur hexafluoride, and nitrogen trifluoride were linked to refrigeration, air-conditioning, and electronics manufacturing (Shirai and Dang 2024).

Emissions trends call for a more nuanced view in developing environmental policies.

As energy systems gradually decarbonize, non-CO_2 emissions—particularly from agriculture, industries, and waste—continue to rise. These sectors, which are already responsible for most methane and nitrous oxide emissions, should become policy priorities as their emissions profiles remain largely unaffected by energy transitions focused on CO_2. However, agriculture and waste sectors currently receive less policy focus and investment than the carbon-intensive utilities and industrial sectors, such as refined fuels, mining, and metal production (UNFCCC 2024). This underscores the need for a broader emissions reduction agenda that includes comprehensive strategies targeting sources of non-CO_2 gases.

Figure 2.11: Emissions by Gas Types and Sector Groupings, 2023

Sectors have distinct emission profiles, with CO_2 dominating overall (except in a few key sectors).

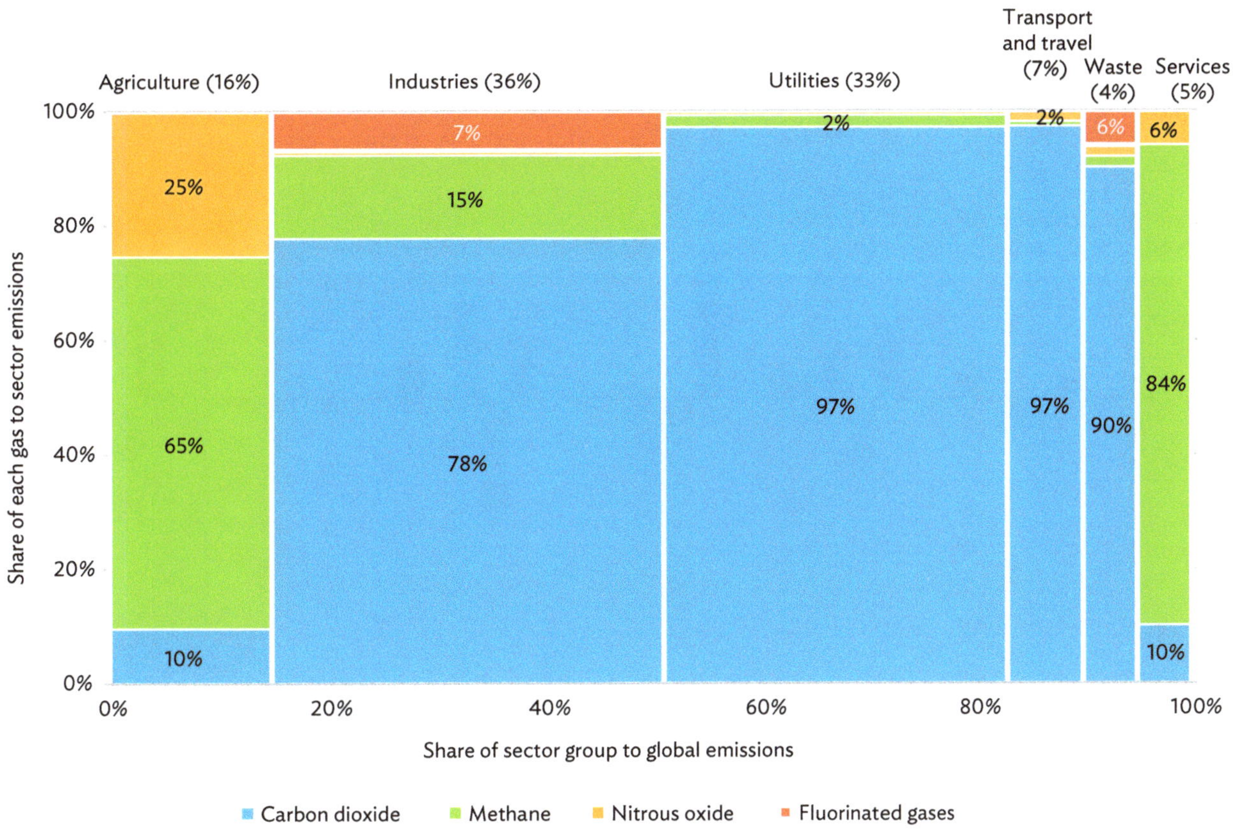

CO_2 = carbon dioxide.

Source: Asian Development Bank analysis using environmentally extended multiregional input-output tables at https://kidb.adb.org/globalization (accessed January 2025).

To effectively target strategies and accurately allocate budget resources, identifying trends in emissions by sectoral grouping and geographic locality is also particularly necessary (Figure 2.12). Targeted reduction of non-CO_2 emissions, especially methane from agriculture and waste, offers a cost-effective opportunity to achieve near-term climate and public health gains. Reducing methane emissions can curb global warming more rapidly due to the gas' high potency and short atmospheric lifespan, while also improving air quality and reducing health risks. However, advancing these efforts require improved data collection, monitoring systems, and innovative solutions to effectively capture the attention of policymakers. This is particularly relevant for emissions related to land use and land-use change, where reliable data on deforestation, soil degradation, and reforestation efforts remain scarce (Box 2.3). Strengthening monitoring systems and integrating land-use data into climate planning will be critical to ensure any neglected sources of emissions are addressed effectively and equitably.

Figure 2.12: Contribution to Global Rise in Emissions by Sectoral Grouping and Region, 2017–2023

Steady growth in agriculture and waste signals increased pressures beyond fossil fuel use.

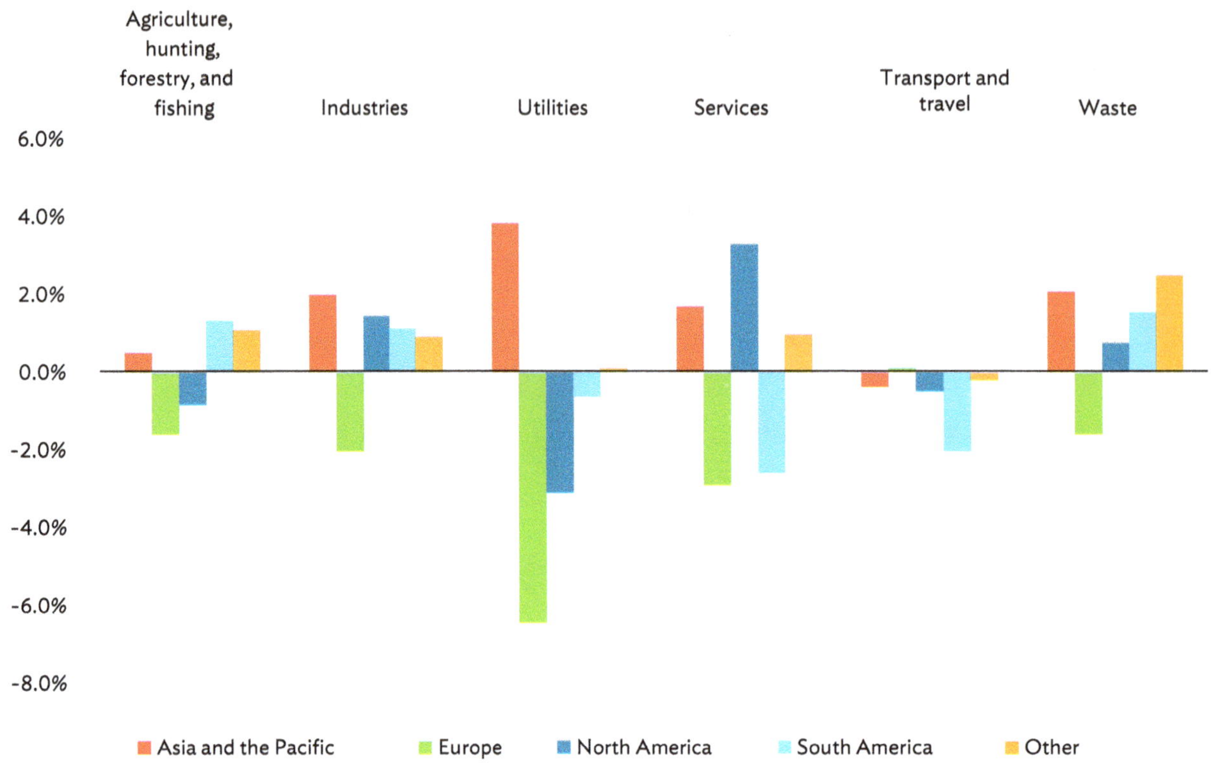

Source: Asian Development Bank analysis using environmentally extended multiregional input-output tables at https://kidb.adb.org/globalization (accessed January 2025).

Box 2.3: Challenges in Tracking Emissions from Land Use and Land-Use Changes

Land Use, Land-Use Change, and Forestry (LULUCF) is an activity grouping that refers to the emission and removal of greenhouse gases resulting from human activities related to land management, such as deforestation, afforestation, and agriculture.

Unlike other sources in emissions inventories, which only emit gases, LULUCF has the unique ability to also function as a "carbon sink," removing carbon dioxide (CO_2) from the atmosphere through processes such as forest regrowth or soil carbon storage in soil. This dual capacity makes LULUCF a critical component of global carbon accounting. Recognizing its importance, many economies have incorporated land-based emissions reductions into their environment-related strategies.

Accurate and comprehensive records on land-use change remain fragmented, outdated, or inconsistent, creating significant uncertainties in emissions estimates. For example, reported uncertainties in LULUCF emissions range from 12% in Colombia to 102% in Cambodia. These discrepancies undermine international confidence in emissions reduction claims, particularly for economies heavily reliant on forestry and agriculture for near-term emissions reduction (McGlynn et al. 2022).

From a conceptual standpoint, LULUCF also challenges the traditional boundaries of Air Emissions Accounts (AEAs). Frameworks such as the System of Environmental-Economic Accounting typically exclude emissions from unmanaged natural land, focusing only on emissions linked directly to economic activities. This exclusion raises concerns when emissions stem from natural environmental processes but are influenced by human interventions, for instance, peatland drainage. Determining whether such changes should be classified as human-induced or natural remains a methodological challenge.

Allocating LULUCF emissions to specific economic sectors further complicates its integration into emissions inventories. While emissions from agricultural land can often be linked directly to farming, those from seminatural areas are harder to allocate as they do not always align with economic production. For example, forest conservation provides a crucial environmental service, yet carbon sequestration is typically not classified as an economic function. Urban settlements introduce additional complexities as emissions stem from multiple overlapping activities, including residential, commercial, and industrial uses. Deforestation emissions are even more challenging to advocate when forest loss is not tied directly to forestry activities but to natural phenomena such as forest fires and droughts (Schenau 2023).

Despite these challenges, integrating LULUCF into AEAs remains crucial for achieving carbon neutrality and ensuring that land-use strategies contribute appropriately to global decarbonization efforts. This can lead to meaningful insights, such as the European Union experiencing a decline in net carbon removals from the LULUCF sector for 2018–2023, primarily due to increased wood harvesting and reduced carbon sequestration in ageing forests. As a result, the union is not on track to meet its 2030 net removal target (EEA 2024).

In Asia and the Pacific, where LULUCF emissions are not closely monitored, the sector offers a crucial pathway to carbon neutrality because improved land management, reforestation, and sustainable agricultural practices could significantly enhance carbon sequestration and offset emissions from other sectors. To fulfil this potential, economies must enhance data collection and monitoring, develop harmonized accounting methodologies, and strengthen international cooperation. By improving statistical accuracy and resolving conceptual ambiguities, the integration of LULUCF into AEAs can become a more effective tool in environmental policymaking, ultimately supporting long-term climate resilience goals.

As economies enhance their LULUCF data systems, there is growing potential to integrate these estimates into the Asian Development Bank's environmentally extended multiregional input-output tables. Such integration would enable a more comprehensive understanding of land-sector emissions and their role in economy-wide emission reduction strategies.

References:

European Environment Agency (EEA). 2024. Greenhouse Gas Emissions from Land Use, Land Use Change and Forestry in Europe. 31 October. https://www.eea.europa.eu/en/analysis/indicators/greenhouse-gas-emissions-from-land?activeAccordion=546a7c35-9188-4d23-94ee-005d97c26f2b.

McGlynn, E., S. Li, M. F. Berger, M. Amend, and K. L. Harper. 2022. Addressing Uncertainty and Bias in Land Use, Land Use Change, and Forestry Greenhouse Gas Inventories. *Climatic Change.* 10 January. https://doi.org/10.1007/s10584-021-03254-2.

Schenau, S. 2023. *LULUCF and SEEA CF.* United Nations System of Environmental Economic Accounting. https://seea.un.org/sites/seea.un.org/files/paper_schenau.pdf

Source: Asian Development Bank analysis.

References

Asian Development Bank (ADB). 2024. *Asian Economic Integration Report 2024: Decarbonizing Global Value Chains*. https://www.adb.org/publications/asian-economic-integration-report-2024.

Arto, I. and E. Dietzenbacher. 2014. Drivers of the Growth in Global Greenhouse Gas Emissions. *Environmental Science and Technology*. 48 (10). pp. 5388–5394. https://doi.org/10.1021/es5005347.

Boulding, K. E. 1966. The Economics of the Coming Spaceship Earth. In: H. Jarrett, ed., *Environmental Quality in a Growing Economy*. pp. 3–14. Resources for the Future and Johns Hopkins University Press.

Baumert, K. A., T. Herzog, and J. Pershing. 2005. *Navigating the Numbers: Greenhouse Gas Data and International Climate Policy*. World Resources Institute. http://pdf.wri.org/navigating_numbers.pdf.

Bashmakov, I.A. 2021. Greenhouse Gas Emissions Caused by Global Steel Industry: The Past, the Present and the Future. *Ferrous Metallurgy Bulletin of Scientific, Technical and Economic Information*. 77 (8). pp. 882–901. https://doi.org/10.32339/0135-5910-2021-9-1071-1086.

Cao, Z., L. Shen, A.N. Løvik, D.B. Müller, and G. Liu. 2017. Elaborating the History of Our Cementing Societies: An In-Use Stock Perspective. *Environmental Science & Technology*. 51 (19). pp. 11468–11475. https://doi.org/10.1021/acs.est.7b03077 .

Cherniwchan, J. 2017. Trade Liberalization and the Environment: Evidence from NAFTA and U.S. Manufacturing. *Journal of International Economics*. 105. pp. 130–149. https://doi.org/10.1016/j.jinteco.2017.01.005.

Copeland, B. R. and M. S. Taylor. 2004. Trade, Growth, and the Environment. *Journal of Economic Literature*. 42 (1). pp. 7–71.

Copeland, B. R., J.S. Shapiro, and M. S. Taylor. 2021. Globalization and the Environment. *NBER Working Paper*. No. 28797. National Bureau of Economic Research. http://www.nber.org/papers/w28797.

Dhakal, S., J. C. Minx, F. L. Toth, A. Abdel-Aziz, M. J. Figueroa Meza, K. Hubacek, I. G. C. Jonckheere, et al. 2022. Emissions Trends and Drivers (Chapter 2). In: A. R. Shukla, J. Skea, R. Slade, R. Fradera, M. Pathak, A. Al Khourdajie, M. Belkacemi, et al., eds, *Climate Change 2022: Mitigation of Climate Change*. Cambridge University Press. pp. 215–294. https://doi.org/10.1017/9781009157926.004

Fei, R. and B. Lin. 2016. Technology Gap and CO_2 Emission Reduction Potential by Technical Efficiency Measures: A Meta-Frontier Modeling for the Chinese Agricultural Sector. *Ecological Indicators*. 73. pp. 653-661. https://doi.org/10.1016/j.ecolind.2016.10.021.

Haberl, H., M. Schmid, W. Haas, D. Wiedenhofer, H. Rau, and V. Winiwarter. 2021. Stocks, Flows, Services and Practices: Nexus Approaches to Sustainable Social Metabolism. *Ecological Economics*. 182 (106949). https://doi.org/10.1016/j.ecolecon.2021.106949.

Hohmann, L., L. Xhaferi-Salihu, and R. Oliveras. 2023. *Fashion Industry Charter for Climate Action: Progress Report 2023*. United Nations Framework Convention on Climate Change. https://unfccc.int/sites/default/files/resource/Fashion%20Industry%20Charter%20For%20Climate%20Action%20Progress%20Report%202023.pdf.

Hubacek, K., K. Feng, J. C. Minx, S. Pfister, and N. Zhou. 2014. Teleconnecting Consumption to Environmental Impacts at Multiple Spatial Scales: Research Frontiers in Environmental Footprinting. *Journal of Industrial Ecology*. 18 (1). pp. 7–9. https://doi.org/10.1111/jiec.12082.

International Energy Agency (IEA). 2019. *Material Efficiency in Clean Energy Transitions*. Organisation for Economic Co-operation and Development. https://www.oecd.org/content/dam/oecd/en/publications/reports/2019/04/material-efficiency-in-clean-energy-transitions_c51a0e7a/aeaaccd8-en.pdf.

Karstensen, J., G. P. Peters, and R. M. Andrew. 2018. Trends of the EU's Territorial and Consumption-Based Emissions from 1990 to 2016. *Climate Change*, 151 (2). pp. 131–142, doi:10.1007/s10584-018-2296-x.

Leontief, W. 1970. Environmental Repercussions and the Economic Structure: An Input-Output Approach. *The Review of Economics and Statistics*. 52 (3). pp. 262–271. https://doi.org/10.2307/1926294.

Manju, G., K. O'Regan, and A. Holst. 2022. Digital Solutions Can Reduce Global Emissions by up to 20%. Here's How. *World Economic Forum*. 23 May 23. https://www.weforum.org/stories/2022/05/how-digital-solutions-can-reduce-global-emissions/

Meadows, D. H., D. L. Meadows, J. Randers, and W. W. Behrens III. 1972. *The Limits to Growth: A Report for the Club of Rome's Project on the Predicament of Mankind*. Universe Books.

Meng, J., J. Huo, Z. Zhang, Y. Liu, Z. Mi, D. Guan, and K. Feng. 2023. The Narrowing Gap in Developed and Developing Country Emission Intensities Reduces Global Trade's Carbon Leakage. *Nature Communications*. 14 (3775). https://doi.org/10.1038/s41467-023-39449-7.

Shapiro, J. S. 2016. Trade Costs, CO_2, and the Environment. *American Economic Journal: Economic Policy*. 8 (4). pp. 220–254. https://www.aeaweb.org/articles?id=10.1257/pol.20150168.

Tapio, P. 2005. Towards a Theory of Decoupling: Degrees of Decoupling in the EU and the Case of Road Traffic in Finland between 1970 and 2001. *Transport Policy*. 12 (2). pp. 137–151. https://doi.org/10.1016/j.tranpol.2005.01.001.

The Journal. 2025. Global Methane Emissions from Energy Are Around 80% Higher Than What Governments Are Reporting. 7 May . https://www.thejournal.ie/global-methane-emissions-from-energy-are-around-80-higher-than-what-governments-are-reporting-6697520-May2025/.

United Nations Environment Programme (UNEP). 2024. *Emissions Gap Report 2024: No More Hot Air .. Please!* DOI 10.59117/20.500.11822/46404

United Nations Framework Convention on Climate Change (UNFCCC). 2024. *Nationally Determined Contributions Under the Paris Agreement: Synthesis Report by the Secretariat* (FCCC/PA/CMA/2024/10). https://unfccc.int/process-and-meetings/the-paris-agreement/nationally-determined-contributions-ndcs/2024-ndc-synthesis-report.

Valayden, A. and D. Chabaud. 2024. Assessing the Evolution of Carbon Emissions of Large Companies: An Index-Based Approach. *Business and Society Review*. 129 (4). pp. 556-586. https://doi.org/10.1111/basr.12372.

Wang, Z. 2017. Measures of Participation in Global Value Chains and Global Business Cycles. *NBER Working Paper*. No. 23222. National Bureau of Economic Research. https://www.nber.org/papers/w23222.

Wiedenhofer, D., T. Fishman, C. Lauk, W. Haas, and F. Krausmann. 2019. Integrating Material Stock Dynamics into Economy-Wide Material Flow Accounting: Concepts, Modelling, and Global Application for 1900–2050. *Ecological Economics*. 156. pp. 121–133. https://doi.org/10.1016/j.ecolecon.2018.09.010.

Wiedmann, T. and M. Lenzen. 2018. Environmental and Social Footprints of International Trade. *Nature Geoscience*. 11. pp. 314–321. https://doi.org/10.1038/s41561-018-0113-9.

World Trade Organization (WTO). 2022. *World Trade Report 2022: Climate Change and International Trade*. https://www.wto.org/english/res_e/booksp_e/wtr22_e/wtr22_e.pdf

Yamano, N. and J. Guilhoto. 2020. CO_2 Emissions Embodied in International Trade and Domestic Final Demand: Methodology and Results Using the OECD Inter-Country Input-Output Database. *OECD Science, Technology and Industry Working Papers*. No. 2020/11. OECD Publishing, https://doi.org/10.1787/8f2963b8-en.

SECTION 3

Sectoral Analyses Through an Environmentally Extended Lens

Input-output analysis gives a detailed sectoral perspective to emissions sources.

While the analytical perspectives presented in Section 2 establish a framework for developing economic and environmental policies through the lenses of emissions intensity, global supply chains, and international trade, effective policymaking requires deeper sectoral analyses.

This section sorts the 35 economic accounting sectors in the Asian Development Bank's multiregional input-output tables (MRIOTs)[1] into six sectoral groupings: (i) Agriculture (including hunting, forestry, and fishing); (ii) Industries; (iii) Utilities; (iv) Transport and Travel; (v) Services; and (vi) Waste. It then provides insights into how these sectoral groupings contribute to the five broad emissions categories defined by the Intergovernmental Panel on Climate Change (IPCC)[2]. These categories are: (i) agriculture, forestry, and land use (AFOLU); (ii) industrial processes and product use; (iii) energy; (iv) waste; and (v) other sectors.

Industries and utilities remain the highest overall emitters and the heaviest users of energy.

The Industries[3] sectoral grouping was the largest contributor (35.6%) to total global emissions in 2023, with 72.5% of its direct (Scope 1) emissions originating from energy combustion (e.g., fuel burned in factories) rather than emissions from industrial processes and product use (Figure 3.1). However, the Utilities grouping was the heaviest

---

1 MRIOT sector categories reflect economic activities that are associated with these emissions. They disaggregate the emissions from each physical source across different sectors, providing insight into which parts of the economy are linked to specific emissions-generating processes.

2 Emissions sources refer to process-based activities, consistent with IPCC classifications, which describe the physical processes that generate greenhouse gas emissions (e.g., fuel combustion, industrial processes).

3 The industries grouping consists of the following sectors based on the MRIOT dataset: Mining, Food and Beverages, Textiles, Leather, Wood, Paper, Petroleum, Chemicals, Rubber and plastics, Nonmetals, Metals, Machinery, Electronics, Transport equipment, Other manufacturing, and Construction.

contributor of emissions from energy. Overall, energy-related emissions constituted 72% of total emissions across all sectors in 2023, underscoring the need for comprehensive and cross-sectoral energy strategies that address environmental risks[4].

In 2023, Industries generated the highest level of emissions at 17.1 gigatons of carbon dioxide equivalent ($GtCO_2e$), followed by the Utilities grouping at 15.8 $GtCO_2e$. Agriculture and Transport and Travel contributed 7.3 $GtCO_2e$ and 3.1 $GtCO_2e$, respectively, while Services and Waste were comparatively lower at 2.4 $GtCO_2e$ and 2.2 $GtCO_2e$. Each of these sectoral groupings faces unique challenges. Agriculture, which is a leading source of methane and nitrous oxide emissions (contributing 50% and 78% of total global emissions, respectively, in 2023), needs to balance food security for a growing population with emissions reduction. Industries and Services contend with growing demand and urbanization, while the Waste grouping struggles with rising consumer demand, and Utilities face the urgent need to decarbonize amid increasing electricity consumption.

Figure 3.1: Volume of Greenhouse Gas Emissions by Source and Sectoral Grouping, 2023

Energy as an emissions source constitute the biggest share of emissions across all the sectoral groupings, besides Agriculture and Waste.

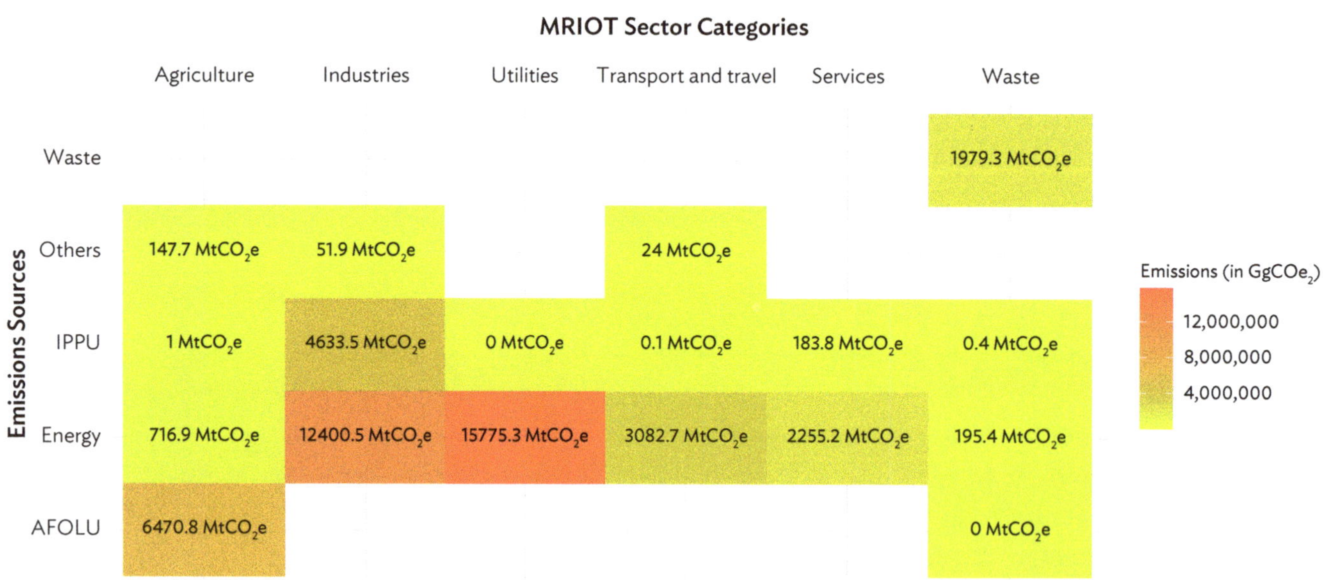

AFOLU = agriculture, forestry, and other land use; $GgCO_2e$ = gigagrams of carbon dioxide equivalent; IPPU = industrial processes and product use, MRIOT = multiregional input-output table, $MtCO_2e$ = megatons of carbon dioxide equivalent.

Note: Sectoral emissions figures exclude emissions from final demand activities and therefore do not sum to the global total.

Source: Asian Development Bank analysis using environmentally extended multiregional input-output tables at https://kidb.adb.org/globalization (accessed January 2025).

[4] Emission sources refer to process-based activities, consistent with IPCC classifications, which describe the physical processes that generate greenhouse gas emissions (e.g., fuel combustion, industrial processes. These are Agriculture, Forestry, and Land Use (AFOLU); Industrial Processes and Product Use (IPPU); Energy; Waste; and Other Sectors.

Trends in sectoral emissions were broadly consistent across regions from 2017 to 2023.

In 2020, the Industries and Utilities sectoral groupings saw emissions volumes fall in response to the coronavirus disease (COVID-19) pandemic, followed by a resurgence in 2021 (Figure 3.2). Transport and Travel experienced the steepest relative decline in emissions during the pandemic, and levels in 2023 were still below those of 2019. Conversely, total emissions from Services increased slightly at the height of the pandemic. Agriculture and Waste showed gradual increases in emissions with minimal year-to-year fluctuations.

The Services grouping's annual emissions rates displayed the widest regional variations, especially by South America and North America. South America's emissions rates in Utilities also fluctuated wildly across the years of the COVID-19 pandemic. By contrast, there was relatively little change to annual emissions rates in all regions for Agriculture and Waste.

Despite the challenges of rising emissions, each sectoral grouping has substantial potential for innovation, decarbonization, and emissions reductions. The following subsections explore sector-specific trends, drivers, and opportunities for environmental resilience, with a focus on the geographic and environmental characteristics of Asian Development Bank (ADB) member economies in Asia and the Pacific.

Figure 3.2: Emissions Volumes and Growth Rates by Sectoral Grouping and Region, 2017–2023

Emissions volumes and growth rates varied by sectoral grouping and geographic region through the years of the COVID-19 pandemic.

COVID-19 = coronavirus disease.

Note: Sectoral emissions figures exclude emissions from final demand activities and therefore do not sum to the global total.

Source: Asian Development Bank analysis using environmentally extended multiregional input-output tables at https://kidb.adb.org/globalization (accessed January 2025).

Sectoral Analysis: Agriculture

Figure 3.3: Key Analyses of Sectoral Emissions in Agriculture

3.3.a. Annual Emission Highlights

Emissions, 2017–2023

7.21

gigatons of CO_2e

Share, 2017–2023

15.6

% of global emissions

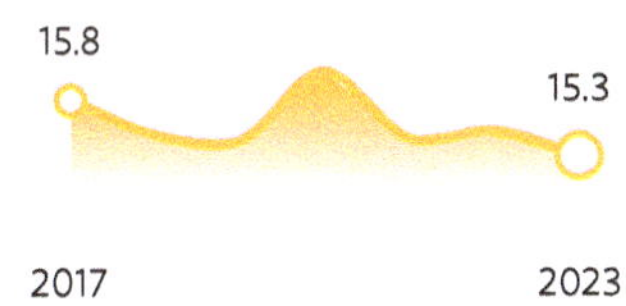

Intensity, 2017–2023

1.10

kilograms of CO_2e/$ of output

3.3.b. Sources of Emissions

Sectoral emissions by Source and Region, 2017–2023

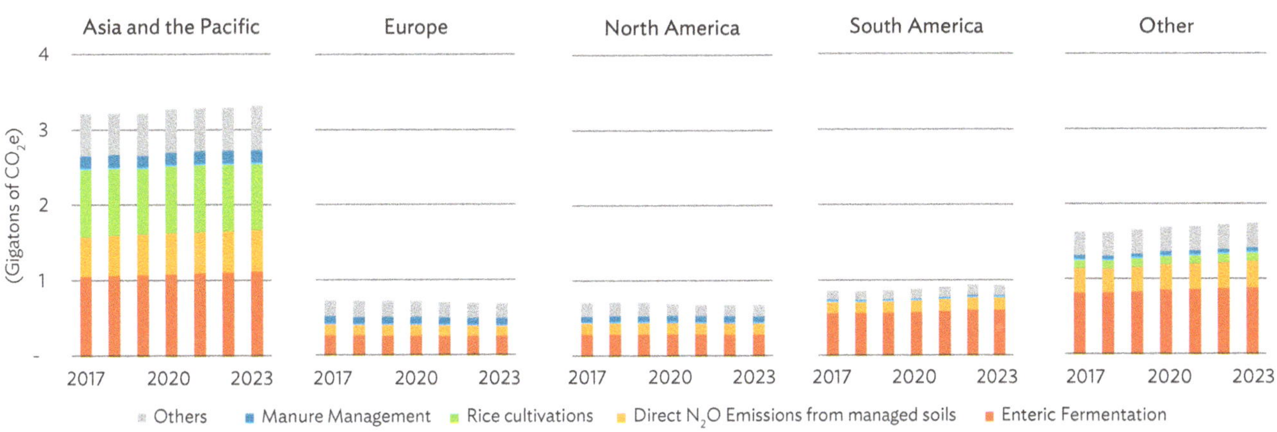

3.3.c. Key Trends and Drivers

Annual growth, 2017–2023

0.53 %

Decoupling index

0.89

Status:

Weak decoupling

Decomposition of emission changes, 2017–2023 (megatons of CO_2e)

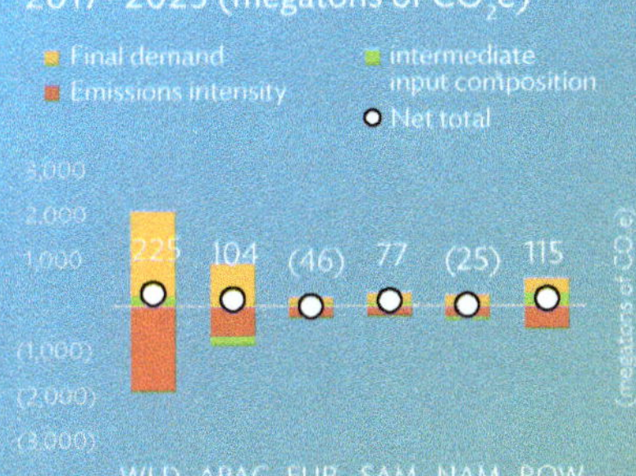

Leading contributors from Asia and the Pacific	Share to global sectoral emissions (%)	Growth, 2017–2023
People's Republic of China	14.0	▼
India	11.5	▲
Pakistan	3.7	▲
Indonesia	2.7	▼
Bangladesh	1.8	▲

3.3.d. Sectoral Decoupling Patterns

Sectoral changes in production-based emissions and GVA, 2017 and 2023

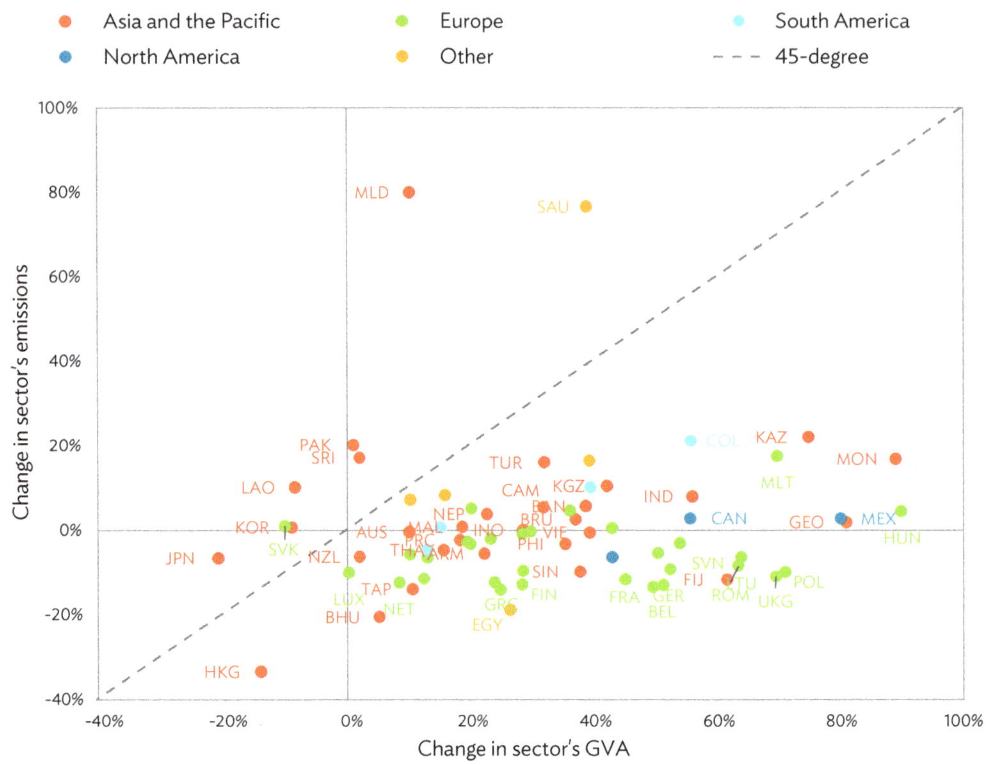

3.3.e. Value Chain Insights

Composition of total emissions footprint, 2023
(in megatons of CO_2-equivalent)

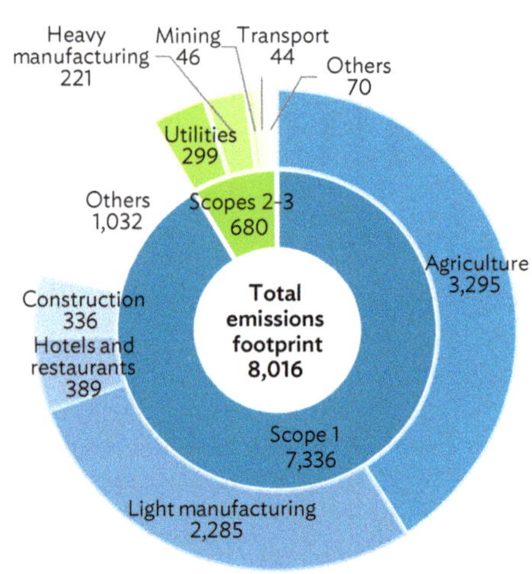

Shares of scopes 1–3 to total footprint, by Region, 2023

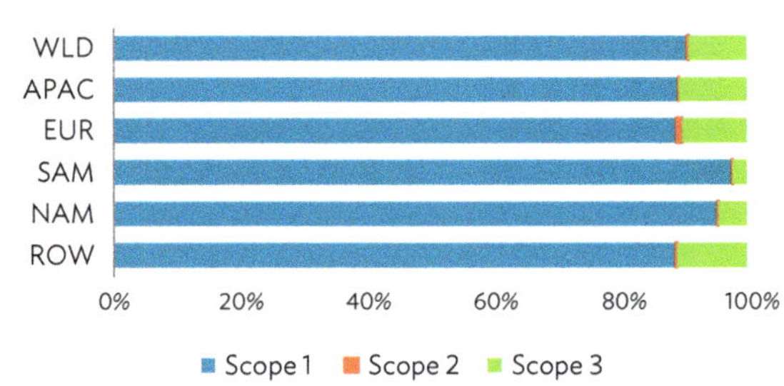

\$ = United States dollars, APAC = Asia and the Pacific, CO_2e = carbon dioxide equivalent, EUR = Europe, GVA = gross value-added, N_2O = nitrous oxide, NAM = North America, ROW = rest of the world, SAM = South America, WLD = world.

Note: As agriculture, hunting, forestry, and fishing are defined as a single sector in the Asian Development Bank's multiregional input-output tables (c1), the sources of emissions are broken down using the definitions of the Intergovernmental Panel on Climate Change.

Source: Asian Development Bank analysis using multiregional input-output tables and environmentally extended multiregional input-Output tables at https://kidb.adb.org/globalization (accessed March 2025).

The Asia and Pacific region is tightly integrated into global agrifood chains. On average, from 2017 to 2023, 45% of the region's agricultural exports traveled beyond its boundaries. Asia and the Pacific also imports large volumes of sectoral inputs from other regions, most notably from Brazil to the People's Republic of China (PRC), Viet Nam, and Japan. This two way trade cements the region's dual role as both a processing hub and a major consumption market. Such tight interdependence makes global agricultural trade highly sensitive to climate shocks that ripple through supply chains, induce price volatility, and disrupt longterm bilateral contracts (OECD and FAO 2025). Recent disruptions to global trade, such as the COVID-19 pandemic, the Russian invasion of Ukraine (a major agricultural supplier), and related supply chain turmoil, pushed the number of people facing acute food insecurity from 135 million in 2019 to 345 million across 82 economies by mid-2022 (World Bank 2022).

Agriculture is the largest source of global methane emissions. The Agriculture sectoral grouping includes hunting, forestry, and fishing. In 2023, methane emissions from livestock management, rice cultivation, biomass burning, and other sources accounted for approximately 65% of total agricultural emissions and 50% of global methane emissions. At the regional level, Asia and the Pacific contributed a significant share (36%) of global emissions from enteric fermentation and manure management, due to the region being home to some of the world's largest cattle populations, namely in India, the PRC, Pakistan, and Bangladesh (Ritchie et al. 2024). The region also accounts for 86% of global emissions from rice cultivation as it represents 90% of the world's cultivated rice area. More specifically, eight economies—India, the PRC, Bangladesh, Indonesia, Viet Nam, Thailand, Myanmar, and the Philippines—collectively account for 86% of the rice cultivation area worldwide (FAO 2024).

Of all nitrous oxide emissions globally, 78% are generated by agriculture. About 26% of agricultural emissions in 2023 came from the use of nitrogen-based fertilizers (liming and urea application), a practice especially prevalent in South Asia. However, overapplication of fertilizers results in nitrogen leaching into groundwater, which fuels algal blooms, oxygen-depleted dead zones, and mass fish kills. This threatens the fishing industry, a key player in food security, by depleting fish stocks and degrading marine habitats (Hawken 2017). Furthermore, soil management practices account for 21% of agricultural emissions and are a significant source of direct and indirect Nitrous Oxide emissions. The IPCC estimates that 5%–14% of AFOLU emissions stem from activities related to deforestation, land-use changes, and peatland degradation, with the global demand for agricultural products driving many exporting economies to alter their natural landscapes significantly, converting ecologically vital ecosystems into farmland. For instance, economies such as the PRC, Thailand, and Viet Nam have converted large swathes of mangrove forests into shrimp and prawn aquafarms, transforming them from carbon sinks to carbon sources (Chang 2022).

The sources of emissions and types of gases emitted can be influenced by geography. Emissions from agriculture stem not only from AFOLU activities, but also from related sources such as energy consumption and industrial process and product use (IPPU). For instance, economies such as Singapore; Hong Kong, China; and Brunei Darussalam exhibit a higher proportion of energy-related CO_2 emissions as geographic conditions constrain major agricultural activities in these economies. On the other hand, Maldives' agricultural emissions are largely CO_2 from fuel used in fishing vessels, rather than being methane or nitrous oxide emissions.

Growth in agricultural emissions exhibits significant disparities across regions and economies. These disparities reflect variations in production systems, land-use practices, and economic development. Asia and the Pacific contributed to 44% of global agricultural emissions from 2017 to 2023, making it the largest regional contributor, growing at an average rate of 3.2%. Meanwhile, sectoral emissions from Europe and North America declined by 6.4% and 3.6%, respectively, over 2017–2023. Some economies have significant dependence on agriculture as a percentage of their gross domestic product (GDP), namely Pakistan (23%), the Lao People's Democratic Republic (16.1%), and the Kyrgyz Republic (9.3%): this compares to the global average of 4%. These economies face substantial challenges in balancing environmental objectives with economic reliance on agriculture. Conversely, a number of agriculture-dependent economies in Asia, including Nepal (21.2%), Cambodia (17.1%), and Viet Nam (12%), have achieved relative decoupling as economic growth outpaced rises in emissions.

While new technologies can lower emissions intensities, demand remains a critical factor. Structural decomposition analysis shows that, globally, technological innovations led to lower emissions intensities in 2023. Without these reductions, total agricultural emissions would have been 5.4% higher than the level actually emitted in 2023. However, higher intermediate and final demand for agricultural products negated the decreases in emissions intensities, which were not enough to offset the emissions generated to meet the additional demand. Therefore, maintaining sustainable growth in agriculture supply chains, coupled with a shift in consumption patterns, is crucial to reducing agricultural emissions.

The vast majority of agricultural emissions are passed on to supply chain partners. Since agriculture mostly supplies raw materials to downstream sectors, its emissions are effectively passed on and embedded in other industries' supply chains. Notably, in 2023, 78% of agriculture's direct emissions supported downstream agri-food industries such as food manufacturing and restaurants, while about 5% were linked to construction through forestry products. As these direct emissions are fundamentally driven by demand from the food and beverages sector, it is important to focus on strategies that address food security through sustainable production and consumption.

Environmental policies should account for involvement in agricultural supply chains. Effective policymaking in agriculture requires comprehensive strategies to address environmental impacts inherent in agricultural supply chains. ADB's environmentally extended multiregional input-output tables provide a direct link between agricultural production and its significant contribution to direct AFOLU emissions, highlighting agriculture's disproportionate share in methane and nitrous oxide emissions. Robust data generated at the economy-sector level allow policymakers to evaluate and refine agricultural, agri-environmental, and agri-production policies; align sectoral growth with lower emissions intensities; and trace the environmental footprint at every stage of agricultural production. This granularity is essential for proposing sustainable practices that strengthen climate resilience and global food security.

Sectoral Analysis: Industries

Figure 3.4: Key Analyses of Sectoral Emissions in Industries

3.4.a. Annual Emission Highlights

Emissions, 2017–2023

16.43

gigatons of CO_2e

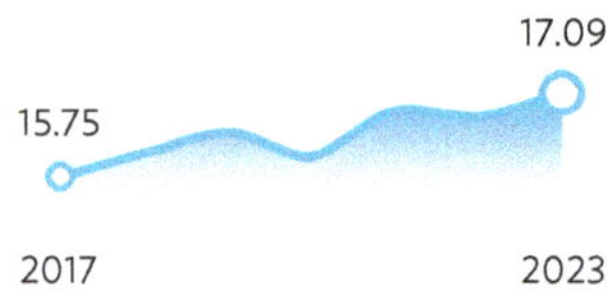

Share, 2017–2023

35.5

% of global emissions

Intensity, 2017–2023

0.22

kilograms of CO_2e/$ of output

3.4.b. Sources of Emissions

Sectoral emissions by Source and Region, 2017–2023

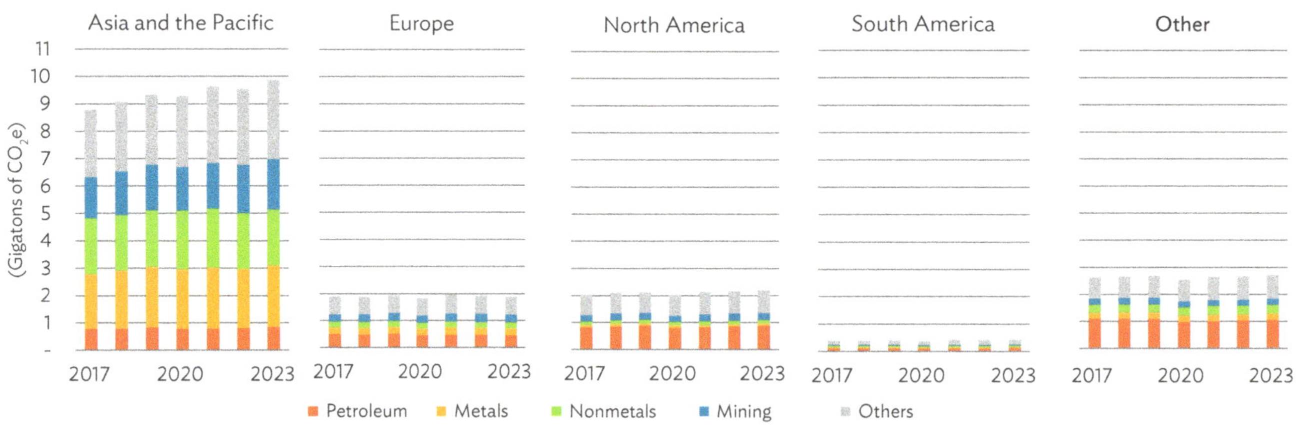

3.4.c. Key Trends and Drivers

Annual growth, 2017–2023

1.42 %

Decoupling index

0.68

Status:

Weak decoupling

Decomposition of emission changes, 2017–2023 (megatons of CO_2e)

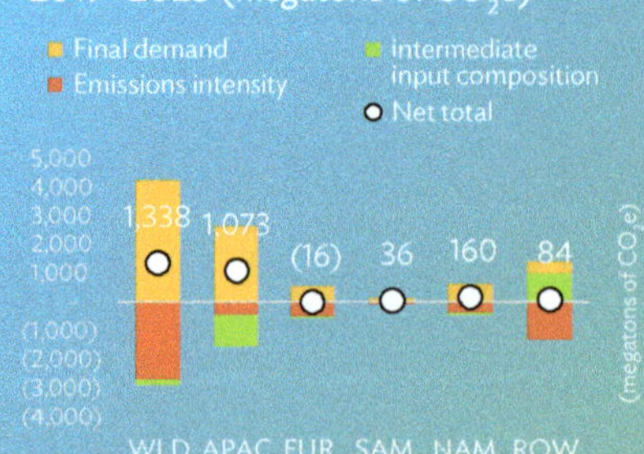

Leading contributors from Asia and the Pacific	Share to global sectoral emissions (%)	Growth, 2017–2023
People's Republic of China	37.2	▲
India	7.1	▲
Indonesia	3.0	▲
Japan	1.7	▼
Republic of Korea	1.2	▼

3.4.d. Sectoral Decoupling Patterns

Sectoral changes in production-based emissions and GVA, 2017 and 2023

3.4.e. Value Chain Insights

Composition of total emissions footprint, 2023
(in megatons of CO_2-equivalent)

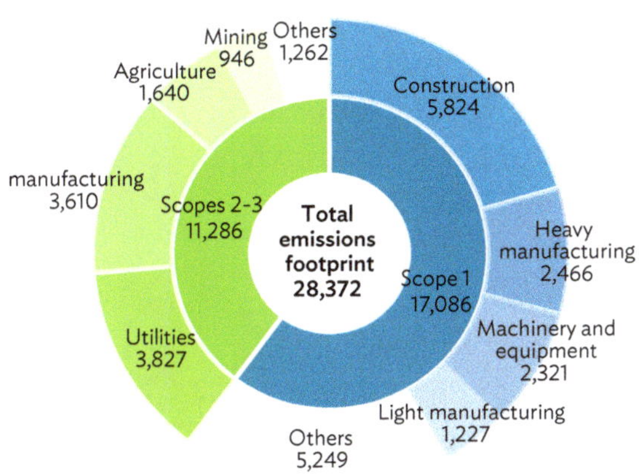

Shares of scopes 1–3 to total footprint, by Region, 2023

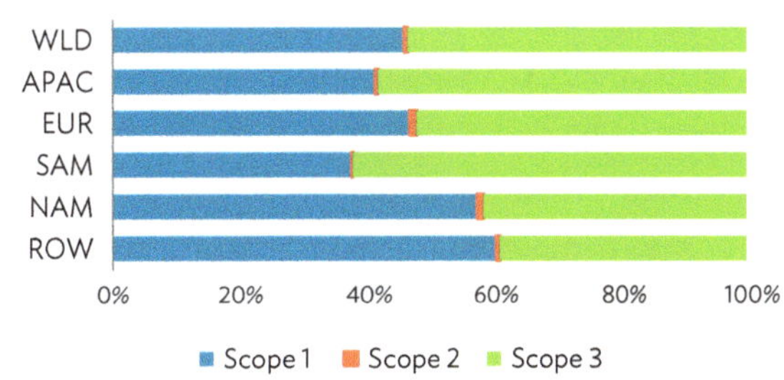

\$ = United States dollars, APAC = Asia and the Pacific, CO_2e = carbon dioxide equivalent, EUR = Europe, GVA = gross value-added, NAM = North America, ROW = rest of the world, SAM = South America, WLD = world.

Note: The industries grouping consists of the following sectors in the Asian Development Bank's multiregional input-output tables: Mining, Food and Beverages, Textiles, Leather, Wood, Paper, Petroleum, Chemicals, Rubber and plastics, Nonmetals, Metals, Machinery, Electronics, Transport equipment, Other manufacturing, and Construction. Sectors with the highest emissions highlighted above.

Source: Asian Development Bank analysis using multiregional input-output tables and environmentally extended multiregional input-output tables at https://kidb.adb.org/globalization (accessed March 2025).

Industries produce many of the materials that underpin modern life. From cement and steel to plastics and refined fuels, the products of industry have a pervasive impact on modern living. Industries are also responsible for the mass production of "green" technologies such as solar panels, wind turbines, and electric vehicles. Just as industrial growth has long underpinned development in many economies, these green technologies can create consumption patterns that support both economic progress and a low-carbon future. The Industries sectoral grouping spans mining, manufacturing, and construction—activities that rely on energy- and resource-intensive processes to transform raw materials. As the largest contributor to carbon emissions, the Industries grouping also holds significant potential for emissions reductions. Such reductions are especially relevant for the industrial production of green technologies.

Asia and the Pacific plays a central role in shaping global industrial emissions. From 2017 to 2023, the Asia and Pacific region was responsible for 58% of global industrial emissions. This reflects the region's position as the world's leading manufacturing base, driven by its integration into global value chains and the outsourcing of production by advanced economies. In 2023, Asia and the Pacific's top industrial emitters were the PRC (emitting 4.5 times as much as the next-highest economy), India, Indonesia, and Japan. Furthermore, 40% of ADB's member economies in the region showed no decoupling on industrial emissions, with only Australia; Kazakhstan; New Zealand; and Taipei,China achieving absolute decoupling. Conversely, all North American and European economies achieved either absolute or relative decoupling on industrial emissions.

The Industries sectoral grouping remains the largest source of global emissions. From 2017 to 2023, industries emitted an average of 16.4 $GtCO_2e$ per year, accounting for approximately one-third of global emissions and far ahead of all other sectoral groupings apart from Utilities. Within the Industries grouping, the heaviest-emitting economic sectors included petroleum refining, nonmetallic mineral production (such as cement and glass), metal production, and mining and quarrying. In 2023, most industrial emissions came from energy use and transformation, which accounted for 73% of direct emissions. The rest originated from industrial processes and product use, particularly cement production (9%) and chemical manufacturing (6%). These process-related emissions are difficult to eliminate through energy-efficient technologies or fuel-switching alone, as they are intrinsic to how modern materials are made. For instance, even if cement kilns run entirely on clean energy, the process emissions from limestone calcination would still occur, requiring additional measures such as carbon capture and storage (IEA 2018). Emissions from many resource-intensive industries are hard to abate because they are inherent to core industrial processes, requiring long-term technological solutions that may be complex or costly to deploy.

Carbon dioxide dominated the industrial grouping's emissions profile at 77%. However, emissions mixes also varied by economy. For example, in Mongolia, methane accounts for 87% of industrial emissions, reflecting the economy's reliance on extractive industries such as coal mining that release methane over CO_2-intensive manufacturing like cement or metal production. Furthermore, industrial activities accounted for 89% of global fluorinated-gas emissions, making the sector a key focus for tackling these high-impact pollutants. Thus, emissions mixes also varied by economy. It is important to identify the emissions makeup of an economy when designing emissions reduction policies.

Value chain emissions significantly expand the scope of environmental initiatives targeting industrial activities. With supply chain emissions included, total emissions from the Industries sectoral grouping reached 28.3 $GtCO_2e$ in 2023, accounting for 59% of total global emissions. On average, Scope 1 emissions accounted for about 60% of each industrial sector's total emissions footprint, while the remaining 40% originated from supply-chain-related (Scope 3) emissions. However, the specific shares varied based on sector characteristics. Energy- and process-intensive upstream sectors—such as mining, cement and steel production, and petroleum refining—typically discharged more than 70% of their emissions on site (Scope 1). Downstream sectors—such as textiles, electronics, machinery, and construction—carried larger upstream (Scope 3) emissions embedded in the goods and services they purchased.

Emissions flows across sectors reflect how value chains are structured. Direct emissions from one sector tend to flow to closely connected sectors that transform or use those same materials. For example, most emissions from the food-processing sector flow into the restaurant services sector; emissions from the textiles sector flow into the apparel manufacturing sector; and emissions from the wood and rubber sector flow into the construction sector. These patterns illustrate how emissions accumulate along the value chain rather than within one sector alone. Meanwhile, the nature of upstream dependencies also differs across economic sectors. In light manufacturing sectors—such as food, paper, and apparel—most of the supply chain footprints come from agricultural inputs and electricity use. In contrast, heavy industries—such as chemicals, metals, nonmetals, and construction—carry significant upstream emissions from extractive industries and energy-intensive processes such as steelmaking and refining.

The Industries sectoral grouping offers significant opportunities for innovation. Despite its challenges, the Industries grouping plays a growing role in producing environmental goods and enabling technologies that support decarbonization across the other sectoral groupings and their individual sectors. Conservative estimates using ADB's MRIOT framework show that the global market for green products reached $492 billion in 2023 (at 2023 prices) and is growing at an annual rate that outpaces global economic growth (Box 3.1 and Appendix 3). With economies in Asia and the Pacific emerging as key players in green manufacturing, the region is well-positioned to leverage its role in global trade to support environmentally sustainable supply chains and accelerate the adoption of green technologies worldwide.

Box 3.1: Measuring the Supply Chain for Green Products

Assessing "green" industries is essential in tracking structural changes in the economy and evaluating policies for environmental resilience and sustainable growth. However, defining "green industry" remains a challenge because current classifications often miss cross-cutting innovations, enabling services, and process improvements. Moreover, it is not sufficient to identify green products in isolation because other nongreen industries may also play critical roles in their value chains. Additionally, products with both environmental and non-environmental uses complicate classification.

To address these issues, the Asian Development Bank (ADB) used its input-output framework to measure direct and indirect contributions to the production of green products. This exercise identified 1,062 unique green products from 14 existing environmental product lists, leading to a narrow set of 12 most frequently listed environmental products based on the 2017 Harmonized System (HS) codes. These 12 products can be classified into renewable energy generation[a], pollution control[b], and energy efficiency[c] products.

The product lists served as the basis for a trade-weighted mapping (by world-export shares) to estimate the share of industrial output linked to the production of environmental goods. This study adapts the United Nations Industrial Development Organization's Green Industrial Performance (GIP) Index methodology (de Alba and Todorov 2022) with key refinements. The exercise draws on United Nations Statistical Division BACI trade data for exports, the United Nations Industrial Development Organization's Industrial Statistics Database for output, and the International Labour Organization's labor force survey for employment. These data were combined to disaggregate ADB's multiregional input-output sectors into green and nongreen production prior to value chain accounting.

Using an input-output approach, the global green products market (based on the 12 most frequently listed environmental products) was valued at $492 billion in 2023, supporting 15 million jobs. Asia and the Pacific contributed $417 billion—about 1.1% of the region's gross domestic product (GDP)–and 13.4 million jobs. The region's green economy grew at 6.6% annually, outpacing global green growth (6.4%) and GDP growth (4.5%). Asia and the Pacific is also in a strong position to meet growing global demand for the critical minerals needed in the energy transition. Globally, the contribution of green products to GDP increased from 0.4% in 2017 to 0.5% in 2023. These statistics highlight the growing significance of green industries in driving environmental resilience and sustainable development, particularly in Asia and the Pacific.

[a] Wind: towers and lattice masts (730820), Electric generating sets - wind-powered (HS 850231); Hydro and tidal: Hydraulic turbines and water wheels (HS 841011), its parts (HS 841090), AC generators (HS 850164); Solar: instantaneous or storage water heaters, non-electric (HS 841919), parts of apparatus for heating or cooling liquids or gases (HS 841990), parts of electrical transformers, static converters, and inductors (HS 850490), boards, panels, consoles, desks, cabinets, and other bases for electric control or distribution of electricity (HS 853710), photosensitive semiconductor devices, photovoltaic cells including solar cells, whether or not assembled into modules or made up into panels, light emitting diodes (HS 854140)

[b] Auxiliary plant for use with steam or vapor generating boilers (HS 840410)

[c] Automatic regulating or controlling instruments and apparatus (HS 903289)

References:

de Alba, J. and V. Todorov. 2022. Measuring and Benchmarking the Green Industrial Performance of Countries and Economies: the GIP Index. *Inclusive and Sustainable Industrial Development Working Paper Series.* No. 1. United Nations Industrial Development Organization.

Source: Asian Development Bank analysis.

Sectoral Analysis: Utilities

Figure 3.5: Key Analyses of Sectoral Emissions in Utilities

3.5.a. Annual Emission Highlights

Emissions, 2017–2023

15.06

gigatons of CO_2e

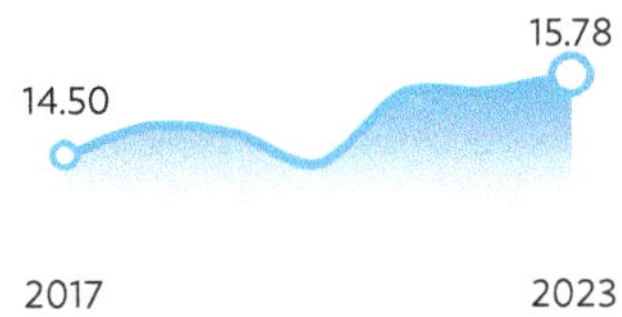

Share, 2017–2023

32.6

% of global emissions

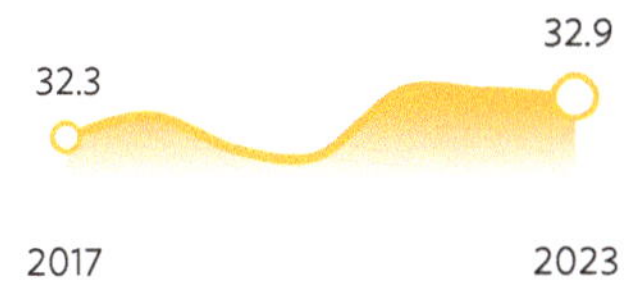

Intensity, 2017–2023

2.47

kilograms of CO_2e/$ of output

3.5.b. Sources of Emissions

Sectoral emissions by Source and Region, 2017–2023

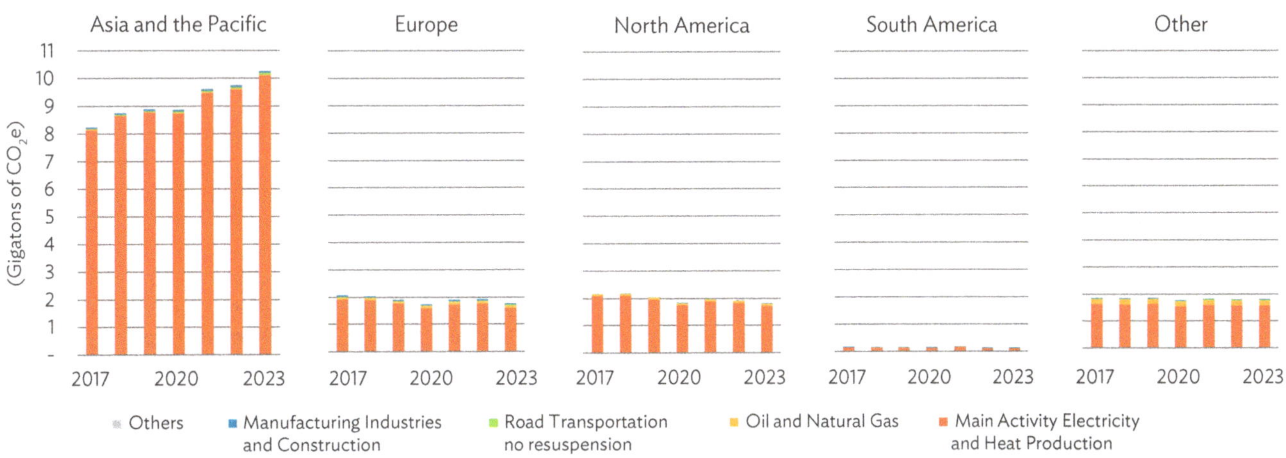

3.5.c. Key Trends and Drivers

Annual growth, 2017–2023

1.47 %

Decoupling index

0.78

Status:

Weak decoupling

Decomposition of emission changes, 2017–2023 (megatons of CO_2e)

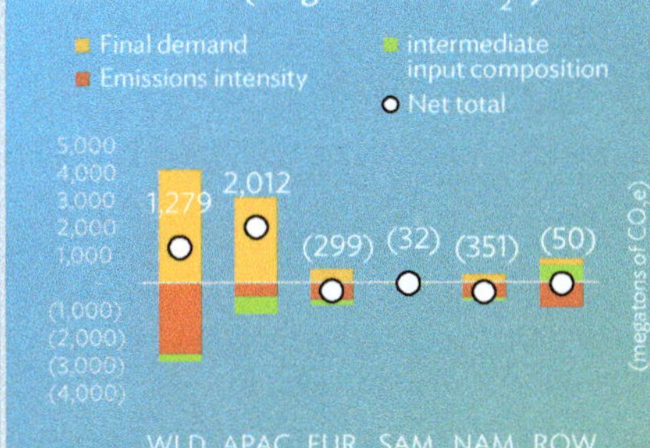

Leading contributors from Asia and the Pacific	Share to global sectoral emissions (%)	Growth, 2017–2023
People's Republic of China	41.9	▲
India	9.0	▲
Japan	2.6	▼
Indonesia	1.8	▲
Republic of Korea	1.6	▼

3.5.d. Sectoral Decoupling Patterns

Sectoral changes in production-based emissions and GVA, 2017 and 2023

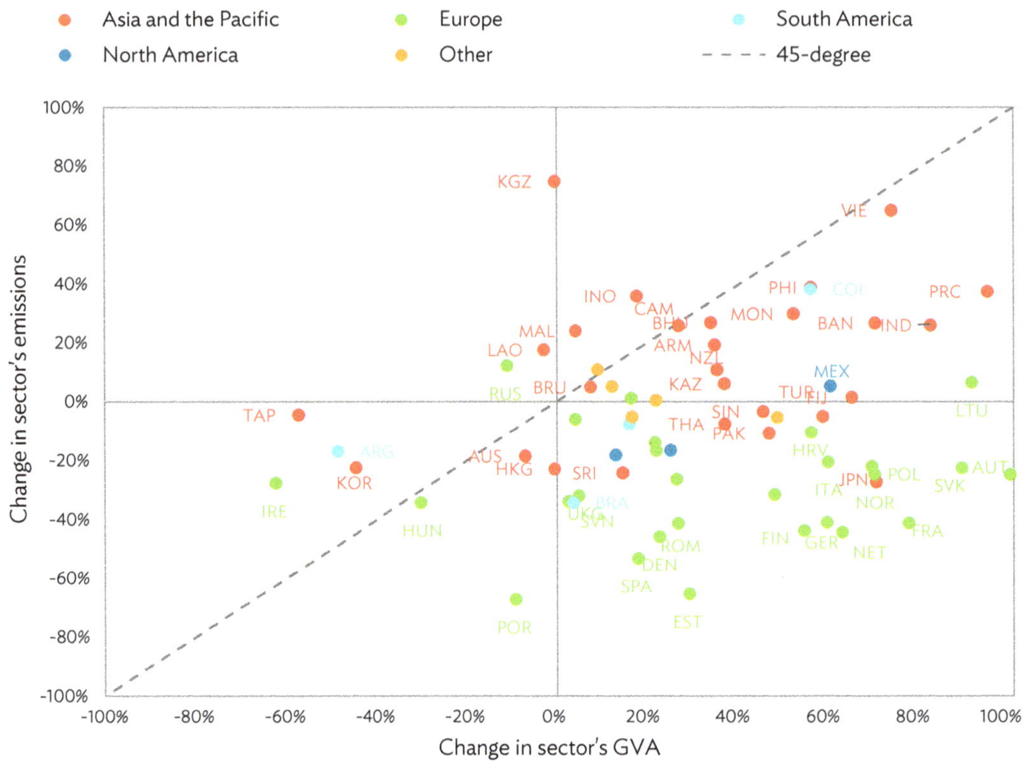

3.5.e. Value Chain Insights

Composition of total emissions footprint, 2023

(in megatons of CO_2-equivalent)

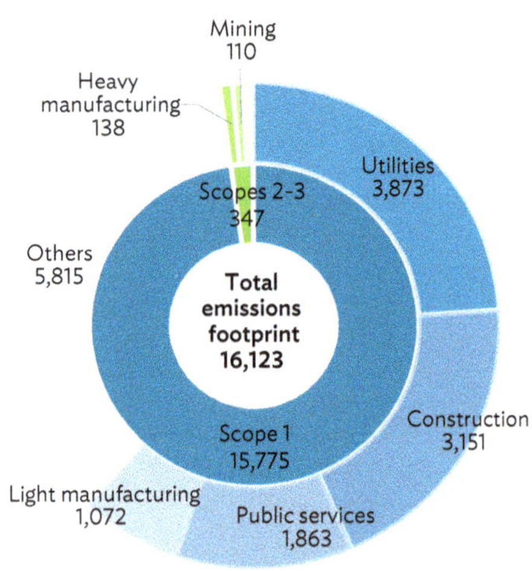

Shares of scopes 1–3 to total footprint,

by Region, 2023

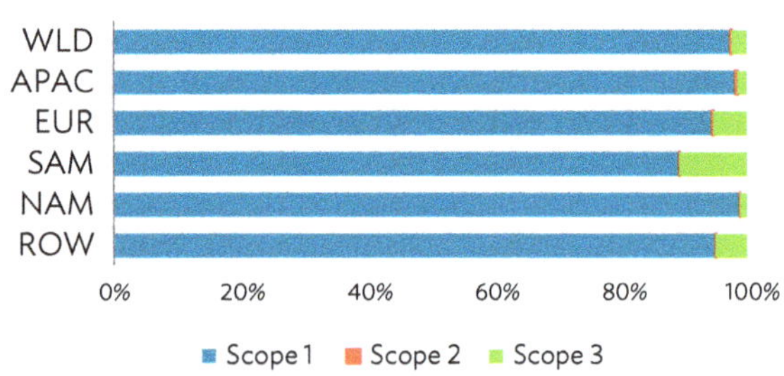

\$ = United States dollars, APAC = Asia and the Pacific, CO_2e = carbon dioxide equivalent, EUR = Europe, GVA = gross value-added, NAM = North America, ROW = rest of the world, SAM = South America, WLD = world.

Note: As utilities are a single sector in the Asian Development Bank's multiregional input-output tables (c17), the sources of emissions are broken down using the definitions of Intergovernmental Panel on Climate Change.

Source: Asian Development Bank analysis using multiregional input-output tables and environmentally extended multiregional input-output tables at https://kidb.adb.org/globalization (accessed March 2025).

The Asia and Pacific region plays a crucial role in the global energy transition and trade. The region produces nearly 70% of the materials needed to generate cleaner energy (KPMG 2024). In particular, the PRC is the world's leading producer of refined cobalt, lithium, and graphite, which are core inputs to producing photovoltaic cells used for solar panels. Enhanced regional cooperation could facilitate further adoption of clean technologies, prevent asymmetric carbon pricing, and foster sustainable energy transitions. Notably, Asia and the Pacific has outpaced the rest of the world in transitioning to renewables, with renewable energy generation in the region growing by 9.6% from 2017 to 2022, driven by solar thermal and biodiesel use. Effective strategies for emissions reductions in the Utilities sectoral grouping therefore require examination of not only the region's energy mix but also the underlying structure of sectors dependent on utilities (Box 3.2). These strategies should consider electricity demand for intermediate uses (such as construction and heavy manufacturing) as well as final consumption across residential, commercial, and public services (IEA 2024a).

Energy use remains the bedrock of economic prosperity. Energy is fundamental to economic growth, powering industries, services, and households the world over. Global electricity access[5] rose from 73.2% in 1992 to 91.6% in 2023 (World Bank 2024) and continued economic growth and urbanization have experts predicting energy demand will almost double by 2030 (ADB 2025a). Coal remained the primary source of global electricity generation at 36%, followed by natural gas at 22%, and hydropower at 15% (WEB 2022)[6]. In 2023, utilities generated 15.06 $GtCO_2e$ of emissions, accounting for approximately 32% of all emissions generated. Assessing data from 2017 to 2023, CO_2 constituted 97% of sectoral emissions as most energy utilities continued to be highly dependent on fossil fuels.

Of all utilities-related emissions, 97% were concentrated within Scope 1. By region, in 2023 North America had the highest proportion of direct (Scope 1) emissions at 98.9%, followed closely by Asia and the Pacific at 98.3%. Energy produced in these regions—and specifically in the United States, the PRC, and India—was directly consumed within the respective regions, without long-distance transportation and grid changes. South America had comparatively lower direct emissions at 89.4%, reflecting higher contributions from hydropower (which has low on-site combustion) and other upstream processes. However, even though the Utilities grouping generated mostly Scope 1 emissions, it is important to note that other economic sectors saw high levels of indirect

---

5 Using the International Energy Agency's definition of electricity access (https://www.iea.org/articles/defining-energy-access-2020-methodology), defined as "a household having reliable and affordable access to both clean cooking facilities and to electricity, which is enough to supply a basic bundle of energy services initially, and then an increasing level of electricity over time to reach the regional average". This energy access definition serves as a benchmark to measure progress towards goal Sustainable Development Goal 7.1 and as a metric for this report's forward-looking analysis. By defining access to modern energy services at the household level, it is recognized that some other categories are excluded, such as electricity access to businesses and public buildings crucial to economic and social development, e.g., schools and hospitals.

6 Latest available data for the energy balance: to be updated for 2023 in the next release.

(Scope 2 and Scope 3) emissions due to their use of energy: approximately 49% in indirect emissions for public services and other services, 20% for construction energy-related emissions, and 7% for light manufacturing.

Energy demand and emissions intensities can be skewed by individual economies. While the COVID-19 pandemic disrupted energy production and consumption in 2020, global demand for electricity quickly rebounded. Global emissions from utilities increased by 5% from 2019 to 2023, outpacing growth rates prior to the pandemic (IEA 2024b). Asia and the Pacific accounted for much of this resurgence, with electricity demand in the region rising 4.8% from 2022 to 2023. The PRC accounted for nearly 70% of this increased demand, driven by its ongoing industrial electrification and rapid growth in electric vehicle charging (IEA 2024b). The PRC's utilities emissions climbed 37% from 2017 to 2023, reaching 6.6 $GtCO_2e$ or about 42% of sectoral emissions globally. Structural decomposition analysis confirms the economy's dominant influence on growth in emissions intensity and rises in total emissions. Excluding the PRC, Asia and the Pacific's emissions intensity declined by 23%, a significant improvement compared to the 6% reduction when the PRC is included. Moreover, without the PRC's contribution total emissions rose by only 6%, rather than 24%, underscoring the disproportionate influence of the PRC on the region's overall emissions profile.

While other regions make progress on decoupling, issues persist for Asia and the Pacific. Increased demand for utilities from 2017 to 2023 was primarily met by clean energy in the form of renewables and low-emission fuels (IEA 2024b). All regions of the world, besides Asia and the Pacific and the Russian Federation, saw either absolute or relative decoupling on utilities emissions. However, the result in the Russian Federation can be at least partly attributed to structural changes caused by shifting trade relations with Europe in oil and gas and by increasing domestic demand. In Asia and the Pacific, 30% of economies in the region exhibited absolute decoupling, 37% relative decoupling, and 33% no decoupling on utilities emissions. For instance, New Zealand, which grew its share of renewable energy from 82% in 2017 to 87% in 2022, achieved only relative decoupling. Even Nepal, powered entirely by renewable energy[7], had not decoupled its utilities emissions from economic output.

Asia and the Pacific faces significant challenges when moving towards renewable energy production as an alternative to carbon-intensive sources. Heavy investments in fossil fuels, especially in coal, limit the ability of many economies to invest in alternative energy sources. This creates an infrastructure lock-in, moving away from which can result in severe financial losses. Additionally, underdeveloped financial markets, inflexible agreements, and lack of investment scalability in emerging markets and developing economies hinder the integration of renewable energy sources (IEA 2024a). While decarbonization efforts have primarily targeted power generation

[7] Hydropower accounts for more than 95% of Nepal's electricity generation (IEA Nepal 2024).

methods, similar investments have not been made to upgrade regional power grids[8], which were not designed for renewable integration. This challenge is evident even in major economies such as the PRC, India, and Japan as they try to expand renewable energy use (IEA 2024a).

One initiative to solve this challenge is the Association of Southeast Asian Nations (ASEAN) Power Grid. The initiative, a partnership between ADB and ASEAN, is designed to connect the electricity networks of the 10 members economies of ASEAN. This will not only establish a fully integrated grid by 2045, but also enable cross-border power trading, ensure a reliable and affordable energy supply for more than 670 million people living in Southeast Asia, bolster scaling-up of renewables in electricity generation, and provide safeguards against environmental and economic shocks. The initiative plans to increase energy transmission capacity from a current 7.7 gigawatts to 17.6 gigawatts by 2040 (ADB 2025b).

8 Power grids are crucial for transmitting electricity from producers to consumers, by managing bidirectional energy flows, inter-grid connectivity, stability, and energy storage (IRENA 2015).

Box 3.2: Energy Transitions – Solutions and Challenges for Utilities

An example of a pointed yet flexible solution to reducing the fossil fuel dependance of utilities is the Energy Transition Mechanism. The Asian Development Bank (ADB) and the Government of Indonesia is actively working on retiring Cirebon-1, a 660-megawatt coal-fired powerplant in Western Java, 7 years ahead of its intended lifespan. By closing the plant in 2035, the initiative aims to reduce the economy's reliance on fossil fuels and avoid emissions that would otherwise occur during that period (ADB 2022).

While the environmental benefits are clear, the transition also carries significant economic and social implications. Retiring a major energy asset affects more than just power generation because it potentially has ripple effects on workers, local businesses, supply chains, and the wider economy. Jobs in coal mining, transportation, and trade, as well as spending across communities linked to these sectors, may all be disrupted. These layers of impact—direct, indirect, and induced—are central to the "just transition" framework laid out in the joint multilateral development banks' *Just Transition High-Level principles* (ADB 2024a).

Motivated by the considerations highlighted in the Preliminary Just Transition Assessment (ADB 2024b), the analysis used ADB's environmentally extended multiregional input-output framework to estimate the economy-wide impacts of Cirebon 1's early closure. Drawing on the 2016 input-output tables of Statistics Indonesia (2021), the plant was found to contribute $137 million in direct value-added, with another $142 million generated in linked industries, and $37 million in induced effects—amounting to a total economic footprint of $317 million. This means that for every dollar generated at the plant, an additional $1.30 was created across the economy. The impact on employment was also similar: while the plant employs around 200 people directly, its linkages to labor-intensive industries supported an estimated 14,000 jobs. The analysis highlights that coal plant retirements have wide-reaching effects beyond the facility itself, with implications for supply chains and livelihoods that must be managed carefully.

On the environmental side, it can be assumed that the plant emits around 4.2 million tons of carbon dioxide annually, primarily from on-site combustion. Retiring the Cirebon 1 plant 7 years early would then impose direct, indirect, and induced economic losses of about $117.6 million in net present value (discounted to 2016), or roughly 0.01% of Indonesia's 2016 gross domestic product under a business-as-usual scenario. However, valuing avoided emissions over the same period at $100 per ton of carbon dioxide, the upper end of the range recommended by the High-Level Commission on Carbon Prices (2017), yields a potential environmental benefit of $156.7 million (also discounted to 2016). The resulting net welfare gain is therefore approximately $39.1 million under an ambitious but policy-relevant carbon price assumption. These illustrative results indicate that early retirement can deliver overall benefits once environmental costs are considered alongside economic ones.

In addition to the above considerations, there remain several other barriers to financing such transitions. Emerging technologies are difficult to assess and rarely pass the threshold for investing, as are the long-term macroeconomic risks associated with them (Sabah et al. 2024). While renewable energy capacities continue to increase in the foreseeable future, the industry faces challenges in the form of high cost of financing, variable profitability, and interregional differences in production, demand, and uptake. The success of energy transitions and deployments by utilities depend on policymaking and implementation necessary to achieving environmental protection and safeguarding goals (IEA Renewables 2023).

References:

Asian Development Bank (ADB). 2022. *ADB and Indonesia Partners Sign Landmark MOU on Early Retirement Plan for First Coal Power Plant.* 14 November. https://www.adb.org/news/adb-and-indonesia-partners-sign-landmark-mou-early-retirement-plan-first-coal-power-plant (accessed 4 April 2025).

ADB. 2024a. *Cirebon Energy Transition Mechanism Pilot Project: Preliminary Poverty and Social Analysis.* https://www.adb.org/projects/documents/ino-56294-001-ipsa (accessed 4 April 2025).

ADB. 2024b. *Cirebon Energy Transition Mechanism Pilot Project: Preliminary Just Transition Assessment.* https://www.adb.org/projects/documents/ino-56294-001-dpta (accessed 4 April 2025).

High-Level Commission on Carbon Prices. 2017. *Report of the High-Level Commission on Carbon Prices.* Washington, D.C.: World Bank Group. https://www.uncclearn.org/wp-content/uploads/library/carbonpricing_fullreport.pdf.

International Energy Agency (IEA). 2023. *Electricity Grids and Secure Energy Transitions.* Paris. https://www.iea.org/reports/electricity-grids-and-secure-energy-transitions (accessed 29 October 2024).

A. Sabah, J. Brown, E. Gratcheva, C. Greig, K. Iychettira, K. Spokas, M. Syed, and K. Waltzer. 2024. *Clean Energy Finance Must Address Three Crucial Challenges to Achieve Ambitious Climate Goals.* https://doi.org/10.2139/ssrn.5016309. Asian Development Bank. *ADB and Indonesia Partners Sign Landmark MOU on Early Retirement Plan for First Coal Power Plant.* November 14, 2022. https://www.adb.org/news/adb-and-indonesia-partners-sign-landmark-mou-early-retirement-plan-first-coal-power-plant.

Statistics Indonesia (BPS). 2021. Input-Output Tables of Indonesia 2016. https://www.bps.go.id/en/publication/2021/03/31/081f6b0af2c15c524d72b660/-input---output-tables-of-indonesia-2016.html (accessed October 2024).

Source: Asian Development Bank analysis.

Sectoral Analysis: Transport and Travel

Figure 3.6: Key Analyses of Sectoral Emissions in Transport and Travel

3.6.a. Annual Emission Highlights

Emissions, 2017–2023

3.07

gigatons of CO_2e

Share, 2017–2023

6.6

% of global emissions

Intensity, 2017–2023

0.23

kilograms of CO_2e/$ of output

3.6.b. Sources of Emissions

Sectoral emissions by Source and Region, 2017–2023

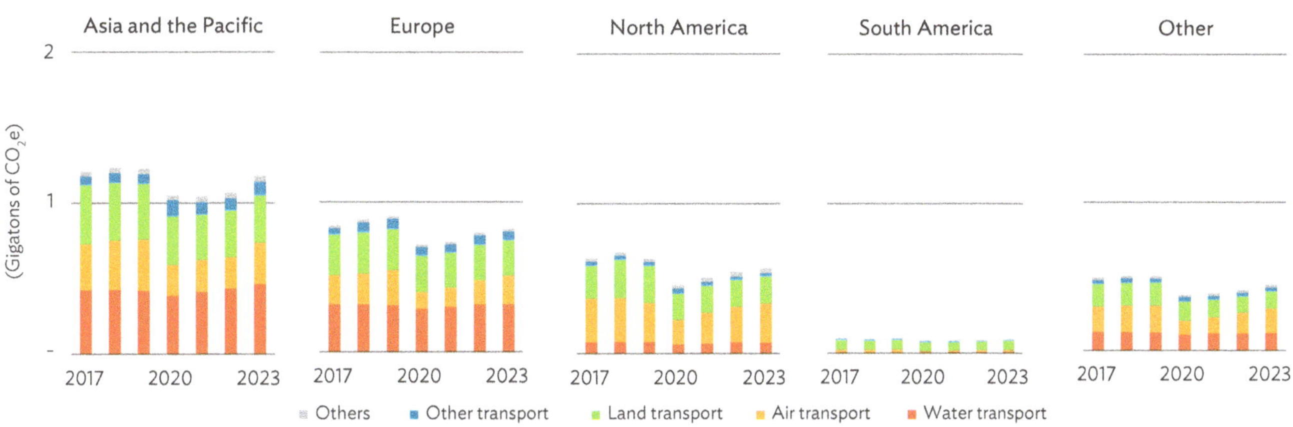

3.6.c. Key Trends and Drivers

Annual growth, 2017–2023

-0.87%

Decoupling index

1.15

Status:

Strong decoupling

Decomposition of emission changes, 2017–2023 (megatons of CO_2e)

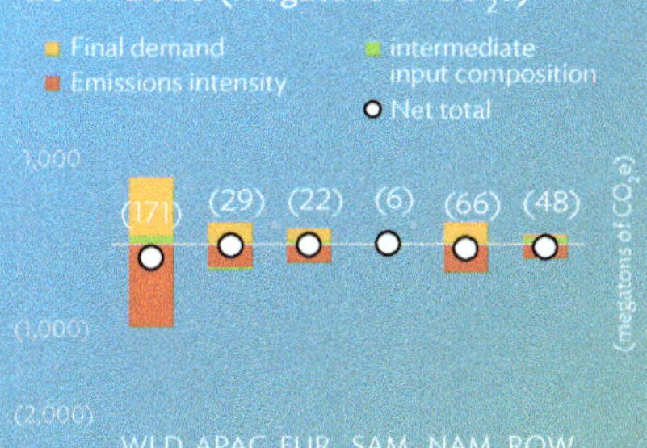

Leading contributors from Asia and the Pacific	Share to global sectoral emissions (%)	Growth, 2017–2023
People's Republic of China	14.6	▲
Japan	3.6	▲
India	2.8	▼
Singapore	2.4	▼
Republic of Korea	2.3	▼

3.6.d. Sectoral Decoupling Patterns

Sectoral changes in production-based emissions and GVA, 2017 and 2023

3.6.e. Value Chain Insights

Composition of total emissions footprint, 2023

(in megatons of CO_2-equivalent)

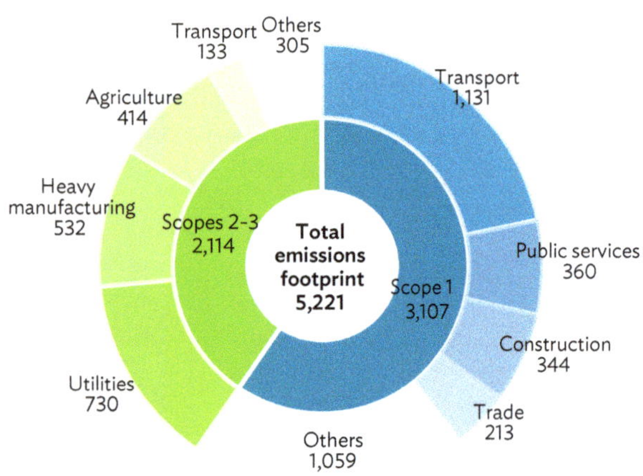

Shares of scopes 1–3 to total footprint, by Region, 2023

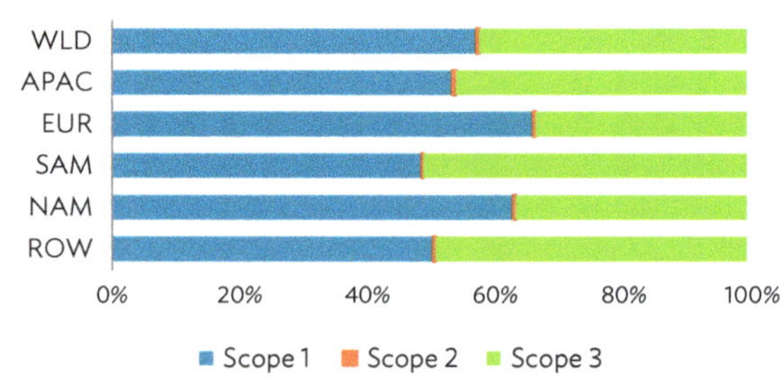

\$ = United States dollars, APAC = Asia and the Pacific, CO_2e = carbon dioxide equivalent, EUR = Europe, GVA = gross value-added, NAM = North America, ROW = rest of the world, SAM = South America, WLD = world.

Note: The Transport and Travel grouping consists of the following sectors in the Asian Development Bank's multiregional input-output tables: Hotels and Restaurants, Land transport, Air transport, Water transport, and Other supporting transport activities.

Source: Asian Development Bank analysis using multiregional input-output tables and environmentally extended multiregional input-output tables at https://kidb.adb.org/globalization (accessed March 2025).

The movement of goods and people, while integral to global trade and mobility, remains a major source of emissions and energy consumption. In 2023, the Transport and Travel sectoral grouping generated 3.1 $GtCO_2e$, accounting for 6.5% of all emissions, with 96% of these emissions generated by burning diesel, petroleum, and other oil-based fuels (IEA 2024). From 2017 to 2023, CO_2 made up 97% of emissions from transport and travel. Without intervention, sectoral emissions are projected to soar due to three main factors: an expected doubling of global transport demand by 2070, a 60% increase in car ownership, and a threefold increase in demand for aviation (IEA 2020a).

Asia and the Pacific was the largest regional contributor, accounting for 35% of sectoral emissions globally. Notably, water transport constituted nearly 40% of the region's sectoral emissions. These emissions were predominantly driven by India and the PRC, which together contributed 40% of the region's water transport emissions (as well as 88% of emissions from supporting and auxiliary transport activities). During the COVID-19 pandemic, with much of the global population in periods of lockdown, transport and travel emissions took one of the sharpest declines among all sectoral groupings. While many economies experienced a strong resurgence in sectoral emissions in 2021, the pandemic underscored the potential to curb the grouping's contribution to global emissions and highlighted its vulnerability to large-scale disruptions (IEA 2020b). From 2017 to 2023, inland transport (road and rail) contributed an average of 33% of all sectoral emissions globally, followed by water transport (31%) and air transport (28%). Supporting and auxiliary transport activities, including travel agencies, contributed 6%, while hotels and restaurants accounted for 2%. Water and air transport exhibited the highest emissions intensities across all regions from 2017 to 2023.

Globally, direct emissions from transport and travel far exceed indirect emissions, but the balance is changing. Direct (Scope 1) emissions dominated the Transport and Travel sectoral grouping in 2023, particularly in water transport (92%) and air transport (82%), where low-carbon fuel alternatives remain limited. However, total direct emissions did decline across most regions (except Europe) from 2017 to 2023, while indirect (Scope 3) emissions increased. This shift suggests that, while measures to control direct emissions might be taking effect, environmental strategies should also focus on reducing emissions embedded in supply chains and outsourced operations. For example, indirect emissions constituted about 92% of emissions by hotels and restaurants, driven by emissions from raw material transportation, supply chain activities, and operational dependencies on procured goods and services. The rising share of indirect (Scope 3) emissions highlights the interconnected nature of global supply chains, reinforcing the need to consider transport emissions beyond direct fuel combustion. A prime example is shipping route disruptions, which not only hinder logistics but also lead to increased emissions (Box 3.3).

Asia and the Pacific lags other regions in decoupling transport and travel emissions. More than half the world's economies achieved absolute or relative decoupling in transport and travel emissions from 2017 to 2023, though significant regional disparities were evident. In the North American region, the United States and Canada achieved absolute decoupling, reducing emissions while achieving growth. In Europe, 48% of economies achieved absolute decoupling and 42% relative decoupling: only Malta and Norway did not decouple during the period under study, suggesting that the region is well-positioned to further reduce sectoral emissions without compromising growth. Conversely, Asia and the Pacific, responsible only for 35% of all sectoral emissions despite its population size, showed mixed results: 40% of its economies achieved absolute decoupling in transport and travel, 37% achieved relative decoupling (including the PRC, which led regional emissions, and India), and 23% saw no decoupling. Some of these results were due to the region's role as a global hub for international trade and logistics, which further increased the demand for commercial and industrial transport and thereby the level of emissions (UNESCAP 2025; Chu et al. 2021).

Accurate accounting of transport and travel emissions can better inform policy responses. Asia and the Pacific had the lowest proportion of direct emissions in all three modes of transport, relative to its total footprint. In particular, direct emissions from inland transport made up just 50% of the total transport footprint in Asia and the Pacific, compared to 70% in other regions. Similarly, Scope 1 emissions in the hotels and restaurants of Asia and the Pacific accounted for only 6% of the total footprint compared to 12% in North America. These patterns underscore how emissions along global supply chains in transport and travel are accounted for: maritime and air transport emissions are disproportionately borne by producer economies, while emissions from inland transport and hotels and restaurants more directly reflect final consumption.

These patterns highlight the environmental costs embedded in global trade and the limitations of relying solely on territorial accounting. Consumption-based accounting from ADB's environmentally extended multiregional input-output tables provides a more comprehensive perspective. It does so by attributing emissions to final consumers, thereby revealing the full carbon emissions of transport-intensive goods and services. These insights can inform more effective policy responses—such as carbon border adjustment mechanisms or targeted demand-side measures—that not only influence consumer choices but also encourage cleaner transport practices along global value chains. Along with improved environmental accounting, technological advancements and focused policy platforms can offer opportunities to decarbonize transport and travel. Inland transport shows strong potential through energy-efficient technologies and sustainable infrastructure development (UNECE 2024). In maritime shipping, aligning with the International Maritime Organization's revised emissions reduction strategy and promoting low-carbon fuels such as hydrogen and ammonia will be key (Tai et al. 2022). Across all transport modes, scaling up low-carbon technologies and sustainable fuels is critical to achieving long-term decarbonization (OECD 2023).

Box 3.3: Impacts of Shipping Route Disruptions on Costs and Emissions.

Shipping route displacements lead to longer wait times, increased costs, and most importantly, higher emissions

In 2023, the shipping industry was responsible for about 3% of global emissions. While there are efforts to decarbonize in the long term, route disruptions have caused an increase in emissions. Conflict in the Red Sea, starting in October 2023, combined with reduced transit capacity in the Panama Canal due to severe drought have forced ships to take longer, more fuel-intensive detours. Containerships that would normally go through the Suez Canal were diverted around the Cape of Good Hope, adding about 6,500 kilometers and 10-12 days to the trip (UNCTAD 2024). Transits around the Cape of Good Hope rose from 300 per week to 605 per week following the Red Sea incidents since November 2023 and remained elevated through March 2024 (ONS 2024).

Given the longer routes, vessel speeds have increased to meet delivery schedules, causing ship fuel consumption to rise rapidly. Research shows that a 1% increase in speed typically results in a 2.2% rise in fuel consumption for large container ships (Meyer et al. 2012). Thus, rerouting increases emissions because of longer distances, which are further exacerbated by increased speeds.

To quantify the impact of the disruptions, carbon dioxide emissions between direct and redirected routes were estimated using Automatic Identification System data and the bottom-up approach from the International Maritime Organization's 4th Greenhouse Gas Study (2020). The analysis focused on vessels with direct voyage between the United States and Asia (the People's Republic of China, Japan, and the Republic of Korea) via the Panama Canal. The vessels were tracked 1 year prior to the period of disruption from July 2022 to July 2023 and during the period of disruption from July 2023 to July 2024, to identify reroutes. Findings show that approximately 20% of the ships chose alternative routes instead of the Panama Canal, with cargo ships choosing to reroute more than tankers. The emissions impact was substantial: rerouted vessels recorded average emissions increases of 17%-66% depending on the vessel type and alternate voyage chosen as shown in the figure below.

While long-term efforts aim to transition the shipping sector to sustainable fuels, immediate action is essential to reduce current environmental impacts. Adoptions such as operational efficiency improvements, digital optimization tools, slow steaming to reduce fuel consumption, and predictive maintenance can offer significant emissions reductions without requiring major fleet overhauls (Mba 2024).

Increases in Emissions Caused by Rerouting Maritime Vessels

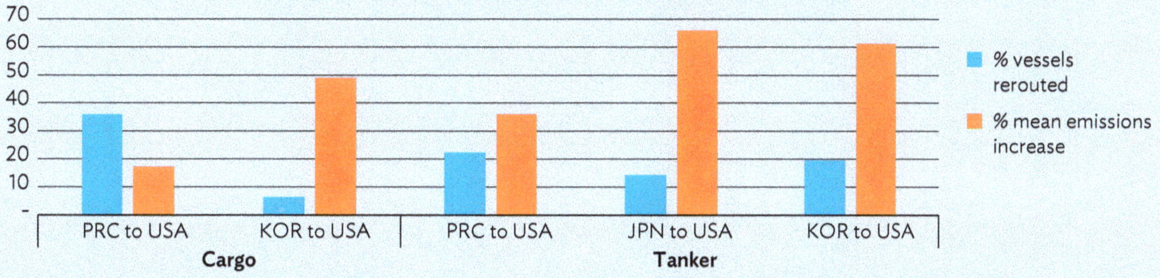

PRC = People's Republic of China; JPN = Japan; KOR = Republic of Korea; USA = United States.

Sources: Automatic Identification System data based on the 4th International Maritime Organization GHG Study Method (accessed March 2025); and Asian Development Bank estimates and analysis.

References:

International Maritime Organization (IMO). 2020. *2020 Fourth Greenhouse Gas Study 2020.* https://www.imo.org/en/ourwork/environment/pages/fourth-imo-greenhouse-gas-study-2020.aspx.

Office for National Statistics (ONS). 2024. *Ship Crossings Through Global Maritime Passages: January 2022 to April 2024.* ONS Statistical Bulletin (released 24 April 2024). https://www.ons.gov.uk/businessindustryandtrade/internationaltrade/bulletins/shipcrossingsthroughglobalmaritimepassages/january2022toapril2024

Mba, U. J. 2024. Advancing Sustainability and Efficiency in Maritime Operations: Integrating Green Technologies and Autonomous Systems in Global Shipping. *International Journal of Sustainable Research and Applications.* https://doi.org/10.30574/ijsra.2024.13.2.2419

Meyer, J., R. Stahlbock, and S. Voß. 2012. Slow Steaming in Container Shipping, *2012 45th Hawaii International Conference on System Sciences.* pp. 1306–1314, doi: 10.1109/HICSS.2012.529.

United Nations Conference on Trade and Development (UNCTAD).). *2024. Navigating Troubled Waters: Impact to Global Trade of Disruption of Shipping Routes in the Red Sea, Black Sea and Panama Canal.* https://unctad.org/system/files/official-document/osginf2024d2_en.pdf.

Source: Asian Development Bank analysis.

Sectoral Analysis: Services

Figure 3.7: Key Analyses of Sectoral Emissions in Services

3.7.a. Annual Emission Highlights

Emissions, 2017–2023

2.39

gigatons of CO_2e

Share, 2017–2023

5.2

% of global emissions

Intensity, 2017–2023

0.03

kilograms of CO_2e/$ of output

3.7.b. Sources of Emissions

Sectoral emissions by Source and Region, 2017–2023

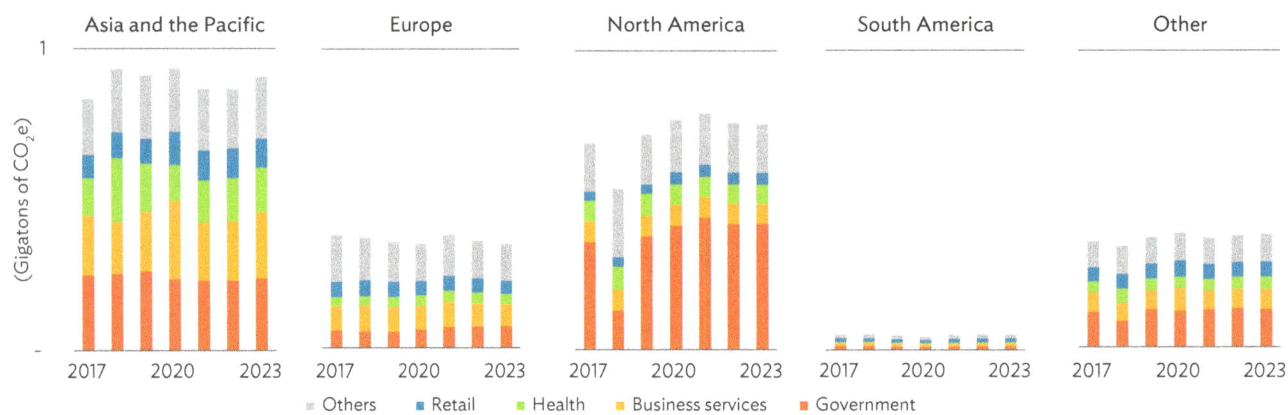

3.7.c. Key Trends and Drivers

Annual growth, 2017–2023

0.95 %

Decoupling index

0.85

Status:

Weak decoupling

Decomposition of emission changes, 2017–2023 (megatons of CO_2e)

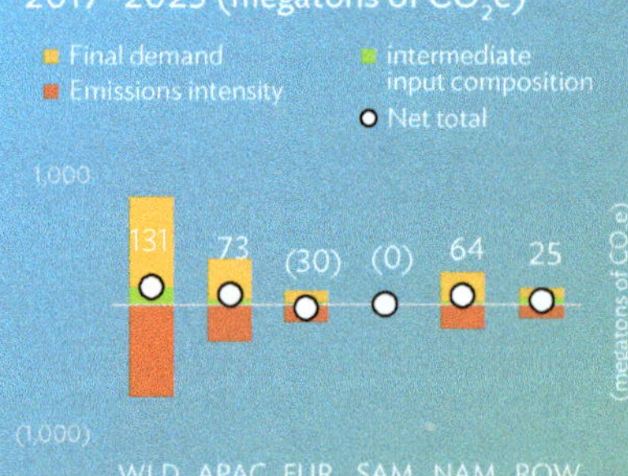

Leading contributors from Asia and the Pacific	Share to global sectoral emissions (%)	Growth, 2017–2023
People's Republic of China	18.4	▲
India	6.0	▲
Japan	3.3	▼
Republic of Korea	2.2	▲
Indonesia	1.1	▼

3.7.d. Sectoral Decoupling Patterns

Sectoral changes in production-based emissions and GVA, 2017 and 2023

3.7.e. Value Chain Insights

Composition of total emissions footprint, 2023
(in megatons of CO_2-equivalent)

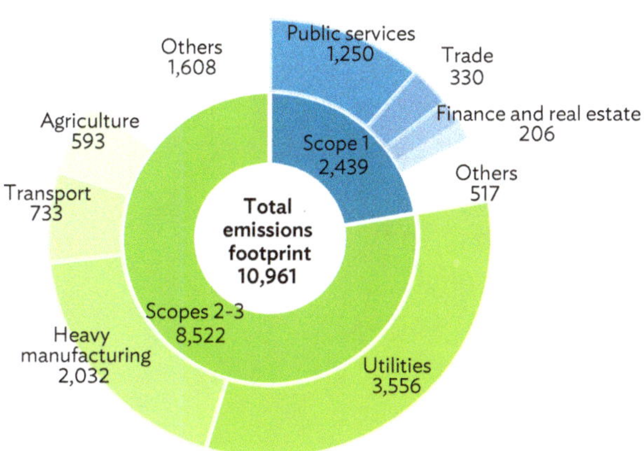

Shares of scopes 1–3 to total footprint, by Region, 2023

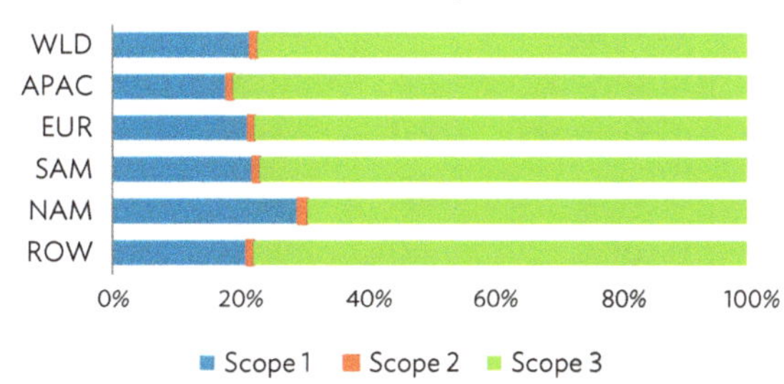

$ = United States dollars, APAC = Asia and the Pacific, CO_2e = carbon dioxide equivalent, EUR = Europe, GVA = gross value-added, NAM = North America, ROW = rest of the world, SAM = South America, WLD = world.

Note: The Services grouping consists of the following sectors in the Asian Development Bank's multiregional input-output tables: Sale of motor vehicle, Wholesale, Retail, Telecommunications, Finance, Real estate, Business services, Government, Education, Health, and Private households. Sectors with the highest emissions highlighted above.

Source: Asian Development Bank analysis using multiregional input-output tables and environmentally extended multiregional input-output tables at https://kidb.adb.org/globalization (accessed March 2025).

Services continue to drive the expansion of the global economy. By 2021, the Services sectoral grouping accounted for two-thirds of global GDP—up from half in 1970—and employed more than 50% of the world's workforce (WTO 2023). Because the grouping has continued to expand faster than agriculture and industries, its share of emissions is correspondingly rising, driven increasingly by the use of carbon-intensive infrastructure and energy sources. When measured by direct (Scope 1) emissions alone, services accounted for just 5% of global emissions from 2017 to 2023. However, because services play a pivotal intermediary role in economic activity, linking producers to final demand, they indirectly drive emissions across other sectors. For this reason, the total emissions footprint of services was almost 11 $GtCO_2e$ (the highest ratio of indirect to direct emissions of all six sectoral groupings).

Asia and the Pacific, at 37%, was the leading regional contributor of global emissions by services in 2023, followed by North America at 30%. The COVID-19 pandemic impacted sectoral emissions differently across regions, largely reflected by the importance of services to their respective regional economies. While emissions from the Services sectoral grouping in Europe and South America decreased in 2020 and increased in 2021, the opposite happened in Asia and the Pacific. Meanwhile, North America saw significant increases in services emissions from 2019 to 2021, led by the United States where services, on average, constituted 77% of GDP over the same period (World Bank 2025). Indeed, Services was the only sectoral grouping to experience an emissions rise during the pandemic in the United States. A similar trend was evident in service-dependent economies such as Australia and Singapore, suggesting that, as economies went into lockdown, an increase in demand for remote digital working solutions and e-commerce activities led to an increase in service-related emissions.

Services sectors generate emissions at different levels for different reasons. Largely attributed to energy consumption, CO_2 dominates services emissions, comprising about 90% of total sectoral emissions from 2017 to 2023. The Services grouping also recorded significant fluorinated-gas emissions (6%) in the study period, owing to widespread air conditioning in commercial and residential buildings. Emissions contributions by individual economic sectors are largely dictated by the nature of their operations. Although considered nonmarket sectors, public administration and defense (34% of sectoral emissions), health and social work (12%), and education (3%) are major consumers of energy and materials. Wholesale and retail trade (20% of sectoral emissions) and renting of machinery and equipment (18%) rely heavily on commercial infrastructure, including energy-intensive buildings, refrigeration, and inventory management systems. Although the telecommunications sector contributed only 3% of sectoral emissions for 2017–2023, it is poised for a substantial rise in emissions with global data usage projected to increase by 60% from 2020 to 2040, driving up energy consumption through data centers and network infrastructure (Deevala et al. 2024). Financial intermediation (3% of sectoral emissions) and real estate services (6%), while not emissions-intensive in their core activities, often operate out of large office spaces and depend on extensive digital infrastructure, contributing to emissions through energy use and carbon embodied in buildings and equipment.

As regions specialize in different services, their emissions profiles also vary. From 2017 to 2023, public administration and defense led services emissions in all regions except Europe. There were, however, wide regional discrepancies: North America averaged 51% of services emissions from public administration and defense, but Asia and the Pacific stood at just 27% and South America reported 24%. Europe, North America, and South America saw a larger share of emissions attributed to financial intermediation (≥ 3.5%) than did Asia and the Pacific (2.7%), reflecting deeper financial ecosystems in the former regions. Regional disparities were also evident in distributive sectors: emissions from wholesale trade dominated in Europe (18% of sectoral emissions), while retail trade emissions were highest in South America (23% of sectoral emissions).

Europe led global progress in decoupling services emissions. In Europe, 70% of the region's economies achieved absolute decoupling of services emissions from 2017 to 2023. Asia and the Pacific exhibited relatively limited progress, with only 50% of economies achieving absolute decoupling in this sectoral grouping. In fact, Cambodia, Fiji, and India posted emissions rises equal to or faster than their economic growth from services. Structural decomposition analysis shows that, while economies in Europe and South America started transitioning to lower-carbon pathways and decreased services emissions by 8% from 2017 to 2023, many in Asia and the Pacific did not reduce their services emissions intensities enough to offset rising final demand.

Direct (Scope 1) emissions are modest while indirect emissions dominate in services. Emissions from purchased electricity (Scope 2) and upstream supply chains (Scope 3) represented the bulk of the carbon emissions of the Services sectoral grouping in 2023. For instance, health and social sectors saw high indirect emissions (86%) as they were particularly reliant on emissions from chemical and pharmaceutical sectors. This suggests that services are carbon-intensive not because of their direct activities, but because of the upstream emissions embodied in the goods, energy, and technologies they mobilize. Moreover, the advent of digital technologies has made services more transferable and scalable, increasing the linkages and spillovers from IT services to other sectors as digitalization improves the quality and efficiency of all production processes (Nayyar et al. 2021). The analysis highlights the importance of looking beyond geography and sector specifics when assessing a region's carbon responsibility, especially in economies where services dominate final consumption and GDP. This pattern was clear in highly service-oriented economies such as Singapore (96% indirect emissions in 2023), Denmark (92%), and Hong Kong, China (91%).

Effective decarbonization of services requires multidimensional strategies. Emissions reduction plans for the Services grouping should prioritize procurement of renewable power, sustainable purchasing protocols, and high-efficiency buildings—measures that target embedded emissions rather than point to sources alone. Enhancing energy efficiency in public and private buildings, developing sustainable digital infrastructures, and adopting sustainable operating models across wholesale and retail operations can avoid indirect emissions. Intentional clean electricity procurement and cross-sector partnerships can amplify these efforts, transferring responsibility for emissions reductions to upstream sectors such as manufacturing, construction, and energy production. Effective decarbonization ultimately depends on recognizing and managing these valuechain interlinkages.

Sectoral Analysis: Waste

Figure 3.8: Key Analyses of Sectoral Emissions in Waste

3.8.a. Annual Emission Highlights

Emissions, 2017–2023

2.07

gigatons of CO_2e

Share, 2017–2023

4.5

% of global emissions

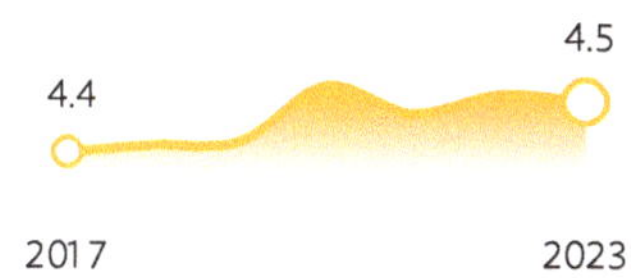

Intensity, 2017–2023

0.38

kilograms of CO_2e/$ of output

3.8.b. Sources of Emissions

Sectoral emissions by Source and Region, 2017–2023

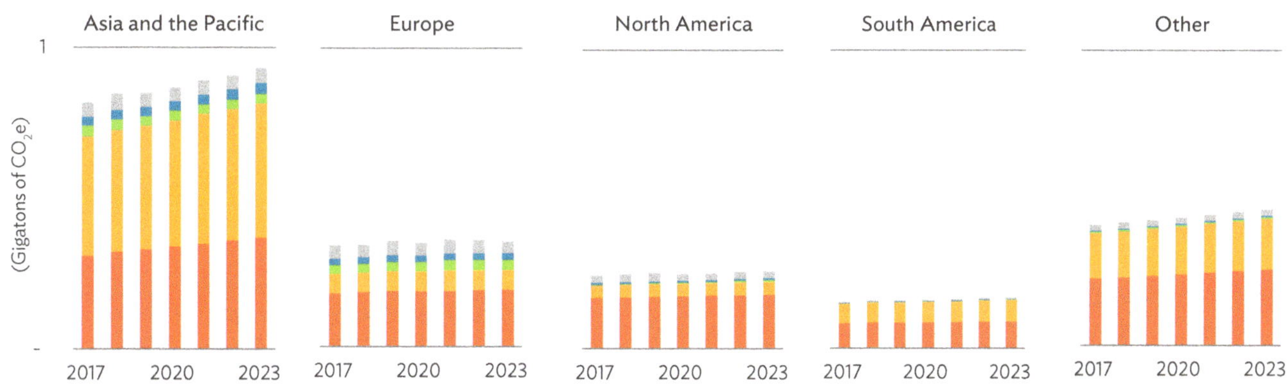

3.8.c. Key Trends and Drivers

Annual growth, 2017–2023

1.76 %

Decoupling index

0.64

Status:

Weak decoupling

Decomposition of emission changes, 2017–2023 (megatons of CO_2e)

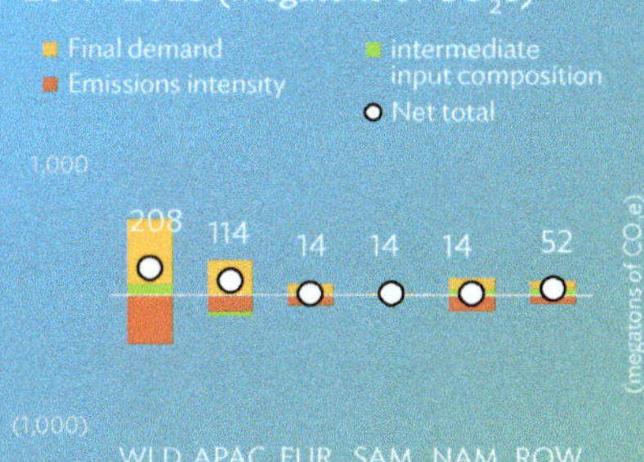

Leading contributors from Asia and the Pacific	Share to global sectoral emissions (%)	Growth, 2017–2023
People's Republic of China	19.4	▲
India	7.0	▲
Indonesia	2.4	▲
Republic of Korea	1.3	▲
Thailand	1.3	▲

3.8.d. Sectoral Decoupling Patterns

Sectoral changes in production-based emissions and GVA, 2017 and 2023

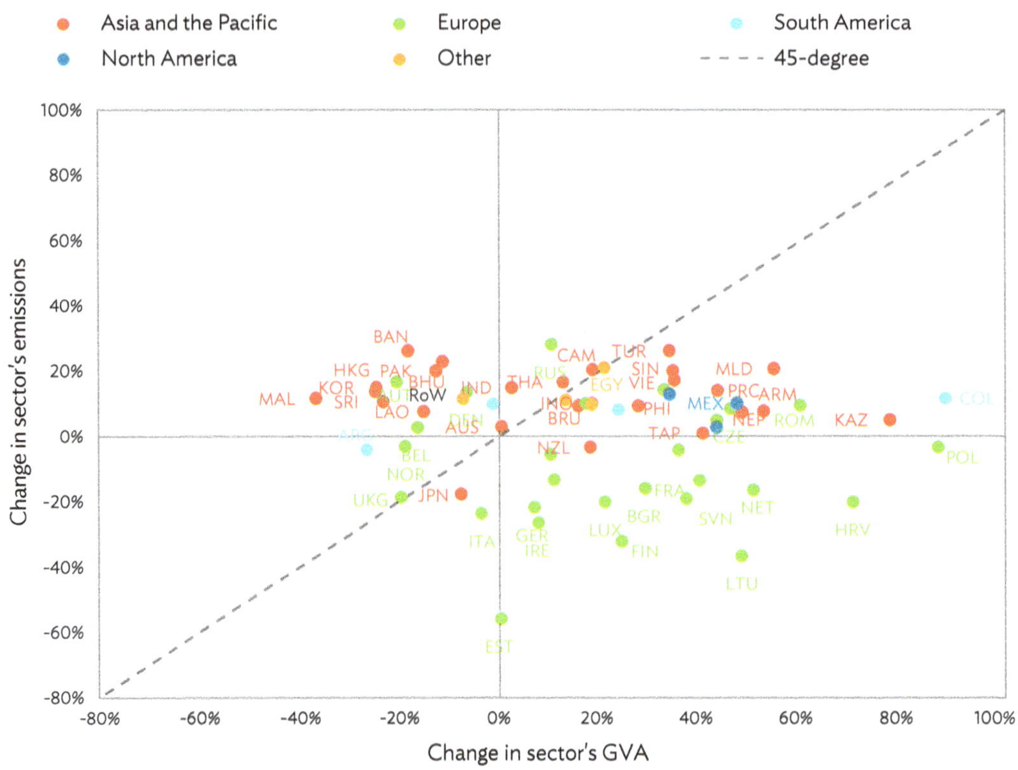

3.8.e. Value Chain Insights

Composition of total emissions footprint, 2023
(in megatons of CO_2-equivalent)

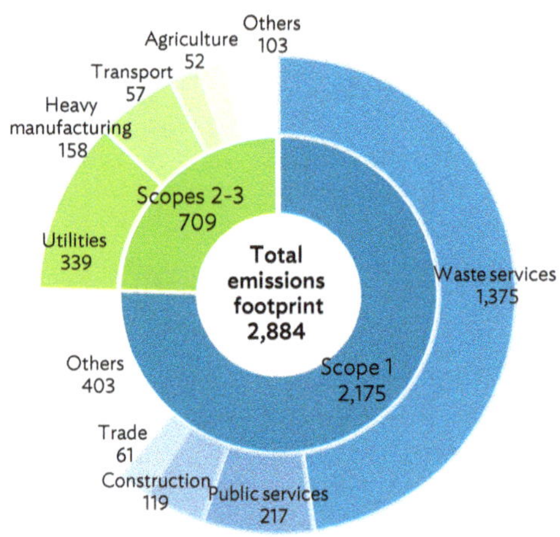

Shares of scopes 1–3 to total footprint, by Region, 2023

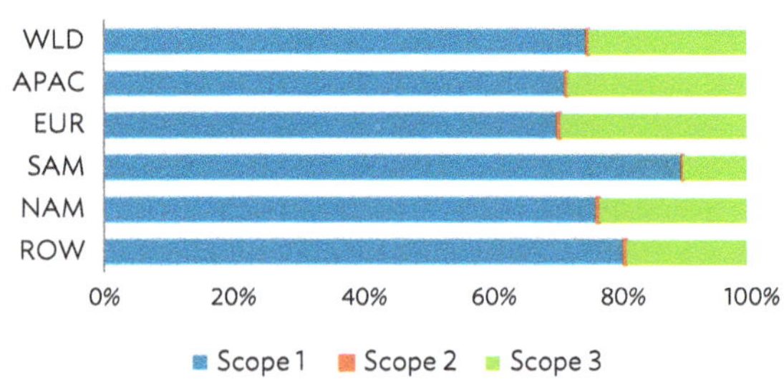

\$ = United States dollars, APAC = Asia and the Pacific, CO_2e = carbon dioxide equivalent, EUR = Europe, GVA = gross value-added, NAM = North America, ROW = rest of the world, SAM = South America, WLD = world.

Note: As the waste sector is a single sector in the Asian Development Bank's multiregional input-output tables (c34), the sources of emissions are broken down using the definitions of Intergovernmental Panel on Climate Change.

Source: Asian Development Bank analysis using multiregional input-output tables and environmentally extended multiregional input-output tables at https://kidb.adb.org/globalization (accessed March 2025).

Waste is now the world's fastest-growing source of emissions. Waste emissions stem from four main sources: (i) solid waste disposal, (ii) biological treatment of waste, (iii) incineration and open burning of waste, and (iv) wastewater treatment and discharge. Methane is released when organic material decomposes in landfills, open dumps, or during wastewater treatment, making waste the third-largest source of methane emissions globally after agriculture and fossil fuels. The Waste[9] sectoral grouping contributed about 4.5% of global emissions annually from 2017 to 2023, emitting an average of 2.1 $GtCO_2e$ per year. Global waste emissions grew at an average annual rate of 1.9% from 2017 to 2023, making it the fastest growing source of emissions. Given this, reducing waste is a pivotal way to slow emissions in the near term.

Globally, solid waste disposal is the highest contributor of sectoral emissions. In 2023 disposal of solid waste was the largest contributor of emissions in the Waste sectoral grouping, accounting for half of all sectoral emissions and approximately 1.0 $GtCO_2e$ annually. This reflects rising material consumption and household demand as economies urbanize and develop (UN 2024). The carbon emissions of waste also points to mounting pressures from industrial sectors, such as construction and other heavy industries, alongside persistent gaps in waste management systems. In Asia and the Pacific, 60% of waste is uncontrolled, i.e., either not collected at all or collected but ultimately dumped and landfilled without proper treatment (UNEP 2024; CEIC 2024; Kaza et al. 2018). Without major improvements, growing volumes of waste from both households and industries risk overwhelming disposal systems, leading to greater "spillover" into the environment and further increases in emissions.

In Asia and the Pacific, wastewater is now the dominant source of sectoral emissions. Inadequate sewerage and sanitation systems, coupled with rising water demand that has outpaced infrastructure investments, have led to large volumes of untreated wastewater in the Asia and Pacific region (ADB 2023; Evans et al. 2012; Arfanuzzaman and Dahiya 2019; UN 2024). Untreated wastewater emits nearly three times more carbon emissions than conventionally treated water (ADB 2023). From 2017 to 2023, wastewater treatment and discharge in Asia and the Pacific generated about 415 megatons of carbon dioxide equivalent ($MtCO_2e$) annually, exceeding the 285 $MtCO_2e$ from solid waste facilities such as landfills and dumpsites, and making it the region's largest contributor of waste emissions. This acceleration in wastewater emissions has in turn contributed to the region's growing share of global waste emissions, rising from around 31% in 1970 (Crippa et al. 2023) to 40% in 2023, led by the populous economies of Bangladesh, the PRC, India, Indonesia, and Pakistan.

---

[9] The Waste sectoral grouping includes sectors such as waste collection, recycling, landfill operations, incineration, and wastewater treatment. In ADB's EE-MRIOT dataset, these are part of a broader services category, "Other Community, Social, and Personal Services," which also covers other unrelated services such as laundry and entertainment. While this limits precision, more than 90% of direct emissions come from waste-related activities. For this reason, and strictly within the context of characterizing emissions, this section refers to the broader category as the "Waste sectoral grouping", while fully acknowledging the limitations of this classification.

Circular economy practices are key to emissions reductions in the Waste grouping. Addressing waste emissions requires both reducing waste generation and improving capacity to manage and treat the waste that is produced. Circular economy practices—such as reuse, repair, rental, and recycling—offer practical ways to extend the life of materials and reduce overall waste. However, these activities are difficult to measure because they often occur outside the formal waste sector (conducted by unregistered waste pickers and small-scale recyclers) or are embedded within other industries (McKinsey & Company 2016; ILO 2013; UN-Habitat 2010; Kaza et al). For a subset of formal industries primarily engaged in circular functions—namely waste collection, recovery, recycling, repair, and rental—estimates suggest they account for a small (about 1%) but growing share of the economy.[10] Yet, without better measurement and stronger policy support, the full potential of circular activities to reduce emissions and ease pressure on waste systems could remain untapped.

Without a broader shift toward circularity, emissions from waste will remain concentrated at the point of disposal, mainly from landfills and wastewater outlets, with a smaller share from energy consumption. In 2023, direct (Scope 1) emissions accounted for approximately 75% of the Waste grouping's total footprint across all regions, or about 2,175 $MtCO_2e$. Indirect (Scope 2 and Scope 3) emissions made up the remaining 25%, primarily from electricity used in facilities such as wastewater aeration systems, along with fuel and chemical inputs. These indirect sources contribute around 708 $MtCO_2e$, bringing waste's total footprint to 2,883 $MtCO_2e$ or roughly 6% of global emissions in 2023.

Asia and the Pacific can play a central role in reducing global waste emissions. Rapid economic development in Asia and the Pacific has placed sustained pressure on waste management systems, resulting in inadequate disposal practices and higher emissions. While waste management remains an essential utility service, this sectoral grouping's growing carbon emissions in the region underscores the role of material producers and consumers in reducing waste at the source. This calls for a shift in focus from a disposal-centric view to one that prioritizes waste prevention and reduction.

10 Calculations by ADB from supply use tables and national accounts data for 2015–2023

References

Arfanuzzaman, M. and B. Dahiya. 2019. Sustainable Urbanization in Southeast Asia and Beyond: Challenges of Population Growth, Land Use Change, and Environmental Health. *Growth and Change*. 50 (2). pp. 725–744.

Asian Development Bank (ADB). 2023. *Decarbonizing the Water Sector in Asia and the Pacific*. https://dx.doi.org/10.22617/TIM230531-2.

ADB. 2025a. *Energy Transition Readiness Assessment for Developing Asia and the Pacific*. https://www.adb.org/sites/default/files/publication/1050701/energy-transition-readiness-developing-asia-pacific.pdf.

ADB. 2025b. ADB and the ASEAN Power Grid. https://www.adb.org/where-we-work/southeast-asia/asean-power-grid.

CEIC. Waste Management: Controlled Solid Waste. https://insights.ceicdata.com/ (accessed October 2024).

Chang, H. 2022. *Edible Economics: A Hungry Economist Explains the World*. Allen Lane.

Chu, F., Y. Li, D. Mohr, Y. Murakami, C. Sun, and H. Yadav. 2021. *Asia:* The Highway of Value for Global Logistics. *McKinsey & Company*. 19 May. https://www.mckinsey.com/featured-insights/asia-pacific/asia-the-highway-of-value-for-global-logistics.

Crippa, M., D. Guizzardi, F. Pagani, M. Banja, M. Muntean, E. Schaaf, W. Becker, et al. 2023. *GHG Emissions of all World Countries*. Publications Office of the European Union.

Deevela, N., B. Singh, B., and T. C. Kandpal. 2024. Assessing the Carbon Footprint of Telecommunication Towers in India: Effect of 4G to 5G Transition and Solar Photovoltaics Based Hybrid Power Systems. *Journal of Cleaner Production*. 440 (140693) https://doi.org/10.1016/j.jclepro.2024.140693.

Dutchen, S. 2023. Confronting Health Care's Carbon Footprint. *Harvard Medicine*. Autumn. https://magazine.hms.harvard.edu/articles/confronting-health-cares-carbon-footprint.

Environmental and Energy Study Institute. 2022. *Climate Impacts of Aviation: Growth in Greenhouse Gas Emissions from Commercial Aviation (Issue Brief)*. https://www.eesi.org/files/IssueBrief_Climate_Impacts_Aviation_2019rev2022.pdf.

Evans, A. E. V., M. A. Hanjra, Y. Jiang, M. Qadir, and P. Drechsel. 2012. Water Quality: Assessment of the Current Situation in Asia. *International Journal of Water Resources Development*. 28 (2). pp. 195–216. https://doi.org/10.1080/07900627.2012.669520.

Food and Agriculture Organization of the United Nations (FAO). 2024. Greenhouse Gas Emissions from Agrifood Systems: Global, Regional and Country Trends, 2000–2022. *FAOSTAT Analytical Brief.* No. 94. https://openknowledge.fao.org/server/api/core/bitstreams/111b7ee8-282b-42ff-ad95-cccecd90f8ea/content.

Hawken, P. 2017. *Drawdown: The Most Comprehensive Plan Ever Proposed to Reverse Global Warming*. Penguin Books.

International Energy Agency (IEA). 2018. *Technology Roadmap: Low-Carbon Transition in the Cement Industry*. https://www.iea.org/reports/technology-roadmap-low-carbon-transition-in-the-cement-industry.

IEA. 2020a. *Energy Technology Perspectives 2020*. https://www.iea.org/reports/energy-technology-perspectives-2020.

IEA. 2021. *Net Zero by 2050*. https://www.iea.org/reports/net-zero-by-2050.

IEA. 2024a. *Renewables 2024: Analysis and Forecast to 2030*. https://iea.blob.core.windows.net/assets/17033b62-07a5-4144-8dd0-651cdb6caa24/Renewables2024.pdf.

IEA. 2024b. Electricity 2024: Analysis and Forecast to 2026. https://www.iea.org/reports/electricity-2024.

IEA. Energy System: Aviation. https://www.iea.org/energy-system/transport/aviation.

IEA. Energy System of Nepal. https://www.iea.org/countries/nepal.

IEA. Energy System: Transport. https://www.iea.org/energy-system/transport.

IEA. World Energy Balances. https://www.iea.org/data-and-statistics/data-product/world-energy-balances. (accessed 1 August 2025).

International Labour Organization (ILO). 2013. *Green Jobs Becoming a Reality: Progress and Outlook 2013*. https://old.adapt.it/adapt-indice-a-z/wp-content/uploads/2013/08/ilo_2013.pdf.

International Maritime Organization (IMO). 2023. *2023 IMO Strategy on Reduction of GHG Emissions from Ships*. https://www.imo.org/en/OurWork/Environment/Pages/2023-IMO-Strategy-on-Reduction-of-GHG-Emissions-from-Ships.aspx.

International Renewable Energy Agency (IRENA). 2015. *Renewable Energy Integration in Power Grids: Technology Brief*. International Energy Agency and IRENA.

Kaza, S., Silpa, L. C. Yao, P. Bhada-Tata, and F. Van Woerden. 2018. *What a Waste 2.0: A Global Snapshot of Solid Waste Management to 2050*. World Bank. https://openknowledge.worldbank.org/entities/publication/d3f9d45e-115f-559b-b14f-28552410e90a

McKinsey & Company. 2016. *The Circular Economy: Moving from Theory to Practice*. https://www.mckinsey.com/capabilities/sustainability/our-insights/the-circular-economy-moving-from-theory-to-practice

Nayyar, G., M. Hallward-Driemeier, and E. Davies. 2021. *At Your Service? The Promise of Services-Led Development*. World Bank. https://hdl.handle.net/10986/35599.

Organisation for Economic Co-operation and Development (OECD). 2023. *ITF Transport Outlook 2023*. https://doi.org/10.1787/b6cc9ad5-en.

Organisation for Economic Co-operation and Development (OECD) and Food and Agriculture Organization of the United Nations (FAO). 2025. *Agricultural Outlook 2025–2034*. OECD Publishing and FAO. https://www.oecd.org/en/publications/2025/07/oecd-fao-agricultural-outlook-2025-2034_3eb15914/full-report.html.

Ritchie, H., M. Roser, and P. Rosado. 2024. Cattle Livestock Count (Number of Heads). *Our World in Data*. https://ourworldindata.org/grapher/cattle-livestock-count-heads (accessed March 2025) .

Tai, H., Y. Chang, C. Chang, and Y. Wang. 2022. Analysis of the Carbon Intensity of Container Shipping on Trunk Routes: Referring to the Decarbonization Trajectory of the Poseidon Principle. *Atmosphere.* 13 (10). pp. 1580. https://doi.org/10.3390/atmos13101580

United Nations (UN). 2024. *The United Nations World Water Development Report 2024: Water for Prosperity and Peace.*

United Nations Conference on Trade and Development (UNCTAD). 2021. *Review of Maritime Transport 2021.* https://unctad.org/system/files/official-document/rmt2021_en_0.pdf.

UNCTAD. 2024. *Review of Maritime Transport 2024.* https://unctad.org/system/files/official-document/rmt2024_en.pdf

United Nations Economic and Social Commission for Asia and the Pacific (UNESCAP). 2025. *Asia-Pacific Trade and Investment Briefs 2024/5: Regional growth outperforms global average.* https://www.unescap.org/news/asia-pacific-trade-and-investment-briefs-20245-regional-growth-outperforms-global-average.

United Nations Economic Commission for Europe (UNECE). 2024. *Report of the Inland Transport Committee on its Eighty-Sixth Session.* https://unece.org/sites/default/files/2024-07/ECE_TRANS_344e.pdf

UNECE. 2024. United Nations Adopts Landmark Global Decarbonization Strategy in Transport by Road, Rail and Inland Waterway. News release. 26 February. https://unece.org/media/press/388574

United Nations Environment Programme (UNEP). 2024. *Global Waste Management Outlook 2024: Beyond an Age of Waste – Turning Rubbish into a Resource.* https://wedocs.unep.org/20.500.11822/44939

United Nations Habitat (UN-Habitat). 2010. *Solid Waste Management in the World's Cities: Water and Sanitation in the World's Cities.* https://unhabitat.org/books/solid-waste-management-in-the-worlds-cities-water-and-sanitation-in-the-worlds-cities-2010-2/

World Bank. 2022. What You Need to Know About Food Security and Climate Change. 17 October. https://www.worldbank.org/en/news/feature/2022/10/17/what-you-need-to-know-about-food-security-and-climate-change.

World Bank 2023. *Greening Public Administration with GovTech – Embracing a Green Digital Transition: Guidance Note – Volume 1.* https://openknowledge.worldbank.org/handle/10986/40594.

World Bank. Access to Electricity (% of Population). https://data.worldbank.org/indicator/EG.ELC.ACCS.ZS (accessed 8 August 2024)

World Bank. Services, Value Added (% of GDP). https://data.worldbank.org/indicator/NV.SRV.TOTL.ZS (accessed May 2025).

World Bank and International Telecommunication Union (ITU). 2024. *Measuring the Emissions & Energy Footprint of the ICT Sector: Implications for Climate Action.* https://documents1.worldbank.org/curated/en/099121223165540890/pdf/P17859712a98880541a4b71d57876048abb.pdf.

World Trade Organization (WTO). 2023. Chapter 1: The Future of Trade Lies in Services: Key Trends. *Trade in Services for Development.* https://www.wto.org/english/res_e/booksp_e/trade_in_serv_devpt_chp1_e.pdf.

SECTION 4

Conclusions

The Asia and Pacific region, accounting for up to 55% of global emissions in 2023, plays a pivotal role in achieving global environmental sustainability and resilience. Utilizing the Asian Development Bank's environmentally extended multiregional input-output tables framework, this report has traced the sources of these emissions and revealed the structural dependence of the region's economies on emissions-intensive activities across six sectoral groupings and, in some cases, the individual economic sectors within those groupings. In summarizing these analyses, four key themes emerge:

Balancing economic growth with environmental sustainability is crucial.

There is ongoing tension between economic growth and environmental sustainability, especially in Asia and the Pacific. Significant structural and economic barriers remain in many of the region's economies and, having built their comparative advantages on energy- and resource-intensive activities, these economies have limited options to advance environmental sustainability. Without disrupting economic stability, decoupling emissions from economic growth can be challenging.

However, the evidence in this report shows that economic growth and emissions reduction can coexist with the advent of low-carbon solutions such as renewable energy and innovative digital and energy-efficient technologies. Globally, improved carbon efficiencies avoided about 9.2 gigatons of carbon emissions from 2017 to 2023. Sectoral groupings such as Utilities and Industries have been at the forefront of this progress, demonstrating that even resource-intensive activities can evolve to reduce their emissions per unit of output. Replicating this technology-driven decoupling in Asia and the Pacific is essential if the costs—and the benefits—of environmental resilience are to be shared equitably.

Policymakers should uncover and target high upstream emissions.

Addressing emissions beyond direct sources is critical as there are significant hidden contributions from other sectors in each supply chain. For example, while construction may have relatively low on-site (Scope 1) emissions, it is heavily reliant on emissions-intensive materials. Similarly, even though services post low direct emissions, they generate substantial indirect emissions from energy consumption and outsourced materials from other sectors. Tracing indirect (Scope 2 and Scope 3) emissions—those linked to energy use, materials, and upstream production—is crucial for understanding the full extent of the challenges.

Geographically, there are also manifest disparities between production-based and consumption-based emissions. Advanced economies with lower territorial emissions often have higher consumption-based emissions, reflecting their reliance on imports from regions such as Asia and the Pacific, where production-based emissions outpace consumption-based emissions. These imbalances can mean that environmental impacts and responsibilities are often displaced across borders.

Regional cooperation can help align global supply-side and demand-side measures.

Sectoral supply chains span different geographical areas, creating opportunities for shared solutions. Coordinated supply-side and demand-side measures tailored to sectoral realities are essential, especially in hard-to-abate sectors. On the supply side, cleaner material inputs and circular economy practices can lower production needs and, consequently, reduce upstream emissions, while structural improvements in developing economies can address carbon leakage risks. These strategies can be aligned with demand-side measures, especially for net importers, who can emphasize environmentally responsible sourcing decisions and cost-sharing of "green" innovation through regional partnerships. In highly interdependent sectoral groupings, such as Utilities and Transport and Travel, cooperation is not merely desirable—it is imperative. Coordinating regional efforts across supply chains can help achieve meaningful environmental sustainability and resilience.

Statisticians must focus on getting the right data—and the data right.

This report emphasizes the importance of robust statistics in carbon emissions accounting, highlighting how data gaps hinder timely and effective environmental policies. While existing information systems are invaluable, they remain disconnected from other statistical frameworks that demonstrate the relationship of the economy with the natural environment. Tools such as environmentally extended multiregional input-output tables help bridge these gaps, integrating emissions within the input-output framework while enhancing the carbon emissions accounting of the economies of Asia and the Pacific.

National statistical systems are the foundation for understanding the environmental impacts of an economy. Integrating environmental and economic data emerges as the most viable entry point for improving environment-related statistics and analysis.

This approach aligns with established statistical frameworks and allows national statistics offices to leverage their existing capacities in economic statistics to support initiatives on environmental sustainability and resilience. However, for national statistical systems to play a more active role in environmental policy, they need adequate resources, tools, and technical expertise.

Addressing capacity gaps in national statistics offices requires investments in statistical capacity building and international collaboration. Enhancing data systems, fostering partnerships between developed and developing economies, and prioritizing harmonization across datasets can strengthen the foundation for effective emissions monitoring.

Ultimately, achieving environmental sustainability and resilience in Asia and the Pacific demands not only bold policies and innovative solutions but also a solid foundation of reliable data, cross-sectoral collaboration, and targeted strategies that balance economic growth with environmental responsibility.

PART II
SDGs and Other Regional Socioeconomic Trends

Goal 1. End poverty in all its forms everywhere

Table 1.1.1: Selected Indicators for Sustainable Development Goal 1—No Poverty

ADB Regional Member	Target 1.1: By 2030, eradicate extreme poverty for all people everywhere, measured as people living below the international poverty line of $2.15 a day (2017 PPP)						
	1.1.1.a: Proportion of Population Living below the $2.15 a Day (2017 PPP) Poverty Line[a,b] (%)		1.1.1.b: Proportion of Employed Population Living below the International Poverty Line, by Age Group and Sex[c,d] (%) 2019				
				Age Group			
				15+		15–24	25+
	2010	2022	Total (2024)	Female	Male		
Developing ADB Member Economies							
Central and West Asia							
Afghanistan	...	...	...	...	...	...	...
Armenia	1.0	0.6 (2023)	0.1	0.4	0.5	0.3	0.5
Azerbaijan[e]	0.0 (2005)	...	0.1	0.1	0.1	0.1	0.1
Georgia	14.4	2.3 (2023)	1.7	2.5	2.6	2.7	2.5
Kazakhstan	0.2	0.0 (2021)	0.1	0.1	0.1	0.2	0.1
Kyrgyz Republic	3.5	0.3	0.3	0.5	0.6	0.8	0.5
Pakistan	9.4	4.9 (2018)	4.2	7.0	3.9	4.4	4.6
Tajikistan	6.8 (2009)	6.1 (2015)	2.1	4.9	3.3	4.2	3.9
Türkiye[g]	0.8	0.4 (2019)	0.1	0.1	0.1	0.1	0.1
Turkmenistan	...	...	2.1	2.8	1.7	2.4	2.3
Uzbekistan	81.5 (2003)	...	1.1	1.1	1.6	1.1	1.4
East Asia							
China, People's Republic of	13.4	0.0 (2021)	0.1	0.1	0.1	0.2	0.1
Hong Kong, China[h]	...	...	0.0	0.0	0.0	0.0	0.0
Korea, Republic of[h]	0.5	0.0 (2021)	0.0	0.0	0.0	0.0	0.0
Mongolia	1.1	0.2	0.1	0.1	0.1	0.2	0.1
Taipei,China	0.2	0.0 (2021)	0.1	0.1	0.1	0.2	0.1
South Asia							
Bangladesh	18.2	5.0	2.6	7.8	6.2	6.7	6.8
Bhutan	1.7 (2012)	0.0	0.1	0.6	0.5	0.7	0.5
India	16.2 (2011)	2.3	8.7	12.4	10.9	13.5	11.0
Maldives	3.8 (2009)	– (2019)	0.1	0.1	0.1	0.1	0.1
Nepal	8.2	0.4	0.2	0.6	0.6	0.6	0.6
Sri Lanka	3.5 (2009)	1.0 (2019)	0.9	0.5	0.6	0.6	0.5
Southeast Asia							
Brunei Darussalam	...	...	...	...	...	...	...
Cambodia[k]	...	...	14.1	18.1	20.8	23.9	18.2
Indonesia	16.5	1.3 (2024)	2.0	4.0	3.9	4.1	3.9
Lao People's Democratic Republic	10.9 (2012)	7.1 (2018)	6.0	7.3	6.7	11.3	5.7
Malaysia	0.1 (2011)	– (2021)	0.1	0.1	0.1	0.1	0.1
Myanmar	...	6.2 (2015)	2.8	1.5	2.0	2.8	1.6
Philippines	11.3 (2009)	1.6 (2023)	1.9	0.1	0.1	0.1	0.1
Singapore	...	...	...	...	...	...	...
Thailand	0.3	– (2023)	0.1	0.0	0.1	0.2	0.0
Timor-Leste	40.9 (2007)	...	16.0	17.6	19.8	22.5	18.0
Viet Nam	2.9	1.0	1.0	1.0	0.9	1.9	0.8
The Pacific							
Cook Islands	...	...	...	...	...	...	...
Fiji	1.0 (2008)	1.3 (2019)	0.0	0.0	0.0	0.0	0.0
Kiribati	14.0 (2006)	1.7 (2019)	...	...	...	...	...
Marshall Islands	...	0.9 (2019)	...	...	...	...	...
Micronesia, Federated States of	16.0 (2013)	...	...	...	...	...	...
Nauru	2.1 (2012)	...	...	...	...	...	...
Niue	...	...	...	...	...	...	...
Palau	...	...	...	...	...	...	...
Papua New Guinea	39.7 (2009)	...	26.6	26.4	26.5	26.7	26.4
Samoa[e]	1.1 (2008)	...	...	...	...	...	...
Solomon Islands	26.6 (2012)	...	30.7	26.0	25.1	27.9	24.7
Tonga	1.3 (2009)	0.0 (2021)	...	...	...	...	...
Tuvalu	3.6	...	...	...	...	...	...
Vanuatu	14.7	10.0 (2019)	...	...	...	...	...
Developed ADB Member Economies							
Australia	...	...	...	...	...	...	...
Japan	...	...	...	...	...	...	...
New Zealand	...	...	...	...	...	...	...

Table 1.1.1: Selected Indicators for Sustainable Development Goal 1—No Poverty *(continued)*

ADB Regional Member	Target 1.2: By 2030, reduce at least by half the proportion of men, women, and children of all ages living in poverty in all its dimensions according to national definitions													
	1.2.1: Proportion of Population Living below the National Poverty Line, by Urban-Rural Location[a] (%)												1.2.2 Proportion of Men, Women and Children of all Ages Living in Poverty in all its Dimensions According to National Definitions (%)	
	2010						2022						2023	
	Total		Urban		Rural		Total		Urban		Rural			
Developing ADB Member Economies														
Central and West Asia														
Afghanistan	38.3	(2011)	..		..		54.5	(2016)	41.6	(2016)	58.6	(2016)	49.40	(2020)
Armenia	35.8		35.7		36.0		23.7	(2023)	21.5	(2023)	27.0	(2023)	17.30	
Azerbaijan[e]	9.1		..		..		5.3	(2024)	4.4	(2024)	6.2	(2024)	...	
Georgia	37.3[f]		32.7[f]		43.3[f]		9.4	(2024)	9.4	(2023)	15.6	(2023)	...	
Kazakhstan	6.5		3.7		10.1		5.0	(2024)	3.8	(2024)	6.9	(2024)	...	
Kyrgyz Republic	33.7		23.6		39.5		29.8	(2023)	...		...		43.60	
Pakistan	36.8		18.2	(2013)	35.6	(2013)	21.9	(2018)	...		...		30.50	(2019)
Tajikistan	36.4	(2012)	..		..		22.5		...		...		...	
Türkiye[g]	16.1		..		..		14.0	(2021)	...		...		30.70	
Turkmenistan	..		..		..		...		...		...		...	
Uzbekistan	..		..		..		8.9	(2024)	...		...		...	
East Asia														
China, People's Republic of	..		..		17.2		...		...		0.0	(2020)	...	
Hong Kong, China[h]	15.7		..		..		17.3	(2020)	...		...		...	
Korea, Republic of[h]	18.6	(2011)	..		..		14.9	(2023)	...		...		...	
Mongolia	38.8		33.2		49.0		27.1		23.0		35.6		...	
Taipei,China	1.2[i]		..		..		1.2[i]	(2023)	...		...		...	
South Asia														
Bangladesh	31.5		21.3		35.2		18.7		...		...		...	
Bhutan	12.0	(2012)	1.8	(2012)	16.7	(2012)	12.4		4.2		17.5		5.80	(2017)
India	21.9[j]	(2011)	13.7[j]	(2011)	25.7[j]	(2011)	15.0	(2019)	...		...		14.96	(2019)
Maldives	..		..		..		5.4	(2019)	...		...		28.40	(2016)
Nepal	25.2		15.5		27.4		20.3		18.3		24.7		17.40	(2019)
Sri Lanka	6.7	(2012)	2.1	(2012)	7.6	(2012)	14.3	(2019)	1.9	(2016)	4.3	(2016)	16.00	(2019)
Southeast Asia														
Brunei Darussalam	..		..		..		...		...		...		...	
Cambodia[k]	21.1		17.0		22.7		17.8	(2019)	12.6	(2019)	22.8	(2019)	...	
Indonesia	13.3		9.9		16.6		9.0	(2024)	7.1	(2024)	11.8	(2023)	...	
Lao People's Democratic Republic	24.6	(2013)	7.9	(2013)	31.4	(2013)	18.3	(2019)	7.0	(2019)	23.8	(2019)	22.00	(2018)
Malaysia	1.7	(2011)	1.0	(2012)	..		6.2	(2021)	0.2	(2016)	1.0	(2016)	...	
Myanmar	..		..		..		...		...		...		...	
Philippines	25.2	(2012)	13.0	(2012)	34.0	(2015)	15.5	(2023)	10.3	(2023)	22.1	(2023)	...	
Singapore	..		..		..		...		...		...		...	
Thailand	16.4		..		..		3.4	(2023)	...		...		11.62	(2021)
Timor-Leste	41.8	(2014)	28.3	(2014)	47.1	(2014)	...		...		...		...	
Viet Nam	14.2		6.9		17.4		3.4	(2023)	1.5		5.9		...	
The Pacific														
Cook Islands	..		..		..		...		...		...		...	
Fiji	28.1[l]	(2013)	19.8[l]	(2013)	36.7[l]	(2013)	29.9	(2019)	20.4	(2019)	41.5	(2019)	...	
Kiribati	..		..		..		21.9	(2019)	...		...		...	
Marshall Islands	..		..		..		7.2	(2019)	2.5	(2019)	21.2	(2019)	...	
Micronesia, Federated States of	41.2[l]	(2013)	..		..		...		...		...		...	
Nauru	24.0[l]	(2013)	..		..		...		...		...		...	
Niue	..		..		..		...		...		...		...	
Palau	..		..		..		...		...		...		...	
Papua New Guinea	..		..		..		37.5	(2017)	...		...		...	
Samoa[e]	18.8[l]	(2013)	..		..		21.9[l]	(2018)	...		...		24.90	(2018)
Solomon Islands	12.7[m]	(2013)	9.1[m]	(2013)	13.6[m]	(2013)	...		...		...		...	
Tonga	27.0	(2015)	..		..		20.6	(2021)	...		...		24.00	(2021)
Tuvalu	19.7[l]		19.8[l]		19.7[l]		...		...		...		...	
Vanuatu	12.7[l]		..		10.0[l]		15.9	(2019)	2.0	(2019)	20.8	(2019)	...	
Developed ADB Member Economies														
Australia	..		..		..		...		...		...		...	
Japan	..		..		..		...		...		...		...	
New Zealand	..		..		..		...		...		...		...	

... = data not available; – = magnitude equals zero; * = provisional, preliminary, estimate; 0.0 = magnitude is less than half of unit employed or true zero; $ = United States dollars; ADB = Asian Development Bank; PPP = purchasing power parity.

a For Indicator 1.1.1.a and Indicator 1.2.1, the year indicated in the table refers to the year when the household survey data were collected. For economies in which the household survey data collection period bridged 2 calendar years, the table reports the first year.
b For Indicator 1.1.1.a, data are consumption-based, except for the Republic of Korea; Malaysia; the Philippines; and Taipei,China, whose estimates are income-based. The World Bank has updated the international poverty lines using 2021 purchasing power parity (PPP), however, 2017-based PPP poverty estimates are still used for SDG monitoring.
c For Indicator 1.1.1.b, the estimates are based on the international poverty line of $2.15 a day (2017 PPP).
d Data are taken from estimates and projections modeled by the International Labour Organization (ILO). These modeled estimates present an internationally comparable series, which consists of economy-sourced estimates and imputations for missing data. Global and regional estimates are updated by the ILO annually.
e For Indicator 1.1.1.a, the latest available estimate for Azerbaijan is for 2005: 0.0%; for Samoa, the latest available estimate is for 2013: 1.2%.
f Refers to absolute poverty or the share of the population under the absolute poverty line.
g Data refer to the percentage of the population living below 50% of median equivalised household disposable income.
h For Indicator 1.2.1 for Hong Kong, China, data refer to the poverty rate after policy intervention (recurrent cash); for the Republic of Korea, data refer to the relative poverty rate.
i Refers to the percentage of the low-income population to the total population.
j Based on the Tendulkar methodology, using mixed reference period.
k The urban and rural poverty estimates refer to other areas excluding Phnom Penh.
l Data refer to the percentage of the population living below the basic-needs poverty line.
m Refers to the poverty headcount ratio using the upper poverty line, which serves as spatial deflator with respect to Honiara (the capital of Solomon Islands).

Sources: For indicator 1.1.1.a: World Bank. Poverty and Inequality Platform. https://pip.worldbank.org/ (accessed 07 June 2025). For indicator 1.1.1.b: International Labour Organization. ILOSTAT. http://www.ilo.org/ilostat (accessed 09 August 2025). For indicator 1.2.1: Economies' official sources; United Nations Statistics Division. Sustainable Development Goals (SDGs), SDG Indicators, Global Database. http://unstats.un.org/sdgs/indicators/database/ (accessed 09 August 2025); and Secretariat of the Pacific Community. National Minimum Development Indicators. https://www.spc.int/nmdi/ (accessed 09 August 2025).

Goal 1. End poverty in all its forms everywhere

Table 1.1.2: Selected Indicators for Sustainable Development Goal 1— Social Protection and Official Development Assistance

ADB Regional Member	Target 1.3: Implement nationally appropriate social protection systems and measures for all, including floors, and by 2030 achieve substantial coverage of the poor and the vulnerable					
	1.3.1.a: Proportion of Population Covered by at least One Social Protection Benefit (%)		1.3.1.b: Proportion of Population above Statutory Pensionable Age Receiving a Pension (%)		1.3.1.c: Proportion of Poor Population Receiving Social Assistance Cash Benefit (%)	
	2015	2023	2015	2023	2016	2023
Developing ADB Member Economies						
Central and West Asia						
Afghanistan	...	7.5 (2019)	10.7 (2010)	24.7 (2019)	...	...
Armenia	47.3	49.2 (2021)	87.6	81.9 (2021)	38.2	32.2 (2021)
Azerbaijan	40.3	35.2	100.0	97.0	100.0	100.0
Georgia	...	94.6 (2022)	91.9	100.0 (2022)	100.0	100.0 (2022)
Kazakhstan	100.0	94.3	82.6	95.7	28.9	100.0 (2022)
Kyrgyz Republic	...	42.9 (2022)	100.0	100.0 (2022)	89.4 (2018)	...
Pakistan	...	20.2 (2022)	2.3 (2010)	17.4 (2022)	69.2 (2018)	74.3 (2022)
Tajikistan	...	29.8 (2021)	92.8	100.0 (2021)	28.1 (2018)	50.7 (2021)
Türkiye	63.9 (2018)	64.0 (2022)	90.0	85.9 (2022)	...	...
Turkmenistan	...	42.7 (2021)	...	77.2 (2021)	...	...
Uzbekistan	...	56.0 (2022)	100.0 (2017)	100.0 (2021)	68.0 (2017)	100.0 (2022)
East Asia						
China, People's Republic of	63.0	75.6 (2021)	100.0	100.0 (2022)	51.6	100.0 (2021)
Hong Kong, China	...	63.3	72.9 (2009)	82.6	...	...
Korea, Republic of	65.7	80.2 (2022)	100.0 (2014)	100.0 (2022)	100.0	100.0 (2022)
Mongolia	72.4	93.5 (2021)	100.0	100.0 (2021)	94.9	...
Taipei,China	...	...	...	...	...	...
South Asia						
Bangladesh	...	22.0 (2021)	33.4	56.9 (2021)	11.0	59.4 (2021)
Bhutan	...	11.9 (2021)	3.2 (2012)	18.8 (2019)	60.2 (2018)	76.5 (2021)
India	19.0	48.8 (2022)	25.2 (2016)	45.9 (2022)	...	100.0 (2022)
Maldives	...	30.1 (2021)	99.7 (2012)	100.0 (2021)	100.0 (2018)	100.0 (2021)
Nepal	...	21.0 (2022)	62.5 (2010)	77.2 (2021)	70.1 (2018)	...
Sri Lanka	30.4	41.3 (2021)	25.2	31.1 (2021)	51.5	100.0 (2020)
Southeast Asia						
Brunei Darussalam	...	36.0 (2021)	81.7 (2011)	100.0 (2021)	...	...
Cambodia	...	20.8 (2022)	3.2	8.1 (2020)	...	12.3 (2020)
Indonesia	...	54.3 (2021)	14.0	31.2 (2021)	100.0 (2018)	100.0 (2021)
Lao People's Democratic Republic	...	15.5 (2021)	5.6 (2010)	7.0 (2021)	...	58.0 (2021)
Malaysia	...	29.2	19.8 (2010)	18.5	100.0 (2018)	17.4 (2020)
Myanmar	...	6.3 (2019)	0.9 (2016)	...	0.8 (2018)	...
Philippines	47.1	34.9 (2022)	39.8	65.6 (2021)	100.0 (2018)	100.0 (2022)
Singapore	...	100.0	- (2011)	37.3 (2021)	...	...
Thailand	...	70.1 (2020)	83.0 (2016)	82.6 (2020)	100.0 (2019)	- (2020)
Timor-Leste	...	23.6	89.7	92.7	...	17.6
Viet Nam	37.9	38.3 (2022)	39.9	40.9 (2019)	100.0 (2018)	76.1 (2020)
The Pacific						
Cook Islands	...	100.0 (2022)	...	67.2 (2022)	...	...
Fiji	...	65.6 (2022)	65.4	100.0 (2022)	68.0 (2018)	55.2 (2022)
Kiribati	...	21.0 (2019)	...	93.8 (2020)	15.9 (2018)	...
Marshall Islands	...	25.2 (2019)	64.2 (2010)	62.8 (2019)	...	- (2022)
Micronesia, Federated States of	...	20.0 (2021)	...	97.0 (2021)	...	...
Nauru	...	65.8 (2020)	100.0 (2018)	...	...	...
Niue	48.6 (2018)	...	100.0 (2018)	...	...	...
Palau	...	93.2 (2019)	...	100.0 (2019)	56.0 (2018)	5.8 (2019)
Papua New Guinea	...	9.1 (2022)	0.9 (2010)	1.9 (2022)	...	- (2022)
Samoa	...	20.2	49.5 (2011)	93.9	69.2 (2018)	...
Solomon Islands	...	17.2 (2019)	...	- (2021)	2.9 (2018)	...
Tonga	...	28.2 (2022)	73.3 (2018)	100.0 (2022)	16.7 (2018)	- (2022)
Tuvalu	...	4.5 (2019)	19.5 (2005)	100.0 (2019)	...	- (2022)
Vanuatu	...	57.4 (2019)	3.5 (2011)	4.1 (2019)	100.0 (2018)	- (2022)
Developed ADB Member Economies						
Australia	82.0	94.0 (2022)	74.3 (2016)	74.4 (2022)	...	69.6 (2022)
Japan	75.4	94.6 (2020)	100.0	100.0 (2020)	...	37.9 (2020)
New Zealand	100.0	100.0	100.0 (2016)	100.0	37.4	86.7

Table 1.1.2: Selected Indicators for Sustainable Development Goal 1— Social Protection and Official Development Assistance *(continued)*

ADB Regional Member	Target 1.3: Implement nationally appropriate social protection systems and measures for all, including floors, and by 2030 achieve substantial coverage of the poor and the vulnerable				Target 1.a: Ensure significant mobilization of resources from a variety of sources, including through enhanced development cooperation, in order to provide adequate and predictable means for developing countries, in particular least developed countries, to implement programmes and policies to end poverty in all its dimensions	
	1.3.1.d: Proportion of Vulnerable Population Receiving Social Assistance Cash Benefit (%)		1.3.1.e: Proportion of Children/ Households Receiving Child/ Family Cash Benefit (%)		1.a.1: Official Development Assistance Grants for Poverty Reduction, by Recipient Countries (percentage of GNI)	
	2015	2023	2015	2023	2015	2023
Developing ADB Member Economies						
Central and West Asia						
Afghanistan	...	5.9 (2019)	...	0.5 (2019)	1.6	4.1 (2022)
Armenia	16.2	21.1 (2021)	21.4	31.8 (2021)	0.1	0.1
Azerbaijan	12.6	10.6	...	10.3	0.0	0.0
Georgia	...	92.1 (2022)	...	30.2 (2022)	0.1	0.1
Kazakhstan	...	75.1 (2022)	...	54.4 (2022)	0.0	0.0
Kyrgyz Republic	...	10.7 (2022)	17.8	16.1 (2022)	0.6	0.3
Pakistan	...	17.2 (2022)	...	5.2 (2021)	0.1	0.1
Tajikistan	...	13.8 (2021)	6.4	15.6 (2021)	0.6	0.7
Türkiye	...	31.7 (2022)	...	37.4 (2022)	0.0	0.0
Turkmenistan	...	10.3 (2021)	...	14.5 (2021)	0.0	0.0
Uzbekistan	16.0 (2017)	40.2 (2022)	22.0 (2017)	51.0 (2022)	0.0	0.1
East Asia						
China, People's Republic of	27.1	38.7 (2021)	2.2	2.9 (2021)	0.0	0.0
Hong Kong, China	...	35.7	...	...	...	...
Korea, Republic of	48.9 (2018)	49.3 (2022)	40.0 (2018)	35.3 (2022)	...	...
Mongolia	35.1	88.4 (2021)	100.0	100.0 (2021)	0.2	0.4
Taipei,China	...	...	...	...	...	...
South Asia						
Bangladesh	4.3	19.2 (2021)	29.4	44.5 (2021)	0.2	0.1
Bhutan	...	6.7 (2021)	...	4.0 (2021)	0.3	0.4 (2022)
India	14.0	38.2 (2022)	...	51.9 (2022)	0.0	0.0
Maldives	...	11.3 (2021)	...	8.2 (2019)	0.1	0.2
Nepal	...	18.6 (2021)	...	27.5 (2021)	0.7	0.3
Sri Lanka	4.5	27.7 (2020)	...	36.1 (2021)	0.0	0.0
Southeast Asia						
Brunei Darussalam	...	15.6 (2021)	...	...	...	...
Cambodia	...	2.7 (2020)	...	7.1 (2020)	0.6	0.4
Indonesia	...	49.5 (2021)	...	43.6 (2021)	0.0	0.0
Lao People's Democratic Republic	...	11.2 (2021)	...	...	0.6	0.6
Malaysia	...	2.0 (2020)	...	1.6 (2021)	0.0	0.0
Myanmar	...	1.1 (2019)	...	2.1 (2019)	0.3	0.3
Philippines	7.8	22.7 (2022)	13.7	9.9 (2021)	0.1	0.0
Singapore	...	100.0	...	27.8	...	...
Thailand	...	59.9 (2020)	18.9	31.8 (2020)	0.0	0.0
Timor-Leste	...	18.1	30.7	16.5	1.0	1.8
Viet Nam	10.0	21.7 (2021)	...	1.4 (2020)	0.0	0.0
The Pacific						
Cook Islands	...	100.0 (2022)	100.0 (2018)	100.0 (2022)	1.8	0.5 (2019)
Fiji	...	39.7 (2022)	...	10.8 (2022)	0.4	0.3
Kiribati	...	5.1 (2020)	1.3 (2018)	1.3 (2019)	3.8	2.7
Marshall Islands	...	1.7 (2020)	...	– (2022)	0.6	3.0
Micronesia, Federated States of	...	2.2 (2019)	...	6.8 (2020)	0.7	0.5
Nauru	...	45.4 (2020)	...	66.0 (2019)	8.1	1.7
Niue	23.8 (2018)	...	84.5 (2018)	...	...	...
Palau	...	17.8 (2020)	...	...	0.4	0.9
Papua New Guinea	...	– (2022)	...	– (2022)	0.3	0.4
Samoa	...	6.8	– (2018)	–	2.7	1.0
Solomon Islands	...	0.4 (2019)	...	...	2.6	1.4
Tonga	...	8.1 (2022)	...	– (2022)	1.4	2.0 (2022)
Tuvalu	...	4.5 (2019)	...	– (2022)	5.4	1.3
Vanuatu	...	53.3 (2019)	...	12.9 (2019)	2.4	1.2
Developed ADB Member Economies						
Australia	82.0	93.6 (2022)	100.0	100.0 (2022)	...	...
Japan	...	69.8 (2020)	85.4 (2018)	85.4 (2019)	...	...
New Zealand	100.0 (2018)	100.0	67.1 (2018)	79.9	...	...

... = data not available, – = magnitude equals zero, 0.0 = magnitude is less than half of unit employed, ADB = Asian Development Bank, GNI = gross national income.

Note: The population covered by at least one social protection benefit (effective coverage) refers to the proportion of the total population receiving at least one contributory or noncontributory cash benefit, or actively contributing to at least one social security scheme. For children, older persons, and the poor and vulnerable, effective coverage is expressed as a share of the respective population.

Source: United Nations. SDG Global Database. https://unstats.un.org/sdgs/dataportal (accessed 18 July 2025).

Goal 2. End hunger, achieve food security and improved nutrition, and promote sustainable agriculture

Table 1.2.1: Selected Indicators for Sustainable Development Goal 2—Zero Hunger

ADB Regional Member	Target 2.1: By 2030, end hunger and ensure access by all people, in particular the poor and people in vulnerable situations, including infants, to safe, nutritious, and sufficient food all year round		Target 2.2: By 2030, end all forms of malnutrition, including achieving, by 2025, the internationally agreed targets on stunting and wasting in children under 5 years of age, and address the nutritional needs of adolescent girls, pregnant and lactating women, and older persons					
	2.1.1: Prevalence of Undernourishment (%)		2.2.1: Prevalence of Stunting among Children under 5 Years of Age[a] (%)		2.2.2.c: Prevalence of Malnutrition (Overweight) among Children under 5 Years of Age[a] (%)		2.2.2.d: Prevalence of Malnutrition (Wasting) among Children under 5 Years of Age (%)	
	2010[b]	2023[c]	2010	2024[d]	2010	2024[d]	2010	2023
Developing ADB Member Economies								
Central and West Asia[d]	...	...	**34.4**	**26.2**	**6.7**	**3.9**	...	...
Afghanistan	17.7	28.1	45.3	42.0	4.9	4.4	9.1 (2004)	3.6 (2022)
Armenia	<2.5	<2.5	16.6	6.2	15.3	12.9	4.1	4.4 (2016)
Azerbaijan	<2.5	<2.5	19.3	6.8	11.8	4.2	6.6 (2011)	3.5
Georgia	8.0	<2.5	10.4	4.7	16.3	4.1	1.3 (2009)	0.6 (2018)
Kazakhstan	3.4	<2.5	12.7	4.4	12.4	8.7	4.1	3.1 (2015)
Kyrgyz Republic	7.7	5.1	17.6	11.0	8.2	9.9	1.4 (2009)	3.0
Pakistan	15.5	16.5	44.9	33.6	4.9	2.1	14.9 (2011)	7.1 (2018)
Tajikistan	24.2	8.4	28.8	13.1	6.1	4.6	4.2 (2009)	6.4
Türkiye	<2.5	<2.5	10.8	5.5	9.9	7.7	1.0 (2008)	1.7 (2018)
Turkmenistan	4.7	4.3	14.4	6.5	5.6	4.8	7.2 (2006)	4.1 (2019)
Uzbekistan	3.6	<2.5	15.4	6.7	8.2	5.5	4.4 (2006)	2.4 (2021)
East Asia[d]	...	...	**8.6**	**4.5**	**6.7**	**11.0**	...	...
China, People's Republic of	<2.5	<2.5	8.8	4.5	6.7	11.1	2.3	1.9 (2017)
Hong Kong, China	<2.5	3.1	...	...	...	...	...	...
Korea, Republic of	<2.5	<2.5	2.0	1.8	6.9	5.5	0.5 (2011)	0.2 (2020)
Mongolia	17.1	<2.5	14.9	7.1	9.9	12.3	1.6	2.7
Taipei,China	4.7	3.8	...	...	...	...	...	...
South Asia[d]	...	...	**43.2**	**31.5**	**2.0**	**3.4**	...	...
Bangladesh	18.2	10.4	41.3	25.1	1.5	1.6	15.7 (2011)	10.7 (2022)
Bhutan	...	...	32.4	17.9	6.6	8.0	5.9	5.1
India	14.6	12.0	43.8	32.9	2.1	3.7	20.0 (2006)	18.7 (2020)
Maldives	...	...	17.9	14.2	5.9	3.0	10.6 (2009)	9.1 (2017)
Nepal	10.8	5.3	42.8	26.0	1.2	1.8	13.7	7.0 (2022)
Sri Lanka	11.0	7.4	17.2	10.1	1.2	0.9	11.8 (2009)	9.3 (2024)
Southeast Asia[d]	...	...	**32.1**	**22.8**	**5.5**	**4.3**	...	...
Brunei Darussalam	...	...	18.4	9.9	8.3	9.5	2.9 (2009)	...
Cambodia	10.0	5.2	37.6	22.0	2.0	5.7	11.0	9.6 (2021)
Indonesia	12.9	6.3	37.0	22.6	7.6	2.6	12.3	8.4
Lao People's Democratic Republic	...	...	42.8	29.9	2.1	3.7	5.9 (2011)	10.7
Malaysia	3.5	<2.5	17.8	24.3	6.2	5.3	13.2 (2006)	11.0 (2022)
Myanmar	9.2	5.4	33.0	24.5	2.3	0.6	7.9 (2009)	7.4 (2018)
Philippines	15.7	3.0	32.7	27.7	3.1	3.3	7.0 (2011)	5.4 (2021)
Singapore	...	...	3.4	2.8	2.6	3.8	3.6 (2000)	...
Thailand	10.2	4.6	15.2	12.3	8.7	9.9	6.7 (2012)	7.2 (2022)
Timor-Leste	19.0	18.7	54.7	45.4	2.8	1.2	18.9 (2009)	8.3 (2020)
Viet Nam	10.4	5.3	27.4	19.2	3.7	10.5	4.1	4.4
The Pacific[d]	...	...	**41.1**	**42.2**	**9.1**	**16.2**	...	...
Cook Islands	...	...	...	...	...	...	...	...
Fiji	7.0	6.8	7.3	7.2	6.1	7.3	6.4 (2004)	4.6 (2021)
Kiribati	3.7	4.1	17.1	14.7	2.0	2.1	...	3.5 (2018)
Marshall Islands	...	...	39.5	30.0	3.9	4.6	...	3.5 (2017)
Micronesia, Federated States of	...	...	...	...	...	...	...	...
Nauru	...	...	22.3	16.0	3.9	8.2	1.0 (2007)	1.3
Niue	...	...	...	...	...	...	...	...
Palau	...	...	...	...	...	...	...	...
Papua New Guinea	29.9	28.7	47.3	47.6	10.1	18.5	14.1	...
Samoa	4.6	3.6	4.8	8.4	5.7	9.4	...	3.1 (2019)
Solomon Islands	14.8	20.0	32.7	29.8	3.2	6.2	4.3 (2007)	8.5 (2015)
Tonga	...	...	8.3	1.6	15.5	9.5	5.2 (2012)	1.1 (2019)
Tuvalu	...	...	8.6	5.3	5.4	4.1	3.3 (2007)	2.8 (2019)
Vanuatu	6.9	7.2	26.6	31.0	4.8	5.5	5.9 (2008)	4.7 (2013)
Developed ADB Member Economies[d]	...	...	**6.0**	**4.6**	**3.7**	**8.7**	...	...
Australia	<2.5	<2.5	3.2	3.1	12.0	26.4	0.2 (2007)	...
Japan	...	...	6.8	5.2	1.5	2.0	2.4	...
New Zealand	<2.5	<2.5	...	...	...	...	...	...
DEVELOPING ADB MEMBER ECONOMIES[d]	...	...	**31.4**	**23.9**	**4.5**	**5.1**	...	...
ALL ADB REGIONAL MEMBERS[d]	...	...	**30.9**	**23.6**	**4.5**	**5.2**	...	...
WORLD	**8.7**	**8.5**	**27.9**	**23.2**	**5.4**	**5.5**	**7.7**	**6.6 (2024)**

... = data not available, < = less than, ADB = Asian Development Bank.

a Refers to modeled estimates from the Joint Child Malnutrition Estimates Database.
b Economy level data refer to the 3-year average for 2009–2011. World estimate refers to annual value.
c Economy level data refer to the 3-year average for 2022–2024. World estimate refers to annual value.
d For indicators 2.2.1 and 2.2.2.c, estimated as weighted averages using total population of children aged 0–5 years from the United Nations' World Population Prospects 2024 as weightings.

Sources: Food and Agriculture Organization of the United Nations. FAOSTAT Database. http://www.fao.org/faostat/en/#data/FS (accessed 29 July 2025). For Indicator 2.2.1, Indicator 2.2.2.c, and Indicator 2.2.2.d: United Nations. SDG Global Database. https://unstats.un.org/sdgs/dataportal (accessed 21 July 2025); and UNICEF/WHO/World Bank Joint Child Malnutrition Estimates - Country Estimates, 2025 edition. https://www.who.int/teams/nutrition-and-food-safety/monitoring-nutritional-status-and-food-safety-and-events/joint-child-malnutrition-estimates (accessed 14 July 2025). For total population of children 0–5 years old used as weightings: United Nations. World Population Prospects: The 2024 Revision. https://population.un.org/dataportal (accessed 3 July 2025).

Table 1.2.2: Selected Indicators for Sustainable Development Goal 2—Improved Agricultural Investment

ADB Regional Member	Target 2.a: Increase investment, including through enhanced international cooperation, in rural infrastructure, agricultural research and extension services, technology development, and plant and livestock gene banks in order to enhance agricultural productive capacity in developing countries (or economies), in particular least developed countries (or economies)					
	2.a.1: The Agriculture Orientation Index for Government Expenditures			2.a.2: Total Official Flows to the Agriculture Sector[a] (constant 2023 $ million)		
	2010	2015	2023	2010	2015	2023
Developing ADB Member Economies						
Central and West Asia	...	...	...	**1,445.4**	**1,487.8**	**1,389.8**
Afghanistan	0.2	0.2	0.1	817.4	382.2	220.2
Armenia	0.3	0.1	0.3	100.8	42.1	26.3
Azerbaijan	0.5	0.5	0.6 (2022)	18.8	59.3	19.3
Georgia	0.1	0.4	0.5	19.4	49.0	69.9
Kazakhstan	0.9	0.9	0.8	61.5	75.1	22.3
Kyrgyz Republic	0.1	0.1	0.1	25.0	28.1	26.3
Pakistan	0.1	0.1	0.1	184.7	335.9	430.3
Tajikistan	0.1	0.0	0.1 (2022)	56.4	38.4	88.4
Türkiye	0.3	0.5	0.5	125.5	398.3	109.7
Turkmenistan	...	0.3	0.2 (2021)	1.2	0.1	0.2
Uzbekistan	0.2 (2011)	0.2	0.1	34.7	79.1	376.8
East Asia[b]	...	...	...	**373.1**	**452.8**	**307.0**
China, People's Republic of	0.9	1.0	0.9	327.6	433.9	267.4
Hong Kong, China	2.7	1.8	2.2 (2022)	...	...	...
Korea, Republic of	2.6	2.1	1.7 (2022)	...	...	...
Mongolia	0.4	0.1	0.2	45.5	18.9	39.5
Taipei,China	...	...	...	...	...	...
South Asia	...	...	...	**1,139.6**	**1,621.1**	**1,346.7**
Bangladesh	0.6	0.6	0.6	206.2	276.2	395.3
Bhutan	0.7	0.8	0.6	6.5	6.2	24.8
India	0.5	0.5	0.4 (2022)	778.4	1,181.4	753.9
Maldives	0.2	0.1	0.1 (2022)	0.0	0.5	12.3
Nepal	0.3	0.3	0.3	112.3	117.4	76.8
Sri Lanka	0.6	0.8	0.4	36.2	39.2	83.6
Southeast Asia[b]	...	...	...	**1,684.2**	**1,014.7**	**1,675.3**
Brunei Darussalam	0.9	0.6	0.7	...	...	...
Cambodia	0.0	0.1	0.1	81.6	126.8	192.3
Indonesia	0.1	0.2	0.2	1,045.4	235.8	571.6
Lao People's Democratic Republic	0.1	0.1	0.1	56.8	75.6	81.0
Malaysia	0.3	0.4	0.2	2.3	5.3	1.1
Myanmar	0.2	0.2	0.2 (2020)	40.3	151.0	61.2
Philippines	0.4	0.4	0.3	130.6	119.8	605.0
Singapore	6.8	7.7	5.4	...	...	...
Thailand	0.4	0.8	0.7	11.0	8.0	7.4
Timor-Leste	0.1	0.1	0.1 (2022)	28.7	25.7	18.1
Viet Nam	0.3	0.4	0.3 (2022)	287.5	266.5	137.7
The Pacific[b]	...	...	...	**58.4**	**90.1**	**113.6**
Cook Islands	0.9	0.9	0.5 (2022)	1.3	0.3	...
Fiji	0.1	0.6	0.4	3.2	23.0	19.9
Kiribati	0.1	0.1	0.1	3.0	2.7	7.4
Marshall Islands	0.2	0.2	...	3.2	1.6	3.3
Micronesia, Federated States of	0.1	0.1	0.2 (2020)	1.0	1.9	0.8
Nauru	...	0.6	0.5 (2022)	0.5	0.4	2.4
Niue	...	...	...	0.2	0.2	0.0
Palau	0.1	0.2	...	0.6	0.7	4.4
Papua New Guinea	0.1	0.1	0.1	22.6	32.6	43.6
Samoa	0.2	0.4	0.4	1.6	4.3	3.3
Solomon Islands	0.1 (2011)	0.1	0.1	11.8	13.9	13.3
Tonga	0.4	0.2	0.2 (2020)	2.3	2.0	2.9
Tuvalu	0.1	0.2	0.2 (2022)	0.9	2.4	3.5
Vanuatu	0.1	0.2	0.2 (2020)	6.3	4.2	8.8
Developed ADB Member Economies	...	...	...	...	...	...
Australia	0.5	0.3	0.4	...	...	...
Japan	2.1	2.2	2.1 (2022)	...	...	...
New Zealand	0.1	0.1	0.0	...	...	...
DEVELOPING ADB MEMBER ECONOMIES[b]	...	...	...	**4,700.7**	**4,666.5**	**4,832.4**

... = data not available, 0.0 = magnitude is less than half of unit employed, $ = United States dollars, ADB = Asian Development Bank.

a Total official flows refer to official development assistance plus other official flows. Data refer to gross disbursements.
b Includes only reporting economies with data corresponding to the year heading.

Source: United Nations. SDG Global Database. https://unstats.un.org/sdgs/dataportal (accessed 18 July 2025).

Goal 3. Ensure healthy lives and promote well-being for all at all ages

Table 1.3.1: Selected Indicators for Sustainable Development Goal 3—Maternal and Child Health

ADB Regional Member	Target 3.1: By 2030, reduce the global maternal mortality ratio to less than 70 per 100,000 live births				Target 3.2: By 2030, end preventable deaths of newborns and children under 5 years of age, with all countries (or economies) aiming to reduce neonatal mortality to at least as low as 12 per 1,000 live births and under-5 mortality to at least as low as 25 per 1,000 live births			
	3.1.1: Maternal Mortality Ratio[a,b] (per 100,000 live births)		3.1.2: Proportion of Births Attended by Skilled Health Personnel[c] (%)		3.2.1: Under-5 Mortality Rate[a,b] (per 1,000 live births)		3.2.2: Neonatal Mortality Rate[a,b] (per 1,000 live births)	
	2010	2023	2010	2023	2010	2023	2010	2023
Developing ADB Member Economies								
Central and West Asia	**251**	**164**			**69**	**46**	**43**	**29**
Afghanistan	893	521	34.3	67.5	88	56	48	34
Armenia	28	19	99.5	99.8 (2016)	19	10	10	5
Azerbaijan	28	18	99.4	99.9	38	19	21	13
Georgia	41	20	99.6	99.8	14	9	10	5
Kazakhstan	22	10	99.4	99.9 (2018)	20	10	12	4
Kyrgyz Republic	71	42	98.3	99.8	30	17	17	11
Pakistan	240	155	43.0 (2011)	68.0 (2020)	87	59	50	38
Tajikistan	26	14	87.7	97.6	37	27	20	13
Türkiye	23	15	91.3 (2008)	97.0 (2019)	18	13	9	5
Turkmenistan	9	5	99.5 (2006)	99.7 (2022)	44	40	23	23
Uzbekistan	34	26	100.0	99.2 (2022)	30	13	17	8
East Asia	**33**	**16**			**16**	**6**	**8**	**3**
China, People's Republic of	34	16	99.6	99.9 (2016)	16	6	8	3
Hong Kong, China	1	3	...	...	...	...	1	1
Korea, Republic of	8	4	99.9 (2009)	100.0 (2021)	4	3	2	1
Mongolia	71	41	98.8	100.0	26	14	11	7
Taipei,China	<[d]	<[d]	...	...	...	...	3	3
South Asia	**198**	**85**			**56**	**28**	**31**	**17**
Bangladesh	275	115	26.5	69.7	49	31	29	18
Bhutan	107	47	64.5	98.5	40	23	22	13
India	188	80	52.3 (2008)	89.4 (2021)	58	28	32	17
Maldives	49	32	98.2	99.5 (2017)	14	6	8	4
Nepal	297	142	36.0 (2011)	80.1 (2022)	48	27	28	17
Sri Lanka	26	18	98.6 (2007)	99.5 (2016)	11	6	6	4
Southeast Asia	**171**	**110**			**32**	**22**	**16**	**12**
Brunei Darussalam	40	36	99.8	99.6	10	9	5	5
Cambodia	234	137	71.0 (2011)	98.7 (2022)	44	23	21	12
Indonesia	242	140	83.1 (2012)	96.8 (2024)	34	21	17	11
Lao People's Democratic Republic	305	112	40.1 (2012)	79.8	68	39	29	20
Malaysia	29	26	98.6	99.8 (2022)	8	8	4	4
Myanmar	259	185	70.6	60.2 (2016)	63	39	28	21
Philippines	117	84	72.2 (2011)	89.6 (2022)	30	27	14	14
Singapore	10	6	99.8	99.5 (2022)	3	2	1	1
Thailand	37	34	99.4 (2009)	99.6 (2022)	14	9	8	5
Timor-Leste	439	192	29.3	68.5 (2016)	71	50	28	22
Viet Nam	62	48	91.9 (2011)	98.0 (2022)	23	20	12	10
The Pacific	**249**	**169**			**52**	**37**	**23**	**19**
Cook Islands	0	0	100.0 (2009)	...	13	14	7	7
Fiji	40	30	99.7	99.8 (2021)	22	29	9	15
Kiribati	102	80	98.3	91.9 (2019)	58	55	24	22
Marshall Islands	212	155	90.0	92.4 (2017)	39	28	18	13
Micronesia, Federated States of	184	129	100.0 (2009)	...	34	23	18	12
Nauru	297	273	97.4 (2007)	98.0	27	9	16	5
Niue	...	...	100.0	...	36	24	19	13
Palau	96	89	99.6	98.7 (2022)	20	22	11	12
Papua New Guinea	289	189	53.0 (2006)	56.4 (2018)	59	40	27	21
Samoa	92	101	80.8 (2009)	88.9 (2020)	19	16	8	6
Solomon Islands	148	123	85.5 (2007)	...	27	21	11	8
Tonga	85	67	99.0	98.3 (2019)	13	10	6	4
Tuvalu	213	170	93.1 (2007)	99.5 (2020)	31	20	16	9
Vanuatu	114	100	89.4 (2013)	90.9	21	17	10	9
Developed ADB Member Economies	**6**	**3**			**4**	**3**	**2**	**1**
Australia	5	2	99.1	98.7 (2021)	5	4	3	2
Japan	6	3	99.8	99.8	3	2	1	1
New Zealand	10	7	96.8	95.8 (2021)	6	5	3	3
DEVELOPING ADB MEMBER ECONOMIES	**160**	**95**			**44**	**27**	**24**	**16**
ALL ADB REGIONAL MEMBERS	**157**	**93**			**43**	**26**	**24**	**16**
WORLD	**253**	**197**	**72.3**	**86.6 (2024)**	**52**	**37**	**23**	**17**

... = data not available, 0 = magnitude is less than half of unit employed, < = small sample size, ADB = Asian Development Bank.

a Regional aggregates are weighted averages estimated using population of annual live births for the respective year headings. The data for maternal, under-5, and neonatal deaths are from United Nations databases. For Taipei,China, maternal and neonatal deaths data are from the Government of Taipei,China's Ministry of Health and Welfare. Aggregates are derived for reporting economies only. For maternal and under-5 mortality rates, aggregates for East Asia exclude Hong Kong, China and Taipei,China. For neonatal mortality rate, aggregates exclude Hong Kong, China.

b Data are estimates as published on the United Nations' SDG Global Database.

c Based on data from national-level household surveys and routine service statistics.

d The number of maternal deaths is fewer than 20, the mortality rate is unreliable due to the small sample size effect.

Sources: For Indicators 3.1.1, 3.1.2, 3.2.1, and 3.2.2: United Nations. SDG Global Database. https://unstats.un.org/sdgs/dataportal (accessed 24 July 2025). For Indicator 3.1.1 for Hong Kong, China: Government of the Hong Kong Special Administrative Region of the People's Republic of China. Centre for Health Protection Statistics. https://www.chp.gov.hk/en/statistics/data/10/27/110.html (accessed 24 July 2025). For Indicator 3.1.1 for Taipei,China: Government of Taipei,China, Directorate-General of Budget, Accounting and Statistics. For Indicator 3.2.2 for Hong Kong, China: Government of the Hong Kong Special Administrative Region of the People's Republic of China, Department of Health. Health Facts of Hong Kong 2024 Edition; past editions. https://www.dh.gov.hk/english/statistics/statistics_hs/files/2024.pdf (accessed 24 July 2025). For Indicator 3.2.2 for Taipei,China: Government of Taipei,China, Ministry of Health and Welfare. 2023 Cause of Death Statistics.

Table 1.3.2: Selected Indicators for Sustainable Development Goal 3—Incidence of Communicable Diseases

ADB Regional Member	Target 3.3: By 2030, end the epidemics of AIDS, tuberculosis, malaria, and neglected tropical diseases; and combat hepatitis, water-borne diseases, and other communicable diseases					
	3.3.1: Number of New HIV Infections[a] (per 1,000 uninfected population)		3.3.2: Tuberculosis Incidence[b] (per 100,000 population)		3.3.3: Malaria Incidence[c] (per 1,000 population)	
	2010	2024	2010	2023	2010	2023
Developing ADB Member Economies						
Central and West Asia						
Afghanistan	<0.1	<0.1	189.0	180.0	13.4	13.3
Armenia	0.12	0.21	61.0	25.0	–	–
Azerbaijan	<0.1[d]	<0.1[d]	104.0	72.0	0.2	–
Georgia	0.12[d]	0.15[d]	127.0	55.0	–	–
Kazakhstan	0.14	0.11	144.0	70.0	–	–
Kyrgyz Republic	0.14	0.13	120.0	112.0	0.0	–
Pakistan	…	…	276.0	277.0	7.4	17.6
Tajikistan	0.14	<0.1	128.0	79.0	0.0	–
Türkiye	…[e]	…[e]		13.0	–	–
Turkmenistan	…[e]	…[e]	79.0	49.0	–	–
Uzbekistan	…[e]	…[e]	97.0	57.0	0.1	–
East Asia						
China, People's Republic of	…[e]	…[e]	76.0	52.0	0.0	–
Hong Kong, China	…	…	80.0	50.0	…	…
Korea, Republic of	…[e]	…[e]	97.0	38.0	0.4	0.2
Mongolia	<0.1[d]	<0.1[d]	428.0	491.0	…	…
Taipei,China	…	…	…	…	…	…
South Asia						
Bangladesh	<0.01	<0.01	221.0	221.0	4.2	1.1
Bhutan	<0.1[d]	0.11[d]	232.0	164.0	0.8	–
India	…	<0.1	276.0	195.0	17.4	1.5
Maldives	<0.01[d]	<0.1[d]	32.0	40.0	…	…
Nepal	<0.1	<0.1	311.0	229.0	0.5	0.0
Sri Lanka	<0.1[d]	<0.1[d]	66.0	62.0	0.1	–
Southeast Asia						
Brunei Darussalam	…[e]	…[e]	69.0	65.0	…	…
Cambodia	0.16	<0.1	438.0	335.0	34.2	0.5
Indonesia	0.20	<0.1	342.0	387.0	8.1	3.9
Lao People's Democratic Republic	0.17	0.16	221.0	132.0	13.3	0.3
Malaysia	0.20	<0.1	75.0	122.0	4.5	–
Myanmar	0.36	0.20	500.0	558.0	35.3	18.0
Philippines	<0.1	0.27	531.0	643.0	1.0	0.2
Singapore	<0.1[d]	<0.1[d](2023)	35.0	42.0	…	…
Thailand	0.27	0.11	181.0	157.0	2.5	0.7
Timor-Leste	0.10	0.11	498.0	498.0	93.5	–
Viet Nam	0.16	<0.1	231.0	182.0	0.3	0.0
The Pacific						
Cook Islands	…	…	–	32.0	…	…
Fiji	<0.1	1.50	27.0	66.0	…	…
Kiribati	…	…	347.0	533.0	…	…
Marshall Islands	…	…	428.0	692.0	…	…
Micronesia, Federated States of	…	…	191.0	234.0	…	…
Nauru	…	…	34.0	174.0	…	…
Niue	…	…	–	48.0	…	…
Palau	…	…	118.0	97.0	…	…
Papua New Guinea	0.79	1.10	432.0	432.0	141.4	147.2
Samoa	…	…	8.3	5.2	…	…
Solomon Islands	<0.01	<0.1	78.0	55.0	173.3	237.0
Tonga	…	…	12.0	8.8	…	…
Tuvalu	0.20	0.26	153.0	296.0	…	…
Vanuatu	<0.1	<0.01	69.0	41.0	88.0	17.9
Developed ADB Member Economies						
Australia	<0.1	<0.1 (2022)	6.6	6.2	…	…
Japan	…[e]	…[e]	20.0	9.3	…	…
New Zealand	<0.1[d]	<0.1[d]	8.0	6.6	…	…

… = data not available, < = less than, – = magnitude equals zero, 0.0 = magnitude is less than half of unit employed, ADB = Asian Development Bank.

a Figures are based on modeled HIV estimates. For more information on the HIV estimates methodology, please see https://www.unaids.org.

b Estimates of tuberculosis incidence are produced through a consultative and analytical process led by the World Health Organization and are published annually. These estimates are based on annual case notifications, assessments of the quality and coverage of tuberculosis notification data, national surveys of the prevalence of tuberculosis disease, and information from death (vital) registration systems. For the period 2000–2019, estimates of incidence for each economy are derived using one or more of the following approaches, depending on available data: (i) incidence = case notifications and/or estimated proportion of cases detected; (ii) capture-recapture modelling, (iii) estimated duration of untreated tuberculosis, applied to prevalence estimates where available. For 2020 and subsequent years, these methods were retained for most countries. However, for countries with large absolute reductions in the reported number of people newly diagnosed with tuberculosis from 2020 onwards, relative to pre-2020 trends, which suggested major disruptions to access to TB diagnosis and treatment during the COVID-19 pandemic, dynamic models were used in replacement of the methods used for 2000-2019.

c Malaria incidence is expressed as the number of new cases per 1,000 population per year with the population of an economy derived from projections made by the UN Population Division and the total proportion at risk estimated by an economy's National Malaria Control Programme. More specifically, the economy estimates what is the total proportion of the population at risk of malaria and then, for each year, the total population at risk is estimated as the UN Population for that year, times the proportion of the population at risk at baseline. The same proportion of the population at risk is used for the entire time series to ensure comparability of estimates through time.

d Children estimates were not available at the time of publication.

e Estimates were not available at the time of publication.

Sources: For Indicator 3.3.1: Joint United Nations Programme on HIV/AIDS (UNAIDS). AIDSinfo. https://aidsinfo.unaids.org/ (accessed 15 July 2025).
For Indicators 3.3.2 and 3.3.3: United Nations. SDG Global Database. https://unstats.un.org/sdgs/dataportal (accessed 15 July 2025).

Goal 3. Ensure healthy lives and promote well-being for all at all ages

Table 1.3.3: Selected Indicators for Sustainable Development Goal 3—Mortality Rates, Reproductive Health

ADB Regional Member	Target 3.4: By 2030, reduce by one-third premature mortality from noncommunicable diseases through prevention and treatment, and promote mental health and well-being					Target 3.6: By 2020, halve the number of global deaths and injuries from road traffic accidents
	3.4.1: Mortality Rate Attributed to Cardiovascular Disease, Cancer, Diabetes, or Chronic Respiratory Disease[a] (%)		3.4.2: Suicide Mortality Rate[a] (per 100,000 population)			3.6.1: Death Rate Due to Road Traffic Injuries[a] (per 100,000 population)
	2010	2021	2021 Total	2021 Female	2021 Male	2021
Developing ADB Member Economies						
Central and West Asia						
Afghanistan	37.6	32.7	3.6	2.4	4.8	24.1
Armenia	24.8	20.6	2.5	1.0	4.2	13.6
Azerbaijan	27.5	17.4	1.6	0.8	2.3	17.2
Georgia	28.2	22.1	5.1	1.3	9.5	12.7
Kazakhstan	31.5	21.2	14.6	5.3	24.4	12.2
Kyrgyz Republic	28.0	18.8	6.8	3.1	10.5	13.3
Pakistan	28.1	25.5	5.6	3.2	8.0	11.9
Tajikistan	26.1	18.1	2.4	1.3	3.6	13.9
Türkiye	18.6	15.4	2.7	1.1	4.3	6.5
Turkmenistan	27.4	25.7	6.8	3.5	10.3	8.0
Uzbekistan	37.8	24.6	8.3	6.1	10.6	9.3
East Asia						
China, People's Republic of	19.4	15.9	8.9	7.5	10.3	17.4
Hong Kong, China	...	...	...	...	...	1.3 (2023)
Korea, Republic of	10.9	6.9	27.5	16.9	38.2	6.9
Mongolia	35.9	26.3	18.5	4.8	32.2	12.4
Taipei,China	...	...	16.7 (2023)	...	...	...
South Asia						
Bangladesh	22.0	18.1	2.8	2.0	3.6	18.6
Bhutan	18.0	15.9	4.9	3.4	6.2	12.2
India	22.6	23.6	12.6	11.2	13.8	15.4
Maldives	20.7	9.0	1.5	0.3	2.2	1.3
Nepal	19.1	19.4	10.1	7.2	13.3	28.2
Sri Lanka	18.2	13.9	14.7	5.9	24.2	11.5
Southeast Asia						
Brunei Darussalam	16.1	14.9	3.0	0.6	5.2	3.6
Cambodia	24.4	22.6	4.5	2.7	6.3	18.8
Indonesia	26.0	21.9	1.2	0.9	1.5	11.3
Lao People's Democratic Republic	29.2	26.5	4.6	2.6	6.5	16.4
Malaysia	19.2	19.9	5.7	2.2	8.8	13.9
Myanmar	28.3	24.0	2.9	1.0	4.8	19.3
Philippines	25.0	31.9	3.5	1.8	5.2	9.7
Singapore	11.0	10.3	8.1	4.9	11.1	1.9
Thailand	15.1	14.5	16.6	5.5	28.2	25.4
Timor-Leste	21.3	20.1	3.6	2.3	4.8	12.0
Viet Nam	21.7	20.1	7.3	4.3	10.4	17.7
The Pacific						
Cook Islands	...	...	...	...	...	17.6
Fiji	41.3	37.9	8.3	5.3	11.2	5.3
Kiribati	42.6	44.1	17.5	4.8	31.0	6.2
Marshall Islands	...	...	...	...	...	11.9
Micronesia, Federated States of	40.1	40.5	19.8	8.6	31.1	14.1
Nauru	...	30.0 (2017)	...	...	...	8.0
Niue	...	18.5 (2016)	...	...	...	-
Palau	...	...	...	...	...	22.2
Papua New Guinea	29.5	28.5	1.8	1.4	2.2	14.9
Samoa	31.0	32.3	12.0	7.0	17.0	9.6
Solomon Islands	39.2	40.6	19.6	9.6	29.2	11.2
Tonga	27.4	26.9	4.7	3.5	6.0	8.5
Tuvalu	...	...	...	...	...	17.9
Vanuatu	38.0	36.8	15.7	6.6	24.7	12.5
Developed ADB Member Economies						
Australia	9.9	8.3	13.1	6.7	19.5	4.5
Japan	9.6	8.0	17.4	11.5	23.6	2.7
New Zealand	11.8	10.3	11.9	6.1	17.9	6.6

Table 1.3.3: Selected Indicators for Sustainable Development Goal 3—Mortality Rates, Reproductive Health *(continued)*

ADB Regional Member	Target 3.7: By 2030, ensure universal access to sexual and reproductive health-care services, including for family planning, information, and education, and the integration of reproductive health into natural strategies and programs				Target 3.8: Achieve universal health coverage, including financial risk protection; access to quality essential health-care services; and access to safe, effective, quality, and affordable essential medicines and vaccines for all	Target 3.9: By 2030, substantially reduce the number of deaths and illnesses from hazardous chemicals and air, water, and soil pollution and contamination	
	3.7.1: Proportion of Women of Reproductive Age (Aged 15–49 Years) Who Have Their Need for Family Planning Satisfied with Modern Methods		3.7.2: Adolescent Birth Rate (Aged 15–19 Years) per 1,000 Women in That Age Group		3.8.1: Coverage of Essential Health Services[b] (index in a unitless scale of 0 to 100)	3.9.1: Mortality Rate Attributed to Household and Ambient Air Pollution (per 100,000 population)	3.9.2: Mortality Rate Attributed to Unsafe Water, Unsafe Sanitation, and Lack of Hygiene (per 100,000 population)
	2010	2022	2010	2022	2021	2019	2019
Developing ADB Member Economies							
Central and West Asia							
Afghanistan	42.1 (2015)	...	107.5 (2011)	62.0 (2021)	41.0	266.0	16.6
Armenia	39.4	...	27.1	11.4	68.0	75.0	5.8
Azerbaijan	21.5 (2006)	...	48.6	37.3	66.0	125.0	3.6
Georgia	52.8[c]	51.3 (2018)	48.4	21.8	68.0	93.0	3.3
Kazakhstan	79.6[c]	73.1[c] (2018)	28.0	17.2 (2023)	80.0	83.0	3.2
Kyrgyz Republic	62.1 (2012)	64.6 (2018)	34.1	29.0 (2023)	69.0	125.0	2.3
Pakistan	47.0 (2012)	48.5[c] (2017)	48.1	41.0 (2021)	45.0	192.0	38.8
Tajikistan	50.8 (2012)	52.1 (2017)	47.5	39.2 (2019)	67.0	204.0	9.0
Türkiye	56.4[c] (2008)	60.2 (2018)	32.0	12.2	76.0	46.0	2.5
Turkmenistan	75.6 (2015)	79.6 (2019)	26.2 (2011)	22.4 (2018)	75.0	88.0	5.7
Uzbekistan	...	81.0 (2021)	23.8	37.3 (2023)	75.0	152.0	2.9
East Asia							
China, People's Republic of	96.6 (2001)	...	5.9	6.1 (2020)	81.0	95.0	2.2
Hong Kong, China	...	...	3.3	1.1	...	...	...
Korea, Republic of	...	74.1 (2021)	1.8	0.4	89.0	19.0	5.2
Mongolia	65.3[c]	63.6 (2018)	18.9	17.0 (2023)	65.0	215.0	3.2
Taipei,China	...	...	...	...	...	...	...
South Asia							
Bangladesh	69.7 (2011)	73.9	118.3	71.2 (2023)	52.0	144.0	18.2
Bhutan	84.6[c]	...	19.6 (2011)	6.1	60.0	94.0	15.7
India	63.9 (2007)	74.3 (2019)	37.2	11.3 (2020)	63.0	139.0	36.4
Maldives	42.7 (2009)	29.2 (2016)	15.6	8.3 (2021)	61.0	32.0	2.3
Nepal	56.2 (2011)	55.1	91.6 (2011)	71.2 (2020)	54.0	178.0	17.8
Sri Lanka	69.4[c] (2006)	74.3 (2016)	23.4	...	67.0	92.0	4.8
Southeast Asia							
Brunei Darussalam	...	...	14.5 (2011)	8.8	78.0	20.0	1.7
Cambodia	51.6	59.5 (2021)	53.8	48.0 (2020)	58.0	163.0	17.1
Indonesia	79.0 (2012)	77.0 (2017)	46.9	36.1 (2016)	55.0	96.0	15.8
Lao People's Democratic Republic	60.5 (2011)	72.3 (2017)	94.4	89.0	52.0	195.0	20.5
Malaysia	...	49.6	14.0	6.0	76.0	76.0	14.4
Myanmar	74.9 (2015)	...	35.1 (2011)	...	52.0	184.0	12.9
Philippines	54.0 (2011)	58.2	68.0	27.0	58.0	203.0	16.9
Singapore	...	...	4.8	1.9	89.0	23.0	8.5
Thailand	89.2 (2012)	87.0	50.1	18.0	82.0	46.0	11.8
Timor-Leste	38.4 (2009)	45.9 (2016)	50.0	...	52.0	186.0	20.4
Viet Nam	73.1[c]	72.0 (2020)	38.0	29.0 (2020)	68.0	103.0	6.9
The Pacific							
Cook Islands	...	...	51.7	31.0 (2023)	46.0	...	...
Fiji	...	51.3 (2021)	38.2	31.0 (2019)	58.0	119.0	10.8
Kiribati	35.8 (2009)	53.1 (2018)	49.9	50.6 (2017)	48.0	247.0	37.4
Marshall Islands	80.5 (2007)	...	82.2	...	59.0	...	...
Micronesia, Federated States of	...	...	33.0 (2009)	...	48.0	254.0	14.0
Nauru	42.5 (2007)	...	69.4	56.1 (2021)	60.0	...	...
Niue	...	...	18.8	–	44.0	...	...
Palau	...	...	30.8 (2012)	36.5 (2020)	65.0	...	...
Papua New Guinea	40.6 (2006)	49.2 (2016)	91.4	67.7 (2016)	30.0	190.0	24.9
Samoa	34.9 (2009)	27.0 (2019)	39.2 (2011)	54.9 (2018)	55.0	145.0	8.2
Solomon Islands	60.0 (2006)	...	61.6 (2009)	49.1 (2019)	47.0	281.0	32.7
Tonga	47.9 (2012)	49.9 (2019)	24.0	30.0 (2017)	57.0	52.0	7.1
Tuvalu	41.0 (2007)	44.9 (2020)	44.2 (2009)	35.7	52.0	...	...
Vanuatu	50.7 (2013)	...	78.0 (2011)	...	47.0	260.0	25.0
Developed ADB Member Economies							
Australia	...	...	16.7	6.7	87.0	10.0	1.9
Japan	...	...	4.6	1.7	83.0	12.0	8.4
New Zealand	...	...	29.0	11.0 (2023)	85.0	12.0	2.1

... = data not available, – = magnitude equals zero, ADB = Asian Development Bank.

a For detailed information regarding the nature of the data, please refer to the United Nations' SDG Global Database at https://unstats.un.org/sdgs/dataportal.

b The universal health coverage service coverage index is calculated as the geometric mean of 14 tracer indicators of health service coverage. The index is reported on a unitless scale of 0 to 100, with 100 being the optimal value. The reported values do not directly translate to the percentage of the population covered by universal health coverage services, but they can be viewed as performance scores.

c For additional information regarding the data, please refer to the United Nations' SDG Global Database at https://unstats.un.org/sdgs/dataportal.

Sources: For Indicators 3.4.1, 3.4.2, 3.6.1, 3.7.1, 3.7.2, 3.8.1, 3.9.1, and 3.9.2: United Nations. SDG Global Database. https://unstats.un.org/sdgs/dataportal (accessed 24 July 2025). For Indicator 3.4.1 for Nauru and Niue: Pacific Community. Pacific Data Hub. Explorer. https://stats.pacificdata.org/ (accessed 24 July 2025). For Indicator 3.4.2 for Taipei,China: Government of Taipei,China, Ministry of Health and Welfare. 2023 Cause of Death Statistics. For Indicator 3.6.1 for Hong Kong, China: Government of the Hong Kong Special Administrative Region of the People's Republic of China. Road Traffic Accident Statistics. https://www.td.gov.hk/en/road_safety/road_traffic_accident_statistics/accident_trend_since_1953/index.html (accessed 24 July 2025).

Goal 3. Ensure healthy lives and promote well-being for all at all ages

Table 1.3.4: Selected Indicators for Sustainable Development Goal 3—Health Workforce and National and Global Health Risks

ADB Regional Member	Target 3.c: Substantially increase health financing and the recruitment, development, training, and retention of the health workforce in developing countries, especially in least developed countries and small island developing states						Target 3.d: Strengthen the capacity of all countries, in particular developing countries, for early warning, risk reduction, and management of national and global health risks
	3.c.1: Health Worker Density, by Type of Occupation[a,b] (per 10,000 population)						3.d.1: International Health Regulations Capacity and Health Emergency Preparedness[c,d,e] (%)
	Density of Medical Doctors			Density of Nursing and Midwifery Personnel			Average of 15 International Health Regulations Core Capacity Scores
	2010	2015	2023	2010	2015	2023	2024
Developing ADB Member Economies							
Central and West Asia	**13.3**	**13.8**	**16.2**	**29.8**	**28.5**	**31.1**	**62**
Afghanistan	2.4	2.9	3.2	6.3 (2009)	1.3	5.5	35
Armenia	27.9	29.2	33.6 (2022)	51.4	49.6	47.5 (2022)	59
Azerbaijan	36.2	33.3	31.9 (2022)	72.6	61.5	55.8 (2022)	67
Georgia	46.8	53.1	56.4	41.6	42.6	59.7	60
Kazakhstan	37.9	37.3	37.5	74.5	70.9	64.9	73
Kyrgyz Republic	23.1	21.8	18.5	55.8	48.1	40.8	49
Pakistan	7.3	8.5	11.6 (2021)	5.0	4.4	5.2 (2021)	52
Tajikistan	16.7	17.5	18.7	38.9	45.9	64.5	60
Türkiye	16.8	17.7	22.4 (2022)	22.5	25.7	34.8 (2022)	75
Turkmenistan	20.8	19.7	19.3	41.3	39.6	34.9	81
Uzbekistan	25.6	23.6	23.1 (2020)	114.3	113.6 (2014)	110.8 (2020)	73
East Asia	**14.8**	**18.2**	**31.0 (2022)**	**16.3**	**24.5**	**38.6**	**84**
China, People's Republic of	14.6	18.0	31.1 (2022)	15.2	23.2	36.7 (2022)	94
Hong Kong, China	...	...	...	...	...	...	...
Korea, Republic of	20.2	22.4	26.1 (2022)	47.1	59.7	90.9 (2022)	99
Mongolia	27.8	32.4	41.3 (2022)	36.6	41.2	42.2 (2018)	60
Taipei,China	...	...	...	...	...	...	...
South Asia	**...**	**5.4**	**7.3 (2021)**	**...**	**13.3**	**16.6**	**66**
Bangladesh	3.5	4.8	7.2	1.8	2.6	6.6	69
Bhutan	2.7 (2012)	3.4	5.5 (2022)	10.3 (2012)	14.5	20.5 (2022)	64
India	...	7.2	7.2 (2020)	8.6	14.3	17.2 (2020)	88
Maldives	14.6	13.2 (2016)	22.4 (2019)	51.8	69.8	50.2 (2020)	58
Nepal	5.1 (2012)	6.8 (2017)	10.1	15.7 (2012)	20.8 (2014)	40.9	49
Sri Lanka	7.0	8.3	11.4	16.9	18.9	22.6	66
Southeast Asia	**4.6**	**5.3**	**7.8**	**19.3**	**21.0**	**32.9**	**70**
Brunei Darussalam	14.4	17.5	18.9 (2021)	74.1	65.3	66.2 (2021)	71
Cambodia	2.3	1.5	2.1 (2019)	8.5	9.3	10.1 (2019)	64
Indonesia	2.4	2.7	5.2	...	12.8	32.4	80
Lao People's Democratic Republic	3.3	4.0	3.3 (2022)	8.5	12.1	10.3	55
Malaysia	11.5	14.9	23.4	32.4	40.1	40.5	87
Myanmar	5.4	6.4 (2016)	7.6 (2019)	9.2	10.7 (2016)	2.1 (2022)	64
Philippines	5.4	6.1	7.9 (2021)	26.5	45.3	47.9 (2021)	62
Singapore	17.8	22.6	28.3 (2022)	57.8	60.8	65.6 (2022)	96
Thailand	3.8	4.5	5.4 (2021)	20.2	23.1	35.7	89
Timor-Leste	...	6.9	7.5 (2020)	11.6	14.7	17.4 (2020)	51
Viet Nam	7.1	8.0	11.1 (2021)	12.4	14.2	...	56
The Pacific	**1.2**	**4.8**	**1.1**	**...**	**...**	**10.3**	**53**
Cook Islands	14.6 (2009)	14.3 (2014)	16.7 (2020)	70.3 (2009)	69.0	76.9 (2020)	70
Fiji	4.1 (2009)	8.1	...	21.6 (2009)	28.5	38.5 (2019)	55
Kiribati	3.8	1.9 (2013)	...	37.2	54.5 (2013)	36.3 (2018)	42
Marshall Islands	6.2	...	...	24.4	...	43.1 (2018)	55
Micronesia, Federated States of	6.7 (2012)	...	9.7 (2020)	...	...	22.2 (2019)	42
Nauru	11.0	12.7	...	69.3 (2011)	63.6	73.0 (2018)	47
Niue	16.7 (2008)	...	...	88.9 (2008)	...	111.1 (2018)	71
Palau	15.8	14.1 (2014)	18.1	64.7	62.7 (2014)	66.1	57
Papua New Guinea	0.5	...	0.6	4.8	...	5.1 (2021)	45
Samoa	3.3	3.3 (2016)	5.6 (2021)	14.8	17.9 (2014)	30.6 (2020)	47
Solomon Islands	2.0 (2011)	1.8 (2016)	2.4	17.5 (2011)	19.2 (2013)	20.0	50
Tonga	5.4	5.1 (2013)	10.1 (2021)	37.2	38.1 (2013)	42.0 (2021)	54
Tuvalu	11.4 (2009)	9.1 (2014)	13.5 (2020)	62.1 (2008)	37.3 (2014)	39.4 (2020)	53
Vanuatu	1.9 (2012)	1.7 (2016)	1.6 (2019)	18.4 (2012)	...	14.6 (2019)	50
Developed ADB Member Economies	**23.9**	**26.0**	**29.2 (2022)**	**103.3**	**116.4**	**130.2 (2022)**	**92**
Australia	33.5	34.9	40.9 (2022)	104.1	121.9	134.5 (2022)	91
Japan	22.1	24.2 (2016)	26.5 (2022)	103.0	115.7 (2016)	129.8 (2022)	99
New Zealand	26.3	30.3	36.1 (2022)	106.3	107.8	123.0	85
DEVELOPING ADB MEMBER ECONOMIES	**...**	**13.5**	**16.5**	**17.6**	**19.9**	**28.2**	**63**
ALL ADB REGIONAL MEMBERS	**...**	**14.1**	**17.0**	**23.0**	**23.6**	**32.0**	**65**
WORLD	**...**	**...**	**18.7 (2022)**	**...**	**...**	**39.4 (2022)**	**64**

... = data not available, ADB = Asian Development Bank.

a Regional aggregates are population weighted averages of the densities of the economies calculated by ADB. The data for number of doctors and nurses and midwifery personnel are from the World Health Organization's Global Health Workforce Database.

b For estimating aggregates, imputation was done for economies with missing data by substituting available data from the nearest years.

c The scores are based on self-assessment and self-reporting by the economy and the World Health Organization (WHO) may need to provide more technical support guidance to ensure data quality. In 2018, WHO introduced a new State Parties Self-Assessment Annual Reporting Tool (SPAR), which has been in use since. For 2021 onward, the tool uses the second edition of the SPAR questionnaire. Historical trends and data analysis of scores for similar capacity titles should be taken with caution.

d Regional aggregates are averages of the scores of the economies calculated by ADB.

e Aggregates are derived for reporting economies only.

Sources: For Indicator 3.c.1: United Nations. SDG Global Database. https://unstats.un.org/sdgs/dataportal (accessed 24 July 2025). For Indicator 3.d.1: World Health Organization. The Global Health Observatory. https://www.who.int/data/gho (accessed 24 July 2025).

Table 1.4.1: Selected Indicators for Sustainable Development Goal 4—Proficiency in Reading and Mathematics

ADB Regional Member	Target 4.1: By 2030, ensure that all girls and boys complete free, equitable, and quality primary and secondary education leading to relevant and effective learning outcomes			
	4.1.1.b: Proportion of Children and Young People at the End of Primary School Achieving at Least a Minimum Proficiency Level (%)		4.1.1.c: Proportion of Children and Young People at the End of Lower Secondary School Achieving at Least a Minimum Proficiency Level (%)	
	Reading	Mathematics	Reading	Mathematics
	2021	2023	2022	2022
Developing ADB Member Economies				
Central and West Asia				
Afghanistan	...	...	...	...
Armenia	...	72.0	...	50.4 (2015)
Azerbaijan	67.4	61.0	30.8	38.1
Georgia	87.2	63.0	33.1	33.6
Kazakhstan	90.7	56.0	36.3	50.4
Kyrgyz Republic[a]	...	...	...	...
Pakistan	...	7.5 (2019)	...	...
Tajikistan	...	...	...	...
Türkiye	85.9	79.0	70.7	59.0 (2023)
Turkmenistan	...	...	...	...
Uzbekistan	69.8	35.0	14.1	19.3
East Asia				
China, People's Republic of	...	...	...	...
Hong Kong, China	98.3	91.0	82.5	86.2
Korea, Republic of	...	93.0	85.3	83.8
Mongolia[b]	...	...	35.9	48.9
Taipei,China	...	...	...	...
South Asia				
Bangladesh	...	...	...	...
Bhutan	...	...	...	...
India	...	...	...	...
Maldives	...	...	...	...
Nepal	...	...	...	...
Sri Lanka	...	...	...	...
Southeast Asia				
Brunei Darussalam	...	...	57.8	58.1
Cambodia	11.0 (2019)	18.0 (2019)	7.9	12.0
Indonesia[c]	...	17.5 (2015)	25.5	18.3
Lao People's Democratic Republic	2.0 (2019)	7.9 (2019)	...	...
Malaysia	58.0 (2019)	64.0 (2019)	41.9	41.0
Myanmar	11.0 (2019)	12.0 (2019)	...	...
Philippines	10.0 (2019)	17.0 (2019)	23.7	16.0
Singapore	96.7	93.0	88.8	89.0 (2023)
Thailand[d]	...	...	34.6	31.7
Timor-Leste	...	...	...	...
Viet Nam	82.0 (2019)	91.0 (2019)	77.1	71.8
The Pacific				
Cook Islands	74.7	62.9 (2021)	...	...
Fiji	59.6	66.4 (2021)	...	...
Kiribati	13.8	53.1 (2021)	...	...
Marshall Islands	39.7	38.1 (2021)	...	...
Micronesia, Federated States of	39.2	44.6 (2021)	...	...
Nauru	...	...	...	...
Niue	81.0	82.0 (2021)	...	...
Palau	93.5	91.7 (2021)	...	...
Papua New Guinea	48.4	55.4 (2021)	...	...
Samoa	...	...	...	...
Solomon Islands	52.8	86.4 (2021)	...	...
Tonga	20.1	75.3 (2021)	...	...
Tuvalu	32.1	54.7 (2021)	...	...
Vanuatu	...	...	...	...
Developed ADB Member Economies				
Australia	...	64.0	78.8	73.7
Japan	...	...	86.3	88.0
New Zealand	89.9	57.0	79.3	71.3

... = data not available, ADB = Asian Development Bank.

a For Indicator 4.1.1.c, the latest available estimates are for 2009: 16.8% (Reading) and 13.4% (Mathematics).
b For Indicator 4.1.1.b, the latest available estimate is for 2007: 33.9% (Mathematics).
c For indicator 4.1.1.b, the latest available estimates for Reading is 2011: 66.2%.
d For Indicator 4.1.1.b, the latest available estimate is for 2011: 43.4% (Mathematics).

Source: United Nations. SDG Global Database. https://unstats.un.org/sdgs/dataportal (accessed 21 July 2025).

Goal 4. Ensure inclusive and equitable quality education and promote lifelong learning opportunities for all

Table 1.4.2: Selected Indicators for Sustainable Development Goal 4—Education Completion

ADB Regional Member	Target 4.1: By 2030, ensure that all girls and boys complete free, equitable, and quality primary and secondary education leading to relevant and effective learning outcomes					
	4.1.2: Completion Rate (Primary Education, Lower Secondary Education, Upper Secondary Education)[a] (%)					
	Primary					
	2010			2022		
	Total	Q1	Q2	Total	Q1	Q2
Developing ADB Member Economies						
Central and West Asia						
Afghanistan	40.73 (2011)	20.70 (2011)	26.24 (2011)	44.24	19.15	26.88
Armenia	99.88 (2011)	99.48 (2011)	100.00 (2011)	99.59	98.63 (2018)	99.39 (2018)
Azerbaijan	97.94 (2006)	94.76 (2006)	98.60 (2006)	98.74 (2023)	97.48 (2023)	98.50 (2023)
Georgia	100.00 (2013)	100.00 (2013)	100.00 (2013)	99.91 (2018)	100.00 (2018)	100.00 (2018)
Kazakhstan	99.78 (2011)	99.36 (2011)	100.00 (2011)	...	...	...
Kyrgyz Republic	99.58 (2012)	99.91 (2012)	99.05 (2012)	99.45 (2023)	98.60 (2023)	99.93 (2023)
Pakistan	60.90 (2012)	24.13 (2012)	49.84 (2012)	60.07 (2021)	28.45 (2018)	47.96 (2018)
Tajikistan	98.02 (2012)	97.47 (2012)	96.57 (2012)	98.56 (2017)	97.80 (2017)	99.39 (2017)
Türkiye	93.65 (2008)	86.75 (2008)	93.45 (2008)	97.70	95.02 (2018)	97.01 (2018)
Turkmenistan	99.65 (2006)	99.67 (2006)	100.00 (2006)	99.35 (2019)	98.78 (2019)	99.88 (2019)
Uzbekistan	100.00 (2006)	100.00 (2006)	100.00 (2006)	99.71	99.69	99.87
East Asia						
China, People's Republic of	96.69	93.16	94.76	99.19 (2020)	98.01 (2020)	99.38 (2020)
Hong Kong, China	...	...	...	...	...	...
Korea, Republic of	100.00 (2012)	100.00 (2012)	100.00 (2012)	...	...	...
Mongolia	96.52	89.50	95.19	97.48 (2020)	96.80 (2018)	99.16 (2018)
Taipei,China	...	...	...	...	...	...
South Asia						
Bangladesh	74.78 (2011)	47.34 (2011)	68.82 (2011)	88.40	81.61	87.18
Bhutan	67.86	42.27	54.78	...	...	...
India	88.35 (2011)	84.02 (2011)	85.24 (2011)	94.15 (2019)	86.73 (2019)	94.08 (2019)
Maldives	96.78 (2008)	93.97 (2008)	95.87 (2008)	98.19 (2017)	96.55 (2017)	95.95 (2017)
Nepal	75.22 (2011)	58.41 (2011)	66.78 (2011)	86.14 (2021)	83.94 (2021)	80.50 (2021)
Sri Lanka	98.38 (2006)	96.44 (2006)	98.83 (2006)	99.06	...	...
Southeast Asia						
Brunei Darussalam	...	...	...	...	...	...
Cambodia	71.07	43.38	60.83	82.32 (2021)	64.26 (2021)	82.62 (2021)
Indonesia	95.24 (2012)	87.09 (2012)	94.86 (2012)	99.05	90.84 (2017)	97.05 (2017)
Lao People's Democratic Republic	67.14 (2012)	27.65 (2012)	54.02 (2012)	83.43 (2017)	57.83 (2017)	79.71 (2017)
Malaysia	...	...	...	...	...	...
Myanmar	48.32 (2000)	20.92 (2000)	36.57 (2000)	83.14 (2016)	64.24 (2016)	83.52 (2016)
Philippines	86.77	60.13 (2008)	82.94 (2008)	95.85	88.23	96.67
Singapore	...	...	...	...	...	...
Thailand	98.14 (2013)	97.86 (2013)	97.19 (2013)	98.81	97.26	98.35
Timor-Leste	60.06 (2009)	39.43 (2009)	47.89 (2009)	80.69 (2016)	59.87 (2016)	71.37 (2016)
Viet Nam	95.53 (2011)	88.77 (2011)	94.66 (2011)	98.29 (2021)	94.51 (2021)	98.87 (2021)
The Pacific						
Cook Islands	...	...	...	...	...	...
Fiji	98.74 (2007)	...	...	98.44 (2021)	98.26 (2021)	96.35 (2021)
Kiribati	...	...	...	94.09 (2018)	88.40 (2018)	93.22 (2018)
Marshall Islands	...	...	...	...	...	...
Micronesia, Federated States of	...	...	...	...	...	...
Nauru	...	...	...	90.29 (2023)	85.00 (2023)	89.58 (2023)
Niue	...	...	...	...	...	...
Palau	...	...	...	...	...	...
Papua New Guinea	...	...	...	67.61	38.56 (2018)	49.45 (2018)
Samoa	...	...	...	98.08 (2019)	97.40 (2019)	97.47 (2019)
Solomon Islands	...	...	...	...	...	...
Tonga	...	...	...	98.21 (2019)	96.91 (2019)	98.31 (2019)
Tuvalu	...	...	...	100.00 (2019)	100.00 (2019)	100.00 (2019)
Vanuatu	81.09 (2007)	63.88 (2007)	81.40 (2007)	81.46 (2023)	58.78 (2023)	72.47 (2023)
Developed ADB Member Economies						
Australia	99.58	98.28	99.62	99.57 (2018)	98.85 (2018)	100.00 (2018)
Japan	...	...	...	...	...	...
New Zealand	...	...	...	...	...	...

Table 1.4.2: Selected Indicators for Sustainable Development Goal 4—Education Completion *(continued)*

ADB Regional Member	Target 4.1: By 2030, ensure that all girls and boys complete free, equitable, and quality primary and secondary education leading to relevant and effective learning outcomes					
	4.1.2: Completion Rate (Primary Education, Lower Secondary Education, Upper Secondary Education)[a] (%)					
	Lower Secondary					
	2010			20212		
	Total	Q 1	Q 2	Total	Q 1	Q 2
Developing ADB Member Economies						
Central and West Asia						
Afghanistan	23.38 (2011)	7.83 (2011)	12.41 (2011)	31.27	10.52	16.21
Armenia	99.28 (2011)	98.32 (2011)	98.76 (2011)	98.43	95.92 (2018)	96.24 (2018)
Azerbaijan	91.66 (2006)	84.28 (2006)	85.89 (2006)	96.35 (2023)	94.67 (2023)	96.86 (2023)
Georgia	98.65 (2013)	97.84 (2013)	96.82 (2013)	99.56 (2023)	93.17 (2018)	97.25 (2018)
Kazakhstan	99.10 (2011)	98.25 (2011)	98.45 (2011)	97.35 (2019)	...	...
Kyrgyz Republic	96.65 (2012)	98.14 (2012)	97.04 (2012)	99.08 (2023)	97.71 (2023)	100.00 (2023)
Pakistan	45.57 (2012)	11.30 (2012)	30.61 (2012)	53.77 (2021)	13.39 (2018)	34.37 (2018)
Tajikistan	88.63 (2012)	82.85 (2012)	85.54 (2012)	94.23 (2017)	93.23 (2017)	91.35 (2017)
Türkiye	86.56 (2008)	66.23 (2008)	85.05 (2008)	95.40	91.59	92.38
Turkmenistan	98.88 (2006)	97.15 (2006)	98.38 (2006)	99.07 (2019)	97.34 (2019)	99.38 (2019)
Uzbekistan	97.12 (2006)	95.39 (2006)	96.32 (2006)	99.06	99.44	98.67
East Asia						
China, People's Republic of	84.94	66.41	85.47	95.74 (2020)	90.51 (2020)	97.54 (2020)
Hong Kong, China	...	...	...	...	...	...
Korea, Republic of	100.00 (2012)	100.00 (2012)	100.00 (2012)	...	...	...
Mongolia	85.13	49.46	84.46 (2014)	98.79	83.34 (2018)	93.32 (2018)
Taipei,China	...	...	...	...	...	...
South Asia						
Bangladesh	50.63 (2011)	16.27 (2011)	36.43 (2011)	71.11	51.98	66.22
Bhutan	38.78	16.01	19.20	...	...	...
India	76.13 (2011)	69.65 (2011)	71.21 (2011)	85.76 (2019)	69.57 (2019)	83.14 (2019)
Maldives	77.87 (2008)	63.50 (2008)	69.93 (2008)	90.73 (2017)	81.94 (2017)	90.51 (2017)
Nepal	59.58 (2011)	35.61 (2011)	48.82 (2011)	77.73 (2021)	66.09 (2021)	67.65 (2021)
Sri Lanka	88.11 (2006)	77.02 (2006)	85.92 (2006)	97.59	...	...
Southeast Asia						
Brunei Darussalam	...	...	...	...	...	...
Cambodia	36.68	11.73	17.82	56.04 (2021)	29.01 (2021)	47.56 (2021)
Indonesia	77.17 (2012)	51.01 (2012)	66.84 (2012)	89.48	66.21 (2017)	82.31 (2017)
Lao People's Democratic Republic	38.14 (2012)	4.21 (2012)	15.84 (2012)	53.57 (2017)	16.41 (2017)	39.35 (2017)
Malaysia	...	...	...	...	...	...
Myanmar	25.94 (2000)	8.64 (2000)	13.65 (2000)	44.84 (2016)	12.91 (2016)	24.04 (2016)
Philippines	71.10	26.77 (2008)	57.36 (2008)	84.16	60.61	80.44
Singapore	...	...	...	...	...	...
Thailand	86.33 (2013)	78.63 (2013)	84.46 (2013)	89.82	79.91	87.29
Timor-Leste	43.87 (2009)	23.83 (2009)	28.70 (2009)	66.04 (2016)	32.92 (2016)	46.67 (2016)
Viet Nam	80.54 (2011)	67.01 (2011)	73.19 (2011)	86.97 (2021)	67.23 (2021)	82.06 (2021)
The Pacific						
Cook Islands	...	...	...	...	...	...
Fiji	83.56 (2007)	...	...	88.99 (2021)	78.40 (2021)	87.34 (2021)
Kiribati	...	...	...	78.36 (2018)	62.15 (2018)	71.91 (2018)
Marshall Islands	...	...	...	...	...	...
Micronesia, Federated States of	...	...	...	...	...	...
Nauru	...	...	...	73.21 (2023)	64.71 (2023)	67.50 (2023)
Niue	...	...	...	...	...	...
Palau	...	...	...	...	...	...
Papua New Guinea	...	...	...	47.62	25.73 (2018)	37.45 (2018)
Samoa	...	...	...	96.99 (2019)	94.87 (2019)	96.74 (2019)
Solomon Islands	...	...	...	...	...	...
Tonga	...	...	...	92.43 (2019)	87.12 (2019)	88.33 (2019)
Tuvalu	...	...	...	85.19 (2019)	75.56 (2019)	83.42 (2019)
Vanuatu	38.27 (2007)	11.16 (2007)	18.49 (2007)	49.52 (2023)	17.02 (2023)	30.59 (2023)
Developed ADB Member Economies						
Australia	99.15	96.56	99.25	99.14 (2018)	97.69 (2018)	100.00 (2018)
Japan	...	...	...	...	...	...
New Zealand	...	...	...	...	...	...

Table 1.4.2: Selected Indicators for Sustainable Development Goal 4—Education Completion *(continued)*

ADB Regional Member	Target 4.1: By 2030, ensure that all girls and boys complete free, equitable, and quality primary and secondary education leading to relevant and effective learning outcomes					
	4.1.2: Completion Rate (Primary Education, Lower Secondary Education, Upper Secondary Education)[a] (%)					
	Upper Secondary					
	2010			2022		
	Total	Q 1	Q 2	Total	Q 1	Q 2
Developing ADB Member Economies						
Central and West Asia						
Afghanistan	13.72 (2011)	2.92 (2011)	4.49 (2011)	26.70	6.08	10.38
Armenia	93.05 (2011)	87.84 (2011)	88.70 (2011)	93.95	75.40 (2018)	73.88 (2018)
Azerbaijan	74.95 (2006)	53.89 (2006)	71.18 (2006)	82.15 (2023)	71.43 (2023)	73.62 (2023)
Georgia	96.01 (2013)	89.14 (2013)	92.75 (2013)	91.80 (2023)	53.50 (2018)	68.68 (2018)
Kazakhstan	91.17 (2011)	85.38 (2011)	87.89 (2011)	97.61 (2019)	...	...
Kyrgyz Republic	85.29 (2012)	88.86 (2012)	84.88 (2012)	86.36 (2023)	86.66 (2023)	78.18 (2023)
Pakistan	19.51 (2012)	3.33 (2012)	8.70 (2012)	27.07 (2021)	1.38 (2018)	7.85 (2018)
Tajikistan	59.54 (2012)	50.86 (2012)	52.27 (2012)	...	...	...
Türkiye	56.49 (2008)	23.98 (2008)	39.28 (2008)	73.21	65.86	68.16
Turkmenistan	20.50 (2015)	9.74 (2015)	14.63 (2015)	...	...	...
Uzbekistan	73.56 (2006)	64.66 (2006)	68.05 (2006)	95.00	89.81	94.84
East Asia						
China, People's Republic of	43.97	26.51	34.93	87.52 (2020)	86.51 (2020)	87.52 (2020)
Hong Kong, China	...	...	...	...	...	...
Korea, Republic of	97.97	94.75	98.30	97.65 (2016)	92.09 (2016)	96.97 (2016)
Mongolia	62.62	26.43	49.69	93.20	50.50 (2018)	62.30 (2018)
Taipei,China	...	...	...	...	...	...
South Asia						
Bangladesh	13.45 (2011)	0.24 (2011)	3.49 (2011)	31.31	12.09	20.79
Bhutan	20.98	6.12	8.19	...	...	...
India	34.98 (2011)	24.02 (2011)	24.12 (2011)	50.63 (2019)	19.68 (2019)	35.21 (2019)
Maldives	13.21 (2008)	4.84 (2008)	4.49 (2008)	40.26 (2017)	18.30 (2017)	28.55 (2017)
Nepal	29.50 (2011)	2.32 (2011)	2.92 (2011)	35.90 (2021)	15.40 (2021)	17.54 (2021)
Sri Lanka	25.03 (2006)	8.29 (2006)	12.68 (2006)	46.30	...	...
Southeast Asia						
Brunei Darussalam	...	...	...	...	...	...
Cambodia	16.98	0.67	3.56	26.65 (2021)	6.09 (2021)	16.48 (2021)
Indonesia	50.65 (2012)	21.76 (2012)	34.51 (2012)	42.99	31.34 (2017)	46.19 (2017)
Lao People's Democratic Republic	24.57 (2012)	1.14 (2012)	5.51 (2012)	31.09 (2017)	4.44 (2017)	16.02 (2017)
Malaysia	...	...	...	...	...	...
Myanmar	6.46 (2000)	0.61 (2000)	2.06 (2000)	16.80 (2016)	1.31 (2016)	5.37 (2016)
Philippines	66.12	21.30 (2008)	48.96 (2008)	67.01	35.85	54.43
Singapore	...	...	...	...	...	...
Thailand	54.15 (2013)	28.66 (2013)	39.16 (2013)	71.05	43.09	63.99
Timor-Leste	50.82 (2009)	27.12 (2009)	33.00 (2009)	51.96 (2016)	19.34 (2016)	28.47 (2016)
Viet Nam	48.39 (2011)	20.09 (2011)	32.54 (2011)	57.89 (2021)	30.29 (2021)	40.78 (2021)
The Pacific						
Cook Islands	...	...	...	...	...	...
Fiji	34.28 (2007)	...	...	54.57 (2021)	29.54 (2021)	41.36 (2021)
Kiribati	...	...	...	16.73 (2018)	3.94 (2018)	5.93 (2018)
Marshall Islands	...	...	...	...	...	...
Micronesia, Federated States of	...	...	...	...	...	...
Nauru	...	...	...	48.13 (2023)	19.35 (2023)	56.67 (2023)
Niue	...	...	...	...	...	...
Palau	...	...	...	...	...	...
Papua New Guinea	...	...	...	20.25	1.67 (2018)	4.10 (2018)
Samoa	...	...	...	56.98 (2019)	38.81 (2019)	43.71 (2019)
Solomon Islands	...	...	...	...	...	...
Tonga	...	...	...	...	...	...
Tuvalu	...	...	...	55.45 (2019)	30.50 (2019)	47.34 (2019)
Vanuatu	7.11 (2007)	– (2007)	0.84 (2007)	23.09 (2023)	2.47 (2023)	7.94 (2023)
Developed ADB Member Economies						
Australia	85.02	73.48	77.22	90.31 (2018)	84.51 (2018)	84.16 (2018)
Japan	...	...	...	...	...	...
New Zealand	...	...	...	...	...	...

... = data not available, – = magnitude equals zero, ADB = Asian Development Bank, Q = wealth quintile.

a Refers to the "percentage of a cohort of children or young people aged 3–5 years above the intended age for the last grade of each level of education who have completed that grade" as defined by the United Nations Educational, Scientific and Cultural Organization (UNESCO) Institute for Statistics.

Source: United Nations. SDG Global Database. https://unstats.un.org/sdgs/dataportal (accessed 21 July 2025).

Table 1.4.3: Selected Indicators for Sustainable Development Goal 4—Early Childhood Education

ADB Regional Member	Target 4.2: By 2030, ensure that all girls and boys have access to quality early childhood development, care, and preprimary education, so that they are ready for primary education — 4.2.2: Participation Rate in Organized Learning (1 Year before the Official Primary Entry Age)[a,b] (%)					
	2010			2023		
	Total	Female	Male	Total	Female	Male
Developing ADB Member Economies						
Central and West Asia						
Afghanistan	...	...	...	...	...	...
Armenia	...	...	...	31.9	31.3	32.4
Azerbaijan	30.4	29.7	30.9	95.6	95.5	95.7
Georgia	47.6 (2007)	48.7 (2007)	46.6 (2007)	...	...	...
Kazakhstan	87.4 (2011)	87.9 (2011)	87.0 (2011)	76.5 (2024)	76.2 (2024)	76.8 (2024)
Kyrgyz Republic	47.9	49.3	46.5	86.2 (2024)	87.2 (2024)	85.3 (2024)
Pakistan	...	...	...	11.4 (2022)	12.4 (2022)	10.5 (2022)
Tajikistan	7.4	6.8	8.0	11.4 (2017)	10.4 (2017)	12.5 (2017)
Türkiye	60.5	59.2	61.8	99.2 (2022)	98.3 (2022)	100.0 (2022)
Turkmenistan	...	...	...	...	...	...
Uzbekistan	32.0	32.7	31.5	65.9 (2022)	66.7 (2022)	65.2 (2022)
East Asia						
China, People's Republic of	...	...	...	...	...	...
Hong Kong, China	96.3	95.7	96.9	99.7	97.6 (2020)	100.0 (2020)
Korea, Republic of	...	...	...	96.7 (2022)	96.7 (2022)	96.7 (2022)
Mongolia	92.8	94.3	91.3	90.6	91.4	89.9
Taipei,China	...	...	...	...	...	...
South Asia						
Bangladesh	33.6	33.8	33.4	18.7 (2022)	19.5 (2022)	18.0 (2022)
Bhutan	4.4 (2000)	4.3 (2000)	4.5 (2000)	42.1 (2020)	43.1 (2020)	41.1 (2020)
India	...	...	...	94.4 (2022)	95.4 (2022)	93.5 (2022)
Maldives	87.7	92.7	83.2	94.1	95.7	92.7
Nepal	82.3 (2011)	86.0 (2011)	78.7 (2011)	80.0 (2024)	75.8 (2024)	84.0 (2024)
Sri Lanka	...	...	...	48.6	49.8	47.4
Southeast Asia						
Brunei Darussalam	97.9	100.0	97.4	73.9	73.0	74.7
Cambodia	35.2	35.8	34.5	60.6	61.2	60.1
Indonesia	90.4	92.4	88.5	89.3	86.0	92.4
Lao People's Democratic Republic	34.6	34.9	34.2	87.7 (2024)	89.3 (2024)	86.2 (2024)
Malaysia	83.5	86.4	80.9	82.9	82.6	83.3
Myanmar	10.2	10.7	9.7	12.1 (2018)	12.3 (2018)	11.8 (2018)
Philippines	39.6 (2009)	40.4 (2009)	38.9 (2009)	74.0	74.2	73.8
Singapore	...	...	...	98.9 (2022)	...	...
Thailand	...	...	...	96.9	97.9	95.9
Timor-Leste	...	...	...	58.9 (2020)	61.7 (2020)	56.2 (2020)
Viet Nam	84.4	...	...	94.4 (2022)	96.6 (2021)	99.4 (2021)
The Pacific						
Cook Islands	...	...	...	100.0	100.0	99.9
Fiji	43.9 (2006)	44.6 (2006)	43.3 (2006)	96.8	95.8	97.8
Kiribati	...	...	...	...	...	...
Marshall Islands	55.5 (2002)	56.5 (2002)	54.5 (2002)	92.2 (2022)	94.8 (2022)	89.7 (2022)
Micronesia, Federated States of	...	...	...	54.7 (2024)	53.6 (2024)	55.8 (2024)
Nauru	85.3 (2012)	74.2 (2012)	96.2 (2012)	96.3	96.4	96.2
Niue	...	...	...	69.0	...	...
Palau	...	...	...	90.5 (2022)	...	...
Papua New Guinea	...	...	...	66.4 (2018)	66.7 (2018)	66.0 (2018)
Samoa	24.3	27.1	21.7	37.0	39.2	35.0
Solomon Islands	...	...	...	45.5	45.3	45.7
Tonga	...	...	...	75.1	77.6	72.8
Tuvalu	...	...	...	95.1	99.2 (2018)	90.0 (2018)
Vanuatu	...	...	...	74.1	75.4	72.9
Developed ADB Member Economies						
Australia	51.4	51.1	51.7	92.2	92.0	92.3
Japan	...	...	...	97.1 (2021)	...	...
New Zealand	...	...	...	84.1	84.5	83.7

... = data not available, ADB = Asian Development Bank.

a According to the United Nations Educational, Scientific and Cultural Organization (UNESCO), this is the percentage of children who participate in one or more organized learning programs, including programs that offer a combination of education and care, 1 year before the official age for entry to primary education (varies by economy). An organized learning program is one that consists of a coherent set or sequence of educational activities designed with the intention of achieving predetermined learning outcomes or the accomplishment of a specific set of educational tasks.

b The figures for the following economies and years are estimates by the UNESCO Institute for Statistics (UIS) as published on the Global SDG Indicators Database: Armenia (2021); Australia (2001–2010 and 2013–2023); Azerbaijan; Bangladesh (2009); Cambodia (2006 and 2015); Hong Kong, China (2002–2004, 2006, 2008–2010, 2012–2013, 2016–2018, and 2020); Indonesia (2009); Japan (2013–2021); Republic of Korea (2013–2022); Nepal (2013); New Zealand (2014–2016 and 2018–2023); Samoa (2000–2001); Singapore (2018–2022); Thailand (2017, 2019, and 2020); Tuvalu (2018); Türkiye (2004–2022); Uzbekistan (2009–2009); and Viet Nam (2013–2014). For the purposes of estimating participation rates by age, the UIS may make one or more of the following: (i) an adjustment to account for over- or under-reporting in enrolments; (ii) an estimate of the number of enrolments in a given age group; (iii) a redistribution of enrolments of unknown age (across known ages); or (iv) for small economies, an estimate of the population in the official age group. In all cases, estimates are based on evidence from the economy itself.

Source: United Nations. SDG Global Database. https://unstats.un.org/sdgs/dataportal (accessed 29 July 2025).

Goal 4. Ensure inclusive and equitable quality education and promote lifelong learning opportunities for all

Table 1.4.4: Selected Indicators for Sustainable Development Goal 4—Teacher Training and Supply

ADB Regional Member	Target 4.c: By 2030, substantially increase the supply of qualified teachers, including through international cooperation for teacher training in developing countries (or economies), especially least developed countries (or economies) and small island developing States															
	Proportion of Teachers Who Have Received at Least the Minimum Organized Teacher Training, by Education Level (% of total teachers)															
	4.c.1.a: Preprimary				4.c.1.b: Primary				4.c.1.c: Lower Secondary				4.c.1.d: Upper Secondary			
	2010		2024		2010		2024		2010		2024		2010		2024	
Developing ADB Member Economies																
Central and West Asia																
Afghanistan	...		...		...		...		...		...		...		...	
Armenia[a,b]	87.8		74.3	(2023)	77.5	(2005)	84.1	(2023)	...		84.1	(2023)	...		85.8	(2023)
Azerbaijan[a,b]	90.9		91.0	(2023)	100.0		99.4	(2023)	...		99.6	(2023)	...		97.7	(2023)
Georgia	96.6	(2003)	...		94.6	(2009)	...		94.6	(2009)	...		94.8	(2009)	...	
Kazakhstan[c,d]	...		100.0		...		100.0		...		...		...		...	
Kyrgyz Republic	82.6		92.7		68.4		95.5		...		...		...		...	
Pakistan[a,b]	...		...		84.2		79.5	(2022)	...		58.0	(2022)	...		76.8	(2022)
Tajikistan	85.2		...		92.9		...		94.0	(2003)	...		94.3	(2003)	...	
Türkiye	...		...		...		...		...		...		...		...	
Turkmenistan[c]	...		...		...		99.5	(2023)	...		...		...		...	
Uzbekistan[a,b]	100.0		100.0	(2023)	100.0		100.0		...		100.0		...		100.0	
East Asia																
China, People's Republic of	...		...		...		...		...		...		...		...	
Hong Kong, China	95.1		97.2	(2023)	95.6		94.2	(2023)	...		...		...		...	
Korea, Republic of[d]	...		100.0	(2022)	100.0		100.0	(2022)	100.0		100.0	(2022)	100.0		100.0	(2022)
Mongolia	89.9		98.0	(2022)	97.6		98.1	(2023)	100.0	(2007)	38.1	(2023)	100.0	(2006)	...	
Taipei,China	...		...		...		...		...		...		...		...	
South Asia																
Bangladesh	...		...		57.7	(2011)	77.3	(2023)	58.5		67.7	(2023)	40.7		63.2	(2023)
Bhutan	93.8	(2000)	100.0		91.5	(2008)	100.0		90.2	(2008)	100.0	(2022)	72.2	(2008)	96.9	(2022)
India[a,b,c,d]	...		92.3		...		91.7		...		92.0		...		92.7	
Maldives	39.0		65.5	(2022)	77.0		86.6	(2022)	97.6		98.3	(2022)	94.5		99.1	(2022)
Nepal	81.5		82.4	(2021)	73.7		96.1		57.2		95.2		72.3		89.8	
Sri Lanka[a,b]	83.1		41.1	(2023)	82.1		86.4	(2023)	...		82.9	(2023)	...		78.0	(2023)
Southeast Asia																
Brunei Darussalam[a,b]	73.0		62.7	(2023)	87.1		85.3	(2023)	...		89.1	(2023)	...		91.6	(2023)
Cambodia	98.3		100.0	(2023)	99.1		100.0	(2023)	99.8		100.0	(2023)	99.8	(2007)	100.0	(2021)
Indonesia[a,b]	...		3.2	(2023)	...		34.9	(2023)	...		36.9	(2023)	...		37.4	(2023)
Lao People's Democratic Republic	97.5		10.8		95.4		65.7		99.3		93.7	(2022)	99.4		93.7	(2022)
Malaysia[d]	...		36.8	(2023)	95.4		89.5	(2023)	...		...		...		87.4	(2023)
Myanmar	58.5		...		99.9		...		98.3		...		100.0		...	
Philippines[a,b]	100.0		100.0	(2022)	100.0		100.0	(2022)	...		100.0	(2022)	...		100.0	(2022)
Singapore	...		...		98.6	(2009)	97.9	(2022)	...		...		...		...	
Thailand[a,b,c,d]	...		100.0		...		100.0		...		100.0		...		100.0	
Timor-Leste	...		...		...		...		...		...		...		...	
Viet Nam[a]	98.5	(2011)	85.8	(2023)	98.3		82.8	(2023)	99.1		90.2	(2023)	...		99.9	(2022)
The Pacific																
Cook Islands	69.7	(2011)	100.0	(2023)	96.6	(2011)	100.0	(2023)	...		94.9	(2023)	...		100.0	(2023)
Fiji[d]	...		91.8	(2023)	100.0	(2011)	96.4	(2023)	...		...		94.8	(2008)	93.3	(2023)
Kiribati[d]	...		94.7	(2023)	85.4	(2008)	92.0	(2023)	79.2	(2008)	77.0	(2023)	33.6	(2008)	52.1	(2023)
Marshall Islands[a,b,c]	100.0	(2002)	...		...		52.5	(2022)	...		68.4	(2022)	...		80.2	(2022)
Micronesia, Federated States of[a,b,c,d]	...		17.0	(2023)	...		27.0	(2023)	...		31.7	(2021)	...		30.3	(2021)
Nauru[a,b]	82.1	(2007)	...		74.2	(2007)	16.1	(2023)	...		100.0	(2022)	...		57.1	(2022)
Niue[a,b,c,d]	...		33.3	(2023)	...		100.0	(2022)	...		100.0	(2022)	...		16.1	(2023)
Palau[a,c]	...		83.3	(2023)	...		94.4	(2023)	...		95.1	(2023)	...		89.2	(2023)
Papua New Guinea	...		...		...		...		...		...		...		...	
Samoa[d]	...		...		...		...		...		...		71.9	(2009)	54.7	(2020)
Solomon Islands	61.3	(2011)	...		58.0		82.4	(2019)	70.8		93.9	(2019)	70.9		...	
Tonga[c,d]	...		80.6	(2023)	...		93.3	(2023)	...		...		...		...	
Tuvalu[a,b,c,d]	...		92.0	(2023)	...		64.6	(2023)	...		29.1	(2022)	...		28.1	(2022)
Vanuatu	100.0	(2007)	100.0	(2022)	100.0	(2007)	100.0	(2022)	...		...		...		...	
Developed ADB Member Economies																
Australia	...		...		...		...		...		...		...		...	
Japan	...		...		...		...		...		...		...		...	
New Zealand	...		...		...		...		...		...		...		...	

... = data not available, ADB = Asian Development Bank.

a For Indicator 4.c.1.d, the earliest available estimate for Armenia is for 2019: 75.4%. For Azerbaijan, the earliest available estimate is for 2018: 94.9%. For Pakistan, the earliest available estimate is for 2019: 77.4%. For Uzbekistan, the earliest available estimate is for 2016: 100%. For India, the earliest available estimate is for 2017: 76.4%. For Sri Lanka, the earliest available estimate is for 2016: 77.3%. For Brunei Darussalam, the earliest available estimate is for 2014: 90.4%. For Indonesia, the earliest available estimate is for 2022: 36.8%. For the Philippines, the earliest available estimate is for 2016: 100%. For Thailand, the earliest available estimate is for 2015: 100%. For Viet Nam, the earliest available estimate is for 2022: 99.9%. For the Marshall Islands, the earliest available estimate is for 2020: 66.9%. For the Federated States of Micronesia, the earliest available estimate is for 2013: 1.7%. For Nauru, the earliest available estimate is for 2016: 100%. For Niue, the earliest available estimate is for 2015: 100%. For Palau, the earliest available estimate is for 2021: 100%. For Tuvalu, the earliest available estimate is for 2016: 34.6%.

b For Indicator 4.c.1.c, the earliest available estimate for Armenia is 2019: 73.6%. For Azerbaijan, the earliest available estimate is for 2016: 91.6%. For Pakistan, the earliest available estimate is for 2015: 61.2%. For Uzbekistan, the earliest available estimate is for 2014: 75.3%. For India, the earliest available estimate is for 2016: 77.0%. For Sri Lanka, the earliest available estimate is for 2013: 72.1%. For Brunei Darussalam, the earliest available estimate is for 2014: 94.0%. For Indonesia, the earliest available estimate is for 2022: 39.7%. For the Philippines, the earliest available estimate is for 2016: 100%. For Thailand, the earliest available estimate is for 2015: 100%. For the Marshall Islands, the earliest available estimate is for 2019: 48.4%. For the Federated States of Micronesia, the earliest available estimate is for 2014: 5.0%. For Nauru, the earliest available estimate is for 2016: 100%. For Niue, the earliest available estimate is for 2015: 100%. For Tuvalu, the earliest available estimate is for 2016: 52.4%.

c For Indicator 4.c.1.b, the earliest available estimate for Kazakhstan is for 2014: 100%. For Turkmenistan, the earliest available estimate is for 2019: 99.2%. For India, the earliest available estimate is for 2017: 69.8%. For Thailand, the earliest available estimate is for 2014: 100%. For the Marshall Islands, the earliest available estimate is for 2021: 51.4%. For the Federated States of Micronesia, the earliest available estimate is for 2018: 39.7%. For Niue, the earliest available estimate is for 2015: 100%. For Palau, the earliest available estimate is for 2021: 100%. For Tonga, the earliest available estimate is for 2013: 99.6%. For Tuvalu, the earliest available estimate is for 2016: 76.6%.

d For Indicator 4.c.1.a, the earliest available estimate for Kazakhstan is for 2014: 100%. For the Republic of Korea, the earliest available estimate is for 2013: 100%. For India, the earliest available estimate is for 2020: 83.8%. For Malaysia, the earliest available estimate is for 2017: 36.8%. For Thailand, the earliest available estimate is for 2021: 100%. For Fiji, the earliest available estimate is for 2020: 93.5%. For Kiribati, the earliest available estimate is for 2020: 97.8%. For the Federated States of Micronesia, the earliest available estimate is for 2018: 26.7%. For Niue, the earliest available estimate is for 2015: 100%. For Samoa, the earliest available estimate is for 2014: 100%. For Tonga, the earliest available estimate is for 2012: 100%. For Tuvalu, the earliest available estimate is for 2014: 74.6%.

Source: United Nations. Sustainable Development Goals Global Database. https://unstats.un.org/sdgs/dataportal (accessed 9 July 2025).

Table 1.5.1: Selected Indicators for Sustainable Development Goal 5—Early Marriage and Women in Leadership

ADB Regional Member	Target 5.3: Eliminate all harmful practices such as child, early, and forced marriage, and female genital mutilation				Target 5.5: Ensure women's full and effective participation in, and equal opportunities for leadership at, all levels of decision-making in political, economic, and public life		
	5.3.1: Proportion of Women Aged 20–24 Years Who Were Married or in a Union (%)				5.5.1.a: Proportion of Seats Held by Women in National Parliaments (%)		5.5.2: Proportion of Women in Managerial Positions (%)
	Before Age 15		Before Age 18				
	2010	2022	2010	2023	2010	2024	2022
Developing ADB Member Economies							
Central and West Asia[a]		...		...	**16.2**	**23.3**	...
Afghanistan	...	9.6 (2023)	...	28.7	27.3	27.0 (2022)	4.9 (2020)
Armenia	...	– (2016)	...	5.3 (2016)	9.2	36.5	26.2
Azerbaijan	1.9 (2011)	0.1 (2023)	11.0 (2011)	15.0	11.4	18.1	35.4
Georgia	...	–	...	9.4 (2022)	5.1	19.3	36.1 (2020)
Kazakhstan	...	0.2 (2015)	...	7.0 (2015)	17.8	19.4	40.8
Kyrgyz Republic	0.9 (2014)	0.3 (2023)	...	9.2	25.6	21.1	42.1
Pakistan	...	3.6 (2018)	...	18.3 (2018)	22.2	20.5	5.7 (2021)
Tajikistan	...	0.1 (2017)	...	8.7 (2017)	17.5	27.0	23.5 (2016)
Türkiye	...	2.0 (2018)	...	14.7 (2018)	9.1	19.9	19.1 (2023)
Turkmenistan	...	0.2 (2019)	...	6.1 (2019)	16.8	25.6	...
Uzbekistan	0.3 (2006)	0.2	7.2 (2006)	3.4 (2022)	22.0	34.6	...
East Asia[a]		...		...	**20.3**	**25.3**	...
China, People's Republic of	...	0.1 (2020)	...	2.8 (2020)	21.3	26.5	...
Hong Kong, China	...	...	...	...	...	...	38.0 (2023)
Korea, Republic of	...	...	...	...	14.7	19.2	16.3 (2023)
Mongolia	...	0.6 (2023)	...	8.1	4.0	18.1	51.2 (2023)
Taipei,China	...	...	...	...	...	...	30.5 (2020)
South Asia[a]		...		...	**18.7**	**22.3**	...
Bangladesh	...	16.7	...	50.7 (2022)	18.6	20.9	6.2 (2023)
Bhutan	6.2	...	25.8	...	8.5	17.4	48.8 (2023)
India	...	4.8 (2021)	...	23.3 (2021)	10.8	14.7	12.6 (2023)
Maldives	0.3 (2009)	– (2017)	...	2.2 (2017)	6.5	5.0	18.7 (2019)
Nepal	...	5.8	...	34.9 (2022)	33.2	33.1	13.2 (2017)
Sri Lanka	...	0.9 (2016)	...	9.8 (2016)	5.8	5.3	22.3
Southeast Asia[a]		...		...	**19.3**	**23.3**	...
Brunei Darussalam	...	...	...	...	...	11.8	39.2 (2023)
Cambodia	1.9 (2014)	1.9	18.5 (2014)	17.9 (2022)	21.1	13.6	26.4 (2023)
Indonesia	...	0.6 (2018)	...	11.2 (2018)	18.0	21.9	33.1 (2023)
Lao People's Democratic Republic	...	6.1 (2023)	...	30.5	25.2	22.0	25.7
Malaysia	...	...	...	...	9.9	13.5	24.6
Myanmar	...	1.9 (2016)	...	16.0 (2016)	4.3 (2011)	15.3 (2022)	27.8 (2020)
Philippines	...	1.5	...	9.4 (2022)	21.0	27.3	48.6
Singapore	...	– (2023)	...	0.1 (2024)	23.4	29.3	39.6 (2023)
Thailand	...	5.5	...	17.0 (2022)	13.3	19.4	38.2 (2023)
Timor-Leste	...	2.6 (2016)	...	14.9 (2016)	29.2	38.5	22.8
Viet Nam	0.9 (2014)	1.1 (2021)	10.6 (2014)	14.6 (2021)	25.8	30.6	27.3 (2023)
The Pacific[a]		...		...	**2.5**	**7.1**	...
Cook Islands	...	...	...	...	...	...	59.8 (2019)
Fiji	...	0.2 (2021)	...	4.0 (2021)	8.5 (2006)	9.1	38.9 (2016)
Kiribati	...	2.4 (2019)	...	18.4 (2019)	4.4	6.7	47.8 (2023)
Marshall Islands	5.5 (2007)	...	26.3 (2007)	...	3.0	12.1	33.3 (2021)
Micronesia, Federated States of	...	...	...	...	–	15.4	20.3 (2014)
Nauru	1.9 (2007)	0.8 (2023)	26.8 (2007)	18.2	–	10.5	57.6 (2021)
Niue	...	...	...	...	...	...	46.9
Palau	...	...	...	...	–	6.3	46.8 (2020)
Papua New Guinea	...	8.0 (2018)	21.3 (2006)	27.3 (2018)	0.9	2.7	19.7
Samoa	...	0.9 (2020)	10.8 (2014)	7.4 (2020)	8.2	13.0	41.4
Solomon Islands	...	5.6 (2015)	...	21.3 (2015)	–	8.0	25.7 (2013)
Tonga	...	0.4 (2019)	5.6 (2012)	10.1 (2019)	3.1	7.1	37.3 (2023)
Tuvalu	– (2007)	– (2020)	9.9 (2007)	1.8 (2020)	–	6.3	35.9
Vanuatu	2.5 (2013)	4.5 (2023)	21.4 (2013)	20.9	3.9	2.0	36.4 (2020)
Developed ADB Member Economies[a]		...		...	**18.1**	**21.8**	...
Australia	...	...	...	...	27.3	38.0	41.1 (2023)
Japan	...	...	...	...	11.3	10.3	14.6 (2023)
New Zealand	...	...	...	...	33.6	45.5	...
DEVELOPING ADB MEMBER ECONOMIES[a]		...		...	**18.2**	**23.0**	...
ALL ADB REGIONAL MEMBERS[a]		...		...	**18.2**	**22.9**	...

... = data not available, – = magnitude equals zero, ADB = Asian Development Bank.

a For proportion of seats held by women in national parliaments, regional aggregates are estimated as weighted averages based on the number of parliament seats in reporting economies.

Sources: United Nations. SDG Global Database. https://unstats.un.org/sdgs/dataportal (accessed 21 July 2025). For Afghanistan, Bangladesh, and Nepal for indicator 5.5.1.a: Inter-Parliamentary Union. Women in National Parliaments. http://archive.ipu.org/wmn-e/classif-arc.htm (accessed 21 July 2025). For indicator 5.5.2: International Labour Organization. ILOSTAT Database. https://ilostat.ilo.org/data (accessed 21 July 2025).

Goal 6. Ensure availability and sustainable management of water and sanitation for all

Table 1.6.1: Selected Indicators for Sustainable Development Goal 6—Clean Water and Sanitation

ADB Regional Member	Target 6.1: By 2030, achieve universal and equitable access to safe and affordable drinking water for all 6.1.1: Proportion of Population Using Safely Managed Drinking Water Services (%)					
	2010			2024		
	Total	Urban	Rural	Total	Urban	Rural
Developing ADB Member Economies						
Central and West Asia						
Afghanistan	19.3	28.1	16.6	30.6	36.4	28.4
Armenia	83.2	...	...	82.1	...	...
Azerbaijan	65.0	90.7	58.0	57.8	76.5	32.0
Georgia	66.1	87.6	39.4	70.5	89.3	40.9
Kazakhstan	77.9	...	...	91.5	...	...
Kyrgyz Republic	57.6	87.6	41.2	73.9	81.0	69.5
Pakistan	38.5	49.8	32.4	45.0	45.4	44.7
Tajikistan	47.4	...	...	65.1	...	...
Türkiye	...	...	...	...	...	...
Turkmenistan	81.8	91.5	72.7	94.9	96.9	92.3
Uzbekistan	66.9	86.5	46.5	81.9	88.9	74.8
East Asia						
China, People's Republic of	...	89.7	...	...	96.4	...
Hong Kong, China	99.4	99.4	...	100.0	100.0	...
Korea, Republic of	97.8	...	...	99.3	...	...
Mongolia	28.7	40.0	5.1	43.4	55.4	16.2
Taipei,China	...	...	...	...	...	...
South Asia						
Bangladesh	55.0	42.4	60.6	59.1	54.3	62.5
Bhutan	26.3	40.9	18.6	65.6	61.5	68.9
India	53.1	73.8	43.8	76.4	83.0	72.6
Maldives	...	...	...	...	...	...
Nepal	29.4	37.9	27.6	16.5	23.6	14.4
Sri Lanka	46.3	88.1	37.0	46.9	80.1	38.9
Southeast Asia						
Brunei Darussalam	...	...	...	...	...	...
Cambodia	22.0	51.1	14.6	30.0	57.2	20.4
Indonesia	26.8	32.9	20.8	30.5	34.7	24.4
Lao People's Democratic Republic	13.7	24.3	9.2	35.2	50.9	25.2
Malaysia	93.3	...	...	94.7	...	...
Myanmar	43.2	67.9	33.1	59.7	74.2	52.8
Philippines	45.2	60.7	32.4	48.5	62.2	35.5
Singapore	100.0	100.0	...	100.0	100.0	...
Thailand	...	...	...	...	...	...
Timor-Leste	...	...	...	...	...	...
Viet Nam	51.3	74.5	41.1	58.6	75.8	47.0
The Pacific						
Cook Islands	...	...	...	...	...	...
Fiji	40.3	52.4	27.1	42.1	52.5	27.0
Kiribati	11.8	18.4	5.8	15.1	20.9	7.0
Marshall Islands	...	...	...	...	...	...
Micronesia, Federated States of	...	...	...	...	...	...
Nauru	18.7	18.7	...	18.7	18.7	...
Niue	97.4	...	...	93.0	...	...
Palau	75.9	82.6	55.8	90.8	97.7	57.3
Papua New Guinea	...	...	...	...	...	...
Samoa	61.0	85.5	54.9	62.5	92.0	56.3
Solomon Islands	...	...	...	...	...	...
Tonga	29.4	50.2	23.1	29.6	50.9	23.2
Tuvalu	8.1	10.4	5.3	8.7	10.4	5.4
Vanuatu	18.3	55.4	12.0	19.2	38.3	12.5
Developed ADB Member Economies						
Australia	...	99.3	...	...	99.6	...
Japan	98.1	...	...	98.7	...	...
New Zealand	89.3	...	...	100.0	...	...

Table 1.6.1: Selected Indicators for Sustainable Development Goal 6—Clean Water and Sanitation *(continued)*

ADB Regional Member	Target 6.2: By 2030, achieve access to adequate and equitable sanitation and hygiene for all and end open defecation, paying special attention to the needs of women and girls and those in vulnerable situations 6.2.1a: Proportion of Population Using Safely Managed Sanitation Services (%)					
	2010			2024		
	Total	Urban	Rural	Total	Urban	Rural
Developing ADB Member Economies						
Central and West Asia						
Afghanistan	16.4	15.9	16.6	24.8	24.9	24.7
Armenia	12.9	3.0	...	10.7	–	...
Azerbaijan	59.7	48.7	56.0	68.0	67.6	68.5
Georgia	34.2	22.9	48.3	63.0	71.1	50.2
Kazakhstan	...	86.9	...	...	75.9	...
Kyrgyz Republic	89.2	81.5	93.5	93.0	89.6	95.1
Pakistan	...	...	19.6	...	...	41.3
Tajikistan	...	...	57.4	...	...	58.7 (2023)
Türkiye	55.5	54.2	58.7	78.9	78.1	81.4
Turkmenistan	...	...	...	...	...	...
Uzbekistan	73.9	64.8	83.3	74.6	63.1	86.3
East Asia						
China, People's Republic of	34.0	53.4	15.3	68.9	85.1	38.1
Hong Kong, China	75.1	75.1	...	94.8	94.8	...
Korea, Republic of	93.5	...	...	99.3	...	...
Mongolia	53.5	62.0	35.9	69.9	77.8	52.3
Taipei,China	...	...	...	...	...	...
South Asia						
Bangladesh	18.2	26.2	14.7	37.3	30.7	41.9
Bhutan	46.2	47.3	45.6	49.5	44.4	53.6
India	25.6	29.7	23.8	62.8	55.8	66.9
Maldives	...	...	...	...	...	...
Nepal	27.0	28.5	26.7	53.4	46.0	55.6
Sri Lanka	...	...	...	...	...	...
Southeast Asia						
Brunei Darussalam	...	...	...	...	...	...
Cambodia	19.5	35.5	15.4	51.6	52.8	51.2
Indonesia	...	...	...	...	...	...
Lao People's Democratic Republic	44.0	55.5	39.1	71.4	69.3	72.7
Malaysia	78.6	...	...	85.8	...	...
Myanmar	61.0	60.8	61.1	60.5	52.7	64.3
Philippines	51.0	49.4	52.3	62.2	54.1	69.9
Singapore	100.0	100.0	...	100.0	100.0	...
Thailand	22.6	25.9	20.0	26.7	30.7	22.0
Timor-Leste	...	...	...	...	...	...
Viet Nam	37.8	40.2	36.8	45.4	41.0	48.3
The Pacific						
Cook Islands	...	...	...	...	...	...
Fiji	46.5	42.6	50.7	48.5	42.5	57.2
Kiribati	22.1	24.9	19.6	24.6	25.3	23.7
Marshall Islands	...	...	...	...	...	...
Micronesia, Federated States of	...	...	...	...	...	...
Nauru	42.7	42.7	...	33.2	33.2	...
Niue	...	...	...	...	...	...
Palau	...	...	...	...	...	...
Papua New Guinea	12.7	29.8	10.2	16.7	31.0	14.4
Samoa	49.2	42.9	50.7	44.1	43.5	44.3
Solomon Islands	...	...	...	...	...	...
Tonga	37.0	29.3	39.4	31.2	22.2	34.0
Tuvalu	43.7	37.4	51.3	39.7	37.4	44.4
Vanuatu	...	37.8	...	...	29.8 (2022)	...
Developed ADB Member Economies						
Australia	94.6	...	...	95.8	...	...
Japan	97.9	...	...	99.2	...	...
New Zealand	86.3	...	...	88.8	...	...

Goal 6: Ensure availability and sustainable management of water and sanitation for all

Table 1.6.1: Selected Indicators for Sustainable Development Goal 6—Clean Water and Sanitation *(continued)*

	Target 6.4: By 2030, substantially increase water-use efficiency across all sectors and ensure sustainable withdrawals and supply of freshwater to address water scarcity and substantially reduce the number of people suffering from water scarcity			Target 6.a: By 2030, expand international cooperation and capacity-building support to developing countries in water- and sanitation-related activities and programmes, including water harvesting, desalination, water efficiency, wastewater treatment, and recycling and reuse technologies		
ADB Regional Member	6.4.2: Level of Water Stress, Freshwater Withdrawal as a Proportion of Available Freshwater Resources (%)			6.a.1: Amount of Water- and Sanitation-Related Official Development Assistance as Part of a Government-Coordinated Spending Plan ($ million)		
	2010	2015	2022	2010	2015	2023
Developing ADB Member Economies						
Central and West Asia						
Afghanistan	54.8	54.8	54.8	116.3	84.1	46.1
Armenia	42.9	66.0	62.0	94.3	43.3	23.4
Azerbaijan	48.4	51.6	57.5	18.8	65.7	1.8
Georgia	5.8	5.3	4.2	59.6	50.1	38.7
Kazakhstan	33.0	30.0	34.6	17.3	0.2	0.3
Kyrgyz Republic	50.0	50.0	50.0	12.4	25.2	28.9
Pakistan	113.7	120.8	110.0	81.9	313.0	426.7
Tajikistan	71.6	68.7	69.9	24.0	45.8	83.9
Türkiye	34.9	39.9	44.1	86.6	159.0	138.0
Turkmenistan	144.1	144.7	135.2	0.0	...	0.0
Uzbekistan	143.1	158.1	121.8	34.0	119.1	120.8
East Asia						
China, People's Republic of	42.9	43.2	41.5	265.9	203.6	40.3
Hong Kong, China	...	...	...	...	...	...
Korea, Republic of	85.2	85.2	85.2	...	...	...
Mongolia	3.9	3.2	3.4	24.3	8.5	64.6
Taipei,China	...	...	...	...	...	...
South Asia						
Bangladesh	5.7	5.7	5.7	187.0	217.2	302.0
Bhutan	1.4	1.4	1.4	2.9	6.4	17.2
India	66.5	66.5	66.5	415.7	437.5	360.6
Maldives	3.4	15.7	15.7	2.1	8.2	10.1
Nepal	8.3	8.3	8.3	80.9	116.5	106.0
Sri Lanka	90.8	90.8	90.8	148.4	155.9	40.2
Southeast Asia						
Brunei Darussalam	3.5	3.5	3.5	...	...	...
Cambodia	1.0	1.0	1.0	40.4	82.3	208.1
Indonesia	24.2	28.8	29.7	263.2	121.6	266.2
Lao People's Democratic Republic	3.8	5.1	4.8	27.7	104.7	63.0
Malaysia	3.1	3.2	3.4	48.0	58.2	1.8
Myanmar	5.8	5.8	5.8	21.9	69.7	30.4
Philippines	25.5	26.4	27.8	44.3	26.8	110.7
Singapore	219.9	84.6	33.3	...	...	...
Thailand	23.0	23.0	23.0	6.2	7.3	2.3
Timor-Leste	28.3	28.3	28.3	18.8	16.7	5.6
Viet Nam	18.1	18.1	18.1	395.1	586.1	282.0
The Pacific						
Cook Islands	...	...	...	0.6	4.5	...
Fiji	0.3	0.3	0.3	1.7	3.5	3.2
Kiribati	...	...	...	0.1	7.3	5.8
Marshall Islands	...	...	...	0.1	1.1	8.0
Micronesia, Federated States of	...	...	...	0.1	1.8	0.2
Nauru	...	...	...	0.1	5.6	0.0
Niue	...	...	...	0.4	0.0 (2016)	0.0 (2022)
Palau	...	...	...	0.1	1.3	0.4
Papua New Guinea	0.1	0.1	0.1	14.5	6.8	23.5
Samoa	...	...	...	16.5	20.3	5.1
Solomon Islands	...	...	...	6.2	8.4	12.1
Tonga	...	...	...	1.0	1.8	0.4
Tuvalu	...	...	...	0.0	2.4	0.1
Vanuatu	...	...	...	0.8	3.3	18.7
Developed ADB Member Economies						
Australia	5.3	3.7	4.7	...	...	...
Japan	37.2	36.7	36.6	...	...	...
New Zealand	4.2	8.1	8.1	...	...	...

... = data not available, – = magnitude equals zero, 0.0 = magnitude is less than half of unit employed, ADB = Asian Development Bank.

Source: United Nations. SDG Global Database. https://unstats.un.org/sdgs/dataportal (accessed 22 July 2025).

Table 1.7.1: Selected Indicators for Sustainable Development Goal 7—Affordable and Clean Energy

ADB Regional Member	Target 7.1: By 2030, ensure universal access to affordable, reliable, and modern energy services								Target 7.2: By 2030, increase substantially the share of renewable energy in the global energy mix		Target 7.3: By 2030, double the global rate of improvement in energy efficiency	
	7.1.1: Proportion of Population with Access to Electricity (%)						7.1.2: Proportion of Population with Primary Reliance on Clean Fuels and Technology (%)		7.2.1: Renewable Energy Share in Total Final Energy Consumption (%)		7.3.1: Energy Intensity Measured in Terms of Primary Energy and GDP (MJ/$ 2021 PPP GDP)	
	Total		Urban		Rural							
	2010	2023	2010	2023	2010	2023	2010	2023	2010	2022	2010	2022
Developing ADB Member Economies												
Central and West Asia												
Afghanistan	42.7	85.3	82.8	96.0	30.2	81.4	19.8	38.6	15.2	20.0	2.0	2.3
Armenia	99.8	100.0	99.7	100.0	100.0	100.0	95.7	98.8	9.4	10.3	3.3	3.2
Azerbaijan	99.9	100.0	100.0	100.0	99.9	100.0	93.5	98.9	4.5	1.3	2.8	3.4
Georgia	100.0	100.0	100.0	100.0	100.0	100.0	66.1	93.2	39.2	22.5	3.1	3.1
Kazakhstan	100.0	100.0	100.0	100.0	100.0	100.0	91.5	94.2	1.5	2.2	6.5	4.5
Kyrgyz Republic	99.0	100.0	99.1	100.0	98.9	100.0	71.3	79.6	25.6	28.1	4.3	4.4
Pakistan	87.1	95.6	96.5	100.0	82.1	92.8	35.6	54.9	47.5	38.0	4.1	3.5
Tajikistan	98.8	100.0	99.4	100.0	98.6	100.0	68.6	87.9	61.8	36.7	4.9	3.7
Türkiye	100.0	100.0	100.0	100.0	100.0	100.0	94.2	95.3	14.2	13.8	3.1	2.3
Turkmenistan	100.0	100.0	100.0	100.0	100.0	100.0	99.9	99.8	0.1	0.0	8.2	11.4
Uzbekistan	99.6	100.0	100.0	100.0	99.2	100.0	85.4	78.1	1.3	1.4	11.6	6.0
East Asia												
China, People's Republic of	99.7	100.0	100.0	100.0	99.4	100.0	57.9	88.7	12.3	15.2	7.8	5.4
Hong Kong, China	100.0	100.0	100.0	100.0	100.0	100.0	...	...	0.2	1.4	1.4	1.0
Korea, Republic of	100.0	100.0	100.0	100.0	100.0	100.0	100.0	100.0	1.3	4.1	5.2	4.2
Mongolia	78.5	100.0	96.1	100.0	41.9	100.0	34.9	55.8	2.7	2.8	6.2	5.2
Taipei,China[a]	...	...	...	...	...	...	...	...	1.6	2.1 (2015)	...	...
South Asia												
Bangladesh	55.3	99.5	90.1	99.5	40.0	99.6	12.6	28.4	40.3	24.3	2.0	1.6
Bhutan	73.3	100.0	99.3	100.0	59.4	100.0	65.8	91.6	84.8	81.0	9.9	8.0
India	76.3	99.5	94.0	100.0	68.4	99.2	35.0	76.7	36.4	34.1	4.4	3.5
Maldives	99.0	100.0	99.6	100.0	98.7	100.0	93.3	99.8	1.4	1.3	2.2	2.8
Nepal	68.6	94.0	95.5	96.1	63.2	93.4	21.7	42.7	87.3	73.9	5.1	4.6
Sri Lanka	85.3	100.0	95.6	100.0	83.0	100.0	22.0	35.4	61.9	52.8	2.0	1.5
Southeast Asia												
Brunei Darussalam	100.0	100.0	100.0	100.0	100.0	100.0	100.0	100.0	–	0.0	3.9	5.2
Cambodia	31.1	95.0	91.3	99.5	15.8	93.4	11.7	58.0	64.8	46.6	3.7	3.3
Indonesia	94.2	99.4	99.0	100.0	89.4	98.6	40.3	90.6	17.1	15.7	3.3	2.9
Lao People's Democratic Republic	70.2	96.5	97.3	98.6	58.6	95.2	3.5	11.1	64.9	56.7	3.2	4.2
Malaysia	99.5	100.0	99.6	100.0	99.0	100.0	96.5	83.8	2.0	7.1	4.5	3.7
Myanmar	48.8	76.8	89.0	94.6	32.5	68.8	9.3	53.5	84.6	62.5	3.6	3.7
Philippines	85.5	98.0	93.9	98.4	78.5	97.6	40.2	59.5	32.7	27.4	2.9	2.4
Singapore	100.0	100.0	100.0	100.0	100.0	100.0	100.0	100.0	0.5	1.3	2.1	2.1
Thailand	99.7	100.0	100.0	100.0	99.5	100.0	73.1	86.8	22.8	19.3	4.3	3.8
Timor-Leste	38.0	100.0	83.4	100.0	20.6	100.0	4.5	19.1	34.8	10.9	0.6	1.0
Viet Nam	97.4	99.8	99.9	100.0	96.4	99.8	50.9	98.7	34.6	24.8	3.9	3.3
The Pacific												
Cook Islands	99.1	100.0	99.0	100.0	...	...	80.8	74.7	7.3	8.5	...	...
Fiji	92.4	99.3	96.9	100.0	87.4	98.3	32.9	54.1	28.0	26.7	2.2	2.3
Kiribati	63.2	95.9	89.5	88.9	39.4	94.3 (2020)	3.0	16.4	50.1	41.9	6.6	4.4
Marshall Islands	89.4	100.0	92.4	100.0	81.1	100.0	56.3	64.8	13.7	11.7	11.1	9.6
Micronesia, Federated States of	64.5	86.9	84.6	97.3	58.8	83.7	11.7	13.3	2.0	2.1	4.3	5.7
Nauru	99.2	100.0	98.4	100.0	100.0 (2015)	100.0	100.0	100.0	0.0	1.8	10.1	6.8
Niue	99.4	100.0	99.7	100.0	...	...	94.0	98.5	1.4	2.8	...	...
Palau	98.8	100.0	99.4	100.0	96.9	100.0	100.0	100.0	–	0.6	11.5	12.4
Papua New Guinea	19.5	20.5	71.2	65.2	11.8	13.4	7.6	10.5	55.2	50.8	5.9	5.3
Samoa	96.4	100.0	98.9	100.0	95.8	100.0	26.6	39.7	41.9	31.8	3.9	4.4
Solomon Islands	35.4	81.3	65.4	81.2	27.9	81.3	8.2	8.7	45.1	50.1	6.3	4.3
Tonga	92.8	100.0	97.9	100.0	91.2	100.0	59.4	90.1	1.0	2.1	3.3	3.2
Tuvalu	96.7	100.0	98.1	100.0	95.1	100.0	44.6	77.0	0.5	5.5	3.7	2.6
Vanuatu	44.1	61.6	82.3	87.5	31.7	54.0	12.9	20.6	38.1	27.6	3.8	4.2
Developed ADB Member Economies												
Australia	100.0	100.0	100.0	100.0	100.0	100.0	100.0	100.0	8.2	13.5	4.5	3.3
Japan	100.0	100.0	100.0	100.0	100.0	100.0	100.0	100.0	4.7	9.3	4.0	2.9
New Zealand	100.0	100.0	100.0	100.0	100.0	100.0	100.0	100.0	29.3	30.4	4.3	3.2
WORLD	**83.6**	**91.7**	**95.9**	**97.8**	**72.9**	**84.0**	**57.2**	**74.1**	**14.9**	**17.9**	**4.8**	**3.9**

... = data not available, – = magnitude equals zero, 0.0 = magnitude is less than half of unit employed, $ = United States dollars, ADB = Asian Development Bank, GDP = gross domestic product, MJ = megajoule, PPP = purchasing power parity.

a Latest available data from World Bank's Sustainable Energy for All database is only up to 2015.

Sources: United Nations. SDG Global Database. https://unstats.un.org/sdgs/dataportal (accessed 24 July 2025). For Indicator 7.2.1 of Taipei,China: World Bank. DataBank: Sustainable Energy for All. https://databank.worldbank.org/source/sustainable-energy-for-all# (accessed 24 July 2025).

Goal 8. Promote sustained, inclusive, and sustainable economic growth; full and productive employment; and decent work for all

Table 1.8.1: Selected Indicators for Sustainable Development Goal 8—Decent Work and Economic Growth

ADB Regional Member	Target 8.1: Sustain per capita economic growth in accordance with national circumstances and, in particular, at least 7% gross domestic product per annum in the least developed countries (or economies)			Target 8.2: Achieve higher levels of economic productivity through diversification, technological upgrading, and innovation, including through a focus on high-value-added and labor-intensive sectors		
	8.1.1: Annual Growth Rate of Real GDP per Capita at Constant 2015 $ (%)			8.2.1: Annual Growth Rate of Real GDP per Employed Person at Constant 2015 $[a] (%)		
	2010	2015	2023	2010	2015	2024
Developing ADB Member Economies						
Central and West Asia						
Afghanistan	–0.5	–5.5	0.5	10.0	–1.4	3.0
Armenia	2.7	3.3	6.4	2.6	4.3	5.3
Azerbaijan	3.8	–0.1	0.9	3.5	–0.9	3.2
Georgia	6.9	3.4	7.1	4.9	1.1	7.3
Kazakhstan	5.9	–0.3	2.8	4.9	0.2	2.8
Kyrgyz Republic	–2.2	3.2	4.4	–2.3	2.0	3.6
Pakistan	–1.0	2.8	–1.5	–2.2	2.4	0.3
Tajikistan	4.3	3.3	6.1	4.0	3.4	4.6
Türkiye	7.1	3.5	4.9	2.0	1.8	0.5
Turkmenistan	13.8	0.7	4.4	7.1	4.6	0.7
Uzbekistan	8.2	5.4	3.9	5.9	6.1	4.4
East Asia						
China, People's Republic of	9.9	6.4	5.4	10.0	7.0	4.9
Hong Kong, China	6.2	1.7	3.6	6.7	1.4	4.0
Korea, Republic of	6.5	2.0	1.5	5.4	1.4	2.1
Mongolia	4.9	–0.9	5.6	5.5	1.1	4.3
Taipei,China	...	...	...	...	...	...
South Asia						
Bangladesh	6.6	7.5	4.5	2.1	5.3	3.6
Bhutan	11.6	5.6	4.2	11.4	3.8	3.6
India	6.9	6.7	7.2	7.9	6.2	3.8
Maldives	3.1	0.4	4.4	–1.0	–2.5	3.8
Nepal	5.6	3.4	2.0	3.0	2.9	3.1
Sri Lanka	8.1	3.3	–2.9	6.5	–0.5	3.9
Southeast Asia						
Brunei Darussalam	0.7	–1.7	0.6	0.8	–1.0	1.6
Cambodia	3.5	5.7	3.7	0.2	5.8	3.8
Indonesia	4.9	3.7	4.2	3.2	4.0	3.6
Lao People's Democratic Republic	6.6	5.7	2.8	5.7	5.6	2.0
Malaysia	5.4	3.3	2.4	4.1	2.7	2.8
Myanmar	9.3	6.1	0.3	8.6	5.9	0.2
Philippines	5.2	4.8	4.7	4.3	4.7	4.4
Singapore	12.1	1.7	–1.4	8.2	0.1	0.8
Thailand	6.8	2.7	1.9	7.0	3.0	3.0
Timor-Leste	7.0	0.8	–19.0	7.0	–0.0	0.9
Viet Nam	10.4	5.7	4.3	3.6	6.2	5.2
The Pacific						
Cook Islands	–7.7	6.3	23.3	...	...	...
Fiji	2.6	4.4	7.0	0.5	5.3	2.2
Kiribati	–0.9	9.8	1.1	...	...	...
Marshall Islands	5.4	4.2	–0.8	...	...	...
Micronesia, Federated States of	2.7	4.3	0.3	...	...	...
Nauru	8.4	0.8	–	...	...	...
Niue	...	...	...	...	...	...
Palau	2.1	8.5	2.1	...	...	...
Papua New Guinea	6.9	3.9	0.8	12.0	2.9	2.3
Samoa	0.8	5.2	9.5	5.6	3.4	9.7
Solomon Islands	6.7	–1.9	0.6	6.3	–2.3	–0.7
Tonga	0.6	1.6	2.5	0.8	2.0	2.8
Tuvalu	–4.7	10.6	5.7	...	...	...
Vanuatu	–1.1	1.7	–0.1	3.9	–0.5	–1.4
Developed ADB Member Economies						
Australia	0.7	1.2	0.5	0.1	0.2	0.5
Japan	4.1	1.7	2.2	4.5	1.3	0.1
New Zealand	–0.1	2.2	–0.1	1.1	1.2	0.2

... = data not available, – = magnitude equals zero, $ = United States dollars, ADB = Asian Development Bank, GDP = gross domestic product.

a Modeled data based on GDP per person engaged, constant 2015 United States dollar.

Source: United Nations. SDG Global Database. https://unstats.un.org/sdgs/dataportal (accessed 10 June 2025).

Table 1.8.2: Selected Indicators for Sustainable Development Goal 8—Unemployment

ADB Regional Member	Target 8.5: By 2030, achieve full and productive employment and decent work for all women and men, including for young people and persons with disabilities, and equal pay for work of equal value 8.5.2.a: Unemployment Rate for Age Group 15+ Years, by Sex (%)					
	2010			2022		
	Total	Female	Male	Total	Female	Male
Developing ADB Member Economies						
Central and West Asia						
Afghanistan	1.7 (2012)	3.3 (2012)	1.4 (2012)	5.7 (2021)	5.5 (2021)	5.7 (2021)
Armenia	19.5	21.7	17.6	8.3 (2023)	9.4 (2023)	7.2
Azerbaijan	5.6	6.9	4.4	5.7 (2022)	6.5 (2022)	4.8 (2022)
Georgia	20.2	17.6	22.5	11.7 (2020)	10.2 (2020)	13.1 (2020)
Kazakhstan	5.8	6.6	4.9	4.9 (2022)	5.5 (2022)	4.3 (2022)
Kyrgyz Republic[a]	8.7	10.0	7.8	3.5 (2023)	4.2 (2023)	3.0
Pakistan	0.7	0.6	0.7	6.3 (2021)	9.2 (2021)	5.5 (2021)
Tajikistan	11.5 (2009)	10.5 (2009)	12.3 (2009)	...	...	...
Türkiye	11.9	13.0	11.4	8.8	11.8	7.1 (2024)
Turkmenistan	4.0	2.3	5.3	...	...	...
Uzbekistan[b]	5.4	6.3	4.6	5.3 (2020)	7.7 (2020)	3.9 (2020)
East Asia						
China, People's Republic of	4.1	3.8 (2000)	3.6 (2000)	5.1 (2021)	...	...
Hong Kong, China	4.3	3.5	5.1	3.0	2.4	3.6 (2024)
Korea, Republic of	3.3	2.8	3.7	2.8	2.8	2.8 (2024)
Mongolia	6.5	5.9	7.1	5.2 (2023)	4.4 (2023)	5.9
Taipei,China	5.2	4.5	5.8	3.8 (2020)	3.8 (2020)	3.9 (2020)
South Asia						
Bangladesh	3.4	4.4	3.0	3.4 (2023)	3.2 (2023)	3.4
Bhutan	3.3	4.0	2.7	3.3	4.1	2.7 (2024)
India	3.1	3.8	2.9	4.2	4.1	4.2 (2024)
Maldives[c]	11.7 (2009)	13.7 (2009)	10.4 (2009)	4.6 (2019)	3.9 (2019)	5.0 (2019)
Nepal	1.3 (2008)	1.1 (2008)	1.6 (2008)	...	...	9.8 (2017)
Sri Lanka[b]	4.8	7.4	3.4	4.5 (2022)	6.2 (2022)	3.6 (2022)
Southeast Asia						
Brunei Darussalam	6.9 (2014)	7.8 (2014)	6.1 (2014)	5.3 (2023)	5.3 (2023)	5.3
Cambodia	0.8	0.8	0.7	0.3 (2023)	0.2 (2023)	0.3
Indonesia	5.6	6.4	5.1	3.3 (2023)	3.1 (2023)	3.5
Lao People's Democratic Republic	0.7	0.7	0.8	1.2 (2022)	0.9 (2022)	1.5 (2022)
Malaysia	3.3	3.3 (2011)	2.9 (2011)	3.9 (2022)	4.1 (2022)	3.8 (2022)
Myanmar	3.9 (2014)	4.0 (2014)	3.8 (2014)	1.5 (2020)	2.1 (2020)	1.0 (2020)
Philippines	3.6	3.8	3.5	2.6 (2022)	2.9 (2022)	2.4 (2022)
Singapore[a]	4.1	4.4	3.9	2.7	2.7	2.8 (2024)
Thailand	0.6	0.6	0.6	0.8	0.8	0.7 (2024)
Timor-Leste	3.3	4.3	2.9	1.5 (2022)	1.6 (2022)	1.5 (2022)
Viet Nam	1.1	1.1	1.1	1.6 (2023)	1.5 (2023)	1.8
The Pacific						
Cook Islands	8.2 (2011)	8.1 (2011)	8.2 (2011)	1.3 (2019)	0.9 (2019)	1.6 (2019)
Fiji	8.9	4.6 (2011)	4.3 (2011)	5.4	7.1	4.5 (2024)
Kiribati	30.6	34.1	27.6	3.1 (2023)	3.8 (2023)	2.5
Marshall Islands	4.7 (2011)	4.5 (2011)	4.9 (2011)	9.8 (2021)	11.5 (2021)	8.9 (2021)
Micronesia, Federated States of	8.9 (2014)	13.9 (2014)	5.4 (2014)	...	...	...
Nauru	23.0 (2011)	25.5 (2011)	21.4 (2011)	5.1 (2021)	5.2 (2021)	4.9 (2021)
Niue	- (2015)	- (2015)	- (2015)	0.6 (2022)	- (2022)	- (2022)
Palau	1.4 (2014)	1.8 (2014)	1.1 (2014)	0.8 (2020)	1.0 (2020)	0.6 (2020)
Papua New Guinea	2.0	1.3	2.7	2.7 (2022)	2.2 (2022)	3.1 (2022)
Samoa	5.7 (2011)	6.8 (2011)	5.2 (2011)	5.0 (2022)	7.8 (2022)	3.5 (2022)
Solomon Islands	2.0 (2009)	1.8 (2009)	2.3 (2009)	...	...	...
Tonga	1.1 (2006)	1.3 (2016)	0.9 (2016)	1.7 (2023)	2.3 (2023)	1.1
Tuvalu	5.5	5.3	5.7	7.3 (2022)	8.3 (2022)	6.7 (2022)
Vanuatu	1.8	1.6	2.1	4.0 (2020)	4.1 (2020)	4.0 (2020)
Developed ADB Member Economies						
Australia	5.2	5.4	5.1	3.9	3.8	4.0 (2024)
Japan	5.1	4.6	5.5	2.5	2.4	2.7 (2024)
New Zealand	6.6	6.9	6.2	4.7	4.9	4.5 (2024)

Goal 8. Promote sustained, inclusive and sustainable economic growth; full and productive employment; and decent work for all

Table 1.8.2: Selected Indicators for Sustainable Development Goal 8—Unemployment *(continued)*

ADB Regional Member	Target 8.5: By 2030, achieve full and productive employment and decent work for all women and men, including for young people and persons with disabilities, and equal pay for work of equal value 8.5.2.b: Unemployment Rate for Age Group 15–24 Years, by Sex (%) 2010			2022		
	Total	Female	Male	Total	Female	Male
Developing ADB Member Economies						
Central and West Asia						
Afghanistan	2.9 (2012)	4.5 (2012)	2.6 (2012)	8.8 (2021)	9.4 (2021)	8.5 (2021)
Armenia	39.0	47.4	32.4	21.2 (2023)	24.9 (2023)	18.4 (2023)
Azerbaijan	14.9	16.0	13.9	13.6 (2022)	15.3 (2022)	12.1 (2022)
Georgia	41.5	45.7	39.1	31.3 (2020)	32.7 (2020)	30.5 (2020)
Kazakhstan	5.2	5.7	4.8	3.8 (2022)	4.9 (2022)	2.8 (2022)
Kyrgyz Republic[a]	16.6	20.1	14.4	8.5 (2023)	7.0 (2023)	9.2 (2023)
Pakistan	1.3	1.1	1.3	11.1 (2021)	14.4 (2021)	10.0 (2021)
Tajikistan	5.9 (2007)	2.9 (2007)	8.4 (2007)	...	...	...
Türkiye	21.7	23.1	21.0	16.4	22.4	13.1
Turkmenistan	...	...	...	...	...	...
Uzbekistan[b]	...	...	...	13.2 (2020)	21.4 (2020)	8.3 (2020)
East Asia						
China, People's Republic of	9.1 (2000)	8.6 (2000)	9.5 (2000)	14.3 (2021)	...	...
Hong Kong, China	12.2	10.3	14.1	9.5	8.6	10.4
Korea, Republic of	8.7	7.8	10.2	6.5	6.5	6.4
Mongolia	14.8	14.2	15.2	11.6 (2023)	9.8 (2023)	12.4 (2023)
Taipei,China	13.1	12.7	13.6	11.6 (2020)	12.1 (2020)	11.3 (2020)
South Asia						
Bangladesh	6.4	7.0	5.9	8.2 (2023)	4.7 (2023)	11.5 (2023)
Bhutan	9.2	11.0	7.1	18.2	19.6	17.0
India	9.6	10.4	9.4	15.6	17.2	15.0
Maldives[c]	25.4 (2009)	21.4 (2009)	29.1 (2009)	13.9 (2019)	9.7 (2019)	17.2 (2019)
Nepal	2.2 (2008)	1.6 (2008)	2.9 (2008)	...	...	...
Sri Lanka[b]	19.0	23.8	16.1	22.1 (2022)	26.0 (2022)	19.8 (2022)
Southeast Asia						
Brunei Darussalam	25.3 (2014)	27.9 (2014)	23.4 (2014)	17.8 (2023)	21.2 (2023)	15.9 (2023)
Cambodia	1.0	0.9	1.0	0.7 (2023)	0.4 (2023)	1.0 (2023)
Indonesia	17.6	18.8	16.7	13.1 (2023)	13.1 (2023)	13.1 (2023)
Lao People's Democratic Republic	1.8	1.7	1.9	2.3 (2022)	2.2 (2022)	2.3 (2022)
Malaysia	9.7 (2011)	10.7 (2011)	9.1 (2011)	11.7 (2022)	13.4 (2022)	10.7 (2022)
Myanmar	9.3 (2014)	9.5 (2014)	9.1 (2014)	4.9 (2020)	5.8 (2020)	4.1 (2020)
Philippines	9.9	12.0	8.7	6.9 (2022)	8.3 (2022)	6.0 (2022)
Singapore[a]	9.9	12.5	7.6	6.6	8.1	5.4
Thailand	2.5	3.1	2.1	4.6	5.9	3.6
Timor-Leste	12.4	19.1	8.7	3.4 (2022)	3.4 (2022)	3.4 (2022)
Viet Nam	3.6	3.5	3.6	6.4 (2023)	6.0 (2023)	6.7 (2023)
The Pacific						
Cook Islands	15.5 (2011)	15.3 (2011)	15.6 (2011)	3.4 (2019)	– (2019)	4.6 (2019)
Fiji	14.2 (2011)	18.4 (2011)	12.1 (2011)	16.5	22.3	13.6
Kiribati	54.0	61.8	47.6	8.4 (2023)	12.1 (2023)	6.2 (2023)
Marshall Islands	...	...	...	24.9 (2021)	25.1 (2021)	24.8 (2021)
Micronesia, Federated States of	18.9 (2014)	29.9 (2014)	10.4 (2014)	...	...	...
Nauru	26.6 (2013)	37.5 (2013)	20.9 (2013)	12.0 (2021)	14.5 (2021)	10.6 (2021)
Niue	– (2015)	– (2015)	– (2015)	– (2022)	– (2022)	– (2022)
Palau	5.6 (2014)	– (2014)	– (2014)	3.3 (2020)	3.5 (2020)	3.1 (2020)
Papua New Guinea	3.6	3.0	4.3	3.8 (2022)	3.0 (2022)	4.6 (2022)
Samoa	16.1 (2011)	22.2 (2011)	13.8 (2011)	13.4 (2022)	23.3 (2022)	8.3 (2022)
Solomon Islands	1.3 (2013)	1.6 (2013)	1.0 (2013)	...	...	...
Tonga	3.1 (2016)	4.0 (2016)	2.7 (2016)	4.8 (2023)	5.9 (2023)	4.0 (2023)
Tuvalu	11.7	11.1	12.2	20.0 (2022)	21.7 (2022)	18.9 (2022)
Vanuatu	4.8	4.8	4.8	9.7 (2020)	9.6 (2020)	9.8 (2020)
Developed ADB Member Economies						
Australia	11.6	11.1	11.9	9.3	8.1	10.5
Japan	9.4	8.1	10.8	4.0	3.7	4.0
New Zealand	17.4	17.8	17.1	14.1	13.7	14.4

Table 1.8.2: Selected Indicators for Sustainable Development Goal 8—Unemployment *(continued)*

ADB Regional Member	Target 8.5: By 2030, achieve full and productive employment and decent work for all women and men, including for young people and persons with disabilities, and equal pay for work of equal value 8.5.2.c: Unemployment Rate for Age Group 25+ Years, by Sex (%)					
	2010			2022		
	Total	Female	Male	Total	Female	Male
Developing ADB Member Economies						
Central and West Asia						
Afghanistan	1.2 (2012)	2.7 (2012)	0.9 (2012)	4.5 (2021)	3.8 (2021)	4.7 (2021)
Armenia	16.4	17.9	15.1	7.2 (2023)	8.3 (2023)	6.2 (2023)
Azerbaijan	4.2	5.6	3.0	4.6 (2022)	5.5 (2022)	3.8 (2022)
Georgia	17.6	14.9	20.1	10.1 (2020)	8.7 (2020)	11.2 (2020)
Kazakhstan	5.9	6.8	5.0	5.0 (2022)	5.6 (2022)	4.4 (2022)
Kyrgyz Republic[a]	6.4	7.4	5.6	2.8 (2023)	3.9 (2023)	2.0 (2023)
Pakistan	0.4	0.5	0.4	4.7 (2021)	7.2 (2021)	3.9 (2021)
Tajikistan	1.9 (2007)	0.9 (2007)	2.5 (2007)	...	...	...
Türkiye	9.8	10.3	9.6	7.4	9.9	6.1
Turkmenistan	...	...	...	...	...	...
Uzbekistan[b]	...	...	...	4.2 (2020)	5.6 (2020)	3.3 (2020)
East Asia						
China, People's Republic of	2.6 (2000)	2.7 (2000)	2.5 (2000)	...	...	...
Hong Kong, China	3.6	2.8	4.3	2.7	2.1	3.3
Korea, Republic of	3.0	2.4	3.4	2.6	2.6	2.7
Mongolia	5.1	4.6	5.6	4.5 (2023)	4.0 (2023)	5.0 (2023)
Taipei,China	4.5	3.5	5.3	3.2 (2020)	3.0 (2020)	3.3 (2020)
South Asia						
Bangladesh	2.5	3.3	2.2	2.1 (2023)	2.6 (2023)	1.8 (2023)
Bhutan	2.1	2.4	1.9	1.6	2.0	1.3
India	1.7	2.4	1.4	2.4	2.5	2.4
Maldives[c]	6.5 (2009)	9.9 (2009)	4.7 (2009)	2.8 (2019)	2.8 (2019)	2.8 (2019)
Nepal	1.0 (2008)	0.9 (2008)	1.1 (2008)	...	...	...
Sri Lanka[b]	2.6	4.6	1.5	2.7 (2022)	4.0 (2022)	2.0 (2022)
Southeast Asia						
Brunei Darussalam	4.1 (2014)	4.9 (2014)	3.4 (2014)	3.8 (2023)	3.6 (2023)	3.9 (2023)
Cambodia	0.7	0.7	0.6	0.1 (2023)	0.2 (2023)	0.1 (2023)
Indonesia	3.1	3.7	2.7	1.7 (2023)	1.4 (2023)	1.9 (2023)
Lao People's Democratic Republic	0.4	0.3	0.4	0.9 (2022)	0.6 (2022)	1.3 (2022)
Malaysia	1.5 (2011)	1.4 (2011)	1.5 (2011)	2.3 (2022)	2.2 (2022)	2.4 (2022)
Myanmar	2.1 (2014)	2.0 (2014)	2.2 (2014)	0.7 (2020)	1.2 (2020)	0.4 (2020)
Philippines	2.0	1.8	2.1	1.9 (2022)	2.1 (2022)	1.8 (2022)
Singapore[a]	3.5	3.5	3.5	2.5	2.4	2.6
Thailand	0.3	0.3	0.4	0.4	0.4	0.4
Timor-Leste	2.2	2.3	2.2	1.2 (2022)	1.2 (2022)	1.2 (2022)
Viet Nam	0.6	0.6	0.6	1.1 (2023)	1.0 (2023)	1.2 (2023)
The Pacific						
Cook Islands	6.5 (2011)	6.5 (2011)	6.4 (2011)	0.8 (2019)	– (2019)	– (2019)
Fiji	2.7 (2011)	2.4 (2011)	2.8 (2011)	3.9	5.1	3.3
Kiribati	20.9	22.8	19.2	2.2 (2023)	2.7 (2023)	1.8 (2023)
Marshall Islands	...	...	...	7.3 (2021)	9.2 (2021)	6.1 (2021)
Micronesia, Federated States of	6.1 (2014)	9.0 (2014)	4.0 (2014)	...	...	...
Nauru	9.1 (2013)	13.1 (2013)	6.1 (2013)	3.3 (2021)	3.4 (2021)	3.3 (2021)
Niue	1.0 (2001)	1.2 (2001)	0.8 (2001)	– (2022)	– (2022)	– (2022)
Palau	1.0 (2014)	1.4 (2014)	0.7 (2014)	0.6 (2020)	0.9 (2020)	0.4 (2020)
Papua New Guinea	1.5	0.7	2.2	2.5 (2022)	2.0 (2022)	2.9 (2022)
Samoa	3.0 (2011)	2.8 (2011)	3.0 (2011)	3.2 (2022)	4.6 (2022)	2.4 (2022)
Solomon Islands	0.5 (2013)	0.4 (2013)	0.6 (2013)	...	...	...
Tonga	0.7 (2016)	0.9 (2016)	0.5 (2016)	1.1 (2023)	1.8 (2023)	0.5 (2023)
Tuvalu	3.9	3.9	3.8	4.8 (2022)	5.7 (2022)	4.1 (2022)
Vanuatu	1.1	0.7	1.5	2.8 (2020)	2.9 (2020)	2.7 (2020)
Developed ADB Member Economies						
Australia	3.8	4.0	3.7	2.9	3.0	2.8
Japan	4.7	4.2	5.0	2.4	2.2	2.5
New Zealand	4.5	4.8	4.2	3.2	3.4	2.9

... = data not available, – = magnitude equals zero, ADB = Asian Development Bank.

a For 2021, data is derived using ILOSTAT microdata processing.
b For 2020, data is derived using ILOSTAT microdata processing.
c For 2009 and 2019, data is derived using ILOSTAT microdata processing

Source: International Labour Organization. ILOSTAT Database. https://ilostat.ilo.org/data (accessed 20 July 2025).

Goal 8. Promote sustained, inclusive and sustainable economic growth; full and productive employment; and decent work for all

Table 1.8.3: Selected Indicators for Sustainable Development Goal 8—Youth Participation in Education and Work, Child Labor

ADB Regional Member	Target 8.6: By 2020, substantially reduce the proportion of youth not in employment, education, or training — 8.6.1: Proportion of Youth (Aged 15–24 Years) not in Education, Employment, or Training[a] (%)		Target 8.7: Take immediate and effective measures to eradicate forced labor, end modern slavery and human trafficking, and secure the prohibition and elimination of the worst forms of child labor, including recruitment and use of child soldiers; and, by 2025, end child labor in all its forms — 8.7.1: Proportion of Children (Aged 5–17 Years) Engaged in Child Labor (%) 2023		
	2010	2023	Total	Female	Male
Developing ADB Member Economies					
Central and West Asia					
Afghanistan	35.1 (2014)	43.8 (2021)	13.3	10.9	15.6
Armenia	38.3	20.2	3.9 (2015)	2.7 (2015)	4.9 (2015)
Azerbaijan	9.6	...	4.8	2.9	6.4
Georgia	32.6 (2012)	24.9 (2020)	1.5 (2015)	0.9 (2015)	2.1 (2015)
Kazakhstan	8.2	9.5 (2016)	...	...	...
Kyrgyz Republic	19.1	19.3	18.0	14.3	21.6
Pakistan	31.1	34.6 (2021)	6.8 [b] (2021)	3.2 [b] (2021)	10.1 [b] (2021)
Tajikistan	42.2 (2009)	41.3 (2016)	...	...	...
Türkiye	32.3	22.4	5.6 (2022)	4.5 (2022)	6.7 (2022)
Turkmenistan	...	...	0.3 (2016)	0.1 (2016)	0.4 (2016)
Uzbekistan	...	...	17.8 (2022)	14.5 (2022)	21.1 (2022)
East Asia					
China, People's Republic of	12.7 (2000)	...	...	...	...
Hong Kong, China	7.0	5.7 (2024)	...	...	...
Korea, Republic of	10.8 (2002)	...	...	...	...
Mongolia	17.6	14.6	6.0	5.1	6.8
Taipei,China	...	...	...	...	...
South Asia					
Bangladesh	30.1	14.3	7.0 (2022)	4.4 (2022)	9.5 (2022)
Bhutan	...	20.2 (2024)	1.7 [c] (2010)	1.7 [c] (2010)	1.6 [c] (2010)
India	28.9	24.2 (2024)	1.0	0.5	1.4
Maldives	32.5 (2009)	26.3 (2019)	...	...	...
Nepal	8.7 (2008)	34.8 (2017)	19.2 (2014)	19.3 (2014)	19.0 (2014)
Sri Lanka	26.7	18.1 (2022)	0.8 (2016)	0.6 (2016)	0.9 (2016)
Southeast Asia					
Brunei Darussalam	17.1 (2014)	16.5	...	...	...
Cambodia	5.3	6.3	10.4 (2021)	9.6 (2021)	11.1 (2021)
Indonesia	26.6	21.4	1.7 (2021)	...	...
Lao People's Democratic Republic	5.1	22.5 (2022)	21.8	21.4	22.2
Malaysia	14.4 (2011)	10.2 (2022)	...	...	...
Myanmar	18.6 (2015)	15.0 (2020)	8.1 [d] (2015)	7.6 [d] (2015)	8.7 [d] (2015)
Philippines	25.3	12.8 (2022)	1.2 (2022)	1.0 (2022)	1.4 (2022)
Singapore	3.7 (2013)	6.0 (2024)	...	...	...
Thailand	12.5	12.8 (2024)	...	...	...
Timor-Leste	19.0	29.1 (2022)	3.7 [b] (2022)	3.5 [b] (2022)	3.8 [b] (2022)
Viet Nam	8.2	10.8	5.7 (2021)	6.2 (2021)	5.2 (2021)
The Pacific					
Cook Islands	...	12.5 (2019)	...	...	...
Fiji	18.4 (2011)	20.1 (2016)	15.6 (2021)	12.3 (2021)	18.8 (2021)
Kiribati	46.9 (2015)	37.7	7.1 (2019)	5.5 (2019)	8.6 (2019)
Marshall Islands	...	40.0 (2021)	...	...	...
Micronesia, Federated States of	28.7 (2014)	...	...	...	...
Nauru	36.4 (2013)	41.0 (2021)	0.7	0.4	1.1
Niue	...	10.8 (2022)	...	...	...
Palau	13.3 (2014)	18.0 (2020)	...	...	...
Papua New Guinea	35.5	27.7 (2022)	...	...	...
Samoa	39.1 (2012)	30.1 (2022)	6.9 (2022)	4.9 (2022)	8.7 (2022)
Solomon Islands	7.0 (2013)	...	13.8 [c] (2015)	13.8 [c] (2015)	13.8 [c] (2015)
Tonga	...	25.6	25.9 (2019)	18.5 (2019)	32.9 (2019)
Tuvalu	38.4	34.3 (2022)	3.7 (2020)	4.0 (2020)	3.4 (2020)
Vanuatu	31.8	47.5 (2020)	26.7	27.4	26.0
Developed ADB Member Economies					
Australia	11.3	8.5 (2024)	...	...	...
Japan	4.3	3.1 (2019)	...	...	...
New Zealand	13.7	12.8 (2024)	...	...	...

... = data not available, ADB = Asian Development Bank.

a For detailed information on data coverage, employment definition, reference period, and repository, please see https://ilostat.ilo.org/data/.
b Refers to children aged 10–17 years.
c Refers to children aged 5–14 years.
d Data differ from published national estimates of child labor from the same source due to different treatment of hazardous working conditions and different hourly thresholds.

Sources: For Indicator 8.6.1: International Labour Organization. ILOSTAT Database. https://ilostat.ilo.org/data/ (accessed 15 July 2025). For Indicator 8.7.1: United Nations. SDG Global Database. https://unstats.un.org/sdgs/dataportal (accessed 15 July 2025).

Goal 8. Promote sustained, inclusive, and sustainable economic growth; full and productive employment; and decent work for all

Table 1.8.4: Access to Banking, Insurance and Financial Services, and Trade

ADB Regional Member	Target 8.10: Strengthen the capacity of domestic financial institutions to encourage and expand access to banking, insurance, and financial services for all					
	8.10.1: Number of Commercial Bank Branches and ATMs per 100,000 Adults				8.10.2: Proportion of Adults (15 Years and Older) with an Account at a Bank or Other Financial Institution or with a Mobile-Money Service Provider (%)	
	Commercial Bank Branches		ATMs			
	2010	2022	2010	2022	2011	2021
Developing ADB Member Economies						
Central and West Asia						
Afghanistan	2.4	1.9 (2019)	0.5	1.6 (2019)	9.0	9.7
Armenia	18.1	24.7	33.2	74.6	17.5	55.4
Azerbaijan	10.0	6.4	27.5	39.9	14.9	46.3 (2022)
Georgia	21.4	31.2	48.7	96.2	33.0	70.5
Kazakhstan	3.3	12.4 (2022)	61.8	89.8 (2022)	42.1	81.1
Kyrgyz Republic	6.2	7.4	7.4	48.4	3.8	45.1
Pakistan	7.9	10.8	4.1	12.0	10.3	21.0
Tajikistan	5.6	3.5 (2022)	4.6	27.2 (2022)	2.5	39.5
Türkiye	17.6	14.4	51.6	80.5	57.6	74.1
Turkmenistan	...	...	...	...	0.4	40.6 (2017)
Uzbekistan	39.2	54.3	8.5 (2014)	104.9	22.5	44.1
East Asia						
China, People's Republic of	7.7 (2012)	8.8	24.9	72.0	63.8	88.7
Hong Kong, China	23.9	18.2	47.1	46.7	88.7	97.8
Korea, Republic of	18.2	12.7	266.3	257.1 (2021)	93.1	98.7
Mongolia	55.1	59.8	18.9	30.8	77.7	98.5
Taipei,China	17.0 (2011)	16.5 (2024)	134.8 (2015)	161.7 (2024)	87.3	94.7
South Asia						
Bangladesh	7.8	8.8	2.1	13.6	31.7	52.8
Bhutan	15.3	20.9 (2021)	8.9	45.2 (2021)	33.7 (2014)	...
India	10.0	14.5	7.2	25.0	35.2	77.5
Maldives	11.9	14.9	16.7	46.1	79.6 (2017)	79.6 (2017)
Nepal	5.1	22.9	7.3 (2011)	22.0	25.3	54.0
Sri Lanka	14.0	17.3	...	...	68.5	89.3
Southeast Asia						
Brunei Darussalam	23.3	16.2 (2021)	82.0	73.1 (2021)	...	...
Cambodia	4.0	14.3	5.1	46.5	3.7	33.4
Indonesia	7.9	11.7	12.8	46.0	19.6	51.8
Lao People's Democratic Republic	2.5	3.1 (2021)	8.5	28.7	26.8	37.3
Malaysia	10.7	8.1	50.3	51.8	66.2	88.4
Myanmar	1.5	5.6 (2019)	0.1 (2012)	6.9 (2019)	22.8 (2014)	47.8
Philippines	7.6	8.8	15.1	28.4	26.6	51.4
Singapore	9.9	6.1	59.3	47.5	98.2	97.6
Thailand	10.8	8.3	80.7	97.9	72.7	95.6
Timor-Leste	1.7	5.4	2.4	16.4	...	...
Viet Nam	3.3	3.1	17.3	27.3	21.4	56.3 (2022)
The Pacific						
Cook Islands	...	...	...	...	...	...
Fiji	10.9	10.2 (2022)	32.4	48.8 (2022)	...	...
Kiribati	6.0 (2011)	...	10.5 (2011)	...	...	...
Marshall Islands	18.6	28.0	3.1	10.5	...	...
Micronesia, Federated States of	14.4	12.4	8.6	12.4	...	...
Nauru	...	...	...	127.8	...	...
Niue	...	...	...	...	...	...
Palau	...	...	33.4	44.9 (2017)	...	...
Papua New Guinea	1.5	1.4 (2022)	5.1	7.4 (2022)	...	...
Samoa	24.4	30.5	24.4	56.0	...	...
Solomon Islands	4.4	3.8	11.0	12.8	...	...
Tonga	21.5	33.0 (2018)	27.7	40.5 (2018)	...	...
Tuvalu	...	...	...	...	...	...
Vanuatu	20.6	21.1 (2021)	28.1	56.6 (2021)	...	...
Developed ADB Member Economies						
Australia	30.8	16.9	168.7	111.4	99.1	99.3
Japan	33.8	33.7	130.7	109.6	96.4	98.5
New Zealand	34.7	16.0	72.6	43.7	99.4	98.8

Goal 8. Promote sustained, inclusive, and sustainable economic growth; full and productive employment; and decent work for all

Table 1.8.4: Access to Banking, Insurance and Financial Services, and Trade *(continued)*

ADB Regional Member	Target 8.10: Strengthen the capacity of domestic financial institutions to encourage and expand access to banking, insurance, and financial services for all — 8.a.1: Aid for Trade (millions of constant 2021 United States dollars)			
	Commitments		Disbursement	
	2010	2022	2010	2022
Developing ADB Member Economies				
Central and West Asia				
Afghanistan	2,070.3	468.2	2,292.5	365.5
Armenia	169.0	48.5	170.0	94.3
Azerbaijan	102.8	29.2	64.5	102.0
Georgia	357.0	94.4	287.1	315.6
Kazakhstan	195.6	11.7	67.4	3.9
Kyrgyz Republic	171.1	242.9	84.4	239.7
Pakistan	824.9	1,312.6	370.1	890.0
Tajikistan	260.0	323.7	175.3	255.7
Türkiye	823.7	244.8	530.8	232.3
Turkmenistan	20.0	2.0	3.3	19.6
Uzbekistan	410.6	761.5	89.4	663.3
East Asia				
China, People's Republic of	646.2	29.6	481.8	285.5
Hong Kong, China	...	...	...	...
Korea, Republic of	...	...	...	...
Mongolia	317.9	167.1	137.0	127.0
Taipei,China	...	...	...	...
South Asia				
Bangladesh	1,098.0	5,788.1	474.5	2,739.9
Bhutan	55.9	61.0	80.1	77.9
India	2,541.5	8,079.1	1,946.8	4,462.4
Maldives	12.6	146.8	29.3	173.2
Nepal	496.3	832.7	247.4	463.6
Sri Lanka	287.8	667.1	294.4	576.6
Southeast Asia				
Brunei Darussalam	...	...	...	...
Cambodia	427.6	621.0	205.8	707.7
Indonesia	660.0	1,667.0	880.6	1,368.4
Lao People's Democratic Republic	271.6	161.8	141.0	153.0
Malaysia	14.3	7.1	27.8	7.0
Myanmar	32.6	60.3	42.1	462.3
Philippines	116.9	3,081.5	320.8	1,377.6
Singapore	...	...	...	...
Thailand	269.4	63.7	142.2	114.2
Timor-Leste	89.5	31.9	43.3	49.4
Viet Nam	1,653.6	880.2	1,521.8	720.7
The Pacific				
Cook Islands	5.2	1.0 (2019)	3.1	5.8 (2019)
Fiji	19.3	83.0	9.0	29.1
Kiribati	4.1	27.1	3.6	35.6
Marshall Islands	0.7	17.5	7.9	22.0
Micronesia, Federated States of	1.2	15.8	10.3	12.2
Nauru	0.2	24.5	0.9	18.0
Niue	4.3	0.4	5.1	11.3
Palau	1.2	18.4	5.7	14.2
Papua New Guinea	250.5	184.7	124.0	273.7
Samoa	25.2	14.9	30.6	25.7
Solomon Islands	40.7	62.1	25.1	98.0
Tonga	28.8	28.9	28.6	33.9
Tuvalu	1.2	64.4	1.4	13.6
Vanuatu	19.5	36.4	38.9	59.0
Developed ADB Member Economies				
Australia	...	...	...	...
Japan	...	...	...	...
New Zealand	...	...	...	...

... = data not available, ADB = Asian Development Bank.

Sources: For indicator 8.10.1: United Nations. SDG Global Database. https://unstats.un.org/sdgs/dataportal (accessed 29 July 2025). For indicator 8.10.1: Commercial bank branches for Taipei,China: Central bank of Taipei,China; and ATMs for Taipei,China: Financial Supervisory Commission, Banking Bureau. For Indicator 8.10.2: World Bank. World Development Indicators. https://data.worldbank.org/indicator (accessed 29 July 2025). For indicator 8.a.1: United Nations. SDG Global Database. https://unstats.un.org/sdgs/dataportal (accessed 29 July 2025).

Goal 9. Build resilient infrastructure, promote inclusive and sustainable industrialization, and foster innovation

Table 1.9.1: Selected Indicators for Sustainable Development Goal 9—Air Transport, Passenger and Freight Volume

ADB Regional Member	Target 9.1: Develop quality, reliable, sustainable, and resilient infrastructure, including regional and transborder infrastructure, to support economic development and human well-being, with a focus on affordable and equitable access for all			
	9.1.2: Passenger Volume, by Air Transport[a] (p-km million)		9.1.2: Freight Volume, by Air Transport[b] (t-km million)	
	2017	2022	2017	2022
Developing ADB Member Economies				
Central and West Asia	**234,853.2**	**328,684.2**	**5,297.0**	**10,472.6**
Afghanistan	1,843.7	2,640.7	21.5	0.8
Armenia	...	2,882.4	...	15.7
Azerbaijan	4,204.1	3,960.8	61.6	1,434.5
Georgia	600.0	786.7	0.5	0.2
Kazakhstan	12,597.2	20,253.2	49.5	53.1
Kyrgyz Republic	2,175.8	1,868.1	0.0	0.7
Pakistan	18,514.6	17,290.6	214.5	309.5
Tajikistan	1,467.7	1,620.9	2.9	131.7
Türkiye	183,397.7	263,040.9	4,800.2	8,367.3
Turkmenistan	2,939.6	1,189.0	19.5	62.7
Uzbekistan	7,112.7	13,150.8	126.8	96.5
East Asia[c]	**1,266,268.0**	**1,374,191.3**	**47,259.0**	**56,674.9**
China, People's Republic of	950,425.2	1,218,208.2	23,323.6	44,354.6
Hong Kong, China	150,193.8	...	12,415.2	...
Korea, Republic of	164,423.6	153,703.3	11,511.8	12,293.8
Mongolia	1,225.4	2,279.9	8.4	26.5
Taipei,China	...	...	...	...
South Asia[c]	**216,727.2**	**275,212.3**	**2,880.2**	**2,231.2**
Bangladesh	9,087.3	10,863.0	61.7	98.9
Bhutan	389.1	289.6	0.5	0.5
India	190,343.5	246,968.3	2,407.1	1,807.0
Maldives	768.7	496.6	7.7	29.5
Nepal	1,970.1	3,882.7	4.6	16.9
Sri Lanka	14,168.5	12,712.0	398.5	278.5
Southeast Asia[c]	**605,563.2**	**586,468.0**	**11,429.0**	**13,670.2**
Brunei Darussalam	3,768.1	2,391.9	132.6	45.9
Cambodia	1,849.6	1,002.0	0.9	2.4
Indonesia	111,371.1	106,320.6	1,052.4	870.5
Lao People's Democratic Republic	860.7	600.3	1.5	–
Malaysia	111,058.6	80,759.1	1,455.2	1,910.1
Myanmar	1,711.2	2,762.4	4.8	9.9
Philippines	63,909.7	61,534.4	753.4	649.2
Singapore	135,587.3	165,636.9	5,063.0	7,604.2
Thailand	119,168.9	85,750.3	2,511.9	1,649.9
Timor-Leste	...	59.2	...	0.0
Viet Nam	56,278.1	79,651.0	453.3	927.9
The Pacific[c]	**8,117.3**	**9,952.7**	**145.5**	**206.3**
Cook Islands	29.8	17.7	0.1	–
Fiji	5,451.8	7,701.4	102.6	156.1
Kiribati	10.7	12.8	–	0.3
Marshall Islands	14.2	7.1	0.2	0.4
Micronesia, Federated States of	...	...	...	...
Nauru	151.2	83.6	7.9	2.9
Niue	...	...	...	...
Palau	...	...	...	...
Papua New Guinea	1,747.6	1,593.4	29.2	7.1
Samoa	21.7	5.7	–	0.0
Solomon Islands	324.6	154.6	3.8	9.1
Tonga	...	...	...	...
Tuvalu	...	...	...	...
Vanuatu	365.8	376.5	1.6	30.3
Developed ADB Member Economies	**381,168.3**	**343,322.8**	**14,003.1**	**10,429.9**
Australia	155,093.0	133,545.6	1,982.6	1,188.1
Japan	191,538.0	183,576.0	10,684.6	8,474.0
New Zealand	34,537.3	26,201.1	1,336.0	767.8
DEVELOPING ADB MEMBER ECONOMIES[c]	**2,331,528.9**	**2,574,508.6**	**67,010.7**	**83,255.3**
ALL ADB REGIONAL MEMBERS[c]	**2,712,697.2**	**2,917,831.5**	**81,013.8**	**93,685.2**

... = data not available, – = magnitude equals zero, 0.0 = magnitude is less than half of unit employed, ADB = Asian Development Bank, p-km = passenger-kilometer, t-km = ton-kilometer.

Note: The numbers shown in the table are modeled estimates as published on the United Nations' SDG Global Database.

a A passenger-kilometer, abbreviated as p-km, is a unit of measurement representing the transport of 1 passenger by a defined mode of transport over 1 kilometer.

b A ton-kilometer, abbreviated as t-km, is a unit of measurement of freight transport representing the transport of 1 metric ton of goods (including packaging and tare weights of intermodal transport units) by a defined mode of transport over 1 kilometer.

c For reporting economies only.

Source: United Nations. SDG Global Database. https://unstats.un.org/sdgs/dataportal (accessed 29 July 2025).

Goal 9. Build resilient infrastructure, promote inclusive and sustainable industrialization, and foster innovation

Table 1.9.2: Selected Indicators for Sustainable Development Goal 9—Growth in Manufacturing

ADB Regional Member	Target 9.2: Promote inclusive and sustainable industrialization; and, by 2030, significantly raise industry's share of employment and GDP, in line with national circumstances, and double its share in least developed countries (or economies)					
	9.2.1: Manufacturing Value-Added (at constant 2015 $)				9.2.2: Manufacturing Employment as a Proportion of Total Employment[a] (%)	
	As a Proportion of GDP (%)		Per Capita			
	2010	2024	2010	2024	2010	2023
Developing ADB Member Economies						
Central and West Asia						
Afghanistan	7.3	7.1	38.7	28.1	6.8 (2012)	6.4 (2021)
Armenia	9.0	10.7	262.5	590.8	5.9	8.2 (2021)
Azerbaijan	4.6	7.7	237.9	442.7	4.8	5.6 (2022)
Georgia	10.6	8.6	317.7	558.7	5.3	5.9 (2020)
Kazakhstan	11.3	11.2	973.3	1,337.8	7.0	6.8 (2022)
Kyrgyz Republic	17.6	14.8	168.8	208.0	8.0	11.5 (2022)
Pakistan	12.1	12.0	150.5	193.7	13.5	14.9 (2021)
Tajikistan	19.2	19.5	155.0	287.1	5.5 (2009)	5.4 (2018)
Türkiye	15.6	16.9	1,303.8	2,498.7	18.7	19.8
Turkmenistan	46.4	29.1	2,354.9	2,165.6	22.3	25.3
Uzbekistan	12.3	13.7	263.3	521.6	11.5	9.0 (2020)
East Asia						
China, People's Republic of	27.5	28.0	1,536.4	3,555.7	...	29.1
Hong Kong, China	1.3	1.0	494.7	473.2	3.8	2.4
Korea, Republic of	27.9	27.4	7,539.6	10,186.2	16.8	15.5 (2024)
Mongolia	9.0	8.0	240.2	374.0	6.3	8.3
Taipei,China	27.8	35.8	5,550.0	11,093.0	28.3	26.6
South Asia						
Bangladesh	15.3	25.2	154.7	590.6	12.4	11.3 (2022)
Bhutan	7.8	5.6	184.3	203.0	3.9	6.7
India	15.3	14.8	193.2	357.6	11.3	12.0
Maldives	2.0	1.9	170.1	228.0	9.1 (2009)	9.7 (2019)
Nepal	5.3	4.8	36.8	54.9	0.2 (2008)	3.1 (2017)
Sri Lanka	18.9	16.0	564.7	634.7	17.1	17.3 (2022)
Southeast Asia						
Brunei Darussalam	14.7	17.6	4,878.3	5,138.0	3.7 (2014)	5.9
Cambodia	19.8	32.2	227.7	695.1	10.7	16.5 (2021)
Indonesia	21.5	19.9	573.6	867.7	12.5	13.7
Lao People's Democratic Republic	8.0	8.8	125.1	252.2	5.1	3.4 (2022)
Malaysia	22.8	23.4	1,851.8	2,768.7	16.8	16.8 (2022)
Myanmar	18.7	22.4	167.8	327.8	10.9 (2015)	12.2 (2020)
Philippines	20.6	18.5	488.4	727.5	8.3 (2012)	7.9 (2022)
Singapore	21.0	20.5	10,244.6	13,953.1	14.6 (2011)	9.0
Thailand	30.1	25.0	1,522.1	1,642.7	14.1	15.7
Timor-Leste	0.9	1.6	10.9	20.3	3.2	1.5 (2022)
Viet Nam	18.7	25.8	379.5	1,023.5	14.3	21.7
The Pacific						
Cook Islands	2.5	1.1	389.2	311.9	3.9 (2011)	3.8 (2019)
Fiji	11.1	8.8	473.8	514.7	9.3 (2011)	5.6 (2016)
Kiribati	4.6	4.6	61.2	95.0	13.2	4.0 (2020)
Marshall Islands	5.7	1.4	194.5	82.6	0.7	4.3 (2021)
Micronesia, Federated States of	0.4	0.6	13.1	18.2	2.4 (2014)	...
Nauru	26.5	20.6	1,404.2	2,173.9	0.5 (2013)	1.4 (2021)
Niue	...	...	...	...	3.2 (2015)	1.5 (2017)
Palau	0.7	1.1	93.2	149.0	3.2 (2008)	1.5 (2020)
Papua New Guinea	2.6	1.7	55.3	43.7	1.8	1.2 (2022)
Samoa	9.3	3.7	364.4	163.0	5.5 (2011)	6.0 (2022)
Solomon Islands	11.7	7.4	241.8	143.5	5.5 (2013)	...
Tonga	6.1	4.1	204.7	183.8	...	13.0
Tuvalu	1.1	0.1	29.2	5.4	...	10.4 (2022)
Vanuatu	5.1	2.9	145.7	75.3	2.3	4.0 (2020)
Developed ADB Member Economies						
Australia	7.5	5.1	3,669.2	2,881.6	8.9	6.2 (2024)
Japan	20.8	21.5	6,847.9	8,023.6	16.8	15.4 (2024)
New Zealand	12.3	8.5	4,347.5	3,619.5	11.6	8.6

... = data not available, $ = United States dollars, ADB = Asian Development Bank, GDP = gross domestic product.

a For detailed information on data coverage, employment definition, reference period, and repository, please see https://unstats.un.org/sdgs/dataportal.

Sources: United Nations. SDG Global Database. https://unstats.un.org/sdgs/dataportal (accessed 15 July 2025). For Taipei,China and Indicator 9.2.2 for Turkmenistan: United Nations Industrial Development Organization. UNIDO Statistics Portal. https://stat.unido.org/ (accessed 15 July 2025).

Table 1.9.3: Selected Indicators for Sustainable Development Goal 9—Carbon Dioxide Emissions

ADB Regional Member	Target 9.4: By 2030, upgrade infrastructure and retrofit industries to make them sustainable, with increased resource-use efficiency and greater adoption of clean and environmentally sound technologies and industrial processes, with all countries (or economies) taking action in accordance with their respective capabilities — 9.4.1: Carbon Dioxide Emissions[a]					
	Per Unit of GDP (PPP) (kg of CO_2 per constant 2021 $)			Per Unit of Manufacturing Value-Added (kg of CO_2 per constant 2015 $)		
	2010	2015	2022	2010	2015	2022
Developing ADB Member Economies						
Central and West Asia						
Afghanistan	...	...	...	...	...	...
Armenia	0.13	0.13	0.13	0.68	0.39	0.34
Azerbaijan	0.13	0.15	0.17	0.58	0.77	0.54
Georgia	0.12	0.16	0.14	0.45	1.12	0.78
Kazakhstan	0.48	0.32	0.34	3.17	1.50	0.87
Kyrgyz Republic	0.23	0.28	0.21	0.65	1.81	0.35
Pakistan	0.15	0.15	0.15	1.27	1.14	1.04
Tajikistan	0.12	0.16	0.18	–	0.07	0.52
Türkiye	0.19	0.16	0.14	0.51	0.33	0.35
Turkmenistan	0.49	0.42	0.64	0.12	0.06	0.97
Uzbekistan	0.74	0.41	0.34	2.27	0.88	0.82
East Asia						
China, People's Republic of	0.57	0.45	0.36	1.32	0.90	0.57
Hong Kong, China	0.11	0.09	0.07	0.54	0.61	0.11
Korea, Republic of	0.29	0.26	0.20	0.25	0.18	0.13
Mongolia	0.54	0.41	0.45	1.88	1.19	1.20
Taipei,China	...	...	...	0.34	0.24	0.13
South Asia						
Bangladesh	0.08	0.08	0.08	0.39	0.30	0.21
Bhutan	...	...	...	...	...	...
India	0.25	0.24	0.21	1.61	1.53	1.36
Maldives	...	...	...	...	...	...
Nepal	0.05	0.05	0.09	1.22	2.15	3.59
Sri Lanka	0.06	0.07	0.06	0.09	0.10	0.06
Southeast Asia						
Brunei Darussalam	0.20	0.17	0.26	0.23	0.22	0.23
Cambodia	0.09	0.10	0.13	0.20	0.08	0.27
Indonesia	0.18	0.16	0.18	0.87	0.53	0.71
Lao People's Democratic Republic	0.08	0.17	0.31	1.12	1.37	0.78
Malaysia	0.29	0.26	0.22	0.57	0.43	0.39
Myanmar	0.05	0.08	0.11	0.28	0.28	0.18
Philippines	0.12	0.12	0.13	0.24	0.20	0.13
Singapore	0.09	0.08	0.06	0.19	0.23	0.16
Thailand	0.19	0.19	0.17	0.47	0.52	0.46
Timor-Leste	...	...	...	...	...	...
Viet Nam	0.20	0.19	0.22	1.25	0.61	0.93
The Pacific						
Cook Islands	...	...	...	...	...	...
Fiji	...	...	...	...	...	...
Kiribati	...	...	...	...	...	...
Marshall Islands	...	...	...	...	...	...
Micronesia, Federated States of	...	...	...	...	...	...
Nauru	...	...	...	...	...	...
Niue	...	...	...	...	...	...
Palau	...	...	...	...	...	...
Papua New Guinea	...	...	...	...	...	...
Samoa	...	...	...	...	...	...
Solomon Islands	...	...	...	...	...	...
Tonga	...	...	...	...	...	...
Tuvalu	...	...	...	...	...	...
Vanuatu	...	...	...	...	...	...
Developed ADB Member Economies						
Australia	0.33	0.28	0.22	0.38	0.37	0.35
Japan	0.22	0.21	0.17	0.23	0.21	0.17
New Zealand	0.17	0.16	0.12	0.26	0.30	0.25

... = data not available, – = magnitude equals zero, $ = United States dollars, ADB = Asian Development Bank, CO_2 = carbon dioxide, GDP = gross domestic product, kg = kilogram, PPP = purchasing power parity.

a Refers to carbon dioxide emissions from fuel combustion.

Sources: United Nations. SDG Global Database. https://unstats.un.org/sdgs/dataportal (accessed 15 July 2025). For CO_2 per unit of manufacturing value-added for Taipei,China: United Nations Industrial Development Organization. UNIDO Data Portal. https://stat.unido.org/sdg (accessed 15 July 2025).

Goal 9. Build resilient infrastructure, promote inclusive and sustainable industrialization, and foster innovation

Table 1.9.4: Selected Indicators for Sustainable Development Goal 9—Research and Development

ADB Regional Member	Target 9.5: Enhance scientific research, upgrade the technological capabilities of industrial sectors in all countries (or economies), in particular developing countries (or economies), including, by 2030, encouraging innovation and substantially increasing the number of research and development workers per 1 million people and public and private research and development spending			
	9.5.1: Research and Development Expenditure as a Proportion of GDP (%)		9.5.2: Researchers (Full-Time Equivalent) (per million inhabitants)	
	2010	2023	2010	2023
Developing ADB Member Economies				
Central and West Asia				
Afghanistan	...	...	...	...
Armenia	0.24	0.18	...	1,040
Azerbaijan	0.22	0.18	...	1,663
Georgia	0.08 (2013)	0.25	600 (2013)	1,768
Kazakhstan	0.15	0.14	360	693
Kyrgyz Republic	0.16	0.06	...	...
Pakistan	0.30 (2011)	0.16	130 (2011)	474
Tajikistan	0.09	0.09 (2020)	...	...
Türkiye	0.79	1.32 (2022)	883	2,479 (2022)
Turkmenistan	...	0.14 (2022)	...	...
Uzbekistan	0.15	0.13	552	542
East Asia				
China, People's Republic of	1.71	2.56 (2022)	899	1,849 (2022)
Hong Kong, China	0.75	1.10	3,063	5,274
Korea, Republic of	3.32	5.21 (2022)	5,429	9,435 (2022)
Mongolia	0.24	0.08 (2022)	...	535 (2022)
Taipei,China	...	...	...	...
South Asia				
Bangladesh	...	...	...	...
Bhutan	...	...	...	...
India	0.79	0.65 (2020)	156	259 (2020)
Maldives	...	...	...	...
Nepal	0.30	...	60 (2002)	...
Sri Lanka	0.13	0.11 (2022)	103	94 (2022)
Southeast Asia				
Brunei Darussalam	0.04 (2004)	0.28 (2018)	291 (2004)	506 (2022)
Cambodia	0.05 (2002)	0.12 (2015)	17 (2002)	30 (2015)
Indonesia	0.08 (2009)	0.28 (2020)	88 (2009)	395 (2020)
Lao People's Democratic Republic	0.04 (2002)	...	16 (2002)	...
Malaysia	1.04	0.95 (2020)	1,453	712 (2020)
Myanmar	0.16 (2002)	0.02	18 (2002)	28
Philippines	0.11 (2011)	0.32 (2018)	83 (2011)	170 (2018)
Singapore	1.93	2.16 (2020)	6,368	7,917 (2021)
Thailand	0.36 (2011)	1.16 (2022)	529 (2011)	1,863 (2022)
Timor-Leste	...	...	...	...
Viet Nam	0.15 (2011)	0.42 (2021)	685 (2013)	768 (2021)
The Pacific				
Cook Islands	...	...	...	...
Fiji	...	...	...	...
Kiribati	...	...	...	...
Marshall Islands	...	...	...	...
Micronesia, Federated States of	...	...	...	...
Nauru	...	...	...	...
Niue	...	...	...	...
Palau	...	...	...	...
Papua New Guinea	...	0.03 (2016)	...	33 (2016)
Samoa	...	...	...	...
Solomon Islands	...	...	...	...
Tonga	...	...	...	...
Tuvalu	...	...	...	...
Vanuatu	...	...	...	...
Developed ADB Member Economies				
Australia	2.37	1.86 (2021)	4,569	...
Japan	3.10	3.41 (2022)	5,117	5,630 (2022)
New Zealand	1.23 (2011)	1.47 (2021)	3,731 (2011)	5,095 (2021)

... = data not available, ADB = Asian Development Bank, GDP = gross domestic product.

Source: United Nations. SDG Global Database. https://unstats.un.org/sdgs/dataportal (accessed 25 July 2025).

Goal 9. Build resilient infrastructure, promote inclusive and sustainable industrialization, and foster innovation

Table 1.9.5: Selected Indicators for Sustainable Development Goal 9—Official International Support and Industry Value-Added

ADB Regional Member	Target 9.a: Facilitate sustainable and resilient infrastructure development in developing countries through enhanced financial, technological, and technical support to African countries, least developed countries, landlocked developing countries and small island developing States — 9.a.1: Total Official International Support to Infrastructure[a] (constant 2023 $ million)		Target 9.b: Support domestic technology development, research, and innovation in developing countries (or economies), including by ensuring a conducive policy environment for, *inter alia*, industrial diversification and value addition to commodities — 9.b.1: Proportion of Medium and High-Tech Industry Value-Added in Total Value-Added[b] (%)	
	2010	2023	2010	2024
Developing ADB Member Economies				
Central and West Asia	**8,898.9**	**7,883.2**		
Afghanistan	1,480.0	133.0	9.5	7.4
Armenia	238.1	167.8	4.4	4.0
Azerbaijan	235.7	219.1	7.7	13.7
Georgia	388.5	975.0	17.0	16.9
Kazakhstan	1,276.4	543.4	9.2	15.7
Kyrgyz Republic	71.8	248.5	4.5	2.3
Pakistan	527.4	1,013.2	17.0	23.4
Tajikistan	130.8	271.1	3.7	4.3
Türkiye	4,456.0	2,504.3	30.6	32.4
Turkmenistan	1.6	193.8	3.5	8.3
Uzbekistan	92.5	1,614.1	16.9	19.4
East Asia[c]	**2,703.2**	**1,583.5**		
China, People's Republic of	2,607.4	1,298.6	41.4	47.1
Hong Kong, China	...	...	22.0	17.3
Korea, Republic of	...	...	61.2	61.8
Mongolia	95.8	284.9	2.1	3.8
Taipei,China	...	...	64.3	73.9
South Asia	**7,109.7**	**15,945.6**		
Bangladesh	467.0	3,792.2	9.7	5.3
Bhutan	93.7	49.7	...	...
India	5,894.3	10,538.0	38.0	43.4
Maldives	29.2	554.3	2.6	2.6
Nepal	189.6	373.7	6.2	10.3
Sri Lanka	435.9	637.8	9.8	8.8
Southeast Asia[c]	**3,552.2**	**9,190.7**		
Brunei Darussalam	...	...	3.3	3.3
Cambodia	131.7	445.2	0.3	0.3
Indonesia	1,104.2	3,623.2	34.2	26.9
Lao People's Democratic Republic	105.3	165.1	3.8	3.9
Malaysia	21.7	8.6	40.6	42.2
Myanmar	4.8	409.4	15.5	40.7
Philippines	256.4	3,381.8	37.2	43.1
Singapore	...	...	78.2	85.5
Thailand	126.7	210.1	43.8	34.5
Timor-Leste	24.4	40.3	...	...
Viet Nam	1,776.9	907.2	20.7	38.1
The Pacific[d]	**245.6**	**650.6**		
Cook Islands	1.7	10.2 (2019)	...	...
Fiji	12.7	40.7	7.3	7.0
Kiribati	1.3	28.1	...	...
Marshall Islands	4.7	18.7	...	...
Micronesia, Federated States of	9.1	11.3	...	...
Nauru	0.2	15.5	...	...
Niue	3.6	5.6	...	...
Palau	5.1	9.8	...	...
Papua New Guinea	105.6	325.1	12.6	12.6
Samoa	23.9	17.9	...	...
Solomon Islands	14.7	82.4	...	...
Tonga	25.6	30.8	17.3	17.3
Tuvalu	0.8	8.9	...	...
Vanuatu	36.5	45.6	...	...
Developed ADB Member Economies	**...**	**...**		
Australia	...	...	27.8	28.9
Japan	...	...	54.5	54.7
New Zealand	...	...	21.5	24.2
DEVELOPING ADB MEMBER ECONOMIES[d]	**22,509.6**	**35,253.6**		

... = data not available, $ = United States dollars, ADB = Asian Development Bank.

a Gross disbursements of total official development assistance and other official flows from all donors in support of infrastructure.
b The indicator is reported in the International Standard Industrial Classification of all Economic Activities (ISIC) revision provided by the economies. This may affect comparability among economies reporting data according to different ISIC revisions – Revision 3 (1990) or Revision 4 (2008).
c Includes only reporting economies with data corresponding to the year heading.
d For estimating aggregates, imputation was done for economies with missing data by substituting available data from the nearest years.

Sources: For Indicator 9.a.1: United Nations. SDG Global Database. https://unstats.un.org/sdgs/dataportal (accessed 15 July 2025). For Indicator 9.b.1: United Nations Industrial Development Organization. UNIDO Statistics Portal. https://stat.unido.org/ (accessed 15 July 2025).

Goal 9. Build resilient infrastructure, promote inclusive and sustainable industrialization, and foster innovation

Table 1.9.6: Selected Indicators for Sustainable Development Goal 9—Coverage by Mobile Networks

ADB Regional Member	Target 9.c: Significantly increase access to information and communications technology and strive to provide universal and affordable access to the internet in least developed countries (or economies) by 2020					
	9.c.1.a: Proportion of Population Covered by 2G Mobile Networks (%)		9.c.1.b: Proportion of Population Covered by 3G Mobile Networks (%)		9.c.1.c: Proportion of Population Covered by LTE Mobile Networks (%)	
	2015	2023	2015	2023	2015	2023
Developing ADB Member Economies						
Central and West Asia						
Afghanistan	89.2	92.3	32.0	67.0	–	34.0
Armenia	100.0	100.0	99.9	100.0	46.5	100.0
Azerbaijan	100.0	100.0	95.5	100.0	39.0	100.0
Georgia	99.0	99.9	99.0	99.9	82.0	99.7
Kazakhstan	96.6	99.0	72.7	97.7	65.5	89.2
Kyrgyz Republic	97.8	99.6	59.0	99.5	1.6	99.3
Pakistan	86.0	91.0	46.0	81.0	16.0	81.0
Tajikistan	60.0	94.3 (2022)	60.0	94.3 (2022)	60.0	80.0 (2022)
Türkiye	98.5	99.9	95.0	99.8	–	99.7
Turkmenistan	93.9	98.0 (2022)	60.0	74.7 (2022)	25.0	67.0 (2022)
Uzbekistan	98.0	99.5	43.0	96.0	10.0	92.0
East Asia						
China, People's Republic of	99.5	100.0	95.0	100.0	85.0	100.0
Hong Kong, China	100.0	100.0	99.0	99.0	99.0	99.0
Korea, Republic of	99.9	99.9	99.0	99.9	99.0	99.9
Mongolia	99.0	100.0	95.0	100.0	6.9 (2016)	99.0
Taipei,China	...	...	...	...	...	...
South Asia						
Bangladesh	99.4	99.6	71.0	98.9	65.0	98.9
Bhutan	98.0	98.0	80.0	97.0	40.0	97.0
India	95.0	99.2	74.0	98.9	4.0	98.8
Maldives	100.0	100.0	100.0	100.0	58.0	100.0
Nepal	82.0	98.3 (2022)	50.0	57.2 (2022)	–	53.3 (2022)
Sri Lanka	99.0	99.5	83.0	97.0	35.0	97.0
Southeast Asia						
Brunei Darussalam	97.0	99.1	91.0	99.1	80.0	99.0
Cambodia	99.0	99.7	70.0	93.1	30.0	93.1
Indonesia	87.9	99.4	60.0	99.0	5.0	99.0
Lao People's Democratic Republic	98.0	97.0	65.0	85.0	5.0	76.0
Malaysia	96.0	98.6	92.0	97.1	71.0	97.1
Myanmar	95.0	96.4	79.3	95.4	–	94.4
Philippines	99.0	99.0	78.0	98.5	39.0	95.5
Singapore	100.0	100.0	100.0	100.0	100.0	100.0
Thailand	97.0	99.0	97.0	99.0	21.0	99.0
Timor-Leste	96.0	96.5	96.0	96.5	–	45.0
Viet Nam	94.0	99.9	70.0	99.9	–	99.9
The Pacific						
Cook Islands	100.0 (2016)	100.0 (2022)	29.7	55.0 (2022)	55.0 (2017)	55.0 (2022)
Fiji	88.0	98.0 (2022)	68.4	96.0 (2022)	17.0	92.9 (2022)
Kiribati	70.0	76.0	19.0	75.0	–	65.0
Marshall Islands	65.0	65.0 (2022)	...	...	...	...
Micronesia, Federated States of	80.0	80.0 (2022)	15.0	50.0 (2022)	–	30.0 (2022)
Nauru	98.0	98.0 (2022)	98.0	98.0 (2022)	–	90.0 (2022)
Niue	...	...	–	70.0 (2022)	20.0 (2019)	90.0
Palau	98.0	98.0 (2022)	88.0	95.0	...	...
Papua New Guinea	89.0	89.0 (2022)	60.0	70.0	35.0	70.0
Samoa	97.0	99.0 (2022)	86.0	99.0 (2022)	–	99.0 (2022)
Solomon Islands	91.0	95.0 (2022)	19.0	45.0 (2022)	11.5	29.5 (2022)
Tonga	92.0	99.0 (2022)	70.0	99.0 (2022)	–	96.0 (2022)
Tuvalu	19.0	59.3 (2022)	19.0	59.3 (2022)	–	27.0 (2022)
Vanuatu	93.0	90.0	51.0	90.0	18.0	90.0
Developed ADB Member Economies						
Australia	99.0	99.6	99.0	99.6	94.0	99.6
Japan	99.9	99.9	99.9	99.9	99.0	96.6
New Zealand	98.0	98.6	98.0	98.6	88.0	97.7

... = data not available, – = magnitude equals zero, 2G = second generation, 3G = third generation, ADB = Asian Development Bank, LTE = Long-Term Evolution.

Source: United Nations. SDG Global Database. https://unstats.un.org/sdgs/dataportal (accessed 16 July 2025).

Table 1.10.1: Selected Indicators for Sustainable Development Goal 10—Household Expenditure or Income Growth

ADB Regional Member	Target 10.1: By 2030, progressively achieve and sustain income growth of the bottom 40% of the population at a rate higher than the national average			
	10.1.1.a: Growth Rates of Household Expenditure or Income per Capita among the Bottom 40% of the Population[a,b] (%)		10.1.1.b: Growth Rates of Household Expenditure or Income per Capita[a,b] (%)	
Developing ADB Member Economies				
Central and West Asia				
Afghanistan	...		...	
Armenia[c]	1.0	(2013–2018)	2.0	(2013–2018)
Azerbaijan	...		...	
Georgia[c]	3.0	(2017–2022)	1.0	(2017–2022)
Kazakhstan[c]	4.0	(2016–2021)	4.0	(2016–2021)
Kyrgyz Republic[c]	2.0	(2017–2022)	2.0	(2017–2022)
Pakistan[c]	1.0	(2013–2018)	1.0	(2013–2018)
Tajikistan[c]	1.0	(2009–2015)	3.0	(2009–2015)
Türkiye[d]	3.0	(2017–2021)	3.0	(2017–2021)
Turkmenistan	...		...	
Uzbekistan	...		...	
East Asia				
China, People's Republic of[c]	5.0	(2015–2020)	4.0	(2015–2020)
Hong Kong, China	...		...	
Korea, Republic of[d]	5.0	(2016–2021)	4.0	(2016–2021)
Mongolia[c]	2.0	(2016–2018)	3.0	(2016–2018)
Taipei,China	...		...	
South Asia				
Bangladesh[c]	1.0	(2010–2016)	2.0	(2010–2016)
Bhutan[c]	2.0	(2012–2017)	2.0	(2012–2017)
India[c]	3.0	(2004–2011)	4.0	(2004–2011)
Maldives	...		...	
Nepal[c]	8.0	(2003–2010)	5.0	(2003–2010)
Sri Lanka[c]	2.0	(2016–2019)	1.0	(2016–2019)
Southeast Asia				
Brunei Darussalam	...		...	
Cambodia	...		...	
Indonesia[c]	3.0	(2018–2023)	2.0	(2018–2023)
Lao People's Democratic Republic[c]	2.0	(2012–2018)	3.0	(2012–2018)
Malaysia[d]	3.0	(2015–2021)	3.0	(2015–2021)
Myanmar[c]	9.0	(2015–2017)	1.0	(2015–2017)
Philippines[d]	3.0	(2015–2021)	1.0	(2015–2021)
Singapore	...		...	
Thailand[c]	1.0	(2017–2021)	1.0	(2017–2021)
Timor-Leste	...		...	
Viet Nam[c]	3.0	(2016–2022)	3.0	(2016–2022)
The Pacific				
Cook Islands	...		...	
Fiji[c]	1.0	(2008–2013)	-1.0	(2008–2013)
Kiribati	...		...	
Marshall Islands	...		...	
Micronesia, Federated States of	...		...	
Nauru	...		...	
Niue	...		...	
Palau	...		...	
Papua New Guinea	...		...	
Samoa	...		...	
Solomon Islands	...		...	
Tonga[c]	8.0	(2015–2021)	5.0	(2015–2021)
Tuvalu	...		...	
Vanuatu	...		...	
Developed ADB Member Economies				
Australia[d]	–	(2014–2018)	–	(2014–2018)
Japan	...		...	
New Zealand	...		...	

... = data not available, – = magnitude equals zero, ADB=Asian Development Bank.

a Refers to the annualized average growth rate in per capita real consumption or income of the bottom 40% of the income distribution or the total population in a country from household surveys over a roughly 5-year period. Data reported are based on consumption, except for Australia, the Republic of Korea, Malaysia, the Philippines, and Türkiye which are based on income. For detailed information, please visit https://unstats.un.org/sdgs/metadata.

b For the data collection periods in brackets, the initial year refers to the most recently conducted survey prior to the latest survey (only surveys conducted between 3 and 7 years before the latest survey are considered). The final year refers to the most recent year of a survey but not earlier than 2018.

c Estimated from individual consumption data.

d Estimated from individual income data.

Source: United Nations. SDG Global Database. https://unstats.un.org/sdgs/dataportal (accessed 15 July 2025).

Goal 11. Make cities and human settlements inclusive, safe, resilient, and sustainable

Table 1.11.1: Selected Indicators for Sustainable Development Goal 11—Sustainable Cities and Environment

ADB Regional Member	Target 11.1: By 2030, ensure access for all to adequate, safe, and affordable housing and basic services, and upgrade slums		Target 11.5: By 2030, significantly reduce the number of deaths and the number of people affected, and substantially decrease the direct economic losses relative to global gross domestic product caused by disasters, including water-related disasters, with a focus on protecting the poor and people in vulnerable situations		Target 11.6: By 2030, reduce the adverse per capita environmental impact of cities, including by paying special attention to air quality and municipal and other waste management	
	11.1.1: Proportion of Urban Population Living in Slums, Informal Settlements, or Inadequate Housing (%)		11.5.2: Direct Economic Loss Attributed to Disasters[a] ($ million)		11.6.2: Annual Mean Levels (μg/m³) of Fine Particulate Matter (e.g., PM2.5 and PM10) in Cities (population weighted)	
					Total	Urban
	2010	2022	2010	2023	2019	2019
Developing ADB Member Economies						
Central and West Asia						
Afghanistan	64.8	71.6	...	– (2020)	62.5	75.2
Armenia	10.4	8.4	7.0	2.2	34.1	36.2
Azerbaijan	26.9 (2008)	...	...	...	24.6	26.2
Georgia	10.9	7.1	14.3 (2015)	0.2	19.1	20.9
Kazakhstan	10.5	0.8	–	4.3 (2022)	26.5	35.4
Kyrgyz Republic	24.8	2.4	81.2	1.0	37.6	39.6
Pakistan	63.6	56.0	1,173.8 (2009)	18.2 (2018)	50.1	51.6
Tajikistan	37.5	17.1	28.8 (2015)	4.9 (2020)	53.6	56.8
Türkiye	17.6	14.1	257.8	2,792.3 (2022)	...	23.3
Turkmenistan	9.8	8.4	...	– (2019)	26.4	26.4
Uzbekistan	15.6	7.1	...	0.3 (2021)	41.0	44.5
East Asia						
China, People's Republic of	...	26.3	...	13,691.6 (2022)	38.2	40.2
Hong Kong, China	...	1.8	...	...	...	...
Korea, Republic of	9.3	4.5	368.3	481.0 (2022)	24.0	24.4
Mongolia	37.7	17.9	41.0	52.2	41.3	50.6
Taipei,China	...	...	...	...	...	...
South Asia						
Bangladesh	55.1	51.5	11,295.3 (2007)	...	46.0	46.8
Bhutan	53.7	44.7	0.5	243.0 (2018)	26.1	...
India	51.8	41.4	...	2,885.1 (2021)	50.2	53.0
Maldives	39.9	34.8	0.2 (2008)	3.3	13.0	12.7
Nepal	51.9	40.1	292.8	62.3 (2021)	36.4	36.9
Sri Lanka	53.7	44.7	– (2009)	115.4 (2020)	23.9	24.8
Southeast Asia						
Brunei Darussalam	28.8	21.6	...	...	6.9	6.8
Cambodia	56.6	42.3	0.0	– (2021)	17.8	18.3
Indonesia	26.9	19.4	859.9	6,859.7	19.3	19.9
Lao People's Democratic Republic	37.3	54.8	120.7	...	21.2	24.2
Malaysia	28.8	21.6	33.0	26.0 (2022)	21.5	23.7
Myanmar	45.4	58.3	14.6	158.2	27.2	27.8
Philippines	42.9	35.9	...	1,305.8	22.5	24.2
Singapore	–	–	...	...	...	13.3
Thailand	12.0	2.0	...	...	24.6	25.5
Timor-Leste	50.0	33.9	29.6	– (2017)	20.5	21.8
Viet Nam	20.6	32.5	988.0	2.3 (2019)	20.9	22.1
The Pacific						
Cook Islands	...	...	...	...	7.8	7.9
Fiji	12.5	9.4	24.6	7.1 (2022)	7.4	8.1
Kiribati	11.8	5.9	0.3 (2014)	22.5 (2021)	7.6	8.0
Marshall Islands	1.4	2.4	– (2011)	7.6 (2022)	7.2	7.6
Micronesia, Federated States of	...	...	– (2009)	0.0 (2021)	7.8	8.1
Nauru	1.4	...	...	– (2022)	7.4	7.4
Niue	...	...	...	...	...	...
Palau	1.1	0.6	– (2011)	2.2 (2022)	7.8	7.9
Papua New Guinea	20.9	22.3	–	1.7 (2020)	8.9	9.5
Samoa	2.6	34.6	27.2 (2009)	2.2	7.8	8.1
Solomon Islands	6.1	1.9	5.8	3.1 (2022)	7.8	8.7
Tonga	1.3	0.3	1.1 (2011)	0.6 (2020)	7.5	7.7
Tuvalu	1.5	50.9	– (2011)	0.1 (2022)	...	...
Vanuatu	4.3	3.1	3.1	– (2021)	8.4	9.1
Developed ADB Member Economies						
Australia	0.1	0.0	106.3	392.9	8.9	9.1
Japan	0.1	0.0	2,048.0 (2015)	716.5	10.8	11.1
New Zealand	...	...	42.2 (2015)	7,278.0	8.6	8.7

... = data not available, – = magnitude equals zero, 0.0 = magnitude is less than half of unit employed, $ = United States dollars, ADB = Asian Development Bank, m^3 = cubic meter, PM = particulate matter, μg = microgram.

a The data are submitted to the United Nation's SDG Global Database by the United Nations Office for Disaster Risk Reduction (UNDRR) and have been extracted from two sources: (a) the Sendai Framework Monitoring System as provided by designated national focal points; and (b) DesInventar disaster loss databases. Some of the data have not undergone an official validation process and may be subject to revision at a later date.

Sources: For Indicator 11.1.1: UN-Habitat. Urban Indicators Database. https://data.unhabitat.org/ (accessed 15 July 2025). For Indicator 11.1.1 for Australia; the People's Republic of China; Hong Kong, China; and the Republic of Korea and Indicator 11.5.2: United Nations. SDG Global Database. https://unstats.un.org/sdgs/dataportal (accessed 15 July 2025). For Indicator 11.6.2: World Health Organization. Datadot. https://data.who.int/ (accessed 15 July 2025). For Indicator 11.6.2 Urban for the Cook Islands, Fiji, Kiribati, the Marshall Islands, Federated States of Micronesia, Nauru, Palau, Singapore, Tonga, and Vanuatu: World Health Organization. The Global Health Observatory. https://www.who.int/data/gho (accessed 15 July 2025).

Table 1.12.1: Selected Indicators for Sustainable Development Goal 12—Responsible Consumption and Production

ADB Regional Member	Target 12.2: By 2030, achieve the sustainable management and efficient use of natural resources								12.c: Rationalize inefficient fossil-fuel subsidies that encourage wasteful consumption by removing market distortions, in accordance with national circumstances, including by restructuring taxation and phasing out those harmful subsidies, where they exist, to reflect their environmental impacts, taking fully into account the specific needs and conditions of developing countries and minimizing the possible adverse impacts on their development in a manner that protects the poor and the affected communities	
	12.2.1: Material Footprint				12.2.2: Domestic Material Consumption				12.c.1: Fossil-fuel subsidies (consumption and production) as a proportion of total GDP (%)	
	All (t million)		Per Capita (t)		All (t million)		Per Capita (t)			
	2010	2024	2010	2024	2010	2024	2010	2024	2010	2023
Developing ADB Member Economies										
Central and West Asia	**2,253.1**	**3,641.7**	...	...	**2,645.3**	**4,562.4**	...	...	...	...
Afghanistan	47.9	52.5	1.7	1.2	46.9	50.6	1.7	1.2	0.2	2.7 (2022)
Armenia	21.5	22.7	7.3	8.2	30.0	60.6	10.2	21.8	0.3	0.1 (2020)
Azerbaijan	63.3	73.6	6.9	7.0	68.5	75.0	7.4	7.2	2.3	8.9
Georgia	34.7	44.7	9.0	12.0	24.8	42.4	6.5	11.4	0.1	0.1
Kazakhstan	244.8	345.3	14.7	17.4	434.5	527.7	26.1	26.6	4.3	6.4
Kyrgyz Republic	15.4	23.3	2.8	3.4	33.6	50.6	6.1	7.4	6.5	13.6 (2022)
Pakistan	547.7	938.9	2.8	3.8	559.5	960.0	2.9	3.9	2.9	2.3
Tajikistan	24.7	37.8	3.2	3.7	17.9	46.3	2.3	4.5	2.0	7.0 (2022)
Türkiye	1,117.2	1,840.0	15.3	21.3	1,150.5	2,355.1	15.7	27.3	0.2	0.2
Turkmenistan	31.1	77.0	5.9	11.7	48.7	61.2	9.2	9.3	25.4	11.4
Uzbekistan	104.9	186.0	3.7	5.2	230.5	332.8	8.1	9.3	22.9	8.5
East Asia	**25,770.8** [a]	**38,260.0** [a]	...	...	**27,542.4**	**39,353.3**	...	...	...	...
China, People's Republic of	24,382.3	36,546.0	18.1	25.6	26,370.7	37,836.1	19.6	26.5	0.5	0.4
Hong Kong, China	293.7	368.9	41.2	47.3 (2022)	38.3	107.4	9.8	17.6 (2023)	...	...
Korea, Republic of	1,046.7	1,258.0	21.4	24.3	746.4	943.6	15.3	18.2	0.1	0.2
Mongolia	48.1	87.2	17.8	24.9	82.1	170.9	30.4	48.9	...	4.0 (2022)
Taipei,China	...	...	...	...	304.9	295.4	...	...	...	...
South Asia	**5,755.6**	**8,940.4** [a]	...	...	**6,154.7**	**9,900.8**	...	...	...	...
Bangladesh	382.7	770.2	2.6	4.4	372.9	664.7	2.5	3.8	3.2	2.1
Bhutan	9.5	20.0	13.5	25.2	13.0	23.4	18.4	29.5	...	0.4 (2022)
India	5,166.1	7,807.7	4.2	5.4	5,597.4	8,896.3	4.5	6.2	1.5	1.9
Maldives	5.2	6.3 (2017)	14.3	13.4 (2017)	2.2	9.2	6.1	17.8	...	2.4 (2022)
Nepal	97.8	253.2	3.6	8.1	89.2	215.1	3.3	6.9	0.1 (2011)	0.0 (2018)
Sri Lanka	94.3	89.4	4.6	4.1	80.0	92.1	3.9	4.2	0.8	1.0
Southeast Asia	**4,358.4** [a]	**6,938.3** [a]	...	...	**4,430.7**	**6,939.9**	...	...	...	...
Brunei Darussalam	8.0	9.4	20.2	20.7	7.5	-1.0	19.1	-2.1	2.7	2.9
Cambodia	97.4	152.3	6.8	8.9	123.4	143.3	8.6	8.4	...	0.5 (2022)
Indonesia	1,375.1	2,220.6	5.6	7.9	1,309.3	2,300.4	5.4	8.2	3.2	3.0
Lao People's Democratic Republic	46.6	76.6	7.4	9.9	53.4	117.9	8.4	15.2	...	0.5 (2022)
Malaysia	430.9	756.4	15.0	21.8	487.2	739.8	17.0	21.3	0.9	1.6
Myanmar	225.0	234.2	4.6	4.3	230.0	192.0	4.7	3.5	0.0 (2013)	0.9 (2022)
Philippines	402.1	1,069.7	4.2	9.0	429.7	1,044.4	4.5	8.8	...	0.3 (2022)
Singapore	195.6	329.2	37.9	54.4	114.4	167.0	22.1	27.6	...	- (2022)
Thailand	747.8	877.7	11.0	12.2	715.7	821.7	10.5	11.4	1.4	0.3
Timor-Leste	...	...	...	...	3.2	6.4	2.9	4.6	...	...
Viet Nam	829.8	1,212.0	9.5	12.2	956.9	1,407.9	10.9	14.2	1.6	1.0
The Pacific	...	...	...	...	**109.3**	**90.3**	...	...	...	...
Cook Islands	...	...	...	...	0.1	0.1	5.2	4.2	...	...
Fiji	5.1	6.5 (2017)	5.7	7.1 (2017)	7.9	6.6	8.7	7.0	...	0.4 (2022)
Kiribati	...	...	...	...	0.6	0.7	5.2	5.4	...	...
Marshall Islands	...	...	...	...	0.1	0.2	2.7	4.1	...	...
Micronesia, Federated States of	...	...	...	...	0.3	0.5	3.7	5.2 (2023)	...	...
Nauru	...	...	...	...	0.4	0.3	42.6	21.9	...	...
Niue	...	...	...	...	0.0	0.0	8.4	9.1	...	...
Palau	...	...	...	...	0.1	0.2	5.9	9.0	...	...
Papua New Guinea	39.8	24.2	5.2	2.3	92.9	73.4	12.3	7.0	...	...
Samoa	1.3	1.6 (2017)	6.9	7.5 (2017)	1.3	1.4	6.5	6.0	...	...
Solomon Islands	...	...	...	...	1.6	4.4	3.0	5.8	...	...
Tonga	...	...	...	...	1.4	0.5	13.4	5.0	...	0.0 (2019)
Tuvalu	...	...	...	...	0.0	0.0	1.4	1.6	...	...
Vanuatu	1.9	2.1 (2017)	7.6	7.2 (2017)	2.5	2.0	10.3	5.9	...	...
Developed ADB Member Economies	**3,407.2**	**3,221.7**	...	...	**2,440.8**	**2,799.2**	...	...	...	...
Australia	829.0	830.9	37.6	31.1	994.1	1,277.8	45.1	47.9	0.7	0.7
Japan	2,460.2	2,217.5	19.2	18.1	1,308.6	1,374.7	10.2	11.2	0.1	1.5
New Zealand	118.0	173.3	27.2	32.9	138.1	146.6	31.8	27.8	...	0.4

... = data not available, - = magnitude equals zero, 0.0 = magnitude is less than half of unit employed, ADB = Asian Development Bank, GDP = gross domestic product, t = metric ton.

a Regional aggregates include reporting economies only.

Sources: For Indicators 12.2.1 and 12.2.2: United Nations Environment Programme. UNEP IRP Global Material Flows Database. https://unep-irp.fineprint.global/ (accessed 24 July 2025). For Indicator 12.2.1 for Fiji; Hong Kong, China; Maldives; Samoa; and Vanuatu and Indicator 12.2.2 for the Federated States of Micronesia and Hong Kong, China: Organisation for Economic Co-operation and Development. OECD Data Explorer - Material Flow Accounts. https://stats.oecd.org/viewhtml.aspx?datasetcode=MATERIAL_RESOURCES&lang=en (accessed 24 July 2025). For Indicator 12.2.2 per capita for the Federated States of Micronesia and Hong Kong, China and Indicator 12.c.1: United Nations. SDG Global Database. https://unstats.un.org/sdgs/dataportal (accessed 24 July 2025).

Goal 13. Take urgent action to combat climate change and its impacts

Table 1.13.1: Selected Indicators for Sustainable Development Goal 13—Impact of Disasters and Risk Reduction Strategies

ADB Regional Member	Target 13.1: Strengthen resilience and adaptive capacity to climate-related hazards and natural disasters in all countries											
	13.1.1.a: Number of Persons Affected by Disaster[a]				13.1.1.b: Number of Deaths Due to Disaster[a]				13.1.2: Countries that Adopt and Implement National Disaster Risk Reduction Strategies in Line with the Sendai Framework for Disaster Risk Reduction 2015–2030[a,b]		13.1.3: Proportion of Local Governments that Adopt and Implement Local Disaster Risk Reduction Strategies in Line with National Disaster Risk Reduction Strategies[a] (%)	
	2010		2022		2010		2022		2023		2022	
Developing ADB Member Economies												
Central and West Asia												
Afghanistan	...		289,693	(2019)	...		368	(2019)	0.73	(2019)	–	(2017)
Armenia	7,641		20,276	(2023)	155		516	(2023)	1.00		64.8	(2023)
Azerbaijan	...		...		...		–	(2017)	–	(2017)	...	
Georgia	79		449	(2023)	54		43	(2023)	0.98		8.8	(2023)
Kazakhstan	1,516	(2011)	1,295		9		1,708		0.78	(2021)	100.0	(2021)
Kyrgyz Republic	76,959		297	(2023)	158		44	(2023)	0.90	(2019)	10.1	(2019)
Pakistan	2,963		404	(2020)	2,199		10,599	(2020)	0.80	(2020)	29.6	(2020)
Tajikistan	11,937	(2015)	2,085	(2020)	35	(2015)	8	(2020)	1.00	(2020)	100.0	
Türkiye	122,296		38,060		179		25		–	(2017)	91.4	(2021)
Turkmenistan	...		–	(2019)	...		–	(2019)	0.75	(2019)	100.0	(2019)
Uzbekistan	...		1,953	(2021)	...		11	(2021)	1.00	(2021)	100.0	(2021)
East Asia												
China, People's Republic of	8,682,611	(2015)	5,798,200		819	(2015)	487		1.00	(2020)	...	
Hong Kong, China	...		...		...		...		...		...	
Korea, Republic of	93,032		77,313		28		5,120	(2021)	1.00	(2021)	100.0	(2021)
Mongolia	9,086		13,399	(2023)	226		237	(2023)	1.00	(2021)	100.0	(2021)
Taipei,China	...		...		...		...		...		...	
South Asia												
Bangladesh	7,674,120	(2007)	206	(2021)	96		389	(2023)	–	(2021)	11.9	(2020)
Bhutan	1,711		244	(2018)	2,763		21	(2019)	0.50	(2018)	51.3	(2018)
India	187,873,332	(2015)	409,904	(2021)	7,489		5,619	(2021)	1.00	(2020)	93.1	
Maldives	84	(2008)	1,171	(2023)	4	(2008)	13		–	(2017)	...	
Nepal	134,309		45,924	(2021)	1,002		508	(2021)	0.08	(2022)	16.9	(2019)
Sri Lanka	1,193,504		94	(2023)	50		51	(2023)	0.93	(2020)	9.4	
Southeast Asia												
Brunei Darussalam	...		15,317	(2021)	...		54	(2021)	0.05	(2018)	...	
Cambodia	5,916		179		91		96		0.65	(2019)	88.0	
Indonesia	333,235		11,625,043	(2023)	1,630		275	(2023)	0.98		53.3	(2023)
Lao People's Democratic Republic	32,952		...		50		...		0.03	(2021)	–	(2021)
Malaysia	9,882		199,244		4		5,412		0.70	(2021)	100.0	(2021)
Myanmar	545,156		441,407	(2023)	55		375	(2023)	0.05	(2022)	100.0	
Philippines	1,489,711		3,112,947	(2023)	192		159	(2023)	1.00		72.1	(2023)
Singapore	...		228,667	(2021)	...		944	(2021)	...		...	
Thailand	117,474	(2015)	2,727,329	(2021)	123	(2015)	154	(2021)	0.80	(2024)	86.2	(2024)
Timor-Leste	19,331		...		10		...		...		...	
Viet Nam	651,751		359	(2019)	60		5	(2019)	...		...	
The Pacific												
Cook Islands	...		...		...		...		...		...	
Fiji	6,644		1,787		3		184		0.98	(2022)	–	
Kiribati	85	(2008)	333	(2021)	...		–	(2021)	0.93	(2021)	26.1	(2021)
Marshall Islands	96	(2008)	52,914		–	(2015)	17		–	(2020)	75.0	
Micronesia, Federated States of	7,600	(2015)	15,010	(2021)	2	(2011)	–	(2021)	0.43	(2021)	11.7	(2021)
Nauru	...		5,393		–	(2015)	1		0.55	(2022)	–	
Niue	...		...		...		...		...		...	
Palau	–	(2011)	780		–	(2015)	9		0.73	(2021)	100.0	(2021)
Papua New Guinea	–		3,297	(2020)	16		651	(2021)	0.78	(2020)	–	(2020)
Samoa	6,332	(2009)	138	(2023)	369	(2009)	29		0.48		3.3	(2023)
Solomon Islands	1,456		20,080		4		144		0.18	(2022)	–	(2021)
Tonga	–		68	(2020)	9	(2009)	17		0.50	(2022)	33.5	
Tuvalu	–	(2011)	7,748		–	(2015)	–	(2021)	0.65	(2022)	100.0	
Vanuatu	500		1,400	(2021)	1	(2011)	–	(2021)	0.60	(2021)	100.0	(2021)
Developed ADB Member Economies												
Australia	23,223		9,322	(2023)	38	(2011)	3,068	(2023)	0.70		57.5	(2023)
Japan	69,117	(2015)	138,524		89		152		1.00		100.0	(2023)
New Zealand	11,759	(2015)	655,814	(2023)	–		941	(2023)	0.90		100.0	(2023)

... = data not available, – = magnitude equals zero, ADB = Asian Development Bank.

a The data are submitted to the SDG Global Database by the United Nations Office for Disaster Risk Reduction have been extracted from two sources: (i) the Sendai Framework Monitoring System as provided by designated national focal points; and (ii) DesInventar disaster loss databases. Some of the data have not undergone an official validation process and may be subject to revision at a later date.

b Economies displaying data in this column have adopted and implemented national disaster risk reduction strategies. Data refer to the score for adoption and implementation of national disaster risk reduction strategies in line with the Sendai Framework. The scores indicate the compliance of alignment of national strategies with the Sendai Framework, based on self-assessments of the economy using 10 criteria for monitoring the progress of national disaster risk reduction strategies. The score ranges are as follows: 1 = comprehensive alignment, 0.75 = substantial alignment, 0.50 = moderate alignment, 0.25 = limited alignment, 0 = no alignment.

Source: United Nations. SDG Global Database. https://unstats.un.org/sdgs/dataportal (accessed 24 July 2025).

Goal 14. Conserve and sustainably use the oceans, seas, and marine resources for sustainable development

Table 1.14.1: Selected Indicators for Sustainable Development Goal 14—Life Below Water

ADB Regional Member	Target 14.5: By 2020, conserve at least 10% of coastal and marine areas, consistent with national and international law and based on the best available scientific information 14.5.1: Average Proportion of Marine Key Biodiversity Areas Covered by Protected Areas (%)						
	2010	2015	2020	2021	2022	2023	2024
Developing ADB Member Economies							
Central and West Asia							
Afghanistan	...	...	...	...	...	...	...
Armenia	...	...	...	...	...	...	...
Azerbaijan	...	...	...	...	...	...	...
Georgia	36.3	36.3	36.3	36.3	36.3	36.3	36.3
Kazakhstan	...	...	...	...	...	...	...
Kyrgyz Republic	...	...	...	...	...	...	...
Pakistan	14.6	14.6	14.6	14.6	14.6	14.6	14.6
Tajikistan	...	...	...	...	...	...	...
Türkiye	3.8	3.8	3.8	3.8	3.8	3.8	3.8
Turkmenistan	...	...	...	...	...	...	...
Uzbekistan	...	...	...	...	...	...	...
East Asia							
China, People's Republic of	6.7	7.0	7.0	7.0	7.0	7.0	7.0
Hong Kong, China	32.5	32.5	32.5	32.5	32.5	32.5	32.5
Korea, Republic of	38.3	38.5	41.7	42.9	42.9	42.9	42.9
Mongolia	...	...	...	...	...	...	...
Taipei,China	...	...	...	...	...	...	...
South Asia							
Bangladesh	34.2	34.3	38.6	38.6	38.6	38.6	38.6
Bhutan	...	...	...	...	...	...	...
India	4.2	4.2	4.2	4.2	4.2	4.2	4.2
Maldives	–	–	–	–	–	–	–
Nepal	...	...	...	...	...	...	...
Sri Lanka	46.3	50.0	50.0	50.0	50.0	50.0	50.0
Southeast Asia							
Brunei Darussalam	5.4	5.4	5.4	5.4	5.4	5.4	5.4
Cambodia	41.2	41.2	51.0	51.0	51.0	51.0	51.0
Indonesia	15.9	22.9	25.9	25.9	25.9	25.9	25.9
Lao People's Democratic Republic	...	...	...	...	...	...	...
Malaysia	16.1	19.7	19.7	19.7	19.7	19.7	19.7
Myanmar	9.3	9.3	19.2	19.2	19.2	19.2	19.2
Philippines	33.3	33.3	46.6	46.6	46.6	46.6	46.6
Singapore	3.3	3.3	3.3	3.3	3.3	3.3	3.3
Thailand	36.3	41.6	44.0	44.0	44.0	44.0	44.0
Timor-Leste	18.7	18.7	19.6	19.6	19.6	19.6	19.6
Viet Nam	18.6	24.5	24.5	24.5	24.5	24.5	24.5
The Pacific							
Cook Islands	19.9	19.9	52.1	52.1	52.1	52.1	52.1
Fiji	16.5	16.5	16.5	16.5	16.5	16.5	16.5
Kiribati	32.9	32.9	32.9	32.9	32.9	32.9	32.9
Marshall Islands	6.7	7.8	7.8	7.8	7.8	7.8	7.8
Micronesia, Federated States of	–	–	–	–	–	–	–
Nauru	–	–	–	–	–	–	–
Niue	...	...	...	...	...	...	...
Palau	56.0	72.3	72.3	72.3	72.3	72.3	72.3
Papua New Guinea	1.9	1.9	1.9	1.9	1.9	1.9	1.9
Samoa	54.2	54.2	54.2	54.2	54.2	54.2	54.2
Solomon Islands	3.1	3.2	3.2	3.2	3.2	3.2	3.2
Tonga	17.6	17.6	17.6	17.6	17.6	17.6	17.6
Tuvalu	...	...	...	...	...	...	...
Vanuatu	3.3	3.3	3.3	3.3	3.3	3.3	3.3
Developed ADB Member Economies							
Australia	53.5	61.4	64.7	65.5	66.2	66.2	66.2
Japan	34.1	58.8	61.6	62.5	66.4	66.4	66.4
New Zealand	46.5	47.1	47.1	47.1	47.1	47.1	47.1

... = data not available, – = magnitude equals zero, ADB = Asian Development Bank.

Source: United Nations. SDG Global Database. https://unstats.un.org/sdgs/dataportal (accessed 10 June 2025).

Goal 15. Protect, restore, and promote sustainable use of terrestrial ecosystems; sustainably manage forests; combat desertification and halt and reverse land degradation; and halt biodiversity loss

Table 1.15.1: Selected Indicators for Sustainable Development Goal 15—Protection of Ecosystems and Biodiversity

ADB Regional Member	Target 15.1: By 2020, ensure the conservation, restoration, and sustainable use of terrestrial and inland freshwater ecosystems and their services, in particular forests, wetlands, mountains, and drylands, in line with obligations under international agreements					
	15.1.1: Forest Area as a Proportion of Total Land Area[a] (%)		15.1.2: Proportion of Important Sites for Terrestrial and Freshwater Biodiversity that are Covered by Protected Areas (%)			
			Terrestrial		Freshwater	
	2010	2020	2010	2024	2010	2024
Developing ADB Member Economies						
Central and West Asia	**3.4**	**3.5**	...	...	...	...
Afghanistan	1.9	1.9	5.8	46.4	–	60.9
Armenia	11.6	11.5	57.1	63.4	66.5	83.5
Azerbaijan	12.5	13.7	55.9	57.4	35.5	39.8
Georgia	40.6	40.6	39.1	54.5	26.1	41.6
Kazakhstan	1.1	1.3	25.8	28.2	19.3	20.0
Kyrgyz Republic	6.4	6.9	23.6	23.6	35.4	35.4
Pakistan	5.3	4.8	27.8	33.6	32.9	35.8
Tajikistan	2.9	3.1	15.8	18.7	27.9	35.1
Türkiye	27.4	28.9	2.2	2.3	4.0	4.2
Turkmenistan	8.8	8.8	14.9	15.9	12.7	14.1
Uzbekistan	7.7	8.4	14.2	22.2	10.1	19.9
East Asia	**20.1**	**21.8**	...	...	...	...
China, People's Republic of	21.3	23.3	8.6	10.1	6.9	9.7
Hong Kong, China	...	...	48.9	48.9	16.6	16.6
Korea, Republic of	65.7	64.4	37.8	40.7	36.6	36.6
Mongolia	9.1	9.1	40.7	45.2	34.9	40.5
Taipei,China	58.1 (2011)	60.8 (2023)	...	...	...	...
South Asia	**24.5**	**25.3**	...	...	...	...
Bangladesh	14.5	14.5	36.9	37.5	–	–
Bhutan	71.0	71.5	45.3	46.9	30.5	34.9
India	23.4	24.3	1.4	6.3	2.6	8.2
Maldives	2.7	2.7	–	–	...	...
Nepal	41.6	41.6	51.7	51.7	35.1	35.1
Sri Lanka	33.6	34.2	41.1	43.7	40.2	43.9
Southeast Asia	**49.7**	**47.1**	...	...	...	...
Brunei Darussalam	72.1	72.1	41.7	41.7	50.0	50.0
Cambodia	60.0	45.7	24.7	54.5	12.9	45.0
Indonesia	53.1	49.1	19.9	26.3	35.5	38.0
Lao People's Democratic Republic	73.4	71.9	26.3	48.5	16.4	30.1
Malaysia	57.7	58.2	31.6	37.0	31.7	32.5
Myanmar	48.1	43.7	18.8	22.3	27.1	27.1
Philippines	22.9	24.1	25.0	42.8	35.4	56.1
Singapore	25.3	21.7	21.1	21.1	...	...
Thailand	39.3	38.9	66.7	68.2	36.3	36.3
Timor-Leste	62.9	61.9	40.7	45.6	...	...
Viet Nam	42.7	46.7	31.0	39.8	29.2	38.2
The Pacific	**78.3**	**77.8**	...	...	...	...
Cook Islands	65.0	65.0	27.3	33.8	...	...
Fiji	58.7	62.4	11.2	11.2	0.1	0.1
Kiribati	1.5	1.5	40.0	40.0	...	...
Marshall Islands	52.2	52.2	8.4	10.1	...	...
Micronesia, Federated States of	91.6	92.0	–	–	...	...
Nauru	–	–	–	–	...	...
Niue	72.2	72.6	95.3	95.3	...	...
Palau	88.2	90.0	46.1	48.1	...	...
Papua New Guinea	79.9	79.2	7.2	7.3	...	...
Samoa	58.8	58.2	47.0	47.1	...	...
Solomon Islands	90.4	90.1	4.6	4.9	...	...
Tonga	12.4	12.4	26.1	26.1	...	...
Tuvalu	33.3	33.3	...	...	...	...
Vanuatu	36.3	36.3	2.8	2.8	...	...
Developed ADB Member Economies	**19.8**	**20.3**	...	...	...	...
Australia	16.9	17.4	45.2	57.7	30.2	37.3
Japan	68.5	68.4	40.9	64.8	41.9	63.6
New Zealand	37.4	37.6	45.5	46.2	23.0	24.2
DEVELOPING ADB MEMBER ECONOMIES	**22.8**	**23.2**	...	...	...	...
ALL ADB REGIONAL MEMBERS	**22.1**	**22.5**	...	...	...	...

Goal 15. Protect, restore, and promote sustainable use of terrestrial ecosystems; sustainably manage forests; combat desertification and halt and reverse land degradation; and halt biodiversity loss

Table 1.15.1: Selected Indicators for Sustainable Development Goal 15—Protection of Ecosystems and Biodiversity *(continued)*

ADB Regional Member	Target 15.4: By 2030, ensure the conservation of mountain ecosystems, including their biodiversity, in order to enhance their capacity to provide benefits that are essential for sustainable development		Target 15.5: Take urgent and significant action to reduce the degradation of natural habitats, halt the loss of biodiversity and, by 2020, protect and prevent the extinction of threatened species	
	15.4.1: Coverage by Protected Areas of Important Sites for Mountain Biodiversity (%)		15.5.1: Red List Index[b]	
	2010	2024	2010	2024
Developing ADB Member Economies				
Central and West Asia	...	...	...	...
Afghanistan	7.6	45.8	0.93	0.92
Armenia	54.6	62.0	0.85	0.84
Azerbaijan	74.8	75.8	0.94	0.94
Georgia	39.6	56.7	0.94	0.93
Kazakhstan	39.3	46.8	0.89	0.88
Kyrgyz Republic	31.5	31.5	0.89	0.89
Pakistan	23.1	32.9	0.88	0.82
Tajikistan	15.8	18.7	0.99	0.99
Türkiye	0.7	0.8	0.90	0.90
Turkmenistan	15.2	15.2	0.98	0.98
Uzbekistan	29.3	36.9	0.97	0.97
East Asia	...	...	...	...
China, People's Republic of	10.3	11.9	0.77	0.72
Hong Kong, China	57.0	57.0	0.89	0.89
Korea, Republic of	...	...	0.74	0.68
Mongolia	45.0	49.3	0.96	0.95
Taipei,China	...	...	...	...
South Asia	...	...	...	...
Bangladesh	–	–	0.79	0.73
Bhutan	45.3	46.9	0.82	0.82
India	1.1	10.0	0.72	0.67
Maldives	...	...	0.90	0.84
Nepal	62.0	62.0	0.85	0.85
Sri Lanka	29.4	30.4	0.60	0.56
Southeast Asia	...	...	...	...
Brunei Darussalam	69.5	69.5	0.86	0.85
Cambodia	60.8	93.8	0.83	0.79
Indonesia	21.6	28.0	0.81	0.75
Lao People's Democratic Republic	31.7	56.8	0.83	0.83
Malaysia	39.8	48.3	0.74	0.69
Myanmar	33.1	37.1	0.83	0.79
Philippines	21.4	43.3	0.72	0.67
Singapore	...	...	0.89	0.84
Thailand	85.7	85.9	0.80	0.76
Timor-Leste	45.4	50.8	0.89	0.84
Viet Nam	34.3	44.6	0.76	0.70
The Pacific	...	...	...	...
Cook Islands	20.8	20.8	0.82	0.79
Fiji	5.5	5.5	0.72	0.69
Kiribati	...	...	0.79	0.74
Marshall Islands	...	...	0.86	0.82
Micronesia, Federated States of	–	–	0.71	0.65
Nauru	...	...	0.85	0.81
Niue	...	...	0.83	0.80
Palau	...	...	0.79	0.66
Papua New Guinea	7.3	7.4	0.87	0.82
Samoa	35.6	35.7	0.78	0.76
Solomon Islands	0.0	0.5	0.80	0.75
Tonga	–	–	0.75	0.72
Tuvalu	...	...	0.87	0.82
Vanuatu	3.8	3.8	0.71	0.66
Developed ADB Member Economies	...	...	...	...
Australia	46.0	67.4	0.85	0.81
Japan	51.8	67.9	0.79	0.75
New Zealand	32.9	34.0	0.67	0.64
DEVELOPING ADB MEMBER ECONOMIES	...	...	...	...
ALL ADB REGIONAL MEMBERS	...	...	...	...

... = data not available, 0.0 = magnitude is less than half of unit employed, – = magnitude equals zero, ADB = Asian Development Bank.

a The regional aggregates are calculated by averaging the combined estimates for each economy. The aggregates for East Asia exclude Hong Kong, China.

b The Red List Index value ranges from 1, which means all species are categorized as "Least Concern" (no species expected to become extinct in the near future), to 0, meaning that all species are categorized as "Extinct". The index therefore indicates how far the set of species has moved overall towards extinction.

Sources: United Nations. SDG Global Database. https://unstats.un.org/sdgs/dataportal (accessed 9 July 2025). For Taipei,China: Government of Taipei,China, Directorate-General of Budget, Accounting and Statistics.

Goal 16. Promote peaceful and inclusive societies for sustainable development; provide access to justice for all; and build effective, accountable, and inclusive institutions at all levels

Table 1.16.1: Selected Indicators for Sustainable Development Goal 16—Peace, Justice, and Strong Institutions

ADB Regional Member	Target 16.1: Significantly reduce all forms of violence and related death rates everywhere — 16.1.1: Number of Victims of Intentional Homicide (per 100,000 population)		Target 16.3: Promote the rule of law at the national and international levels and ensure equal access to justice for all — 16.3.2: Unsentenced Detainees as a Proportion of Overall Prison Population (%)		Target 16.5: Substantially reduce corruption and bribery in all their forms — 16.5.2: Proportion of Firms Experiencing at least One Bribe Payment Request (%)	Target 16.9: By 2030, provide legal identity for all, including birth registration — 16.9.1: Proportion of Children Under 5 Years of Age Whose Births have been Registered with a Civil Authority[a] (%)
	2010	2023	2015	2023	2023	2023
Developing ADB Member Economies						
Central and West Asia						
Afghanistan	3.5	4.0 (2021)	29.5	27.7 (2018)	46.8 (2014)	47.8
Armenia	1.9	2.2	27.9	68.6	1.5 (2020)	98.7 (2016)
Azerbaijan	2.3	2.2	18.6	20.7 (2024)	12.1 (2019)	100.0
Georgia	4.8	2.0 (2019)	13.5	19.3 (2024)	1.0	98.5 (2017)
Kazakhstan	8.2	2.6 (2022)	13.8	20.3 (2022)	11.6 (2019)	99.7 (2015)
Kyrgyz Republic	16.8	1.8 (2020)	18.0	25.6 (2022)	31.4	99.5
Pakistan	6.6	4.3	69.1	67.7 (2021)	15.9 (2022)	42.2 (2018)
Tajikistan	2.4	0.9 (2020)	...	...	11.1 (2019)	95.8 (2017)
Türkiye	4.2	3.2	14.6	14.9 (2024)	1.4 (2019)	98.4 (2018)
Turkmenistan	1.9	1.0 (2015)	...	...	...	99.9 (2019)
Uzbekistan	3.0 (2008)	1.4 (2021)	...	...	5.9 (2019)	100.0 (2022)
East Asia						
China, People's Republic of	1.0	0.5 (2020)	...	...	11.6 (2012)	96.7 (2020)
Hong Kong, China	0.5	0.4	18.8	40.6	2.6	...
Korea, Republic of	1.0	0.5	43.9	35.3	...	...
Mongolia	8.9	5.9	17.6	19.0 (2024)	24.7 (2019)	99.6 (2018)
Taipei,China	0.8	0.8 (2015)	5.5	5.2 (2018)	...	...
South Asia						
Bangladesh	2.6	2.3 (2018)	73.8	75.6 (2022)	23.0 (2022)	41.8 (2022)
Bhutan	2.3	2.5 (2020)	26.9 (2017)	14.2 (2019)	0.3 (2024)	99.9 (2010)
India	3.7	2.8 (2022)	67.2	75.8 (2022)	27.2 (2022)	89.1 (2021)
Maldives	1.7	0.6 (2019)	...	...	...	98.8 (2017)
Nepal	3.0	2.1 (2020)	...	53.0 (2022)	6.2	73.2 (2022)
Sri Lanka	3.7	3.3 (2019)	52.8	66.2 (2024)	10.0 (2011)	98.9 (2019)
Southeast Asia						
Brunei Darussalam	0.3	...	7.1	7.1 (2018)	...	99.9 (2020)
Cambodia	2.3	...	49.3	26.6 (2024)	27.1	91.7 (2022)
Indonesia	0.4	0.3 (2022)	33.2	21.3 (2024)	20.3	85.1 (2024)
Lao People's Democratic Republic	...	...	...	...	40.3 (2018)	65.0
Malaysia	1.9	0.7	25.8	33.0	0.4 (2019)	97.7 (2022)
Myanmar	1.6	2.6	15.1 (2016)	22.0 (2020)	29.3 (2016)	81.3 (2016)
Philippines	9.0	4.4	69.1	65.2 (2022)	8.3	94.0 (2022)
Singapore	0.4	0.1	10.7	14.4	0.6	99.9
Thailand	5.3	2.6 (2017)	18.6	11.5	9.9 (2016)	99.8 (2022)
Timor-Leste	3.6	4.1 (2015)	78.3	23.2 (2018)	9.9 (2021)	60.4 (2016)
Viet Nam	1.5	...	17.6	11.5 (2022)	31.1	99.0
The Pacific						
Cook Islands	3.6 (2012)	...	21.6	14.6 (2018)	...	100.0 (2017)
Fiji	2.2	2.1	27.4	19.9 (2021)	10.5 (2009)	86.6 (2021)
Kiribati	3.7	...	9.8	5.4 (2018)	...	91.6 (2019)
Marshall Islands	...	...	...	...	...	83.8 (2017)
Micronesia, Federated States of	...	0.9 (2019)	...	...	4.6 (2009)	...
Nauru	...	...	...	34.2	...	99.1
Niue	...	...	...	...	...	...
Palau	...	11.2 (2018)	...	...	...	...
Papua New Guinea	9.3	...	37.9	42.9	26.4 (2015)	13.4 (2018)
Samoa	8.3	6.3 (2018)	5.2	23.2 (2019)	2.4	66.9 (2020)
Solomon Islands	3.7 (2008)	...	61.3	46.8 (2018)	43.8 (2015)	88.0 (2015)
Tonga	0.9	1.0 (2019)	7.4	33.0 (2022)	10.7 (2024)	97.7 (2019)
Tuvalu	9.4	– (2019)	...	...	...	87.2 (2020)
Vanuatu	...	0.3 (2020)	12.1	32.3 (2021)	23.5	76.7
Developed ADB Member Economies						
Australia	1.0	0.9	26.4	39.9 (2024)	...	100.0 (2022)
Japan	0.4	0.2	11.0	14.4	...	100.0 (2021)
New Zealand	1.0	1.1 (2021)	25.0	42.3 (2024)	4.0	100.0

... = data not available, – = magnitude equals zero, ADB = Asian Development Bank.

a Data from household surveys like the Multiple Indicator Cluster Surveys (MICS) or Demographic and Health Surveys (DHS) sometimes refer only to children with a birth certificate. UNICEF methodically notes this difference when publishing country-level / economy-level estimates for global SDG monitoring.

Sources: For Indicator 16.1.1: United Nations Office on Drugs and Crime. dataUNODC. https://dataunodc.un.org/ (accessed 17 July 2025). For Indicator 16.3.2: United Nations. SDG Global Database. https://unstats.un.org/sdgs/dataportal (accessed 17 July 2025). For Indicator 16.5.2: World Bank. World Development Indicators. https://data.worldbank.org/indicator (accessed 17 July 2025). For Indicator 16.9.1: United Nations Children's Fund (UNICEF). UNICEF Data Warehouse. https://data.unicef.org/dv_index/ (accessed 17 July 2025).

Goal 17. Strengthen the means of implementation and revitalize the Global Partnership for Sustainable Development

Table 1.17.1: Selected Indicators for Sustainable Development Goal 17—Financial Sustainability of Developing Economies

ADB Regional Member	Target 17.4: Assist developing countries in attaining long-term debt sustainability through coordinated policies aimed at fostering debt financing, debt relief, and debt restructuring, as appropriate, and address the external debt of highly indebted poor countries to reduce debt distress		Target 17.9: Enhance international support for implementing effective and targeted capacity-building in developing countries to support national plans to implement all the Sustainable Development Goals, including through North-South, South-South, and triangular cooperation	
	17.4.1: Debt Service as a Proportion of Exports of Goods and Services (%)		17.9.1: Dollar Value of Financial and Technical Assistance Committed to Developing Countries[a] (constant 2022 $ million)	
	2010	2022	Average, 2000–2010	Average, 2011–2022
Developing ADB Member Economies				
Central and West Asia			**4,393.3**	**3,814.1**
Afghanistan	0.3	2.2 (2020)	1,670.6	272.7
Armenia	2.7	5.5	63.6	38.3
Azerbaijan	1.1	4.1	58.9	31.2
Georgia	6.3	4.5	77.1	248.5
Kazakhstan	0.5	3.5	534.5	277.7
Kyrgyz Republic	3.7	8.5	58.5	89.8
Pakistan	11.7	37.0	609.1	754.0
Tajikistan	2.7	5.1	57.4	126.3
Türkiye	8.0	6.6	1,225.5	956.3
Turkmenistan	...	...	6.2	144.4
Uzbekistan	3.3	7.0	31.8	874.9
East Asia[b]			**660.9**	**615.9**
China, People's Republic of	0.8	1.5	591.0	546.2
Hong Kong, China	...	...	...	...
Korea, Republic of	...	...	...	...
Mongolia	4.3	12.5	70.0	69.7
Taipei,China	...	...	...	...
South Asia			**2,475.2**	**4,250.4**
Bangladesh	4.5	8.0	300.9	1,409.5
Bhutan	14.4	16.0	23.0	44.0
India	1.7	2.8	1,821.7	2,148.9
Maldives	3.0	8.4	16.4	58.2
Nepal	10.4	9.4	151.1	371.4
Sri Lanka	10.7	10.3	162.2	218.3
Southeast Asia[b]			**3,754.3**	**4,311.9**
Brunei Darussalam	...	...	...	...
Cambodia	1.0	1.8	117.5	344.5
Indonesia	6.6	8.8	2,200.2	1,560.1
Lao People's Democratic Republic	4.0	6.8	100.8	82.9
Malaysia	...	...	32.4	11.0
Myanmar	3.1	6.8	12.4	99.3
Philippines	16.0	5.2	193.5	1,735.4
Singapore	...	...	...	...
Thailand	0.4	1.5	49.1	65.7
Timor-Leste	–	2.0	53.8	34.7
Viet Nam	2.1	1.2	994.5	378.2
The Pacific			**500.4**	**479.1**
Cook Islands	...	...	2.3	...
Fiji	1.3	4.7	17.4	93.5
Kiribati	...	...	5.0	20.8
Marshall Islands	...	...	1.7	15.6
Micronesia, Federated States of	...	...	1.6	15.7
Nauru	...	...	17.2	5.7
Niue	...	...	3.3	4.9
Palau	...	...	1.5	2.8
Papua New Guinea	1.4	3.8	168.7	181.2
Samoa	5.0	9.8	40.5	29.0
Solomon Islands	3.1	2.2	205.7	64.7
Tonga	9.3	11.0	18.5	15.7
Tuvalu	...	...	1.8	6.8
Vanuatu	1.4	4.8	15.2	22.9
Developed ADB Member Economies			**...**	**...**
Australia	...	...	...	...
Japan	...	...	...	...
New Zealand	...	...	...	...
DEVELOPING ADB MEMBER ECONOMIES[b]			**11,784.1**	**13,471.3**

... = data not available, – = magnitude equals zero, $ = United States dollars, ADB = Asian Development Bank.

a Technical assistance includes assistance through North-South, South-South, and triangular cooperation. The United Nations dataset and metadata refer to this indicator as total official development assistance (gross disbursements) for technical cooperation.

b For reporting economies only.

Source: United Nations. SDG Global Database. https://unstats.un.org/sdgs/dataportal (accessed 29 July 2025).

Goal 17. Strengthen the means of implementation and revitalize the Global Partnership for Sustainable Development

Table 1.17.2: Selected Indicators for Sustainable Development Goal 17—Statistical Capacity Building

ADB Regional Member	Target 17.18: By 2020, enhance capacity-building support to developing countries (or economies), including for least developed countries (or economies) and small island developing states, to increase significantly the availability of high-quality, timely, and reliable data disaggregated by income, gender, age, race, ethnicity, migratory status, disability, geographic location, and other characteristics relevant in national contexts	Target 17.19: By 2030, build on existing initiatives to develop measurements of progress on sustainable development that complement gross domestic product and support statistical capacity-building in developing countries (or economies)	
	17.18.3: Availability of National Statistical Plan[a]	17.19.1: Dollar Value of All Resources Made Available to Strengthen Statistical Capacity in Developing Countries (or Economies) (million United States dollars)	17.19.2: Have Conducted at Least One Population and Housing Census in the Last 10 Years[b]
	2022	2021	2020
Developing ADB Member Economies			
Central and West Asia			
Afghanistan	B (2023)	0.1	...
Armenia	A, B, C, D	0.1	2022
Azerbaijan	A, B, C	2.2	2019
Georgia	A, B, C, D	1.6	2022
Kazakhstan	A, B, C	0.1	2020
Kyrgyz Republic	A, B	4.8	2022
Pakistan	A, B, C	3.3	2023
Tajikistan	A, B, C, D	2.1	2020
Türkiye	A, B, C	9.7	2021
Turkmenistan	...	0.4	2022
Uzbekistan	A, B, C	1.0	...
East Asia			
China, People's Republic of	A, B, C	0.3	2020
Hong Kong, China	A, B (2023)	...	2021
Korea, Republic of	A, B, C	...	2020
Mongolia	A, B, C, D	0.2	2020
Taipei,China	...	...	2020
South Asia			
Bangladesh	B	2.7	2022
Bhutan	A, B, C, D	0.1	2017
India	B (2023)	10.5	...
Maldives	B	0.3	2022
Nepal	B, C, D	16.0	2021
Sri Lanka	B (2023)	1.5	...
Southeast Asia			
Brunei Darussalam	A, B, C	...	2021
Cambodia	B	4.0	2019
Indonesia	B, C, E	4.6	2020
Lao People's Democratic Republic	B, C, D	8.6	2015
Malaysia	A, B, C	0.2	2020
Myanmar	B, C	2.6	2014
Philippines	B, C	1.4	2020
Singapore	A, B, C	...	2020
Thailand	A, B, C	0.2	...
Timor-Leste	B, C, D	0.7	2022
Viet Nam	A, B, C	21.0	2019
The Pacific			
Cook Islands	B	0.3 (2019)	2021
Fiji	C, D	0.2	2017
Kiribati	...	0.3	2020
Marshall Islands	...	0.2	2021
Micronesia, Federated States of	...	0.0 (2018)	2023
Nauru	C (2019)	0.0 (2020)	2021
Niue	...	0.1 (2021)	2022
Palau	C (2019)	0.0 (2020)	2020
Papua New Guinea	B	0.3 (2021)	...
Samoa	A, B, C	0.3	2021
Solomon Islands	B	0.1 (2021)	2019
Tonga	A, B	0.2	2021
Tuvalu	B	0.0	2022
Vanuatu	B	0.1	2020
Developed ADB Member Economies			
Australia	A, B (2023)	...	2021
Japan	A, B, C	...	2020
New Zealand	A, B, C	...	2023

... = data not available, 0.0 = magnitude is less than half of unit employed, ADB = Asian Development Bank.

a A = a national statistical plan fully funded, B = a national statistical plan under implementation, C = a national statistical plan with funding from government, D = a national statistical plan with funding from donors, E = a national statistical plan with funding from others.
b Refers to the most recent year in which a population and housing census was conducted.

Sources: United Nations. SDG Global Database. https://unstats.un.org/sdgs/dataportal/database (accessed 29 July 2025). For 17.19.2: For Australia: Australian Bureau of Statistics. Population Census. https://www.abs.gov.au/statistics/people/population/population-census/latest-release (accessed 29 July 2025); For Georgia: National Statistics Office of Georgia. https://www.geostat.ge/en/modules/categories/735/population-census (accessed 29 July 2025); For Japan: Statistics Bureau of Japan. Monthly Report. https://www.stat.go.jp/english/data/jinsui/tsuki/index.html (accessed 29 July 2025); For Maldives: Maldives Bureau of Statistics. https://statisticsmaldives.gov.mv/census-in-2022 (accessed 29 July 2025); For Myanmar: Department of Population. https://www.dop.gov.mm/en/population-censuses-myanmar (accessed 29 July 2025); For the Philippines: Philippine Statistics Authority. Census of Population and Housing. https://psa.gov.ph/content/2020-census-population-and-housing-2020-cph-population-counts-declared-official-president (accessed 29 July 2025); For Taipei,China: Government of Taipei,China, Directorate-General of Budget, Accounting and Statistics; For Timor-Leste: National Institute Of Statistics Timor-Leste. Census Population. https://inetl-ip.gov.tl/census-population/ (accessed 29 July 2025); and for Turkmenistan: State Statistics Committee of Turkmenistan. https://turkmenistan.gov.tm/en/post/68763/population-and-housing-census-took-start-turkmenistan (accessed 29 July 2025).

Data Gaps and Other Data-Related Issues

New and huge data demands. The approved global framework for monitoring the Sustainable Development Goals (SDGs) consists of 234 unique indicators with greater disaggregation and across a wider spectrum of topics than the Millennium Development Goals. With international development support, governments are strengthening their national statistical systems to address data demands across all SDG indicators.

Limited data availability for Sustainable Development Goal indicators. While there have been many improvements to data availability and timeliness since the launch of the SDGs in 2015, there is more to be done. Since March 2020, all SDG indicators have been supported by well-defined and internationally agreed methodologies, a significant improvement from the 39% of indicators lacking such standards in 2016. Additionally, the percentage of indicators that are conceptually clear and are broadly available increased from 36% in 2016 to 68% in 2024. Further, trend data—at least two data points since 2015—are now available for 51% of indicators in more than half of all economies. Despite these advances, there remain significant data gaps concerning geographic coverage, timeliness, and the level of disaggregation.

Differing priorities among national statistics offices with regard to economic data production result in disparities in data availability. Most national statistics offices across Asia and the Pacific conduct population and housing censuses every decade. Such sources provide baseline socioeconomic data that overlap SDG indicators with economic and social dimensions. Depending on the frequency of data collection, administrative reporting systems and household surveys—such as labor force surveys, household income and expenditure surveys, demographic and health surveys, establishment surveys, and agriculture surveys—can be other good sources of data for SDG indicators.

Gaps in data granularity. Many SDG indicators require disaggregation by location, sex, gender, age, income, ethnicity, migration status, disability status, and other relevant dimensions. Granular data can illustrate disparities within and across economies.

However, the extent to which specific groups are disproportionately vulnerable and/or in need of targeted development initiatives is difficult to determine given the lack of data disaggregation and interlinkages across indicators. Sex disaggregation—even for basic indicators such as extreme poverty rates, whether based on national definitions or the international poverty line of $3.00 a day (at 2021 purchasing power parity) level—is not readily available for many economies. Similarly, poverty numbers are not widely available for vulnerable groups, such as people with disabilities or Indigenous Peoples, since the surveys on which these poverty calculations are based may not have adequate sample sizes to ensure accurate representation of these groups. Investments are needed (e.g., to finance and conduct special surveys) to obtain poverty data on vulnerable groups that make up only a small proportion of the total population.

Innovative data sources, such as big data and crowdsourced data, can potentially address data gaps and strengthen the monitoring of SDG indicators. However, some types of big data may require significant assumptions or may not represent the underlying groups of interest. Therefore, it is necessary to ensure that reliable statistical inferences can be made when complementing surveys and other conventional data sources with big data (Cox, Kartsonaki, and Keogh 2018).

Lack of data comparability. Differences in definitions mean that SDG indicators, such as the proportion of the population with access to safely managed drinking water services, rely on data related to housing conditions, which may not be fully comparable across economies. Likewise, comparisons of SDG indicators across economies are difficult for urban–rural disaggregation due to various definitions of "urban" and "rural" across time and economies.

Sparse data and irregular frequency. Some indicators that provide a useful description of income inequality—such as the growth in household expenditure among those in an economy's bottom 40th percentile of income distribution in relation to national averages are only currently available for a few economies. In another example, despite agreed definition of global minimum proficiency level in reading and mathematics, patchy data posed a challenge in monitoring and assessing progress made.

Frequency is also of concern as some indicators, such as the coverage of protected areas in relation to marine areas, are not regularly collected. Indicators on material footprint and domestic material consumption, which are widely accepted as strategic sustainability indicators of production and consumption, are not produced annually.

Further, some protected areas are not assigned management categories. While access to remote sensing data has improved in recent years, forest regrowth cannot easily be detected with remote-sensing techniques.

Data limitations. The indicators included in the framework for monitoring the SDGs, while carefully chosen, may have some limitations.

For example, in the absence of a household survey with an employment module, data for the labor share in gross domestic product may not include information about the self-employed (who comprise a sizeable portion of the working population in many economies) when employment data are sourced from establishment surveys.

In addition, while the indicator on participation in learning programs tracks the percentage of children participating in organized learning, it fails to capture critical details such as the duration and quality of time spent by children in such programs. This highlights a significant data gap that limits the understanding of how much children are actually learning.

The many challenges facing cities—pollution, traffic congestion, and inadequate housing for the poor—can be exacerbated by migration and population growth, changes in family structures, inequality of opportunity for excluded groups, and rising insecurity. Currently available data do not allow for a simple assessment of these issues.

The Red List Index is a composite index aggregated across multiple taxonomic groups. While it can be updated annually, the index does not adequately capture the deteriorating status of common species that are abundant and widespread yet declining gradually. Data on other indicators for monitoring many targets under SDG 15 are also sparsely available. Limited data availability and the lack of good-quality data must be carefully addressed.

Measurement errors. The quality of data for all SDG indicators needs to be considered when identifying trends and drawing inferences. For example, self-reporting of land area and production by farmers is known to have significant biases (Dillon and Rao 2018). The calculation of under-5 mortality rates requires complete counts of live births and child deaths by a precise age, which are not always available in economies of Asia and the Pacific that lack civil registration systems. Maternal deaths are likewise not always accounted for, given incomplete or inaccurate records on causes of death. Anthropometric measures of malnutrition (including stunted heights) are subject to measurement errors and issues around reference standards (i.e., local versus international standards). Access to safely managed drinking water and sanitation services, and information on hygiene all depend on more and better data, particularly nationally representative surveys and administrative data sources (WHO and UNICEF).

A complete stocktaking of all statistical capacity development programs cannot be guaranteed in the data compiled by PARIS21 for measuring the dollar-value support for statistics development. Double counting of projects can occur, or the data may also be inflated by the inaccurate inclusion of multisector projects. Further, donor commitments do not always lead to actual disbursements to recipient economies.

Ultimately, the reliability of data on SDG indicators depends on the quality of the underlying data sources. Governments across Asia and the Pacific need to increase investment, look for innovative data sources, and form strategic partnerships with a range of stakeholders to enhance data quality, comparability, measurement, and timeliness. Reliable and comprehensive data supports evidence-based policymaking that leads to better development outcomes.

Table 2.1.1: Midyear Population

ADB Regional Member	Population (million)								Population Growth Rates[a] (%)							
	2010	2015	2019	2020	2021	2022	2023	2024	2010	2015	2019	2020	2021	2022	2023	2024
Developing ADB Member Economies																
Central and West Asia[b]	**350.3**	**383.0**	**420.7**	**427.9 |**	**436.2 |**	**444.0 |**	**458.9**	**461.3**	**1.9**	**1.8**	**1.8**	**1.7 |**	**1.9 |**	**1.8 |**	**1.9**	**1.9**
Afghanistan[c,d]	24.5	27.1	30.7	31.4 |	32.9	33.6	34.3	35.0	2.1	2.1	2.2	2.2 |	4.8	2.1	2.1	2.1
Armenia[c]	3.1	3.0	3.0	3.0	3.0	3.0 |	2.9	3.0	-0.7	-0.2	-0.2	-0.2	0.1	-0.1 |	...	1.8
Azerbaijan	9.1	9.6	9.9	10.0	10.0	10.1	10.2	10.2	1.2	1.2	-0.1	0.7	0.4	0.5	1.0	–
Georgia	3.8	3.7	3.7	3.7	3.7	3.7	3.7	3.7	-0.7	0.2	-0.2	0.1	-0.4	0.1	0.1	-0.4
Kazakhstan	16.1	17.5	18.5	18.8	19.0 |	19.6	19.9	20.2	1.7	1.5	1.3	1.4	1.3 |	3.2	1.4	1.3
Kyrgyz Republic[c]	5.5	6.0	6.6	6.7	6.9	7.0	7.1	7.2	1.4	2.3	2.3	2.1	1.9	1.8	1.8	1.7
Pakistan	173.5	191.7	216.1	220.4	224.8	229.2	241.5	...	2.1	2.0	2.0	2.0	2.0	2.0	2.6	...
Tajikistan	7.5	8.5	9.2	9.4	9.8	10.0	10.2	10.4	2.5	2.4	2.2	2.0	1.7	1.9	2.0	2.2
Türkiye	73.1	78.2	82.6	83.4	84.1	85.0	85.3	85.5	1.5	1.3	1.4	1.0	0.9	1.0	0.4	0.2
Turkmenistan	5.6	6.2	6.8	6.9	7.1	7.2	7.4	7.5	2.1	2.3	2.2	2.1	2.0	1.9	1.9	1.8
Uzbekistan	28.6	31.3	33.6	34.2	34.9	35.6	36.4	37.2	2.9	1.8	1.9	1.9	2.0	2.1	2.1	2.1
East Asia[b]	**1,423.4**	**1,468.1**	**1,496.2**	**1,498.3**	**1,498.7**	**1,497.4**	**1,495.8**	**1,494.5**	**0.5**	**0.5**	**0.3**	**0.1**	**0.0**	**-0.1**	**-0.1**	**-0.1**
China, People's Republic of[c]	1,340.9	1,383.3	1,410.1	1,412.1	1,412.6	1,411.8	1,409.7	1,408.3	0.5	0.5	0.3	0.1	0.0	-0.1	-0.1	-0.1
Hong Kong, China	7.0	7.3	7.5	7.5	7.4	7.3	7.5	7.5	0.7	0.9	0.7	-0.4	-0.9	-0.9	2.6	-0.2
Korea, Republic of	49.6	51.0	51.8	51.8	51.8	51.7	51.7	51.8	0.5	0.5	0.3	0.1	-0.1	-0.2	0.1	0.1
Mongolia	2.7	3.0	3.3	3.3	3.4	3.4	3.5	3.5	1.6	2.1	1.8	1.8	1.6	1.4	1.4	1.1
Taipei,China	23.1	23.5	23.6	23.6	23.5	23.2	23.4	23.4	0.3	0.3	0.1	-0.0	-0.4	-1.3	0.8	0.2
South Asia[b]	**1,382.6**	**1,492.0**	**1,559.7**	**1,576.1**	**1,591.3**	**1,607.7**	**1,621.0**	**1,633.9**	**1.4**	**1.3**	**1.1**	**1.1**	**1.0**	**1.1**	**0.9**	**1.0**
Bangladesh	148.6	158.9	166.5	168.1	170.1	171.7	172.9	...	1.4	1.4	1.3	1.3	1.3	1.4	1.3	...
Bhutan	0.7	0.8	0.7	0.7	0.8	0.8	0.8	0.8	1.8	1.6	1.0	1.0	1.0	0.9	0.9	0.9
India[c]	1,186.0	1,283.0	1,341.0	1,355.4	1,368.6	1,383.0	1,395.0	1,408.0	1.4	1.3	1.1	1.1	1.0	1.1	0.9	0.9
Maldives	0.4	0.5	0.5	0.6	0.6	0.6	0.6	0.6	2.3	3.9	4.3	4.4	2.0	1.9	1.9	1.9
Nepal	26.3	28.0	29.1	29.4	29.2	29.4	29.7	...	1.4	1.4	0.9	0.9	0.9	0.9	0.9	...
Sri Lanka	20.7	21.0	21.8	21.9	22.2	22.2	22.0	21.9	1.0	0.9	0.6	0.5	1.1	0.1	-0.6	-0.5
Southeast Asia[b]	**588.1 |**	**627.6**	**655.6 |**	**662.8**	**668.1**	**674.1**	**680.8**	**687.5**	**1.2 |**	**1.3**	**1.1 |**	**0.9**	**0.9**	**0.9**	**1.0**	**1.0**
Brunei Darussalam	0.4	0.4	0.5	0.4	0.4	0.4	0.5	0.5	1.8	1.2	3.3	-2.0	-0.2	1.1	1.1	1.1
Cambodia	14.1	15.1	16.0	16.2	16.6	16.8	17.1	17.3	1.3	1.4	1.4	1.4	1.5	1.5	1.5	1.2
Indonesia	237.6	255.6	266.9	270.2	272.7	275.7	278.7	281.6	1.5	1.4	1.3	1.3	1.2	1.2	1.1	1.1
Lao People's Democratic Republic	6.0	6.5	7.1	7.2	7.3	7.4	7.6	7.6	1.5	1.4	1.6	1.5	1.5	1.4	1.4	1.3
Malaysia	28.6	31.2	32.5	32.4	32.6	32.7	33.4	34.1	1.8	1.6	0.4	-0.2	0.4	0.4	2.1	2.0
Myanmar[c]	49.0	51.1	52.6	53.0	53.4	53.8	54.1	54.5	0.8	0.8	0.7	0.7	0.7	0.7	0.7	0.7
Philippines	93.1 |	100.8	107.2 |	109.2	110.1	110.9	111.9	112.9	1.0 |	1.7(2016)	1.5 |	...	0.8	0.8	0.9	0.9
Singapore[c]	5.1	5.5	5.7	5.7	5.5	5.6	5.9	6.0	1.8	1.2	1.2	-0.3	-4.1	3.4	5.0	2.0
Thailand	65.9	68.0	69.3	69.5	69.7	69.9	70.0	70.2	0.6	0.6	0.3	0.3	0.3	0.2	0.2	0.2
Timor-Leste	1.1	1.2	1.3	1.3	1.3	1.3	1.4	1.4	2.2	1.8	1.5	1.5	1.6	1.5	1.5	2.9
Viet Nam	87.1	92.2	96.5	97.6	98.5	99.5	100.3	101.3	1.2	1.1	1.2	1.1	1.0	1.0	0.8	1.0
The Pacific[b,e]	**9.3**	**10.6**	**11.8***	**12.1***	**14.4***	**14.8***	**15.2* |**	**15.6***	**2.7**	**2.7**	**2.7***	**2.7***	**2.8***	**2.8***	**2.8* |**	**2.8**
Cook Islands	23.7	18.4	20.2	16.5	18.2	20.5	21.6	24.5	4.9	0.1	–	-18.3	10.3	12.6	5.4	13.4
Fiji	850.7	869.5	889.3	891.4	893.5	899.5	897.3	882.6	0.6	0.4	0.6	0.6	0.6	0.6	0.6	-0.1
Kiribati[c]	103.1	110.1	117.5	119.4	121.4*	123.4*	125.4*	...	2.2	1.3	1.6	1.6	1.6*	1.6*	1.6*	...
Marshall Islands	52.9	49.9	44.2	43.9	42.4	41.4	40.4	39.5	1.1	-2.0	-2.6	-0.5	-3.5	-2.4	-2.4	-2.2
Micronesia, Federated States of[c]	102.8	103.7	104.5*	104.6*	104.8*	105.0*	105.2*	105.4*	-0.5	0.2	0.2*	0.2*	0.2*	0.2*	0.2*	0.2*
Nauru	10.0	10.9	11.5	11.7	11.8	11.9	12.0	12.1	-0.2	1.6	0.9	1.6	1.2	0.8	0.7	0.8
Niue[c]	1.6	1.7	1.7	1.7	1.7	1.7	1.7	1.7	-0.2	1.1	-0.4	-0.4	-0.4	-0.5	-0.4	-0.4
Palau	18.3	17.7	17.5	17.6	17.6	17.6	17.6 |	17.9	-1.9	1.8	-0.5	0.9	-0.1	-0.1	0.3 |	1.2
Papua New Guinea	7,055.4	8,225.6	9,300.0	9,589.9	11,781.6	12,148.8	12,527.4	12,917.8	3.1	3.1	3.1	3.1	3.1	3.1	3.1	3.1
Samoa	185.9	193.8	200.3	201.9	204.5	206.7	208.6	210.7	0.8	0.8	0.8	0.8	1.4	0.9	1.0	1.0
Solomon Islands	573.0	651.4	721.0	725.1	739.6	754.1	768.7	783.3	2.6	2.6	2.6	...	2.0	2.0	1.9	1.9
Tonga	102.9	101.4	100.4	100.3	100.2	100.1	100.0	99.9	0.2	-0.5	-0.1	-0.1	-0.1	-0.1	-0.1	-0.1
Tuvalu	11.1	10.7	10.3	10.2	10.3	10.6	10.1	10.0	0.5	-0.3	-2.8	-0.7	0.7	3.1	-4.7	-0.9
Vanuatu	239.7	268.6	291.7	300.0	307.0	314.0	321.5	334.7	2.4	2.3	2.3	2.8	2.2	2.3	2.2	4.1
Developed ADB Member Economies[b]	**154.5**	**155.6**	**156.6**	**156.6**	**156.5**	**156.2**	**156.4**	**156.5**	**0.3**	**0.2**	**0.1**	**-0.0**	**-0.1**	**-0.1**	**0.1**	**0.1**
Australia	22.0	23.8	25.3	25.6	25.7	26.0	26.7	27.2	1.6	1.5	1.5	1.2	0.1	1.3	2.5	2.0
Japan	128.1	127.1	126.3	125.8	125.7	125.1	124.5	124.0	0.0	-0.1	-0.2	-0.3	-0.1	-0.4	-0.5	-0.4
New Zealand	4.4	4.6	5.0	5.1	5.1	5.1	5.2	5.3	1.1	2.1	1.4	2.1	0.2	-0.1	2.3	1.7
DEVELOPING ADB MEMBER ECONOMIES[b]	**3,753.7 |**	**3,980.4**	**4,144.1* |**	**4,177.3***	**4,208.6* |**	**4,238.0* |**	**4,271.7* |**	**4,292.7***	**1.1 |**	**1.0**	**0.9* |**	**0.8* |**	**0.7* |**	**0.7* |**	**0.7* |**	**0.7**
ALL ADB REGIONAL MEMBERS[b]	**3,908.1 |**	**4,135.9**	**4,300.6* |**	**4,333.9***	**4,365.0* |**	**4,394.2* |**	**4,428.0* |**	**4,449.2***	**1.0 |**	**1.0**	**0.9* |**	**0.8* |**	**0.7* |**	**0.7* |**	**0.7* |**	**0.7**
WORLD	**7,021.7**	**7,470.5**	**7,811.3**	**7,887.0**	**7,954.4**	**8,021.4**	**8,091.7**	**8,162.0**	**1.3**	**1.2**	**1.1**	**1.0**	**0.9**	**0.8**	**0.9**	**0.9**

... = data not available; | = marks break in series; * = provisional, preliminary, estimate; (-/+) 0.0 = magnitude is less than half of unit employed; – = magnitude equals zero; ADB = Asian Development Bank.

a The annual population growth rate is calculated as the percentage change in population when comparing the reference year with the year prior. For example, the population growth rates under the column heading "2020" refer to population growth from 2019 to 2020.
b Regional population totals include only reporting economies with data corresponding to the year heading, while regional population growth rates are estimated as a weighted average of the annual population growth rates of the reporting economies. Weights are based on the total population of the region for the years in which the reporting economies have published the annual growth rates.
c Estimates of population size are as of 1 January for the Kyrgyz Republic and Armenia; 10 June for Afghanistan; 30 June for Niue and Singapore; 30 September for the Federated States of Micronesia; 1 October for India and Myanmar; 7 November for Kiribati; and 31 December for the People's Republic of China.
d Prior 2021, total population refers to resident population. It excludes the nomadic population and populations in Daikunkdi, Helmand, Paktika, and Zabul provinces.
e The total population for the Pacific subregion is expressed in millions, while estimates of population size for ADB developing member economies in the Pacific are expressed in thousands.

Sources: Economies' official sources. For Afghanistan (2021–2024), the Lao People's Democratic Republic (2000–2004), Niue, Papua New Guinea (2001–2010, 2012–2020, 2022–2024), and Türkiye: Asian Development Bank estimates using data from the economies' official sources. For Nauru: Pacific Data Hub. Stat Data Explorer. Population projections. https://stats.pacificdata.org/ (accessed 3 February 2025). For Myanmar, Turkmenistan, and World: United Nations. World Population Prospects 2024. https://population.un.org/wpp/Download/Standard/Population/ (accessed 8 and 30 May 2025, and 2 June 2025).

Population

Table 2.1.2: Migration and Urbanization

ADB Regional Member	Net International Migration Rate[a] (per 1,000 population)								Urban Population[b] (% of total population)							
	2010	2015	2019	2020	2021	2022	2023	2024	2010	2015	2019	2020	2021	2022	2023	2024
Developing ADB Member Economies																
Central and West Asia	...	...	...	...	...	...	...	...	**45.8**	**47.6**	**46.5**	**46.6** |	**46.6**	**46.9** |	**47.7**	**48.0**
Afghanistan[c]	-5.9	-8.5	0.2	3.7	-13.7	-16.0	-1.2	-1.0	23.2	24.7	25.3	25.6 |	24.4	24.7	25.0	25.3
Armenia	-10.2	-5.2	-4.9	-4.5	-6.8	13.2	25.5	-10.1	63.5	63.5	63.9	63.9	64.0	63.9 |	63.8	64.0
Azerbaijan	0.2	0.1	0.0	0.1	0.1	0.9	-8.2	1.1	53.0	53.1	55.0	54.9	54.7	54.6	54.5	54.4
Georgia	-9.4	-3.5	-1.4	-0.7	-0.7	7.1	0.5	0.5	56.5	57.5	58.9	59.2	59.5	60.0	60.7	61.3
Kazakhstan	-0.4	-0.1	0.1	-0.4	-0.5	2.3	-0.2	-0.4	53.8	56.8	58.3	58.8	59.2	61.6	61.9	62.7
Kyrgyz Republic	-1.2	-0.8	7.3	8.2	6.8	1.8	0.8	0.5	33.9	33.3	33.5	33.6	34.2	34.8	34.9	41.6
Pakistan	-2.2	-10.0	-5.1	-2.4	-2.4	-5.4	-6.5	-5.6	36.9	39.2	36.7	36.8	36.8	36.9	38.8	...
Tajikistan	-4.4	-0.9	-0.9	-0.4	-0.4	-1.7	-1.9	-2.0	26.4	26.4	26.3	26.3	26.3	28.8	28.8	28.9
Türkiye[d]	0.8	13.3	-0.2	0.4	0.2	-3.5	-3.6	-3.2	70.8	73.6	75.6	76.1	76.6	77.0	77.5	77.9
Turkmenistan[d]	1.2	1.6	2.9	2.9	2.5	2.0	2.0	2.0	48.5	50.3	52.0	52.5	53.0	53.5	54.0	54.5
Uzbekistan	-0.7	-0.5	-0.3	-0.3	-0.3	-0.1	-0.2	-0.2	51.5	50.8	50.5	50.6	50.7	50.9	51.0	51.0
East Asia	...	...	...	...	...	...	...	...	**51.5**	**58.5**	**63.5**	**64.6**	**65.4**	**65.9**	**66.8**	**67.6***
China, People's Republic of	-0.1	-0.5	-0.5	-0.1	-0.3	-0.2	-0.4	-0.2	50.0	57.3	62.7	63.9	64.7	65.2	66.2	67.0
Hong Kong, China[d]	1.2	1.4	-1.0	-0.2	-0.5	-0.5	-0.5	-2.6	100.0	100.0	100.0	100.0	100.0	100.0	100.0	100.0
Korea, Republic of[d]	1.1	5.4	2.5	2.2	-0.3	1.7	1.7	1.5	81.9	81.6	81.4	81.4	81.4	81.4	81.5	81.5
Mongolia	-2.4	1.4	2.7	–	–	–	–	0.0	69.2	68.6	68.5	69.0	69.4	70.1	70.8	71.2*
Taipei,China[e]	0.8	0.5	0.7	-0.9	-6.2	-1.1	-1.4	-1.1	59.3	60.9	61.0	61.1	61.1	60.7	61.0	61.5
South Asia	...	...	...	...	...	...	...	...	**29.0**	**32.4**	**34.0**	**35.1**	**35.5**	**35.9**	**35.6**	**35.9**
Bangladesh[d]	-7.3	-5.7	-6.2	-6.0	-5.9	-3.2	-3.2	-2.7	25.9	34.3	37.4	38.2	38.9	39.7	40.5	41.2
Bhutan[d]	-1.3	0.6	0.4	0.4	0.4	0.4	0.4	-0.4	34.8	38.9	40.9	42.3	43.0	40.9	44.4	45.0
India	-0.0	-0.5	-0.7	-0.1	-0.2	-1.0	-0.7	-0.4	29.9	32.7	34.1	34.4	34.7	35.1	35.4	35.7
Maldives	17.7	21.8	19.8	19.2	18.2	-5.1	-5.5	-4.6	36.4	38.7	40.4	40.8	41.3	41.7	42.1	42.6
Nepal[f]	-9.9	-7.9	6.4	5.6	4.4	-12.8	-13.8	-13.5	16.6	18.5	21.4	62.4	63.2	66.1	27.9	...
Sri Lanka[d]	-4.7	-1.4	-1.3	-1.3	-1.3	-1.2	-1.2	-1.2	18.2	18.3	18.6	18.7	18.9	19.0	19.2	19.4
Southeast Asia	**0.1**	**-0.5**	**0.0**	**-0.2**	**-0.0**	**0.0**	**-0.2**	**-0.2**	**44.2**	**47.3**	**49.5**	**50.2**	**50.7**	**51.2**	**51.8**	**52.4**
Brunei Darussalam[d]	6.3	0.8	1.0	1.0	–	–	–	–	75.0	76.7	77.9	78.3	78.6	78.9	79.1	79.4
Cambodia[d]	-3.4	-3.7	-3.5	–	-1.6	-1.8	-1.8	-1.9	20.3	22.2	23.8	24.2	24.7	25.1	25.6	26.0
Indonesia[d]	-0.2	-0.1	-0.1	-0.1	-0.0	-0.1	-0.1	-0.1	49.9	53.3	56.0	56.6	57.3	57.9	58.6	59.2
Lao People's Democratic Republic[d]	-4.7	-1.9	-1.4	-1.4	-1.4	-1.3	-1.3	-1.3	30.1	33.1	35.6	36.3	36.9	37.6	38.2	38.9
Malaysia	5.5	6.0	6.1	3.0	5.5	5.4	5.2	4.9	71.0	74.3	76.2	75.1	75.3	75.5	75.7	76.0
Myanmar[d]	-2.4	-1.8	-1.9	-1.2	-0.7	-0.7	-0.6	-0.7	28.9	29.9	30.9	31.1	31.4	31.8	32.1	32.5
Philippines[d]	0.1	-3.7	-0.1	-0.4	-0.8	-1.9	-1.4	-1.4	45.3	46.3	47.1	47.4	47.7	48.0	48.3	48.6
Singapore[d]	14.3	7.6	0.2	-25.9	-7.9	38.0	4.7	3.4	100.0	100.0	100.0	100.0	100.0	100.0	100.0	100.0
Thailand[g]	0.8	0.5	0.1	0.5	-0.0	0.3	0.3	0.3	42.0	48.6	53.6	54.8	56.0	57.1	58.2	59.3
Timor-Leste[d]	0.4	-0.0	3.0	2.9	2.3	-4.0	-4.1	-1.8	27.7	29.5	30.9	31.3	31.7	32.1	32.5	32.8
Viet Nam	-0.1	-0.1	-0.0	-0.1	-0.1	-0.8	-0.8	-0.6	30.4	33.5	35.0	36.8	37.1	37.5	38.1	38.5
The Pacific	...	...	...	...	...	...	...	...	**18.5**	**18.5**	**18.8**	**18.9**	**19.0**	**19.1**	**19.3**	**19.5**
Cook Islands	18.9	-13.8	-36.2	-37.3	-33.6	-38.0	-39.2	-36.8	73.3	74.4	75.3	75.5	75.7	75.9	76.2	76.4
Fiji	-11.4	-11.3	-13.0	-6.6	-6.6	-3.9	-3.6	-3.5	52.2	54.7	56.8	57.2	57.7	58.2	58.7	59.2
Kiribati[d]	-4.2	-8.7	-5.7	–	-2.7	-3.0	-3.7	-3.5	47.4	51.6	54.8	55.6	56.3	57.1	57.8	58.4
Marshall Islands[d]	-23.5	-40.2	-46.1	-46.9	-48.7	-45.6	-47.2	-47.0	73.6	75.8	77.4	77.8	78.2	78.5	78.9	79.2
Micronesia, Federated States of[d]	-16.7	-13.0	-12.3	-6.1	-10.7	-10.3	-10.1	-9.8	22.3	22.5	22.8	22.9	23.1	23.2	23.4	23.6
Nauru[d]	-24.5	-7.9	-14.7	-18.3	-11.7	-12.2	-12.5	-10.1	100.0	100.0	100.0	100.0	100.0	100.0	100.0	100.0
Niue[d]	-8.2	2.8	3.3	3.9	7.2	–	–	5.3	38.7	42.6	45.5	46.2	46.9	47.6	48.2	48.9
Palau	-21.3	-0.6	-2.6	–	-1.2	-1.1	-1.1	-0.8	77.0	78.7	...	78.9	...	...	...	77.9
Papua New Guinea[d]	6.6	3.5	2.4	1.1	1.1	-0.1	-0.1	-0.1	13.0	13.0	13.2	13.3	13.5	13.6	13.7	13.9
Samoa	-16.6	-15.2	-11.0	-10.8	-13.4	-13.2	-13.0	-12.6	19.9	19.2	18.8	18.8	17.6	17.3	17.0	...
Solomon Islands	9.5	9.2	-2.7	2.1	2.0	2.0	2.0	2.0	20.3	23.8	27.6	29.1	30.2	31.4	32.6	33.9
Tonga	-19.5	-24.6	-16.8	-17.1	-21.0	-21.1	-20.8	-20.6	23.4	23.2	22.1	21.7	21.3	20.9	20.5	...
Tuvalu[d]	2.1	-16.3	-32.4	-34.1	-35.9	-32.0	-32.9	-29.1	54.8	59.7	63.2	64.0	64.8	65.5	66.2	66.9
Vanuatu	-5.9	-5.0	-2.2	-0.7	-0.7	–	–	-0.1	24.4	24.6	25.1	25.2	21.7	21.2	21.4	...
Developed ADB Member Economies	...	...	...	...	...	...	...	...	**90.0**	**90.5**	**90.8**	**90.8**	**90.9**	**90.9**	**91.0**	**91.1**
Australia	7.5	8.9	8.1	1.7	4.5	5.4	5.3	5.2	86.2	86.8	87.3	87.3	87.2	87.3	87.4	87.5
Japan[d]	1.0	1.3	2.5	0.3	-0.3	1.4	1.4	1.2	90.8	91.4	91.7	91.8	91.9	92.0	92.0	92.1
New Zealand	1.5	15.4	14.0	8.3	-2.9	4.2	4.1	3.6	84.2	84.3	84.5	84.4	84.3	84.1	84.2	...
DEVELOPING ADB MEMBER ECONOMIES	...	...	...	...	...	...	...	...	**41.5**	**45.8**	**48.3**	**49.2** |	**49.7**	**50.0** |	**50.4**	**50.8***
ALL ADB REGIONAL MEMBERS	...	...	...	...	...	...	...	...	**43.4**	**47.5**	**49.9**	**50.7** |	**51.1**	**51.5** |	**51.8**	**52.2***
WORLD	–	–	–	–	–	–	–	–	**51.7**	**53.9**	**55.7**	**56.2**	**56.6**	**57.0**	**57.5**	**57.9**

... = data not available; | = marks break in series; (-/+) 0.0 = magnitude is less than half of unit employed; * = provisional, preliminary, estimate; – = magnitude equals zero; ADB = Asian Development Bank.

a Refers to annual average migration over the period shown. United Nations population estimates and projections are based on all available sources of data on population size and levels of fertility, mortality, and international migration. Statistics on international migration are sourced from population registers and other administrative sources. These estimates and projections are made for 237 distinct national economies or areas comprising the total population of the world.

b In estimating the aggregates for Asia and the Pacific, imputation was done for economies with missing data by substituting available data from the nearest years. The aggregates were derived using data on total population and percentage of urban population from economies' official sources and the United Nations' World Urbanization Prospects 2018 and World Population Prospects 2024.

c From 2000 to 2020, the urban population ratio was computed as the proportion of the total resident population residing in urban areas, excluding nomadic groups. From 2021 onward, this metric was revised to include nomadic populations.

d For urban population, refers to data from World Urbanization Prospects 2018 for: 2013–2024 for Bangladesh; 2023–2024 for Bhutan; and the whole data series for Brunei Darussalam; Cambodia; Hong Kong, China; Indonesia; Japan; Kiribati; the Republic of Korea; the Lao People's Democratic Republic; the Marshall Islands; the Federated States of Micronesia; Myanmar; Nauru; Niue; Papua New Guinea; the Philippines; Singapore; Sri Lanka; Timor-Leste; Türkiye; Turkmenistan; and Tuvalu.

e For urban population, refers to localities of 100,000 or more inhabitants.

f For 2000, the figure is an estimate based on the 2001 census. For 2002–2010 and 2012 onward, the figures are estimates based on the 2011 census and refer to 58 urban municipalities. For 2020 onward, data refer to 293 urban municipalities.

g For urban population, data for 2010 onward include non-Thai citizens who are listed in the civil registration.

Sources: For net international migration rate: United Nations. World Population Prospects 2024. https://population.un.org/wpp/Download/Standard/Migration/ (accessed 2 June 2025).
For urban population: economies' official sources; and United Nations. World Urbanization Prospects 2018. https://population.un.org/wup/Download/ (accessed 30 June 2025).

Table 2.1.3: Proportion of Total Population by Age Bracket, and Age Dependency Ratio

ADB Regional Member	Population Aged 0–14 Years (% of total population)				Population Aged 15–64 Years (% of total population)			
	2010	2015	2023	2024	2010	2015	2023	2024
Developing ADB Member Economies								
Central and West Asia	**34.9**	**34.3**	**33.3**	**33.0**	**60.4**	**60.9**	**61.1**	**61.2**
Afghanistan	48.5	46.3	43.2	42.9	49.2	51.4	54.4	54.7
Armenia	19.3	20.1	19.5	19.2	70.0	69.0	67.2	67.1
Azerbaijan	22.3	23.5	22.3	21.8	71.8	70.8	69.6	69.6
Georgia	18.6	19.4	21.0	20.8	67.7	66.4	63.6	63.6
Kazakhstan	25.4	27.7	29.5	29.4	68.1	65.6	62.2	62.0
Kyrgyz Republic	30.3	31.8	32.7	32.3	65.3	63.2	61.9	62.0
Pakistan	39.3	38.8	37.0	36.7	57.0	57.4	58.8	59.0
Tajikistan	36.8	36.3	36.5	36.3	60.0	60.7	59.8	59.9
Türkiye	25.9	23.9	21.8	21.4	66.9	68.5	68.2	68.3
Turkmenistan	30.3	29.7	31.7	31.5	65.9	66.7	64.1	64.0
Uzbekistan	28.9	28.3	30.9	31.1	66.3	67.0	63.4	63.0
East Asia	**18.3**	**18.1**	**16.3**	**15.8**	**72.9**	**71.7**	**69.1**	**69.3**
China, People's Republic of	18.5	18.3	16.6	16.0	72.9	71.6	69.1	69.3
Hong Kong, China	12.2	11.5	10.7	10.5	74.6	73.1	67.7	66.8
Korea, Republic of	16.4	13.8	11.0	10.6	72.6	73.3	70.7	70.2
Mongolia	27.9	29.5	32.6	32.2	68.3	66.6	62.5	62.7
Taipei,China	15.5	13.7	11.9	11.7	73.7	73.9	69.7	69.1
South Asia	**31.6**	**29.2**	**25.4**	**25.0**	**63.5**	**65.4**	**67.7**	**67.9**
Bangladesh	34.1	31.2	28.4	28.0	61.7	63.9	65.3	65.5
Bhutan	29.4	27.0	21.5	20.9	65.5	67.4	72.2	72.6
India	31.3	28.9	25.1	24.6	63.7	65.6	68.0	68.2
Maldives	25.7	23.2	20.0	19.6	69.9	72.8	75.6	75.8
Nepal	36.0	33.0	28.7	28.4	59.3	61.5	64.9	65.1
Sri Lanka	25.4	24.7	22.4	22.0	67.2	66.3	65.9	65.9
Southeast Asia	**27.9**	**26.6**	**24.3**	**23.9**	**66.4**	**67.2**	**67.9**	**68.0**
Brunei Darussalam	25.3	23.6	21.0	20.8	71.2	72.3	72.5	72.3
Cambodia	33.3	31.9	30.1	29.8	62.8	63.5	63.9	64.0
Indonesia	27.9	27.0	24.9	24.6	66.2	67.0	68.0	68.1
Lao People's Democratic Republic	36.3	33.2	30.6	30.2	59.9	62.6	64.9	65.1
Malaysia	27.9	25.8	22.3	21.8	67.1	68.5	70.3	70.5
Myanmar	28.2	26.5	24.5	24.3	66.5	67.9	68.4	68.4
Philippines	35.6	33.5	28.6	27.9	61.1	62.7	66.1	66.6
Singapore	14.1	12.7	11.8	11.7	78.5	78.3	75.1	74.7
Thailand	20.1	18.1	15.1	14.7	71.3	71.6	70.2	69.9
Timor-Leste	41.6	39.1	34.2	33.7	54.0	55.6	60.4	61.1
Viet Nam	24.6	24.0	23.6	23.2	69.4	69.6	67.8	67.7
The Pacific	**37.0**	**35.9**	**33.8**	**33.4**	**59.9**	**60.9**	**62.5**	**62.7**
Cook Islands	27.0	25.1	24.8	24.3	64.7	65.1	62.3	61.9
Fiji	30.8	29.6	27.4	27.1	64.7	65.2	66.3	66.4
Kiribati	36.6	35.2	34.9	34.7	59.8	61.1	61.0	61.1
Marshall Islands	39.7	37.5	34.7	34.5	58.3	59.7	60.9	60.9
Micronesia, Federated States of	35.7	34.0	32.1	31.8	61.1	62.1	62.1	62.2
Nauru	36.3	38.2	38.2	37.8	62.4	60.3	59.1	59.4
Niue	26.1	26.1	23.4	22.9	61.3	61.3	60.7	60.8
Palau	21.0	20.3	18.5	18.2	72.9	72.1	70.6	70.4
Papua New Guinea	37.5	36.2	33.8	33.5	59.8	61.0	62.8	63.1
Samoa	38.4	38.1	38.7	38.5	56.7	57.1	55.6	55.7
Solomon Islands	41.0	40.0	37.4	37.0	55.5	56.5	59.0	59.4
Tonga	37.6	36.7	35.6	35.4	56.6	57.3	57.8	57.9
Tuvalu	32.8	31.9	32.6	32.9	61.8	62.7	61.1	60.4
Vanuatu	38.2	38.5	38.6	38.3	58.6	57.7	57.2	57.4
Developed ADB Member Economies	**14.4**	**14.0**	**13.0**	**12.8**	**64.2**	**61.3**	**60.0**	**59.9**
Australia	19.1	18.9	18.0	17.8	67.4	66.2	64.6	64.4
Japan	13.4	12.8	11.6	11.4	63.5	60.2	58.8	58.8
New Zealand	20.9	19.9	18.4	18.1	66.2	65.6	64.8	64.7
DEVELOPING ADB MEMBER ECONOMIES	**26.5**	**25.3**	**23.0**	**22.5**	**67.1**	**67.5**	**67.5**	**67.6**
ALL ADB REGIONAL MEMBERS	**26.0**	**24.9**	**22.6**	**22.2**	**67.0**	**67.3**	**67.2**	**67.4**
WORLD	**27.3**	**26.6**	**25.0**	**24.7**	**65.2**	**65.1**	**65.0**	**65.1**

continued on next page

Table 2.1.3: Proportion of Total Population by Age Bracket, and Age Dependency Ratio *(continued)*

ADB Regional Member	Population Aged 65 Years and Older (% of total population)				Age Dependency Ratio for Total Population			
	2010	2015	2023	2024	2010	2015	2023	2024
Developing ADB Member Economies								
Central and West Asia	**4.7**	**4.8**	**5.6**	**5.8**	**65.6**	**64.3**	**63.7**	**63.4**
Afghanistan	2.3	2.4	2.4	2.4	103.1	94.6	83.8	82.8
Armenia	10.7	10.9	13.2	13.7	42.9	45.0	48.7	49.1
Azerbaijan	5.9	5.8	8.0	8.6	39.3	41.3	43.6	43.6
Georgia	13.8	14.1	15.3	15.6	47.7	50.5	57.1	57.3
Kazakhstan	6.5	6.8	8.3	8.7	46.8	52.5	60.9	61.4
Kyrgyz Republic	4.4	5.0	5.4	5.7	53.1	58.2	61.5	61.4
Pakistan	3.7	3.8	4.2	4.3	75.5	74.2	70.2	69.4
Tajikistan	3.2	3.0	3.7	3.9	66.7	64.7	67.1	67.0
Türkiye	7.2	7.6	10.0	10.3	49.5	45.9	46.7	46.5
Turkmenistan	3.8	3.6	4.3	4.5	51.7	49.9	56.1	56.3
Uzbekistan	4.8	4.7	5.7	5.9	50.9	49.3	57.6	58.6
East Asia	**8.8**	**10.2**	**14.5**	**14.9**	**37.2**	**39.4**	**44.6**	**44.2**
China, People's Republic of	8.7	10.1	14.3	14.7	37.2	39.6	44.7	44.2
Hong Kong, China	13.2	15.4	21.6	22.7	34.1	36.8	47.8	49.6
Korea, Republic of	11.0	13.0	18.3	19.3	37.7	36.5	41.5	42.5
Mongolia	3.8	3.8	4.9	5.1	46.5	50.1	60.0	59.6
Taipei,China	10.8	12.4	18.3	19.2	35.6	35.3	43.4	44.7
South Asia	**4.9**	**5.5**	**6.9**	**7.1**	**57.5**	**53.0**	**47.8**	**47.4**
Bangladesh	4.2	4.9	6.3	6.5	62.0	56.5	53.1	52.6
Bhutan	5.1	5.6	6.4	6.5	52.8	48.3	38.6	37.7
India	4.9	5.5	6.9	7.1	56.9	52.4	47.0	46.6
Maldives	4.4	4.0	4.3	4.6	43.1	37.4	32.3	32.0
Nepal	4.7	5.5	6.4	6.5	68.7	62.7	54.0	53.7
Sri Lanka	7.4	9.0	11.7	12.1	48.9	50.8	51.7	51.8
Southeast Asia	**5.6**	**6.1**	**7.8**	**8.1**	**50.6**	**48.7**	**47.2**	**47.0**
Brunei Darussalam	3.4	4.2	6.5	6.9	40.4	38.4	38.0	38.3
Cambodia	3.9	4.6	6.0	6.2	59.1	57.5	56.4	56.1
Indonesia	5.9	6.1	7.0	7.3	51.1	49.4	47.0	46.8
Lao People's Democratic Republic	3.8	4.1	4.5	4.7	66.9	59.7	54.1	53.5
Malaysia	4.9	5.7	7.5	7.7	49.0	46.0	42.3	41.9
Myanmar	5.2	5.6	7.1	7.3	50.4	47.3	46.2	46.2
Philippines	3.3	3.8	5.3	5.5	63.8	59.5	51.2	50.1
Singapore	7.3	9.0	13.1	13.7	27.3	27.7	33.1	33.9
Thailand	8.6	10.3	14.7	15.4	40.3	39.7	42.5	43.1
Timor-Leste	4.4	5.3	5.3	5.3	85.2	79.8	65.5	63.8
Viet Nam	6.0	6.5	8.6	9.0	44.2	43.8	47.6	47.6
The Pacific	**3.0**	**3.2**	**3.7**	**3.8**	**66.8**	**64.2**	**59.9**	**59.4**
Cook Islands	8.3	9.8	12.9	13.7	54.5	53.5	60.5	61.4
Fiji	4.5	5.2	6.3	6.5	54.4	53.5	50.9	50.6
Kiribati	3.6	3.7	4.1	4.2	67.3	63.5	64.1	63.7
Marshall Islands	2.1	2.8	4.4	4.6	71.6	67.4	64.2	64.2
Micronesia, Federated States of	3.3	3.9	5.7	5.9	63.7	61.1	60.9	60.8
Nauru	1.3	1.5	2.7	2.9	60.4	65.9	69.1	68.4
Niue	12.6	12.7	15.9	16.3	63.1	63.2	64.6	64.5
Palau	6.1	7.5	10.9	11.3	37.2	38.6	41.6	42.0
Papua New Guinea	2.7	2.8	3.3	3.5	67.2	64.0	59.1	58.6
Samoa	4.9	4.9	5.7	5.9	76.4	75.3	80.0	79.7
Solomon Islands	3.5	3.5	3.6	3.6	80.1	76.9	69.5	68.4
Tonga	5.8	6.0	6.6	6.7	76.5	74.6	73.1	72.8
Tuvalu	5.4	5.4	6.3	6.7	61.9	59.6	63.6	65.6
Vanuatu	3.2	3.7	4.2	4.3	70.8	73.2	74.9	74.2
Developed ADB Member Economies	**21.4**	**24.7**	**27.1**	**27.3**	**55.9**	**63.1**	**66.7**	**66.8**
Australia	13.5	14.9	17.4	17.7	48.4	51.1	54.8	55.2
Japan	23.1	26.9	29.6	29.8	57.4	66.0	70.1	70.1
New Zealand	13.0	14.6	16.8	17.2	51.2	52.5	54.3	54.6
DEVELOPING ADB MEMBER ECONOMIES	**6.4**	**7.2**	**9.5**	**9.8**	**49.0**	**48.2**	**48.2**	**47.8**
ALL ADB REGIONAL MEMBERS	**7.0**	**7.9**	**10.2**	**10.4**	**49.3**	**48.7**	**48.8**	**48.4**
WORLD	**7.6**	**8.3**	**10.0**	**10.2**	**53.5**	**53.5**	**53.9**	**53.7**

ADB = Asian Development Bank.

Notes:
1. All figures presented in this table are ADB estimates using data from the United Nations' World Population Prospects 2024.
2. United Nations population estimates are based on all available sources of data on population size and levels of fertility, mortality, and international migration for 237 distinct economies or areas comprising the total population of the world.

Source: United Nations. World Population Prospects 2024. https://population.un.org/wpp/ (accessed 2 June 2025).

Table 2.1.4: Labor Force Participation Rates
(%)

ADB Regional Member	2010	2015	2019	2020	2021	2022	2023	2024
Developing ADB Member Economies								
Central and West Asia								
Afghanistan[a,b]	49.8 (2011)	55.4 (2013)	53.9 (2017)	41.9	...	...	...	...
Armenia[c]	61.2	62.5	59.9	58.5	57.8	58.8	60.3	...
Azerbaijan[c]	64.8	65.4	65.7	65.8	65.8	65.7	65.5	...
Georgia[c]	51.5	55.5	51.8	50.5	50.9	51.9	53.3	55.0
Kazakhstan[c]	71.2	69.7	70.1	69.2	69.3	68.7	68.5	68.2
Kyrgyz Republic	64.2	62.4	60.2	60.1	60.3	60.1	58.7	...
Pakistan	45.9	45.2	44.8	...	44.9	...	...	...
Tajikistan	50.1	47.1	45.2	45.6	45.4	45.2	45.2	...
Türkiye	46.3	51.1	52.9	49.1	51.4	53.1	53.3	54.2
Turkmenistan[d]	49.8	48.2	47.8	46.5	46.7	47.8	47.7	47.6
Uzbekistan[c]	70.7	71.9	75.0	73.8	74.1	73.7	72.9	72.3
East Asia								
China, People's Republic of[d]	71.0	69.3	67.4	66.0	67.1	65.8	65.8	65.4
Hong Kong, China	59.6	61.1	60.7	59.7	59.4	58.2	57.3	57.0
Korea, Republic of	61.1	62.8	63.3	62.5	62.8	63.9	64.3	64.5
Mongolia[c]	61.6	61.5	62.8	61.1	59.1	60.3	59.5	61.3
Taipei,China	58.1	58.7	59.2	59.1	59.0	59.2	59.2	59.3
South Asia								
Bangladesh	59.3	57.1 (2013)	58.2 (2017)	...	...	61.2	60.9	...
Bhutan[e]	68.6	63.1	66.4	67.8	69.1	63.1	65.0	63.9
India	57.1	...	50.2	53.5	54.9	55.2	57.9	60.1
Maldives[f]	52.1	63.8 (2014)	60.2	...	...	64.2	...	...
Nepal[c]	74.3 (2012)	72.2 (2014)	38.5 (2018)	...	...	...	...	...
Sri Lanka	48.6	53.8	52.3	50.6	49.9	49.8	48.6	...
Southeast Asia								
Brunei Darussalam[c]	68.9 (2011)	65.6 (2014)	64.6	65.5	63.8	62.7	63.6	64.1
Cambodia	87.0	82.7	87.4	...	84.0	...	...	...
Indonesia	67.7	65.8	67.5	67.8	67.8	68.6	69.5	70.6
Lao People's Democratic Republic[c]	79.2	...	40.8 (2017)	...	...	47.1	...	...
Malaysia[c]	63.7	67.9	68.7	68.4	68.6	69.3	70.0	70.6
Myanmar	67.0	64.7	63.2	59.9	60.3	60.7	...	...
Philippines	64.1	63.7	61.3	59.5	63.3	64.7	64.9	64.4
Singapore[g]	66.2	68.3	68.0	68.1	70.5	70.0	68.6	68.2
Thailand[h]	72.3	69.8	67.5	67.8	67.8	68.1	68.6	68.2
Timor-Leste[c]	24.0	30.6 (2013)	...	...	30.5	...	...	...
Viet Nam[c]	76.7	77.4	76.8	74.4	67.8	68.6	68.9	68.1
The Pacific								
Cook Islands	71.0 (2011)	...	70.4	...	68.1	...	...	...
Fiji[i]	62.0	58.2	57.4	55.5	55.4	57.6	...	51.2
Kiribati	59.3	66.0	...	53.0	...	...	...	...
Marshall Islands	41.7 (2011)	...	...	...	...	...	...	...
Micronesia, Federated States of	57.3	56.9 (2014)	...	...	...	...	...	...
Nauru[b,d]	64.0 (2011)	68.7 (2013)	63.0	...	67.0	...	...	...
Niue	68.9 (2011)	...	68.6 (2017)	...	...	70.7	...	...
Palau	68.1 (2012)	77.4	...	76.9	...	...	...	...
Papua New Guinea[d]	48.3	49.7	50.9	50.8	51.4	52.0	52.0	52.0
Samoa[b]	41.3 (2011)	...	43.3 (2017)	...	43.4	43.8	...	...
Solomon Islands	62.9 (2009)	...	55.4	...	...	...	...	...
Tonga	52.3 (2011)	...	46.7 (2018)	...	48.5	...	44.7	...
Tuvalu	59.4 (2012)	...	...	...	...	...	...	...
Vanuatu[d]	64.4	61.2	58.6	58.0	57.9	58.7	58.7	58.4
Developed ADB Member Economies								
Australia	65.4	65.0	65.8	64.7	65.6	66.4	66.7	66.9
Japan	59.6	59.6	62.1	62.0	62.1	62.5	62.9	63.3
New Zealand	67.6	68.8	70.5	70.2	70.8	71.3	72.1	71.3

... = data not available, ADB = Asian Development Bank.

Note: Based on varying concepts and definitions of "labor force" across economies.

a For 2017, data cover the period from April 2016 to April 2017. For 2020, data cover the period from October 2019 to September 2020.
b Figures for different years may not be directly comparable with each other due to changes in methodology and labor concepts adopted.
c Recommendations from the 19th International Conference of Labour Statisticians were adopted by: Armenia, beginning 2018; Azerbaijan, beginning 2015; Brunei Darussalam, beginning 2017; Georgia, beginning 2010; Kazakhstan, beginning 2015; the Lao People's Democratic Republic, for 2017; Malaysia, beginning 2019; Mongolia, beginning 2019; Nepal, for 2018; Timor-Leste, beginning 2010; Uzbekistan, beginning 2017; and Viet Nam, beginning 2021. Hence, data for these years may not be directly comparable with data in other years. The 19th conference provided the statistical concept of work for reference purposes; and the operational concepts, definitions, and guidelines for (i) three distinct subsets of work activities, referred to as forms of work, which include own-use production work, employment work, and volunteer work; (ii) related classifications of the population according to their labor force status and main work status; and (iii) measures of labor underutilization. The concept of employment has also been refined to refer to work for pay or profit.
d Data refer to estimates modeled by the International Labour Organization.
e For 2017, data are from the census of population. For all other years, data are from labor force surveys. Thus, data prior to and after the census year may not be directly comparable with 2017 data.
f Includes local population only.
g Refers to Singapore residents only.
h Includes the seasonally inactive labor force.
i For 2017, the reported number of employed people excludes those who are engaged in unpaid employment as of end of June. Hence, data for 2014 and 2016 are not comparable with data for 2017 because the former years include unpaid employment.

Sources: Economies' official sources. For Nauru (2013), Papua New Guinea, the People's Republic of China, Turkmenistan, and Vanuatu: International Labour Organization. ILOSTAT Database. http://www.ilo.org/ilostat/ (accessed 8 July 2025). For Tuvalu (2016): Pacific Data Hub. Explorer: National Minimum Development Indicators. https://stats.pacificdata.org/vis?lc=en&df[ds]=SPC2&df[id]=DF_NMDI&df[ag]=SPC&df[vs]=1.0&dq=A..NMDI0014%2BOTH._T._T._T..&pd=2010%2C2020&ly[rw]=GEO_PICT&ly[cl]=TIME_PERIOD&fs[0]=Development%20indicators%2C0%7CNational%20Minimum%20Development%20Indicators%23NMDI%23&pg=0&fc=Development%20indicators&lo=1 (accessed 8 July 2025).

Labor Force and Employment

Table 2.1.5: Employment in Agriculture, Industry, and Services
(% of total employment)

ADB Regional Member	Agriculture						
	2010	2015	2020	2021	2022	2023	2024
Developing ADB Member Economies							
Central and West Asia							
Afghanistan[a]	69.6 (2004)	43.6 (2017)	44.5	…	…	…	…
Armenia[b]	38.6	35.3	21.8	21.8	22.0	19.2	…
Azerbaijan[b]	38.2	36.4	35.9	35.9	35.8	35.8	35.4
Georgia[b,c]	26.2	23.0	19.8	18.9	17.9	16.5	16.0
Kazakhstan	28.3	16.2	13.5	13.4	12.4	11.9	11.2
Kyrgyz Republic	31.2	29.3	18.3	18.3	17.8	17.1	…
Pakistan	45.0	42.3	39.2 (2019)	37.5	…	…	…
Tajikistan	65.9	64.9	60.9	60.6	63.2	61.7	…
Türkiye	23.3	20.2	17.7	17.2	15.8	14.8	14.8
Turkmenistan	31.2	26.7	23.5	23.3	22.8	22.2	…
Uzbekistan[b]	26.8	27.6	26.4	25.2	25.1	23.9	22.9
East Asia							
China, People's Republic of[d]	36.7	28.1	23.6	22.9	24.1	22.8	22.2
Hong Kong, China[e]	–	–	–	–	–	–	–
Korea, Republic of	6.6	5.1	5.4	5.3	5.4	5.3	5.2
Mongolia[b]	33.5	28.5	28.2	28.7	27.3	27.9	22.5
Taipei,China	5.2	5.0	4.8	4.7	4.6	4.4	4.3
South Asia							
Bangladesh	47.5	42.7 (2016)	…	…	45.4	44.4	…
Bhutan	59.4	58.0	49.9	49.2	43.5	…	41.7
India	49.6	…	…	…	…	…	…
Maldives[f]	4.3	9.0 (2016)	7.4 (2019)	…	4.8	…	…
Nepal[b]	73.9 (2008)	64.0 (2011)	21.5 (2018)	…	…	…	…
Sri Lanka[g]	32.5	28.7	27.1	27.3	26.5	26.1	…
Southeast Asia							
Brunei Darussalam[b]	1.4 (2001)	0.5 (2014)	1.3	1.4	1.5	1.3	…
Cambodia	72.3	64.3 (2014)	33.1 (2019)	35.7	…	…	…
Indonesia	38.3	32.9	29.8	28.3	28.6	28.2	28.2
Lao People's Democratic Republic[b]	72.2	31.3 (2017)	…	…	56.8	…	…
Malaysia[b]	13.6	12.5	9.9	9.5	9.3	9.1	9.0
Myanmar	…	51.7	45.3 (2019)	…	…	…	…
Philippines	33.2	29.2	24.8	24.2	23.1	23.2	…
Singapore[h]	0.1	0.1	0.1	0.1	0.1	0.0	0.1
Thailand	38.2	32.3	31.3	31.9	30.4	30.2	28.9
Timor-Leste[b]	26.3	31.6 (2016)	…	28.4	…	…	…
Viet Nam[i]	48.6	43.6	33.1	29.1	27.5	26.9	26.0
The Pacific							
Cook Islands[j]	4.9 (2006)	5.3 (2016)	2.5 (2019)	3.8	…	…	…
Fiji[k]	1.7	19.2 (2016)	3.6	…	…	…	23.3
Kiribati[l]	22.1	24.3	23.2	…	…	…	…
Marshall Islands	0.9	0.9	0.8	0.7	0.7	…	…
Micronesia, Federated States of	52.2 (2000)	1.7	2.4	2.1	1.9	2.2	…
Nauru	…	…	0.7 (2019)	1.6	…	…	…
Niue	15.9 (2006)	8.7 (2017)	…	…	10.4	…	…
Palau[m]	7.8 (2005)	6.4	5.1	…	…	…	…
Papua New Guinea	25.7	30.1	36.1	37.3	38.7	38.7	…
Samoa	35.4 (2006)	41.9 (2016)	…	35.3	30.0	…	…
Solomon Islands[n]	41.5 (2009)	…	68.4 (2019)	…	…	…	…
Tonga	27.9 (2006)	24.1 (2016)	20.0 (2018)	7.9	…	12.9	…
Tuvalu	…	…	…	…	…	…	…
Vanuatu	…	…	…	…	…	…	…
Developed ADB Member Economies							
Australia	3.2	2.6	2.8	2.5	2.2	2.2	2.2
Japan	4.0	3.6	3.2	3.1	3.0	2.9	2.8
New Zealand	6.7	6.2	6.0	6.1	6.0	5.6	5.5

continued on next page

Table 2.1.5: Employment in Agriculture, Industry, and Services *(continued)*
(% of total employment)

ADB Regional Member	Industry						
	2010	2015	2020	2021	2022	2023	2024
Developing ADB Member Economies							
Central and West Asia							
Afghanistan[a]	6.2 (2004)	...	18.1	...	...	...	...
Armenia[b]	17.4	15.9	21.0	22.1	21.9	23.4	...
Azerbaijan[b]	13.7	14.1	15.1	15.3	15.4	15.7	16.1
Georgia[b,c]	10.5	10.1	18.2	19.0	20.3	21.0	21.7
Kazakhstan	18.7	21.0	19.7	19.7	19.8	19.4	18.8
Kyrgyz Republic	21.1	20.9	25.9	26.7	26.3	25.9	...
Pakistan	20.9	23.6	24.0 (2019)	25.4	...	...	...
Tajikistan	7.9	6.7	9.1	9.0	9.1	9.0	...
Türkiye	27.7	27.4	26.3	27.5	27.7	27.5	27.3
Turkmenistan	28.5	31.0	33.2	33.3	33.3	33.7	...
Uzbekistan[b]	22.7	22.9	23.5	23.7	22.8	23.8	21.8
East Asia							
China, People's Republic of[d]	28.7	29.7	28.7	29.1	28.8	29.1	29.0
Hong Kong, China[e]	11.2	11.4	11.1	11.4	11.6	11.9	11.9
Korea, Republic of	25.0	25.4	24.7	24.6	24.5	24.0	23.7
Mongolia[b]	16.2	20.3	20.2	22.2	23.4	22.8	22.9
Taipei,China	35.9	36.0	35.4	35.5	35.4	35.1	34.9
South Asia							
Bangladesh	17.6	...	...	...	17.0	17.3	...
Bhutan	6.6	9.6	14.9	15.4	15.1	...	16.3
India	20.0	...	...	...	...	...	...
Maldives[f]	9.4	...	18.0 (2019)	...	17.1	...	...
Nepal[b]	10.8 (2008)	...	30.8 (2018)	...	...	...	...
Sri Lanka[g]	24.6	25.8	26.9	26.0	26.5	25.5	...
Southeast Asia							
Brunei Darussalam[b]	21.4 (2001)	...	23.5	23.6	21.5	20.5	...
Cambodia	9.2	...	27.0 (2019)	27.3	...	...	...
Indonesia	19.3	22.2	21.6	22.3	22.2	22.2	22.2
Lao People's Democratic Republic[b]	8.1	...	...	...	10.2	...	...
Malaysia[b]	28.3	27.5	26.4	26.2	26.4	26.2	26.4
Myanmar	...	15.8	15.7 (2019)	...	...	...	...
Philippines	15.0	16.2	18.3	18.4	18.2	17.5	...
Singapore[h]	14.1	10.5	9.2	9.5	9.4	8.5	8.6
Thailand	20.8	23.7	22.6	22.2	22.2	21.9	22.2
Timor-Leste[b]	14.3	...	...	14.2	...	...	...
Viet Nam[i]	21.7	23.0	30.8	33.1	33.4	33.5	32.9
The Pacific							
Cook Islands[j]	14.2 (2006)	...	11.3 (2019)	11.9	...	...	...
Fiji[k]	23.9	...	24.7	...	...	...	14.5
Kiribati[l]	16.1	18.2	5.6	...	...	...	...
Marshall Islands	21.8	14.8	14.4	12.8	12.3	...	...
Micronesia, Federated States of	...	9.0	8.2	7.7	7.5	8.0	...
Nauru	...	...	12.0 (2019)	20.7	...	...	...
Niue	17.1 (2006)	...	...	...	11.7	...	...
Palau[m]	2.6 (2005)	11.7	14.8	...	...	...	...
Papua New Guinea	7.5	7.6	7.5	7.6	7.6	7.9	...
Samoa	21.8 (2006)	...	...	10.3	13.2	...	...
Solomon Islands[n]	13.7 (2009)	...	6.5 (2019)	...	...	...	...
Tonga	27.8 (2006)	...	29.7 (2018)	16.7	...	26.7	...
Tuvalu	...	...	...	...	...	...	...
Vanuatu	...	...	...	...	...	...	...
Developed ADB Member Economies							
Australia	21.0	19.4	19.4	18.9	18.7	19.1	18.9
Japan	25.4	24.6	23.5	23.3	23.2	23.3	22.9
New Zealand	20.7	21.7	20.4	20.0	20.8	20.5	20.1

continued on next page

Table 2.1.5: Employment in Agriculture, Industry, and Services *(continued)*
(% of total employment)

ADB Regional Member	Employment in Services (% of total employment)						
	2010	2015	2020	2021	2022	2023	2024
Developing ADB Member Economies							
Central and West Asia							
Afghanistan[a]	24.2 (2004)	…	36.7	…	…	…	…
Armenia[b]	44.0	48.8	57.2	56.0	56.1	57.4	…
Azerbaijan[b]	48.1	49.6	49.0	48.8	48.8	48.5	48.5
Georgia[b,c]	63.3	66.8	61.9	62.1	61.8	62.4	62.3
Kazakhstan	53.0	62.8	66.8	66.9	67.8	68.7	70.1
Kyrgyz Republic	47.7	49.8	55.9	54.9	55.8	57.0	…
Pakistan	34.2	34.2	36.8 (2019)	37.2	…	…	…
Tajikistan	26.3	28.4	30.0	30.4	27.7	29.3	…
Türkiye	49.0	52.4	55.9	55.3	56.5	57.6	57.9
Turkmenistan	40.3	42.4	43.4	43.4	44.0	44.1	…
Uzbekistan[b]	50.5	49.5	50.0	51.0	52.1	52.3	55.4
East Asia							
China, People's Republic of[d]	34.6	42.3	47.7	48.0	47.1	48.1	48.8
Hong Kong, China[e]	88.9	88.5	88.6	88.6	88.3	87.9	88.0
Korea, Republic of	68.4	69.5	70.0	70.1	70.1	70.7	71.1
Mongolia[b]	50.2	51.3	51.7	49.1	49.3	49.3	54.7
Taipei,China	58.8	59.0	59.8	59.8	60.0	60.5	60.8
South Asia							
Bangladesh	35.3	…	…	…	37.7	38.3	…
Bhutan	33.7	32.4	35.2	35.4	41.4	…	42.0
India	23.6	…	…	…	…	…	…
Maldives[f]	86.3	…	74.6 (2019)	…	78.1	…	…
Nepal[b]	15.3 (2008)	…	47.7 (2018)	…	…	…	…
Sri Lanka[g]	42.9	45.6	46.0	46.7	47.0	48.4	…
Southeast Asia							
Brunei Darussalam[b]	77.2 (2001)	…	75.1	75.0	77.0	78.2	…
Cambodia	18.6	…	39.8 (2019)	37.0	…	…	…
Indonesia	42.3	44.9	48.7	49.3	49.2	49.6	49.6
Lao People's Democratic Republic[b]	19.7	…	…	…	33.0	…	…
Malaysia[b]	58.1	60.0	63.7	64.3	64.3	64.7	64.6
Myanmar	…	32.5	39.0 (2019)	…	…	…	…
Philippines	51.8	54.6	56.9	57.4	58.7	59.3	…
Singapore[h]	50.2	50.5	52.9	56.0	54.9	52.7	51.9
Thailand	41.0	44.0	46.1	45.9	47.4	47.9	48.8
Timor-Leste[b]	59.4	…	…	62.8	…	…	…
Viet Nam[i]	29.7	33.4	36.1	37.8	39.0	39.6	39.4
The Pacific							
Cook Islands[j]	80.9 (2006)	…	86.3 (2019)	84.3	…	…	…
Fiji[k]	74.4	…	71.6	…	…	…	62.2
Kiribati[l]	61.8	57.5	71.2	…	…	…	…
Marshall Islands	75.5	84.3	84.8	85.7	86.1	…	…
Micronesia, Federated States of	…	89.3	89.3	90.2	90.6	89.8	…
Nauru	…	…	86.3 (2019)	77.7	…	…	…
Niue	66.9 (2006)	…	…	…	78.1	…	…
Palau[m]	89.6 (2005)	82.0	80.1	…	…	…	…
Papua New Guinea	66.7	62.3	56.4	55.1	53.8	53.4	…
Samoa	42.8 (2006)	…	…	54.4	56.9	…	…
Solomon Islands[n]	44.8 (2009)	…	25.2 (2019)	…	…	…	…
Tonga	44.3 (2006)	…	50.3 (2018)	75.4	…	60.4	…
Tuvalu	…	…	…	…	…	…	…
Vanuatu	…	…	…	…	…	…	…
Developed ADB Member Economies							
Australia	75.9	78.0	77.9	78.6	79.1	78.8	78.9
Japan	70.5	71.8	73.3	73.6	73.8	73.8	74.2
New Zealand	72.6	72.1	73.6	73.9	73.2	73.8	74.4

… = data not available, 0.0 = magnitude is less than half of unit employed, – = magnitude equals zero, ADB = Asian Development Bank.

Note: Data are based on varying labor force concepts and definitions adopted by different economies. Some values may not add up to 100% due to limitations on data availability.

a For 2017, data cover the period from April 2016 to April 2017. For 2020, data cover the period from October 2019 to September 2020. For 2011 onward, different methodologies were used in surveys for labor force estimation, therefore, data are not directly comparable overtime.
b Recommendations from the 19th International Conference of Labour Statisticians have been adopted by: Armenia, beginning 2018; Azerbaijan, beginning 2015; Brunei Darussalam, beginning 2017; Georgia, beginning 2010; the Lao People's Democratic Republic, for 2017; Malaysia, beginning 2019; Mongolia, beginning 2019; Nepal, for 2018; Timor-Leste, beginning 2010; and Uzbekistan, beginning 2017. Hence, data for these years may not be directly comparable with data for other years. The 19th conference provided the statistical concept of work for reference purposes; and the operational concepts, definitions, and guidelines for (i) three distinct subsets of work activities, referred to as forms of work, which include own-use production work, employment work, and volunteer work; (ii) related classifications of the population according to their labor force status and main work status; and (iii) measures of labor underutilization. The concept of employment has also been refined to refer to work for pay or profit.
c Prior to 2017, employment in services includes people who were engaged in construction industries.
d Refers to persons engaged in social labor and receiving remuneration or earning business income.
e Employment in services includes people who are engaged in electricity and gas supply; water supply; and sewerage, waste management, and remediation activities.
f Figures include local population only. For 2010, employment in services includes people who were engaged in industries other than agriculture, forestry, and fishing; mining and quarrying; or manufacturing.
g Some data may not add up because data for 2010 exclude the northern and eastern provinces.
h Refers to Singapore residents only.
i Refers to total number of persons engaged in any activity regardless of age.
j Covers all wage and salary earners from all islands.
k For 2010 and 2018, the reported number of employed people excludes those who are engaged in unpaid employment as of end of June. For 2016, figures are not comparable with other years because they include unpaid employment.
l Refers to cash work and unpaid village work. For 2010, employment in agriculture includes people who were engaged in mining and quarrying.
m For 2005, employment in services includes people who were engaged in electricity, gas, water, and construction industries.
n For 2009, the figure refers to paid employment.

Source: Asian Development Bank estimates using data from economies' official sources.

Table 2.1.6: Poverty and Inequality

ADB Regional Member	Proportion of Population Living on Less Than $3.00 a Day (2021 PPP)[a] (%)			Proportion of Population Living on Less Than $4.20 a Day (2021 PPP)[a] (%)			Income Ratio of Highest 20% to Lowest 20%[b]			Gini Coefficient[c]		
	2010	2015	2022	2010	2015	2022	2010	2015	2022	2010	2015	2022
Developing ADB Member Economies												
Central and West Asia												
Afghanistan	...	...	...	...	...	...	...	...	...	...	...	...
Armenia	2.9	2.9	1.9(2023)	14.1	9.5	8.4(2023)	4.3	5.0	3.9(2023)	0.300	0.324	0.272(2023)
Azerbaijan[d]	0.0(2005)	...	...	0.3(2005)	...	...	3.5(2005)	...	...	0.266(2005)	...	...
Georgia	23.6	10.6	5.8(2023)	39.5	23.8	14.0(2023)	8.0	6.5	6.0(2023)	0.395	0.365	0.348(2023)
Kazakhstan	0.5	0.1	0.0(2021)	3.0	0.7	0.3(2021)	4.0	3.7	4.0(2021)	0.280	0.268	0.292(2021)
Kyrgyz Republic	12.6	11.0	4.5	32.9	34.6	22.1	4.5	4.1	3.6	0.301	0.290	0.264
Pakistan[e]	26.7	16.9	16.5(2018)	57.2	44.8	44.7(2018)	3.9	4.4	4.1(2018)	0.288	0.313	0.296(2018)
Tajikistan	15.8(2009)	13.3	...	37.1(2009)	29.8	...	4.7(2009)	5.6	...	0.308(2009)	0.340	...
Türkiye	2.8	1.3	1.2(2019)	6.5	4.1	3.7(2019)	7.7	8.8	9.4	0.388	0.429	0.419(2019)
Turkmenistan	...	...	...	...	...	...	...	...	...	...	...	...
Uzbekistan	93.3(2003)	...	...	97.2(2003)	...	...	5.8(2003)	...	6.5(2023)	0.352(2003)	...	...
East Asia												
China, People's Republic of	20.6	3.0	0.0(2021)	34.9	10.9	0.3(2021)	9.6	7.1	5.9(2021)	0.437	0.386	0.357(2021)
Hong Kong, China	...	...	...	...	...	...	...	...	...	...	...	...
Korea, Republic of	0.5	0.2(2014)	0.2(2021)	1.0	0.5(2014)	0.2(2021)	5.4	5.2(2014)	5.2(2016)	0.320	0.312(2014)	0.329(2021)
Mongolia	3.5	0.8(2014)	0.4	12.1	4.0(2014)	2.3	5.3	5.0(2014)	4.9	0.331	0.320(2014)	0.314
Taipei,China	0.2	0.2(2013)	0.0(2021)	0.2	0.2(2013)	0.0(2021)	4.3	3.9	3.8(2023)	0.332	0.325(2013)	0.316(2021)
South Asia												
Bangladesh	25.1	...	8.0	52.1	...	24.4	4.7	...	5.1	0.321	...	0.334
Bhutan	12.0(2007)	3.6(2012)	0.0	26.8(2007)	12.1(2012)	0.5	6.7(2007)	6.9(2012)	4.2	0.381(2007)	0.388(2012)	0.285
India[e]	27.1(2011)	...	5.3	57.7(2011)	...	23.9	4.0(2011)	...	3.5	0.288(2011)	...	0.255
Maldives[e]	13.1(2009)	...	0.0(2019)	25.9(2009)	...	0.0(2019)	7.0(2009)	...	4.3(2019)	0.384(2009)	...	0.293(2019)
Nepal[e]	21.5	...	2.4	44.1	...	9.1	5.0	...	4.5	0.328	...	0.300
Sri Lanka	7.8(2009)	6.4(2012)	2.7(2019)	24.2(2009)	20.1(2012)	11.5(2019)	5.7(2009)	6.4(2012)	6.2(2019)	0.361(2009)	0.387(2012)	0.377(2019)
Southeast Asia												
Brunei Darussalam	...	...	...	...	...	...	...	...	...	...	...	...
Cambodia	...	...	...	...	...	...	...	...	...	...	...	...
Indonesia	34.1	21.6	5.4(2024)	56.7	43.4	19.9(2024)	5.3	6.3	5.4(2024)	0.346	0.382	0.349(2024)
Lao People's Democratic Republic[e]	36.0(2007)	21.7(2012)	15.7(2018)	61.1(2007)	43.2(2012)	35.0(2018)	5.5(2007)	5.8(2012)	6.6(2018)	0.354(2007)	0.360(2012)	0.388(2018)
Malaysia	0.4(2011)	0.1	0.0(2021)	1.9(2011)	0.4	0.1(2021)	9.5(2011)	8.2	7.9(2021)	0.439(2011)	0.411	0.407(2021)
Myanmar	...	18.2	...	...	40.6	...	...	6.3	4.5(2017)	...	0.381	...
Philippines[f]	22.0(2009)	14.6	5.3(2023)	38.9(2009)	30.7	16.9(2023)	9.9(2009)	9.1	6.8(2023)	0.463(2009)	0.446	0.393(2023)
Singapore	...	...	...	...	...	...	...	...	...	...	...	...
Thailand	0.7	0.1	0.0(2023)	3.8	0.8	0.2(2023)	7.0	5.8	5.3(2023)	0.394	0.360	0.335(2023)
Timor-Leste	60.3(2007)	44.2(2014)	...	81.9(2007)	71.6(2014)	...	3.9(2007)	4.1(2014)	...	0.278(2007)	0.287(2014)	...
Viet Nam	5.2	3.4(2014)	1.6	13.7	8.6(2014)	4.2	7.1	5.9(2014)	6.4	0.393	0.348(2014)	0.361
The Pacific												
Cook Islands	...	...	...	...	...	...	...	...	...	...	...	...
Fiji[e]	3.8(2008)	1.6(2013)	4.7(2019)	11.5(2008)	7.9(2013)	15.1(2019)	7.2(2008)	6.0(2013)	4.7(2019)	0.404(2008)	0.367(2013)	0.307(2019)
Kiribati	21.3(2006)	...	6.1(2019)	40.0(2006)	...	22.0(2019)	6.7(2006)	...	3.9(2019)	0.370(2006)	...	0.278(2019)
Marshall Islands	...	...	2.1(2019)	...	...	6.7(2019)	...	...	6.0(2019)	...	...	0.355(2019)
Micronesia, Federated States of	15.8(2005)	26.1(2013)	...	29.2(2005)	43.8(2013)	...	8.7(2005)	8.4(2013)	...	0.424(2005)	0.401(2013)	...
Nauru	...	9.7(2012)	...	...	21.7(2012)	...	...	5.1(2012)	...	...	0.324(2012)	...
Niue	...	...	...	...	...	...	...	...	...	...	...	...
Palau	...	...	...	...	...	...	...	...	...	...	...	...
Papua New Guinea[e]	52.2(2009)	...	...	69.4(2009)	...	...	9.3(2009)	...	...	0.419(2009)	...	...
Samoa[e]	3.7(2008)	4.5(2013)	...	12.3(2008)	11.5(2013)	...	7.7(2008)	6.8(2013)	...	0.420(2008)	0.387(2013)	...
Solomon Islands	62.2(2005)	40.3(2012)	...	75.9(2005)	62.9(2012)	...	10.4(2005)	6.4(2012)	...	0.461(2005)	0.371(2012)	...
Tonga	3.6(2009)	4.0	0.4(2021)	10.8(2009)	15.1	1.8(2021)	6.7(2009)	5.4	3.9(2021)	0.375(2009)	0.335	0.271(2021)
Tuvalu	9.0	...	...	21.2	...	...	7.0	...	...	0.391	...	...
Vanuatu	25.7	...	19.5(2019)	44.4	...	36.9(2019)	6.5	...	5.3(2019)	0.374	...	0.323(2019)
Developed ADB Member Economies												
Australia	...	...	...	...	...	...	5.8	5.5(2014)	5.6(2018)	0.347	0.344(2014)	0.343(2018)
Japan	...	...	...	...	...	...	5.1	4.8	5.7(2020)	0.315	0.307	0.323(2020)
New Zealand[g]	...	...	...	...	...	...	...	...	...	0.335	0.325	0.326

... = Data not available, 0.0 = magnitude is less than half the unit employed or true zero value, $ = United States dollars, ADB = Asian Development Bank, PPP = purchasing power parity.

a Poverty estimates are consumption-based, except for the Republic of Korea; Malaysia; the Philippines; and Taipei,China, whose estimates are income-based. The World Bank has updated the international poverty lines using 2021 purchasing power parity (PPP), however, 2017-based PPP poverty estimates are still released for SDG monitoring.
b Derived from income or expenditure share of the highest 20% and lowest 20% groups by income.
c Inequality estimates are consumption-based, except for the Republic of Korea; Malaysia; the Philippines; and Taipei,China, whose estimates are income-based.
d The most recent year data are for 2005: 0.0% for proportion of population below $3.00 a day (2021 PPP); 0.3% for proportion of population below $4.20 a day (2021 PPP); 3.5 for income ratio of highest 20% to lowest 20%; and 0.266 for Gini coefficient.
e Household income and expenditure surveys for these economies were conducted in overlapping years. The table adopts the approach of the World Bank's World Development Indicators of using the initial year of the survey as the reference period for the poverty estimates.
f Income-based poverty estimates were used. However, consumption-based estimates are also available for $3.00 poverty line, 23.4% (2009), 18.9% (2015), and 11.5% (2023); and for $4.20 poverty line 42.4% (2009), 37.7% (2015), and 29.3% (2023).
g The Gini coefficient data are based on disposable income post taxes and transfers using the new definition.

Sources: World Bank. World Development Indicators. https://databank.worldbank.org/source/world-development-indicators# (accessed 07 August 2025) and Poverty and Inequality Platform. https://pip.worldbank.org/ (accessed 07 June 2025). For New Zealand's Gini coefficient: Organisation for Economic Co-operation and Development. Income Distribution and Poverty. https://stats.oecd.org/index.aspx?queryid=66670# (accessed 07 August 2025). For Taipei,China's income ratio coefficient: Government of Taipei,China, Directorate-General of Budget, Accounting and Statistics.

Table 2.1.7: Human Development Index

ADB Regional Member	2010	2015	2019	2020	2021	2022	2023	Rank in 2023[a]
Developing ADB Member Economies								
Central and West Asia	**0.677**	**0.709**	**0.725**	**0.716**	**0.719**	**0.732**	**0.735**	
Afghanistan	0.465	0.496	0.507	0.501	0.486	0.495	0.496	181
Armenia	0.747	0.777	0.796	0.761	0.786	0.801	0.811	69
Azerbaijan	0.744	0.771	0.780	0.757	0.765	0.784	0.789	81
Georgia	0.770	0.807	0.830	0.822	0.819	0.838	0.844	57
Kazakhstan	0.781	0.819	0.834	0.826	0.816	0.831	0.837	60
Kyrgyz Republic	0.668	0.695	0.708	0.700	0.704	0.717	0.720	117
Pakistan	0.500	0.527	0.540	0.536	0.537	0.544	0.544	168
Tajikistan	0.639	0.658	0.673	0.664	0.672	0.687	0.691	128
Türkiye	0.750	0.821	0.841	0.838	0.841	0.853	0.853	51
Turkmenistan	0.700	0.725	0.741	0.744	0.754	0.761	0.764	95
Uzbekistan	0.681	0.707	0.730	0.723	0.727	0.737	0.740	107
East Asia	**0.821**	**0.848**	**0.867**	**0.866**	**0.868**	**0.868**	**0.859**	
China, People's Republic of	0.710	0.750	0.781	0.786	0.794	0.796	0.797	78
Hong Kong, China	0.912	0.937	0.952	0.950	0.961	0.950	0.955	8
Korea, Republic of	0.894	0.914	0.927	0.928	0.933	0.928	0.937	20
Mongolia	0.714	0.753	0.758	0.741	0.727	0.742	0.747	104
Taipei,China	0.873	0.885	0.916	0.923	0.926	0.925	...	...
South Asia	**0.622**	**0.660**	**0.687**	**0.685**	**0.687**	**0.700**	**0.705**	
Bangladesh	0.561	0.621	0.656	0.663	0.663	0.680	0.685	130
Bhutan	0.593	0.637	0.680	0.688	0.691	0.695	0.698	125
India	0.590	0.633	0.651	0.652	0.647	0.676	0.685	130
Maldives	0.689	0.725	0.749	0.730	0.745	0.764	0.766	93
Nepal	0.551	0.575	0.604	0.599	0.596	0.605	0.622	145
Sri Lanka	0.748	0.769	0.781	0.780	0.777	0.777	0.776	89
Southeast Asia	**0.688**	**0.712**	**0.729**	**0.729**	**0.727**	**0.730**	**0.735**	
Brunei Darussalam	0.830	0.839	0.835	0.836	0.835	0.825	0.837	60
Cambodia	0.543	0.562	0.593	0.595	0.594	0.602	0.606	151
Indonesia	0.670	0.701	0.714	0.710	0.707	0.726	0.728	113
Lao People's Democratic Republic	0.556	0.604	0.615	0.616	0.613	0.614	0.617	147
Malaysia	0.779	0.800	0.812	0.810	0.802	0.810	0.819	67
Myanmar	0.515	0.566	0.610	0.609	0.605	0.606	0.609	150
Philippines	0.669	0.690	0.708	0.699	0.690	0.714	0.720	117
Singapore	0.932	0.935	0.942	0.944	0.948	0.942	0.946	13
Thailand	0.742	0.788	0.800	0.798	0.800	0.792	0.798	76
Timor-Leste	0.645	0.628	0.642	0.650	0.644	0.633	0.634	142
Viet Nam	0.686	0.717	0.744	0.755	0.754	0.764	0.766	93
The Pacific	**0.637**	**0.660**	**0.675**	**0.673**	**0.672**	**0.677**	**0.680**	
Cook Islands	...	...	...	...	...	...	...	...
Fiji	0.697	0.715	0.727	0.718	0.705	0.726	0.731	111
Kiribati	0.600	0.623	0.635	0.632	0.631	0.642	0.644	140
Marshall Islands	0.666 (2011)	0.691	0.722	0.722	0.723	0.732	0.733	108
Micronesia, Federated States of	0.603	0.604	0.611	0.609	0.611	0.614	0.615	149
Nauru	0.616	0.660	0.678	0.684	0.692	0.700	0.703	124
Niue	...	...	...	...	...	...	...	...
Palau	0.779	0.802	0.806	0.799	0.789	0.786	0.786	84
Papua New Guinea	0.503	0.543	0.566	0.567	0.567	0.572	0.576	160
Samoa	0.708	0.708	0.708	0.708	0.706	0.703	0.708	122
Solomon Islands	0.564	0.576	0.583	0.579	0.577	0.583	0.584	156
Tonga	0.724	0.743	0.763	0.765	0.763	0.764	0.769	92
Tuvalu	0.636	0.658	0.681	0.681	0.681	0.686	0.689	129
Vanuatu	0.582	0.599	0.622	0.617	0.615	0.621	0.621	146
Developed ADB Member Economies	**0.921**	**0.930**	**0.936**	**0.937**	**0.938**	**0.935**	**0.940**	
Australia	0.929	0.938	0.947	0.950	0.954	0.952	0.958	7
Japan	0.907	0.917	0.922	0.922	0.922	0.921	0.925	23
New Zealand	0.926	0.934	0.938	0.940	0.939	0.933	0.938	17
DEVELOPING ADB MEMBER ECONOMIES	**0.679**	**0.706**	**0.723**	**0.720**	**0.720**	**0.728**	**0.727**	
ALL ADB REGIONAL MEMBERS	**0.694**	**0.720**	**0.737**	**0.734**	**0.734**	**0.741**	**0.741**	
WORLD[b]	**0.707**	**0.731**	**0.745**	**0.742**	**0.742**	**0.752**	**0.756**	

... = data not available, ADB = Asian Development Bank.

Notes:

1. Regional indexes are calculated as an arithmetic average of the indexes of reporting economies with data corresponding to the year heading.
2. The Human Development Index (HDI) is calculated by the Human Development Report Office of the United Nations Development Programme (UNDP) using the most recently revised historical data from national and international agencies, which continually improve their data series. Hence, the HDI values and ranks presented in this table are not comparable to those published in previous editions. More information is available at the UNDP website, https://hdr.undp.org/content/human-development-report-2025.

a Rank in 2023 among the 193 national economies presented in the Human Development Report 2025 of the UNDP.
b Calculated by the UNDP Human Development Report Office (HDRO) by applying the human development index formula to the weighted group averages of component indicators.

Sources: United Nations Development Programme. Human Development Data (1990–2023). https://hdr.undp.org/sites/default/files/2025_HDR/HDR25_Composite_indices_complete_time_series.csv (accessed 4 June 2025). For Taipei,China: Government of Taipei,China, Directorate-General of Budget, Accounting and Statistics.

Table 2.1.8: Life Expectancy at Birth
(years)

ADB Regional Member	Both Sexes 2010	Both Sexes 2024	Female 2010	Female 2024	Male 2010	Male 2024
Developing ADB Member Economies						
Central and West Asia	...	...	...	...	...	...
Afghanistan	60.7	66.3	62.3	67.8	59.1	64.7
Armenia	72.9	75.8	76.7	79.6	68.8	71.6
Azerbaijan	70.3	74.6	73.1	77.3	67.3	71.7
Georgia	71.7	74.7	76.4	79.2	66.9	69.7
Kazakhstan	68.3	74.5	73.8	78.5	62.8	70.3
Kyrgyz Republic	67.5	71.8	71.7	75.4	63.5	68.3
Pakistan	64.4	67.8	66.7	70.3	62.3	65.5
Tajikistan	68.4	71.9	71.1	74.1	65.7	69.7
Türkiye	75.0	77.4	78.2	80.3	71.9	74.6
Turkmenistan	68.6	70.2	71.8	73.0	65.2	67.0
Uzbekistan	69.8	72.5	72.7	75.5	67.0	69.6
East Asia	...	...	...	...	...	...
China, People's Republic of	75.7	78.0	78.3	81.0	73.2	75.2
Hong Kong, China	82.9	85.6	85.8	88.3	80.0	83.0
Korea, Republic of	80.7	84.4	84.2	87.3	77.1	81.3
Mongolia	67.1	72.0	71.6	76.7	63.0	67.5
Taipei,China	79.2	80.2 (2023)	82.5	83.7 (2023)	76.1	76.9 (2023)
South Asia	...	...	...	...	...	...
Bangladesh	68.0	74.9	69.7	76.7	66.5	73.3
Bhutan	68.8	73.3	70.5	75.3	67.3	71.6
India	67.2	72.2	68.8	73.9	65.6	70.7
Maldives	76.8	81.3	78.4	83.0	75.5	79.9
Nepal	66.8	70.6	68.4	72.1	65.2	69.1
Sri Lanka	74.5	77.7	78.2	80.7	70.9	74.4
Southeast Asia[a]	**69.8**	**72.3**	**72.6**	**75.3**	**67.1**	**69.3**
Brunei Darussalam	74.8	75.5	77.1	77.7	72.9	73.5
Cambodia	67.3	70.8	69.4	73.4	65.1	68.1
Indonesia	68.4	71.3	70.2	73.4	66.6	69.2
Lao People's Democratic Republic	63.7	69.2	66.1	71.5	61.4	67.0
Malaysia	75.4	76.8	78.1	79.5	73.0	74.4
Myanmar	63.5	67.1	66.5	70.4	60.7	64.0
Philippines	68.9	69.9	72.1	73.0	65.5	67.0
Singapore	81.6	83.9	83.9	86.4	79.3	81.4
Thailand	75.0	76.6	78.7	81.0	71.4	72.3
Timor-Leste	63.7	67.9	65.3	69.7	62.1	66.3
Viet Nam	73.6	74.7	78.4	79.4	68.8	70.1
The Pacific	...	...	...	...	...	...
Cook Islands	72.8	75.5	77.0	79.2	69.2	72.1
Fiji	66.8	67.5	68.9	69.5	64.8	65.5
Kiribati	65.9	66.6	67.4	68.3	64.1	64.7
Marshall Islands	64.5	67.1	66.7	69.5	62.7	65.0
Micronesia, Federated States of	64.9	67.4	68.0	71.3	62.0	63.6
Nauru	60.1	62.3	63.6	64.2	57.5	60.4
Niue	67.7	70.1	70.9	72.9	64.8	67.5
Palau	68.3	69.4	72.2	71.9	65.2	67.3
Papua New Guinea	63.1	66.3	65.5	69.2	61.2	63.8
Samoa	71.5	71.8	74.1	73.8	69.0	70.0
Solomon Islands	68.7	70.7	70.7	72.2	66.9	69.4
Tonga	71.3	73.1	75.2	76.5	67.9	69.5
Tuvalu	64.8	67.3	67.8	70.9	61.9	63.9
Vanuatu	69.6	71.7	72.5	74.1	67.6	69.6
Developed ADB Member Economies	...	...	...	...	...	...
Australia	82.0	84.1	84.2	85.8	79.8	82.3
Japan	82.9	84.9	86.2	87.9	79.5	81.8
New Zealand	81.1	82.2	82.9	83.9	79.1	80.6
DEVELOPING ADB MEMBER ECONOMIES	...	...	...	...	...	...
ALL ADB REGIONAL MEMBERS	...	...	...	...	...	...
WORLD[a]	**70.1**	**73.3**	**72.7**	**76.0**	**67.6**	**70.7**

... = data not available, ADB = Asian Development Bank.

a Aggregate age-specific mortality rates by single year of age were computed by dividing aggregated deaths by age and sex by aggregated sex- and age-specific person-years of exposure. Complete life tables and related indicators were then derived from those mortality rates.

Sources: United Nations. World Population Prospects 2024. https://population.un.org/wpp/Download/Standard/Population/ (accessed 2 June 2025).
For Taipei,China: Government of Taipei,China, Ministry of the Interior.

Table 2.1.9: Births, Deaths, and Fertility Rates

ADB Regional Member	Crude Birth Rate (per 1,000 people)		Crude Death Rate (per 1,000 people)		Total Fertility Rate (births per woman)	
	2010	2024	2010	2024	2010	2024
Developing ADB Member Economies						
Central and West Asia	...	...	...	...	...	...
Afghanistan	41.8	35.0	8.4	5.7	6.2	4.8
Armenia	15.0	12.2	9.7	9.3	1.6	1.7
Azerbaijan	18.5	11.7	7.0	6.6	1.9	1.7
Georgia	15.6	11.3	12.9	11.8	2.0	1.8
Kazakhstan	22.6	19.5	8.9	6.7	2.6	3.0
Kyrgyz Republic	27.3	20.9	7.4	6.0	3.1	2.8
Pakistan	33.5	27.4	7.7	6.4	4.4	3.5
Tajikistan	32.0	25.3	5.7	4.6	3.5	3.0
Türkiye	17.2	12.1	6.0	6.6	2.1	1.6
Turkmenistan	25.7	20.9	6.1	5.8	2.8	2.7
Uzbekistan	22.4	25.6	6.2	6.0	2.4	3.5
East Asia	...	...	...	...	...	...
China, People's Republic of	13.3	6.2	6.5	8.2	1.7	1.0
Hong Kong, China	9.8	5.4	6.2	7.7	1.1	0.7
Korea, Republic of	9.2	4.7	5.2	6.9	1.2	0.7
Mongolia	23.7	18.2	6.8	5.9	2.5	2.6
Taipei,China	7.2	5.8	6.3	8.6	0.9	0.9
South Asia	...	...	...	...	...	...
Bangladesh	21.9	20.0	6.0	5.1	2.4	2.1
Bhutan	18.9	12.5	6.6	6.1	2.3	1.4
India	21.6	16.0	7.2	6.6	2.6	2.0
Maldives	20.9	10.6	3.3	2.4	2.3	1.6
Nepal	22.9	19.0	7.0	7.0	2.5	2.0
Sri Lanka	17.1	13.9	6.4	7.1	2.1	2.0
Southeast Asia[a]	**19.8**	**14.7**	**6.8**	**7.3**	**2.4**	**1.9**
Brunei Darussalam	16.6	13.3	3.8	5.3	1.9	1.7
Cambodia	25.0	20.3	6.3	6.5	2.9	2.5
Indonesia	20.4	15.8	7.5	7.6	2.5	2.1
Lao People's Democratic Republic	27.2	20.9	7.9	6.2	3.1	2.4
Malaysia	16.9	12.4	4.3	5.3	2.1	1.5
Myanmar	19.4	16.5	9.2	9.2	2.3	2.1
Philippines	26.6	15.9	5.5	6.4	3.3	1.9
Singapore	8.4	8.4	3.9	5.0	0.9	1.0
Thailand	12.0	8.1	6.6	9.0	1.6	1.2
Timor-Leste	31.5	21.8	8.0	7.2	4.8	2.6
Viet Nam	17.4	13.4	5.9	6.6	1.9	1.9
The Pacific	...	...	...	...	...	...
Cook Islands	17.8	11.6	7.2	9.7	2.5	2.0
Fiji	22.3	17.9	7.8	9.5	2.7	2.3
Kiribati	31.2	25.3	6.9	7.1	3.9	3.1
Marshall Islands	30.9	20.1	6.5	7.1	3.7	2.9
Micronesia, Federated States of	25.2	22.3	7.2	7.7	3.3	2.7
Nauru	36.1	24.6	8.2	7.6	4.0	3.3
Niue	17.4	14.0	13.2	14.8	3.0	2.5
Palau	13.7	10.7	9.3	11.7	1.9	1.9
Papua New Guinea	30.7	24.3	7.3	6.6	3.9	3.1
Samoa	30.5	25.0	5.8	6.2	4.5	3.8
Solomon Islands	33.2	26.7	5.8	5.1	4.3	3.5
Tonga	28.0	23.0	6.3	6.4	3.9	3.1
Tuvalu	22.2	22.0	9.4	9.3	3.4	3.2
Vanuatu	33.0	27.7	5.5	5.0	4.1	3.6
Developed ADB Member Economies	...	...	...	...	...	...
Australia	13.6	11.4	6.5	6.7	1.9	1.6
Japan	8.4	6.1	9.6	12.4	1.4	1.2
New Zealand	14.6	11.3	6.6	7.4	2.2	1.7
DEVELOPING ADB MEMBER ECONOMIES	...	...	...	...	...	...
ALL ADB REGIONAL MEMBERS	...	...	...	...	...	...
WORLD[a]	**20.4**	**16.2**	**7.7**	**7.6**	**2.6**	**2.2**

... = data not available, ADB = Asian Development Bank.

a Aggregate age-specific fertility rates were computed by dividing aggregated (summed) births by mothers' single-year of age by aggregated exposures of women by age. Total fertility and other fertility indicators for the economy grouping were then derived from those age-specific fertility rates. Similarly, aggregate age-specific mortality rates by single year of age were computed by dividing aggregated deaths by age and sex by aggregated sex- and age-specific person-years of exposure. Complete life tables and related indicators were then derived from those mortality rates.

Sources: United Nations. World Population Prospects 2024. https://population.un.org/wpp/Download/Standard/Population/ (accessed 2 June 2025). For Taipei,China: Government of Taipei,China, Ministry of the Interior.

Table 2.1.10: Adult (15 Years and Older) Literacy Rate
(%)

ADB Regional Member	Both Sexes 2010		Both Sexes 2023		Female 2010		Female 2023		Male 2010		Male 2023	
Developing ADB Member Economies												
Central and West Asia												
Afghanistan	31.0	(2011)	37.0	(2021)	17.0	(2011)	26.6[a]	(2022)	45.0	(2011)	52.0	(2021)
Armenia	100.0	(2011)	99.8[a]	(2022)	100.0	(2011)	99.9[a]	(2022)	100.0	(2011)	99.7[a]	(2022)
Azerbaijan	100.0[b]		100.0		100.0[b]		100.0		100.0[b]		100.0	
Georgia	100.0	(2014)	99.6		100.0	(2014)	99.6		100.0	(2014)	99.5	
Kazakhstan	100.0	(2009)	...		100.0	(2009)	...		100.0	(2009)	...	
Kyrgyz Republic	99.0	(2009)	...		99.0	(2009)	...		100.0	(2009)	...	
Pakistan	55.0		58.9	(2021)	41.0		48.5	(2021)	69.0		69.1	(2021)
Tajikistan	99.0	(2000)	...		99.0	(2000)	94.6[a]	(2017)	100.0	(2000)	...	
Türkiye	93.0		97.0	(2021)	88.0		95.0	(2021)	97.0		99.0	(2021)
Turkmenistan	...		...		...		99.6[a]	(2019)	...		...	
Uzbekistan	100.0	(2013)	100.0	(2022)	100.0	(2013)	100.0	(2022)	100.0	(2013)	100.0	(2022)
East Asia												
China, People's Republic of	95.0		97.0	(2020)	93.0		95.0	(2020)	97.0		98.0	(2020)
Hong Kong, China	...		...		...		...		...		...	
Korea, Republic of	98.0	(2008)	...		98.0	(2008)	...		98.0	(2008)	...	
Mongolia	98.0		98.7	(2022)	98.0		98.9	(2022)	98.0		98.5	(2022)
Taipei,China	...		...		...		...		...		...	
South Asia												
Bangladesh	59.0	(2011)	79.0	(2022)	55.0	(2011)	77.0	(2022)	62.0	(2011)	81.0	(2022)
Bhutan	55.0	(2012)	67.0	(2017)	45.0	(2012)	57.0	(2017)	66.0	(2012)	75.0	(2017)
India	69.0	(2011)	82.0		59.0	(2011)	75.0		79.0	(2011)	88.0	
Maldives	99.0	(2014)	98.2	(2019)	99.0	(2014)	98.3	(2019)	99.0	(2014)	98.2	(2019)
Nepal	60.0	(2011)	68.7[a]	(2019)	49.0	(2011)	59.4[a]	(2019)	72.0	(2011)	79.7[a]	(2019)
Sri Lanka	91.0		93.0		90.0		92.0		93.0		93.0	
Southeast Asia												
Brunei Darussalam	96.0	(2011)	...		95.0	(2011)	...		97.0	(2011)	...	
Cambodia	76.0	(2009)	71.9[a]	(2021)	69.0	(2009)	63.6[a]	(2021)	84.0	(2009)	81.5[a]	(2021)
Indonesia	93.0	(2011)	96.0	(2020)	90.0	(2011)	95.0	(2020)	96.0	(2011)	97.0	(2020)
Lao People's Democratic Republic	73.0	(2005)	85.0	(2015)	63.0	(2005)	79.0	(2015)	82.0	(2005)	90.0	(2015)
Malaysia	93.0		96.0	(2022)	91.0		95.0	(2022)	95.0		97.0	(2022)
Myanmar	90.0	(2014)	89.0	(2019)	87.0	(2014)	86.0	(2019)	93.0	(2014)	92.0	(2019)
Philippines	95.0	(2008)	98.0	(2020)	96.0	(2008)	97.0[a]	(2022)	95.0	(2008)	98.0	(2020)
Singapore	96.0		98.0	(2021)	94.0		96.0	(2021)	98.0		99.0	(2021)
Thailand	96.0		91.1[a]	(2022)	96.0		91.5[a]	(2022)	96.0		90.7[a]	(2022)
Timor-Leste	58.0		65.8[a]	(2016)	53.0		59.6[a]	(2016)	64.0		72.2[a]	(2016)
Viet Nam	94.0	(2009)	96.0	(2022)	91.0	(2009)	95.0	(2022)	96.0	(2009)	97.0	(2022)
The Pacific												
Cook Islands	...		...		...		...		...		...	
Fiji	...		...		...		92.4[a]	(2021)	...		...	
Kiribati	...		98.0[a]	(2018)	...		98.6[a]	(2018)	...		97.3[a]	(2018)
Marshall Islands	98.0	(2011)	...		98.0	(2011)	...		98.0	(2011)	...	
Micronesia, Federated States of	...		...		...		...		...		...	
Nauru	...		96.6[a]		...		99.7[a]		...		93.4[a]	
Niue	...		...		...		...		...		...	
Palau	100.0[a]	(2013)	97.0	(2015)	100.0[a]	(2013)	96.0	(2015)	99.0[a]	(2013)	97.0	(2015)
Papua New Guinea	57.0	(2000)	70.1[a]	(2017)	51.0	(2000)	61.6	(2017)	63.0	(2000)	78.4[a]	(2017)
Samoa	99.0	(2011)	98.0[a]	(2019)	99.0	(2011)	97.7[a]	(2019)	99.0	(2011)	98.3[a]	(2019)
Solomon Islands	...		...		...		...		...		...	
Tonga	99.0	(2011)	91.1[a]	(2019)	99.0	(2011)	97.6[a]	(2019)	99.0	(2011)	83.8[a]	(2019)
Tuvalu	...		...		...		...		...		...	
Vanuatu	...		88.0[a]		...		88.2[a]		...		87.7[a]	
Developed ADB Member Economies												
Australia	...		...		...		...		...		...	
Japan	...		...		...		...		...		...	
New Zealand	...		...		...		...		...		...	
WORLD	**84.2**		**87.4**		**80.0**		**84.1**		**88.5**		**90.6**	

... = data not available, ADB = Asian Development Bank.

a UNESCO Institute for Statistics estimates.
b National estimate.

Source: United Nations Educational, Scientific and Cultural Organization (UNESCO) Institute for Statistics. UIS.Stat Database. https://databrowser.uis.unesco.org (accessed 11 June 2025).

Table 2.1.11: Years of Schooling

ADB Regional Member	Expected[a]					
	Both Sexes		Female		Male	
	2010	2023	2010	2023	2010	2023
Developing ADB Member Economies						
Central and West Asia						
Afghanistan	9.6 (2011)	10.6[c] (2018)	7.5 (2011)	8.0[c] (2018)	11.6 (2011)	13.0 (2018)
Armenia	13.1[c]	13.8	13.1[c]	14.1	13.1[c]	13.6
Azerbaijan	11.7[c]	12.9[d]	11.5[c]	12.9[d]	11.8[c]	12.9[d]
Georgia	14.5[c] (2009)	16.4	13.7[c] (2008)	16.6	14.4[c] (2008)	16.3
Kazakhstan	13.7	13.7 (2024)	13.8	13.8 (2024)	13.5	13.6 (2024)
Kyrgyz Republic	12.3[d]	12.6 (2024)	12.6[d]	12.9 (2024)	12.1[d]	12.2 (2024)
Pakistan	6.0[c] (2011)	7.5 (2022)	5.3[c] (2011)	6.9 (2022)	6.5[c] (2011)	8.0 (2022)
Tajikistan	11.0	11.6 (2024)	9.9	11.1 (2024)	12.3	12.1 (2024)
Türkiye	14.0[c]	19.8[d] (2022)	13.5[c]	19.7[d] (2022)	14.4[c]	19.9[d] (2022)
Turkmenistan	...	12.9[c]	...	12.4 (2022)	...	12.4 (2022)
Uzbekistan	11.6[d]	12.6 (2024)	11.5[d]	12.7 (2024)	11.7[d]	12.5 (2024)
East Asia						
China, People's Republic of	12.9[c]	...	13.1[c]	...	12.8[c]	...
Hong Kong, China	15.8[c]	16.9[c]	15.4[c]	16.9[c]	15.5[c]	16.9[c]
Korea, Republic of	16.8[d]	16.6[d] (2022)	15.9[d]	16.2[d] (2022)	17.6[d]	16.9[d] (2022)
Mongolia	14.5[c]	13.6	15.3[c]	14.4	13.8[c]	12.9
Taipei,China	16.7 (2012)	16.8 (2024)	16.8 (2012)	17.0 (2024)	16.7 (2012)	16.7 (2024)
South Asia						
Bangladesh	8.6[d] (2009)	11.1	8.6[d] (2009)	11.6	8.6[d] (2009)	10.6
Bhutan	11.8	13.2 (2022)	12.4	14.1 (2022)	11.3	12.3 (2022)
India	11.1[c]	13.4 (2024)	10.8[c]	13.4 (2024)	11.4[c]	13.3 (2024)
Maldives	12.0 (2003)	12.7 (2022)	12.5 (2003)	14.9 (2022)	11.5 (2003)	11.2 (2022)
Nepal	11.8[c]	13.5	11.8[c]	13.5	11.9[c]	13.5
Sri Lanka	13.1[c]	12.9	13.4[c]	13.5	12.9[c]	12.4
Southeast Asia						
Brunei Darussalam	14.4[c]	13.6	14.9[c]	14.1	13.9[c]	13.2
Cambodia	10.5[c] (2008)	10.8	9.9[c] (2008)	11.0	11.0[c] (2008)	10.7
Indonesia	12.5	13.1	12.6	13.4	12.4	12.9
Lao People's Democratic Republic	9.8	8.9	9.2	8.7	10.5	9.0
Malaysia	12.8	11.7	13.3	12.3	12.3	11.2
Myanmar	8.7 (2007)	11.7 (2018)	9.3 (2007)	12.1 (2018)	8.1 (2007)	11.2 (2018)
Philippines	10.8 (2009)	12.3 (2021)	11.1 (2009)	12.5 (2021)	10.5 (2009)	12.1 (2021)
Singapore	17.8[c] (2009)	16.7[d] (2022)	17.8[c] (2009)	16.9[d] (2022)	17.8[c] (2009)	16.6[d] (2022)
Thailand	13.5[c]	15.9	13.9[c]	16.2	13.2[c]	15.6
Timor-Leste	13.2	...	12.9	...	13.4	...
Viet Nam	10.9 (2001)	14.4 (2022)	...	13.9 (2022)	...	14.8 (2022)
The Pacific						
Cook Islands	15.3 (2012)	15.1	14.6 (2012)	15.0	16.0 (2012)	15.2
Fiji	12.4 (2004)	...	12.5 (2004)	...	12.3 (2004)	...
Kiribati	...	...	...	...	...	...
Marshall Islands	12.5[c] (2002)	14.4 (2022)	12.5[c] (2002)	15.0 (2022)	12.6[c] (2002)	13.9 (2022)
Micronesia, Federated States of	...	...	...	...	...	...
Nauru	...	...	...	...	...	...
Niue	...	...	...	...	...	...
Palau	14.4[c] (2000)	15.0	15.3[c] (2000)	16.0	13.6[c] (2000)	14.0
Papua New Guinea	...	...	...	...	...	...
Samoa	11.9 (2000)	...	12.2[c] (2000)	...	11.7[c] (2000)	...
Solomon Islands	...	...	...	...	...	...
Tonga	14.1[c] (2003)	17.6[d] (2020)	13.6[c] (2002)	18.8[d] (2020)	13.0[c] (2002)	16.4[d] (2020)
Tuvalu	...	...	...	...	...	...
Vanuatu	10.2[c] (2004)	...	9.8[c] (2004)	...	10.7[c] (2004)	...
Developed ADB Member Economies						
Australia	...	20.6[d]	...	21.4[d]	...	19.9[d]
Japan	...	15.5[d] (2022)	...	15.5[d] (2022)	...	15.5[d] (2022)
New Zealand	19.5[c] (2011)	19.1[d]	20.3[c] (2011)	19.6[d]	18.7[c] (2011)	18.7[d]
WORLD	**11.3**	**12.7[c]**	**11.1**	**12.8[c]**	**11.4**	**12.7[c]**

continued on next page

Table 2.1.11: Years of Schooling (*continued*)

ADB Regional Member	Mean[b]					
	Both Sexes		Female		Male	
	2010	2023	2010	2023	2010	2023
Developing ADB Member Economies						
Central and West Asia						
Afghanistan	...	2.5 (2022)	...	1.2 (2022)	...	3.9 (2022)
Armenia	11.2 (2011)	11.3 (2020)	11.2 (2011)	11.3 (2020)	11.2 (2011)	11.3 (2020)
Azerbaijan	10.6	11.1	10.3	11.0	10.9	11.2
Georgia	12.5 (2012)	12.7 (2022)	12.4 (2012)	12.8 (2022)	12.6 (2012)	12.6 (2022)
Kazakhstan	11.0 (2009)	12.2 (2018)	11.0 (2009)	12.2 (2018)	11.0 (2009)	12.2 (2018)
Kyrgyz Republic	10.9 (2009)	11.7	10.9 (2009)	11.8	10.8 (2009)	11.6
Pakistan	4.7	5.0 (2021)	3.0	3.9 (2021)	6.2	6.1 (2021)
Tajikistan	10.8 (2000)	11.4 (2017)	10.3 (2000)	10.8 (2017)	11.3 (2000)	12.0 (2017)
Türkiye	7.1	8.6 (2019)	6.2	7.9 (2019)	8.0	9.4 (2019)
Turkmenistan	...	11.1 (2019)	...	10.8 (2019)	...	11.4 (2019)
Uzbekistan	...	11.9 (2022)	...	11.8 (2022)	...	12.1 (2022)
East Asia						
China, People's Republic of	7.0	7.9 (2020)	6.6	7.6 (2020)	7.4	8.3 (2020)
Hong Kong, China	11.4	12.4 (2022)	11.0	12.0 (2022)	11.9	12.8 (2022)
Korea, Republic of	11.6	12.1 (2015)	10.9	11.4 (2015)	12.5	12.9 (2015)
Mongolia	9.9	9.4 (2020)	10.2	9.9 (2020)	9.6	8.9 (2020)
Taipei,China	...	...	...	...	...	...
South Asia						
Bangladesh	5.2 (2011)	6.8 (2021)	4.4 (2011)	6.2 (2021)	6.0 (2011)	7.3 (2021)
Bhutan	2.2 (2012)	4.1 (2017)	1.5 (2012)	3.3 (2017)	3.0 (2012)	4.8 (2017)
India	5.3 (2011)	7.3	4.0 (2011)	6.2	6.5 (2011)	8.5
Maldives	3.8 (2006)	6.8 (2017)	3.5 (2006)	6.8 (2017)	4.1 (2006)	6.8 (2017)
Nepal	3.5 (2011)	4.5 (2021)	2.3 (2011)	3.5 (2021)	4.9 (2011)	5.8 (2021)
Sri Lanka	10.5 (2009)	10.8 (2022)	10.4 (2009)	10.7 (2022)	10.7 (2009)	10.8 (2022)
Southeast Asia						
Brunei Darussalam	11.6 (2011)	...	11.3 (2011)	...	11.8 (2011)	...
Cambodia	3.9 (2009)	5.2 (2021)	3.1 (2009)	4.4 (2021)	5.0 (2009)	6.2 (2021)
Indonesia	7.5 (2011)	8.6 (2020)	7.0 (2011)	8.2 (2020)	8.0 (2011)	8.9 (2020)
Lao People's Democratic Republic	...	5.7 (2017)	...	4.6 (2017)	...	6.8 (2017)
Malaysia	9.7	11.1 (2022)	9.4	11.0 (2022)	10.0	11.2 (2022)
Myanmar	...	6.4 (2019)	...	6.1 (2019)	...	6.7 (2019)
Philippines	8.9	8.9 (2020)	9.0	9.1 (2020)	8.8	8.7 (2020)
Singapore	10.9	12.0 (2022)	10.5	11.7 (2022)	11.4	12.3 (2022)
Thailand	7.6	9.0 (2022)	7.4	8.9 (2022)	7.8	9.2 (2022)
Timor-Leste	5.3	5.3 (2016)	4.7	4.6 (2016)	6.0	6.0 (2016)
Viet Nam	7.5 (2009)	9.0 (2022)	7.0 (2009)	8.5 (2022)	8.1 (2009)	9.5 (2022)
The Pacific						
Cook Islands	9.9 (2006)	...	9.8 (2006)	...	10.0 (2006)	...
Fiji	9.2 (2007)	10.4 (2021)	9.2 (2007)	10.4 (2021)	9.3 (2007)	10.3 (2021)
Kiribati	...	9.0 (2018)	...	9.1 (2018)	...	9.0 (2018)
Marshall Islands	10.9 (2011)	...	10.7 (2011)	...	11.1 (2011)	...
Micronesia, Federated States of	...	...	...	...	...	...
Nauru	...	10.0	...	10.2	...	9.9
Niue	...	...	...	...	...	...
Palau	...	12.8 (2013)	...	12.9 (2013)	...	12.8 (2013)
Papua New Guinea	...	4.9 (2018)	...	4.1 (2018)	...	5.6 (2018)
Samoa	10.0 (2011)	11.4 (2019)	10.1 (2011)	11.8 (2019)	9.9 (2011)	11.0 (2019)
Solomon Islands	...	...	...	...	...	...
Tonga	10.9 (2011)	10.9 (2019)	10.9 (2011)	10.9 (2019)	10.9 (2011)	10.8 (2019)
Tuvalu	...	10.5 (2019)	...	10.3 (2019)	...	10.7 (2019)
Vanuatu	...	7.1	...	6.9	...	7.2
Developed ADB Member Economies						
Australia	12.0	12.9 (2022)	12.0	12.9 (2022)	12.0	12.8 (2022)
Japan	12.4	12.9 (2020)	12.1	12.5 (2020)	12.8	13.2 (2020)
New Zealand	12.8 (2011)	12.9 (2020)	12.6 (2011)	12.9 (2020)	12.9 (2011)	12.9 (2020)
WORLD	...	...	...	...	...	...

... = data not available, ADB = Asian Development Bank.

a Refers to the expected number of years of schooling from primary to tertiary level of education.
b Refers to the average number of completed years of education among the population aged 25 years and older (excluding years spent repeating individual grades), by highest level of education attained.
c UNESCO Institute for Statistics estimate.
d National estimate.

Sources: United Nations Educational, Scientific and Cultural Organization (UNESCO) Institute for Statistics. UIS.Stat Database. https://databrowser.uis.unesco.org/browser/EDUCATION/UIS-EducationOPRI (accessed 16 June 2025). For expected years of schooling for Taipei,China: Government of Taipei,China, Ministry of Education. Gender Statistics.

Table 2.1.12: Education Resources

ADB Regional Member	Pupil/Trained Teacher Ratio[a]				Pupil/Qualified Teacher Ratio[b]			
	Primary		Secondary		Primary		Secondary	
	2010	2023	2010	2023	2010	2023	2010	2023
Developing ADB Member Economies								
Central and West Asia								
Afghanistan	...	...	...	...	...	60.4 (2019)	...	42.1 (2018)
Armenia	27.4 (2005)	23.6	...	13.7	...	19.9	...	11.6
Azerbaijan	11.0	16.0	...	9.3	...	15.9	...	9.2
Georgia	9.4[c] (2009)	...	8.0[c] (2009)	...	...	...	...	...
Kazakhstan	...	14.0	...	9.5	...	14.0	...	9.5
Kyrgyz Republic	35.5	25.0	18.8	14.0 (2017)	48.8 (2002)	...	...	...
Pakistan	48.0	65.0 (2022)	...	16.5 (2022)	...	...	...	...
Tajikistan	27.1	22.3 (2017)	17.0 (2004)	...	...	23.0 (2017)	...	...
Türkiye	...	...	...	...	...	...	...	...
Turkmenistan	...	26.0	...	10.1 (2021)	...	25.9	...	12.2
Uzbekistan	17.8	21.0	13.0	13.1	15.4 (2012)	21.0	13.1 (2012)	13.1
East Asia								
China, People's Republic of	...	...	...	...	...	16.2	...	14.0
Hong Kong, China	15.9	12.5	17.7[d]	11.7	...	11.8	...	10.6
Korea, Republic of	20.9	15.8 (2022)	17.6	11.5 (2022)	20.9	15.8 (2022)	17.6	11.5 (2022)
Mongolia	31.0	33.1	14.8	15.1 (2019)	...	33.1	...	13.9 (2019)
Taipei,China	...	...	...	...	...	...	...	...
South Asia								
Bangladesh	78.3[c] (2009)	54.7	57.2 (2011)	44.1	...	42.3	...	28.6
Bhutan	32.7 (2008)	29.1 (2022)	28.5 (2008)	10.6 (2022)	...	29.1 (2022)	...	10.6 (2022)
India	...	29.6	...	21.7	...	28.7	...	21.5
Maldives	15.3	11.0 (2022)	18.4 (2002)	8.5 (2022)	...	9.5 (2022)	...	8.4 (2022)
Nepal	43.3	23.2	49.1[d]	38.3	...	23.3	...	37.5
Sri Lanka	29.1	24.9	21.9	20.3	...	21.9	...	17.1
Southeast Asia								
Brunei Darussalam	13.0	11.8	10.9 (2011)	8.9	...	10.9	...	8.9
Cambodia	48.9	49.0	29.1 (2007)	9.9 (2021)	...	49.0	...	...
Indonesia	...	56.1	...	54.4	...	20.4	...	20.7
Lao People's Democratic Republic	30.2	43.3	20.4[d]	17.7 (2022)	...	24.8 (2018)	...	22.4 (2017)
Malaysia	13.2	13.6	14.6	12.6	...	12.1	...	11.0
Myanmar	28.3	25.6 (2018)	34.5	30.6 (2018)	...	26.7 (2018)	...	28.1 (2018)
Philippines	...	24.3 (2022)	...	26.3 (2022)	...	24.3 (2022)	...	26.3 (2022)
Singapore	18.5 (2009)	14.3 (2022)	16.3 (2009)	12.1 (2022)	18.2 (2009)	14.0 (2022)	16.2 (2009)	11.9 (2022)
Thailand	...	14.4	...	22.7	...	14.4	...	22.7
Timor-Leste	...	...	...	...	...	33.7 (2020)	...	31.0 (2020)
Viet Nam	20.2	29.3	...	23.1 (2022)	...	29.3	...	23.1 (2022)
The Pacific								
Cook Islands	16.5 (2011)	15.6	15.6 (2011)	18.2	...	34.2	...	26.4
Fiji	30.8 (2011)	18.1	26.5 (2011)	...	...	17.5	...	...
Kiribati	47.9 (2012)	26.0	...	...	25.7	24.0	...	...
Marshall Islands	...	23.8 (2022)	...	17.3 (2022)	...	18.7 (2022)	...	16.2 (2022)
Micronesia, Federated States of	...	56.6	...	...	...	17.4	...	...
Nauru	26.8 (2007)	204.1	57.4 (2007)	63.7 (2022)	...	39.3	...	75.7
Niue	...	17.8 (2021)	...	45.4	...	10.2	...	7.3
Palau	...	12.0	...	10.1	...	17.5	...	11.8
Papua New Guinea	...	...	27.4 (2012)	...	...	...	...	...
Samoa	...	...	...	...	...	22.5	...	...
Solomon Islands	34.4	29.9 (2019)	39.6	...	...	29.9 (2019)	...	...
Tonga	...	21.2	...	24.8 (2015)	...	20.2	...	18.3 (2015)
Tuvalu	...	23.1	...	17.6	...	42.1	...	29.8
Vanuatu	23.8 (2007)	26.2 (2022)	...	24.8 (2021)	...	25.3	...	43.0
Developed ADB Member Economies								
Australia	...	...	...	...	...	...	...	...
Japan	...	...	...	...	...	...	...	...
New Zealand	...	...	...	...	...	...	...	...
WORLD	**26.9**[d]	**26.5**[d]	...	**19.0**[d]	...	**25.4**[d]	...	**18.3**[d]

... = data not available, ADB = Asian Development Bank.

a The UNESCO Institute for Statistics (UIS) defines a trained teacher as one who has received at least the minimum organized pedagogical teacher training pre-service and in-service required for teaching at the relevant level in a given economy in a given academic year.

b The UIS defines a qualified teacher as one who has at least the minimum academic qualifications required for teaching their subjects at the relevant level in a given economy in a given academic year.

c National estimate.

d UNESCO Institute for Statistics estimate.

Source: United Nations Educational, Scientific and Cultural Organization (UNESCO) Institute for Statistics. UIS.Stat Database. https://databrowser.uis.unesco.org/browser/EDUCATION/UIS-SDG4Monitoring (accessed 19 June 2025).

Table 2.1.13: Health Care Resources
(per 1,000 population)

ADB Regional Member	Physicians		Hospital Beds	
	2010	2022	2010	2022
Developing ADB Member Economies				
Central and West Asia				
Afghanistan	0.25	0.25 (2020)	0.4	0.4 (2021)
Armenia	2.78	3.12 (2019)	4.1	4.6 (2020)
Azerbaijan	3.58	3.09 (2020)	4.5	3.9 (2019)
Georgia	4.75	5.61	3.5	4.9 (2020)
Kazakhstan	3.84	4.03 (2020)	7.2	6.7 (2020)
Kyrgyz Republic	2.31	2.15 (2021)	5.1	4.2 (2021)
Pakistan	0.75	1.08 (2019)	0.4	0.5 (2019)
Tajikistan	1.68	2.13 (2021)	5.0	4.3 (2021)
Türkiye	1.69	2.17 (2021)	2.7	3.0 (2020)
Turkmenistan	2.20	2.14 (2021)	3.9	4.0 (2021)
Uzbekistan	2.54	2.81 (2021)	4.9	4.9 (2021)
East Asia				
China, People's Republic of	1.46	2.52 (2021)	2.5	5.0 (2020)
Hong Kong, China	...	...	...	...
Korea, Republic of	2.01	2.52 (2021)	8.9	12.8 (2021)
Mongolia	2.77	3.87 (2021)	6.6	10.6 (2021)
Taipei,China[a]	1.96 (2011)	2.64 (2023)	6.9 (2011)	7.3 (2023)
South Asia				
Bangladesh	0.36	0.67 (2021)	0.6	0.9 (2019)
Bhutan	0.27 (2012)	0.55	1.7	2.2 (2021)
India	...	0.73 (2020)	1.8	1.6 (2021)
Maldives	1.45	2.16 (2019)	3.9 (2009)	5.0 (2020)
Nepal	0.51 (2012)	0.87 (2021)	0.3	0.4 (2021)
Sri Lanka	0.71	1.19 (2021)	3.5	4.0 (2020)
Southeast Asia				
Brunei Darussalam	1.42	1.91 (2021)	2.8	3.9 (2021)
Cambodia	0.23	0.21 (2019)	0.8	0.7 (2018)
Indonesia	0.14	0.69	0.7	1.4 (2021)
Lao People's Democratic Republic	0.33	0.33 (2021)	1.1	1.3 (2021)
Malaysia	1.15	2.32 (2021)	1.9	2.0 (2021)
Myanmar	0.54	0.75 (2019)	0.9	1.1 (2020)
Philippines	0.55	0.79 (2021)	1.0	1.0 (2021)
Singapore	1.75	2.60 (2021)	2.2	2.7 (2021)
Thailand	0.38	0.93 (2020)	2.0	2.3 (2021)
Timor-Leste	0.08	0.77 (2020)	5.9	...
Viet Nam	0.72	...	2.0	2.6 (2017)
The Pacific				
Cook Islands	1.46 (2009)	1.43 (2019)	...	...
Fiji	0.41 (2009)	...	2.2	1.9 (2017)
Kiribati	0.38	...	1.3	...
Marshall Islands	0.60	...	2.7	...
Micronesia, Federated States of	0.19 (2009)	0.96 (2020)	3.2 (2009)	...
Nauru	1.08	...	4.9	...
Niue	2.22 (2006)	...	...	...
Palau	1.57	1.78 (2020)	4.3	...
Papua New Guinea	0.05	0.06 (2021)	...	0.2 (2019)
Samoa	0.33	0.55 (2021)	1.0 (2007)	...
Solomon Islands	0.20 (2011)	...	1.7 (2011)	...
Tonga	0.54	1.01 (2021)	2.5	...
Tuvalu	1.15 (2009)	1.26 (2020)	4.2 (2001)	...
Vanuatu	0.18 (2012)	0.16 (2019)	1.7 (2008)	...
Developed ADB Member Economies				
Australia	3.36	3.98 (2021)	3.8	...
Japan	2.21	2.61 (2020)	13.5	12.7 (2020)
New Zealand	2.63	3.57	2.8	2.7 (2021)
WORLD	**1.47**	**1.71** (2020)	**2.7**	**3.3** (2020)

... = data not available, ADB = Asian Development Bank.

a Physicians include doctors of Chinese medicine.

Sources: World Bank. World Development Indicators. https://databank.worldbank.org/source/world-development-indicators (accessed 29 May 2025); and World Health Organization. Global Health Observatory. https://www.who.int/data/gho (accessed 29 May 2025). For Taipei,China: Government of Taipei,China, Directorate-General of Budget, Accounting and Statistics.

Table 2.1.14: Adults Aged 15 Years and Older Living with HIV
('000)

ADB Regional Member	All Adults		Women	
	2010	2023	2010	2023
Developing ADB Member Economies				
Central and West Asia				
Afghanistan	4.0	12.0	0.7	1.6
Armenia	1.7	6.3	0.5	2.0
Azerbaijan	7.8	10.0	1.5	2.8
Georgia	2.6	8.9	0.8	2.6
Kazakhstan	16.0	39.0	6.0	13.0
Kyrgyz Republic	3.7	11.0	1.4	4.7
Pakistan	79.0	290.0	9.6	54.0
Tajikistan	8.3	14.0	2.9	4.8
Türkiye	...	...	...	...
Turkmenistan	...	...	...	...
Uzbekistan	19.0	59.0	8.4	27.0
East Asia				
China, People's Republic of	...	...	...	...
Hong Kong, China	...	...	...	...
Korea, Republic of	...	...	...	...
Mongolia	0.5	0.7	0.1	0.2
Taipei,China	...	...	...	...
South Asia				
Bangladesh	7.0	15.0	2.1	5.0
Bhutan	0.8	1.2	0.5	0.6
India	...	2,500.0	...	1,100.0
Maldives	...	...	...	...
Nepal	32.0	29.0	11.0	13.0
Sri Lanka	4.3	4.7	1.3	1.1
Southeast Asia				
Brunei Darussalam	...	...	...	...
Cambodia	78.0	74.0	41.0	36.0
Indonesia	410.0	550.0	120.0	180.0
Lao People's Democratic Republic	9.1	19.0	3.6	7.0
Malaysia	74.0	85.0	12.0	16.0
Myanmar	240.0	270.0	94.0	110.0
Philippines	18.0	190.0	1.4	13.0
Singapore	4.0	8.1	0.5	0.7
Thailand	700.0	570.0	330.0	240.0
Timor-Leste	0.9	1.6	0.5	0.6
Viet Nam	210.0	250.0	63.0	77.0
The Pacific				
Cook Islands	...	...	...	...
Fiji	0.6	2.5	0.5	1.2
Kiribati	...	...	...	...
Marshall Islands	...	...	...	...
Micronesia, Federated States of	...	...	...	...
Nauru	...	...	...	...
Niue	...	...	...	...
Palau	...	...	...	...
Papua New Guinea	30.0	72.0	17.0	44.0
Samoa	...	...	...	...
Solomon Islands	...	...	...	...
Tonga	...	...	...	...
Tuvalu	...	...	...	...
Vanuatu	...	...	...	...
Developed ADB Member Economies				
Australia	20.0	29.0	2.5	3.7
Japan	...	...	...	...
New Zealand	2.3	3.6	0.5	0.6
WORLD	**29,600.0**	**38,600.0**	**15,400.0**	**20,500.0**

... = data not available, ADB = Asian Development Bank.

Note: Figures reported in this table are based on modelled HIV estimates. According to the Joint United Nations Programme on HIV/AIDS, modelled HIV estimates provide a scientifically appropriate way of describing HIV epidemic levels and trends, and are required because it is impossible to count the exact number of people living and newly infected with HIV, or people who have died from AIDS-related causes, in any given economy. Doing so would require regularly testing every person for HIV and investigating all deaths, which is logistically impossible and ethically problematic.

Source: Joint United Nations Programme on HIV/AIDS (UNAIDS). AIDSInfo. https://aidsinfo.unaids.org/ (accessed 29 May 2025).

Data Issues and Comparability

Demographic data are based on vital registration records, censuses, and surveys. Since vital registration records in many developing Asian Development Bank member economies are incomplete, they cannot be used for statistical purposes. In most economies, population censuses, which are used to provide more accurate estimates of population sizes, are conducted every 10 years. Population numbers in between census years are products of imputation methods that use various population distributional assumptions.

The United Nations Department of Economics and Social Affairs' Population Division uses future trends on fertility, mortality, and international migration to project population numbers through to 2100. The medium-fertility variant included in the United Nations' World Population Prospects 2024 assumes, over the remainder of the century, a decline of fertility in economies where large families are still prevalent, a slight increase of fertility in several economies where women have fewer than 2.1 live births on average over a lifetime, and special considerations for the impact on mortality of crises such as the coronavirus disease (COVID-19) pandemic as well as the HIV epidemic.

Urban population statistics are compiled according to each economy's national definition, as there is no agreed international standard for defining an urban area, which poses constraints in comparability of urban and city indicators across economies. Data from World Urbanization Prospects were used when national estimates were not available.

Household surveys, which are the best source of labor force data, are not carried out in all economies on a regular basis. Some economies rely on census data supplemented by enterprise surveys and unemployment registration records, which are often incomplete and may refer only to formal employment. Furthermore, a breakdown by economic activities also may not be available. An initiative is underway to adopt new standards for work and employment statistics, following the recommendations of the 19th International Conference of Labour Statisticians in 2013. The 19th conference provided the statistical concept of work for reference purposes; and the operational concepts, definitions, and guidelines for (i) three distinct subsets of work activities, referred to as forms of work, which include own-use production work, employment work, and volunteer work; (ii) related classifications of the population according to their labor force status and main work status; and (iii) measures of labor underutilization. The concept of employment has also been refined to refer to work for pay or profit. These recommendations were adopted by Armenia, beginning 2018; Azerbaijan, beginning 2015; Brunei Darussalam, beginning 2017; Georgia, beginning 2010; Kazakhstan, beginning 2015; the Lao People's Democratic Republic, beginning 2017; Malaysia, beginning 2019; Mongolia, beginning 2019; Nepal, beginning 2018;

Timor-Leste, beginning 2010; and Uzbekistan, beginning 2017. Hence, data for these years may not be directly comparable with data in other years. For all other economies, the conceptual definitions used are based on the old framework.

When comparing educational indicators across economies, caution is necessary due to differences in academic year length and education quality. The effects of grade repetition are not directly accounted for, complicating comparisons between economies with automatic promotion and those allowing repetition. Enrolment data might exclude various types of continuing education and training, while distinctions between full-time and part-time enrolment may be unclear. Degrees and qualifications may not be classified at the same levels under the International Standard Classification of Education, despite similar ages or years of schooling. This indicator focuses on years of schooling, which does not necessarily reflect the quality of education.

The ideal pupil–trained teacher ratios depend on various factors, including the age and academic needs of pupils as well as the experience and effectiveness of teachers. Part-time teaching, school shifts, and multigrade classes can affect the precision of pupil–teacher ratios. Converting part-time teachers to full-time equivalents and counting double-shift teachers twice can improve accuracy. Pupil–teacher ratios are not equivalent to average class size and national teacher training requirements vary. The UNESCO Institute for Statistics is developing an international classification of teacher training programs for better cross-economy comparisons.

Table 2.2.1: Gross Domestic Product at Purchasing Power Parity
(current international dollars, million)

ADB Regional Member	2010	2015	2019	2020	2021	2022	2023	2024
Developing ADB Member Economies								
Central and West Asia	**2,814,553**	**4,042,231**	**...**	**...**	**...**	**...**	**...**	**...**
Afghanistan	51,355	79,629	97,801	100,898	105,222	83,983	86,713	...
Armenia	21,604	29,315	44,366	43,553	47,165	56,894	63,833	69,234
Azerbaijan	135,185	145,466	167,158	153,048	203,884	228,718	240,157	255,979
Georgia	29,202	45,708	62,388	62,509	70,151	83,388	93,155	104,403
Kazakhstan	313,869	406,611	551,108	565,757	650,470	719,144	783,018	834,233
Kyrgyz Republic	16,815	25,087	34,956	34,834	39,302	45,880	51,815	57,865
Pakistan	754,259	973,520	1,162,667	1,186,294	1,285,343	1,442,775	1,494,096	1,579,724
Tajikistan	17,532	25,719	32,973	35,624	39,727	45,964	51,571	57,254
Türkiye	1,268,554	2,022,940	2,350,308	2,391,489	2,637,031	3,322,806	3,611,521	...
Turkmenistan	49,921	79,153	...	...	...	...	...	...
Uzbekistan	156,258	209,082	281,653	283,863	316,674	359,610	395,989	431,926
East Asia	**15,485,500**	**22,150,205**	**28,931,559**	**30,106,553**	**34,166,564**	**37,597,119**	**40,755,658**	**43,729,022**
China, People's Republic of	12,589,327	18,577,515	24,777,566	25,777,239	29,438,240	32,525,464	35,520,435	38,190,083
Hong Kong, China	345,574	408,627	459,644	435,301	488,412	503,958	538,875	565,931
Korea, Republic of	1,640,278	2,030,372	2,407,645	2,481,996	2,677,430	2,845,652	2,898,616	3,038,656
Mongolia	20,626	31,656	44,457	45,560	50,053	56,320	62,677	67,315
Taipei,China	889,695	1,102,036	1,242,247	1,366,457	1,512,429	1,665,725	1,735,054	1,867,036
South Asia	**5,877,717**	**8,226,566**	**11,378,613**	**11,297,414**	**13,102,175**	**15,044,298**	**16,916,565**	**...**
Bangladesh	407,273	668,950	997,250	1,104,316	1,247,561	1,431,395	1,568,542	1,674,316
Bhutan	5,084	7,565	9,873	9,606	10,437	11,764	12,782	...
India	5,230,655	7,204,581	9,932,851	9,771,021	11,384,368	13,124,053	14,845,911	16,173,667
Maldives	4,303	6,783	9,871	6,129	8,621	10,618	11,114	...
Nepal	58,491	82,283	121,063	122,690	134,000	151,638	159,657	169,970
Sri Lanka	171,911	256,404	307,705	283,652	317,188	314,829	318,559	342,604
Southeast Asia	**5,169,376**	**6,794,592**	**8,816,200**	**8,679,805**	**9,391,734**	**10,652,671**	**...**	**...**
Brunei Darussalam	31,207	26,476	30,701	31,223	35,347	37,250	39,026	41,648
Cambodia	43,335	69,268	101,426	99,390	105,674	119,016	129,472	139,597
Indonesia	2,057,501	2,625,202	3,266,186	3,223,405	3,530,633	3,983,083	4,334,734	4,662,895
Lao People's Democratic Republic	22,606	41,395	56,043	58,547	61,016	65,811	67,467	74,329
Malaysia	578,658	766,028	967,568	931,107	1,022,399	1,192,353	1,279,178	1,377,111
Myanmar	164,140	227,990	300,151	318,055	263,613	308,131	...	...
Philippines	528,817	726,056	988,832	923,367	1,001,824	1,154,612	1,262,175	1,366,276
Singapore	382,788	482,410	600,787	577,214	723,237	806,629	850,876	909,690
Thailand	886,887	1,113,922	1,427,827	1,372,919	1,451,960	1,595,615	1,686,385	1,770,791
Timor-Leste[a]	2,121	3,745	4,923	5,946	3,972	4,097	5,763	...
Viet Nam	471,315	712,101	1,071,756	1,138,633	1,192,059	1,386,075	1,508,682	1,654,735
The Pacific[b]	**32,465**	**48,241**	**57,519**	**54,778**	**56,224**	**64,890**	**...**	**...**
Cook Islands	...	...	...	...	...	...	...	...
Fiji	6,806	10,778	12,095	10,280	9,795	12,571	14,003	...
Kiribati	187	270	342	342	388	434	462	...
Marshall Islands	181	201	266	262	277	294	292	...
Micronesia, Federated States of	330	359	411	408	440	458	474	...
Nauru	59	130	124	128	143	158	164	171
Niue	...	...	...	...	...	...	...	...
Palau	242	319	324	309	279	294	311	...
Papua New Guinea	21,319	32,085	39,011	38,277	39,820	45,094	48,497	51,704
Samoa	1,015	1,213	1,408	1,289	1,404	1,564	1,851	2,004
Solomon Islands	1,163	1,505	1,829	1,791	1,921	2,107	...	...
Tonga	480	581	686	707	742	777	821	...
Tuvalu	31	39	55	54	56	59	61	...
Vanuatu	651	759	968	932	959	1,081	...	...
Developed ADB Member Economies	**5,529,000**	**6,475,934**	**6,963,973**	**6,972,225**	**7,314,414**	**7,918,096**	**8,374,820**	**...**
Australia	867,453	1,101,817	1,334,463	1,384,652	1,494,437	1,713,615	1,879,380	1,936,798
Japan	4,525,401	5,200,905	5,404,462	5,356,711	5,574,651	5,929,963	6,212,963	6,407,673
New Zealand	136,146	173,212	225,048	230,862	245,325	274,519	282,478	...

... = data not available, ADB = Asian Development Bank.

Note: Gross domestic product figures in local currency units are obtained from the economies' official sources and converted into a common currency using the purchasing power parity (PPP) from the World Bank's World Development Indicators. For 2011, 2017, and 2021, PPP figures are based on results from the 2011, 2017 and 2021 benchmark cycles of the International Comparison Program (ICP). For 2010 (and years prior featured in the Key Indicators Database), PPPs are extrapolated from the reference year 2011. For 2012–2016, figures are interpolated from the PPPs of the two ICP reference years, 2011 and 2017. For 2018–2020, figures are interpolated from the PPPs of the two ICP reference years, 2017 and 2021. For 2022–2024, figures are extrapolated from the 2021 ICP PPPs or imputed based on a regression model.

a From September 2019, following the new Timor-Leste Australia Maritime Boundary Treaty, oil revenue from the Joint Petroleum Development Area is included in the national accounts. The National Institute of Statistics Timor-Leste (INETL) disaggregates the accounts into 'oil' and 'non-oil' components. To better assess the performance of the domestic economy, this publication presents GDP on a non-oil basis, which reflects the primary analytical approach used by INETL.

b For reporting economies only.

Source: Asian Development Bank estimates based on data from the economies' official sources.

National Accounts

Table 2.2.2: Gross Domestic Product
(current $ million)

ADB Regional Member	2010	2015	2019	2020	2021	2022	2023	2024
Developing ADB Member Economies								
Central and West Asia	**1,295,428**	**1,585,471**	**...**	**...**	**...**	**...**	**...**	**...**
Afghanistan	16,078	20,607	18,904	20,143	18,525	13,843	15,567	19,119
Armenia	9,260 |	10,553	13,619	12,642	13,879	19,514	24,086	25,787
Azerbaijan	52,906	53,076	48,174	42,693	54,825	78,807	72,429	74,316
Georgia	12,425	15,218	17,639	16,011	18,853	24,990	30,779	33,774*
Kazakhstan	148,052 |	184,387	181,666	171,084	197,056	225,342	261,757	285,983*
Kyrgyz Republic	4,778	6,633 |	9,370	8,275	9,254	12,137	15,173	17,468*
Pakistan	196,982	300,384	321,834	300,832	348,933	375,643	338,450	373,332
Tajikistan	5,642 |	8,271	8,301	8,134	8,938	10,714	12,244	14,206*
Türkiye	776,967	864,314	761,006	720,338	819,865	907,118	1,118,253	...
Turkmenistan	22,582	35,855	...	...	...	...	...	...
Uzbekistan	49,756	86,172	67,277	66,433	77,336	90,087	102,622	114,962*
East Asia	**8,066,390**	**13,673,113**	**17,322,369**	**17,782,826**	**21,297,348**	**21,286,910**	**21,365,042**	**22,038,523***
China, People's Republic of	6,193,268	11,279,165	14,581,031	15,003,237	18,194,561	18,346,944	18,366,936	18,943,335*
Hong Kong, China	228,644	309,376	363,071	344,952	368,919	358,653	381,095	407,150
Korea, Republic of	1,193,040	1,538,480	1,750,610	1,744,390	1,941,520	1,798,660	1,839,410	1,868,880
Mongolia	7,193 |	11,618	14,204	13,312	15,286	17,124	20,325	23,585*
Taipei,China	444,245	534,474	613,453	676,935	777,062	765,529	757,276	795,573
South Asia	**1,879,243**	**2,495,508**	**3,337,699**	**3,177,238**	**3,742,182**	**4,005,670**	**4,233,233***	**...**
Bangladesh	130,410	232,945	351,251	373,959	416,264	460,219	451,534	450,461
Bhutan	1,709	2,188	2,736	2,457	2,768	2,898	3,019	...
India	1,669,620	2,146,759	2,854,799	2,679,381	3,192,375	3,420,984	3,646,847*	3,952,683*
Maldives	2,588	4,115	5,712	3,703	5,238	6,157	6,899	...
Nepal	16,281	24,361	34,186	33,434	36,927	40,828	41,211	42,660*
Sri Lanka	58,636	85,141	89,015	84,304	88,609	74,584	83,723	98,963
Southeast Asia	**2,032,591**	**2,534,004**	**3,255,061**	**3,105,608**	**3,401,693**	**3,687,190***	**...**	**...**
Brunei Darussalam	13,707	12,930	13,469	12,006	14,006	16,682	15,095	15,463
Cambodia	14,248	24,355	36,344	34,835	36,726	39,491	42,317	46,148
Indonesia	756,534	861,658	1,119,096	1,060,971	1,186,459	1,319,305	1,371,109*	1,396,849*
Lao People's Democratic Republic	6,747	14,426	18,741	19,116	19,074	15,363	15,008	15,085
Malaysia	255,018	301,355	365,178	337,456	373,785	407,606	399,705	421,972*
Myanmar	80,011 (2012)	62,543 |	69,329	81,621	66,972 |	64,857	...	...
Philippines	208,369	306,446	376,823	361,751	394,087	404,353	437,056	461,618*
Singapore	239,809	308,004	376,150	349,303	436,423	508,932	505,314	547,482
Thailand	340,628	401,269	543,935	500,361	506,138	495,590*	515,838*	526,386*
Timor-Leste[a]	882	1,590	1,688	1,581	1,563	1,676	1,802	...
Viet Nam	147,107	239,427	334,308	346,606	366,460	413,336	433,673	476,279
The Pacific	**21,145**	**31,077**	**35,846**	**33,664**	**36,096***	**42,392***	**...**	**...**
Cook Islands	241	302	357	283	328	286	366*	...
Fiji	3,140	4,682	5,444	4,432	4,305	4,970	5,442*	...
Kiribati	183	186	219	247	276	264	297*	...
Marshall Islands	161	184	233	242	259 |	253*	259*	...
Micronesia, Federated States of	292	312	395	373	392	416	441*	...
Nauru	50	76	125	125	176	152	152	161
Niue	18 |	21	27	26	26	24	26	30*
Palau	184	283	282	259	236	256 |	282	310*
Papua New Guinea	14,251	21,723	24,751	23,848	26,109	31,653	30,816	...
Samoa	699	826	913	829	897	936	1,136	1,253
Solomon Islands	898	1,308	1,619	1,536 |	1,523*	1,566*	...	...
Tonga	366	437	494	497	520	518	509	...
Tuvalu	31	35	54	53	62	64	...	...
Vanuatu	630	701	935	913	989	1,034	...	...
Developed ADB Member Economies	**7,102,410**	**5,843,331**	**6,684,709**	**6,630,860**	**6,859,971**	**6,128,072**	**6,174,145**	**...**
Australia	1,196,451	1,220,176	1,353,709	1,363,763	1,566,845	1,616,416	1,705,772	1,763,715
Japan	5,759,072	4,444,931	5,117,994	5,054,068	5,039,148	4,262,146	4,213,167	4,026,211
New Zealand	146,888	178,224	213,006	213,030	253,978	249,510	255,206	...

... = data not available; | = marks break in the series; * = provisional, preliminary, estimate; $ = United States dollars; ADB = Asian Development Bank.

Note: Data on gross domestic product (GDP) in United States (US) dollars are sourced from economies' official sources. For Afghanistan, Australia, Malaysia, Myanmar, New Zealand, Niue, the Philippines, Sri Lanka, Türkiye, Turkmenistan, and Tuvalu, GDP figures in local currency units are obtained from the economies' official sources and converted to US dollars using the official exchange rates from the International Monetary Fund. The exchange rates used are expressed as the average rate for a period of time (average of period), calculated as annual averages based on the monthly averages (local currency units relative to the US dollar). For Pakistan and the People's Republic of China, exchange rates used to convert GDP figures in local currency units to US dollars are from the economies' official sources. For Myanmar, the 2010 figure for GDP in US dollars was converted from the domestic currency using the World Bank's alternative conversion factor to calculate the aggregate for Southeast Asia.

a From September 2019, following the new Timor-Leste Australia Maritime Boundary Treaty, oil revenue from the Joint Petroleum Development Area is included in the national accounts. The National Institute of Statistics Timor-Leste (INETL) disaggregates the accounts into 'oil' and 'non-oil' components. To better assess the performance of the domestic economy, this publication presents GDP on a non-oil basis, which reflects the primary analytical approach used by INETL.

Sources: Economies' official sources and Asian Development Bank estimates based on data from the economies' official sources. For Nauru: IMF's World Economic Outlook Database.

Table 2.2.3: Gross Domestic Product per Capita at Purchasing Power Parity
(current international dollars)

ADB Regional Member	2010	2015	2019	2020	2021	2022	2023	2024
Developing ADB Member Economies								
Central and West Asia	**8,035**	**10,555**	**...**	**...**	**...**	**...**	**...**	**...**
Afghanistan	2,097	2,938	3,183	3,214	3,199	2,502	2,531	...
Armenia	7,071	9,737	14,962	14,715	15,916	19,212	21,730	23,146
Azerbaijan	14,930	15,075	16,832	15,305	20,298	22,656	23,545	25,096
Georgia	7,712	12,270	16,770	16,791	18,916	22,461	25,177	28,217
Kazakhstan	19,436	23,180	29,777	30,157	34,218	36,650	39,349	41,381
Kyrgyz Republic	3,076	4,153	5,304	5,179	5,736	6,578	7,298	8,037
Pakistan	4,347	5,078	5,381	5,382	5,718	6,294	6,187	...
Tajikistan	2,332	3,043	3,579	3,786	4,054	4,604	5,056	5,505
Türkiye	17,344	25,863	28,461	28,680	31,338	39,101	42,326	...
Turkmenistan	8,972	12,734	...	...	...	...	...	...
Uzbekistan	5,471	6,680	8,387	8,292	9,070	10,088	10,875	11,620
East Asia	**10,879**	**15,088**	**19,337**	**20,093**	**22,798**	**25,108**	**27,247**	**29,260**
China, People's Republic of	9,389	13,430	17,572	18,254	20,840	23,039	25,198	27,118
Hong Kong, China	49,198	56,043	61,221	58,187	65,885	68,602	71,506	75,216
Korea, Republic of	33,101	39,800	46,511	47,881	51,718	55,071	56,052	58,717
Mongolia	7,532	10,458	13,605	13,693	14,792	16,402	18,005	19,233
Taipei,China	38,451	46,972	52,658	57,940	64,393	71,841	74,232	79,744
South Asia	**4,251**	**5,514**	**7,295**	**7,168**	**8,234**	**9,358**	**10,436**	**...**
Bangladesh	2,741	4,210	5,989	6,570	7,336	8,335	9,071	...
Bhutan	7,306	9,992	13,312	12,826	13,803	15,412	16,594	...
India	4,410	5,615	7,407	7,209	8,318	9,490	10,642	11,487
Maldives	10,933	14,927	18,488	10,996	15,168	18,329	18,827	...
Nepal	2,228	2,943	4,157	4,175	4,595	5,152	5,374	...
Sri Lanka	8,315	12,227	14,113	12,941	14,316	14,194	14,456	15,633
Southeast Asia	**8,791**	**10,826**	**13,447**	**13,096**	**14,058**	**15,802**	**...**	**...**
Brunei Darussalam	80,680	64,200	68,074	70,673	80,203	83,633	86,627	91,434
Cambodia	3,068	4,590	6,356	6,145	6,369	7,066	7,575	8,069
Indonesia	8,660	10,271	12,237	11,930	12,948	14,447	15,554	16,558
Lao People's Democratic Republic	3,742	6,376	7,868	8,097	8,315	8,842	8,936	9,720
Malaysia	20,241	24,563	29,750	28,696	31,385	36,466	38,299	40,432
Myanmar	3,348	4,463	5,702	5,999	4,938	5,732	...	...
Philippines	5,678	7,201	9,222	8,456	9,101	10,408	11,278	12,102
Singapore	75,401	87,156	105,335	101,518	132,617	143,095	143,786	150,689
Thailand	13,454	16,386	20,599	19,752	20,835	22,843	24,091	25,220
Timor-Leste[a]	1,948	3,106	3,845	4,574	3,007	3,056	4,236	...
Viet Nam	5,413	7,721	11,108	11,668	12,101	13,935	15,040	16,329
The Pacific[b]	**3,479**	**4,537**	**4,862**	**4,514**	**3,917**	**4,398**	**...**	**...**
Cook Islands	...	...	...	...	...	...	...	...
Fiji	8,001	12,397	13,600	11,532	10,963	13,975	15,605	...
Kiribati	1,819	2,451	2,914	2,862	3,194	3,521	3,684	...
Marshall Islands	3,416	4,034	6,019	5,970	6,542	7,098	7,239	...
Micronesia, Federated States of	3,210	3,461	3,930	3,903	4,200	4,361	4,507	...
Nauru	5,890	11,951	10,740	10,911	12,061	13,221	13,665	14,157
Niue	...	...	...	...	...	...	...	...
Palau	13,249	18,075	18,583	17,543	15,822	16,736	17,610	...
Papua New Guinea	3,022	3,901	4,195	3,991	3,380	3,712	3,871	4,003
Samoa	5,460	6,261	7,031	6,382	6,865	7,563	8,874	9,512
Solomon Islands	2,030	2,310	2,537	2,470	2,597	2,794	...	...
Tonga	4,661	5,726	6,829	7,049	7,408	7,760	8,215	...
Tuvalu	2,742	3,682	5,370	5,269	5,440	5,528	6,001	...
Vanuatu	2,717	2,827	3,318	3,106	3,124	3,442	...	...
Developed ADB Member Economies	**35,797**	**41,628**	**44,478**	**44,535**	**46,752**	**50,685**	**53,558**	**...**
Australia	39,373	46,264	52,673	53,984	58,182	65,872	70,513	71,220
Japan	35,335	40,907	42,803	42,569	44,355	47,392	49,897	51,685
New Zealand	31,293	37,578	45,278	45,513	48,249	54,021	54,323	...

... = data not available, ADB = Asian Development Bank.

Note: The figures in the table are calculated as gross domestic product (GDP) at purchasing power parity (PPP) divided by the midyear population. GDP figures in local currency units are obtained from the economies' official sources and converted into a common currency using the purchasing power parity (PPP) from the World Bank's World Development Indicators. For 2011, 2017, and 2021, PPP figures are based on results from the 2011, 2017 and 2021 benchmark cycles of the International Comparison Program (ICP). For 2010 (and years prior featured in the Key Indicators Database), PPPs are extrapolated from the reference year 2011. For 2012–2016, figures are interpolated from the PPPs of the two ICP reference years, 2011 and 2017. For 2018–2020, figures are interpolated from the PPPs of the two ICP reference years, 2017 and 2021. For 2022–2024, figures are extrapolated from the 2021 ICP PPPs or imputed based on a regression model.

a From September 2019, following the new Timor-Leste Australia Maritime Boundary Treaty, oil revenue from the Joint Petroleum Development Area is included in the national accounts. The National Institute of Statistics Timor-Leste (INETL) disaggregates the accounts into 'oil' and 'non-oil' components. To better assess the performance of the domestic economy, this publication presents GDP on a non-oil basis, which reflects the primary analytical approach used by INETL.

b For reporting economies only.

Source: Asian Development Bank estimates based on data from the economies' official sources.

Table 2.2.4: Gross National Income per Capita, Atlas Method
(current $)

ADB Regional Member	2010	2015	2019	2020	2021	2022	2023	2024
Developing ADB Member Economies								
Central and West Asia[a]	**3,252**	**4,039**	**3,503**	**3,271**	**3,482**	**3,739**	**4,012**	**4,355**
Afghanistan	530	590	520	490	380	370	370	...
Armenia	3,280	3,910	4,650	4,230	4,580	5,680	6,840	7,780
Azerbaijan	5,400	6,610	4,510	4,480	4,910	5,670	6,670	7,310
Georgia	3,220	4,500	4,780	4,330	4,760	5,690	6,710	8,200
Kazakhstan	7,210	11,040	8,500	8,380	8,540	9,420	10,690	12,150
Kyrgyz Republic	850	1,160	1,240	1,210	1,270	1,540	1,840	2,150
Pakistan	1,000	1,280	1,520	1,370	1,420	1,510	1,460	1,430
Tajikistan	910	1,230	1,050	1,030	1,130	1,360	1,400	1,650
Türkiye	10,380	12,080	9,800	9,160	10,010	10,640	11,730	13,150
Turkmenistan	3,720	6,300	6,450	6,740	7,200	7,780	8,250	8,390
Uzbekistan	1,420	2,790	2,150	2,000	2,250	2,500	2,750	3,020
East Asia[a]	**5,416**	**9,147**	**11,764**	**11,957**	**13,506**	**14,473**	**14,991**	**14,938**
China, People's Republic of	4,410	8,040	10,510	10,740	12,220	13,170	13,730	13,660
Hong Kong, China	33,620	41,180	50,480	48,550	54,380	54,000	54,910	57,100
Korea, Republic of	22,280	28,720	33,830	33,040	35,180	36,160	35,490	...
Mongolia	1,990	3,770	3,800	3,690	3,690	4,340	4,870	5,350
Taipei,China	19,334	22,731	26,885	28,076	31,773	34,636	34,100	34,165
South Asia[a]	**1,171**	**1,562**	**2,105**	**1,957**	**2,223**	**2,438**	**2,603**	**2,663**
Bangladesh	780	1,200	2,220	2,320	2,600	2,850	2,880	2,820
Bhutan	2,180	2,740	3,370	3,040	3,300	3,600	3,740	...
India	1,210	1,580	2,070	1,900	2,170	2,390	2,580	2,650
Maldives	6,000	8,210	10,730	7,050	9,350	10,570	11,090	11,650
Nepal	530	870	1,240	1,190	1,250	1,380	1,430	1,470
Sri Lanka	2,360	3,920	4,220	3,880	4,010	3,620	3,530	3,860
Southeast Asia[b]	**2,986**	**4,027**	**4,740**	**4,536**	**4,792**	**5,191**	**5,429**	**5,589**
Brunei Darussalam	35,370	38,180	31,550	30,810	29,890	30,970	34,390	36,150
Cambodia	910	1,430	2,100	2,050	2,120	2,270	2,390	2,520
Indonesia	2,490	3,390	4,020	3,850	4,130	4,520	4,810	4,910
Lao People's Democratic Republic	990	1,960	2,520	2,470	2,500	2,300	2,110	2,000
Malaysia	8,130	10,350	10,750	10,110	10,520	11,610	11,710	11,670
Myanmar	880	1,230	1,380	1,320	1,240	1,290	1,230	1,220
Philippines	2,310	3,280	3,760	3,350	3,570	4,010	4,320	4,470
Singapore	44,930	53,160	58,430	55,780	65,010	66,910	69,850	74,750
Thailand	4,490	5,560	7,060	6,900	7,090	7,210	7,190	7,120
Timor-Leste	2,870	2,180	2,170	2,040	2,050	1,820	2,020	1,560
Viet Nam	1,370	2,460	3,290	3,400	3,540	3,980	4,150	4,490
The Pacific[a]	**1,966**	**2,826**	**2,837**	**2,725**	**2,684**	**3,020**	**3,134**	**3,244**
Cook Islands	9,349	17,121	18,768	13,805	15,066	18,821	19,613	...
Fiji	3,450	4,820	5,620	4,680	4,520	5,440	5,680	5,680
Kiribati	2,030	3,490	3,610	3,070	3,150	3,320	3,690	3,620
Marshall Islands	3,820	4,980	6,770	6,610	6,660	7,500	7,860	8,380
Micronesia, Federated States of	2,780	3,500	4,050	3,990	4,040	4,050	4,130	4,250
Nauru	5,060	12,160	15,790	17,210	19,400	22,540	23,750	21,260
Niue	10,611	17,580	15,589	15,699	15,132	15,342	16,022	17,233
Palau	10,180	14,030	16,220	15,440	13,830	14,050	14,070	...
Papua New Guinea	1,660	2,520	2,420	2,410	2,370	2,690	2,800	2,940
Samoa	3,430	3,970	4,270	4,060	3,910	3,780	4,220	4,650
Solomon Islands	1,600	2,010	2,210	2,170	2,140	2,120	2,110	2,080
Tonga	3,270	4,220	4,940	5,130	5,240	5,260	5,520	...
Tuvalu	4,480	5,650	6,880	6,880	7,510	8,100	8,770	...
Vanuatu	2,580	2,980	3,740	3,390	3,520	3,850	3,830	3,940
Developed ADB Member Economies[b]	**43,916**	**42,653**	**44,093**	**43,030**	**45,979**	**45,848**	**43,726**	**40,991**
Australia	46,750	60,520	54,890	53,630	57,180	60,710	63,160	62,550
Japan	43,910	39,380	41,970	40,930	43,710	42,640	39,360	36,030
New Zealand	29,750	40,670	43,050	41,710	45,560	48,820	48,600	46,280
DEVELOPING ADB MEMBER ECONOMIES[a]	**3,224**	**4,936**	**6,088**	**6,025**	**6,713**	**7,201**	**7,486**	**7,527**
ALL ADB REGIONAL MEMBERS[a]	**4,790**	**6,324**	**7,449**	**7,341**	**8,096**	**8,554**	**8,748**	**8,686**
WORLD	**9,402**	**10,574**	**11,545**	**11,099**	**12,173**	**12,954**	**13,333**	**13,439**

... = data not available, $ = United States dollars, ADB = Asian Development Bank.

Note: The Atlas method refers to a conversion factor that averages the exchange rate for a given year and the two preceding years, adjusted for differences in rates of inflation between the member economy and the G5 economies (France, Germany, Japan, the United Kingdom, and the United States).

a Aggregates are weighted averages estimated using midyear population. For estimating aggregates, imputation was done for economies with missing data by substituting available data from the nearest years.

b Aggregates are weighted averages estimated using midyear population.

Sources: World Bank. World Development Indicators. https://databank.worldbank.org/source/world-development-indicators (accessed 2 July 2025).
For the Cook Islands; Niue; and Taipei,China: Asian Development Bank estimates using the Atlas method based on economies' official sources.

Table 2.2.5: Gross Domestic Product per Capita
(current $)

ADB Regional Member	2010	2015	2019	2020	2021	2022	2023	2024
Developing ADB Member Economies								
Central and West Asia	**3,698**	**4,140**	**...**	**...**	**...**	**...**	**...**	**...**
Afghanistan	561	566	497	511	356	357	416	...
Armenia	3,041 |	3,512	4,597	4,269	4,685	6,661	8,125	8,501
Azerbaijan	5,843	5,501	4,851	4,269	5,458	7,806	7,133	7,284
Georgia	3,282	4,087	4,741	4,301	5,084	6,730	8,120	9,144*
Kazakhstan	9,071 |	10,511	9,813	9,122	10,371	11,477	13,153	14,187*
Kyrgyz Republic	920	1,163 |	1,422	1,230	1,351	1,740	2,137	2,419*
Pakistan	1,140	1,538	1,504	1,378	1,568	1,655	1,462	1,582
Tajikistan	750 |	979	901	864	912	1,073	1,202	1,368*
Türkiye	10,629	11,085	9,208	8,600	9,601	10,659	13,243	15,463
Turkmenistan	4,058	5,768	...	...	...	...	...	...
Uzbekistan	1,742	2,753	2,003	1,941	2,215	2,527	2,818	3,093*
East Asia	**5,667**	**9,314**	**11,577**	**11,868**	**14,211**	**14,216**	**14,284**	**14,747***
China, People's Republic of	4,619	8,154	10,341	10,625	12,880	12,996	13,029	13,451*
Hong Kong, China	32,551	42,431	48,358	46,110	49,766	48,822	50,569	54,113
Korea, Republic of	24,075	30,158	33,819	33,652	37,503	34,809	35,570	36,113
Mongolia	2,727 |	3,920	4,450	4,128	4,657	5,126	6,008	6,898*
Taipei,China	19,197	22,780	25,998	28,705	33,111	32,827	32,442	33,983
South Asia	**1,359**	**1,671**	**2,137**	**2,014**	**2,350**	**2,492**	**2,611***	**...**
Bangladesh	882	1,475	2,122	2,234	2,462	2,687	2,643	2,625
Bhutan	2,405	2,847	3,689	3,281	3,661	3,833	3,920	...
India	1,408	1,673	2,129	1,977	2,333	2,474	2,614*	2,807*
Maldives[a]	6,576	9,056	10,698	6,644	9,213	10,639	11,141	...
Nepal	620	871	1,204	1,167	1,277	1,411	1,389	1,434*
Sri Lanka	2,836	4,060	4,083	3,846	3,999	3,363	3,799	4,516
Southeast Asia	**3,456**	**4,037**	**4,965**	**4,686**	**5,092**	**5,470***	**...**	**...**
Brunei Darussalam	35,437	31,354	29,865	27,175	31,781	37,453	33,507	33,948
Cambodia	1,025	1,616	2,260	2,132	2,213	2,345	2,476	2,666
Indonesia	3,172	3,373	4,193	3,927	4,351	4,785	4,920*	4,960*
Lao People's Democratic Republic	1,117	2,222	2,631	2,644	2,599	2,064	1,988	1,973
Malaysia	8,920	9,663	11,228	10,400	11,474	12,466	11,975	12,389*
Myanmar[b]	1,605 (2012)	1,224 |	1,317	1,540	1,254 |	1,206	...	...
Philippines	2,237	3,039	3,512	3,313	3,580	3,645	3,905	4,089
Singapore	47,237	55,647	65,950	61,434	80,025	90,284	85,392	90,689
Thailand	5,167	5,902	7,847	7,199	7,263	7,095*	7,365*	7,497*
Timor-Leste[c]	810	1,319	1,318	1,216	1,183	1,250	1,324	...
Viet Nam	1,690	2,596	3,465	3,552	3,720	4,155	4,323	4,700
The Pacific	**2,266**	**2,923**	**3,030**	**2,774**	**2,515***	**2,873***	**...**	**...**
Cook Islands	10,160	16,388	17,663	17,175	17,996	13,966	16,954*	...
Fiji	3,691	5,386	6,122	4,973	4,818	5,525	6,065*	...
Kiribati	1,779	1,691	1,861	2,070	2,270	2,138	2,370*	...
Marshall Islands[d]	3,043	3,681	5,275	5,502	6,103	6,119	6,417*	...
Micronesia, Federated States of	2,836	3,011	3,777	3,563	3,736	3,961	4,197*	...
Nauru	5,844	8,100 |	10,567	10,346	14,303	12,153	11,866	12,318
Niue	11,983 |	14,155	17,337	16,654	15,427	14,960	15,792	18,364*
Palau	10,044	15,788	16,154	14,653	13,309	14,526*	15,971*	17,351*
Papua New Guinea	2,020	2,642	2,662	2,488	2,642	3,107	2,934	...
Samoa	4,072	4,250	4,543	4,094	4,363	4,511	5,433	5,849
Solomon Islands	1,587	2,035	2,274	2,103 |	2,032*	2,038*	...	...
Tonga	3,564	4,300	4,915	4,954	5,182	5,170	5,090	...
Tuvalu	2,816	3,275	5,088	4,933	5,865	5,970	...	...
Vanuatu	2,630	2,610	3,205	3,059	3,240	3,312	...	...
Developed ADB Member Economies	**45,984**	**37,562**	**42,695**	**42,354**	**43,847**	**39,227**	**...**	**...**
Australia	54,306	51,233	53,433	53,170	61,001	62,135	64,000	64,856
Japan	44,968	34,961	40,534	40,164	40,094	34,063	33,836	32,476
New Zealand	33,668	38,425	42,494	41,795	49,667	48,518	...	...

... = data not available; | = marks break in the series; * = provisional, preliminary, estimate; $ = United States dollars; ADB = Asian Development Bank.

Note: The figures in the table are calculated as gross domestic product (GDP) in current United States (US) dollars divided by the midyear population. GDP figures in US dollars are sourced from economies' official sources. For Australia, Malaysia, Myanmar, Nauru, New Zealand, Niue, the Philippines, Sri Lanka, Türkiye, Turkmenistan, and Tuvalu, GDP figures in local currency units are obtained from the economies' official sources and converted to US dollars using the official exchange rates from the International Monetary Fund. The exchange rates used are expressed as the average rate for a period of time (average of period), calculated as annual averages based on the monthly averages (local currency units relative to the US dollar). For Pakistan and the People's Republic of China, exchange rates used to convert GDP figures in local currency units to US dollars are from the economies' official sources. For Myanmar, the 2010 figure for GDP in US dollars was converted from the domestic currency using the World Bank's alternative conversion factor to calculate the aggregate for Southeast Asia.

a Data refer to per capita GDP of population including expatriates.
b For 2000–2011, figures are not computed due to the official exchange rates being pegged to the special drawing rights.
c From September 2019, following the new Timor-Leste Australia Maritime Boundary Treaty, oil revenue from the Joint Petroleum Development Area is included in the national accounts. The National Institute of Statistics Timor-Leste (INETL) disaggregates the accounts into 'oil' and 'non-oil' components. To better assess the performance of the domestic economy, this publication presents GDP on a non-oil basis, which reflects the primary analytical approach used by INETL.
d For 2021 onward, per capita GDP was calculated using an estimated population size of 55.2 million derived based on average annual population growth rate.

Sources: Economies' official sources and Asian Development Bank estimates based on data from the economies' official sources. For Afghanistan, World Bank. World Development Indicators. https://databank.worldbank.org/source/world-development-indicators# (accessed 7 May 2025). For Nauru, data for 2016 onward are sourced from the IMF's World Economic Outlook Database.

Table 2.2.6: Agriculture, Industry, and Services Value-Added
(% of GDP)

ADB Regional Member	Agriculture Value-Added				Industry Value-Added				Services Value-Added			
	2010	2015	2020	2024	2010	2015	2020	2024	2010	2015	2020	2024
Developing ADB Member Economies												
Central and West Asia												
Afghanistan	28.8	22.7	28.1	35.5 (2023)	21.3	22.7	14.7	16.9 (2023)	49.8	54.7	57.2	47.5 (2023)
Armenia	18.8	18.9	12.4	8.6	36.3	28.2	29.3	25.1	45.0	52.9	58.2	66.4
Azerbaijan	5.9	6.8	7.4	6.3	64.1	49.3	46.3	47.2	30.0	43.9	46.2	46.5
Georgia	10.1	9.6	9.5	6.2*	19.1	22.3	24.1	21.9*	70.8	68.1	66.3	71.9*
Kazakhstan	4.7	5.0	5.7	4.2*	41.9	32.5	35.0	33.9*	53.4	62.5	59.3	61.9*
Kyrgyz Republic	18.8	15.4	13.6	10.1*	28.2	27.5	30.0	28.9*	53.1	57.1	56.5	61.0*
Pakistan	23.6	24.4	23.2	25.0	21.8	20.5	19.8	21.3	54.7	55.1	57.0	53.7
Tajikistan	21.8	23.7	24.7	25.2*	27.9	33.2	36.8	27.6*	50.3	43.1	38.4	47.2*
Türkiye	10.2	7.8	7.5	6.9 (2023)	27.8	31.6	31.5	32.0 (2023)	62.0	60.6	61.0	61.0 (2023)
Turkmenistan	11.5	9.3	...	...	60.0	56.9	...	...	28.5	33.8	...	...
Uzbekistan	30.6	32.1	24.1	19.2*	24.1	24.8	34.3	33.4*	45.3	43.1	41.6	47.4*
East Asia												
China, People's Republic of	9.4	8.5	7.9	7.2*	45.9	40.2	37.1	36.8*	44.6	51.2	54.9	56.1*
Hong Kong, China	0.1	0.1	0.1	0.0 (2023)	7.0	7.3	6.4	6.4 (2023)	93.0	92.7	93.4	93.5 (2023)
Korea, Republic of	2.2	2.1	1.7	1.6	37.7	38.1	36.3	37.0	60.1	59.8	62.0	61.4
Mongolia	11.6	14.0	12.8	7.3*	36.1	34.1	40.2	40.3*	52.4	52.0	47.0	52.4*
Taipei,China	1.6	1.8	1.6	1.5	33.4	36.3	39.0	39.8	65.0	62.0	59.4	58.7
South Asia												
Bangladesh	17.2	14.7	12.4	11.5	27.6	31.9	34.1	35.3	55.3	53.4	53.4	53.2
Bhutan	12.4	12.0	15.7	15.0 (2023)	39.3	38.5	31.8	29.6 (2023)	48.3	49.5	52.5	55.5 (2023)
India	18.4	17.7	20.4	17.9*	33.1	30.0	27.4	27.1*	48.5	52.3	52.3	54.9*
Maldives	5.6	5.5	7.6	5.1 (2023)	9.4	10.7	12.6	9.7 (2023)	77.7	72.4	70.8	70.6 (2023)
Nepal	35.4	29.4	25.2	24.1*	15.1	14.6	13.7	13.0*	49.5	56.0	61.2	62.9*
Sri Lanka	10.1	8.9	8.7	9.1	30.9	32.1	29.9	28.0	59.0	58.9	61.3	62.9
Southeast Asia												
Brunei Darussalam	0.7	1.1	1.2	1.2	67.4	60.2	58.1	60.7	31.9	38.7	40.7	38.1
Cambodia	29.8	21.5	18.2	17.8	27.8	33.5	40.0	44.0	42.4	45.0	41.8	38.2
Indonesia	14.3	13.9	14.2	13.2*	43.9	41.4	39.7	41.1*	41.8	44.7	46.1	45.7*
Lao People's Democratic Republic	30.6	19.7	18.4	24.4	29.8	31.0	37.2	35.3	39.6	49.4	44.4	40.2
Malaysia	10.2	8.3	8.2	8.2*	40.9	38.4	35.9	37.1*	48.9	52.0	54.8	53.6*
Myanmar	36.9	26.8	20.9	22.3 (2022)	26.5	34.5	38.6	38.2 (2022)	36.7	38.8	40.5	39.4 (2022)
Philippines	13.7	11.0	10.2	9.1*	32.3	30.5	28.4	27.7*	53.9	58.5	61.4	63.2*
Singapore	0.0	0.0	0.0	0.0	28.2	25.8	24.4	22.7	71.8	74.2	75.6	77.3
Thailand[a]	10.5	8.9	8.7	8.7*	37.1	33.4	30.6	29.7*	52.4	57.7	60.7	61.6*
Timor-Leste[b]	24.7	17.8	18.5	19.1 (2023)	8.8	18.4	14.0	12.0 (2023)	66.5	63.8	67.5	68.9 (2023)
Viet Nam	15.4	14.5	12.7	11.9*	33.0	34.3	36.7	37.6*	40.6	42.2	41.8	42.4*
The Pacific												
Cook Islands	3.4	3.2	3.1	2.7 (2023)	7.9	11.3	9.7	4.6 (2023)	88.7	85.4	87.2	92.6 (2023)
Fiji	11.0	10.0	16.9	14.5 (2023)	20.9	19.3	20.3	17.5 (2023)	68.1	70.6	62.8	68.0 (2023)
Kiribati	24.8	23.4	26.1	25.7*(2023)	12.0	15.1	9.5	10.8* (2023)	63.2	61.5	64.4	63.5*(2023)
Marshall Islands	11.3	12.9	20.2	20.1 (2023)	15.6	11.7	13.5	11.4 (2023)	76.5	78.7	69.8	72.8 (2023)
Micronesia, Federated States of	27.1	28.2	...	...	8.1	7.0	...	...	64.8	64.9	...	...
Nauru	6.3	4.0	4.7	3.3*	32.7	6.1	7.5	15.0*	61.0	89.9	73.3	74.0*
Niue	23.0	20.8	...	...	4.0	2.3(2014)	...	...	73.0	77.0(2014)	...	...
Palau	4.5	3.4	3.6	3.4 (2023)	11.0	9.0	14.0	11.2 (2023)	87.0	89.1	84.3	87.3 (2023)
Papua New Guinea	20.2	18.3	19.6	17.9*	34.2	36.4	34.5	38.8*	45.5	45.3	45.9	43.3*
Samoa	9.5	9.2	11.0	10.1	16.2	16.2	12.4	11.2	74.4	74.6	76.6	78.7
Solomon Islands	34.6	33.3	34.1	33.8* (2022)	13.8	15.6	17.2	18.7* (2022)	51.6	51.2	48.6	47.3*(2022)
Tonga	18.7	19.6	20.8	21.6 (2023)	20.5	18.1	18.0	16.7 (2023)	60.9	62.2	61.2	61.8 (2023)
Tuvalu	27.3	21.4	8.9	9.2 (2023)	5.7	12.7	15.2	14.5 (2023)	67.0	65.9	75.9	76.3 (2023)
Vanuatu	20.8	24.0	24.4	26.8 (2022)	13.7	10.6	11.0	8.1 (2022)	65.6	65.4	64.6	65.1 (2022)
Developed ADB Member Economies												
Australia	2.4	2.5	2.1	2.4	27.1	25.5	27.1	27.7	70.5	72.1	70.8	70.0
Japan	1.1	1.0	1.1	0.9 (2023)	28.3	28.8	29.2	28.8 (2023)	70.6	70.2	69.8	70.3 (2023)
New Zealand	7.1	4.9	6.2	5.0 (2022)	23.2	23.2	21.7	21.4 (2022)	69.7	72.0	72.1	73.6 (2022)

... = data not available; 0.0 = magnitude is less than half of the unit employed; * = provisional, preliminary, estimate; ADB = Asian Development Bank; GDP = gross domestic product.

a Value-added for construction is included under services.

b From September 2019, following the new Timor-Leste Australia Maritime Boundary Treaty, oil revenue from the Joint Petroleum Development Area is included in the national accounts. The National Institute of Statistics Timor-Leste (INETL) disaggregates the accounts into 'oil' and 'non-oil' components. To better assess the performance of the domestic economy, this publication presents GDP on a non-oil basis, which reflects the primary analytical approach used by INETL.

Source: Economies' official sources.

Table 2.2.7: Household and Government Consumption Expenditure
(% of GDP)

ADB Regional Member	Household Consumption				Government Consumption			
	2010	2015	2020	2024	2010	2015	2020	2024
Developing ADB Member Economies								
Central and West Asia[a]	**61.5**	**62.0**	**61.2**	**63.2**	**13.4**	**12.6**	**14.0**	**12.0**
Afghanistan	97.4	82.9	91.8	96.3	14.0	12.1	21.2	21.2
Armenia[b]	82.0	77.9	75.3	66.5	13.1	13.1	15.0	10.7
Azerbaijan	38.9	56.3	60.5	53.6 (2023)	10.9	12.4	16.2	13.8 (2023)
Georgia	76.8	73.9	77.8	70.0*	17.3	14.6	14.6	13.4*
Kazakhstan[b]	45.4	53.7	53.0	53.2*	10.8	11.6	12.7	11.0*
Kyrgyz Republic[b]	84.6	90.5	76.4	88.3 (2023)	18.1	17.8	18.4	16.0 (2023)
Pakistan[b]	79.0	80.2	80.5	84.4	10.9	9.8	11.8	8.5
Tajikistan[b]	84.7	71.2	77.6	89.0 (2023)	11.3	11.6	11.6	10.7 (2023)
Türkiye	62.4	59.7	56.4	59.1 (2023)	14.9	13.8	15.0	13.1 (2023)
Turkmenistan[b]	5.0	9.3 (2013)	...	...	9.3	9.1 (2013)	...	...
Uzbekistan[b]	61.5	64.9	64.4	68.0*	12.5	13.6	14.6	13.9*
East Asia	**39.3**	**41.2**	**40.8**	**40.8**	**14.8**	**16.1**	**17.7**	**16.3**
China, People's Republic of	34.6	38.1	38.2	39.9	14.8	16.3	17.6	16.6
Hong Kong, China[b]	61.4	66.4	66.3	67.4	8.9	9.6	12.7	12.8
Korea, Republic of	49.8	48.1	45.8	46.4	13.5	14.3	17.0	17.2
Mongolia[b]	55.2	61.9	59.8	49.7*	12.7	14.9	15.6	16.3*
Taipei,China[b]	53.2	51.5	48.3	47.1	15.1	13.9	13.9	13.3
South Asia	**56.8**	**61.3**	**62.1**	**62.3**	**16.8**	**17.3**	**19.2**	**15.7**
Bangladesh	70.8	69.4	67.0	70.1	5.4	5.4	6.0	5.9
Bhutan[b]	42.1	51.0	54.3	59.4 (2023)	21.2	19.1	22.3	20.3 (2023)
India[b]	54.7	59.0	61.1	61.4*	11.0	10.4	11.6	10.0*
Maldives	...	40.9	59.4	51.4 (2023)	...	18.1	23.0	17.1 (2023)
Nepal[b]	78.6	83.6	85.2	86.1*	10.0	8.8	9.1	6.3*
Sri Lanka	68.5	63.9	62.9	68.7	8.5	8.9	10.4	7.0
Southeast Asia	**51.0**	**54.0**	**54.9**	**53.9**	**10.6**	**11.5**	**12.1**	**10.6**
Brunei Darussalam[b]	14.7	19.8	23.8	28.5	22.2	25.1	25.4	23.0
Cambodia[b]	80.2	74.2	64.3	60.1	6.5	5.5	5.4	5.8
Indonesia[b]	56.2	57.5	58.9	55.4*	9.0	9.7	9.7	7.7*
Lao People's Democratic Republic	65.1 (2012)	55.7	47.9	63.3 (2023)	12.1 (2012)	16.6	13.6	10.3 (2023)
Malaysia[b]	48.1	53.9	61.0	60.7*	12.6	13.1	13.0	12.0*
Myanmar[c]	67.3	74.0	71.9	72.8 (2022)				
Philippines[b]	70.2	72.5	75.1	76.1*	9.7	10.9	15.3	14.5*
Singapore	36.3	37.2	32.1	31.5	9.7	10.2	12.3	10.6
Thailand	51.7	49.7	52.2	57.5*	16.0	16.9	17.8	16.7*
Timor-Leste[d]	68.7	55.1	67.0	78.8 (2023)	103.2	58.9	60.8	61.1 (2023)
Viet Nam	58.4	59.3	56.0	53.9*	10.4	10.7	9.5	8.9*
The Pacific	**...**	**...**	**...**	**...**	**...**	**...**	**...**	**...**
Cook Islands	...	...	...	...	...	...	...	...
Fiji[e]	72.6	60.9	76.3	69.5*(2023)	15.0	20.2	23.6	20.8*(2023)
Kiribati	85.8	87.6	87.6	111.2*(2023)	57.9	55.6	54.5	55.9*(2023)
Marshall Islands	73.8	76.2	60.0	62.6 (2023)	55.3	56.7	54.3	48.9 (2023)
Micronesia, Federated States of	...	...	...	...	...	...	...	...
Nauru	...	...	...	...	...	...	...	...
Niue	...	...	...	...	...	...	...	...
Palau	67.6	63.4	72.7	...	37.3	28.2	42.0	...
Papua New Guinea[b]	48.0 (2005)	...	...	...	16.1 (2005)	...	...	...
Samoa	66.9	63.2	76.5	63.7	13.9	14.4	16.9	19.2
Solomon Islands	61.6	60.5	59.6	57.9*(2022)	31.5	29.6	25.1	29.2*(2022)
Tonga	87.0	87.7	78.4	101.5 (2023)	18.8	21.3	22.5	29.1 (2023)
Tuvalu	...	...	...	...	...	...	...	...
Vanuatu	62.6	66.9	70.1	75.6 (2022)	18.3	16.5	23.4	23.9 (2022)
Developed ADB Member Economies	**55.6**	**54.9**	**52.6**	**52.5**	**19.2**	**19.5**	**21.1**	**21.2**
Australia	55.3	56.1	52.3	51.2	18.8	19.2	21.9	22.2
Japan[b]	56.9	55.8	54.1	54.1	19.2	19.6	21.0	20.6
New Zealand	56.4	56.2	56.0	56.6 (2023)	19.7	18.5	20.4	21.3 (2023)
DEVELOPING ADB MEMBER ECONOMIES[a]	**45.9**	**47.0**	**46.4**	**46.9**	**14.3**	**15.4**	**17.0**	**15.3**
ALL ADB REGIONAL MEMBERS[a]	**49.3**	**48.8**	**47.7**	**47.8**	**16.0**	**16.3**	**17.8**	**16.2**
WORLD	**48.8**	**48.3**	**46.3**	**...**	**14.9**	**16.1**	**17.1**	**...**

.... = data not available, * = provisional or preliminary, ADB = Asian Development Bank, GDP = gross domestic product.

Note: Figures in the table are calculated as a percentage of GDP at current prices.

a For estimating aggregates, GDP figures in domestic currencies were converted to United States dollars using official exchange rates, and imputation was done for economies with missing data by substituting available data from the nearest years.

b Data for household consumption includes nonprofit institutions serving households.

c Data refer to total final consumption expenditure.

d From September 2019, following the new Timor-Leste Australia Maritime Boundary Treaty, oil revenue from the Joint Petroleum Development Area is included in the national accounts. The National Institute of Statistics Timor-Leste (INETL) disaggregates the accounts into 'oil' and 'non-oil' components. To better assess the performance of the domestic economy, this publication presents GDP on a non-oil basis, which reflects the primary analytical approach used by INETL.

e For years prior to 2005 (as featured in the Key Indicators Database), data for household consumption includes nonprofit institutions serving households.

Sources: Economies' official sources. For "World": World Bank. World Development Indicators. https://databank.worldbank.org/source/world-development-indicators (accessed 7 July 2025).

Table 2.2.8: Gross Capital Formation and Changes in Inventories
(% of GDP)

ADB Regional Member	Gross Capital Formation			Changes in Inventories		
	2010	2015	2024	2010	2015	2024
Developing ADB Member Economies						
Central and West Asia[a]	**24.9**	**26.1**	**26.5**	...	...	...
Afghanistan[b,c]	17.5	19.0	15.2	5.3	28.1	...
Armenia	32.9	20.7	22.2	-0.6	0.1	0.5
Azerbaijan	18.1	27.9	17.7 (2023)	-0.1	0.1	0.3 (2023)
Georgia	20.9	26.9	22.8*	2.3	3.0	0.8*
Kazakhstan	25.4	27.9	27.7*	1.0	5.0	2.9*
Kyrgyz Republic[d]	28.1	33.0	22.0 (2023)	-0.7	1.7	12.4 (2023)
Pakistan	16.0	15.8	12.9	1.6	1.6	1.6
Tajikistan	23.8	44.7	31.7 (2023)	-0.6	6.0	3.4 (2023)
Türkiye	26.8	28.2	30.0 (2023)	2.1	-1.4	-1.9 (2023)
Turkmenistan	51.9	50.3 (2013)	...			...
Uzbekistan	27.2	26.3	33.3*	4.6	4.3	-3.8*
East Asia	**43.1**	**40.8**	**38.4**	...	...	...
China, People's Republic of	46.1	42.7	40.6	2.6	1.1	0.7
Hong Kong, China	23.9	21.5	15.7	2.1	-0.9	-0.5
Korea, Republic of	32.8	29.3	30.4	2.3	0.1	-0.3
Mongolia	42.1	24.5	34.6*	7.6	6.2	7.8*
Taipei,China	25.1	21.7	26.5	1.4	0.3	1.0
South Asia	**39.0**	**32.5**	**29.0**	...	...	...
Bangladesh[b,e]	28.5	29.7	30.7			
Bhutan	62.9	56.4	45.2 (2023)	-0.5	0.2	0.6 (2023)
India[f]	39.8	32.1	31.4* (2023)	4.4	1.9	1.5*
Maldives	...	31.9	33.0 (2023)	...	-1.4	-2.0 (2023)
Nepal[g]	38.3	31.3	30.5*	16.1	3.7	6.1*
Sri Lanka	30.4	34.3	27.0	5.9	5.6	7.7
Southeast Asia	**106.9**	**28.4**	**26.7**	...	...	...
Brunei Darussalam	23.7	35.2	28.4	0.2	0.2	0.2
Cambodia	22.3	29.9	32.4	1.0	0.9	0.6
Indonesia	32.9	34.1	31.4*	1.9	1.3	2.3*
Lao People's Democratic Republic	32.5 (2012)	30.9	27.2 (2023)		...	...
Malaysia[h]	23.4	25.4	21.9*	1.0	-0.4	1.3*
Myanmar	23.2	34.8	29.2 (2022)	0.3	0.2	1.0 (2022)
Philippines	20.4	21.3	23.7*	0.0	-0.9	0.1*
Singapore	27.7	25.4	22.2	2.1	-1.9	0.3
Thailand	25.6	22.1	21.6*	1.4	-2.1	-0.7*
Timor-Leste[i]	42.7	36.9	21.1 (2023)	0.0	1.3	2.8 (2023)
Viet Nam	37.1	32.1	30.6*	1.9	1.9	1.5*
The Pacific	...	...	...	...	...	...
Cook Islands	...	...	...	...	...	...
Fiji	18.8	22.4	18.6* (2023)	2.9	2.6	1.2* (2023)
Kiribati	15.9	37.8	25.8* (2023)	0.3	-0.8	0.4* (2023)
Marshall Islands	41.2	17.5	18.0 (2023)	-1.0	-0.6	-0.4 (2023)
Micronesia, Federated States of	...	...	...	...	...	...
Nauru	...	...	...	...	...	...
Niue	...	...	...	...	...	...
Palau	24.5	25.0	39.5* (2021)	0.7	-1.9	-0.6* (2021)
Papua New Guinea	17.5 (2005)	...	...	1.0 (2005)	...	...
Samoa	39.1	34.9	30.5	1.1	0.4	2.6
Solomon Islands	17.9	16.0	24.4* (2022)	-1.4 (2012)	-0.0	-1.0* (2022)
Tonga	29.2	24.6	27.0 (2023)	0.5	2.0	-0.3 (2023)
Tuvalu	...	...	...	...	...	...
Vanuatu	37.0	32.9	38.8 (2022)	1.6	0.8	0.4 (2022)
Developed ADB Member Economies	**23.3**	**25.3**	**24.6**	...	...	...
Australia	26.8	26.3	24.4	-0.2	0.1	0.2
Japan	22.6	25.2	26.2	-0.0	0.2	0.1
New Zealand	20.4	23.2	23.8 (2023)	0.4	0.3	-0.9 (2023)
DEVELOPING ADB MEMBER ECONOMIES[a]	**50.7**	**37.0**	**34.9**	...	...	...
ALL ADB REGIONAL MEMBERS[a]	**41.1**	**34.3**	**33.3**	...	...	...
WORLD	**25.2**	**25.5**	...	...	...	...

... = data not available, (-/+) 0.0 = magnitude is less than half of unit employed, * = provisional or preliminary, ADB = Asian Development Bank, GDP = gross domestic product.

Note: Figures in the table are calculated as a percentage of GDP at current prices.

a For estimating aggregates, GDP figures in domestic currencies were converted to United States dollars using official exchange rates, and imputation was done for economies with missing data by substituting available data from the nearest years.
b Refers to gross fixed capital formation.
c Changes in inventories include valuables and statistical discrepancy.
d Refers to gross fixed capital formation and acquisitions less disposals of valuables.
e Includes data on changes in inventories.
f Refers to gross capital formation, which refers to the sum of gross fixed capital formation, valuables, increases in stocks, and errors and omissions.
g Changes in inventories were derived residually; hence, statistical discrepancies or errors are included in this entry.
h Changes in inventories include valuables and statistical discrepancy.
i From September 2019, following the new Timor-Leste Australia Maritime Boundary Treaty, oil revenue from the Joint Petroleum Development Area is included in the national accounts. The National Institute of Statistics Timor-Leste (INETL) disaggregates the accounts into 'oil' and 'non-oil' components. To better assess the performance of the domestic economy, this publication presents GDP on a non-oil basis, which reflects the primary analytical approach used by INETL.

Sources: Economies' official sources. For "World": World Bank. World Development Indicators. https://databank.worldbank.org/source/world-development-indicators (accessed 17 July 2025).

Table 2.2.9: Exports and Imports of Goods and Services
(% of GDP)

ADB Regional Member	Exports of goods and services			Imports of goods and services		
	2010	2015	2024	2010	2015	2024
Developing ADB Member Economies						
Central and West Asia[a]	**26.6**	**23.2**	**26.3**	**15.5**	**12.9**	**3.3**
Afghanistan	9.8	6.9	16.9	43.9	49.0	50.7
Armenia	20.8	29.7	76.3	45.3	42.0	75.8
Azerbaijan	54.3	37.8	49.0 (2023)	20.7	34.8	34.5 (2023)
Georgia	32.5	40.1	48.4*	49.2	56.9	56.0*
Kazakhstan	44.2	28.5	32.2*	29.9	24.5	26.0*
Kyrgyz Republic	51.6	35.2	36.9 (2023)	81.7	75.8	95.5 (2023)
Pakistan	12.6	10.0	10.4	19.4	16.7	17.1
Tajikistan	26.8	9.8	17.2 (2023)	59.0	40.1	48.4 (2023)
Türkiye	21.2	24.5	31.9 (2023)	25.5	26.6	34.4 (2023)
Turkmenistan	76.3	74.8 (2013)	...	44.5	44.1 (2013)	...
Uzbekistan	24.3	13.8	22.8*	25.0	17.0	38.0*
East Asia	**37.7**	**29.1**	**26.7**	**34.0**	**25.2**	**23.4**
China, People's Republic of	26.7	20.9	20.0	23.1	17.8	17.1
Hong Kong, China[b]	205.3	195.9	181.7	199.4	193.5	177.7
Korea, Republic of	45.3	41.0	44.6	42.8	34.4	40.7
Mongolia	46.7	44.2	69.1*	56.7	45.5	69.7*
Taipei,China	79.6	71.3	63.5	73.0	58.4	50.3
South Asia	**21.6**	**19.3**	**20.0**	**26.4**	**22.3**	**23.0**
Bangladesh	14.2	14.5	10.5	19.3	19.3	16.3
Bhutan	39.4	31.5	28.3 (2023)	65.6	58.1	53.2 (2023)
India	22.4	19.8	21.2*	26.9	22.1	23.5*
Maldives	...	76.4	74.4 (2023)	...	67.3	75.7 (2023)
Nepal	9.6	10.2	7.9*	36.4	36.5	33.7*
Sri Lanka	19.6	19.9	19.9	26.8	27.0	22.5
Southeast Asia	**29.4**	**59.3**	**65.5**	**24.4**	**54.2**	**59.7**
Brunei Darussalam	67.4	52.2	74.3	28.0	37.7	58.9
Cambodia	50.2	56.0	70.1	59.8	66.1	72.5
Indonesia	24.3	21.2	22.2*	22.4	20.8	20.4*
Lao People's Democratic Republic	34.9 (2012)	28.9	38.5 (2023)	44.6 (2012)	32.2	39.4 (2023)
Malaysia	86.9	69.4	71.4*	71.0	61.9	66.0*
Myanmar	19.6	17.4	30.1 (2022)	15.1	27.9	31.6 (2022)
Philippines	32.9	27.2	25.8*	33.2	31.9	40.1*
Singapore	198.0	178.4	178.8	171.7	151.1	143.6
Thailand	67.1	66.8	70.2*	61.3	56.5	66.8*
Timor-Leste[c]	8.6	3.1	3.3 (2023)	125.8	57.0	66.3 (2023)
Viet Nam	54.2	72.9	90.2*	59.8	72.0	83.7*
The Pacific	**...**	**...**	**...**	**...**	**...**	**...**
Cook Islands	...	...	...	...	...	...
Fiji	57.4	48.8	57.0* (2023)	63.8	52.4	69.2* (2023)
Kiribati	11.6	14.0	5.9* (2023)	74.1	95.9	101.7* (2023)
Marshall Islands	35.0	44.6	35.6 (2023)	105.3	95.1	65.1 (2023)
Micronesia, Federated States of	...	...	...	...	...	...
Nauru	...	...	...	...	...	...
Niue	...	...	...	...	...	...
Palau	49.6	57.7	4.6* (2021)	76.8	74.8	76.2* (2021)
Papua New Guinea	74.5 (2005)	...	...	56.1 (2005)	...	...
Samoa	28.2	28.7	26.3	53.8	46.0	45.7
Solomon Islands	35.2	40.4	26.3* (2022)	61.0	47.8	51.7* (2022)
Tonga	12.5	16.9	18.8 (2023)	58.3	64.4	75.4 (2023)
Tuvalu	...	...	...	...	...	...
Vanuatu	48.7	46.0	9.6 (2022)	55.1	67.0	55.5 (2022)
Developed ADB Member Economies	**16.1**	**18.3**	**23.3**	**15.1**	**19.0**	**23.5**
Australia	19.8	20.1	24.7	20.7	21.6	22.6
Japan	14.9	17.4	22.7	13.6	18.0	23.7
New Zealand	30.2	27.9	23.6 (2023)	27.9	26.9	26.5 (2023)
DEVELOPING ADB MEMBER ECONOMIES[a]	**31.9**	**31.3**	**30.6**	**28.1**	**27.6**	**28.0**
ALL ADB REGIONAL MEMBERS[a]	**27.7**	**28.4**	**29.4**	**24.7**	**25.7**	**27.3**
WORLD	**28.5**	**28.1**	**29.0**	**27.7**	**27.3**	**28.1**

... = data not available, * = provisional or preliminary, ADB = Asian Development Bank, GDP = gross domestic product.

Note: Figures in the table are calculated as a percentage of GDP at current prices.

a For estimating aggregates, imputation was done for economies with missing data by substituting available data from the nearest years.
b The statistics for trade in goods and services were compiled based on the change of ownership principle in recording goods sent abroad for processing and merchanting under the standards stipulated in the System of National Accounts 2008.
c From September 2019, following the new Timor-Leste Australia Maritime Boundary Treaty, oil revenue from the Joint Petroleum Development Area is included in the national accounts. The National Institute of Statistics Timor-Leste (INETL) disaggregates the accounts into 'oil' and 'non-oil' components. To better assess the performance of the domestic economy, this publication presents GDP on a non-oil basis, which reflects the primary analytical approach used by INETL.

Sources: Economies' official sources. For "World": World Bank. World Development Indicators. https://databank.worldbank.org/source/world-development-indicators (accessed 24 July 2025).

Table 2.2.10: Gross Domestic Saving
(% of GDP)

ADB Regional Member	2010	2015	2019	2020	2021	2022	2023	2024
Developing ADB Member Economies								
Central and West Asia[a]	**27.1**	...	...	...	...	...	...	...
Afghanistan	-11.4	5.0 |	-19.9	-15.5 |	-14.4	-9.7	-19.5	-19.3
Armenia	4.9 |	9.0	4.0	9.7	15.1	21.4	20.5	22.7
Azerbaijan	49.8	30.9	31.4	22.9	33.8	45.0	32.2	...
Georgia	4.2	10.1	18.0	5.5	4.4	14.3	16.4	15.2*
Kazakhstan	43.8 |	34.6	38.6	34.3	37.1	40.1	37.1	...
Kyrgyz Republic	-2.7	-8.3 |	7.0	5.2	-2.2	-5.5	-4.3	...
Pakistan	9.2	9.1	5.4	6.7	5.6	3.6	6.4	6.3
Tajikistan	4.0 |	17.2	12.6	10.8	8.7	2.2	2.3	...
Türkiye	...	...	...	...	...	...	...	...
Turkmenistan	85.6	81.6 (2013)	...	...	...	...	...	...
Uzbekistan	26.0	21.5	20.1	21.0	19.2	16.6	17.1	18.1*
East Asia[a]	**46.6**	**43.6**	**41.6**	**42.6**	**43.9**	**43.8**	**41.4**	...
China, People's Republic of	50.6	45.7	43.5	44.2	45.3	45.6	43.2	43.4
Hong Kong, China	29.8	23.9	19.7	20.9	22.3	19.3	16.7	19.8
Korea, Republic of	35.3	35.9	33.8	35.2	35.9	33.3	32.5	...
Mongolia	32.1 |	23.2	29.6	23.7	32.1	34.2	42.5	33.9*
Taipei,China	31.5	34.4	32.9	36.9	41.5	40.0	36.1	39.2
South Asia	...	...	...	...	...	...	...	...
Bangladesh	23.8	25.2	26.9	27.1	25.3	25.2	25.8	24.0
Bhutan	36.7	29.9	32.9	23.4	25.2	21.4	20.3	...
India	...	...	...	...	...	...	...	...
Maldives	...	...	...	...	...	...	...	...
Nepal	11.5 |	7.6	15.3	5.7	6.4	6.6	7.4	7.6*
Sri Lanka	22.3	27.1	28.3	26.7	29.3	23.7	22.4	24.3
Southeast Asia	...	...	...	...	...	...	...	...
Brunei Darussalam	63.1	55.2	54.5	50.8	52.7	56.6	49.5	48.5
Cambodia	13.3	20.3	28.5	30.2	30.6	34.1	33.6	34.0
Indonesia	34.8	32.8	31.1	31.9	31.0	31.4	30.5*	...
Lao People's Democratic Republic	...	...	...	...	...	...	...	...
Malaysia	39.3	33.0	28.6	26.0	29.4	30.8	27.6	27.2*
Myanmar	32.7	23.4 |	28.3	...	...	...	...	...
Philippines	...	...	...	...	...	...	...	...
Singapore	54.0	52.7	53.9	54.3	60.3	62.1	58.7	57.4
Thailand	31.1	32.8	33.2	28.9	28.5	25.7*	24.5*	24.9*
Timor-Leste[b]	-74.6	-17.0	-1.7	6.9	96.6	46.5	-8.7	...
Viet Nam	31.2	30.0	33.6	34.6	34.9	36.5	36.8	...
The Pacific	...	...	...	...	...	...	...	...
Cook Islands	...	...	...	...	...	...	...	...
Fiji	12.4	18.9	9.2	0.0	-3.5	-0.5	6.8*	...
Kiribati	-46.3	-45.5	-52.6	-44.4	-50.0	-70.8	-69.2*	...
Marshall Islands	28.6	25.4	42.6	47.5	58.1	50.9	43.1	...
Micronesia, Federated States of	...	...	...	...	...	...	...	...
Nauru	...	...	...	...	...	...	...	...
Niue	...	...	...	...	...	...	...	...
Palau	-7.5	5.0	-0.3	-18.7	-26.4	...	...	...
Papua New Guinea	35.9 (2005)	...	...	...	...	...	...	...
Samoa	10.7	19.3	17.1	5.1	-0.2	1.7	8.9	8.1
Solomon Islands	...	...	...	...	...	...	...	...
Tonga	-12.6	-15.6	-10.6	-7.2	-18.2	-7.8	-36.8	...
Tuvalu	...	...	...	...	...	...	...	...
Vanuatu	28.2	25.3 (2014)	...	...	...	...	...	...
Developed ADB Member Economies[a]	**25.2**	**25.6**	**26.5**	**26.2**	**26.6**	**25.5**	**26.5**	...
Australia	25.9	24.7	25.5	25.8	26.7	29.0	28.3	26.6
Japan	25.1	25.9	26.8	26.5	26.8	24.5	26.1	26.7
New Zealand	22.7	24.2	24.0	22.5	21.2	20.9	20.8	...

... = data not available; | = marks break in series; 0.0 = magnitude is less than half of unit employed; * = provisional, preliminary, estimate; ADB = Asian Development Bank; GDP = gross domestic product.

Note: Figures in the table are calculated as a percentage of GDP at current prices.

a For estimating aggregates, GDP figures in domestic currencies were converted to United States dollars using official exchange rates.

b From September 2019, following the new Timor-Leste Australia Maritime Boundary Treaty, oil revenue from the Joint Petroleum Development Area is included in the national accounts. The National Institute of Statistics Timor-Leste (INETL) disaggregates the accounts into 'oil' and 'non-oil' components. To better assess the performance of the domestic economy, this publication presents GDP on a non-oil basis, which reflects the primary analytical approach used by INETL.

Source: Economies' official sources and Asian Development Bank estimates based on data from the economies' official sources.

Table 2.2.11: Growth Rates of Real Gross Domestic Product
(%)

ADB Regional Member	2010	2015	2019	2020	2021	2022	2023	2024
Developing ADB Member Economies								
Central and West Asia								
Afghanistan	3.2	-1.8|	3.9	-2.4|	-2.1	-20.7	-6.2	2.3
Armenia	2.2|	3.2	7.6	-7.2	5.8	12.6	8.3	5.9
Azerbaijan	5.0	1.1	2.5	-4.2	5.6	4.7	1.4	4.1
Georgia	6.2	3.4	5.4	-6.3	10.6	11.0	7.8	9.4*
Kazakhstan	7.3|	1.2	4.5	-2.5	4.3	3.2	3.5	4.8*
Kyrgyz Republic	-0.5	3.9	4.6|	-7.1	5.5	9.0	9.0	9.0*
Pakistan	2.3	3.8	3.1	-0.9	5.8	6.2	-0.2	2.5
Tajikistan	6.5	6.0|	7.4	4.4	9.4	8.0	8.3	...
Türkiye	8.4	6.1	0.8	1.9	11.4	5.5	5.1	...
Turkmenistan	16.2	10.3 (2014)	...	...	5.0	6.2	6.3	6.3
Uzbekistan	7.1	7.2	6.8	1.6	8.0	6.0	6.3	6.5*
East Asia								
China, People's Republic of	10.6	7.0	6.1	2.3	8.6	3.1	5.4	5.0*
Hong Kong, China	6.8	2.4	-1.7	-6.5	6.5	-3.7	3.2	2.5
Korea, Republic of	7.0	2.9	2.3	-0.7	4.6	2.7	1.4	2.0
Mongolia	6.4|	2.4	5.6	-4.6	1.6	5.0	7.4	4.9*
Taipei,China	10.3	1.5	3.1	3.4	6.7	2.7	1.1	4.6
South Asia								
Bangladesh	6.7	7.6	7.9	3.5	6.9	7.1	5.8	4.2
Bhutan	12.0	6.7	5.8	-10.2	4.4	5.2	4.9	...
India	8.5	8.0	3.9	-5.8	9.7	7.6	9.2*	6.5*
Maldives	6.8	3.9	6.9	-32.9	37.5	13.8	4.7	...
Nepal	4.8|	4.0	6.7	-2.4	4.8	5.6	2.0	3.9*
Sri Lanka	8.0	4.2	-0.2	-4.6	4.2	-7.3	-2.3	5.0
Southeast Asia								
Brunei Darussalam	3.7 (2011)	-0.4	3.9	1.1	-1.6	-1.6	1.1	4.2
Cambodia	5.1	7.2	7.9	-3.6	3.1	5.1	5.3	6.0
Indonesia	6.2	4.9	5.0	-2.1	3.7	5.3	5.0*	5.0*
Lao People's Democratic Republic	8.1	7.3	5.5	3.3	3.5	4.4	4.2	4.3
Malaysia	7.4	5.1	4.4	-5.5	3.3	8.9	3.6	5.1*
Myanmar	9.6	7.0	6.8	3.2	-5.9	3.4	0.8*	-0.7*
Philippines	7.3	6.3	6.1	-9.5	5.7	7.6	5.5	5.7*
Singapore	14.5	3.0	1.3	-3.8	9.8	4.1	1.8	4.4
Thailand	7.5	3.1	2.1	-6.1	1.6	2.6*	2.0*	2.5*
Timor-Leste[a]	9.3	2.5	2.7	-8.5	3.0	4.0	2.4	...
Viet Nam	6.4	7.0	7.4	2.9	2.6	8.5	5.1	7.1*
The Pacific								
Cook Islands	-4.9	5.7	4.8	-35.1	-4.3	30.8	16.8*	...
Fiji	3.0	4.5	-0.6	-17.0	-4.9	19.8	7.5*	...
Kiribati	1.2	11.3	3.3	-1.5	8.5	4.6	2.7*	...
Marshall Islands	5.6	1.9	10.5	-2.8	1.2	-1.1	-3.9	...
Micronesia, Federated States of	2.0	4.5	3.4	-2.0	3.1	-2.9	0.5	...
Nauru	13.6	2.8|	8.5	2.0	7.2	3.0	0.6	1.8
Niue	0.6|	4.0	-1.7	-1.6	-6.7	0.1	6.1	8.7*
Palau	-3.0	8.6	0.3	-6.0	-11.9	-0.5	1.2	12.0*
Papua New Guinea	10.1	6.6	4.5	-3.2	-0.5	5.7	3.8	4.1*
Samoa	3.1	6.1	2.8	-10.1	4.4	5.7	11.9	2.8
Solomon Islands	9.7	1.7	1.7	-3.4|	2.6*	2.4*	...	...
Tonga	0.8	1.1	-0.2	1.8	0.4	-2.3	2.1	...
Tuvalu	-3.3	9.2	13.4	-3.7	-0.5	-2.3	7.9	...
Vanuatu	1.3	0.4	3.2	-5.0	-1.6	5.2	...	...
Developed ADB Member Economies								
Australia	2.2	2.2	2.2	-0.1	2.1	4.2	3.4	1.4
Japan	4.1	1.6	-0.4	-4.2	2.7	0.9	1.5	0.1
New Zealand	1.5	3.7	2.3	-0.3	4.5	3.5	1.4	...

... = data not available; | = marks break in series; * = provisional, preliminary, estimate; ADB = Asian Development Bank.

a From September 2019, following the new Timor-Leste Australia Maritime Boundary Treaty, oil revenue from the Joint Petroleum Development Area is included in the national accounts. The National Institute of Statistics Timor-Leste (INETL) disaggregates the accounts into 'oil' and 'non-oil' components. To better assess the performance of the domestic economy, this publication presents GDP on a non-oil basis, which reflects the primary analytical approach used by INETL.

Sources: Economies' official sources and Asian Development Bank estimates based on data from the economies' official sources. For Nauru, data for 2016 onward are sourced from the IMF's World Economic Outlook Database.

Table 2.2.12: Growth Rates of Real Gross Domestic Product per Capita
(%)

ADB Regional Member	2010	2015	2019	2020	2021	2022	2023	2024
Developing ADB Member Economies								
Central and West Asia								
Afghanistan	1.2	-3.8 |	1.7	-4.5 |	-6.6	-22.3	-8.1	0.2
Armenia	2.9 |	3.5	7.9	-7.0	5.7	12.7 |	...	4.0
Azerbaijan	3.8	-0.1	2.6	-4.9	5.2	4.1	0.4	4.1
Georgia	7.0	3.2	5.6	-6.4	11.0	10.9	7.7	9.8*
Kazakhstan	5.5 |	-0.3	3.2	-3.8	2.9 |	-0.0	2.0	3.4*
Kyrgyz Republic	-1.9	1.6	2.3 |	-9.0	3.6	7.0	7.1	7.2*
Pakistan	0.2	1.8	1.1	-2.9	3.7	4.1	-2.7	...
Tajikistan	3.9	3.5 |	5.1	2.3	7.6	6.0	6.2	...
Türkiye	6.8	4.7	-0.6	0.9	10.4	4.5	4.7	...
Turkmenistan	13.8	7.8 (2014)	...	...	2.9	4.2	4.4	4.5
Uzbekistan	4.1	5.4	4.8	-0.4	5.9	3.8	4.1	4.4*
East Asia								
China, People's Republic of	10.1	6.5	5.7	2.2	8.6	3.2	5.6	5.1*
Hong Kong, China	6.0	1.5	-2.4	-6.1	7.5	-2.8	0.6	2.7
Korea, Republic of	6.5	2.4	1.9	-0.8	4.7	2.9	1.3	1.9
Mongolia	4.7 |	0.3	3.7	-6.3	0.0	3.6	5.9	3.7*
Taipei,China	9.9	1.2	3.0	3.5	7.2	4.0	0.3	4.4
South Asia								
Bangladesh	5.3	6.1	6.5	2.1	5.6	5.6	4.4	...
Bhutan	10.0	5.0	4.7	-11.1	3.4	4.2	3.9	...
India	7.0	6.6	2.7	-6.8	8.6	6.5	8.2*	5.5*
Maldives	4.4	0.0	2.5	-35.7	34.9	11.7	2.8	...
Nepal	3.4 |	2.6	5.7	-3.3	3.9	4.7	1.0	...
Sri Lanka	6.9	3.2	-0.8	-5.1	3.1	-7.4	-1.7	5.5
Southeast Asia								
Brunei Darussalam	2.0 (2011)	-1.6	0.6	3.2	-1.3	-2.7	-0.0	3.1
Cambodia	3.7	5.7	6.5	-4.8	1.6	3.6	3.7	4.7
Indonesia	4.7 |	3.5	3.7	-3.3	2.5	4.1	3.9*	3.9*
Lao People's Democratic Republic	6.6	5.7	3.8	1.7	2.0	2.9	2.7	3.0
Malaysia	5.5	3.4	4.0	-5.3	2.9	8.4	1.4	3.1*
Myanmar	8.8	6.2	6.0	2.4	-6.5	2.7	0.1*	-1.4*
Philippines	6.3 |	5.4 (2016)	4.6 |	...	4.9	6.7	4.6	4.8*
Singapore	12.5	1.8	0.1	-3.5	14.5	0.7	-3.0	2.4
Thailand	6.9	2.5	1.8	-6.3	1.3	2.3*	1.8*	2.3*
Timor-Leste[a]	7.0	0.7	1.2	-9.9	1.3	2.4	0.9	...
Viet Nam	5.1	5.8	6.1	1.7	1.6	7.5	4.2	6.0*
The Pacific								
Cook Islands	-9.3	5.7	4.8	-20.6	-13.2	16.1	10.8*	...
Fiji	2.3	4.1	-1.2	-17.5	-5.5	19.1	6.9*	...
Kiribati	-0.9	9.8	1.6	-3.0	6.7*	2.9*	1.0*	...
Marshall Islands	4.4	4.0	13.5	-2.3	4.9	1.3	-1.5	...
Micronesia, Federated States of	2.6	4.3	3.2*	-2.1*	2.9*	-3.1*	0.3*	...
Nauru	13.8	1.2 |	7.5	0.4	5.9	2.1*	-0.1*	1.0*
Niue	0.7 |	2.9	-1.3	-1.2	-6.3	0.6	6.6	9.2*
Palau	-1.2	6.7	0.8	-6.8	-11.9	-0.4	0.9	10.7*
Papua New Guinea	6.8	3.4	1.3	-6.1	-3.5	2.5	0.7	0.9*
Samoa	2.3	5.2	2.0	-10.8	3.0	4.7	10.8	1.8
Solomon Islands	6.9	-0.9	-0.8	... |	0.6*	0.4*	...	...
Tonga	0.6	1.6	-0.1	1.9	0.5	-2.2	2.2	...
Tuvalu	-3.8	9.5	16.7	-3.0	-1.2	-5.3	13.3	...
Vanuatu	-1.2	-1.9	0.9	-7.6	-3.7	2.8	...	...
Developed ADB Member Economies								
Australia	0.6	0.7	0.7	-1.3	2.0	2.9	0.9	-0.6
Japan	4.1	1.7	-0.2	-3.8	2.8	1.4	2.0	0.5
New Zealand	0.3	1.6	0.9	-2.3	4.3	3.6	-0.9	...

... = data not available; | = marks break in the series; (-/+) 0.0 = magnitude is less than half of unit employed; * = provisional, preliminary, estimate; ADB = Asian Development Bank.

a From September 2019, following the new Timor-Leste Australia Maritime Boundary Treaty, oil revenue from the Joint Petroleum Development Area is included in the national accounts. The National Institute of Statistics Timor-Leste (INETL) disaggregates the accounts into 'oil' and 'non-oil' components. To better assess the performance of the domestic economy, this publication presents GDP on a non-oil basis, which reflects the primary analytical approach used by INETL.

Source: Asian Development Bank estimates based on data from the economies' official sources.

Table 2.2.13: Growth Rates of Agriculture Real Value-Added
(%)

ADB Regional Member	2010	2015	2017	2018	2019	2020	2021	2022	2023	2024
Developing ADB Member Economies										
Central and West Asia										
Afghanistan	-18.0	-16.9	6.4	-4.4	17.5	5.9	4.4	-9.8	-6.6	2.2
Armenia	-16.0	13.2	-5.1	-6.9	-5.8	-3.7	-0.8	-2.8	2.9	1.0
Azerbaijan	-4.7	6.6	4.2	4.6	7.3	1.9	3.3	3.4	3.0	1.4
Georgia	-4.2	0.3	-2.2	13.1	1.4	6.7	2.3	-1.8	-3.4	4.4*
Kazakhstan	-12.9	3.5	6.9	3.8	-0.1	5.9	-2.2	9.1	-16.4	13.3*
Kyrgyz Republic	-2.6	6.2	2.2	2.6	2.5	0.9	-4.5	7.3	0.6	6.3*
Pakistan	0.3	1.8	2.2	3.9	0.9	3.9	3.5	4.2	2.2	6.2
Tajikistan	6.8	3.4	7.6	7.0	7.0	7.9	-0.3	-4.5	13.8	...
Türkiye	7.7	9.3	4.9	2.3	3.0	5.8	-3.0	1.3	0.2	...
Turkmenistan	25.3	1.7 (2014)	...	...	...	...	...	...	...	...
Uzbekistan	6.1	6.1	1.2	0.3	3.1	2.9	4.0	3.6	4.1	3.1*
East Asia										
China, People's Republic of	4.3	3.9	4.0	3.5	3.1	3.1	7.1	4.2	4.1	3.5*
Hong Kong, China[a]	3.9	-6.8	-5.2	-1.8	-0.8	3.8	-2.5	-15.8	1.5	-9.3
Korea, Republic of	-3.6	-0.3	1.2	-0.8	2.9	-6.7	3.4	0.8	-2.6	0.8
Mongolia	-16.6	10.7	-0.3	6.5	5.2	5.8	-5.5	12.0	-8.9	-28.7*
Taipei,China	2.1	-7.7	8.6	4.8	-0.7	-1.2	-4.1	-4.2	-0.8	-0.5
South Asia										
Bangladesh	7.4	4.0	3.2	3.5	3.3	3.4	3.2	3.1	3.4	3.3
Bhutan	1.0	5.2	3.1	2.9	1.7	4.0	1.4	-1.1	1.4	...
India	8.8	0.6	6.6	2.1	6.2	4.0	4.6	6.3	2.7*	4.6*
Maldives	-3.9	-0.5	8.2	4.9	-8.1	6.6	-0.8	6.2	3.2	...
Nepal	2.0	1.2	5.2	2.6	5.2	2.4	2.8	2.4	2.8	3.0*
Sri Lanka	7.0	5.4	-1.8	6.3	0.5	-0.9	1.0	-4.1	1.6	1.2
Southeast Asia										
Brunei Darussalam	-2.6 (2011)	6.4	-1.6	-1.6	-1.4	14.4	16.9	-3.3	-11.6	4.1
Cambodia	4.4	0.2	1.7	1.1	-0.4	0.6	1.5	0.6	1.1	0.8
Indonesia	3.0	3.8	3.9	3.9	3.6	1.8	1.9	2.3	1.3*	0.7*
Lao People's Democratic Republic	3.2	3.6	2.9	1.3	1.2	1.2	2.5	3.4	3.7	1.4
Malaysia	2.4	1.4	5.9	0.1	1.9	-2.4	-0.3	1.3	0.7	3.1*
Myanmar	4.7	3.4	-1.5	0.1	1.6	1.6	1.0	2.8	-1.8*	-2.3*
Philippines	1.3	0.7	4.2	1.1	1.2	-0.2	-0.3	0.5	1.2	-1.5*
Singapore[a]	2.8	-0.4	2.9	3.1	6.9	-4.2	11.2	-7.7	2.9	3.0
Thailand	-0.5	-6.5	4.8	6.1	-1.0	-3.2	2.2	2.4*	2.0*	-1.0*
Timor-Leste	4.4	-4.4	-2.9	2.9	2.5	0.6	5.5	5.4	2.3	...
Viet Nam	3.3	2.5	3.2	4.1	2.7	3.0	3.7	3.7	3.9	3.3*
The Pacific										
Cook Islands	0.4	-2.2	3.2	-2.5	-3.0	-11.3	1.1	1.8	-4.1*	...
Fiji	-2.6	2.9	10.8	3.7	4.5	3.1	0.8	4.0	4.7*	...
Kiribati	-7.2	-7.3	21.1	-10.6	8.9	-0.0	1.4	-5.4	2.4*	...
Marshall Islands	14.0	5.9	6.1	20.9	54.5	-6.4	11.4	-15.4	-4.3	...
Micronesia, Federated States of	-3.2	9.2	...	...	...	...	...	...	...	...
Nauru	3.7	5.2	42.1	-14.4	34.3	1.6*	-26.6	2.9*	0.7*	4.6*
Niue	-0.4	0.2 (2014)	3.5	1.6	1.2	-4.1	5.2	0.9	1.5	0.1*
Palau	-4.9	-5.6	10.8	-3.9	-5.6	-10.1	-3.8	-0.1	0.5	-2.2*
Papua New Guinea	2.8	-2.6	2.4	4.6	2.3	1.9	1.1	3.1	1.0	3.6*
Samoa	-9.0	1.9	7.1	-12.4	2.3	-5.8	-0.1	-5.6	2.5	3.7
Solomon Islands	13.0	3.2	3.6	0.4	0.1	-3.8	1.7*	-3.0*	...	...
Tonga	4.7	-1.7	-2.5	2.6	5.2	3.1	-0.9	2.8	16.4	...
Tuvalu	12.8	-1.8	0.0	2.7	-7.0	-6.6	2.8	-1.8	-2.5	...
Vanuatu	4.6	-5.7	0.2	0.9	6.2	-2.7	2.7	3.9	...	...
Developed ADB Member Economies										
Australia	-0.7	1.5	9.4	-2.8	-10.5	-9.6	21.8	17.1	4.6	4.6
Japan	-5.2	-4.2	0.7	-6.7	4.4	-3.7	5.8	3.9	1.1	...
New Zealand	-7.9	2.2	-3.9	6.6	-2.4	2.7	-2.6	3.5	7.5	...

... = data not available; (+/-) 0.0 = magnitude is less than half of the unit employed; * = provisional, preliminary, estimate; ADB = Asian Development Bank.

a Refers to other goods industries comprising agriculture, forestry, and fishing; and mining and quarrying.

Source: Economies' official sources.

Table 2.2.14: Growth Rates of Industry Real Value-Added
(%)

ADB Regional Member	2010	2015	2017	2018	2019	2020	2021	2022	2023	2024
Developing ADB Member Economies										
Central and West Asia										
Afghanistan	6.3	4.5	9.2	11.1	4.8	-4.6	-5.6	-12.8	-5.7	1.8
Armenia	5.7	2.8	9.0	3.7	10.5	-2.5	2.6	9.8	2.7	6.2
Azerbaijan	3.7	-1.9	-3.1	-0.7	1.0	-5.0	3.2	0.4	-0.3	2.1
Georgia[a]	8.2	7.9	8.8	-0.1	-0.2	-3.4	1.0	15.1	4.3	4.7*
Kazakhstan	9.5	-0.4	7.7	4.4	5.5	1.5	4.4	2.7	6.0	4.6*
Kyrgyz Republic	2.5	2.9	8.6	5.9	8.0	-9.5	2.5	11.1	10.0	9.4*
Pakistan	4.0	5.4	4.6	9.2	0.3	-5.8	8.2	7.0	-3.8	-1.7
Tajikistan	2.8	16.3	7.3	17.0	10.3	17.3	13.2	9.2	14.3	...
Türkiye	...	...	...	...	...	...	...	...	...	...
Turkmenistan	12.8	11.6 (2014)	...	...	...	...	...	...	...	...
Uzbekistan	5.5	8.3	5.4	10.9	9.3	3.5	8.1	5.6	6.7	7.3*
East Asia										
China, People's Republic of	12.7	5.9	5.9	5.8	4.6	2.1	8.2	2.3	4.4	5.3*
Hong Kong, China[a,b]	7.7	2.4	-0.7	2.5	-6.4	-11.2	1.3	5.1	6.9	3.4
Korea, Republic of[a]	...	...	...	...	...	...	...	...	...	...
Mongolia	4.3	9.9	1.4	8.5	3.1	-4.4	-2.2	-4.5	12.9	6.5*
Taipei,China[a]	21.5	0.9	6.4	3.5	2.2	8.2	14.9	2.3	-6.6	7.2
South Asia										
Bangladesh	9.7	12.2	8.3	10.2	11.6	3.6	10.3	9.9	8.4	3.5
Bhutan	12.7	8.5	2.8	-4.0	-1.3	-14.4	3.9	5.6	-0.0	...
India	7.9	9.6	5.9	5.3	-1.4	-0.4	12.2	2.5	10.8*	5.9*
Maldives	7.3	20.7	13.3	17.4	2.6	-34.1	-4.6	19.6	3.3	...
Nepal	4.0	2.0	17.1	10.4	7.4	-4.0	6.9	10.7	1.4	1.3*
Sri Lanka	8.4	1.1	13.0	-1.1	-4.1	-5.3	5.7	-16.0	-9.2	11.0
Southeast Asia										
Brunei Darussalam	3.2 (2011)	-0.0	1.5	-0.4	4.2	2.9	-4.2	-4.9	-1.9	5.7
Cambodia	5.7	12.6	13.1	14.8	13.0	-2.2	8.4	8.2	6.0	10.4
Indonesia	4.9	3.0	4.1	4.3	3.8	-2.8	3.4	4.1	5.0*	5.2*
Lao People's Democratic Republic	17.5	7.0	11.6	7.8	5.6	9.2	6.1	4.4	3.1	4.7
Malaysia	8.4	5.2	4.7	3.3	2.6	-6.1	5.7	6.7	1.3	4.9*
Myanmar	18.6	8.3	8.7	8.3	8.4	3.8	-9.6	1.7	2.2*	-0.1*
Philippines	9.8	6.5	7.0	7.3	5.5	-13.1	8.5	6.5	3.6	5.6*
Singapore[a,b]	24.1	-2.5	6.8	5.6	-1.0	-0.2	15.5	3.9	-2.7	4.2
Thailand[a,c]	10.6	1.9	2.2	2.9	-0.1	-5.8	3.7	0.6*	-1.9*	0.9*
Timor-Leste	7.9	22.2	-26.5	5.3	4.8	-22.9	-11.2	7.7	-2.0	...
Viet Nam	7.2	9.2	8.3	9.0	8.2	4.4	3.2	8.2	3.7	8.2*
The Pacific										
Cook Islands	-8.9	25.4	19.1	7.0	10.5	-15.5	-26.2	-89.7	242.0*	...
Fiji	6.5	6.9	4.2	5.5	-0.9	-10.2	-6.7	8.4	-4.9*	...
Kiribati	7.1	23.2	-9.1	-7.4	-5.3	-2.4*	15.0*	2.9	14.4*	...
Marshall Islands	7.8	-13.7	0.4	8.2	14.6	-5.3	-6.2	9.7	-2.8	...
Micronesia, Federated States of	17.7	-7.4	...	...	...	...	...	...	...	...
Nauru	39.4	-17.1	-27.4	-41.8	-15.1	-3.6*	105.4	12.2*	7.2*	-8.4*
Niue	14.4	6.2 (2014)	-12.8	198.8	-16.6	28.3	-0.2	-13.2	-2.5	35.9*
Palau	3.8	27.6	-8.5	-1.7	29.0	-4.2	1	-19.2	-19.7	37.2*
Papua New Guinea	12.0	26.4	4.7	-7.5	7.5	-7.5	-7.9	6.6	1.6	3.6*
Samoa	7.2	8.6	-8.6	-4.8	10.8	-15.3	-0.2	-5.4	2.5	6.2
Solomon Islands	13.2	-4.0	9.5	1.3	3.5	-3.8	-0.3*	4.7*	...	...
Tonga	4.1	-0.5	9.6	-14.7	4.6	0.7	19.0	-12.3	-11.1	...
Tuvalu	-41.6	36.7	9.5	-5.2	61.9	-28.7	-3.4	-24.3	20.1	...
Vanuatu	12.2	38.5	10.1	4.9	-8.3	4.0	-1.3	-19.7	...	...
Developed ADB Member Economies										
Australia[a]	...	...	...	...	...	...	...	...	...	...
Japan[a]	...	...	...	...	...	...	...	...	...	...
New Zealand[a]	...	...	...	...	...	...	...	...	...	...

... = data not available; -0.0 = magnitude is less than half of unit employed; * = provisional, preliminary, estimate; ADB = Asian Development Bank.

a National accounts are compiled using chain volume measures.

b Industry data refer to manufacturing, construction, and utilities comprising electricity, gas, steam, and air-conditioning supply; water supply; and sewerage, waste management, and remediation activities.

c Industry data refer to mining and quarrying; manufacturing; electricity, gas, steam, and air-conditioning supply; water supply; and sewerage, waste management, and remediation activities.

Source: Economies' official sources.

Table 2.2.15: Growth Rates of Services Real Value-Added
(%)

ADB Regional Member	2010	2015	2017	2018	2019	2020	2021	2022	2023	2024
Developing ADB Member Economies										
Central and West Asia										
Afghanistan	18.1	1.4	-0.7	1.9	-1.4	-5.9	-4.6	-30.1	-6.5	1.5
Armenia	4.7	1.0	10.4	9.2	9.8	-8.7	7.6	17.8	12.2	8.8
Azerbaijan	8.8	4.4	3.2	3.8	3.8	-4.4	7.8	9.8	2.9	6.4
Georgia[a]	8.2	2.2	5.0	8.0	8.6	-6.8	17.9	9.9	10.8	12.0*
Kazakhstan	6.0	3.1	6.4	3.9	4.4	-5.3	4.4	2.5	3.0	4.7*
Kyrgyz Republic	-1.3	3.5	3.3	2.9	3.2	-7.9	6.9	6.8	7.9	9.3*
Pakistan	2.6	4.2	5.6	6.0	5.0	-1.2	5.9	6.7	-0.0	2.3
Tajikistan	7.3	1.9	6.2	4.5	7.3	-1.8	14.3	15.7	3.9	...
Türkiye	...	...	...	...	...	...	...	...	...	...
Turkmenistan	21.1	-13.2 (2014)	...	...	...	...	...	...	...	...
Uzbekistan	9.6	7.6	6.0	5.5	7.7	-0.8	10.9	9.1	7.1	7.7*
East Asia										
China, People's Republic of	9.6	8.6	8.1	8.0	7.6	2.4	9.0	3.5	6.3	5.0*
Hong Kong, China[a,b]	6.9	1.7	3.5	3.1	-0.6	-6.7	5.9	-3.4	3.4	2.2
Korea, Republic of[a]	5.1	3.1	2.8	4.2	3.8	-0.4	4.3	3.8	2.1	1.6
Mongolia	9.8	0.6	7.1	5.1	6.4	-6.5	3.9	6.9	9.9	9.8*
Taipei,China[a]	6.4	1.2	2.2	2.2	2.8	0.5	2.3	3.2	4.9	4.7
South Asia										
Bangladesh	6.0	6.0	6.4	6.6	6.9	3.9	5.7	6.3	5.4	5.1
Bhutan	11.5	5.6	1.2	9.8	11.8	-10.9	5.5	6.6	8.6	...
India	7.8	9.4	6.3	7.2	6.4	-8.4	9.2	10.3	9.0*	7.2*
Maldives	7.3	3.9	5.9	7.7	9.5	-31.7	43.4	14.7	...	...
Nepal	5.8	5.4	8.4	9.3	6.8	-4.5	4.7	5.3	2.4	4.5*
Sri Lanka	8.0	5.3	3.6	4.3	2.9	-1.9	3.4	-2.6	-0.2	2.4
Southeast Asia										
Brunei Darussalam	4.9 (2011)	-1.1	1.1	0.8	3.4	-2.1	2.5	3.8	5.9	2.1
Cambodia	5.1	6.9	7.0	7.1	6.6	-6.7	-1.8	3.6	6.0	4.1
Indonesia	8.4	5.5	5.7	5.8	6.4	-1.5	3.5	6.5	6.1*	6.2*
Lao People's Democratic Republic	7.6	8.0	4.5	6.8	6.9	-1.2	1.4	5.0	5.6	5.1
Malaysia	7.4	5.3	6.5	7.0	6.2	-5.4	2.2	11.4	5.2	5.4*
Myanmar	9.5	8.7	8.1	8.7	8.3	3.4	-6.3	5.2	1.0*	-0.5*
Philippines	7.6	7.4	7.4	6.7	7.2	-9.1	5.4	9.2	7.1	6.7*
Singapore[a,c]	11.4	4.2	3.6	3.1	2.0	-4.1	7.8	4.9	3.3	4.4
Thailand[a,d]	7.0	5.9	5.4	4.7	3.8	-6.6	0.3	3.7*	4.2*	3.9*
Timor-Leste	10.2	4.5	2.6	-1.4	0.3	-7.2	6.4	2.4	3.3	...
Viet Nam	7.2	7.0	7.1	7.5	8.1	2.0	1.7	10.7	6.9	7.4*
The Pacific										
Cook Islands	-5.8	2.4	6.6	5.1	6.4	-38.6	-3.1	43.5	16.0*	...
Fiji	2.9	3.0	3.6	1.7	0.0	-16.9	-3.1	12.7	8.6*	...
Kiribati	1.5	8.5	6.6	5.1	8.0	-1.8	4.4	8.5	5.0*	...
Marshall Islands	2.6	4.6	4.2	2.7	-0.0	-0.6	-0.9	2.1	-2.4	...
Micronesia, Federated States of	2.2	3.0	...	...	...	...	...	...	...	...
Nauru	4.2	11.6	2.2	6.3	3.9	1.0*	9.7	-1.5*	1.7*	4.1*
Niue	0.4	5.2 (2014)	4.0	5.7	-2.0	-5.9	-12.0	3.7*	9.5	7.2*
Palau	-3.6	8.7	-3.1	0.4	-2.1	-6.3	-12.8	1.3	4.7	8.9*
Papua New Guinea	12.4	-2.3	1.4	5.1	2.5	-0.2	4.5	6.3	5.0	5.7*
Samoa	2.9	7.3	1.4	5.4	1.4	-6.4	3.2	4.9	14.1	1.6
Solomon Islands	5.1	2.5	1.2	4.8	2.0	-3.0	3.9*	4.6*	...	...
Tonga	0.8	1.2	1.6	3.3	-2.5	2.6	-5.2	-1.9	-3.0	...
Tuvalu	2.3	7.1	2.1	4.0	5.0	3.5	-0.1	1.8	6.5	...
Vanuatu	2.7	-2.5	4.6	0.8	6.1	-6.7	0.4	7.8	...	...
Developed ADB Member Economies										
Australia[a]	...	...	...	...	...	...	...	...	...	...
Japan[a]	...	...	...	...	...	...	...	...	...	...
New Zealand[a]	...	...	...	...	...	...	...	...	...	...

... = data not available; (-/+) 0.0 = magnitude is less than half of unit employed; * = provisional, preliminary, estimate; ADB = Asian Development Bank.

a National accounts are compiled using chain volume measures.
b Services data refer to import, export, wholesale, and retail trades; accommodation and food services; transportation, storage, postal, and courier services; information and communications; financing and insurance; real estate, professional, and business services; public administration, social services, and personal services; and ownership of premises.
c Services data refer to services-producing industries, including ownership of dwellings.
d Services data include construction.

Source: Economies' official sources.

Table 2.2.16: Growth Rates of Real Household Final Consumption
(%)

ADB Regional Member	2010	2015	2017	2018	2019	2020	2021	2022	2023	2024
Developing ADB Member Economies										
Central and West Asia										
Afghanistan	...	...	-6.2	26.2	11.3	0.0 |	-1.0	-24.4	0.5	6.8
Armenia[a]	3.9	-7.5	14.0	4.8	11.5	-14.0	2.7	5.6	5.6	6.8
Azerbaijan[a]	10.8	10.3	0.8	4.6	5.9	-8.7	3.6	4.5	5.2	...
Georgia[a]	8.7 (2011)	3.8	8.5	3.1	5.2	10.1	12.3	-2.8	4.7	11.0*
Kazakhstan[a]	11.5 |	1.8	4.6	6.1	6.1	-3.7	6.3	4.0	7.6	6.7*
Kyrgyz Republic[a]	2.7	-0.9	6.3	5.0	0.8 |	-6.2	18.8	17.0	18.6	...
Pakistan[a]	2.2	3.0	6.9	7.2	5.6	-2.9	9.5	7.1	2.7	6.4
Tajikistan[a]	10.5	-15.1 |	4.6	4.0	5.0	3.1	4.3	15.7	9.2	...
Türkiye	11.0	5.2	5.9	0.6	1.5	3.2	15.4	19.0	13.6	...
Turkmenistan[a]	-61.4	...	...	...	...	...	...	...	...	...
Uzbekistan[a]	10.3	11.8	4.2	6.1	6.0	-2.4	11.6	11.2	7.0	7.5*
East Asia										
China, People's Republic of	...	...	...	...	...	...	...	...	...	...
Hong Kong, China[a]	6.1	4.8	5.5	5.3	-0.8	-10.6	5.6	-2.2	6.8	-0.6
Korea, Republic of	4.7	2.5	2.8	3.1	2.2	-4.7	3.8	4.2	1.7	1.0
Mongolia[a]	15.8 (2011)	8.1	4.3	11.7	5.8	2.1	-5.9	8.1	9.7	12.9*
Taipei,China	3.7	2.9	3.0	2.3	2.5	-2.4	-0.1	4.0	7.9	...
South Asia										
Bangladesh	6.3	5.3	6.3	9.4	4.9	3.0	8.0	7.5	2.0	6.0
Bhutan[a]	2.5	13.3	2.6	7.9	-1.9	3.1	-2.4	6.0	7.6	...
India[a]	6.7	7.9	6.2	7.1	5.2	-5.3	11.7	7.5	5.6*	7.2*
Maldives	...	1.4	12.8	10.3	7.0	-15.9	9.3	15.1	11.1	...
Nepal[a]	6.2	2.6	0.8	6.2	8.1	3.6	8.0	6.8	0.7	1.1*
Sri Lanka	9.9 (2011)	3.7 (2014)	-0.6	4.7	3.8	-5.8	2.7	1.2	-1.9	4.0
Southeast Asia										
Brunei Darussalam[a]	5.4 (2011)	5.2	4.7	2.2	6.1	21.5	5.6	8.3	11.1	5.9
Cambodia[a]	9.3	5.7	6.7	5.5	3.4	-1.9	-2.4	5.2	4.6	2.4
Indonesia[a]	4.7	4.8	5.0	5.1	5.2	-2.7	2.0	5.0	4.9*	5.1*
Lao People's Democratic Republic	...	...	...	...	...	...	...	...	...	...
Malaysia[a]	6.9	6.0	6.9	8.0	7.7	-4.0	1.8	11.3	4.7	5.1*
Myanmar[b]	2.6	4.7	4.1	4.5	1.7	7.1	-4.6	...	...	...
Philippines[a]	3.6	6.4	6.0	5.8	5.9	-8.0	4.2	8.3	5.5	4.9*
Singapore	4.4	5.2	3.1	4.4	3.3	-13.6	7.2	9.7	4.9	4.8
Thailand[a]	5.5	2.6	3.1	4.6	4.0	-0.8	0.6	6.2*	6.9*	4.4*
Timor-Leste	5.2	1.2	6.4	2.5	4.8	-1.5	-3.0	14.6	3.8	...
Viet Nam	8.2	8.8	7.2	6.9	7.0	0.4	2.2	7.9	3.4	6.7*
The Pacific										
Cook Islands	...	...	...	...	...	...	...	...	...	...
Fiji	...	...	...	...	...	...	...	...	...	...
Kiribati	0.4	14.0	3.7	1.6	10.6	-4.8	29.5	10.5	4.4*	...
Marshall Islands	0.4	-0.7	10.3	-0.9	6.7	-3.0	-3.8	4.6	-9.2	...
Micronesia, Federated States of	...	...	...	...	...	...	...	...	...	...
Nauru	...	...	...	...	...	...	...	...	...	...
Niue	...	...	...	...	...	...	...	...	...	...
Palau	-3.1	4.2	-0.5	5.2	-0.3	1.0	-4.4	-1.3	-6.6	...
Papua New Guinea[a]	9.8 (2005)	...	...	...	...	...	...	...	...	...
Samoa	1.6	3.2	0.6	-3.7	5.6	6.9	10.9	-6.2	10.3	1.4
Solomon Islands	8.7	2.5	0.0	7.7	2.3	-14.6 |	0.2*	4.1*	...	...
Tonga	-5.3	7.6	0.8	4.5	0.8	1.9	13.3	-22.4	33.9	...
Tuvalu	...	...	...	...	...	...	...	...	...	...
Vanuatu	2.7	1.0	-1.9	3.4	0.4	7.7	5.9	8.2	...	...
Developed ADB Member Economies										
Australia	3.5	2.6	2.4	2.8	1.7	-3.3	0.9	4.3	6.3	1.0
Japan	2.3	-0.3	1.0	0.4	-0.7	-4.9	0.8	2.3	0.8	-0.1
New Zealand	2.5	4.3	4.9	4.7	2.4	0.0	6.3	3.3	0.8	...

... = data not available; 0.0 = magnitude is less than half of unit employed; | = marks break in series; * = provisional, preliminary, estimate; ADB = Asian Development Bank.

a Includes expenditure of nonprofit institutions serving households.
b Data refers to total final consumption expenditure.

Source: Economies' official sources.

Table 2.2.17: Growth Rates of Real Government Consumption Expenditure
(%)

ADB Regional Member	2010	2015	2017	2018	2019	2020	2021	2022	2023	2024
Developing ADB Member Economies										
Central and West Asia										
Afghanistan	...	...	-6.4	-5.6	28.4	-13.0 |	7.8	-25.4	-1.2	0.7
Armenia	3.9	4.7	-2.1	-3.0	12.9	9.2	-6.2	-2.2	28.3	-22.3
Azerbaijan	3.4	1.4	1.1	-3.9	2.2	3.4	4.0	0.8	-2.1	...
Georgia	-9.5 (2011)	0.4	0.3	0.2	2.6	6.6	7.1	-0.8	7.5	24.7*
Kazakhstan	2.7	2.4	1.8	-14.1	15.5	12.8	-2.4	4.3	7.4	1.0*
Kyrgyz Republic	-1.1	0.9	1.3	1.3	0.5 |	0.7	0.5	4.4	0.2	...
Pakistan	-3.1	1.9	4.5	5.5	-1.6	8.5	1.8	-1.3	-3.9	-11.8
Tajikistan	0.9	3.3 |	10.9	4.5	0.7	2.3	4.6	-0.7	-9.1	...
Türkiye	1.7	3.9	5.0	5.9	3.9	2.2	3.0	4.2	2.4	...
Turkmenistan	3.7	...	...	...	...	...	...	...	...	...
Uzbekistan	7.0	6.7	1.5	4.8	5.7	1.4	3.1	3.5	1.1	1.1*
East Asia										
China, People's Republic of	...	...	...	...	...	...	...	...	...	...
Hong Kong, China	3.4	3.4	2.8	4.2	5.1	7.9	5.9	8.0	-3.9	1.0
Korea, Republic of	5.7	3.9	3.7	5.4	6.4	5.2	5.6	4.0	1.3	1.8
Mongolia	15.3 (2011)	-4.7	-2.4	1.1	12.3	14.6	9.2	6.9	3.2	18.3*
Taipei,China	1.2	-0.1	-0.4	4.0	0.6	2.7	3.7	5.2	0.4	2.5
South Asia										
Bangladesh	6.5	9.8	7.2	5.3	13.4	2.0	6.9	6.2	8.5	9.8
Bhutan	7.5	10.8	4.4	3.7	9.7	4.5	6.4	-2.3	1.4	...
India	5.2	7.5	11.9	6.7	3.9	-0.8	0.0	4.3	8.1*	2.3*
Maldives	...	12.6	-10.8	9.1	17.6	-6.2	6.5	-4.9	2.0	...
Nepal	1.3 |	11.5	21.4	2.1	9.8	3.8	-1.7	9.6	-21.2	-4.2*
Sri Lanka	-2.1 (2011)	6.0 (2014)	5.5	18.7	6.6	0.0	-2.8	1.4	-5.4	-1.8
Southeast Asia										
Brunei Darussalam	5.3 (2011)	-3.6	7.4	1.6	1.8	-9.6	2.6	6.9	-2.4	0.7
Cambodia	13.2	4.4	8.3	5.9	8.8	9.2	12.3	-1.2	7.5	3.4
Indonesia	0.3	5.3	2.1	4.8	3.3	2.1	4.3	-4.4	3.0*	6.6*
Lao People's Democratic Republic	...	...	...	...	...	...	...	...	...	...
Malaysia	3.4	4.5	5.7	3.4	1.5	4.1	5.8	5.1	3.3	4.7*
Myanmar[a]								...	...	...
Philippines	4.2	7.9	6.5	13.4	9.1	10.5	7.2	5.1	0.3	7.3*
Singapore	10.2	8.9	3.4	2.9	3.6	13.2	3.9	-2.3	1.8	8.3
Thailand	8.9	2.5	0.3	2.7	1.6	1.4	3.7	0.1*	-4.7*	2.5*
Timor-Leste	2.1	3.6	-5.8	-0.3	3.2	4.9	2.9	-0.3	-0.8	...
Viet Nam	12.3	7.8	5.6	4.7	5.4	1.2	4.5	3.0	4.6	5.8*
The Pacific										
Cook Islands	...	...	...	...	...	...	...	...	...	...
Fiji	...	...	...	...	...	...	...	...	...	...
Kiribati	-7.6	-1.6	3.9	2.7	1.2	-6.5	-6.7	26.9	-2.2*	...
Marshall Islands	-0.9	3.1	2.1	8.8	12.9	-6.2	3.6	-7.3	-9.8	...
Micronesia, Federated States of	...	...	...	...	...	...	...	...	...	...
Nauru	...	...	...	...	...	...	...	...	...	...
Niue	...	...	...	...	...	...	...	...	...	...
Palau	-1.5	1.3	-0.9	4.4	10.5	10.5	-5.9	-4.8	-0.6	...
Papua New Guinea	1.1 (2005)	...	...	...	...	...	...	...	...	...
Samoa	17.9	-4.6	8.3	20.9	5.5	0.5	2.8	18.9	-6.0	12.1
Solomon Islands	10.0	4.9	-5.5	14.4	6.1	-13.3 |	-15.2*	-12.0*	...	...
Tonga	4.0	3.1	1.5	1.1	9.8	11.1	22.8	0.6	1.0	...
Tuvalu	...	...	...	...	...	...	...	...	...	...
Vanuatu	5.0	16.9	19.5	4.5	2.6	3.7	-0.0	7.8	...	...
Developed ADB Member Economies										
Australia	1.6	2.2	4.9	3.5	5.0	7.4	6.6	6.9	1.7	3.8
Japan	1.9	1.9	0.1	1.0	1.9	2.4	3.4	1.4	-0.3	0.9
New Zealand	2.0	2.0	3.8	3.3	5.5	7.0	7.9	2.8	2.1	...

... = data not available; (-/+) 0.0 = magnitude is less than half of unit employed; | = marks break in series; * = provisional, preliminary, estimate; ADB = Asian Development Bank.

a For 2000–2019, real government consumption expenditure data are included in real household consumption expenditure.

Source: Economies' official sources.

Table 2.2.18: Growth Rates of Real Gross Capital Formation
(%)

ADB Regional Member	2010	2015	2019	2020	2021	2022	2023	2024
Developing ADB Member Economies								
Central and West Asia								
Afghanistan[a]	...	8.2 (2017)	-17.3	33.4 |	-20.4	-9.4	29.2	-5.7
Armenia	0.5	-3.2	-14.3	-0.5	21.5	11.8	5.9	11.4
Azerbaijan	2.0	-8.2	1.1	-7.3	-4.5	0.8	17.5	...
Georgia	19.1 (2011)	8.4	0.5	-15.9	-16.1	35.7	19.5	2.2*
Kazakhstan	2.0 |	5.5	12.2	-1.0	1.5	2.1	16.4	5.6*
Kyrgyz Republic	-5.2	-2.3	7.9 |	-29.2	21.5	58.5	20.9	...
Pakistan	-6.8	12.5	-9.7	-6.1	4.0	4.6	-13.6	-2.6
Tajikistan	7.5	25.2	8.9	-4.6	12.0	11.9	-9.9	...
Türkiye	22.0	9.3	-12.5	7.3	7.2	1.3	8.4	...
Turkmenistan	21.5	...	...	...	...	...	...	...
Uzbekistan	...	...	...	...	...	...	...	...
East Asia								
China, People's Republic of	...	...	...	...	...	...	...	...
Hong Kong, China	11.3	-8.1	-16.9	-1.4	-2.3	-11.7	12.7	4.1
Korea, Republic of	17.7	6.5	-1.4	0.8	4.1	0.1	0.8	-2.3
Mongolia	62.8 (2011)	-26.5	0.2	-40.7	80.7	11.2	-3.4	22.2*
Taipei,China	35.6	2.6	7.0	8.3	19.1	3.4	-10.1	12.5
South Asia								
Bangladesh[b,c]	6.1	9.4	6.9	4.0	8.1	11.7	2.2	3.3
Bhutan	44.2	16.5	-7.4	-21.8	20.0	28.8	-12.6	...
India[d]	20.1	7.0	-6.0*	-10.6	25.4	3.5	7.3*	...
Maldives	...	11.8	-2.9	-55.4	-4.2	30.9	-3.1	...
Nepal	34.4 |	7.0	11.1	-26.7	30.9	11.7	-13.3	12.3*
Sri Lanka	20.2 (2011)	12.0 (2016)	-11.9	-0.6	6.4	-40.6	-5.7	21.1
Southeast Asia								
Brunei Darussalam	37.0 (2011)	6.6	-4.4	-9.3	-13.8	-1.8	0.2	-2.3
Cambodia	-6.7	9.9	14.5	-1.8	4.7	5.4	-0.4	1.0
Indonesia	8.8	3.0	2.4	-6.9	4.1	4.0	5.2*	7.5*
Lao People's Democratic Republic	...	...	...	...	...	...	...	...
Malaysia	25.3	6.7	-3.8	-12.1	8.4	7.4	5.6	6.0*
Myanmar	34.6	16.1	1.5	3.3	-16.8	...	...	...
Philippines	30.5	13.4	3.5	-34.2	20.0	13.7	6.3	7.7*
Singapore	22.5	-9.8	-0.6	-12.6	22.9	3.5	-12.7	10.1
Thailand	32.0	2.1	-3.4	-4.7	12.8	-7.6*	-15.4*	...
Timor-Leste	2.8	-5.0 |	-14.7	-42.3	-14.1	32.5	11.8	...
Viet Nam[e]	10.4	9.6	7.5	4.1	3.3	5.7	4.1	7.2*
The Pacific								
Cook Islands	...	...	...	...	...	...	...	...
Fiji	...	...	...	...	...	...	...	...
Kiribati	-5.5	48.9	-14.8	-7.3	40.0	10.7	37.3*	...
Marshall Islands	19.5	-16.6	141.4	-59.2	5.0	21.5*	-27.6*	...
Micronesia, Federated States of	...	...	...	...	...	...	...	...
Nauru	...	...	...	...	...	...	...	...
Niue	...	...	...	...	...	...	...	...
Palau	3.3	0.3	24.8	14.6	-23.0	9.5	-15.5	...
Papua New Guinea	-9.8 (2005)	...	...	...	...	...	...	...
Samoa	54.7	3.8	17.4	-20.8	3.8	11.6	-7.4	11.3
Solomon Islands[a]	85.2	19.9	20.0	-12.6 |	-5.7*	36.0*	...	...
Tonga	29.0	9.8	13.6	-5.1	48.0	-28.4	2.6	...
Tuvalu	...	...	...	...	...	...	...	...
Vanuatu	-4.7	46.5	-3.6	30.1	13.1	-9.1	...	...
Developed ADB Member Economies								
Australia	...	...	...	...	...	...	...	...
Japan	2.9	3.3	0.1	-5.4	2.2	0.3	0.2	0.1
New Zealand	7.4	1.7	1.7	-2.4	11.7	5.1	-7.7	...

... = data not available, | = marks break in series; * = provisional, preliminary, estimate; ADB = Asian Development Bank.

a Refers to gross fixed capital formation.
b Refers to gross fixed capital formation, which includes data on changes in inventories.
c For 2000–2006, data refer to previous growth rates calculated using the base year 1995/1996; for 2007–2016, using the base year 2005/2006; and for 2017–2021, using the base year 2015/2016.
d Refers to gross capital formation, which refers to the sum of gross fixed capital formation, valuables, increases in stocks, and errors and omissions.
e For 2000–2004, gross domestic product data are based on unreassured/unreevaluated scale. For 2005 onward, methodology was revised and 2010 base year was used.

Source: Economies' official sources.

Table 2.2.19: Growth Rates of Real Exports of Goods and Services
(%)

ADB Regional Member	2010	2015	2019	2020	2021	2022	2023	2024
Developing ADB Member Economies								
Central and West Asia								
Afghanistan	...	...	-21.5	-35.6 |	41.4	7.2	18.6	-12.1
Armenia	26.5 |	4.9	16.0	-33.5	18.6	59.3	30.7	35.6
Azerbaijan	9.1	-0.2	-4.3	-11.5	13.8	13.0	-0.1	...
Georgia	11.6 (2011)	3.2	10.9	-37.6	23.5	37.4	9.5	5.9*
Kazakhstan	3.1 |	-4.1	2.1	-11.3	2.3	9.6	1.8	0.3*
Kyrgyz Republic	-11.7	-5.6	16.2 |	-27.2	16.4	59.2	-3.0	...
Pakistan	7.9	-3.8	13.2	1.5	6.5	5.9	3.2	-1.1
Tajikistan	23.0	–	21.5	21.8	55.4	-24.0	13.4	...
Türkiye	1.7	3.2	5.3	-14.6	25.1	9.9	-2.8	...
Turkmenistan	11.7	...	...	...	...	...	...	...
Uzbekistan	1.7	2.2	16.4	-20.1	13.4	19.0	17.3	-5.9*
East Asia								
China, People's Republic of	...	...	...	...	...	...	...	...
Hong Kong, China[a]	17.6	-1.4	-6.1	-6.7	17.0	-12.5	-6.5	4.7
Korea, Republic of	13.1	–	-0.2	-1.7	10.8	3.9	3.6	7.0
Mongolia	18.2 | (2011)	0.1	12.0	-5.3	-14.6	32.3	33.2	0.7*
Taipei,China	27.6	0.4	0.0	-0.5	15.1	2.8	-4.1	8.7
South Asia								
Bangladesh[b]	-0.2	-4.0	11.5	-17.5	9.2	29.4	8.0	-17.1
Bhutan	7.5	-3.2	26.1	-19.7	1.0	-9.1	30.7	...
India	19.5	-5.6	-3.4	-7.0	29.6	10.3	2.2*	6.3*
Maldives	...	-3.1	4.0	-49.2	129.3	18.1	4.4	...
Nepal	-10.4 |	2.3	5.5	-15.9	-21.3	34.1	3.3	18.1*
Sri Lanka	10.2 (2011)	4.9 (2016)	1.7	-29.6	10.1	9.8	13.2	12.5
Southeast Asia								
Brunei Darussalam	-3.0 (2011)	-9.9	14.9	7.6	8.4	7.2	-2.2	4.0
Cambodia	20.0	8.6	12.3	-12.2	6.1	21.3	-0.4	14.4
Indonesia	15.3	-2.1	-0.5	-8.4	18.0	16.2	1.3*	6.5*
Lao People's Democratic Republic	...	...	...	...	...	...	...	...
Malaysia	11.1	0.3	-1.0	-8.6	18.5	14.5	-8.1	8.5*
Myanmar	10.9	15.1	26.8	-7.6	-19.1	...	...	...
Philippines	20.3	10.0	2.6	-16.1	8.0	11.0	1.3	3.3*
Singapore	17.8	5.0	0.1	-0.4	8.8	4.9	5.7	5.4
Thailand	14.0	1.0	-3.0	-19.7	11.1	6.2*	2.4*	7.8*
Timor-Leste[c]	28.0	-28.3 |	-23.2	-47.3	79.3	30.3	31.9	...
Viet Nam[d]	14.6	13.9	6.2	4.1	14.8	4.2	-3.2	15.4*
The Pacific								
Cook Islands	...	...	...	...	...	...	...	...
Fiji	...	...	...	...	...	...	...	...
Kiribati	-20.8	35.2	72.9	-33.6	-62.3	106.1	-18.8*	...
Marshall Islands	35.5	-0.9	11.9	-4.7	22.2	-18.9*	0.5*	...
Micronesia, Federated States of	...	...	...	...	...	...	...	...
Nauru	...	...	...	...	...	...	...	...
Niue	...	...	...	...	...	...	...	...
Palau	5.7	12.7	-19.8	-43.0	-73.5	119.0	76.2	...
Papua New Guinea	6.8 (2005)	...	...	...	...	...	...	...
Samoa	3.1	7.2	15.4	-61.1	-19.0	77.0	46.5	3.5
Solomon Islands	32.7	-6.5	-2.8	-21.8 |	-1.0*	-1.5*	...	...
Tonga	-9.5	8.1	-3.3	-1.9	-47.7	-3.0	101.2	...
Tuvalu	...	...	...	...	...	...	...	...
Vanuatu	1.0	4.9	-3.7	-60.1	-52.8	103.4	...	...
Developed ADB Member Economies								
Australia	4.7	6.9	3.9	-1.7	-8.5	-0.4	6.7	3.8
Japan	24.9	3.2	-1.5	-11.6	11.9	5.5	3.0	1.0
New Zealand	2.8	6.7	0.1	-18.0	2.5	5.6	8.6	...

... = data not available; | = marks break in series; * = provisional, preliminary, estimate; – = magnitude equals zero; 0.0 = magnitude is less than half of unit employed; ADB = Asian Development Bank.

a The statistics for trade in goods and services are compiled based on the change of ownership principle in recording goods sent abroad for processing and merchanting under the standards stipulated in the 2008 SNA.

b For 2000–2006, data refer to previous growth rates calculated using the base year 1995/1996; for 2007–2016, using the base year 2005/2006; and for 2017 onward, using the base year 2015/2016.

c From September 2019, following the new Timor-Leste Australia Maritime Boundary Treaty, oil revenue from the Joint Petroleum Development Area is included in the national accounts. The National Institute of Statistics Timor-Leste (INETL) disaggregates the accounts into 'oil' and 'non-oil' components. To better assess the performance of the domestic economy, this publication presents GDP on a non-oil basis, which reflects the primary analytical approach used by INETL.

d For 2000, data refer to exports less imports of goods and services. Annual growth rate cannot be calculated separately for exports and imports for 2001.

Source: Economies' official sources.

Table 2.2.20: Growth Rates of Real Imports of Goods and Services
(%)

ADB Regional Member	2010	2015	2019	2020	2021	2022	2023	2024
Developing ADB Member Economies								
Central and West Asia								
Afghanistan	...	...	16.5	-7.1 |	-14.3	-21.3	36.7	0.7
Armenia	12.8 |	-15.3	11.6	-31.5	12.9	34.5	30.2	31.4
Azerbaijan	12.4	8.4	-3.2	-17.1	3.0	13.5	9.7	...
Georgia	10.2 (2011)	5.3	6.8	-16.6	8.8	16.9	10.0	8.5*
Kazakhstan	2.9 |	-0.1	14.9	-9.0	-0.3	13.1	15.6	2.1*
Kyrgyz Republic	-6.9	-13.2	6.1 |	-27.4	38.8	66.7	37.6	...
Pakistan	-2.3	-1.0	7.6	-5.1	14.5	11.0	1.8	4.1
Tajikistan	8.0	–	6.4	-0.4	20.0	4.0	-4.3	...
Türkiye	19.4	0.7	-5.0	6.8	1.7	8.6	11.8	...
Turkmenistan	7.3	...	...	...	...	...	...	...
Uzbekistan	0.4	-10.6	13.4	-14.9	23.4	13.6*	15.3*	-1.5
East Asia								
China, People's Republic of	...	...	...	...	...	...	...	...
Hong Kong, China[a]	18.2	-1.8	-7.2	-6.9	15.8	-12.2	-5.2	3.5
Korea, Republic of	17.8	1.9	-2.0	-3.3	10.2	4.2	3.5	2.5
Mongolia	49.5 | (2011)	-11.4	8.6	-15.5	13.6	29.1	18.9*	17.7
Taipei,China	30.1	1.3	-0.2	-5.2	16.1	5.2	-5.5	11.4
South Asia								
Bangladesh[b]	-0.7	-5.0	0.5	-11.4	15.3	31.2	-9.8	-4.6
Bhutan	28.7	17.2	-3.4	-9.1	9.0	17.0	-0.6	...
India	15.8	-5.9	-0.8	-12.6	22.1	8.9	13.8*	-3.7*
Maldives	...	-4.2	-0.4	-43.5	33.5	35.9	0.7	...
Nepal	28.3 |	9.6	5.8	-20.8	18.8	16.4	-18.7*	-2.3
Sri Lanka	23.6 (2011)	7.0 (2016)	-3.5	-20.1	4.1	-19.9	8.9	22.5
Southeast Asia								
Brunei Darussalam	33.7 (2011)	-8.9	13.8	-1.9	27.0	11.5	-7.8	0.2
Cambodia	18.3	8.2	10.5	-8.3	1.9	18.6	-2.2	7.5
Indonesia	17.3	-6.2	-7.1	-17.6	24.9	15.0*	-1.6*	7.9
Lao People's Democratic Republic	...	...	...	...	...	...	...	...
Malaysia	15.6	0.8	-2.4	-7.9	21.2	16.0	-7.4	8.9
Myanmar	51.9	21.6	5.8	-3.3	-26.0	...	...	...
Philippines	20.7	15.0	2.3	-21.6	12.8	14.0	1.0	4.2
Singapore	16.3	3.4	0.2	-2.0	8.9	5.8	5.3	6.6
Thailand	23.0	0.0	-5.2	-13.9	17.9*	3.4*	-2.5*	6.3
Timor-Leste[c]	-1.8	-7.4 |	-6.5	-7.0	-8.8	22.9	4.9	...
Viet Nam[d]	13.7	15.7	4.9	3.3	16.7	1.7	-5.2	16.1
The Pacific								
Cook Islands	...	...	...	...	...	...	...	...
Fiji	...	...	...	...	...	...	...	...
Kiribati	-7.3	18.8	14.1	-18.2	20.6	37.7*	3.7	...
Marshall Islands	9.7	0.2	38.2	-30.7	-5.8	-0.9*	-8.9	...
Micronesia, Federated States of	...	...	...	...	...	...	...	...
Nauru	...	...	...	...	...	...	...	...
Niue	...	...	...	...	...	...	...	...
Palau	0.9	2.5	-0.1	-0.4	-19.6	7.8	-5.4*	...
Papua New Guinea	4.7 (2005)	...	...	...	...	...	...	...
Samoa	27.4	-5.6	12.0	-20.1	9.6	12.3	9.2	0.5
Solomon Islands	52.2	0.8	8.1	-37.1 |	22.2*	51.4*	...	...
Tonga	3.0	22.6	4.8	-0.3	-2.9	-1.7	11.5	...
Tuvalu	...	...	...	...	...	...	...	...
Vanuatu	1.2	26.2	-15.1	1.8	-3.9	13.6	...	...
Developed ADB Member Economies								
Australia	7.0	1.6	0.5	-6.6	-3.1	7.3	12.2	6.3
Japan	11.3	0.4	1.0	-6.8	5.2	8.3	-1.5	1.3
New Zealand	11.5	3.1	1.5	-15.9	17.2	4.4	-1.3	...

... = data not available; | = marks break in series; * = provisional, preliminary, estimate; – = magnitude equals zero; ADB = Asian Development Bank.

a The statistics for trade in goods and services are compiled based on the change of ownership principle in recording goods sent abroad for processing and merchanting under the standards stipulated in the System of National Accounts 2008.

b For 2000–2006, data refer to previous growth rates calculated using the base year 1995/1996; for 2007–2016, using the base year 2005/2006; and for 2017 onward, using the base year 2015/2016.

c From September 2019, following the new Timor-Leste Australia Maritime Boundary Treaty, oil revenue from the Joint Petroleum Development Area is included in the national accounts. The National Institute of Statistics Timor-Leste (INETL) disaggregates the accounts into 'oil' and 'non-oil' components. To better assess the performance of the domestic economy, this publication presents GDP on a non-oil basis, which reflects the primary analytical approach used by INETL.

d For 2000, data refer to exports less imports of goods and services. Annual growth rate cannot be calculated separately for exports and imports for 2001.

Source: Economies' official sources.

Table 2.2.21: Growth Rates of Agriculture Production Index
(%)

ADB Regional Member	2010	2015	2019	2020	2021	2022	2023	2024
Developing ADB Member Economies								
Central and West Asia								
Afghanistan	-0.7	-5.7	12.9	3.0	1.6	-2.5	4.4	...
Armenia	-13.4	9.5	-2.6	4.9	-1.5	-1.6	-1.8	...
Azerbaijan	-2.2	6.6	7.2	2.0	3.4	3.4	3.0	1.5
Georgia	-4.5	2.0	1.4	10.0	0.9	-3.6	-4.1	...
Kazakhstan[a]	-10.4	3.4	-0.1	5.7	-2.3	9.1	-7.7	13.8
Kyrgyz Republic	-1.7	8.2	2.1	0.4	-4.4	7.1	0.4	...
Pakistan	-1.9	-4.8	-13.4	1.2	...	...	...	...
Tajikistan	5.0	10.1	7.1	-1.7	1.1	-1.1	-0.4	...
Türkiye	3.2	5.5	3.9	4.7	0.4	7.6	-1.7	...
Turkmenistan	6.3	3.2	5.2	5.1	0.2	-0.3	-7.3	...
Uzbekistan	6.3	6.1	3.3	2.7	3.9	3.6	4.0	...
East Asia								
China, People's Republic of	2.9	3.3	0.6	1.0	4.1	2.4	2.1	...
Hong Kong, China	–	–	-0.6	1.7	-2.2	-0.6	-0.6	-10.2
Korea, Republic of	-4.5	-2.4	0.9	-1.5	2.6	-1.2	0.2	...
Mongolia	-21.8	30.7	3.8	27.8	-24.4	23.8	-6.8	...
Taipei,China[b]	2.2	-3.3	-3.9	0.3	-1.8	-3.0	-1.3	...
South Asia								
Bangladesh	6.0	2.9	1.4	3.5	5.4	3.1	3.1	...
Bhutan	4.3	3.0	7.8	9.0	-11.4	-22.2	-1.5	...
India	10.5	-1.3	2.7	3.0	4.8	3.6	3.0	...
Maldives	-4.2	1.7	4.2	2.2	-12.2	-0.4	4.7	...
Nepal	1.0	–	5.4	3.1	2.6	2.5	-1.9	...
Sri Lanka	25.1	7.4	1.8	9.4	8.4	-16.3	2.4	...
Southeast Asia								
Brunei Darussalam	5.0	-2.0	-1.6	7.2	7.7	1.9	-2.3	...
Cambodia	7.6	2.5	-0.5	1.5	6.5	-1.1	6.8	...
Indonesia	5.2 (2011)	2.5	8.5	1.5	-0.3	5.9	3.3	...
Lao People's Democratic Republic	9.5	15.8	3.5	2.9	0.7	8.4	8.9	...
Malaysia	1.8	4.0	-0.7	0.1	-2.9	1.5	-0.5	...
Myanmar	2.9	3.0	-1.4	-0.3	2.3	2.0	-3.2	...
Philippines	-1.1	-0.1	-0.2	-0.5	-0.7	-0.1	1.2	...
Singapore	3.2	4.2	10.6	0.4	8.0	-1.7	-1.0	...
Thailand	0.9	-2.5	-0.3	-3.8	1.6	1.6	2.1	-1.0
Timor-Leste	-0.3	3.4	-3.2	0.2	-3.4	16.2	-3.7	...
Viet Nam	2.7	3.8	-0.7	1.2	4.5	1.5	2.8	...
The Pacific								
Cook Islands	-2.1	-2.2	-3.6	-1.7	-2.5	-0.2	-2.2	...
Fiji	-19.6	1.6	2.1	-5.1	-0.1	21.2	8.1	...
Kiribati	0.7	0.7	-12.1	0.1	0.1	2.9	3.6	...
Marshall Islands	-5.0	8.0	20.0	2.8	-13.5	18.8	-4.8	...
Micronesia, Federated States of	-1.0	-0.6	-0.1	0.4	0.1	0.1	1.1	...
Nauru	1.1	0.7	0.9	-0.6	0.2	0.1	0.1	...
Niue	2.9	-4.3	0.4	-1.2	-0.2	-0.1	-0.1	...
Palau	...	...	...	...	...	...	...	...
Papua New Guinea	-1.7	0.9	0.9	-2.3	2.1	0.3	1.7	...
Samoa	1.7	-26.2	-8.7	-1.4	8.2	-1.6	-0.6	...
Solomon Islands	-25.4	1.3	0.3	0.7	2.8	-0.2	1.1	...
Tonga	-0.8	-2.2	0.2	0.7	0.7	0.9	0.9	...
Tuvalu	-1.4	1.4	10.9	-0.1	0.8	0.2	-1.9	...
Vanuatu	28.5	-7.2	1.0	-1.9	2.4	83.9	-1.6	...
Developed ADB Member Economies								
Australia	-0.1	-1.3	-8.8	-7.9	26.2	7.3	10.1	...
Japan	-2.3	-1.2	0.7	-0.1	0.4	-0.3	-1.9	...
New Zealand	–	2.1	0.3	1.2	-0.1	-2.8	0.9	...

... = data not available, – = magnitude equals zero, ADB = Asian Development Bank.

Note: Data refer to the gross production index (2014–2016 = 100), except for Azerbaijan; Hong Kong, China; Indonesia; Kazakhstan; Pakistan; Taipei,China; Thailand; and Uzbekistan.

a Refers to the index of physical volume of the gross production (services) of agriculture.
b Refers to the index of agricultural, forestry, and fishery production.

Sources: Asian Development Bank estimates using data from the Food and Agriculture Organization of the United Nations. FAOSTAT Database. http://www.fao.org/faostat/en/#home (accessed 30 June 2025). For Azerbaijan; Hong Kong, China; Indonesia; Kazakhstan; Nepal; Pakistan; Taipei,China; Thailand; and Uzbekistan: Asian Development Bank estimates based on data from the economies' official sources.

Production

Table 2.2.22: Growth Rates of Manufacturing Production Index
(%)

ADB Regional Member	2010	2015	2019	2020	2021	2022	2023	2024
Developing ADB Member Economies								
Central and West Asia								
Afghanistan	...	...	...	...	...	...	...	...
Armenia	...	...	...	...	...	...	...	...
Azerbaijan	9.4	7.0	11.5	10.6	19.6	4.3	9.8	2.2*
Georgia	14.0 (2011)	-9.7	2.0	-5.9	7.1	13.4	3.1	2.1
Kazakhstan	13.9	0.2	5.8	4.1	4.7	3.6	4.0	5.9
Kyrgyz Republic	10.1	-7.8	8.3	-7.2	7.0	16.4	2.0	4.4*
Pakistan	0.5	3.4	3.4	-11.0	11.6	11.8	-10.3	0.9
Tajikistan	673.7	4.8	0.2	2.2	0.3	-6.5	0.6	0.9
Türkiye[a]	14.4	6.6	-0.7	2.5	17.3	6.1	2.1	-0.3
Turkmenistan	...	...	...	...	...	...	...	...
Uzbekistan	8.9	5.9	6.6	7.9	8.3	5.4	7.4	7.7*
East Asia								
China, People's Republic of[b]	16.6	7.0	6.0	3.4	9.8	3.0	5.0	6.1
Hong Kong, China[c]	3.5	-1.6	0.4	-5.8	5.4	0.2	3.8	0.8
Korea, Republic of	16.7	-0.3	0.4	-0.2	8.7	1.0	-2.6	4.2
Mongolia	...	...	...	...	...	...	...	...
Taipei,China	29.2	-1.0	1.0	9.2	15.6	-2.0	-12.8	12.3
South Asia								
Bangladesh	16.9 (2011)	10.7	14.9	0.9	11.6	12.5	8.8	2.5
Bhutan	...	...	...	...	...	...	...	...
India[d]	9.0	3.0	-1.4	-9.6	11.8	4.7	5.5	3.3
Maldives	...	...	...	...	...	...	...	...
Nepal	-3.6	-9.8 (2016)	7.2	-8.9	4.5	5.9	-2.3	-0.2
Sri Lanka	...	...	...	...	...	...	...	...
Southeast Asia								
Brunei Darussalam	...	...	...	...	...	...	...	...
Cambodia	...	...	...	...	...	...	...	...
Indonesia	4.1 (2011)	4.8	4.1	-10.1	7.5	4.0	2.4	2.6*
Lao People's Democratic Republic	...	...	...	...	...	...	...	...
Malaysia	11.1	4.8	3.6	-2.7	9.5	8.2	0.7	4.4
Myanmar[e]	10.1 (2011)	10.2	7.3	...	...	...	...	...
Philippines	23.2	0.5	-8.8	-40.5	52.6	15.1	4.9	0.9
Singapore[f]	29.7	-5.1	-1.5	7.5	13.3	2.7	-4.2	3.8
Thailand	14.2	0.0	-3.4	-9.5	...	1.5	-3.6	-1.3
Timor-Leste	...	...	...	...	...	...	...	...
Viet Nam	...	1.6	-1.6	-5.1	1.0	1.7	-5.7	8.0
The Pacific								
Cook Islands	...	...	...	...	...	...	...	...
Fiji	7.6	8.9	12.5	-5.1	-2.3	4.3	-2.3	3.3
Kiribati	...	...	...	...	...	...	...	...
Marshall Islands	...	...	...	...	...	...	...	...
Micronesia, Federated States of	...	...	...	...	...	...	...	...
Nauru	...	...	...	...	...	...	...	...
Niue	...	...	...	...	...	...	...	...
Palau	...	...	...	...	...	...	...	...
Papua New Guinea	...	...	...	...	...	...	...	...
Samoa[g]	15.2	3.2 (2013)	...	...	...	...	...	...
Solomon Islands	...	...	...	...	...	...	...	...
Tonga	...	...	...	...	...	...	...	...
Tuvalu	...	...	...	...	...	...	...	...
Vanuatu	...	...	...	...	...	...	...	...
Developed ADB Member Economies								
Australia	0.4	-1.6	-1.0	-1.9	1.8	2.4	0.2	0.3
Japan	15.6	-1.1	-2.7	-10.4	5.4	-0.1	-1.2	-2.4
New Zealand	4.6	1.8	1.1	-4.4	4.1	-5.3	-5.2	...

... = data not available; 0.0 = magnitude is less than half of unit employed; * = provisional, preliminary, estimate; ADB = Asian Development Bank.

a Figures are derived as averages of the monthly unadjusted index.
b Data include only industrial enterprises above a designated size (annual revenue from principal business of over 20 million yuan).
c Starting from the reference year 2008, the index of industrial production and producer price index for manufacturing industries are compiled based on the Hong Kong Standard Industrial Classification Version 2.0 of Hong Kong, China, which adopts the basic framework and principles of the International Standard Industrial Classification of All Economic Activities Revision 4.
d For the fiscal year beginning 1 April.
e For 2010–2015, fiscal year is April–March. For 2016 onward, fiscal year is October–September.
f Refers to index of industrial production.
g Refers to volume indices of industrial production.

Source: Asian Development Bank estimates based on data from the economies' official sources.

Data Issues and Comparability

Indicators in this theme were derived from national accounts statistics compiled in accordance with the United Nations System of National Accounts. As national statistical offices gradually adopt the latest 2008 System of National Accounts framework with regard to data compilation and methodologies, these indicators will become more consistent across economies. Currently, economies in the region have varying reference periods (e.g., calendar year versus fiscal year) and price valuation methods. Due to a lack of reliable data and limited technical and financial resources dedicated for national accounts compilation, some economies with small statistical offices are not able to provide timely estimates, while some are dependent upon the estimates of external institutions.

Table 2.3.1: Growth Rates of Consumer Price Index
(%)

ADB Regional Member	2010	2015	2018	2019	2020	2021	2022	2023	2024
Developing ADB Member Economies									
Central and West Asia									
Afghanistan	4.9	-0.7	0.6	2.3	5.6	...	7.8	10.6	-7.7
Armenia	8.2	3.7	2.5	1.4	1.2	7.2	8.6	2.0	0.3
Azerbaijan	5.7	4.0	2.3	2.6	2.8	6.7	13.9	8.8	2.2
Georgia	7.1	4.0	2.6	4.9	5.2	9.6	11.9	2.5	1.1
Kazakhstan	7.1	6.6	6.0	5.3	6.8	8.0	15.0	14.5	8.7
Kyrgyz Republic	8.0	6.5	1.5	1.1	6.3	11.9	13.9	10.8	5.0
Pakistan	10.1	4.5	4.7	6.8	10.7	8.9	12.2	29.2	23.4
Tajikistan	9.8	5.1	5.4	8.0	9.4	8.0	4.2	3.8	3.6
Türkiye	8.6	7.7	16.3	15.2	12.3	19.6	72.3	53.9	58.5
Turkmenistan	4.4	7.4	13.2	5.1	6.1	19.5	11.2	-1.6	6.3
Uzbekistan[a]	7.6	5.5	17.5	14.5	12.9	10.8	11.4	10.0	9.6
East Asia									
China, People's Republic of	3.3	1.4	2.1	2.9	2.5	0.9	2.0	0.2	0.2
Hong Kong, China	2.4	3.0	2.4	2.9	0.3	1.6	1.9	2.1	1.7
Korea, Republic of	2.9	0.7	1.5	0.4	0.5	2.5	5.1	3.6	2.3
Mongolia[b]	13.0	2.0	8.1	5.2	2.6	13.9	13.2	7.9	9.0
Taipei,China	1.0	-0.3	1.4	0.6	-0.2	2.0	3.0	2.5	2.2
South Asia									
Bangladesh	6.8	6.4	5.8	5.5	5.7	5.6	6.2	9.0	9.7
Bhutan	7.0	4.5	2.7	2.7	5.6	7.3	5.6	4.2	2.8
India[c]	10.4	4.9	3.4	4.8	6.5	5.1	6.6	5.4	4.6
Maldives[d]	6.1	1.0	-0.1	0.2	-1.4	0.5	2.3	2.9	1.4
Nepal	9.6	7.2	4.2	4.6	6.2	3.6	6.3	7.7	5.4
Sri Lanka[e]	6.2	2.2	4.3	4.3	4.6	6.0	...	17.4	1.2
Southeast Asia									
Brunei Darussalam	0.4	-0.5	1.0	-0.4	1.9	1.7	3.7	0.4	-0.4
Cambodia[e]	4.0	1.2	2.5	1.9	2.9	2.9	5.1	2.4	0.8
Indonesia[f]	5.1	6.4	3.2	2.8	2.0	1.6	4.2	3.7	1.6
Lao People's Democratic Republic	6.0	1.3	2.0	3.3	5.1	3.8	23.0	31.2	23.1
Malaysia	1.7	2.1	1.0	0.7	-1.2	2.5	3.3	2.5	1.8
Myanmar	7.7	10.0	11.4	5.4	3.5	11.8	...	...	...
Philippines	3.8	0.7	5.2	2.4	2.4	3.9	5.8	6.0	3.2
Singapore	2.8	-0.5	0.4	0.6	-0.2	2.3	6.1	4.8	2.4
Thailand	3.3	-0.9	1.1	0.7	-0.8	1.2	6.1	1.2	0.4
Timor-Leste	5.2	0.6	2.3	0.9	0.5	3.8	7.0	8.4	2.1
Viet Nam[g]	9.2	0.6	3.5	2.8	3.2	1.8	3.1	3.3	3.6
The Pacific									
Cook Islands	1.5	1.1	0.1	0.4	1.0	1.9	9.5	9.1	3.1
Fiji	3.7	1.4	4.1	1.8	-2.6	0.2	4.3	2.4	4.5
Kiribati	-3.9	0.6	0.6	-1.8	2.6	2.1	5.3	8.8	2.6
Marshall Islands[e]	1.8	-2.2	0.8	-0.1	-0.7	2.2	2.7	7.5	...
Micronesia, Federated States of	3.6	0.0 |	1.5	1.9	0.6	3.2	5.3	4.5	6.4
Nauru	-3.1 |	2.6 (2016)	2.6	2.8	1.1	1.1	3.5	4.3	...
Niue[h]	5.3 |	1.8	9.6	2.3	2.3	3.5	3.2	8.3	1.6
Palau	1.4	0.9	2.2	0.2	0.1	2.0	13.9	11.6	2.4
Papua New Guinea	4.4 (2011)	6.0	4.4	3.9	4.9	4.5	5.3	2.3	0.6
Samoa	0.8 |	0.7	4.2	1.0	-1.6	3.1	11.0	7.9	2.2
Solomon Islands[i]	0.9	-0.6	3.5	2.2	3.0	0.1	5.4	5.1	4.2
Tonga	3.5	-1.1	6.1	1.2	-0.3	4.2	10.9	10.2	5.1
Tuvalu	-1.9	3.1	2.2	3.5	1.6	6.7	12.2	7.1	1.2
Vanuatu[j]	3.1	2.5 |	2.3	2.8	5.3	2.3	6.7	11.2	1.2
Developed ADB Member Economies									
Australia	2.3	1.7	1.9	1.6	1.3	1.6	4.4	7.0	4.2
Japan	-0.7	0.8	1.0	0.5	-0.0	-0.2	2.5	3.2	2.7
New Zealand	2.3	0.3	1.6	1.6	1.7	3.9	7.2	5.7	2.9

... = data not available, | = marks break in series, (-/+) 0.0 = magnitude is less than half of unit employed, ADB = Asian Development Bank.

Note: Data refer to the whole of each economy, unless otherwise indicated. In general, the consumer price index (CPI) data of economies are grouped according to the Classification of Individual Consumption According to Purpose (COICOP) adopted by the United Nations Statistical Commission in 1999. Other economies have switched to the most recent version, COICOP 2018. For more information on COICOP versions, please refer to United Nations' Classification of Economic Statistics available at https://unstats.un.org/unsd/classifications/econ/.

a For 2003–2015, the calculation for the CPI includes weights in horticulture goods. Prior to 2016, values were calculated based on the variable weights' method, while 2016 onward uses the fixed weights method. For 2021 onward, the CPI commodity grouping is based on the COICOP 2018.
b For 2000–2005, figures are based on COICOP 1999. For 2006 onward, figures are based on COICOP 2018.
c Prior to 2011, data refer to CPI for industrial workers. From 2011 onward, data refer to the new CPI series (national combining rural and urban).
d For 2019 onward, the CPI follows the COICOP 2018.
e Data refer to capital city.
f For 2000–2002, data refer to the CPI for 43 cities; for 2003–2007, 45 cities; for 2008–2013, 66 cities; for 2014–2018, 82 cities; for 2019–2023, 90 cities; and for 2024, 150 districts/cities. For 2019 onward, the CPI commodity grouping also changed based on COICOP 2018.
g For 2000–2023, figures are based on COICOP 1999. Starting 2024, figures are based on COICOP 2018.
h For 2011 onward, CPI period averages are ADB estimates based on the Niue Consumer Price Index Statistical Releases.
i Prior to 2010, data refer to the CPI for Honiara. For 2010 onward, separate CPI for four towns (Auki, Gizo, Honiara, and Noro) were produced then aggregated as a weighted average for the national index.
j Vanuatu Bureau of Statistics used COICOP 1999 from 2000–2017 and COICOP 2018 from 2018 onward.

Sources: Economies' official sources. For Afghanistan, 2016 onward: Official statistics and Asian Development Bank (ADB) estimates based on official statistics from national and international sources. For Nauru, 2014: International Monetary Fund's (IMF's) Republic of Nauru Article IV Consultation-Press Release Staff Report. For Turkmenistan, 2000–2017: IMF's World Economic Outlook, and 2018–2024: ADB's Asian Development Outlook (ADO).

Table 2.3.2: Growth Rates of Food and Nonalcoholic Beverages Consumer Price Index
(%)

ADB Regional Member	2010	2015	2018	2019	2020	2021	2022	2023	2024
Developing ADB Member Economies									
Central and West Asia									
Afghanistan	3.5	-0.8	-1.0	3.8	10.0	...	9.4	14.0	-11.7
Armenia	9.4	3.1	2.3	1.9	0.3	11.2	13.0	-0.5	-2.0
Azerbaijan	7.5	4.8	2.0	3.3	4.6	8.2	20.1	9.8	1.1
Georgia	11.7	4.2	2.2	8.1	10.5	10.8	17.9	3.7	-0.1
Kazakhstan	5.9	5.7	4.7	8.1	10.5	10.8	19.2	15.1	5.6
Kyrgyz Republic	6.5	3.7	-2.2	1.3	11.7	18.0	16.2	8.4	1.7
Pakistan[a]	12.9	3.5	6.7	-4.6	15.5	13.2	13.4	39.0	20.8
Tajikistan	...	3.8	4.9	11.4	13.6	7.3	5.2	3.5	2.7
Türkiye	10.6	11.1	18.0	19.5	13.8	24.3	85.6	65.8	56.9
Turkmenistan	...	...	...	...	...	...	...	...	...
Uzbekistan[b]	4.9	2.7	20.1	17.0	17.5 |	14.4	15.0	11.6	4.1
East Asia									
China, People's Republic of[c]	7.2	2.3	1.8	9.2	10.6	-1.4	2.8	-0.3	-0.6
Hong Kong, China	3.5	3.4	4.3	9.9	7.7	1.4	4.5	0.5	-0.3
Korea, Republic of	6.4	1.6	2.8	0.0	4.4	5.9	5.9	5.5	3.9
Mongolia[d]	18.6	-5.9	9.1	8.3	9.0	21.0	15.4	12.2	8.8
Taipei,China	1.1	3.8	0.5	2.0	0.4	3.4	5.6	3.9	4.4
South Asia									
Bangladesh[e]	7.7 (2012)	6.7	7.1	5.5	5.5	5.7	6.1	8.7	10.7
Bhutan	9.4	3.3	4.9	3.6	11.2	9.0	4.2	3.9	0.5
India	...	4.7	0.4	6.6	8.0	3.7	6.5	7.3	7.5
Maldives[f,g]	7.5	0.5	-1.1 |	-0.8	2.7	1.8	4.8	5.8	5.8
Nepal[h]	15.5	9.6	2.7	3.1	8.2	5.0	5.7	6.6	6.5
Sri Lanka[i]	6.9	5.5	3.3	0.8	11.4	11.7	...	12.1	1.6
Southeast Asia									
Brunei Darussalam	-0.0 (2011)	1.0	1.9	-0.7	2.5	2.4	5.1	2.7	0.5
Cambodia[i]	4.3	4.0	2.5	2.1	4.6	2.7	5.6	2.6	1.2
Indonesia[j]	9.4	7.2	4.2	3.0	3.4	2.7	6.0	4.9	1.9
Lao People's Democratic Republic	8.3	4.5	1.2	4.7	8.6	3.0	22.0	38.0	22.3
Malaysia	2.5	3.6	1.6	1.7	1.3	1.7	5.8	4.8	2.0
Myanmar	7.4	13.9	10.8	3.9	2.1	11.6	...	...	...
Philippines	4.0	1.9	6.8	1.6	2.9	4.2	5.9	7.9	4.4
Singapore[k]	2.3	1.2	1.3	1.1	2.9	1.6	5.3	5.1	1.2
Thailand	5.4	1.1	0.4	2.3	1.2	-0.1	6.9	2.6	0.8
Timor-Leste	6.4	0.3	1.7	0.9	0.9	5.8	7.5	10.2	4.3
Viet Nam[l]	10.7	1.5	3.2	4.1	10.0	0.7	2.6	3.4 |	4.0
The Pacific									
Cook Islands[i,m]	2.6	0.1	0.6	1.3	2.5	2.9	14.9	14.5	3.0
Fiji	4.1	4.8	3.4	4.9	-2.4	6.4	6.1	7.5	7.1
Kiribati[n]	-7.0	-0.6	-1.1	-1.9	3.7	2.4	6.9	10.3	1.6
Marshall Islands[i,o]	-0.9	2.3	1.5	0.5	-0.6	3.3	2.6	10.5	...
Micronesia, Federated States of	2.2	0.8 |	-1.0	1.3	0.7	1.6	6.7	9.5	8.6
Nauru	-0.4 |	0.8 (2016)	3.8	6.6	1.7	2.6	0.6	6.9	...
Niue[p]	8.2 |	2.7	0.6	4.7	5.1	0.8	3.1	14.1	4.7
Palau	1.8	1.7	4.0	0.6	2.2	4.2	13.7	16.2	-0.3
Papua New Guinea	-1.0 (2011)	4.9	0.8	3.0	2.2	4.4	7.2	7.0	4.6
Samoa	-6.6 |	3.3	5.6	1.0	-1.5	3.4	15.5	15.9	4.0
Solomon Islands[q]	-2.9	-3.0	1.9	-0.2	1.5	-3.1	7.4	6.7	3.2
Tonga	3.0	1.8	6.7	1.7	1.9	...	...	...	...
Tuvalu	-5.9	4.0	3.3	3.5	0.6	5.9	17.5	8.1	-2.8
Vanuatu[r]	4.5	3.6 |	4.1	5.4	11.4	4.6	9.9	19.1	1.7
Developed ADB Member Economies									
Australia[s]	1.6	2.1	-0.0	2.0	3.1	1.8	3.4	8.4	4.1
Japan	-0.3	3.6	1.6	0.2	1.2	–	4.9	8.6	4.8
New Zealand	1.0	-0.1	-0.2	1.1	3.2	1.8	8.7	9.9	-0.1

... = data not available, | = marks break in series, – = magnitude equals zero, (-/+) 0.0 = magnitude is less than half of unit employed, ADB = Asian Development Bank.

Note: Data refer to the whole of each economy, unless otherwise indicated.

a For 2010 onward, growth rates were calculated using price indexes with base year 2007/2008 = 100 (for 2010–2019) and base year 2015/2016 = 100 (for 2020 onward) for food and nonalcoholic beverages only.
b Prior to 2016, values were calculated based on the variable weights' method, while 2016 onward uses the fixed weights method. For 2021 onward, the consumer price index (CPI) commodity grouping is based on the Classification of Individual Consumption According to Purpose (COICOP) 2018.
c For 2016 onward, excludes nonalcoholic beverages.
d For 2000–2005, figures are based on COICOP 1999. For 2006 onward, figures are based on COICOP 2018.
e Refers to food, beverages, and tobacco.
f Refers to food (including fish) and nonalcoholic beverages.
g For 2019 onward, the CPI follows the COICOP 2018.
h Includes alcoholic beverages, tobacco, and narcotics; and restaurants and hotels.
i Refers to capital city.
j For 2010–2018, data refer to Indonesia's consumer price index group "Foodstuff" consisting of cereals, cassava, and related products; meat and related products; fresh fish; preserved fish; eggs, milk, and related products; vegetables; beans and nuts; fruits; spices; fats and oils; and other food items. The group does not include alcoholic and nonalcoholic beverages. For 2019 onward, data refer to food, beverages, and tobacco. Both alcoholic and nonalcoholic beverages are included in this group.
k Refers to food excluding food-serving services.
l For 2000–2023, figures are based on COICOP 1999. Starting 2024, figures are based on COICOP 2018.
m Refers to fruits and vegetables; meat, poultry, and fish; cereal products; soft drink and sweets; farm products; fats and oils; other food; and prepared food.
n Data refer to the weighted average of food and nonalcoholic drinks price indexes.
o Refers to food.
p For 2010, refers to food.
q Refers to weighted average of four towns (Audi, Gizo, Honiara, and Noro).
r Vanuatu Bureau of Statistics used COICOP 1999 from 2000–2017 and COICOP 2018 from 2018 onward.
s Includes restaurants and hotels.

Sources: Economies' official sources. For Afghanistan, 2016 onward: Official statistics and Asian Development Bank (ADB) estimates based on official statistics from national and international sources. For Türkiye, ADB estimates using data from economy sources.

Table 2.3.3: Growth Rates of Wholesale and/or Producer Price Indexes
(%)

ADB Regional Member	2010	2015	2018	2019	2020	2021	2022	2023	2024
Developing ADB Member Economies									
Central and West Asia									
Afghanistan	...	...	...	...	...	...	...	...	...
Armenia	22.6	-0.8	1.6	0.5	2.4	9.9	2.6	1.5	3.6
Azerbaijan	30.5	-30.6	26.0	3.2	-24.8	69.6	84.3	-11.0	0.0
Georgia	11.3	7.5	6.1	7.2	11.8	16.7	11.4	-2.9	6.2
Kazakhstan	25.2	-20.5	19.0	5.1	-8.0	32.5	27.1	-2.1	5.0
Kyrgyz Republic	22.8	8.8	1.5	4.3	21.3	11.5	5.1	9.3	13.5
Pakistan	13.8	-0.3	5.3	16.0	10.2	9.4	24.9	32.8	20.2
Tajikistan	27.2	3.0	1.8	1.1	5.4	5.9	-3.4	-0.1	6.9
Türkiye	8.5	5.3	27.0	17.6	12.2	43.9	128.5	49.9	41.1
Turkmenistan	...	...	...	...	...	...	...	...	...
Uzbekistan	15.6	13.5	31.8	43.2	14.9	9.3	16.8	12.5	17.9
East Asia									
China, People's Republic of	5.5	-5.2	3.5	-0.3	-1.8	8.1	4.1	-3.0	-2.2
Hong Kong, China[a]	6.0	-2.7	2.0	1.0	2.3	1.2	0.8	1.6	2.9
Korea, Republic of	3.8	-4.0	1.9	0.0	-0.5	6.4	8.4	1.6	1.7
Mongolia	...	15.7 (2016)	-7.3	23.4	-0.9	37.3	19.8	0.5	-12.2
Taipei,China[b]	5.5	-8.9	3.6	-2.3	-7.8	... |	10.5	-0.6	1.4
South Asia									
Bangladesh[c]	8.9 (2006)	... |	4.8	3.1	3.4	4.0	6.7	4.6	5.4
Bhutan	4.9 (2012)	0.5	4.7	-3.7	2.0	10.9	...	...	...
India	9.6	-3.7	4.3	1.7	1.3	13.0	9.4	-0.7	2.3
Maldives	3.9	-2.4	...	...	...	...	...	...	...
Nepal	12.2	6.1	1.7	6.2	6.9	7.6	9.5	8.5	3.9
Sri Lanka[d]	2.6	1.0	3.4	3.4	5.4 |	10.9	74.0	11.5	-0.0
Southeast Asia									
Brunei Darussalam	...	...	...	...	...	...	...	...	...
Cambodia	...	...	...	...	...	...	...	...	...
Indonesia	4.8	4.4	5.5	1.0	1.3	2.6	4.7	4.2	2.8
Lao People's Democratic Republic	...	...	...	...	...	...	...	...	...
Malaysia[e]	12.3 (2011)	-7.4	-1.1	-1.4	-2.7	9.5	7.8	-1.9	0.3
Myanmar	...	...	...	...	...	...	...	...	...
Philippines[f]	5.9	1.6	1.9	1.6	2.5	3.1	7.3	4.9	2.5
Singapore[g]	4.7	-15.3	6.4	-3.3	-8.7	15.2	18.6	-6.7	-1.3
Thailand	9.4	-1.2 (2016)	0.5	-0.7	-1.6	4.7	10.4	-2.4	1.7
Timor-Leste	...	...	...	...	...	...	...	...	...
Viet Nam	12.6	-0.6	3.1	1.3	-0.6	2.9	4.2	-0.9	0.6
The Pacific									
Cook Islands	...	...	...	...	...	...	...	...	...
Fiji	...	...	...	...	...	...	...	...	...
Kiribati	...	...	...	...	...	...	...	...	...
Marshall Islands	...	...	...	...	...	...	...	...	...
Micronesia, Federated States of	...	...	...	...	...	...	...	...	...
Nauru	...	...	...	...	...	...	...	...	...
Niue	...	...	...	...	...	...	...	...	...
Palau	...	...	...	...	...	...	...	...	...
Papua New Guinea	...	...	...	...	...	...	...	...	...
Samoa	...	...	...	...	...	...	...	...	...
Solomon Islands	...	...	...	...	...	...	...	...	...
Tonga	...	...	...	...	...	...	...	...	...
Tuvalu	...	...	...	...	...	...	...	...	...
Vanuatu	...	...	...	...	...	...	...	...	...
Developed ADB Member Economies									
Australia	-0.1	1.0	1.6	2.0	1.0	0.5	4.3	5.3	4.2
Japan[h]	-0.1	-2.3	2.6	0.2	-1.2	4.6	9.8	4.3	2.3
New Zealand	3.5	-1.4	3.8	1.9	0.1	6.5	8.3	2.1	3.5

... = data not available, | = marks break in series, 0.0 = magnitude is less than half of unit employed, ADB = Asian Development Bank.

a Refers to manufacturing industries.
b Starting from 2022, the series of wholesale price index (WPI) and annual change were replaced with PPI (Producer Price Index; 2021=100).
c For 2000–2006, data refer to the annual change in WPI for agricultural and industrial products only. For 2017 onward, data refer to the annual change in PPI.
d For 2000–2020, data refer to the annual change in WPI. For 2021 onward, data refer to the annual change in PPI.
e Data refer to the PPI for local production.
f Refers to manufacturing sector only. PPI for agriculture sector is also available at https://psa.gov.ph/tags/producer-price-index-agriculture.
g Refers to the domestic supply price index. The domestic supply price index measures the changes in prices of imported and locally manufactured products retained for use in the economy.
h Refers to domestic corporate goods price index.

Source: Economies' official sources.

Table 2.3.4: Growth Rates of Gross Domestic Product Deflator
(%)

ADB Regional Member	2010	2015	2018	2019	2020	2021	2022	2023	2024
Developing ADB Member Economies									
Central and West Asia									
Afghanistan[a]	14.3	5.1	2.1	6.5	7.8	-8.0	2.8	9.4	2.9
Armenia[b]	7.8 |	1.2	2.8	1.0	1.8	6.9	8.0	2.7	1.1
Azerbaijan[c]	13.6	-8.8	12.2	-0.2	-7.5	21.6	37.3	-9.4	-1.4
Georgia[d]	8.5 |	5.4	3.5	4.0	6.8	10.2	8.1	2.9	3.8
Kazakhstan[e]	19.6	1.9	9.2	7.6	4.2	13.9	19.7	11.2	7.3*
Kyrgyz Republic[f]	10.0	3.4	3.4 |	3.9	5.3	16.0	19.7	19.9	4.7*
Pakistan	10.6	4.4	3.8	9.0	9.9	10.3	13.9	26.0	21.9
Tajikistan	12.4	5.5 (2014)	2.5	3.6	1.7	10.0	8.2	3.7	...
Türkiye	7.0	7.8	16.5	13.9	14.8	29.0	96.0	68.2	...
Turkmenistan	-3.9	-4.9	...	...	...	...	...	...	...
Uzbekistan[g]	19.9	10.5	25.9	17.6	10.6	13.7	14.5	13.8	13.3
East Asia									
China, People's Republic of	6.9	0.1	3.5	1.4	0.6	4.6	2.1	-0.3	...
Hong Kong, China	0.3	3.6	3.7	2.0	0.6	0.7	1.7	2.9	3.8
Korea, Republic of	2.7	3.2	0.6	-0.6	1.6	3.2	1.8	1.9	4.1
Mongolia	15.1 (2011)	3.0 (2016)	8.0	10.0	3.7	14.4	17.7	21.7	8.2*
Taipei,China	-1.3	3.4	-0.6	-0.1	2.1	1.9	2.1	2.3	3.5
South Asia									
Bangladesh[h]	7.2	7.2	5.8	3.7	3.8	4.1	5.0	6.9	6.9
Bhutan[h]	7.5	3.2	1.2	3.1	5.3	7.6	5.8	4.4	...
India	10.5	2.3	3.9	2.4	4.7	8.5	5.9	2.6	3.1
Maldives[i]	3.3	7.3	3.3	-1.3	-3.4	2.7	3.2	...	...
Nepal	14.4	4.5	3.1	4.3	5.1	3.7	8.8	8.8	2.9
Sri Lanka	7.3	3.0	4.3	3.9	3.1	8.0	47.5	16.6	3.9
Southeast Asia									
Brunei Darussalam	5.3	-17.6	9.2	-3.3	-10.9	15.5	24.2	-12.8	-2.2
Cambodia	6.3	3.1	3.8	2.8	-0.8	2.6	3.5	0.8	1.6
Indonesia[j]	7.3	4.0	3.8	1.6	-0.4	6.0	9.6	1.5*	0.9*
Lao People's Democratic Republic	3.1	2.3	1.9	1.2	2.9	3.4	11.6	18.2	17.4
Malaysia	5.4 (2011)	-0.4	0.6	0.1	-0.8	5.7	6.4	-1.9	0.7
Myanmar	7.0	4.1	5.4	6.3	3.8	1.9	...	...	...
Philippines	4.4	-0.7	3.7	0.7	1.7	2.2	5.5	4.5	3.1
Singapore	1.1	3.1	3.6	-0.4	-2.4	11.0	14.9	-5.0	3.3
Thailand	3.9	0.2	1.3	0.6	-1.1	1.7	4.4	1.0	...
Timor-Leste[k]	11.0	7.2	-1.4	5.7	2.4	-4.0	3.2	5.0	...
Viet Nam	12.1	-1.7	3.6	2.4	1.5	2.9	4.4	2.1	4.2
The Pacific									
Cook Islands	1.9	6.4 |	2.0	-1.4	24.4	10.7	-25.4	13.1	...
Fiji	2.5	2.5	1.4	2.2	-1.2	-3.4	2.5	...	...
Kiribati	-0.9	3.1	3.9	-3.3	4.4	9.1	-2.0	8.7*	...
Marshall Islands	0.9	-3.1	-2.4	-4.2	6.7	5.9	-1.0	6.5	...
Micronesia, Federated States of	3.2	-5.5	8.9	-3.3	-3.6	1.9	9.4	5.7	...
Nauru	-18.1	-8.3 |	18.5	-4.7	4.3	18.1	-13.4	6.6	6.8*
Niue	7.6 |	0.6 (2016)	12.2	4.4	0.3	-3.6	5.6	4.1	8.5*
Palau	3.2	6.3	-0.2	-2.5	-2.3	3.3	8.9	8.9	-1.8
Papua New Guinea	10.0	-1.4	10.0	1.1	1.6	11.9	15.5	-3.8	6.8*
Samoa	4.1	4.4	-0.2	1.6	1.6	-0.7	4.0	10.4	7.9
Solomon Islands[l]	1.7	3.4	7.9	1.2	-1.3	-5.5	2.0	...	...
Tonga	7.7	5.2	4.9	4.7	0.4	2.5	2.1	-0.0	...
Tuvalu	2.5	4.6	7.2	6.6	1.1	8.8	10.0	-1.1	...
Vanuatu	1.5	5.9	3.2	3.3	2.8	4.1	5.1	...	...
Developed ADB Member Economies									
Australia	1.2	-0.6	1.9	3.5	1.9	3.1	7.2	6.5	2.6
Japan	-1.9	2.1	-0.0	0.6	0.9	-0.2	0.4	4.1	2.9
New Zealand	3.7	1.0	1.4	3.0	1.5	4.5	5.4	4.7	...

... = data not available; | = marks break in series; * = provisional, preliminary, estimate; (-/+) 0.0 = magnitude is less than half of unit employed; ADB = Asian Development Bank.

a For 2016 onward, there are changes in basic concepts in line with the changing of the base year to 2016 producer's prices and the adoption of the System of National Accounts (SNA) 2008.
b For 2000–2011, estimates are based on SNA 1993. For 2012 onward, estimates are based on SNA 2008.
c For 2000–2009, estimates are based on SNA 1993. From 2010, transition to the 2008 SNA began, although a global revision of the GDP and sectoral accounts series according to the 2008 SNA has yet to be fully implemented.
d For 2010 onward, there are changes in basic concepts in line with the changing of the base year to 2015 chain-linked series and the adoption of SNA 2008.
e For 2011 onward, estimates are in accordance with SNA 2008, where financial intermediation services indirectly measured are no longer compiled as a notional industry. For 2017 onward, the calculations were made in accordance with the new methodology for assessing the unobserved economy, registered in the Ministry of Justice of the Republic of Kazakhstan No.19215 of 08.08.2019.
f For 2019 onward, data are calculated according to the international standard of SNA 2008.
g From 2010 onward, data are in accordance with the international methodology "SNA 2008." Since 2017, the non-observed economy has been measured in accordance with the 2008 SNA methodology.
h Rebased to 2017 from the previous base year of 2000 and adopted SNA 2008.
i For 2011 onward, GDP at current prices includes some product taxes that were not included in the calculation of GDP at constant prices, hence, the implicit GDP deflators may be overestimated.
j For 2010 onward, data are based on SNA 2008. Base year was also changed from 2000 to 2010.
k From September 2019, following the new Timor-Leste Australia Maritime Boundary Treaty, oil revenue from the Joint Petroleum Development Area is included in the national accounts. The National Institute of Statistics Timor-Leste (INETL) disaggregates the accounts into 'oil' and 'non-oil' components. To better assess the performance of the domestic economy, this publication presents GDP on a non-oil basis, which reflects the primary analytical approach used by INETL.
l For 2003 onward, there are changes in basic concepts in line with the changing of the base year to 2012 and a closer consistency with SNA 2008. Improvements to methodologies, data sources, concepts, and revisions to benchmark estimates have been implemented.

Sources: Economies' official sources and Asian Development Bank estimates based on data from the economies' official sources. For Nauru, data for 2016 onward are sourced from the IMF's World Economic Outlook Database.

Table 2.3.5: Growth Rates of Money Supply
(%)

ADB Regional Member	2010	2015	2017	2018	2019	2020	2021	2022	2023	2024
Developing ADB Member Economies										
Central and West Asia										
Afghanistan	39.3	3.7 |	4.1	2.6	5.7	12.1 |	-6.5	-3.5	-0.7	...
Armenia	11.8	10.8	18.5	7.4	11.2	9.0	13.1	16.1	17.4	13.7
Azerbaijan[a]	24.3	-1.3	9.0	5.7	20.0	1.1	18.7	23.6	5.3	3.2
Georgia[a]	30.1	17.3	14.6	13.9	17.6	24.6	11.4	11.4	14.9	14.5
Kazakhstan	23.1	8.0	7.5	7.1	11.0	19.2	24.1	18.0	16.8	19.9
Kyrgyz Republic	21.1	14.9	17.9	5.5	12.8	23.9	19.1	30.6	15.0	31.9*
Pakistan	13.0	12.8	13.9	9.5	10.8	18.3	14.7	13.1	16.7	16.7*
Tajikistan	18.6	18.7	21.8	5.1	17.0	18.4	8.2	40.4	-0.8	28.8
Türkiye	19.0	16.3	15.5	19.0	26.9	34.0	52.7	62.6	65.7	38.9
Turkmenistan[a]	74.2	18.0	11.4	8.4	12.9	11.8	-1.4	1.0	6.3	6.0
Uzbekistan	52.4	24.3	40.2	14.1	13.9	17.7	29.7	30.2	12.2	30.6
East Asia										
China, People's Republic of	18.9	13.3	9.0	8.1	8.7	10.1	9.0	11.8	9.7	7.3
Hong Kong, China	8.1	5.5	10.0	4.3	2.8	5.8	4.3	1.6	4.0	7.3
Korea, Republic of	6.0	8.2	5.1	6.7	7.9	9.8	12.9	4.0	3.9	6.6
Mongolia	62.5	-5.5	30.5	22.8	8.2	16.2	13.8	6.5	26.8	15.2
Taipei,China	5.5	5.8	3.6	2.7	4.5	9.4	7.4	6.7	5.6	5.4
South Asia										
Bangladesh	22.4	12.4	10.9	9.2	9.9	12.6	13.6	9.5	10.5	7.8
Bhutan	30.1	7.8	31.5	10.4	5.6	19.3	24.4	9.4	9.8	0.9
India[a]	16.1	10.1	9.2	10.5	8.9	12.2	8.8	9.0	11.6*	9.4*
Maldives	14.6	12.1	5.2	3.4	9.5	14.2	26.2	6.0	7.0	-0.1
Nepal	14.1	19.9	15.5	19.4	15.8	18.1	22.7	6.8	11.4	12.9
Sri Lanka	18.0	17.2	17.5	13.5	7.6	22.9	13.5	8.9	9.4	10.2
Southeast Asia										
Brunei Darussalam	4.8	-1.8	-0.4	2.8	4.3	-0.4	2.7	1.3	2.7	3.6
Cambodia	21.3	17.0	23.1	26.6	18.2	15.3	16.4	8.2	12.5	17.5
Indonesia	15.4	9.0	8.3	6.3	6.5	12.5	14.0	8.4	3.5	4.8
Lao People's Democratic Republic	39.5	14.7	12.2	8.4	18.9	16.3	24.0	36.9	33.3	17.8
Malaysia[a]	6.8	3.0	4.9	9.1	3.5	4.0	6.4	4.3	6.0	3.6
Myanmar	...	30.0	21.4	18.6	15.4	15.0	11.4	-0.7	...	...
Philippines[a]	10.0	9.4	11.9	9.5	11.5	9.6	7.9	6.9	6.3	7.7*
Singapore	8.6	1.5	3.2	3.9	5.0	13.2 |	...	1.8	4.6	6.0
Thailand	10.9	4.4	5.0	4.7	3.6	10.2	4.8	3.9	1.9	3.4
Timor-Leste	18.2	7.1	12.1	3.1	-7.1	10.2	28.7	8.6	2.7	7.3
Viet Nam	33.3	16.2	15.0	12.4	14.8	14.5	10.7	6.2	12.5	12.0
The Pacific										
Cook Islands	0.1	9.5	6.4	9.9	7.9	17.1	-5.3	7.2	5.0	6.8
Fiji[a]	3.5	13.9	8.1	2.5	3.2	1.0	11.4	5.1	9.1	7.7
Kiribati	...	...	...	...	...	...	...	...	...	...
Marshall Islands	9.4	28.6	23.9	-3.3	-4.9	21.8	11.7	9.2	-7.0	...
Micronesia, Federated States of	...	...	...	...	...	...	...	...	...	...
Nauru	...	...	...	...	...	...	...	...	...	...
Niue	...	...	...	...	...	...	...	...	...	...
Palau	12.0 (2011)	30.9	0.3	0.3	-3.2	10.3	-1.2	-1.0	-5.7	...
Papua New Guinea[a]	11.4	8.0	-0.7	-4.0	4.4	7.0	11.7	14.8	11.5	-6.4
Samoa	6.4	6.0	15.2	8.8	4.6	5.4	1.7	7.3	13.7	8.9
Solomon Islands[a]	13.3	15.5	3.5	6.8	-3.1	6.6	1.9	5.3	6.1	3.8
Tonga	5.1	9.3	13.7	7.6	4.3	1.2	26.0	10.7	-0.6	7.6
Tuvalu	...	...	...	...	...	...	...	...	...	...
Vanuatu	1.3	11.4	9.3	13.1	7.0	-0.7	8.9	7.3	5.9	9.6
Developed ADB Member Economies										
Australia[a]	4.5	6.7	7.8	1.9	4.0	8.5	7.7	9.9	4.1	5.3
Japan[a]	1.9	2.5	2.9	2.2	2.0	7.7	3.3	2.3	1.8	1.0
New Zealand[b]	3.2	8.1 |	7.3	6.4	4.7	12.2	7.1	1.8	3.6	4.1

... = data not available; | = marks break in series; * = provisional, preliminary, estimate; ADB = Asian Development Bank.

Note: Data are based on money supply M2 (M2), unless otherwise stated.

a Refers to money supply M3 (M3).
b Refers to M3 prior to 2016 and M2 for 2016 onward.

Source: Economies' official sources.

Table 2.3.6: Money Supply
(% of GDP)

ADB Regional Member	2010	2015	2017	2018	2019	2020	2021	2022	2023	2024
Developing ADB Member Economies										
Central and West Asia										
Afghanistan	30.3	29.7 |	36.9	36.6	35.0	37.2 |	35.1	41.5	40.2	...
Armenia	26.3	36.8	46.4	46.1	47.2	54.4	54.4	51.9	54.8	58.2
Azerbaijan[a]	24.8	39.1	32.4	30.0	35.2	40.2	37.2	32.0	36.6	36.8
Georgia[a]	28.4	38.7	44.7	46.5	49.5	61.7	56.4	52.6	53.8	54.3
Kazakhstan	30.1	21.0	24.9	23.4	23.1	27.1	28.3	27.0	27.4	29.0*
Kyrgyz Republic	31.4	33.3	36.5	35.8	35.2	44.6	43.4	43.5	38.3	44.2*
Pakistan	37.7	40.2	40.5	40.2	39.8	43.4	42.4	40.2	37.2	34.5*
Tajikistan	18.0 |	21.2	28.0	26.7	28.0	31.3	28.1	33.7	30.2	33.2
Türkiye	54.6	54.8	55.9	55.4	61.2	70.2	74.6	58.6	54.9	...
Turkmenistan[a,b]	17.3	48.2	...	...	...	...	...	...	...	...
Uzbekistan	17.7	19.1	20.5	17.6	16.0	16.8	17.7	19.0	17.6	19.0
East Asia										
China, People's Republic of	173.1	198.2	199.5	195.2	197.5	211.3	203.0	215.9	225.8	232.4
Hong Kong, China	401.7	484.4	517.2	506.0	518.3	583.3	567.4	588.7	576.3	581.0
Korea, Republic of	120.4	129.1	130.8	134.5	142.8	155.4	162.6	161.7	162.6	163.2
Mongolia	48.0	43.9	56.6	59.8	55.7	65.4	64.0	55.1	53.4	54.2
Taipei,China	220.2	233.9	237.4	238.4	241.9	250.6	247.4	252.0	257.5	250.6
South Asia										
Bangladesh	45.5	52.0	43.7	42.1	41.3	43.3	44.3	43.1	42.6	40.8
Bhutan	53.5	48.7	61.7	65.1	63.0	79.6	88.1	86.6	86.9	78.4
India[a]	85.2	84.4	81.7	81.7	83.6	94.9	86.8	83.1	82.8*	82.5*
Maldives	47.9	48.1	43.2	39.8	41.1	72.5	64.7	58.3	58.4	54.3
Nepal	60.3	77.5	84.2	89.5	92.8	108.8	119.3	111.4	115.5	122.2
Sri Lanka	27.3	35.1	39.4	41.9	43.4	54.3	54.7	43.6	41.9	42.3
Southeast Asia										
Brunei Darussalam	67.3	80.8	86.7	81.6	84.7	93.6	84.6	70.1	81.6	83.0
Cambodia	33.9	54.1	66.6	74.7	79.5	95.8	105.4	104.8	111.2	120.5
Indonesia	36.0	39.5	39.9	38.8	38.8	44.7	46.4	43.5	42.2	41.8
Lao People's Democratic Republic	38.0	51.2	53.1	53.1	59.1	64.7	75.0	88.0	95.3	91.6
Malaysia[a]	132.2	136.3	126.5	130.9	129.7	143.9	140.2	126.3	131.8	128.9
Myanmar	...	44.7 |	55.5	58.7	59.7	64.1	74.4	63.8	...	...
Philippines[a]	47.7	60.5	64.2	63.7	66.5	79.2	79.0	74.5	71.7	71.1*
Singapore	123.3	122.9	122.3	118.5	123.3	148.6 |	125.0	106.4	115.1	113.2
Thailand	109.0	127.7	124.0	122.8	123.4	146.6	148.6	143.8	142.2	143.4
Timor-Leste[c]	33.5	40.4	51.9	54.5	46.7	54.9	71.6	72.5	69.3	...
Viet Nam	101.8	116.0	130.2	131.4	137.2	150.5	157.9	147.9	155.0	155.6
The Pacific										
Cook Islands	83.1	59.3	56.2	57.3	59.9	86.8	77.6	85.4	67.9	...
Fiji[a]	67.6	73.3	74.1	72.1	73.7	91.0	109.4	93.6	91.3	89.0
Kiribati	...	...	...	...	...	...	...	...	...	...
Marshall Islands	63.4	83.3	106.3	99.9	89.7	105.2	109.8	122.5	111.3	...
Micronesia, Federated States of	...	...	...	...	...	...	...	...	...	...
Nauru	...	...	...	...	...	...	...	...	...	...
Niue	...	...	...	...	...	...	...	...	...	...
Palau	46.0	71.1	81.8	82.5	81.7	98.1	106.5	97.3	83.2	...
Papua New Guinea[a]	34.0	33.6	30.7	26.9	26.6	28.9	29.1	27.5	30.9	27.4
Samoa	43.8	41.1	48.5	51.3	51.4	59.3	58.1	56.8	52.2	51.3
Solomon Islands[a]	28.6	40.4	42.3	40.8	38.4	42.9	45.2	45.5	45.5	44.0
Tonga	41.2	47.4	52.6	53.6	53.4	52.9	64.8	71.9	70.1	...
Tuvalu	...	...	...	...	...	...	...	...	...	...
Vanuatu	83.3	78.6	82.9	88.3	88.8	90.1	92.0	91.8	90.9	93.2*
Developed ADB Member Economies										
Australia[a]	93.1	108.0	113.9	110.6	108.6	117.8	120.6	118.5	112.2	113.4
Japan[a]	216.6	232.5	240.2	243.8	248.2	276.3	278.5	281.1	271.0	265.8
New Zealand[d]	111.2	121.4 |	102.0	102.9	101.9	112.9	110.9	103.4	100.2	102.0

... = data not available; | = marks break in series; * = provisional, preliminary, estimate; ADB = Asian Development Bank; GDP = gross domestic product.

Note: Data are based on money supply M2 (M2), unless otherwise stated.

a Refers to money supply M3 (M3).
b GDP data is not available from 2016 onward.
c From September 2019, following the new Timor-Leste Australia Maritime Boundary Treaty, oil revenue from the Joint Petroleum Development Area is included in the national accounts. The National Institute of Statistics Timor-Leste (INETL) disaggregates the accounts into 'oil' and 'non-oil' components. To better assess the performance of the domestic economy, this publication presents GDP on a non-oil basis, which reflects the primary analytical approach used by INETL.
d Refers to money supply M3 (M3) prior to 2016 and M2 for 2016 onward.

Source: Economies' official sources.

Money and Finance

Table 2.3.7: Interest Rates on Savings and Time Deposits
(% per annum, period averages)

ADB Regional Member	Savings Deposits									Time Deposits								
	2010	2015	2018	2019	2020	2021	2022	2023	2024	2010	2015	2018	2019	2020	2021	2022	2023	2024
Developing ADB Member Economies																		
Central and West Asia																		
Afghanistan	5.4	3.1	1.6	1.5	0.8	...	...	...	...	8.2	5.2	2.3	3.4	2.4	...	...	...	...
Armenia	...	...	...	...	...	...	...	...	...	10.7	15.4	9.4	9.3	9.2	9.2	9.2	9.2	9.1
Azerbaijan	...	...	...	...	...	...	...	...	...	11.0	8.2	9.8	9.4	8.6	8.8	9.0	8.4	8.9
Georgia[a]	8.7	5.3	4.3	4.7	5.2	4.9	5.5	6.2	6.5	11.6	7.0	5.8	5.7	6.6	6.6	7.5	8.1	8.7
Kazakhstan[b]	...	...	...	...	...	...	...	...	...	9.8	7.5	10.5	9.1	8.6	8.6	11.1	13.4	13.0
Kyrgyz Republic	...	...	...	...	...	...	...	...	...	11.5	14.5	10.3	9.5	9.8	11.0	12.9	12.3	12.6
Pakistan	5.0	4.7	4.1	8.6	5.9	5.0	10.7	16.8	18.0	7.2	5.9	4.6	8.0	6.2	5.2	9.1	14.7	11.3
Tajikistan	4.6	0.3	1.1	0.5	0.8	0.9	0.5	0.3	0.2	17.7	15.0	12.8	11.3	11.5	11.5	13.9	14.4	13.3
Türkiye	...	...	...	...	...	...	...	...	...	9.0	10.7	22.3	14.6	13.5	17.9	16.4	36.3	50.1
Turkmenistan	...	...	...	...	...	...	...	...	...	11.3(2004)	...	...	...	...	...	...	...	...
Uzbekistan[c]	...	...	...	11.6	16.2	17.7	18.3	18.8	20.2	...	18.3	16.4	18.6	19.2	18.7	19.8	20.6	20.9
East Asia																		
China, People's Republic of	0.4	0.4	0.4	0.4	0.4	0.4	0.4	0.4	0.4	2.3	2.1	1.5	1.5	1.5	1.5	1.5	1.5	1.5
Hong Kong, China	0.1(2008)	...	0.0	0.1	0.0	0.0	0.1	0.7	0.7	0.2	0.1	0.2	0.3	0.2	0.1	0.1	0.6	0.6
Korea, Republic of[d]	3.2	1.7	1.8	1.7	1.0	1.1	2.7	3.7	3.5	3.9	1.8	2.0	1.9	1.2	1.2	3.1	3.8	3.5
Mongolia[e]	10.7	13.0	11.2	10.5	8.4	5.8	10.9	11.6	11.9	...	...	11.8	10.9	8.8	6.2	11.1	11.8	12.1
Taipei,China	0.2	0.3	0.2	0.2	0.1	0.1	0.4	0.7	0.8	1.0	1.3	1.1	1.1	0.8	0.8	1.2	1.5	1.7
South Asia																		
Bangladesh[f]	4.9	4.5	3.3	3.3	2.8	2.2	2.3	2.5	2.7	9.0	9.0	7.4	8.2	6.5	5.7	6.2	7.3	9.9
Bhutan[g]	4.8	5.3	5.3	5.4	5.4	5.3	5.2	5.2	4.8	6.8	6.8	7.8	7.8	7.6	7.8	7.0	6.6	5.1
India	3.5	4.0	...	...	...	...	...	...	...	7.5	6.2	...	...	...	...	...	...	...
Maldives[h]	2.3	2.2	1.5	1.5	1.5	1.5	1.5	1.5	1.4	4.3	4.0	3.7	3.3	3.8	3.6	4.0	4.1	3.9
Nepal	7.0	2.9	4.6	5.0	4.2	3.0	6.2	5.8	3.7	8.1	6.5	10.4	9.8	9.0	7.3	10.1	10.2	7.1
Sri Lanka	5.0	5.0	4.0	4.0	3.5	3.5	3.0	3.0	3.0	8.5	7.3	10.5	9.8	5.3	5.5	12.0	8.0	7.0
Southeast Asia																		
Brunei Darussalam	0.4	0.3	0.3	0.3	0.1	0.1	0.2	0.2	0.4	0.7	0.8	0.8	0.8	0.3	0.2	0.4	0.6	0.7
Cambodia	1.2	1.2	0.6	0.6	0.6	1.0	0.9	0.8	0.8	6.6	7.4	6.2	6.3	6.3	6.2	7.6	7.5	5.7
Indonesia	3.9	1.7	1.3	1.1	0.8	0.7	0.7	0.7	0.7	7.9	8.5	6.5	6.8	5.7	3.8	4.7	5.7	5.2
Lao People's Democratic Republic	3.4	2.6	1.8	1.8	1.7	1.7	1.7	1.8	1.7	9.1	7.6	5.4	5.4	5.4	5.3	5.4	5.5	6.1
Malaysia	0.9	1.1	1.0	1.0	0.6	0.5	0.7	0.9	0.9	2.8	3.3	3.3	3.2	2.1	1.7	2.1	2.8	2.8
Myanmar	...	...	10.0	10.0	7.4	5.0	5.0	...	...	...	...	...	...	...	...	...	...	...
Philippines[i]	1.6	0.7	0.9	1.2	0.2*	0.1*	0.3*	1.6*	1.8*	2.1	3.1	3.5	4.6	2.1*	1.7*	3.6*	4.4*	4.9*
Singapore	0.1	0.1	0.2	0.2	0.1	0.2	0.5	0.5	0.5	0.5	0.3	0.5	0.6	0.3	0.3	1.7	2.3	2.2
Thailand	0.5	0.5	0.5	0.5	0.3	0.3	0.4	0.4	0.3	1.6	1.4	1.4	1.3	0.5	0.5	1.0	1.7	1.5
Timor-Leste	0.8	0.8	0.4	0.5	0.5	0.5	0.5	0.5	0.5	1.3	1.3	0.7	0.7	0.6	0.6	0.7	0.7	0.7
Viet Nam[j]	3.0	0.7	0.5	0.5	0.2	0.1	0.4	0.2	0.2	11.5	6.3	7.1	7.3	6.8	5.5	6.6	6.9	4.9
The Pacific																		
Cook Islands	...	...	...	...	...	...	...	...	...	...	...	...	...	...	...	...	...	...
Fiji	1.0	0.9	1.3	1.2	0.9	0.5	0.4	0.4	0.4	5.6	2.6	3.4	4.6	3.3	2.3	1.3	1.1	2.0
Kiribati	...	...	...	...	...	...	...	...	...	...	...	...	...	...	...	...	...	...
Marshall Islands	0.5	0.3	0.2	0.2	0.2	0.1	...	...	...	3.5	1.5	1.1	0.9	0.8	0.7	...	...	...
Micronesia, Federated States of	...	...	...	...	...	...	...	...	...	...	...	...	...	...	...	...	...	...
Nauru	...	...	...	...	...	...	...	...	...	...	...	...	...	...	...	...	...	...
Niue	...	...	...	...	...	...	...	...	...	...	...	...	...	...	...	...	...	...
Palau	0.9	0.1	0.1	0.1	...	...	...	...	...	0.8	0.2	0.4	0.4	...	...	...	...	...
Papua New Guinea	1.0	0.4	0.7	1.0	0.9	0.3	1.5	2.3	1.5	4.8	2.1	2.0	12.9	9.5	1.5	1.9	2.2	2.9
Samoa	1.0	1.0	1.0	1.0	1.0	1.0	1.0	1.0	1.0	2.9	2.9	2.9	2.9	2.9	2.9	2.9	2.9	2.9
Solomon Islands	0.3	0.3	0.4	0.6	0.5	0.6	0.6	0.5	0.8	5.0	0.7	1.3	1.5	1.6	1.2	1.4	1.8	1.4
Tonga	1.5	2.5	2.4	2.5	2.6	2.5	2.3	2.4	2.5	3.0	4.9	5.2	4.8	4.8	4.0	3.5	3.9	3.7
Tuvalu	...	...	...	...	...	...	...	...	...	...	...	...	...	...	...	...	...	...
Vanuatu	1.8	0.9	–	–	–	0.1	0.5	0.5	0.5	6.0	3.4	2.3	2.0	2.0	1.9	2.0	2.2	3.5
Developed ADB Member Economies																		
Australia[k]	4.4	2.0	1.0	0.7	0.3	0.1	0.3	2.0	1.8	6.0	2.5	2.2	1.8	0.8	0.3	0.8	4.3	4.5
Japan[l]	0.0	0.0	0.0	0.0	0.0	0.0	0.0	0.0	0.0	0.1	0.1	0.0	0.0	0.0	0.0	0.0	0.0	0.1
New Zealand[m]	...	...	...	...	...	...	...	...	...	4.7	3.3	3.3	2.6	0.8	1.5	4.5	...	...

... = data not available; – = magnitude equals zero; * = provisional, preliminary, estimate; 0.0 = magnitude is less than half of unit employed; ADB = Asian Development Bank.

a Refers to deposits allocated with maturity of more than 1 year.
b Refers to interest rates on deposits of more than 12 months.
c Refers to weighted average interest rate on all time household savings deposits and time deposits from 181 to 365 days.
d Refers to weighted averages of interest rates on newly extended time and savings deposits of commercial and specialized banks.
e Rates for savings deposits include both demand and time deposits. Rates for time deposits refer to the time deposit rate.
f Refers to savings bank accounts with checking facilities.
g For savings deposits, actual range of rates for 2015–2016 is 5.0%–7.0%; for 2017, 5.0%–6.0%; for 2019 and 2020, 5.0%–5.75%; and for 2021, from 5.0% to 5.6%. For time deposits, rate refers to fixed deposits of 1 year to less than 2 years for 2010 and actual range of rates is 4.5%–6.5%; for 2015–2017, 6.5%–7.5%; for 2018 and 2019, 6.0%–9.5%; for 2020, 6.0%–9.1%; and for 2021, 6.5%–9.1%.
h Refers to time deposits of 6 months to 1 year (local currency). Figures represent a weighted average.
i Rates for savings deposits refer to the annual percentage equivalent of commercial banks' actual monthly interest expenses on peso-savings deposits to the total outstanding levels of these deposits. Rates for time deposits refer to rates charged on interest-bearing deposits with maturities of over 1 year.
j For 2010, the rate for time deposit refers to maximum interest per annum for state enterprise deposits.
k Refers to interest rates of online savings deposits.
l Refers to savings deposits of at least ¥0.3 million, calculated as the arithmetic average of weekly figures. Refers to time deposits from 12 months to less than 2 years, calculated as the arithmetic average of the monthly figures.
m Refers to interest rate on time deposits of 6 months.

Sources: Economies' official sources. For the People's Republic of China: CEIC Database. https://www.ceicdata.com/en (accessed 16 June 2025).

Table 2.3.8: Yield on Short-Term Treasury Bills and Lending Interest Rates
(% per annum, period averages)

ADB Regional Member	Yield on Short-Term Treasury Bills[a]							Lending Interest Rates						
	2010	2015	2020	2021	2022	2023	2024	2010	2015	2020	2021	2022	2023	2024
Developing ADB Member Economies														
Central and West Asia														
Afghanistan	...	...	...	...	...	...	...	15.6	15.0	...	...	...	...	...
Armenia[a]	10.6	12.9	5.8	7.8	10.6	11.1	9.4	19.2	17.6	11.6	11.8	11.7	12.4	13.1
Azerbaijan	1.8	13.0 (2016)	...	...	...	...	...	20.7	17.5	17.2	16.4	14.6	14.0	14.7
Georgia	9.6	8.8	8.6	8.9	10.2	9.5	8.0	15.8	12.5	11.8	12.5	13.7	13.5	12.0
Kazakhstan[b]	3.2	4.0	10.7	86.3	12.6	15.6	11.9	...	...	...	...	...	...	...
Kyrgyz Republic	10.4	12.8	5.9	7.1	8.1	8.5	...	23.7	23.6	17.0	16.6	18.7	19.1	19.8
Pakistan[c]	12.5	7.1	8.6	7.6	...	...	...	14.0	10.2	10.8	8.7	...	...	...
Tajikistan[d]	6.7	0.8	...	...	...	...	...	23.4	25.8	23.5 (2019)	...	...	...	...
Türkiye	...	...	...	...	...	...	...	...	...	...	...	...	...	...
Turkmenistan	...	...	...	...	...	...	...	...	...	...	...	...	...	...
Uzbekistan	...	...	13.9	13.3	16.4	17.0	16.3	...	13.8	22.3	21.4	21.7	22.2	23.1
East Asia														
China, People's Republic of[e]	2.6	3.7	2.9	2.9	2.8	2.8	...	5.8	4.4	4.4	4.4	4.4	4.4	4.4
Hong Kong, China[f]	0.2	0.0	0.4	0.0	1.6	3.9	4.0	5.0	5.0	5.0	5.0	5.1	5.8	5.7
Korea, Republic of[g]	2.7	1.8	0.9	0.9	2.5	3.7	...	5.5	3.5	2.8	2.9	4.3	5.2	4.7
Mongolia[h]	12.9 (2012)	14.5	...	...	...	...	...	20.1	19.6	16.9	16.0	...	...	...
Taipei,China[i]	0.3	0.4	0.3	0.2	0.4	1.1	1.2	2.7	2.8	2.4	2.4	2.8	...	...
South Asia														
Bangladesh[d]	4.5	5.8	4.8	1.3	5.0	7.7	11.5	12.2	11.7	8.3	7.3	7.1	7.6	9.9
Bhutan[d]	2.0	0.1	3.5	6.0	0.3	3.1	3.3	13.9	14.9	14.0	14.0	14.0	12.3	10.5
India[d,j]	6.2	7.4	3.3	3.5	5.8	6.9	6.6	8.3	10.0	9.2	8.7	8.6	...	...
Maldives[k]	4.9	6.8	3.5	3.5	3.5	3.5	3.5	10.4	11.1	11.6	11.6	10.9	11.7	11.6
Nepal[d]	6.9	0.7	1.9	3.1	8.8	7.5	3.0	...	...	...	...	...	...	...
Sri Lanka[l]	8.6	6.7	9.1 (2019)	...	...	...	...	10.2	7.0	11.2 (2019)	...	...	...	...
Southeast Asia														
Brunei Darussalam	...	...	...	...	...	...	...	5.5	5.5	5.5	5.5	5.5	5.5	5.5
Cambodia	...	...	...	...	...	...	...	...	...	...	...	...	...	...
Indonesia	7.0	8.3	5.5	3.7	3.2	4.6	...	13.3	12.7	9.5	8.9	8.5	8.9	8.8
Lao People's Democratic Republic[m]	8.0	...	...	...	...	...	...	22.6	...	...	...	...	...	...
Malaysia	2.6	3.1	2.0	1.8	...	...	...	5.0	4.6	3.9	3.4	3.9	5.3	5.3
Myanmar	...	...	...	...	...	...	...	20.9	16.0	14.8	...	...	...	...
Philippines[d]	3.5	1.7	2.0	1.1	2.2	5.4	5.7	7.7	5.6	7.1 (2019)	...	...	...	...
Singapore	0.3	0.3 (2013)	...	...	...	...	...	5.4	5.4	5.3	5.3	...	...	...
Thailand[d]	1.4	1.6	0.6	0.4	0.7	1.8	2.2	4.3	4.7	3.3	3.1	3.1	4.3	4.2
Timor-Leste	...	...	...	...	...	...	...	...	13.5	14.1	11.2	11.0	10.7	10.6
Viet Nam[n]	11.1	4.2	...	...	...	...	...	13.1	7.1	7.6	7.8	8.0	9.3	...
The Pacific														
Cook Islands	...	...	...	...	...	...	...	...	...	...	...	...	...	...
Fiji[d]	3.4	1.2	1.8	0.6	0.0	0.0	0.1	7.5	5.8	6.2	5.9	5.4	5.0	4.6
Kiribati	...	...	...	...	...	...	...	...	...	...	...	...	...	...
Marshall Islands	...	...	...	...	...	...	...	...	...	...	...	...	...	...
Micronesia, Federated States of	...	...	...	...	...	...	...	15.1	15.7	14.5	12.6	...	...	...
Nauru	...	...	...	...	...	...	...	...	...	...	...	...	...	...
Niue	...	...	...	...	...	...	...	...	...	...	...	...	...	...
Palau	...	...	...	...	...	...	...	...	...	...	...	...	...	...
Papua New Guinea[o]	4.6	5.3	6.9	4.0	2.8	2.3	...	10.4	8.7	7.7	7.6	8.0	8.3	...
Samoa	...	...	...	...	...	...	...	10.7	9.5	8.7	8.5	8.3	8.3	8.4
Solomon Islands[d]	3.7	0.5	0.5	0.5	0.5	0.5	...	14.4	10.5	10.7	5.2	...	...	...
Tonga	...	...	...	...	...	...	...	...	8.2	7.8	7.8	7.9	7.7	7.8
Tuvalu	...	...	...	...	...	...	...	...	...	...	...	...	...	...
Vanuatu	...	...	...	...	...	...	...	...	10.2	9.8	9.3	8.8	8.9	8.6
Developed ADB Member Economies														
Australia[p]	4.7	2.3	0.3	0.0	1.6	4.0	4.4	7.3	5.6	5.1 (2019)	...	...	...	...
Japan	0.4	0.2	-0.0	-0.1	-0.0	0.0	0.2	1.6	1.1	...	...	...	...	...
New Zealand	3.0	3.2	0.5	0.5	2.8	5.5	5.3	6.3	5.8	– (2018)	...	...	...	...

... = data not available, – = magnitude equals zero, (-/+) 0.0 = magnitude is less than half of unit employed, ADB = Asian Development Bank.

a Refers to average yield on 9-month to 12-month Treasury bills since March 2001.
b Refers to short-term Treasury bills with maturities of 3, 6, 9, and 12 months.
c Refers to weighted average yield on 6-month Treasury securities.
d Refers to 91-day Treasury bills.
e Refers to 3-month Treasury bonds trading rate.
f Refers to annualized yields on 91-day Exchange Fund bills.
g Refers to 91-day certificates of deposit.
h Refers to weighted average rate on Treasury bills of all maturities. From December 2012 onward, refers to yield on 12-week Treasury bills.
i Refers to prime lending rates.
j Figures are for fiscal year ending March.
k Refers to rate on 28-day Treasury bills.
l Refers to weighted average rate on the last monthly issuance of 364-day Treasury bills since December 2001.
m Refers to weighted average auction rate for 12-month Treasury bills.
n Refers to average monthly yield on 360-day Treasury bills sold at auction.
o Refers to rate on 182-day Treasury bills.
p Refers to estimated closing yield in the secondary market on 13-week Treasury notes.

Sources: International Monetary Fund. International Financial Statistics. http://data.imf.org/ (accessed 30 June 2025); For Australia, the People's Republic of China, Japan, the Republic of Korea, and New Zealand: Organisation for Economic Co-operation and Development. Main Economic Indicators. https://stats.oecd.org/ (accessed 30 June 2025). For Bhutan; India; Kazakhstan; and Taipei,China: Economies' official sources. For Malaysia: Bank Negara Malaysia. Monthly Highlights and Statistics. https://www.bnm.gov.my/-/monthly-highlights-statistics-in-may-2025 (accessed 1 July 2025).

Money and Finance

Table 2.3.9: Domestic Credit Provided by Financial Sector, and Bank Nonperforming Loans

ADB Regional Member	Domestic Credit Provided by Financial Sector[a] (% of GDP)								Bank Nonperforming Loans[b] (% of total gross loans)							
	2010	2015	2019	2020	2021	2022	2023	2024	2010	2015	2019	2020	2021	2022	2023	2024
Developing ADB Member Economies																
Central and West Asia																
Afghanistan	...	...	...	...	...	...	...	...	49.9	12.1	...	...	...	...	...	...
Armenia	27.8	48.3	65.4	83.4	74.5	65.0	68.8	79.3	3.0	7.9	5.5	6.6	1.8	2.4	...	...
Azerbaijan	...	...	14.6	15.4	16.3	14.7	20.4	21.0	...	...	...	...	...	2.6	1.9	...
Georgia	33.3	51.2	68.4	82.4	76.5	66.3	69.3	73.9	5.9	2.7	1.9	2.3	1.9	1.5	1.5	...
Kazakhstan	...	45.7	35.0	40.2	39.0	37.8	40.1	42.6	20.9	8.0	8.1	6.9	3.3	3.4	2.9	...
Kyrgyz Republic	...	...	...	...	...	...	...	...	14.8	6.7	7.7	10.1	10.8	12.5	8.9	...
Pakistan	...	...	...	...	...	...	...	...	...	11.4	8.6	9.2	7.9	6.5	6.6	...
Tajikistan	7.6	19.7	15.5	13.6	10.4	8.8	11.1	...	6.1	26.3	27.0	23.8	13.7	...	...	...
Türkiye	67.6	77.1	82.8	100.2	95.3	74.1	66.0	59.6	3.5	3.0	5.0	3.9	3.0	2.0	1.5	...
Turkmenistan	...	...	...	...	...	...	...	...	...	...	...	...	...	...	...	...
Uzbekistan	...	...	6.6	10.5	14.9	18.2	23.8	...	1.0	1.5	1.5	2.1	5.1	3.5	3.5	...
East Asia																
China, People's Republic of	...	...	...	...	...	...	...	...	1.1	1.7	1.9	1.8	1.7	...	...	...
Hong Kong, China	...	...	...	...	...	...	...	...	0.8	0.7	0.6	0.9	0.9	1.0	1.2	...
Korea, Republic of	...	...	...	...	...	...	...	...	0.6	0.5	0.3	0.2	0.2	0.2	...	...
Mongolia	...	...	...	...	...	...	...	...	...	...	...	...	...	...	...	...
Taipei,China[c]	0.9	...	...	...	...	...	...	...	0.6	0.2	0.2	0.2	0.2	0.1	0.1	0.1
South Asia																
Bangladesh	...	...	...	...	...	...	...	...	...	8.4	8.9	7.7	8.0	8.7	9.6	...
Bhutan	...	...	...	...	89.8	90.6	97.9	78.5	5.2	6.6	8.5	11.7	6.7	3.0	...	...
India	...	...	...	...	...	...	...	...	...	5.9	9.2	7.9	6.5	4.8	1.7	...
Maldives	76.9	61.0	63.5	125.9	97.8	93.1	98.4	99.3	...	12.9	11.6	18.8	12.6	9.4	8.3	...
Nepal	...	...	...	...	...	...	...	...	...	...	1.7	1.7	1.2	2.4	3.8	...
Sri Lanka	...	...	...	...	...	...	...	...	...	3.2	4.7	4.9	4.5	12.0	...	...
Southeast Asia																
Brunei Darussalam	22.7	40.0	29.5	66.1	54.2	43.5	62.0	64.6	6.9	4.0	3.9	3.9	3.1	2.8	...	...
Cambodia	...	...	...	...	...	...	...	...	3.1	1.6	1.6	1.8	1.7	2.7	5.1	...
Indonesia	34.2	46.8	47.1	53.7	54.3	51.1	50.4	50.1	2.3	2.3	2.3	2.6	2.6	2.1	2.0	...
Lao People's Democratic Republic	...	...	...	...	...	...	...	...	...	...	...	...	...	...	...	...
Malaysia	...	...	...	...	...	...	...	...	3.4	1.6	1.5	1.6	1.7	1.7	1.7	...
Myanmar	...	...	...	...	...	...	...	...	...	...	...	...	...	...	...	...
Philippines	...	...	86.5	100.3	100.8	98.5	98.7	99.8	3.3	1.9	2.0	3.5	4.0	3.1	3.2	...
Singapore	...	...	...	...	...	...	...	...	1.4	0.9	1.3	...	...	...	...	...
Thailand	133.4	171.2	169.1	194.4	203.6	196.2	197.4	196.5	3.9	2.7	3.1	3.2	3.1	2.8	2.8	...
Timor-Leste	...	...	...	...	...	...	...	...	...	...	...	...	...	...	...	...
Viet Nam	...	...	...	...	...	...	...	...	2.1	2.8	1.8	1.9	1.6	2.3	...	...
The Pacific																
Cook Islands	...	...	...	...	...	...	...	...	...	...	...	...	...	...	...	...
Fiji	131.7	111.4	136.6	175.0	195.5	170.4	165.9	166.4	4.4	1.4	3.8	6.2	8.5	...	...	...
Kiribati	...	...	...	...	...	...	...	...	...	...	...	...	...	...	...	...
Marshall Islands	...	...	...	...	...	...	...	...	...	...	...	...	...	...	...	...
Micronesia, Federated States of	...	...	...	...	...	...	...	...	...	0.2	0.3	0.1	0.3	...	...	...
Nauru	...	...	...	...	...	...	...	...	...	...	...	...	...	...	...	...
Niue	...	...	...	...	...	...	...	...	...	...	...	...	...	...	...	...
Palau	...	...	...	...	...	...	...	...	...	...	...	...	...	...	...	...
Papua New Guinea	23.7	40.5	37.3	41.7	38.8	32.6	36.5	...	1.9	3.1	3.8	5.3	6.2	4.8	5.4	...
Samoa	60.0	72.5	77.0	76.5	86.1	85.5	68.7	61.1	...	...	4.0	3.8	3.6	5.0	5.4	...
Solomon Islands	20.3	21.5	25.6	27.5	30.6	32.8	33.3	32.6	9.3	4.1	10.4	10.7	10.4	9.5	9.4	...
Tonga	...	...	...	...	...	...	...	...	...	7.7	3.2	3.7	3.5	8.3	11.2	...
Tuvalu	...	...	...	...	...	...	...	...	...	...	...	...	...	...	...	...
Vanuatu	...	...	...	...	...	...	...	...	4.8	12.3	...	...	...	...	...	...
Developed ADB Member Economies																
Australia	...	...	...	...	...	...	...	...	2.1	0.9	1.0	1.1	0.9	0.7	...	...
Japan[d]	311.7	341.1	363.3	393.6	390.9	385.4	379.4	372.0	2.5	1.5	1.1	1.1	1.2	1.2	1.2	1.2
New Zealand	...	160.0	167.9	184.6	178.9	165.5	158.2	...	2.0	0.7	0.5	0.7	0.5	0.4	0.5	0.7

... = data not available, ADB = Asian Development Bank, GDP = gross domestic product.

a Domestic credit provided by the financial sector includes all credit to various sectors on a gross basis, with the exception of credit to the central government, which is net. The financial sector includes monetary authorities and deposit money banks, as well as other financial corporations where data are available (including corporations that do not accept transferable deposits, but do incur such liabilities as time and savings deposits). Examples of other financial corporations are finance and leasing companies, money lenders, insurance corporations, pension funds, and foreign exchange companies.

b Bank nonperforming loans to total gross loans are the value of nonperforming loans divided by the total value of the loan portfolio (including nonperforming loans before the deduction of specific loan-loss provisions). The loan amount recorded as nonperforming should be the gross value of the loan as recorded on the balance sheet, not just the amount that is overdue.

c Before 1 July 2005, nonperforming loans include loans in which payment of principal is past due for three months or more, repayment of interest is past due for six months or more, and installment repayment loans for medium to long-term is past due for six months or more. Starting 1 July 2005, includes loans in which repayment of principal or interest has been overdue for more than 3 months and any loan of which the principal debtors and surety have been sued for non-payment or the underlying collateral has been disposed, although the repayment of principal or interest has not been overdue for more than 3 months.

d Refers to end-September nonperforming loans data for all banks, as defined by the Financial Reconstruction Act (FRA) of Japan.

Sources: International Monetary Fund. Financial Soundness Indicators. http://data.imf.org/ (accessed 8 July 2025); World Bank. World Development Indicators. https://databank.worldbank.org/source/world-development-indicators (accessed 8 July 2025). For Taipei,China: Central bank of Taipei,China. For nonperforming loans (% of total gross loans) of New Zealand: Reserve Bank of New Zealand. https://www.rbnz.govt.nz/statistics (accessed 23 June 2025). For nonperforming loans (% of total gross loans) of Japan for 2023-2024: Financial Services Agency. https://www.fsa.go.jp/en/index.html (accessed 23 June 2025).

Table 2.3.10: Growth Rates of Stock Market Price Index
(%)

ADB Regional Member	2010	2015	2019	2020	2021	2022	2023	2024
Developing ADB Member Economies								
Central and West Asia								
Afghanistan	…	…	…	…	…	…	…	…
Armenia	…	…	…	…	…	…	…	…
Azerbaijan	…	…	…	…	…	…	…	…
Georgia	…	…	…	…	…	…	…	…
Kazakhstan	…	…	…	…	…	…	…	…
Kyrgyz Republic	…	…	…	…	…	…	…	…
Pakistan[a]	28.2	2.1	…	…	…	…	…	…
Tajikistan	…	…	…	…	…	…	…	…
Türkiye	58.5	7.2	…	…	…	…	…	…
Turkmenistan	…	…	…	…	…	…	…	…
Uzbekistan	…	…	-42.7	8.6	40.0	-19.5	-11.2	5.5
East Asia								
China, People's Republic of	3.4	66.0	…	…	…	…	…	…
Hong Kong, China	19.3	4.8	-4.3	-8.4	7.3	-24.8	-6.6	-5.4
Korea, Republic of	23.6	1.4	-9.4	5.4	40.1	-18.9	-1.0	5.3
Mongolia	88.7	-14.6	-0.8	-13.0	100.2	…	…	…
Taipei,China	23.1	-0.4	1.6	11.9	40.3	-7.8	4.9	30.5
South Asia								
Bangladesh[a]	82.8	-4.8	-17.3	21.3	25.1	-8.1	0.6	-16.5
Bhutan	…	…	…	…	…	…	…	…
India	29.8	10.9	…	…	…	…	…	…
Maldives	-20.4	8.9	5.2	7.7	0.0	32.2	45.3	8.4
Nepal	…	…	…	…	…	…	…	…
Sri Lanka[a]	96.0	-5.5	1.3	…	…	…	…	…
Southeast Asia								
Brunei Darussalam	…	…	…	…	…	…	…	…
Cambodia	…	…	…	…	…	…	…	…
Indonesia[a]	46.1	-12.1	1.7	-5.1	10.1	4.1	6.2	-3.2
Lao People's Democratic Republic	…	…	…	…	…	…	…	…
Malaysia	27.1	-6.1	-8.4	-7.3	3.3	-3.7	-4.4	10.5
Myanmar	…	…	…	…	…	…	…	…
Philippines	43.1	5.5	2.8	-21.1	8.5	-13.7	-2.5	5.4
Singapore	30.3	-2.5	…	…	…	…	…	…
Thailand	45.6	0.2	-4.7	-18.1	17.6	3.2	-6.1	-9.6
Timor-Leste	…	…	…	…	…	…	…	…
Viet Nam[a]	12.2	6.1	…	…	…	…	…	…
The Pacific								
Cook Islands	…	…	…	…	…	…	…	…
Fiji	-11.1	22.0	45.0	1.5	-11.2	-4.3	3.5	7.4
Kiribati	…	…	…	…	…	…	…	…
Marshall Islands	…	…	…	…	…	…	…	…
Micronesia, Federated States of	…	…	…	…	…	…	…	…
Nauru	…	…	…	…	…	…	…	…
Niue	…	…	…	…	…	…	…	…
Palau	…	…	…	…	…	…	…	…
Papua New Guinea	26.2	-6.3	-2.9	…	…	…	…	…
Samoa	…	…	…	…	…	…	…	…
Solomon Islands	…	…	…	…	…	…	…	…
Tonga	…	…	…	…	…	…	…	…
Tuvalu	…	…	…	…	…	…	…	…
Vanuatu	…	…	…	…	…	…	…	…
Developed ADB Member Economies								
Australia[a]	-2.6	-2.1	…	…	…	…	…	…
Japan	2.0	22.7	…	…	…	…	…	…
New Zealand	9.7	12.7	18.0	12.3	10.8	-9.4	0.4	4.5

… = data not available, 0.0 = magnitude is less than half of unit employed, ADB = Asian Development Bank.

Note: All data in the table refer to growth rates of stock market prices (period average), unless otherwise indicated.

a Refers to growth rates of end-of-period stock market prices.

Sources: Asian Development Bank estimates using data from the International Monetary Fund's International Financial Statistics. http://data.imf.org/IFS (accessed 17 June 2025). For Taipei,China: Annual statistics from the stock exchange corporation in Taipei,China.

Table 2.3.11: Stock Market Capitalization

ADB Regional Member	Stock Market Capitalization ($ million)								Stock Market Capitalization (% of GDP)							
	2010	2015	2019	2020	2021	2022	2023	2024	2010	2015	2019	2020	2021	2022	2023	2024
Developing ADB Member Economies																
Central and West Asia																
Afghanistan	...	...	...	...	...	...	...	...	...	...	...	...	...	...	...	...
Armenia	...	...	55.0	27.0	29.5	252.7	279.9	4,847.1	...	...	0.4	0.2	0.2	1.3	1.2	18.8
Azerbaijan	...	...	2,173.9	1,434.4	1,595.3	1,468.0	1,577.3	1,635.3	...	...	4.5	3.4	2.9	1.9	2.2	2.2
Georgia	...	...	...	...	...	...	...	...	...	...	...	...	...	...	...	...
Kazakhstan	26,672.7	34,891.9	40,678.8	38,252.8	65,789.6	45,788.5	59,078.4	62,818.0	18.0	18.9	22.4	22.4	33.4	20.3	22.6	21.8
Kyrgyz Republic	...	...	...	...	...	...	...	...	...	...	...	...	...	...	...	...
Pakistan	38,007.2	...	50,561.9	50,278.5	43,096.6	28,713.9	32,255.8	52,073.6	19.3	...	15.8	16.7	12.4	7.7	9.5	14.0
Tajikistan	...	...	...	...	...	...	...	...	...	...	...	...	...	...	...	...
Türkiye	302,443.1	188,861.9	184,966.1	237,473.6	138,395.2	330,011.0	337,585.0	378,961.2	38.9	21.9	24.3	33.0	16.9	36.4	30.2	28.6
Turkmenistan	...	...	...	...	...	...	...	...	...	...	...	...	...	...	...	...
Uzbekistan	...	...	...	5,230.0	5,194.0	8,426.8	13,721.6	18,799.6	...	...	...	7.9	6.7	9.4	13.4	16.4
East Asia																
China, People's Republic of	4,027,840.3	8,188,019.3	8,569,512.2	12,276,766.3	14,437,446.2	11,469,346.1	10,935,845.6	11,755,758.0	65.0	72.6	58.9	81.9	79.3	62.6	59.9	62.7
Hong Kong, China	2,711,316.2	3,184,874.2	4,899,234.6	6,130,420.4	5,434,177.1	4,566,809.1	3,974,783.5	4,549,720.8	1,185.9	1,029.4	1,349.4	1,777.2	1,472.9	1,273.2	1,043.1	1,117.6
Korea, Republic of	1,091,911.5	1,231,199.8	1,484,840.3	2,176,189.5	2,218,658.1	1,644,507.6	1,967,998.3	1,557,487.6	95.5	84.0	89.9	132.3	122.0	98.2	114.9	...
Mongolia	...	...	...	...	...	...	...	...	...	...	...	...	...	...	...	...
Taipei,China	752,520.1	768,179.4	1,177,469.7	1,518,132.7	2,008,469.9	1,486,585.8	1,824,771.7	2,301,557.2	169.4	143.7	191.9	224.3	258.5	194.0	240.9	289.2
South Asia																
Bangladesh	41,616.9	65,484.9	64,416.5	89,773.7	109,263.9	115,230.3	111,557.4	87,941.6	36.1	33.6	18.3	24.0	26.2	25.0	25.5	19.5
Bhutan	219.0	374.0	615.2	622.3	711.0	684.9	728.8	...	12.8	17.1	22.5	25.3	25.7	23.6	24.1	...
India	1,762,461.9	1,745,169.2	2,162,702.9	2,552,463.8	3,548,018.5	3,387,366.7	4,340,130.8	5,131,397.4	105.2	83.0	76.3	95.4	112.0	101.2	119.3	131.1
Maldives	...	...	...	...	...	...	...	...	...	...	...	...	...	...	...	...
Nepal	...	...	...	...	...	...	...	...	...	...	...	...	...	...	...	...
Sri Lanka	19,923.9	20,804.1	15,720.5	15,981.9	27,056.9	10,598.2	13,122.1	19,501.3	34.0	24.4	17.7	19.0	30.6	14.3	15.7	19.7
Southeast Asia																
Brunei Darussalam	...	...	...	...	...	...	...	...	...	...	...	...	...	...	...	...
Cambodia	...	...	...	...	...	...	...	...	...	...	...	...	...	...	...	...
Indonesia	360,388.1	353,271.0	523,321.9	496,086.1	578,631.4	610,288.4	758,301.8	...	47.7	41.0	46.8	46.8	48.8	46.3	55.3	...
Lao People's Democratic Republic	...	...	...	...	...	...	...	...	...	...	...	...	...	...	...	...
Malaysia	408,689.1	382,976.7	403,957.4	436,537.9	414,285.3	381,207.2	378,054.6	449,470.4	160.3	127.1	110.6	129.4	110.8	93.5	94.6	106.5
Myanmar	...	...	...	...	...	...	...	...	...	...	...	...	...	...	...	...
Philippines	157,320.5	238,819.9	275,366.7	272,790.3	285,423.3	238,581.1	236,456.1	251,828.4	75.5	77.9	73.1	75.4	72.4	59.0	54.1	54.6
Singapore	647,226.4	639,955.9	697,271.3	652,614.7	663,388.5	619,361.7	608,306.3	637,630.3	269.9	207.8	185.4	186.9	151.9	121.7	120.4	116.5
Thailand	277,731.7	348,798.0	569,228.3	543,164.6	598,908.3	604,355.0	519,600.2	519,672.0	81.4	86.9	104.6	108.5	118.3	121.9	100.7	98.7
Timor-Leste	...	...	...	...	...	...	...	...	...	...	...	...	...	...	...	...
Viet Nam	36,855.0	58,734.0	149,817.3	186,008.5	278,794.1	170,152.3	187,818.3	204,615.9	25.0	24.5	44.8	53.7	76.1	41.2	43.3	43.0
The Pacific																
Cook Islands	...	...	...	...	...	...	...	...	...	...	...	...	...	...	...	...
Fiji	...	...	...	...	...	...	...	...	...	...	...	...	...	...	...	...
Kiribati	...	...	...	...	...	...	...	...	...	...	...	...	...	...	...	...
Marshall Islands	...	...	...	...	...	...	...	...	...	...	...	...	...	...	...	...
Micronesia, Federated States of	...	...	...	...	...	...	...	...	...	...	...	...	...	...	...	...
Nauru	...	...	...	...	...	...	...	...	...	...	...	...	...	...	...	...
Niue	...	...	...	...	...	...	...	...	...	...	...	...	...	...	...	...
Palau	...	...	...	...	...	...	...	...	...	...	...	...	...	...	...	...
Papua New Guinea	11,027.3	1,718.9	...	...	...	...	...	...	77.4	7.9	...	...	...	...	...	...
Samoa	...	...	...	...	...	...	...	...	...	...	...	...	...	...	...	...
Solomon Islands	...	...	...	...	...	...	...	...	...	...	...	...	...	...	...	...
Tonga	...	...	...	...	...	...	...	...	...	...	...	...	...	...	...	...
Tuvalu	...	...	...	...	...	...	...	...	...	...	...	...	...	...	...	...
Vanuatu	...	...	...	...	...	...	...	...	...	...	...	...	...	...	...	...
Developed ADB Member Economies																
Australia	1,454,490.6	1,187,083.5	1,487,598.5	1,720,556.2	1,887,400.8	1,679,171.9	1,788,726.0	1,737,106.3	126.6	87.8	106.8	129.5	121.2	99.3	103.5	99.1
Japan	3,827,774.2	4,894,919.1	6,191,073.3	6,718,219.6	6,544,303.5	5,380,475.5	6,149,200.2	6,310,681.4	66.5	110.1	121.0	132.9	129.9	126.2	146.0	156.7
New Zealand	...	74,350.5	107,879.8	132,198.5	122,933.8	97,545.7	96,578.1	92,866.7	...	41.7	50.6	62.1	48.4	39.1	37.8	35.7

... = data not available, $ = United States dollars, ADB = Asian Development Bank, GDP = gross domestic product.

Sources: World Bank. World Development Indicators. https://databank.worldbank.org/source/world-development-indicators (accessed 9 July 2025). For Bhutan and Taipei,China: ADB estimates using data from economies' official sources.

Table 2.3.12: Official Exchange Rates

ADB Regional Member	2010	2015	2017	2018	2019	2020	2021	2022	2023	2024
Developing ADB Member Economies										
Central and West Asia										
Afghanistan	46.5	61.1	68.0	72.1	77.7	76.8	83.6	90.4*	82.4*	70.7*
Armenia	373.7	477.9	482.7	483.0	480.4	489.0	503.8	435.7	392.5	392.7
Azerbaijan	0.8	1.0	1.7	1.7	1.7	1.7	1.7	1.7	1.7	1.7
Georgia	1.8	2.3	2.5	2.5	2.8	3.1	3.2	2.9	2.6	2.7
Kazakhstan	147.4	221.7	326.0	344.7	382.7	413.0	425.9	460.2	456.2	469.0
Kyrgyz Republic	46.0	64.5	68.9	68.8	69.8	77.3	84.6	84.1	87.9	87.2
Pakistan	85.2	102.8	105.5	121.8	150.0	161.8	162.9	204.9	280.4	278.6
Tajikistan	4.4	6.2	8.5	9.2	9.5	10.3	11.3	11.0	10.8	10.8
Türkiye	1.5	2.7	3.6	4.8	5.7	7.0	8.9	16.5	23.7	32.8
Turkmenistan	2.9	3.5	3.5	3.5	3.5	3.5	3.5	3.5	3.5	3.5
Uzbekistan[a]	1,586.5	2,775.3	8,101.3	8,320.8	9,521.9	10,454.3	10,806.2	11,242.1	12,335.9	12,875.0
East Asia										
China, People's Republic of	6.8	6.2	6.8	6.6	6.9	6.9	6.4	6.7	7.1	7.2
Hong Kong, China	7.8	7.8	7.8	7.8	7.8	7.8	7.8	7.8	7.8	7.8
Korea, Republic of	1,156.5	1,131.0	1,131.0	1,100.2	1,165.4	1,180.3	1,144.0	1,291.4	1,305.7	1,363.4
Mongolia	1,357.1	1,970.3	2,439.8	2,472.5	2,663.5	2,813.3	2,849.3	3,140.7	3,465.7	3,390.0
Taipei,China	31.6	31.9	30.4	30.2	30.9	29.6	28.0	29.8	31.2	32.1
South Asia										
Bangladesh	69.6	77.9	80.4	83.5	84.5	84.9	85.1	91.7	106.3	115.6
Bhutan	45.7	64.2	65.1	68.4	70.4	74.1	73.9	78.6	82.6	83.7
India	45.7	64.2	65.1	68.4	70.4	74.1	73.9	78.6	82.6	83.7
Maldives	12.8	15.4	15.4	15.4	15.4	15.4	15.4	15.4	15.4	15.4
Nepal	73.3	102.4	104.5	108.9	112.6	118.3	118.1	125.2	132.1	133.7
Sri Lanka	113.1	135.9	152.4	162.5	178.7	185.6	198.8	322.6	327.5	302.1
Southeast Asia										
Brunei Darussalam	1.4	1.4	1.4	1.3	1.4	1.4	1.3	1.4	1.3	1.3
Cambodia	4,184.9	4,067.8	4,050.6	4,051.2	4,061.1	4,092.8	4,098.7	4,102.0	4,110.7	4,072.4
Indonesia	9,090.4	13,389.4	13,380.8	14,236.9	14,147.7	14,582.2	14,308.1	14,849.9	15,236.9	15,855.4
Lao People's Democratic Republic	8,254.2	8,127.6	8,244.8	8,401.3	8,679.4	9,045.8	9,697.9	14,035.2	17,688.9	21,564.2
Malaysia	3.2	3.9	4.3	4.0	4.1	4.2	4.1	4.4	4.6	4.6
Myanmar[b]	5.6	1,162.6	1,360.4	1,429.8	1,518.3	1,381.6	1,615.7	1,932.5	...	...
Philippines	45.1	45.5	50.4	52.7	51.8	49.6	49.3	54.5	55.6	57.3
Singapore	1.4	1.4	1.4	1.3	1.4	1.4	1.3	1.4	1.3	1.3
Thailand	31.7	34.2	33.9	32.3	31.0	31.3	32.0	35.1	34.8	35.3
Timor-Leste[c]	1.0	1.0	1.0	1.0	1.0	1.0	1.0	1.0	1.0	1.0
Viet Nam	18,612.9	21,697.6	22,370.1	22,602.1	23,050.2	23,208.4	23,159.8	23,271.2	23,787.3	24,164.9
The Pacific										
Cook Islands[d]	1.4	1.4	1.4	1.4	1.5	1.5	1.4	1.6	1.6	1.7
Fiji	1.9	2.1	2.1	2.1	2.2	2.2	2.1	2.2	2.3	2.3
Kiribati	1.1	1.3	1.3	1.3	1.4	1.5	1.3	1.4	1.5	1.5
Marshall Islands[c]	1.0	1.0	1.0	1.0	1.0	1.0	1.0	1.0	1.0	1.0
Micronesia, Federated States of[c]	1.0	1.0	1.0	1.0	1.0	1.0	1.0	1.0	1.0	1.0
Nauru	1.1	1.3	1.3	1.3	1.4	1.5	1.3	1.4	1.5	1.5
Niue[d]	1.4	1.4	1.4	1.4	1.5	1.5	1.4	1.6	1.6	1.7
Palau[c]	1.0	1.0	1.0	1.0	1.0	1.0	1.0	1.0	1.0	1.0
Papua New Guinea	2.7	2.8	3.2	3.3	3.4	3.5	3.5	3.5	3.6	3.9
Samoa	2.5	2.6	2.6	2.6	2.6	2.7	2.6	2.7	2.7	2.8
Solomon Islands	8.1	7.9	7.9	8.0	8.2	8.2	8.0	8.2	8.4	8.5
Tonga	1.9	2.1	2.2	2.2	2.3	2.3	2.3	2.3	2.4	2.4
Tuvalu[e]	1.1	1.3	1.3	1.3	1.4	1.5	1.3	1.4	1.5	1.5
Vanuatu	96.9	109.0	107.8	110.2	114.7	115.4	109.5	115.4	119.1	119.2
Developed ADB Member Economies										
Australia	1.1	1.3	1.3	1.3	1.4	1.5	1.3	1.4	1.5	1.5
Japan	87.8	121.0	112.2	110.4	109.0	106.8	109.8	131.5	140.5	151.4
New Zealand	1.4	1.4	1.4	1.4	1.5	1.5	1.4	1.6	1.6	1.7

... = data not available; * = provisional, preliminary, estimate; $ = United States (US) dollars; ADB = Asian Development Bank.

a Data show weighted averages of the official, bank, and parallel market rates.
b Beginning 1 April 2012, the Central Bank of Myanmar adopted the managed float exchange rate regime for kyat vis-à-vis the US dollar.
c Unit of currency is the US dollar.
d Unit of currency is the New Zealand dollar.
e Unit of currency is the Australian dollar.

Sources: International Monetary Fund. Exchange Rates. https://data.imf.org/en/datasets/IMF.STA:ER (accessed 30 June 2025). For Afghanistan for 2021–2024: Asian Development Bank estimates based on statistics from the bank's Afghanistan Resident Mission. For the Republic of the Marshall Islands: Economic Policy, Planning and Statistics Office. Official communication, 6 May 2025. For Sri Lanka for 2024: Central Bank of Sri Lanka. https://www.cbsl.gov.lk/en/rates-and-indicators/exchange-rates (accessed 29 May 2025). For Taipei,China: Central bank of Taipei,China. Official communication, 25 April 2025. For Turkmenistan for 2000–2008: United Nations Statistics Division. UN National Accounts Main Aggregates Database. https://unstats.un.org/unsd/snaama/countryprofile (accessed 30 May 2023), and for 2009–2024: ADB estimates using data from the Central Bank of Turkmenistan. For Uzbekistan: Central Bank of Uzbekistan. Official communication, 29 May 2025.

Exchange Rates

Table 2.3.13: Purchasing Power Parity Conversion Factor
(local currency units per $, period averages)

ADB Regional Member	2010	2011	2017	2018	2019	2020	2021	2022	2023	2024
Developing ADB Member Economies										
Central and West Asia										
Afghanistan	14.54	16.61	15.42	14.86	15.03	15.34	14.59	14.90	14.80	...
Armenia	160.17	163.65	154.79	157.38	147.49	141.94	148.24	149.43	148.09	146.27
Azerbaijan	0.31	0.38	0.50	0.53	0.49	0.47	0.46	0.59	0.51	0.49
Georgia	0.76	0.81	0.81	0.81	0.80	0.80	0.87	0.87	0.87	0.88
Kazakhstan	69.51	82.09	121.61	130.11	126.17	124.88	129.06	144.29	152.54	160.93
Kyrgyz Republic	13.11	15.73	16.98	18.49	18.71	18.36	19.92	22.25	25.74	26.32
Pakistan	21.89	24.96	33.25	34.68	37.67	40.07	43.44	46.20	56.19	66.86
Tajikistan	1.41	1.56	2.35	2.49	2.40	2.36	2.54	2.57	2.57	2.68
Türkiye	0.92	0.97	1.38	1.63	1.84	2.11	2.75	4.52	7.35	11.55
Turkmenistan	1.29	1.43	1.54	1.49	1.50	1.53	1.50	1.56	1.45	1.47
Uzbekistan	505.17	602.00	1,432.91	1,799.89	2,111.32	2,353.38	2,591.11	2,768.48	3,041.71	3,367.64
East Asia										
China, People's Republic of	3.33	3.52	4.04	4.09	4.06	4.01	3.99	3.79	3.64	3.53
Hong Kong, China	5.14	5.23	6.07	6.25	6.19	6.15	5.87	5.57	5.54	5.61
Korea, Republic of	840.99	854.59	872.62	854.87	847.55	829.36	829.87	816.61	828.39	838.90
Mongolia	473.02	533.53	801.67	824.53	851.15	822.06	870.18	956.17	1,123.87	1,187.79
Taipei,China	15.80	15.15	15.57	15.57	15.27	14.65	14.40	13.70	13.60	13.68
South Asia										
Bangladesh	22.15	23.41	29.35	29.40	29.60	28.71	28.30	27.75	28.63	29.88
Bhutan	15.37	16.40	19.16	19.43	19.51	18.96	19.61	19.37	19.51	...
India	14.60	15.55	20.46	20.47	20.24	20.32	20.73	20.49	20.29	20.45
Maldives	7.14	7.86	8.18	8.03	7.83	8.47	8.21	7.93	7.79	7.66
Nepal	20.39	25.25	30.48	31.11	31.88	31.70	32.48	32.82	33.50	33.56
Sri Lanka	38.56	39.29	49.27	49.97	51.71	55.16	55.53	76.43	86.07	87.27
Southeast Asia										
Brunei Darussalam	0.60	0.71	0.63	0.64	0.60	0.53	0.53	0.62	0.52	0.50
Cambodia	1,333.51	1,371.24	1,464.89	1,468.92	1,468.90	1,433.77	1,426.96	1,378.47	1,344.13	1,342.77
Indonesia	3,336.15	3,512.75	4,756.17	4,833.60	4,847.45	4,791.01	4,808.43	4,917.92	4,819.74	4,747.91
Lao People's Democratic Republic	2,463.64	2,666.53	2,808.07	2,855.98	2,902.38	2,953.51	3,031.70	3,276.33	3,934.87	4,376.34
Malaysia	1.42	1.47	1.61	1.58	1.56	1.52	1.51	1.50	1.43	1.40
Myanmar	242.33	261.78	366.64	343.60	350.69	354.56	410.47	406.77	435.00	475.94
Philippines	17.77	18.10	19.70	19.96	19.74	19.44	19.38	19.08	19.26	19.36
Singapore	0.85	0.85	0.88	0.87	0.85	0.83	0.81	0.87	0.80	0.80
Thailand	12.19	12.39	12.39	12.15	11.83	11.41	11.15	10.89	10.65	10.49
Timor-Leste	0.42	0.45	0.37	0.34	0.34	0.27	0.39	0.41	0.31	0.28
Viet Nam	5,813.19	6,915.34	7,211.60	7,275.83	7,191.19	7,064.95	7,120.01	6,941.45	6,840.61	6,956.93
The Pacific										
Cook Islands	...	...	...	...	...	...	...	...	...	...
Fiji	0.89	0.95	0.94	0.96	0.97	0.94	0.91	0.87	0.87	0.89
Kiribati	0.96	0.96	0.94	0.96	0.91	0.94	0.98	0.90	0.94	0.94
Marshall Islands	0.89	0.94	0.97	0.93	0.88	0.92	0.93	0.86	0.89	0.91
Micronesia, Federated States of	0.88	0.88	0.95	1.01	0.96	0.91	0.89	0.91	0.93	0.96
Nauru	0.95	1.00	1.30	1.51	1.42	1.46	1.65	1.33	1.37	1.43
Niue	...	...	...	...	...	...	...	...	...	...
Palau	0.76	0.75	0.92	0.91	0.87	0.84	0.85	0.87	0.91	...
Papua New Guinea	1.82	1.86	2.01	2.16	2.15	2.16	2.30	2.47	2.28	2.40
Samoa	1.71	1.66	1.74	1.72	1.72	1.71	1.63	1.61	1.68	1.72
Solomon Islands	6.23	6.37	6.89	7.26	7.24	7.05	6.37	6.06	6.21	6.33
Tonga	1.48	1.45	1.55	1.59	1.64	1.62	1.59	1.52	1.46	...
Tuvalu	1.12	1.11	1.29	1.35	1.41	1.41	1.47	1.51	1.55	1.58
Vanuatu	99.80	100.51	108.30	109.27	111.02	112.62	112.10	110.00	120.98	117.20
Developed ADB Member Economies										
Australia	1.50	1.51	1.48	1.47	1.46	1.43	1.40	1.36	1.37	1.38
Japan	111.71	107.45	105.10	104.16	103.23	100.74	99.21	94.51	95.27	95.11
New Zealand	1.50	1.49	1.43	1.47	1.44	1.42	1.46	1.43	1.47	1.46

... = data not available, $ = United States dollars, ADB = Asian Development Bank.

Notes: For 2011, 2017, and 2021, purchasing power parity (PPP) figures are based on results from the 2011, 2017 and 2021 benchmark cycles of the International Comparison Program (ICP). For 2010 (and years prior featured in the Key Indicators Database), PPPs are extrapolated from the reference year 2011. For 2012–2016, figures are interpolated from the PPPs of the two ICP reference years, 2011 and 2017. For 2018–2020, figures are interpolated from the PPPs of the two ICP reference years, 2017 and 2021. For 2022–2024, figures are extrapolated from the 2021 ICP PPPs or imputed based on a regression model.

Sources: World Bank. World Development Indicators. https://databank.worldbank.org/source/world-development-indicators (accessed 9 July 2025). For Taipei,China: for 2000–2010; and 2024, Asian Development Bank estimates using data from the economy's official sources and World Bank data; for 2011, World Bank. DataBank: ICP 2011. https://databank.worldbank.org/source/international-comparison-program-(icp)-2011 (accessed 9 July 2025); for 2012–2016, International Comparison Program (ICP), Global Office at the World Bank (July 2024); for 2017–2023, World Bank. DataBank: ICP 2021. https://databank.worldbank.org/source/icp-2021# (accessed 9 July 2025).

Table 2.3.14: Price Level Indexes
(PPPs to official exchange rates, period averages, United States = 100)

ADB Regional Member	2010	2011	2017	2018	2019	2020	2021	2022	2023	2024
Developing ADB Member Economies										
Central and West Asia										
Afghanistan	31.8	34.8	22.5	20.2	19.2	19.9	16.6	16.8	18.8	...
Armenia	42.9	43.9	32.1	32.6	30.7	29.0	29.4	34.3	37.7	37.2
Azerbaijan	39.1	48.6	29.0	31.0	28.8	27.9	26.9	34.5	30.2	29.0
Georgia	42.6	48.1	32.2	32.0	28.3	25.6	26.9	30.0	33.0	32.4
Kazakhstan	47.2	56.0	37.3	37.7	33.0	30.2	30.3	31.4	33.4	34.3
Kyrgyz Republic	28.5	34.1	24.7	26.9	26.8	23.7	23.5	26.4	29.3	30.2
Pakistan	26.1	29.2	31.7	31.5	27.6	25.3	27.1	26.0	22.6	23.6
Tajikistan	32.2	33.9	27.5	27.2	25.2	22.8	22.5	23.3	23.7	24.8
Türkiye	61.2	57.7	37.9	33.8	32.4	30.1	31.1	27.3	31.0	35.2
Turkmenistan	45.2	50.0	43.9	42.6	43.0	43.7	42.9	44.5	41.5	42.0
Uzbekistan	31.8	35.1	28.0	22.3	23.9	23.4	24.4	25.1	25.9	26.6
East Asia										
China, People's Republic of	49.2	54.5	59.8	61.9	58.8	58.2	61.8	56.3	51.4	49.1
Hong Kong, China	66.2	67.2	77.9	79.7	79.0	79.2	75.5	71.2	70.7	71.9
Korea, Republic of	72.7	77.1	77.2	77.7	72.7	70.3	72.5	63.2	63.4	61.5
Mongolia	34.9	42.2	32.9	33.3	32.0	29.2	30.5	30.4	32.4	35.0
Taipei,China	49.9	51.4	51.2	51.6	49.4	49.5	51.4	46.0	43.7	42.6
South Asia										
Bangladesh	32.0	32.9	37.1	35.8	35.2	33.9	33.4	32.1	27.9	26.9
Bhutan	33.6	35.1	29.4	28.4	27.7	25.6	26.5	24.6	23.6	...
India	32.0	32.4	31.7	29.3	28.5	27.4	27.8	25.5	24.5	24.2
Maldives	55.8	53.8	53.2	52.2	50.9	55.1	53.4	51.5	50.7	49.8
Nepal	27.4	34.9	28.7	29.8	28.2	27.3	27.6	27.2	25.6	25.2
Sri Lanka	34.1	35.5	32.3	30.7	28.9	29.7	27.9	23.6	26.3	28.9
Southeast Asia										
Brunei Darussalam	43.9	56.1	45.5	47.6	43.9	38.5	39.6	44.8	38.7	37.1
Cambodia	31.9	33.8	36.2	36.3	36.2	35.0	34.8	33.6	32.7	33.0
Indonesia	36.7	40.1	35.5	34.0	34.3	32.9	33.6	33.1	31.6	29.9
Lao People's Democratic Republic	29.8	33.2	34.1	34.0	33.4	32.7	31.3	23.3	22.2	21.7
Malaysia	44.1	47.9	37.3	39.2	37.7	36.2	36.6	34.2	31.2	30.6
Myanmar	30.2	33.9	27.0	23.3	23.4	26.0	24.0	20.2	20.7	22.7
Philippines	39.4	41.8	39.1	37.9	38.1	39.2	39.3	35.0	34.6	33.8
Singapore	62.6	67.3	64.0	64.3	62.6	60.5	60.4	63.1	59.4	60.2
Thailand	38.5	40.6	36.5	37.6	38.1	36.5	34.9	31.1	30.6	29.7
Timor-Leste	41.6	45.5	36.6	34.2	34.3	26.6	39.3	40.9	31.3	28.2
Viet Nam	31.2	33.7	32.2	32.2	31.2	30.4	30.7	29.8	28.8	28.8
The Pacific										
Cook Islands	...	...	...	...	...	...	...	...	...	...
Fiji	46.1	53.0	45.5	46.0	45.0	43.1	44.0	39.5	38.9	39.2
Kiribati	88.3	99.2	72.3	71.6	63.4	64.6	73.6	62.2	62.5	61.8
Marshall Islands	89.1	93.9	97.3	92.9	87.5	92.3	93.3	86.2	88.7	91.1
Micronesia, Federated States of	88.3	87.9	94.8	101.2	96.1	91.3	88.9	90.8	93.1	95.9
Nauru	83.3	98.5	98.4	117.1	101.3	97.8	122.9	96.6	92.2	93.7
Niue	...	...	...	...	...	...	...	...	...	...
Palau	76.1	74.9	91.8	90.6	86.9	83.8	84.6	86.8	90.7	...
Papua New Guinea	66.8	78.4	63.2	65.6	63.4	62.3	65.6	70.2	63.5	62.9
Samoa	67.4	69.6	68.6	67.0	65.6	63.6	63.5	61.8	61.5	62.5
Solomon Islands	77.2	83.4	87.3	91.3	88.5	85.8	79.3	74.3	74.1	74.8
Tonga	76.5	79.3	70.1	72.5	72.1	70.3	69.8	66.7	61.9	...
Tuvalu	102.7	114.5	98.6	100.8	98.2	97.1	110.3	104.4	103.2	...
Vanuatu	103.0	112.3	100.4	99.2	96.8	97.6	102.4	95.4	101.6	98.3
Developed ADB Member Economies										
Australia	132.4	149.0	111.4	114.0	104.4	95.9	104.2	98.7	91.9	90.5
Japan	127.3	134.6	93.7	94.3	94.7	94.4	90.4	71.9	67.8	62.8
New Zealand	107.9	117.4	101.7	101.7	94.6	92.3	103.5	90.9	90.3	88.5

... = data not available, ADB = Asian Development Bank, PPP = purchasing power parity.

Sources: World Bank. World Development Indicators. https://databank.worldbank.org/source/world-development-indicators (accessed 8 July 2025). For Taipei,China: Asian Development Bank estimates using data from the economy's official sources, International Comparison Program (ICP), Global Office at the World Bank (July 2024); and World Bank DataBank: ICP 2021. https://databank.worldbank.org/source/icp-2021# (accessed 9 July 2025).

Data Issues and Comparability

Not all reporting economies meet the standards and classifications of the International Monetary Fund on the compilation of monetary and financial statistics available on the fund's Dissemination Standards Bulletin Board.[1]

Consumer price index coverage differs across economies. Most economies try to follow the Classification of Individual Consumption by Purpose guidelines, but the implementation varies across economies. In some instances, the basket of goods and services in the index is outdated or represents only urban areas (or the capital city). Other price measurements, such as the wholesale price index and the producer price index, are not available in Pacific economies.

Broad money supply in most economies relates to M2, which includes cash, checking deposits, savings deposits, money market securities, mutual funds, and other time deposits. However, 12 of the 45 economies with available data reported M3, thereby posing limits to comparability as M3 also includes less liquid financial assets. Not all economies publish the same types of aggregates, and even when aggregates have the same name (i.e., M1, M2, M3, etc.), their asset composition often differs significantly. For example, the definition of M2 in one economy may include time deposits with maturities of 1 year or less, whereas another economy's M2 definition may include time deposits with maturities of 2 years or less.

Finally, some economies use the central bank policy rate, while others use commercial bank rates in measuring banks' average deposit and lending rates.

1 For more information on the IMF's standards and classifications on the compilation of monetary and financial statistics, go to https://dsbb.imf.org/sdds/statistical-methodology.

Table 2.4.1: Trade in Goods Balance
(% of GDP)

ADB Regional Member	2010	2015	2019	2020	2021	2022	2023	2024
Developing ADB Member Economies								
Central and West Asia								
Afghanistan[a,b]	-27.3	-32.4	-28.0	-25.3 |	-27.7	-27.7	-33.8	-32.9
Armenia	-22.3	-11.2	-12.6	-10.9	-10.8	-9.6	-10.4	...
Azerbaijan	37.3	11.0	17.7	5.9	20.6	36.5	17.7	11.9
Georgia	-21.5	-26.4	-21.7	-20.0	-20.3	-20.9	-20.0	-19.2*
Kazakhstan	20.1	4.2	10.1	3.5	12.3	15.5	7.6	6.7
Kyrgyz Republic[b]	-27.9	-33.5	-28.0	-17.5	-26.2	-56.6	-54.7	-37.0*
Pakistan[b]	-5.8	-5.8	-8.6	-7.0	-8.2	-10.4	-7.3	-5.9*
Tajikistan[b]	-43.9	-27.7	-23.1	-17.8	-19.2	-27.6	-27.5	-31.8
Türkiye	-7.2	-5.7	-2.2	-5.3	-3.6	-9.9	-7.7	...
Turkmenistan[c]	9.9	-5.3	...	...	...	...	...	...
Uzbekistan[c]	1.3	-2.4	-11.7	-9.7	-11.5	-13.2	-15.2	-12.0*
East Asia								
China, People's Republic of	3.8	5.1	2.7	3.4	3.1	3.6	3.3	4.1
Hong Kong, China	1.4	-7.4	-4.2	-1.5	0.9	-1.4	-4.2	-0.5
Korea, Republic of	4.0	7.8	4.6	4.6	3.9	0.9	2.0	5.4
Mongolia	-2.4	4.8	8.2	13.2	9.0	7.2	22.4	13.1
Taipei,China	8.3	13.7	9.4	11.1	11.3	9.0	12.6	12.7
South Asia								
Bangladesh	-4.0	-3.0	-4.5	-5.0	-5.7	-7.2	-6.1	-5.0
Bhutan[b]	-15.9	-19.1	-15.0	-12.2	-6.0	-20.2	-24.5	-14.1
India[b]	-7.6	-6.2	-5.6	-3.8	-6.0	-7.9	-6.7*	-7.3*
Maldives[b]	-40.9	-40.1	-41.6	-39.1	-40.1	-47.2	-43.6	...
Nepal[d]	-25.0	-28.2	-33.2	-28.0	-31.2	-34.6	-26.4	-24.5
Sri Lanka[b]	-8.2	-9.9	-9.0	-7.1	-9.2	-7.0	-5.9	-6.1
Southeast Asia								
Brunei Darussalam[b]	45.3	22.4	16.4	11.5	19.1	30.9	25.2	24.0
Cambodia[b]	-18.8	-16.2	-20.0	-5.8	-30.5	-22.4	-7.1	-9.7
Indonesia[b]	4.1	1.6	0.3	2.7	3.7	4.8	3.4	2.9*
Lao People's Democratic Republic[b]	-4.7	-14.0	-2.5	3.9	7.4	6.2	4.8*	4.8*
Malaysia[b]	15.1	9.3	8.2	9.7	11.5	10.4	7.5	6.1
Myanmar[b]	0.1	-6.1	...	...	...	...	...	...
Philippines[b]	-8.1	-7.6	-13.1	-9.3	-13.4	-17.2	-15.1	-14.9*
Singapore	26.4	30.1	25.2	29.5	27.8	31.5	31.1	27.1
Thailand	7.8	6.5	4.9	8.1	6.3	2.7	3.8*	3.7*
Timor-Leste[b,e]	-31.8	-40.0 |	9.9	68.1	143.9	60.4	-7.8	...
Viet Nam[b]	-3.5	3.0	6.3	8.9	4.3	7.1	10.1	9.0
The Pacific								
Cook Islands	-13.1	-26.3	-31.1	-30.1	-30.1	-40.9	...	...
Fiji[b]	-23.5	-19.5	-25.5	-14.8	-19.5	-33.0	-32.7*	...
Kiribati[b]	-38.6	-46.8	-43.5	-44.1	-47.5	-61.8	-63.8*	...
Marshall Islands	-51.5	-29.4	-59.5	-23.3	-13.4	-21.6	-19.0	...
Micronesia, Federated States of	-44.0	-40.9	...	...	...	...	...	...
Nauru	12.0	-47.8	-43.3	-53.2*	-43.8*	-41.5	-37.6	...
Niue	-60.3	-45.8	-42.3	-36.2	-41.6	-41.1	-49.4*	-25.4*
Palau	-45.6	-48.3	-50.0	-57.8	-53.9	-61.5	-57.6	-55.4*
Papua New Guinea[b]	15.5	25.7	27.2	23.0	24.8	27.6	24.1	27.3*
Samoa[b]	-36.7	-32.0	-33.6	-29.8	-34.4	-38.9	-34.0	-32.3
Solomon Islands[b]	-15.2	-1.3	-2.3	-1.7	-6.4	-13.2	-12.3	-5.8
Tonga[c]	-53.0	-64.5	-81.4	-80.0	-87.2	-98.7	-122.1	...
Tuvalu[c]	-54.3	-88.5	-57.7	-51.7	-51.7	-41.8	-55.7	...
Vanuatu[b]	-28.3	-36.8	-24.0	-23.5	-24.6	-29.3	-30.5*	-27.4*
Developed ADB Member Economies								
Australia	-0.7	-0.8	2.7	3.6	3.6	6.2	5.9	3.4
Japan	1.9	-0.2	0.0	0.5	0.3	-2.8	-1.1	-0.6
New Zealand	1.4	-1.0	-1.0	0.4	-2.0	-3.5	-2.6	...

... = data not available, | = marks break in series due to change in compilation methodology and/or reference year, (-/+) 0.0 = magnitude is less than half of unit employed, * = provisional or preliminary, ADB = Asian Development Bank, GDP = gross domestic product.

a Change in reference year from beginning March for 2002–2011 and 2021–2024 to ending 20 December for 2012–2020.

b Change in compilation methodology from the International Monetary Fund's Balance of Payments Manual (fifth edition) [BPM5] to the International Monetary Fund's Balance of Payments and International Investment Position Manual (sixth edition) [BPM6].

c Change in compilation methodology from BPM4 to BPM6.

d Based on BPM5.

e From September 2019, following the new Timor-Leste Australia Maritime Boundary Treaty, oil revenue from the Joint Petroleum Development Area is included in the national accounts. The National Institute of Statistics Timor-Leste (INETL) disaggregates the accounts into 'oil' and 'non-oil' components. To better assess the performance of the domestic economy, this publication presents GDP on a non-oil basis, which reflects the primary analytical approach used by INETL.

Source: Economies' official sources.

Table 2.4.2: Trade in Services Balance
(% of GDP)

ADB Regional Member	2010	2015	2019	2020	2021	2022	2023	2024
Developing ADB Member Economies								
Central and West Asia								
Afghanistan[a,b]	6.1	-1.4	-2.9	-2.0 |	-2.5	-2.9	-6.1	-5.2
Armenia	-2.8	-0.9	-0.7	1.0	2.8	8.8	9.6	...
Azerbaijan	-3.3	-8.0	-5.4	-6.7	-3.9	-3.4	-3.2	-2.8
Georgia	4.5	9.4	12.5	0.8	3.9	10.9	11.3	11.5*
Kazakhstan	-4.9	-2.6	-2.1	-1.9	-1.1	-0.7	-0.6	-0.4
Kyrgyz Republic[b]	-4.2	-3.3	0.7	-2.1	-2.4	-0.9	-4.3	-0.6*
Pakistan[b]	-0.9	-1.0	-1.5	-1.1	-0.7	-1.6	-0.3	-0.8*
Tajikistan[b]	-0.5	-2.5	-3.0	-3.3	-4.3	-5.1	-4.2	-5.5
Türkiye	2.2	4.2	5.6	2.1	4.0	5.8	5.1	...
Turkmenistan[c]	...	...	...	...	...	...	...	...
Uzbekistan[c]	-2.5	-0.8	-3.6	-3.0	-3.6	-3.4	-2.8	-3.5*
East Asia								
China, People's Republic of	-0.2	-1.9	-1.8	-1.0	-0.6	-0.5	-1.1	-1.2
Hong Kong, China	4.4	9.8	5.8	3.5	4.7	5.5	4.8	4.5
Korea, Republic of	-1.2	-1.0	-1.5	-0.8	-0.3	-0.4	-1.5	-1.3
Mongolia	-4.2	-6.2	-14.0	-10.9	-11.0	-13.8	-12.8	-14.1
Taipei,China	-2.5	-2.0	-0.8	0.5	1.6	1.6	-1.3	-1.6
South Asia								
Bangladesh	-0.9	-1.4	-0.9	-0.7	-0.7	-0.9	-0.7	-0.9
Bhutan[b]	-4.2	-3.1	-1.9	-3.6	-4.2	-6.2	-6.2	0.3
India[b]	2.6	3.3	3.0	3.3	3.4	4.3	4.5*	4.8*
Maldives[b]	34.8	49.2	35.7	21.2	49.6	49.7	42.1	...
Nepal[d]	-1.3	1.2	-0.4	0.0	-1.7	-2.2	-1.5	-1.0
Sri Lanka[b]	1.2	2.7	3.2	1.0	1.8	2.8	3.6	3.5
Southeast Asia								
Brunei Darussalam[b]	-5.9	-7.8	-8.8	-7.1	-5.0	-5.1	-8.6	-8.6
Cambodia[b]	7.1	7.0	7.7	-0.7	-3.9	-1.1	3.1	4.1
Indonesia[b]	-1.3	-1.0	-0.7	-0.9	-1.2	-1.5	-1.3	-1.3*
Lao People's Democratic Republic[b]	2.4	-1.6	-0.4	-0.5	-0.7	-2.2	2.5*	3.1*
Malaysia[b]	0.8	-1.8	-0.7	-3.3	-4.2	-3.2	-2.4	-0.7
Myanmar[b]	-0.0	2.2	...	...	...	...	...	...
Philippines[b]	2.8	1.8	3.5	3.8	3.6	3.9	4.2	3.2*
Singapore[b]	-0.1	-2.8	4.2	2.1	8.5	8.4	6.3	8.1
Thailand	-2.1	3.9	4.5	-2.9	-6.4	-4.8	-1.7*	-0.3*
Timor-Leste[b,e]	-107.7	-36.6 |	-25.4	-51.0	-33.4	-26.3	-18.1	...
Viet Nam[b]	-1.7	-1.7	-0.3	-3.0	-4.2	-3.4	-2.0	-2.6
The Pacific								
Cook Islands	21.5	51.2	59.2	-0.1	-0.5	54.2	...	...
Fiji[b]	17.1	16.0	15.0	0.2	1.4	13.7	21.3*	...
Kiribati[b]	-24.0	-35.2	-23.3	-13.2	-19.5	-30.7	-31.9*	...
Marshall Islands	-21.8	-20.6	-19.5	-13.8	-11.7	-15.8	-13.8	...
Micronesia, Federated States of	-15.2	-10.8	...	...	...	...	...	...
Nauru	-7.3	-15.9	8.2	5.3*	-5.3	-17.7	-18.4	...
Niue	-40.5	14.8	19.0	9.5	-12.7	-10.2	6.7*	14.1*
Palau	15.6	27.9	11.5	0.4	-12.5	-10.1	7.1	4.5*
Papua New Guinea[b]	-17.2	-8.4	-7.3	-6.7	-7.2	-7.7	-7.9	-7.1*
Samoa[b]	14.3	15.1	20.5	-1.5	-2.6	2.9	15.1	15.9
Solomon Islands[b]	-10.7	-5.8	-7.7	-6.6	-7.1	-9.0	-8.2	-6.9
Tonga[c]	-2.1	1.2	6.6	3.8	-4.8	-15.7	-17.0	...
Tuvalu[c]	-4.1	-82.3	-60.9	-51.4	-43.1	-48.2	-35.5	...
Vanuatu[b]	22.3	10.4	6.5	-10.6	-19.2	-16.0	2.1*	-8.7*
Developed ADB Member Economies								
Australia	-0.2	-0.7	-0.6	-0.2	0.2	-1.0	-1.5	-1.3
Japan	-0.5	-0.4	-0.2	-0.7	-0.8	-1.0	-0.5	-0.4
New Zealand	0.9	2.0	1.2	-1.0	-1.9	-1.9	-0.4	...

... = data not available, | = marks break in series due to change in compilation methodology and/or reference year, (-/+) 0.0 = magnitude is less than half of unit employed, * = provisional or preliminary, ADB = Asian Development Bank, GDP = gross domestic product.

a Change in reference year from beginning March for 2002–2011 and 2021–2024 to ending 20 December for 2012–2020.

b Change in compilation methodology from the International Monetary Fund's Balance of Payments Manual (fifth edition) [BPM5] to the International Monetary Fund's Balance of Payments and International Investment Position Manual (sixth edition) [BPM6].

c Change in compilation methodology from BPM4 to BPM6.

d Based on BPM5.

e From September 2019, following the new Timor-Leste Australia Maritime Boundary Treaty, oil revenue from the Joint Petroleum Development Area is included in the national accounts. The National Institute of Statistics Timor-Leste (INETL) disaggregates the accounts into 'oil' and 'non-oil' components. To better assess the performance of the domestic economy, this publication presents GDP on a non-oil basis, which reflects the primary analytical approach used by INETL.

Source: Economies' official sources.

Table 2.4.3: Current Account Balance
(% of GDP)

ADB Regional Member	2010	2015	2019	2020	2021	2022	2023	2024
Developing ADB Member Economies								
Central and West Asia								
Afghanistan[a,b]	-4.6	-19.9	-20.1	-15.5 |	-17.3	-19.9	-26.0	-27.0
Armenia	-13.6	-2.7	-7.1	-4.0	-3.5	0.3	-2.3	...
Azerbaijan	28.4	-0.4	9.1	-0.5	15.1	29.8	11.5	6.3
Georgia	-9.8	-11.8	-5.9	-12.5	-10.4	-4.1	-4.3	-4.4*
Kazakhstan	1.8	-5.4	-3.9	-6.5	-1.4	2.8	-3.6	-1.3
Kyrgyz Republic[b]	-9.8	-16.0	-11.4	4.5	-8.0	-42.1	-45.0	-25.2*
Pakistan[b]	-2.0	-0.9	-4.2	-1.5	-0.8	-4.7	-1.0	-0.5*
Tajikistan[b]	-10.3	-5.8	-2.2	4.3	8.2	15.3	4.8	6.2
Türkiye	-5.7	-2.5	2.0	-4.3	-0.8	-5.1	-3.6	...
Turkmenistan[c]	-8.9	-16.7	...	...	6.5	7.1	4.7	4.0
Uzbekistan[c]	4.6	1.0	-5.4	-4.7	-6.4	-3.2	-8.0	-5.1*
East Asia								
China, People's Republic of	3.8	2.6	0.7	1.7	1.9	2.4	1.4	2.3
Hong Kong, China	7.0	3.3	5.9	7.0	11.8	10.2	8.5	12.9
Korea, Republic of	2.3	6.8	3.4	4.4	4.4	1.4	1.8	5.3
Mongolia	-12.3	-8.2	-15.2	-5.1	-13.8	-13.5	0.6	-10.5
Taipei,China	8.3	13.6	11.1	14.5	15.2	13.3	14.0	14.3
South Asia								
Bangladesh	2.9	1.5	-1.3	-1.5	-1.1	-4.0	-2.6	-1.5
Bhutan[b]	-18.8	-25.6	-18.8	-14.9	-10.4	-27.9	-33.0	-16.9
India[b]	-2.9	-1.1	-0.9	0.9	-1.2	-2.0	-0.7*	-0.6*
Maldives[b]	-13.8	-7.3	-25.8	-35.7	-8.6	-16.9	-21.2	...
Nepal[d]	-2.3	4.5	-6.9	-1.0	-7.7	-13.0	-0.9	3.9
Sri Lanka[b]	-1.8	-2.2	-2.1	-1.4	-3.7	-1.9	1.7	1.2
Southeast Asia								
Brunei Darussalam[b]	36.5	16.6	6.6	4.5	11.2	19.6	12.9	14.5
Cambodia[b]	-6.9	-6.6	-8.1	-1.0	-29.7	-19.2	1.3	0.5
Indonesia[b]	0.7	-2.0	-2.7	-0.4	0.3	1.0	-0.1	-0.6*
Lao People's Democratic Republic[b]	0.4	-15.7	-7.0	-1.6	2.3	-3.0	2.7*	3.5*
Malaysia[b]	10.1	3.0	3.5	4.2	3.9	3.2	1.5	1.7
Myanmar[b]	0.0	-4.9 |	0.4*	-2.5*	-1.3*	-3.0*	-2.4*	-2.2*
Philippines[b]	3.4	2.4	-0.8	3.2	-1.5	-4.5	-2.8	-3.8*
Singapore	22.9	18.7	15.4	17.5	19.8	18.4	17.7	17.5
Thailand	3.4	6.9	7.0	4.2	-2.1	-3.5	1.4*	2.1*
Timor-Leste[b,e]	180.2	12.8 |	26.3	32.6	108.6	24.3	-9.8	...
Viet Nam[b]	-2.9	-0.7	3.7	4.3	-2.2	0.3	5.9	5.9
The Pacific								
Cook Islands	8.1	31.1	34.3	-18.9	-13.8	22.3	...	...
Fiji[b]	-4.7	-3.5	-12.8	-11.6	-6.8	-15.5	-6.7*	...
Kiribati[b]	0.1	29.3	40.0	32.1	7.2	-11.7	-2.1*	...
Marshall Islands	-18.1	11.4	-31.2	14.9	22.7	10.0	16.8	...
Micronesia, Federated States of	-17.9	4.5	...	...	...	...	...	...
Nauru	46.2	-18.5	4.6	2.5	3.7	2.0	1.3	...
Niue	-53.9	12.6	30.6	6.0	9.0	0.3	0.3*	29.2*
Palau	-11.8	-13.1	-30.1	-43.5	-40.2	-45.7	-47.3	-26.5*
Papua New Guinea[b]	-4.4	11.1	14.4	14.4	12.6	14.4	9.1	15.5*
Samoa[b]	-4.8	-1.5	3.8	-9.1	-12.7	-7.8	3.6	5.2
Solomon Islands[b]	-16.0	-2.7	-9.5	-1.6	-5.1	-14.4	-10.6	-3.9
Tonga[c]	-8.7	-75.8	-42.9	10.7	21.7	13.8	0.6	...
Tuvalu[c]	-3.8	-35.3	-22.2	16.2	28.2	-0.2	32.3	...
Vanuatu[b]	-5.6	-15.7	5.2	-6.4	-11.3	-18.0	-6.7*	-19.0*
Developed ADB Member Economies								
Australia	-5.0	-3.7	-1.3	1.1	2.5	1.3	0.0	-1.3
Japan	3.8	3.1	3.5	3.0	3.9	2.0	3.8	4.8
New Zealand	-2.8	-2.4	-2.4	-2.7	-6.8	-8.6	-6.6	...

... = data not available, | = marks break in series due to change in compilation methodology, reference year, and/or data source, 0.0 = magnitude is less than half of unit employed, * = provisional or preliminary, ADB = Asian Development Bank, GDP = gross domestic product.

a Change in reference year from beginning March for 2002–2011 and 2021–2024 to ending 20 December for 2012–2020.
b Change in compilation methodology from the International Monetary Fund's Balance of Payments Manual (fifth edition) [BPM5] to the International Monetary Fund's Balance of Payments and International Investment Position Manual (sixth edition) [BPM6].
c Change in compilation methodology from BPM4 to BPM6.
d Based on BPM5.
e From September 2019, following the new Timor-Leste Australia Maritime Boundary Treaty, oil revenue from the Joint Petroleum Development Area is included in the national accounts. The National Institute of Statistics Timor-Leste (INETL) disaggregates the accounts into 'oil' and 'non-oil' components. To better assess the performance of the domestic economy, this publication presents GDP on a non-oil basis, which reflects the primary analytical approach used by INETL.

Sources: Economies' official sources. For Myanmar (2019–2024): ADB. 2025. Asian Development Outlook 2025: Statistical Tables. Current account balance (% of GDP at current producer prices). https://www.adb.org/outlook/editions/april-2025 (accessed 17 June 2025).

Balance of Payments

Table 2.4.4: Total Remittances, Inflows—Dollar Amounts
($ million)

ADB Regional Member	2010	2015	2019	2020	2021	2022	2023	2024
Developing ADB Member Economies								
Central and West Asia	**23,098**	**34,360**	**43,070**	**44,809**	**53,606**	**65,591**	**57,429**	**66,050**
Afghanistan	378	349	829	789	320	320	320	...
Armenia	1,669	1,491	1,528	1,327	1,557	2,031	1,452	1,182
Azerbaijan	1,410	1,270	1,275	1,403	1,527	3,950	1,913	1,352
Georgia	1,184	1,459	2,258	2,110	2,644	3,854	4,201	3,999
Kazakhstan	226	294	506	374	310	481	304	240
Kyrgyz Republic	1,266	1,688	2,698	2,631	3,012	3,225	2,850	...
Pakistan	9,690	19,306	22,252	26,089	31,312	30,176	26,558	34,914
Tajikistan	2,021	2,259	2,322	2,187	2,922	5,346	4,634	6,802
Türkiye	1,819	1,401	856	816	726	696	1,029	982
Turkmenistan	–	–	–	–	–	–	–	...
Uzbekistan	3,435	4,843	8,546	7,084	9,277	15,512	14,169	16,579
East Asia	**20,596**	**41,131**	**28,319**	**29,185**	**33,106**	**36,890**	**39,624**	**41,693**
China, People's Republic of	13,636	33,105	18,294	18,876	22,480	26,094	29,484	31,411
Hong Kong, China	340	387	451	427	453	419	454	462
Korea, Republic of	5,854	6,464	7,166	7,435	7,742	7,815	7,035	7,449
Mongolia	266	261	561	549	471	399	455	...
Taipei,China	500	915	1,846	1,899	1,960	2,164	2,196	2,371
South Asia	**71,929**	**97,958**	**116,750**	**120,237**	**125,407**	**145,717**	**158,226**	**179,098**
Bangladesh	10,850	15,296	18,364	21,752	22,206	21,505	22,168	27,122
Bhutan	8	20	57	83	73	96	108	110
India	53,480	68,910	83,332	83,149	89,375	111,222	119,526	137,675
Maldives	3	4	4	5	5	5	5	6
Nepal	3,464	6,730	8,244	8,108	8,226	9,069	10,396	14,185
Sri Lanka	4,123	7,000	6,749	7,140	5,522	3,819	6,023	...
Southeast Asia	**42,429**	**58,418**	**73,056**	**70,537**	**73,618**	**79,154**	**83,323**	**70,555**
Brunei Darussalam	–	–	–	1	1	1	1	...
Cambodia	557	1,185	2,654	2,588	2,539	2,616	2,782	2,828
Indonesia	6,916	9,659	11,666	9,651	9,402	13,089	14,467	16,038
Lao People's Democratic Republic	42	189	297	232	220	240	287	...
Malaysia	1,103	1,644	1,597	1,427	1,552	1,618	1,704	1,605
Myanmar	115	1,934	2,553	2,672	1,282	1,261	1,100	...
Philippines	21,557	29,799	35,167	34,883	36,685	38,049	39,097	40,279
Singapore	–	–	–	–	–	–	–	...
Thailand	4,433	5,895	8,162	8,257	9,065	8,917	9,692	9,584
Timor-Leste	137	62	74	113	150	164	193	220
Viet Nam	7,569	8,051	10,885	10,715	12,722	13,200	14,000	...
The Pacific[a]	**479**	**655**	**915**	**947**	**1,191**	**1,341**	**1,334**	**...**
Cook Islands	...	...	...	...	...	...	...	...
Fiji	176	252	287	317	394	459	500	...
Kiribati	16	14	20	15	13	28	12	...
Marshall Islands	22	27	32	33	34	34	34	...
Micronesia, Federated States of	18	23	23	23	23	23	23	...
Nauru	0	10	4	2	1	1	1	...
Niue	...	...	...	...	...	...	...	...
Palau	2	2	2	2	2	2	2	...
Papua New Guinea	4	4	29	2	3	15	11	...
Samoa	139	131	155	204	248	280	265	282
Solomon Islands	14	19	25	28	51	81	85	95
Tonga	74	129	182	190	218	217	254	257
Tuvalu	4	3	2	2	3	2	3	...
Vanuatu	12	40	152	127	200	198	145	...
Developed ADB Member Economies	**3,919**	**6,031**	**6,625**	**6,514**	**6,892**	**7,292**	**7,256**	**6,528**
Australia	1,864	2,175	1,763	1,197	936	1,307	1,727	1,884
Japan	1,684	3,325	4,389	4,888	5,294	5,408	4,712	4,644
New Zealand	371	532	474	428	661	577	816	...
DEVELOPING ADB MEMBER ECONOMIES[a]	**158,531**	**232,522**	**262,110**	**265,716**	**286,928**	**328,693**	**339,937**	**358,030**
ALL ADB REGIONAL MEMBERS[a]	**162,451**	**238,553**	**268,735**	**272,229**	**293,820**	**335,985**	**347,193**	**364,558**
WORLD[a]	**421,425**	**552,612**	**659,353**	**661,682**	**740,974**	**793,778**	**822,680**	**740,508**

... = data not available, – = magnitude equals zero, $ = United States dollars, ADB = Asian Development Bank.

Note: Figures are based on the International Monetary Fund's Balance of Payments and International Investment Position Manual (sixth edition).

a Includes only reporting economies with data corresponding to the year heading.

Sources: World Bank. World Development Indicators. https://databank.worldbank.org/source/world-development-indicators (accessed 9 July 2025). For Taipei,China: Ministry of Finance. Official communication, 10 June 2025.

Table 2.4.5: Total Remittances, Inflows—Proportion of Economic Activity
(% of GDP)

ADB Regional Member	2010	2015	2019	2020	2021	2022	2023	2024
Developing ADB Member Economies								
Central and West Asia[a]	**1.8**	**2.2**	**3.0**	**3.3**	**3.4**	**3.4**	**2.9**	**...**
Afghanistan	2.4	1.8	4.4	4.0	2.2	2.2	1.9	...
Armenia	18.0	14.1	11.2	10.5	11.2	10.4	6.0	4.6
Azerbaijan	2.7	2.4	2.6	3.3	2.8	5.0	2.6	1.8
Georgia	9.5	9.6	12.8	13.2	14.0	15.4	13.7	11.8
Kazakhstan	0.2	0.2	0.3	0.2	0.2	0.2	0.1	0.1
Kyrgyz Republic	26.4	25.3	28.8	31.8	32.6	26.6	18.8	...
Pakistan	4.9	6.4	6.9	8.7	9.0	8.0	7.9	9.4
Tajikistan	35.8	27.3	28.0	26.9	32.7	49.9	37.8	47.9
Türkiye	0.2	0.2	0.1	0.1	0.1	0.1	0.1	0.1
Turkmenistan	–	–	–	–	–	–	–	...
Uzbekistan	6.9	5.6	12.7	10.7	12.0	17.2	13.8	14.4
East Asia	**0.3**	**0.3**	**0.2**	**0.2**	**0.2**	**0.2**	**0.2**	**0.2**
China, People's Republic of	0.2	0.3	0.1	0.1	0.1	0.1	0.2	0.2
Hong Kong, China	0.1	0.1	0.1	0.1	0.1	0.1	0.1	0.1
Korea, Republic of	0.5	0.4	0.4	0.5	0.4	0.5	0.4	...
Mongolia	3.7	2.2	3.9	4.1	3.1	2.3	2.2	...
Taipei,China	0.1	0.2	0.3	0.3	0.3	0.3	0.3	0.3
South Asia[a]	**3.8**	**3.9**	**3.5**	**3.8**	**3.4**	**3.7**	**3.8**	**4.0**
Bangladesh	9.4	7.8	5.2	5.8	5.3	4.7	5.1	6.0
Bhutan	0.5	0.9	2.1	3.4	2.6	3.3	3.6	...
India	3.2	3.3	2.9	3.1	2.8	3.3	3.3	3.5
Maldives	0.1	0.1	0.1	0.1	0.1	0.1	0.1	0.1
Nepal	21.6	27.6	24.1	24.3	22.3	22.0	25.3	33.1
Sri Lanka	7.0	8.2	7.6	8.5	6.2	5.2	7.2	...
Southeast Asia[a]	**0.4**	**2.6**	**2.5**	**2.5**	**2.3**	**2.4**	**2.4**	**2.1**
Brunei Darussalam	–	–	–	0.0	0.0	0.0	0.0	...
Cambodia	4.0	4.9	7.2	7.4	6.9	6.5	6.6	6.1
Indonesia	0.9	1.1	1.0	0.9	0.8	1.0	1.1	1.1
Lao People's Democratic Republic	0.6	1.3	1.6	1.2	1.2	1.5	1.8	...
Malaysia	0.4	0.5	0.4	0.4	0.4	0.4	0.4	0.4
Myanmar	0.2	3.2	3.4	3.4	1.9	2.0	1.6	...
Philippines	10.3	9.7	9.3	9.6	9.3	9.4	8.9	8.7
Singapore	–	–	–	–	–	–	–	...
Thailand	1.3	1.5	1.5	1.6	1.8	1.8	1.9	1.8
Timor-Leste	15.5	3.9	3.6	5.2	4.1	5.1	9.3	11.7
Viet Nam	5.1	3.4	3.3	3.1	3.5	3.2	3.2	...
The Pacific[a]	**2.3**	**2.1**	**2.6**	**2.8**	**3.3**	**3.2**	**2.8**	**...**
Cook Islands	...	...	...	...	...	...	...	...
Fiji	5.6	5.4	5.3	7.2	9.1	9.2	9.2	...
Kiribati	9.5	7.3	9.3	6.8	4.7	10.4	4.0	...
Marshall Islands	13.8	14.9	13.9	13.8	13.3	13.6	13.3	...
Micronesia, Federated States of	6.1	7.4	5.9	6.3	6.0	5.6	5.3	...
Nauru	...	...	...	...	...	...	...	...
Niue	...	...	...	...	...	...	...	...
Palau	0.9	0.8	0.8	0.9	0.8	0.8	0.7	...
Papua New Guinea	0.0	0.0	0.1	0.0	0.0	0.0	0.0	...
Samoa	20.4	15.9	17.0	23.5	29.4	33.6	28.2	26.4
Solomon Islands	1.6	1.4	1.6	1.8	3.4	5.2	5.1	5.4
Tonga	20.2	29.5	36.8	38.2	42.0	41.9	50.0	...
Tuvalu	12.2	7.2	4.4	4.3	4.9	4.2	4.2	...
Vanuatu	1.8	5.2	16.2	14.0	20.3	19.2	12.9	...
Developed ADB Member Economies[a]	**0.1**	**0.1**	**0.1**	**0.1**	**0.1**	**0.1**	**0.1**	**0.1**
Australia	0.2	0.2	0.1	0.1	0.1	0.1	0.1	0.1
Japan	0.0	0.1	0.1	0.1	0.1	0.1	0.1	0.1
New Zealand	0.3	0.3	0.2	0.2	0.3	0.2	0.3	...
DEVELOPING ADB MEMBER ECONOMIES[a]	**0.8**	**1.1**	**1.0**	**1.0**	**0.9**	**1.1**	**1.1**	**1.2**
ALL ADB REGIONAL MEMBERS[a]	**0.6**	**0.9**	**0.8**	**0.8**	**0.8**	**0.9**	**0.9**	**1.0**

... = data not available, – = magnitude equals zero, 0.0 = magnitude is less than half of unit employed, ADB = Asian Development Bank, GDP = gross domestic product.

a Aggregate percentages calculated using only reporting economies with data available for both remittances and GDP in the years specified in the column headings.

Sources: World Bank. World Development Indicators. https://databank.worldbank.org/source/world-development-indicators (accessed 9 July 2025). Aggregates by ADB based on data from WDI and Economy Tables. For Taipei,China: Ministry of Finance. Official communication, 10 June 2025; past communication.

Table 2.4.6: Foreign Direct Investment, Net Inflows—Dollar Amounts
($ million)

ADB Regional Member	2010	2015	2019	2020	2021	2022	2023	2024
Developing ADB Member Economies								
Central and West Asia[a]	**29,428**	**39,332**	**23,284**	**20,777**	**23,196**	**22,938**	**25,119**	**18,008**
Afghanistan	191	169	23	13	...	...	...	...
Armenia	529	184	100	59	366	976	580	139
Azerbaijan	3,353	4,048	1,504	507	–1,708	–4,474	253	231
Georgia	916	1,735	1,398	544	1,271	2,287	2,087	1,368
Kazakhstan	7,456	6,578	3,731	7,206	4,567	5,082	5,818	–682
Kyrgyz Republic	473	1,144	404	–402	226	55	...	...
Pakistan	2,022	1,673	2,234	2,057	2,147	1,462	2,048	2,568
Tajikistan	94	454	213	107	84	174	141	291
Türkiye	9,099	19,263	9,507	7,522	12,674	13,784	10,657	11,257
Turkmenistan	3,632	3,043	1,854	1,436	1,287	936	1,378	...
Uzbekistan	1,663	1,041	2,316	1,728	2,280	2,657	2,156	2,836
East Asia[a]	**340,093**	**430,126**	**265,787**	**387,085**	**510,916**	**351,521**	**201,073**	**161,900**
China, People's Republic of	243,703	242,489	187,170	253,096	344,075	190,204	51,338	18,556
Hong Kong, China	82,709	181,047	58,299	117,452	137,191	122,408	121,986	117,027
Korea, Republic of	9,497	4,104	9,634	8,765	22,060	25,045	19,042	15,226
Mongolia	1,691	94	2,443	1,719	2,173	2,504	2,248	...
Taipei,China	2,492	2,391	8,240	6,053	5,416	11,360	6,459	11,092
South Asia[a]	**29,486**	**47,877**	**54,422**	**66,886**	**47,889**	**53,265**	**31,030**	**30,017**
Bangladesh	1,232	2,831	1,908	1,525	1,724	1,635	1,385	1,506
Bhutan	75	6	13	–3	7	8	12	23
India	27,397	44,009	50,611	64,362	44,727	49,940	28,079	27,609
Maldives	216	298	961	441	643	732	767	806
Nepal	88	52	186	127	196	66	75	73
Sri Lanka	478	680	743	434	592	884	712	...
Southeast Asia[a]	**107,932**	**132,976**	**177,415**	**125,819**	**234,291**	**232,445**	**201,647**	**235,650**
Brunei Darussalam	...	171	373	566	206	–290	–56	29
Cambodia	1,404	1,823	3,663	3,625	3,483	3,579	3,959	4,395
Indonesia	15,292	19,779	24,994	19,175	21,213	24,702	21,543	24,130
Lao People's Democratic Republic	279	1,078	756	968	1,072	726	1,781	...
Malaysia	10,886	9,857	9,155	4,059	20,245	15,028	7,919	15,593
Myanmar	901	4,084	1,736	–	–	–	–	–
Philippines	1,070	5,639	8,671	6,822	11,983	9,492	8,925	8,930
Singapore	55,322	69,775	106,573	79,753	145,405	149,724	132,496	151,941
Thailand	14,747	8,928	5,534	–4,294	15,390	11,855	6,516	10,230
Timor-Leste	30	43	–158	–654	–367	–270	63	232
Viet Nam	8,000	11,800	16,120	15,800	15,660	17,900	18,500	20,170
The Pacific[a]	**435**	**369**	**787**	**456**	**495**	**1,423**	**...**	**...**
Cook Islands	...	...	...	...	...	...	...	...
Fiji	178	205	322	239	410	104	...	...
Kiribati	–7	–1	–1	3	1	4	5	...
Marshall Islands	–9	–5	5	3	0	...	...	...
Micronesia, Federated States of	–	20 (2014)	...	...	...	...	...	...
Nauru	–	–	2	–3	7	–9	1	...
Niue	...	...	...	...	...	...	...	...
Palau	3	35	45	43	31	72	...	...
Papua New Guinea	36	30	336	113	–34	1,193	83	...
Samoa	0	27	–2	4	9	5	2	4
Solomon Islands	166	32	33	9	28	41	79	33
Tonga	5	15	–6	4	0	3	5	–12
Tuvalu	0	–	–	–	–	–	–	...
Vanuatu	63	31	53	41	43	11	...	...
Developed ADB Member Economies	**43,282**	**52,072**	**81,621**	**84,697**	**71,086**	**126,859**	**56,904**	**74,510**
Australia	35,555	46,893	38,745	17,977	31,519	70,365	33,132	54,188
Japan	7,441	5,252	39,961	62,585	35,027	48,154	20,180	17,174
New Zealand	286	–73	2,916	4,135	4,540	8,340	3,592	3,147
DEVELOPING ADB MEMBER ECONOMIES[a]	**507,374**	**650,680**	**521,695**	**601,024**	**816,788**	**661,593**	**459,044**	**...**
ALL ADB REGIONAL MEMBERS[a]	**550,656**	**702,752**	**603,316**	**685,720**	**887,874**	**788,452**	**515,948**	**...**
WORLD[a]	**1,842,150**	**2,792,083**	**1,939,138**	**1,199,499**	**2,384,047**	**1,827,629**	**820,399**	**...**

... = data not available; – = magnitude equals zero; 0 = magnitude is less than half of unit employed; $ = United States dollars; ADB = Asian Development Bank.

Note: For any given year, a negative value for net inflows of foreign direct investment shows that the value of disinvestment by foreign investors was more than the value of capital newly invested in the reporting economy.

a Includes only reporting economies with data corresponding to the year heading.

Sources: International Monetary Fund. Balance of Payments and International Investment Position Statistics. https://data.imf.org/ (accessed 30 June 2025) and World Bank. World Development Indicators. https://databank.worldbank.org/ (accessed 30 June 2025). For Taipei,China: Central bank of Taipei,China.

Table 2.4.7: Foreign Direct Investment, Net Inflows—Proportion of Economic Activity
(% of GDP)

ADB Regional Member	2010	2015	2019	2020	2021	2022	2023	2024
Developing ADB Member Economies								
Central and West Asia[a]	**2.3**	**2.5**	**1.5**	**1.4**	**1.4**	**1.3**	**1.2**	**...**
Afghanistan	1.2	0.8	0.1	0.1	...	...	...	...
Armenia	5.7	1.7	0.7	0.5	2.6	5.0	2.4	0.5
Azerbaijan	6.3	7.6	3.1	1.2	-3.1	-5.7	0.3	0.3
Georgia	7.4	11.4	7.9	3.4	6.7	9.2	6.8	4.0
Kazakhstan	5.0	3.6	2.1	4.2	2.3	2.3	2.2	-0.2
Kyrgyz Republic	9.9	17.2	4.3	-4.9	2.4	0.5	...	...
Pakistan	1.0	0.6	0.7	0.7	0.6	0.4	0.6	0.7
Tajikistan	1.7	5.5	2.6	1.3	0.9	1.6	1.1	2.1
Türkiye	1.2	2.2	1.2	1.0	1.5	1.5	1.0	...
Turkmenistan	16.1	8.5	...	...	...	...	...	...
Uzbekistan	3.3	1.2	3.4	2.6	2.9	2.9	2.1	2.5
East Asia[a]	**4.2**	**3.1**	**1.5**	**2.2**	**2.4**	**1.7**	**0.9**	**0.7**
China, People's Republic of	3.9	2.1	1.3	1.7	1.9	1.0	0.3	0.1
Hong Kong, China	36.2	58.5	16.1	34.0	37.2	34.1	32.0	28.7
Korea, Republic of	0.8	0.3	0.6	0.5	1.1	1.4	1.0	0.8
Mongolia	23.5	0.8	17.2	12.9	14.2	14.6	11.1	...
Taipei,China	0.6	0.4	1.3	0.9	0.7	1.5	0.9	1.4
South Asia[a]	**1.6**	**1.9**	**1.6**	**2.1**	**1.3**	**1.3**	**0.7**	**0.7**
Bangladesh	0.9	1.2	0.5	0.4	0.4	0.4	0.3	0.3
Bhutan	4.4	0.3	0.5	-0.1	0.2	0.3	0.4	...
India	1.6	2.1	1.8	2.4	1.4	1.5	0.8	0.7
Maldives	8.4	7.2	16.8	11.9	12.3	11.9	11.1	...
Nepal	0.5	0.2	0.5	0.4	0.5	0.2	0.2	0.2
Sri Lanka	0.8	0.8	0.8	0.5	0.7	1.2	0.9	...
Southeast Asia[a]	**5.4**	**5.2**	**5.5**	**4.1**	**6.9**	**6.3**	**5.4**	**6.0**
Brunei Darussalam	3.0 (2009)	1.3	2.8	4.7	1.5	-1.7	-0.4	0.2
Cambodia	9.9	7.5	10.1	10.4	9.5	9.1	9.4	9.5
Indonesia	2.0	2.3	2.2	1.8	1.8	1.9	1.6	1.7
Lao People's Democratic Republic	4.1	7.5	4.0	5.1	5.6	4.7	11.9	...
Malaysia	4.3	3.3	2.5	1.2	5.4	3.7	2.0	3.7
Myanmar	1.7 (2012)	6.5	2.5	–	–	–	...	...
Philippines	0.5	1.8	2.3	1.9	3.0	2.3	2.0	1.9
Singapore	23.1	22.7	28.3	22.8	33.3	29.4	26.2	27.8
Thailand	4.3	2.2	1.0	-0.9	3.0	2.4	1.3	1.9
Timor-Leste[b]	3.4	2.7	-9.4	-41.4	-23.5	-16.1	3.5	...
Viet Nam	5.4	4.9	4.8	4.6	4.3	4.3	4.3	4.2
The Pacific[a]	**2.1**	**1.2**	**2.2**	**1.4**	**1.4**	**3.4**	**...**	**...**
Cook Islands	...	...	...	...	...	...	...	...
Fiji	5.7	4.4	5.9	5.4	9.5	2.1	...	...
Kiribati	-3.6	-0.4	-0.3	1.1	0.4	1.6	1.7	...
Marshall Islands	-5.8	-2.9	2.2	1.3	0.2	...	...	...
Micronesia, Federated States of	–	6.4 (2014)	...	...	...	...	...	...
Nauru	–	–	1.8	-2.7	3.8	-5.9	1.0	...
Niue	...	...	...	...	...	...	...	...
Palau	1.5	12.2	15.9	16.6	13.3	28.2	...	...
Papua New Guinea	0.2	0.1	1.4	0.5	-0.1	3.8	0.3	...
Samoa	0.0	3.3	-0.2	0.5	1.0	0.5	0.2	0.3
Solomon Islands	18.5	2.5	2.0	0.6	1.8	2.6	...	...
Tonga	1.3	3.4	-1.2	0.8	0.0	0.6	1.0	...
Tuvalu	1.4	–	–	–	–	–	...	...
Vanuatu	10.0	4.4	5.7	4.5	4.4	1.0	...	...
Developed ADB Member Economies[a]	**0.6**	**0.9**	**1.2**	**1.3**	**1.0**	**2.1**	**0.9**	**1.2**
Australia	3.0	3.8	2.9	1.3	2.0	4.4	1.9	3.1
Japan	0.1	0.1	0.8	1.2	0.7	1.1	0.5	0.4
New Zealand	0.2	-0.0	1.4	1.9	1.8	3.3	1.4	...
DEVELOPING ADB MEMBER ECONOMIES[a]	**3.8**	**3.2**	**2.0**	**2.4**	**2.7**	**2.1**	**1.5**	**...**
ALL ADB REGIONAL MEMBERS[a]	**2.7**	**2.7**	**1.9**	**2.1**	**2.4**	**2.1**	**1.4**	**...**

... = data not available, – = magnitude equals zero, (-/+) 0.0 = magnitude is less than half of unit employed, ADB = Asian Development Bank, GDP = gross domestic product.

a Aggregate percentages calculated using only reporting economies with data available for both foreign direct investment and GDP in the years specified in the column headings.

b From September 2019, following the new Timor-Leste Australia Maritime Boundary Treaty, oil revenue from the Joint Petroleum Development Area is included in the national accounts. The National Institute of Statistics Timor-Leste (INETL) disaggregates the accounts into 'oil' and 'non-oil' components. To better assess the performance of the domestic economy, this publication presents GDP on a non-oil basis, which reflects the primary analytical approach used by INETL.

Sources: Economies' official sources; International Monetary Fund. Balance of Payments and International Investment Position Statistics. https://data.imf.org/ (accessed 30 June 2025) and World Bank. World Development Indicators. https://databank.worldbank.org/ (accessed 30 June 2025). For Taipei,China: Central bank of Taipei,China.

External Trade

Table 2.4.8: Merchandise Exports
($ million)

ADB Regional Member	2010	2015	2019	2020	2021	2022	2023	2024
Developing ADB Member Economies								
Central and West Asia[a]	**248,403**	**267,193**	**320,492**	**287,419**	**375,350**	**461,662**	**450,677**	**464,188**
Afghanistan	388	571	864	777	850 |	1,838	...	...
Armenia	1,041	1,485	2,649	2,537	3,016	5,419	8,552	...
Azerbaijan	26,374	15,586	19,868	12,588	21,692	42,207	29,202	25,992
Georgia	1,677	2,204	3,797	3,341	4,242	5,582	6,086	6,560
Kazakhstan	60,271	45,956	58,066	47,541	60,321	84,593	79,139	81,618
Kyrgyz Republic	1,756	1,483	1,986	1,973	2,752	2,255	3,385	3,828*
Pakistan	18,986	23,329	20,850	20,822	24,811	27,633	24,466	31,137
Tajikistan	1,195	891	1,174	1,407	2,150	2,142	2,449	1,947*
Türkiye	114,012	151,016	181,188	171,049	228,571	255,534	257,381	262,455
Turkmenistan	9,679	12,164	12,592*	...	10,282	14,727	13,310	13,313
Uzbekistan	13,023	12,508	17,459	15,102	16,663	19,733	24,870	26,948
East Asia	**2,713,931**	**3,552,572**	**3,887,606**	**3,961,142**	**5,053,978**	**5,296,691**	**4,992,803**	**5,333,206**
China, People's Republic of	1,577,754	2,273,468	2,499,482	2,589,952	3,316,022	3,544,434	3,379,044	3,577,222
Hong Kong, China	390,134	465,092	509,026	506,303	638,170	578,650	533,541	582,069
Korea, Republic of	466,384	526,757	542,233	512,498	644,400	683,585	632,226	683,609
Mongolia	2,909	4,669	7,620	7,576	9,241	12,539	15,187	15,783
Taipei,China	276,750	282,585	329,246	344,813	446,144	477,483	432,806	474,522
South Asia	**274,793**	**310,212**	**368,206**	**335,089**	**477,103**	**522,723**	**492,632**	**496,258**
Bangladesh	16,099	30,588	39,404	32,087	36,783	46,376	40,524	39,216
Bhutan	535	561	610	632	718	736	676	698
India	248,648	267,550	315,229	291,371	425,745	460,731	438,175*	442,345*
Maldives	62	144	158	157	150	156	162	92
Nepal	830	833	862	826	1,195	1,598	1,189	1,139
Sri Lanka	8,618	10,536	11,943	10,016	12,512	13,126	11,906	12,767
Southeast Asia[a]	**1,048,328**	**1,172,149**	**1,422,434**	**1,394,639**	**1,725,181**	**1,957,947**	**1,816,081**	**1,938,998**
Brunei Darussalam	8,887	6,338	7,247	6,611	10,518	14,231	10,994	11,253
Cambodia	3,903	9,336	14,986	19,055	19,521	23,179	23,564	26,752
Indonesia	157,779	150,366	167,683	163,192	231,609	291,690	258,774	264,703*
Lao People's Democratic Republic	1,746	3,653	5,806	6,115	7,695	8,198	8,370*	9,386*
Malaysia	198,325	199,041	240,212	234,050	299,525	352,189	312,590	329,445
Myanmar	8,872	11,432	18,118	16,937	...	...	...	...
Philippines	51,498	58,827	70,927	65,215	74,693	79,574	73,617	73,269*
Singapore	352,553	357,730	390,361	373,725	457,081	514,966	475,439	504,781
Thailand	192,511	213,397	242,686	226,861	270,977	284,918	280,948*	296,814*
Timor-Leste	16	11	141	249	458	351	127	...
Viet Nam	72,237	162,017	264,267	282,629	336,167	371,715	354,721	405,532
The Pacific[a]	**7,012**	**10,064**	**12,721**	**10,624**	**12,421**	**16,403**	**14,726**	**...**
Cook Islands	5	14	18	19	15	11	7	13
Fiji	837	982	1,027	828	873*	1,053*	1,068*	1,133*
Kiribati	4	10	12	9	9	9	8	8*
Marshall Islands	44	60	69	72	63	106	...	...
Micronesia, Federated States of	30	40	41	125	115	...	...	...
Nauru	32	11	14	12	31	43	38*	...
Niue	1	1	2	1	1	1	1	...
Palau	16	18	4	7	2	8	7	5
Papua New Guinea	5,737	8,418	10,947	9,073	10,842	14,615	12,838	13,393*
Samoa	23	34	51	38	29	41	43	42
Solomon Islands	227	421	461	379	371	340	431	510
Tonga	8	18	20	15	16	13	10	...
Tuvalu	1	0	0	0	0	0	0	0
Vanuatu	48	39	56	46	54	50	54	70*
Developed ADB Member Economies	**1,011,217**	**846,359**	**1,016,296**	**928,709**	**1,146,148**	**1,204,140**	**1,131,273**	**1,091,506**
Australia	212,027	187,525	271,101	249,626	344,170	411,930	371,131	341,164
Japan	767,826	624,681	705,733	640,594	757,067	746,578	718,003	707,495
New Zealand	31,365	34,152	39,463	38,489	44,910	45,632	42,139	42,847
DEVELOPING ADB MEMBER ECONOMIES[a]	**4,292,466**	**5,312,190**	**6,011,459**	**5,988,913**	**7,644,032**	**8,255,426**	**7,766,920**	**8,248,096**
ALL ADB REGIONAL MEMBERS[a]	**5,303,684**	**6,158,549**	**7,027,755**	**6,917,622**	**8,790,180**	**9,459,567**	**8,898,193**	**9,339,602**
WORLD[b]	**15,226,919**	**16,443,471**	**18,843,030**	**17,402,634**	**22,093,720**	**24,702,224**	**23,548,298**	**24,061,710**

... = data not available; | = marks break in series; 0 = magnitude is less than half of unit employed; * = provisional, preliminary, estimate; $ = United States dollars; ADB = Asian Development Bank.

a For estimating aggregates, imputation was done for economies with missing data by substituting available data from the nearest years.
b The world aggregate includes estimates derived from reports of partner economies for nonreporting and slow-reporting economies.

Sources: Economies' official sources; and International Monetary Fund (IMF). International Financial Statistics. http://data.imf.org/ (accessed 30 June 2025).
For "World": IMF. International Trade in Goods (by partner country/economy). https://data.imf.org/ (accessed 30 June 2025).

Table 2.4.9: Growth Rates of Merchandise Exports
(%)

ADB Regional Member	2010	2015	2019	2020	2021	2022	2023	2024
Developing ADB Member Economies								
Central and West Asia[a]	**18.6**	**-21.7**	**1.4**	**-10.3**	**30.6**	**23.0**	**-2.4**	**3.0**
Afghanistan	-3.7	0.2	-1.3	-10.1	9.4 |	116.2	...	...
Armenia	46.6	-4.0	9.8	-4.2	18.9	79.7	57.8	...
Azerbaijan	25.3	-44.8	-4.5	-36.6	72.3	94.6	-30.8	-11.0
Georgia	48.0	-23.0	12.3	-12.0	27.0	31.6	9.0	7.8
Kazakhstan	39.5	-42.2	-5.0	-18.1	26.9	40.2	-6.4	3.1
Kyrgyz Republic	5.0	-21.3	8.1	-0.7	39.5	-18.1	50.1	13.1*
Pakistan	12.1	-8.7	-0.6	-0.1	19.2	11.4	-11.5	27.3
Tajikistan	18.3	-8.9	9.5	19.8	52.8	-0.4	14.3	-20.5*
Türkiye	11.5	-9.4	1.8	-5.6	33.6	11.8	0.7	2.0
Turkmenistan	3.8	-38.5	8.1*	...	...	43.2	-9.6	0.0
Uzbekistan	10.6	-7.7	24.8	-13.5	10.3	18.4	26.0	8.4
East Asia	**29.8**	**-4.3**	**-1.9**	**1.9**	**27.6**	**4.8**	**-5.7**	**6.8**
China, People's Republic of	31.3	-2.9	0.5	3.6	28.0	6.9	-4.7	5.9
Hong Kong, China	22.5	-1.8	-4.0	-0.5	26.0	-9.3	-7.8	9.1
Korea, Republic of	28.3	-8.0	-10.4	-5.5	25.7	6.1	-7.5	8.1
Mongolia	54.3	-19.1	8.7	-0.6	22.0	35.7	21.1	3.9
Taipei,China	35.1	-11.2	-1.4	4.7	29.4	7.0	-9.4	9.6
South Asia	**38.2**	**-12.2**	**-4.7**	**-9.0**	**42.4**	**9.6**	**-5.8**	**0.7**
Bangladesh	3.7	2.6	10.4	-18.6	14.6	26.1	-12.6	-3.2
Bhutan	6.5	4.1	6.3	3.7	13.6	2.5	-8.1	3.2
India	42.3	-13.9	-6.6	-7.6	46.1	8.2	-4.9*	1.0*
Maldives	-63.6	-0.6	-13.1	-0.2	-4.5	3.7	3.7	-43.0
Nepal	-4.9	-11.6	15.5	-4.3	44.7	33.7	-25.6	-4.2
Sri Lanka	21.7	-5.3	0.4	-16.1	24.9	4.9	-9.3	7.2
Southeast Asia[a]	**29.7**	**-9.7**	**-1.7**	**-2.0**	**23.7**	**13.5**	**-7.2**	**6.8**
Brunei Darussalam	23.9	-40.2	10.2	-8.8	59.1	35.3	-22.7	2.4
Cambodia	24.4	14.3	15.6	27.2	2.4	18.7	1.7	13.5
Indonesia	35.4	-14.6	-6.8	-2.7	41.9	25.9	-11.3	2.3*
Lao People's Democratic Republic	65.9	11.5	7.4	5.3	25.8	6.5	2.1*	12.1*
Malaysia	26.5	-14.9	-3.4	-2.6	28.0	17.6	-11.2	5.4
Myanmar	32.4	-0.2	8.5	-6.5	...	...	...	...
Philippines	34.0	-5.3	2.3	-8.1	14.5	6.5	-7.5	-0.5*
Singapore	30.5	-13.8	-5.2	-4.3	22.3	12.7	-7.7	6.2
Thailand	27.2	-5.8	-3.4	-6.5	19.4	5.1	-1.4*	5.6*
Timor-Leste	100.0	-21.4	513.0	76.6	83.9	-23.4	-63.8	...
Viet Nam	26.5	7.9	8.4	6.9	18.9	10.6	-4.6	14.3
The Pacific[a]	**30.4**	**-6.3**	**9.3**	**-16.5**	**16.9**	**32.1**	**-10.2**	**...**
Cook Islands	88.0	-20.3	0.6	10.8	-24.4	-28.0	-31.0	77.8
Fiji	25.1	-19.5	2.0	-19.4	5.5*	20.6*	1.4*	6.1*
Kiribati	-38.0	-1.5	49.3	-24.2	-1.6	-6.4	-6.0	5.8*
Marshall Islands	27.4	-13.9	8.1	3.6	-12.4	0.7	...	...
Micronesia, Federated States of	63.5	23.0	-13.2	208.7	-8.5	...	...	...
Nauru	249.5	-51.7	49.7	-13.6	146.3	40.2	-12.4*	...
Niue	1.0	-20.2	-7.7	-66.5	39.2	28.2	25.1	...
Palau	15.9	-5.3	-4.4	55.8	-70.1	295.0	-12.0	-23.7
Papua New Guinea	30.9	-4.2	11.4	-17.1	19.5	34.8	-12.2	4.3*
Samoa	114.4	23.8	18.9	-24.3	-24.3	41.3	5.9	-2.5
Solomon Islands	37.4	-7.6	-14.0	-17.7	-2.0	-8.5	26.8	18.4
Tonga	7.1	-6.5	56.1	-24.0	2.8	-15.7	-22.5	...
Tuvalu	76.5	-12.0	51.6	-83.0	591.0	-84.2	226.3	-88.6
Vanuatu	-14.8	-33.5	-9.0	-17.6	17.3	-7.7	8.8	29.7*
Developed ADB Member Economies	**33.6**	**-12.9**	**-1.8**	**-8.6**	**23.4**	**5.1**	**-6.1**	**-3.5**
Australia	38.3	-21.8	5.3	-7.9	37.9	19.7	-9.9	-8.1
Japan	32.6	-9.5	-4.4	-9.2	18.2	-1.4	-3.8	-1.5
New Zealand	26.6	-17.8	-0.4	-2.5	16.7	1.6	-7.7	1.7
DEVELOPING ADB MEMBER ECONOMIES[a]	**29.6**	**-7.1**	**-1.8**	**-0.4**	**27.6**	**8.0**	**-5.9**	**6.2**
ALL ADB REGIONAL MEMBERS[a]	**30.3**	**-7.9**	**-1.8**	**-1.6**	**27.1**	**7.6**	**-5.9**	**5.0**
WORLD[b]	**22.8**	**-12.6**	**-2.7**	**-7.6**	**27.0**	**11.8**	**-4.7**	**2.2**

... = data not available; 0.0 = magnitude is less than half of unit employed; | = marks break in series; * = provisional, preliminary, estimate; ADB = Asian Development Bank.

Note: Growth rates are based on the value of exports in United States dollars.

a For estimating aggregates, imputation was done for economies with missing data by substituting available data from the nearest years.
b The world aggregate includes estimates derived from reports of partner economies for nonreporting and slow-reporting economies.

Sources: Economies' official sources; and International Monetary Fund (IMF). International Financial Statistics. http://data.imf.org/ (accessed 30 June 2025).
For "World": Asian Development Bank estimates using data from the IMF's International Trade in Goods (by partner country/economy). https://data.imf.org/ (accessed 30 June 2025).

External Trade

Table 2.4.10: Merchandise Imports
($ million)

ADB Regional Member	2010	2015	2019	2020	2021	2022	2023	2024
Developing ADB Member Economies								
Central and West Asia[a]	**294,783**	**350,795**	**371,048**	**366,363**	**444,726**	**580,606**	**583,246**	**579,748**
Afghanistan	5,154	7,723	6,777	6,538	5,308 |	7,006	...	...
Armenia	3,749	3,239	5,538	4,564	5,362	8,776	12,758	...
Azerbaijan	6,662	9,774	11,335	10,077	10,419	13,509	16,397	17,167
Georgia	5,236	7,304	9,518	8,049	10,099	13,548	15,604	16,924
Kazakhstan	31,127	30,568	39,709	38,929	41,415	50,935	60,412	59,787
Kyrgyz Republic	3,223	4,154	4,989	3,719	5,580	9,803	12,518	12,214*
Pakistan	34,169	45,190	49,610	43,437	55,139	69,671	48,057	55,575
Tajikistan	2,657	3,436	3,349	3,151	4,210	5,168	5,880	7,008*
Türkiye	185,427	212,940	210,524	220,496	275,437	364,234	358,201	344,233
Turkmenistan	8,204	14,051	5,406*	...	6,250	7,188	7,754	8,090
Uzbekistan	9,176	12,417	24,292	21,154	25,508	30,768	38,659	38,986
East Asia	**2,512,923**	**2,876,639**	**3,437,056**	**3,375,368**	**4,365,910**	**4,502,344**	**4,153,579**	**4,253,126**
China, People's Republic of	1,396,244	1,679,565	2,078,409	2,065,962	2,679,412	2,706,507	2,556,941	2,585,067
Hong Kong, China	433,102	522,001	563,487	550,421	682,828	629,192	593,262	630,729
Korea, Republic of	425,212	436,499	503,343	467,633	615,093	731,370	642,572	631,767
Mongolia	3,200	3,798	6,128	5,299	6,846	8,704	9,250	11,612
Taipei,China	255,165	234,777	285,689	286,054	381,731	426,571	351,554	393,950
South Asia	**409,681**	**455,084**	**568,858**	**473,064**	**716,231**	**847,078**	**776,956**	**824,234**
Bangladesh	21,245	37,528	55,159	50,636	60,483	77,654	65,989	60,783
Bhutan[b]	810	977	1,012	939	887	1,325	1,407	1,238
India	368,166	388,189	477,270	393,519	618,628	731,485	677,110*	727,855*
Maldives	909	1,890	2,875	1,828	2,551	3,492	3,479	3,627
Nepal	5,110	7,565	12,597	10,113	13,035	15,339	12,199	11,912
Sri Lanka	13,441	18,935	19,945	16,029	20,649	17,783	16,771	18,819
Southeast Asia[a]	**934,493**	**1,089,693**	**1,369,411**	**1,249,854**	**1,592,458**	**1,842,672**	**1,684,352**	**1,842,672**
Brunei Darussalam	2,536	3,235	5,100	5,319	7,234	9,184	7,451	7,301
Cambodia[b]	6,588	13,285	22,242	21,066	30,726	32,005	26,551	31,247
Indonesia	135,663	142,695	171,276	141,569	196,190	237,447	221,886	233,659*
Lao People's Democratic Republic[b]	2,060	5,675	6,272	5,370	6,275	7,244	7,649*	8,663*
Malaysia	164,177	175,593	205,049	190,433	238,299	293,976	265,654	299,544
Myanmar	4,866	16,913	18,611	17,965	...	...	...	...
Philippines	54,933	71,067	111,593	89,812	116,885	137,221	126,209	127,597*
Singapore	312,669	307,968	358,985	328,661	406,318	475,413	422,500	457,524
Thailand	165,988	187,079	216,052	186,372	239,054	271,650	261,317*	277,597*
Timor-Leste	175	406	536	497	542	786	812	...
Viet Nam	84,839	165,776	253,697	262,791	332,970	359,780	326,358	380,764
The Pacific[a]	**7,058**	**7,292**	**9,080**	**7,396**	**8,795**	**11,485**	**11,419**	**...**
Cook Islands	91	110	136	105	119	148	174	175
Fiji	1,806	2,268	2,358	1,731	2,022*	2,999*	3,103*	3,097*
Kiribati	73	103	112	109	146	167	192	227*
Marshall Islands	125	112	200	126	135	138	...	...
Micronesia, Federated States of	168	160	215	213	254	...	...	...
Nauru	13	93	63	68	96	88	70*	...
Niue	9	13	14	12	13	16	19	...
Palau	103	156	193	150	156	208	196	249
Papua New Guinea[b]	3,522	2,837	4,223	3,584	4,368	5,880	5,402	4,574*
Samoa	280	298	357	285	338	405	429	448
Solomon Islands	405	485	553	452	526	615	713	688
Tonga	158	209	267	229	246	269	268	...
Tuvalu	22	37	33	34	34	34	43	39
Vanuatu	284	411	357	300	340	266	419	422*
Developed ADB Member Economies	**915,836**	**885,006**	**977,235**	**875,951**	**1,071,320**	**1,245,348**	**1,111,246**	**1,074,073**
Australia	193,071	200,643	213,797	202,055	248,068	289,250	274,961	283,726
Japan	692,242	647,744	721,032	636,957	773,318	901,177	785,780	742,742
New Zealand	30,523	36,619	42,405	36,939	49,933	54,920	50,505	47,604
DEVELOPING ADB MEMBER ECONOMIES[a]	**4,158,938**	**4,779,502**	**5,755,453**	**5,472,045**	**7,128,121**	**7,784,185**	**7,209,551**	**7,510,447**
ALL ADB REGIONAL MEMBERS[a]	**5,074,774**	**5,664,507**	**6,732,688**	**6,347,996**	**8,199,441**	**9,029,533**	**8,320,797**	**8,584,520**
WORLD[c]	**15,457,220**	**16,531,494**	**19,269,514**	**17,655,417**	**22,408,276**	**25,412,805**	**24,059,152**	**24,574,008**

... = data not available; | = marks break in series; * = provisional, preliminary, estimate; $ = United States dollars; ADB = Asian Development Bank.

a For estimating aggregates, imputation was done for economies with missing data by substituting available data from the nearest years.

b The Key Indicators Database features a longer time series on trade in goods. The compilation methodology shifted from cost, insurance, and freight to free on board from 2004 onward for Bhutan; from 2005 onward for Cambodia; from 2017 onward for the Lao People's Democratic Republic; and from 2010 onward for Papua New Guinea.

c The world aggregate includes estimates derived from reports of partner economies for nonreporting and slow-reporting economies.

Sources: Economies' official sources; and International Monetary Fund (IMF). International Financial Statistics. http://data.imf.org/ (accessed 30 June 2025). For "World": IMF. International Trade in Goods (by partner country/economy). https://data.imf.org/ (accessed 30 June 2025).

Table 2.4.11: Growth Rates of Merchandise Imports
(%)

ADB Regional Member	2010	2015	2019	2020	2021	2022	2023	2024
Developing ADB Member Economies								
Central and West Asia[a]	**21.0**	**-14.2**	**-2.4**	**-1.3**	**21.4**	**30.6**	**0.5**	**-0.6**
Afghanistan	54.5	-0.1	-8.5	-3.5	-18.8 |	32.0	...	...
Armenia	12.9	-26.8	11.3	-17.6	17.5	63.7	45.4	...
Azerbaijan	6.9	4.7	3.5	-11.1	3.4	29.7	21.4	4.7
Georgia	17.0	-15.1	1.7	-15.4	25.5	34.2	15.2	8.5
Kazakhstan	9.6	-26.0	18.0	-2.0	6.4	23.0	18.6	-1.0
Kyrgyz Republic	6.0	-27.6	-5.7	-25.5	50.1	75.7	27.7	-2.4*
Pakistan	2.5	-1.3	-9.7	-12.4	26.9	26.4	-31.0	15.6
Tajikistan	3.4	-20.1	6.3	-5.9	33.6	22.8	13.8	19.2*
Türkiye	32.0	-15.1	-6.7	4.7	24.9	32.2	-1.7	-3.9
Turkmenistan	-8.8	-15.5	1.6*	...	...	15.0	7.9	4.3
Uzbekistan	-2.8	-11.2	25.0	-12.9	20.6	20.6	25.6	0.8
East Asia	**35.5**	**-13.2**	**-3.6**	**-1.8**	**29.3**	**3.1**	**-7.7**	**2.4**
China, People's Republic of	38.8	-14.3	-2.7	-0.6	29.7	1.0	-5.5	1.1
Hong Kong, China	24.7	-4.1	-6.4	-2.3	24.1	-7.9	-5.7	6.3
Korea, Republic of	31.6	-16.9	-6.0	-7.1	31.5	18.9	-12.1	-1.7
Mongolia	49.7	-27.5	4.3	-13.5	29.2	27.2	6.3	25.5
Taipei,China	44.4	-16.2	0.3	0.1	33.4	11.7	-17.6	12.1
South Asia	**29.1**	**-11.6**	**-7.8**	**-16.8**	**51.4**	**18.3**	**-8.3**	**6.1**
Bangladesh	5.1	2.5	3.0	-8.2	19.4	28.4	-15.0	-7.9
Bhutan	40.7	4.5	4.2	-7.2	-5.6	49.4	6.2	-12.0
India	30.7	-13.4	-9.2	-17.5	57.2	18.2	-7.4*	7.5*
Maldives	-5.6	-4.9	-2.6	-36.4	39.5	36.9	-0.4	4.2
Nepal	39.3	3.3	10.2	-19.7	28.9	17.7	-20.5	-2.4
Sri Lanka	31.8	-2.5	-10.2	-19.6	28.8	-13.9	-5.7	12.2
Southeast Asia[a]	**31.1**	**-11.0**	**-2.6**	**-8.7**	**27.4**	**15.7**	**-8.6**	**9.4**
Brunei Darussalam	5.6	-10.0	22.3	4.3	36.0	26.9	-18.9	-2.0
Cambodia	35.0	10.5	18.3	-5.3	45.9	4.2	-17.0	17.7
Indonesia	40.1	-19.9	-9.2	-17.3	38.6	21.0	-6.6	5.3*
Lao People's Democratic Republic	41.0	14.1	-0.7	-14.4	16.8	15.4	5.6*	13.3*
Malaysia	33.1	-15.9	-6.0	-7.1	25.1	23.4	-9.6	12.8
Myanmar	11.0	4.3	-3.8	-3.5	...	...	...	...
Philippines	27.5	8.7	-1.1	-19.5	30.1	17.4	-8.0	1.1*
Singapore	26.9	-18.5	-3.2	-8.4	23.6	17.0	-11.1	8.3
Thailand	38.2	-10.7	-5.6	-13.7	28.3	13.6	-3.8*	6.2*
Timor-Leste	-1.7	-9.6	3.3	-7.3	9.1	45.0	3.3	...
Viet Nam	21.3	12.1	6.9	3.6	26.7	8.1	-9.3	16.7
The Pacific[a]	**18.9**	**-14.8**	**2.2**	**-18.5**	**18.9**	**30.6**	**-0.6**	**...**
Cook Islands	11.2	-9.3	1.1	-23.0	13.3	24.5	17.3	0.5
Fiji	17.0	-14.6	-12.1	-26.6	16.8*	48.3*	3.5*	-0.2*
Kiribati	5.4	-3.7	8.7	-2.4	34.4	14.1	15.0	18.0*
Marshall Islands	-21.2	-10.7	58.6	-37.2	7.5	0.0	...	...
Micronesia, Federated States of	-1.8	-0.3	8.6	-0.9	19.2	...	...	...
Nauru	-47.3	-18.0	-1.8	9.2	40.8	-8.1	-20.9*	...
Niue	28.5	-15.4	-23.7	-14.2	13.9	17.5	19.3	...
Palau	9.3	4.4	9.3	-22.4	4.3	33.0	-5.7	27.3
Papua New Guinea	23.0	-22.4	10.7	-15.1	21.9	34.6	-8.1	-15.3*
Samoa	36.6	-12.7	7.2	-20.1	18.4	19.9	6.0	4.3
Solomon Islands	51.2	-4.1	-6.7	-18.3	16.5	16.9	15.9	-3.5
Tonga	10.3	-4.4	17.2	-14.4	7.7	9.2	-0.2	...
Tuvalu	59.2	66.4	28.1	3.9	1.0	-1.3	27.3	-8.0
Vanuatu	-2.5	12.9	-8.6	-15.9	13.3	-21.9	57.7	0.8*
Developed ADB Member Economies	**25.1**	**-18.2**	**-4.2**	**-10.4**	**22.3**	**16.2**	**-10.8**	**-3.3**
Australia	23.4	-11.9	-5.9	-5.5	22.8	16.6	-4.9	3.2
Japan	25.8	-20.1	-3.7	-11.7	21.4	16.5	-12.8	-5.5
New Zealand	21.5	-13.9	-3.4	-12.9	35.2	10.0	-8.0	-5.7
DEVELOPING ADB MEMBER ECONOMIES[a]	**32.7**	**-12.6**	**-3.7**	**-4.9**	**30.3**	**9.2**	**-7.4**	**4.2**
ALL ADB REGIONAL MEMBERS[a]	**31.2**	**-13.5**	**-3.8**	**-5.7**	**29.2**	**10.1**	**-7.8**	**3.2**
WORLD[b]	**21.5**	**-12.5**	**-2.6**	**-8.4**	**26.9**	**13.4**	**-5.3**	**2.1**

... = data not available; | = marks break in series; 0.0 = magnitude is less than half of unit employed; * = provisional, preliminary, estimate; ADB = Asian Development Bank.

Note: Growth rates are based on the value of imports in United States dollars.

a For estimating aggregates, imputation was done for economies with missing data by substituting available data from the nearest years.
b The world aggregate includes estimates derived from reports of partner economies for nonreporting and slow-reporting economies.

Sources: Economies' official sources; and International Monetary Fund (IMF). International Financial Statistics. http://data.imf.org/ (accessed 30 June 2025).
For "World": Asian Development Bank estimates using data from the IMF's International Trade in Goods (by partner country/economy). https://data.imf.org/ (accessed 30 June 2025).

Table 2.4.12: Trade in Goods
(% of GDP)

ADB Regional Member	2010	2015	2019	2020	2021	2022	2023	2024
Developing ADB Member Economies								
Central and West Asia[a]	**41.9**	**39.0**	**46.6**	**...**	**...**	**...**	**...**	**...**
Afghanistan	34.5	40.2	40.4	36.3	33.2	63.9	...	...
Armenia	51.7	44.8	60.1	56.2	60.4	72.7	88.5	...
Azerbaijan	62.4	47.8	64.8	53.1	58.6	70.7	63.0	58.1
Georgia	55.6	62.5	75.5	71.1	76.1	76.6	70.5	69.5
Kazakhstan	61.7	41.5	53.8	50.5	51.6	60.1	53.3	49.4
Kyrgyz Republic	104.2	85.0	74.4	68.8	90.0	99.3	104.8	91.8
Pakistan	27.0	22.8	21.9	21.4	22.9	25.9	21.4	23.2
Tajikistan	68.3	52.3	54.5	56.0	71.1	68.2	68.0	63.0
Türkiye	38.5	42.1	51.5	54.4	61.5	68.3	55.0	...
Turkmenistan	79.2	73.1	...	...	...	...	**...**	...
Uzbekistan	44.6	28.9	62.1	54.6	54.5	56.1	**61.9**	57.4
East Asia	**64.8**	**47.0**	**42.3**	**41.3**	**44.2**	**46.0**	**42.8**	**43.5**
China, People's Republic of	48.0	35.0	31.4	31.0	33.0	34.1	32.3	32.5
Hong Kong, China	360.1	319.1	295.4	306.3	358.1	336.8	295.7	297.9
Korea, Republic of	74.7	62.6	59.7	56.2	64.9	78.7	69.3	70.4
Mongolia	84.9	72.9	96.8	96.7	105.2	124.1	120.2	116.2
Taipei,China	119.7	96.8	100.2	93.2	106.5	118.1	103.6	109.2
South Asia[a]	**36.4**	**30.7**	**28.1**	**25.4**	**31.9**	**34.2**	**30.0**	**...**
Bangladesh	28.6	29.2	26.9	22.1	23.4	27.0	23.6	22.2
Bhutan[b]	78.7	70.3	59.3	64.0	58.0	71.1	69.0	...
India	36.9	30.5	27.8	25.6	32.7	34.9	30.6	29.6
Maldives	37.5	49.4	53.1	53.6	51.6	59.3	52.8	...
Nepal	36.5	34.5	39.4	32.7	38.5	41.5	32.5	30.6
Sri Lanka	37.6	34.6	35.8	30.9	37.4	41.4	34.3	31.9
Southeast Asia[a]	**96.1**	**89.3**	**85.8**	**85.2**	**...**	**...**	**...**	**...**
Brunei Darussalam	83.3	74.0	91.7	99.4	126.7	140.4	122.2	120.0
Cambodia[b]	73.6	92.9	102.4	115.2	136.8	139.7	118.4	125.7
Indonesia	38.8	34.0	30.3	28.7	36.1	40.1	35.1	35.7
Lao People's Democratic Republic[b]	56.4	64.7	64.4	60.1	73.2	100.5	106.7	119.7
Malaysia	142.1	124.3	121.9	125.8	143.9	158.5	144.7	149.1
Myanmar	22.6 (2012)	45.3	53.0	42.8	...	...	...	...
Philippines	51.1	42.4	48.4	42.9	48.6	53.6	45.7	43.5
Singapore	277.4	216.1	199.2	201.1	197.8	194.6	177.7	175.8
Thailand	105.2	99.8	84.3	82.6	100.8	112.3	105.1	109.1
Timor-Leste[c]	21.7	26.2	40.1	47.2	64.0	67.8	52.1	...
Viet Nam	106.8	136.9	154.9	157.4	182.6	177.0	157.0	165.1
The Pacific[a]	**66.5**	**55.8**	**60.8**	**53.5**	**58.8**	**...**	**...**	**...**
Cook Islands	39.8	40.9	43.1	43.9	40.8	55.4	49.4	...
Fiji	84.2	69.4	62.2	57.7	67.3	81.5	76.6	...
Kiribati	42.0	60.8	56.6	47.8	56.4	66.5	67.3	...
Marshall Islands	104.5	93.5	115.7	81.6	76.5	96.1	...	...
Micronesia, Federated States of	67.8	64.0	64.8	90.7	94.1	...	...	...
Nauru	88.5	137.0	61.7	64.7	72.2	86.5	70.8	...
Niue	56.5	67.0	57.1	47.1	55.3	68.8	77.0	...
Palau	64.4	61.4	69.9	60.3	67.0	84.3	71.9	82.1
Papua New Guinea[b]	65.0	51.8	61.3	53.1	58.3	64.7	59.2	...
Samoa	43.3	40.2	44.7	39.0	40.9	47.6	41.6	39.1
Solomon Islands	70.4	69.2	62.6	54.1	58.9	61.0	...	...
Tonga	45.5	51.9	58.2	49.1	50.5	54.5	54.7	...
Tuvalu	72.7	105.7	60.7	64.5	55.3	53.1	...	...
Vanuatu	52.7	64.2	44.2	37.9	39.8	30.5	...	...
Developed ADB Member Economies[a]	**27.1**	**29.6**	**29.8**	**27.2**	**32.3**	**40.0**	**36.3**	**...**
Australia	33.9	31.8	35.8	33.1	37.8	43.4	37.9	35.4
Japan	25.4	28.6	27.9	25.3	30.4	38.7	35.7	36.0
New Zealand	42.1	39.7	38.4	35.4	37.3	40.3	36.3	...
DEVELOPING ADB MEMBER ECONOMIES[a]	**63.4**	**49.7**	**46.3**	**...**	**...**	**...**	**...**	**...**
ALL ADB REGIONAL MEMBERS[a]	**50.8**	**45.2**	**42.8**	**...**	**...**	**...**	**...**	**...**

... = data not available, ADB = Asian Development Bank, GDP = Gross Domestic Product.

Note: Trade in goods is calculated as the sum of merchandise exports and imports in United States dollars.

a For estimating aggregates prior to 2020, imputation was done for economies with missing data by substituting available data from the nearest years.

b The Key Indicators Database features a longer time series on trade in goods. The compilation methodology shifted from cost, insurance, and freight to free on board from 2004 onward for Bhutan; from 2005 onward for Cambodia; from 2017 onward for the Lao People's Democratic Republic; and from 2010 onward for Papua New Guinea.

c From September 2019, following the new Timor-Leste Australia Maritime Boundary Treaty, oil revenue from the Joint Petroleum Development Area is included in the national accounts. The National Institute of Statistics Timor-Leste (INETL) disaggregates the accounts into 'oil' and 'non-oil' components. To better assess the performance of the domestic economy, this publication presents GDP on a non-oil basis, which reflects the primary analytical approach used by INETL.

Sources: Economies' official sources; and International Monetary Fund. International Financial Statistics. http://data.imf.org/ (accessed 30 June 2025).

Table 2.4.13: International Trade in Goods (by partner country/economy): Merchandise Exports
(% of total merchandise exports)

To / From / ADB Regional Member	Asia and the Pacific		Europe		North and Central America		Middle East		South America		Africa		Rest of the World	
	2010	2024	2010	2024	2010	2024	2010	2024	2010	2024	2010	2024	2010	2024
Developing ADB Member Economies														
Central and West Asia[a]	**20.0**	**19.2**	**52.0**	**44.5**	**6.4**	**5.8**	**14.9**	**10.9**	**0.7**	**0.7**	**2.8**	**3.3**	**3.2**	**15.5**
Afghanistan	72.0	83.1	12.5	4.0	1.1	1.4	13.5	11.4	0.0	0.0	0.0	0.1	0.9	0.0
Armenia	10.5	25.2	67.0	30.8	11.5	0.5	9.5	43.3	0.3	0.0	0.1	0.0	1.1	0.2
Azerbaijan	20.5	22.9	59.1	71.7	9.5	0.5	10.7	3.5	0.0	0.4	0.3	1.1	0.0	0.0
Georgia	46.7	69.0	29.1	23.5	18.6	2.3	4.6	3.7	0.4	0.9	0.6	0.6	0.0	0.0
Kazakhstan	26.3	19.9	62.3	29.4	6.0	1.6	4.5	0.4	0.1	0.1	0.1	0.2	0.7	48.3
Kyrgyz Republic	20.7	31.0	46.9	62.2	6.8	0.2	19.9	3.8	0.0	0.0	0.0	0.0	5.7	2.7
Pakistan	27.6	26.3	21.9	35.0	16.3	20.0	13.0	10.9	1.4	1.1	5.1	6.5	14.7	0.2
Tajikistan	81.2	72.6	7.3	14.8	0.0	0.1	8.0	10.9	0.0	0.0	3.6	0.1	0.0	1.5
Türkiye	9.9	10.8	55.4	55.8	4.2	7.9	22.1	17.1	1.1	1.1	4.5	5.6	2.8	1.8
Turkmenistan	65.3	94.5	25.0	4.2	1.9	0.3	7.1	0.0	0.0	0.9	0.7	0.0	0.0	0.0
Uzbekistan	68.4	31.2	22.5	23.6	0.0	0.8	9.0	2.1	0.1	0.1	0.0	0.1	0.0	42.1
East Asia[a]	**53.3**	**53.1**	**18.3**	**16.9**	**18.3**	**19.0**	**4.1**	**4.6**	**2.8**	**3.1**	**2.5**	**3.2**	**0.7**	**0.1**
China, People's Republic of	44.2	45.6	22.4	20.6	21.7	19.5	4.6	5.7	3.4	4.2	3.3	4.4	0.4	0.1
Hong Kong, China	72.4	80.3	12.4	7.9	12.4	7.5	1.4	3.1	0.9	0.7	0.5	0.5	0.1	0.0
Korea, Republic of	57.4	59.3	14.0	12.0	15.1	23.0	5.7	2.8	3.4	1.4	2.6	1.5	1.9	0.0
Mongolia	82.2	88.1	7.1	5.9	4.9	0.2	0.4	0.4	0.0	0.1	0.0	0.0	5.5	5.3
Taipei,China	71.1	63.5	10.6	8.1	13.0	25.8	2.3	1.2	1.3	0.4	0.8	0.3	1.0	0.5
South Asia[a]	**32.9**	**26.6**	**22.5**	**25.7**	**13.7**	**21.1**	**19.4**	**14.7**	**2.4**	**2.6**	**6.4**	**8.0**	**2.8**	**1.3**
Bangladesh	12.1	16.7	46.5	57.6	23.4	21.5	2.1	2.0	0.4	1.2	0.7	0.8	14.7	0.1
Bhutan	99.7	99.2	0.1	0.6	0.1	0.1	0.0	0.0	0.0	0.0	0.0	0.0	0.0	0.1
India	34.6	27.4	20.3	22.8	12.7	21.1	21.2	16.3	2.6	2.8	7.1	8.9	1.5	0.8
Maldives	59.8	55.0	35.3	40.4	0.7	2.0	3.1	1.5	0.0	0.0	0.5	1.1	0.7	0.0
Nepal	73.0	69.0	10.8	8.7	7.0	10.1	0.4	0.3	0.1	0.0	0.1	0.2	8.5	11.7
Sri Lanka	22.4	19.8	34.2	27.2	21.4	22.8	9.9	7.3	1.0	1.6	0.9	1.7	10.2	19.6
Southeast Asia[a]	**69.6**	**65.8**	**12.3**	**10.6**	**11.7**	**18.5**	**3.1**	**2.6**	**1.0**	**1.0**	**1.9**	**1.4**	**0.4**	**0.2**
Brunei Darussalam	99.6	93.3	0.2	0.1	0.2	3.7	0.0	0.0	0.0	2.9	0.0	0.0	0.0	0.0
Cambodia	41.7	33.1	17.5	18.9	39.7	42.9	0.3	0.0	0.4	0.0	0.1	0.0	0.2	5.1
Indonesia	71.6	72.7	11.8	8.9	10.2	11.6	3.2	4.0	1.5	1.2	1.7	1.6	0.0	0.0
Lao People's Democratic Republic	93.0	94.9	5.4	4.2	1.2	0.8	0.4	0.0	0.0	0.0	0.1	0.0	0.0	0.0
Malaysia	70.6	71.2	11.5	8.8	11.1	15.3	4.3	2.3	0.7	0.5	1.7	1.9	0.1	0.0
Myanmar	95.4	72.6	1.3	18.1	0.1	3.6	1.7	1.1	0.1	0.3	1.3	1.3	0.1	3.1
Philippines	67.0	66.6	14.7	12.7	16.0	18.7	1.1	1.2	0.5	0.6	0.4	0.2	0.4	0.0
Singapore	74.6	76.8	10.5	7.8	9.8	11.1	2.1	2.0	0.5	0.5	1.8	1.7	0.6	0.1
Thailand	63.4	60.0	13.9	11.1	12.1	21.0	5.0	3.8	2.1	1.8	3.0	2.0	0.5	0.3
Timor-Leste	54.4	68.6	21.9	11.6	0.2	13.6	7.8	0.4	0.1	0.4	11.1	2.1	4.5	3.4
Viet Nam	51.6	46.7	21.4	15.7	22.4	33.5	1.7	2.2	1.1	1.4	1.5	0.5	0.4	0.0
The Pacific[a]	**67.6**	**75.1**	**21.7**	**11.5**	**3.7**	**2.6**	**0.1**	**0.5**	**0.1**	**0.2**	**0.2**	**2.8**	**6.7**	**7.1**
Cook Islands	78.9	90.9	0.0	0.0	2.0	0.4	0.0	0.0	0.0	0.0	0.0	0.0	19.1	8.7
Fiji	49.9	41.0	5.2	1.8	13.0	15.2	0.2	0.2	0.0	0.0	0.6	0.1	31.1	41.8
Kiribati	98.6	68.6	1.4	0.0	0.0	16.0	0.0	0.0	0.0	0.0	0.0	0.0	0.0	15.4
Marshall Islands	0.3	13.6	95.4	44.6	4.2	3.0	0.0	5.5	0.0	1.6	0.1	31.6	0.0	0.0
Micronesia, Federated States of	71.0	90.7	2.1	0.1	7.4	0.9	0.0	0.0	0.0	1.2	0.1	0.0	19.4	7.0
Nauru	97.6	76.5	0.2	0.1	0.6	2.2	1.2	0.4	0.0	1.9	0.4	18.8	0.0	0.0
Niue	...	...	...	...	...	...	...	...	...	...	...	...	...	...
Palau	91.4	2.8	1.9	86.7	6.4	6.5	0.2	1.2	0.1	0.1	0.0	0.0	0.0	2.6
Papua New Guinea	72.7	85.7	22.8	9.3	1.9	1.0	0.0	0.0	0.1	0.0	0.1	0.0	2.4	3.9
Samoa	96.9	70.5	0.0	0.0	3.0	13.2	0.0	0.0	0.0	0.0	0.0	0.0	0.1	16.3
Solomon Islands	81.5	74.8	17.7	23.9	0.4	0.2	0.0	0.0	0.0	0.2	0.0	0.0	0.4	0.8
Tonga	71.6	78.2	0.0	0.0	14.4	21.8	0.0	0.0	0.0	0.0	0.0	0.0	14.0	0.0
Tuvalu	74.9	71.1	14.8	9.1	5.5	4.2	0.8	1.1	2.1	14.1	2.0	0.3	0.0	0.0
Vanuatu	83.4	91.0	4.9	0.0	6.1	8.8	1.1	0.0	0.0	0.0	0.0	0.0	4.6	0.2
Developed ADB Member Economies[a]	**63.6**	**65.3**	**12.5**	**10.0**	**16.9**	**18.1**	**3.4**	**3.6**	**1.6**	**1.1**	**1.4**	**1.0**	**0.5**	**0.8**
Australia	80.2	82.9	8.7	5.7	5.0	5.4	2.9	2.6	1.0	0.6	1.3	0.7	0.9	2.2
Japan	58.9	56.7	13.6	12.2	20.5	24.4	3.5	4.1	1.8	1.4	1.3	1.1	0.3	0.0
New Zealand	65.8	66.1	11.9	8.4	11.2	15.5	4.8	4.5	1.7	0.7	2.6	2.2	2.1	2.4
DEVELOPING ADB MEMBER ECONOMIES[a]	**54.3**	**52.4**	**18.9**	**17.7**	**15.7**	**18.2**	**5.3**	**5.1**	**2.2**	**2.4**	**2.6**	**3.1**	**0.9**	**1.2**
ALL ADB REGIONAL MEMBERS[a]	**56.1**	**53.9**	**17.7**	**16.8**	**16.0**	**18.2**	**5.0**	**4.9**	**2.1**	**2.3**	**2.4**	**2.9**	**0.8**	**1.1**
WORLD[a]	**32.1**	**34.0**	**39.0**	**35.6**	**17.1**	**19.3**	**4.6**	**4.5**	**2.8**	**2.5**	**2.8**	**2.7**	**1.6**	**1.3**

... = data not available, 0.0 = magnitude is less than half of unit employed, ADB = Asian Development Bank.

a Aggregates include estimates derived from reports of partner economies for nonreporting and slow-reporting economies.

Sources: Asian Development Bank estimates using data from the International Monetary Fund's International Trade in Goods (by partner country/economy). https://data.imf.org/ (accessed 30 June 2025). For the Cook Islands: Economies' official sources; and for Taipei,China: Government of Taipei,China, Ministry of Finance.

Table 2.4.14: International Trade in Goods (by partner country/economy): Merchandise Imports
(% of total merchandise imports)

From / To ADB Regional Member	Asia and the Pacific		Europe		North and Central America		Middle East		South America		Africa		Rest of the World	
	2010	2024	2010	2024	2010	2024	2010	2024	2010	2024	2010	2024	2010	2024
Developing ADB Member Economies														
Central and West Asia[a]	**29.7**	**33.6**	**47.9**	**40.5**	**6.4**	**5.0**	**10.8**	**7.7**	**1.6**	**1.8**	**2.2**	**1.7**	**1.4**	**9.7**
Afghanistan	67.3	66.9	12.6	5.7	2.0	0.8	9.8	26.3	0.5	0.0	0.4	0.1	7.4	0.1
Armenia	27.5	22.7	58.8	65.9	3.8	2.7	7.4	5.4	2.0	0.8	0.4	0.6	0.1	1.9
Azerbaijan	35.8	48.3	53.1	36.6	3.8	9.6	3.7	3.7	3.2	1.5	0.3	0.3	0.0	0.0
Georgia	43.3	38.8	45.7	42.5	3.9	12.7	4.6	4.6	1.9	1.1	0.6	0.2	0.0	0.0
Kazakhstan	29.6	30.6	60.1	15.6	7.0	3.6	1.2	0.7	1.4	0.5	0.4	0.3	0.2	48.7
Kyrgyz Republic	42.0	65.8	45.0	26.7	6.2	2.5	0.8	0.9	0.3	0.3	0.1	0.1	5.6	3.7
Pakistan	39.2	47.9	12.8	8.6	5.5	3.5	34.1	32.8	1.2	1.1	3.1	5.5	4.2	0.7
Tajikistan	52.6	59.4	32.5	30.0	4.6	3.0	8.8	2.3	1.4	1.3	0.0	0.1	0.0	3.9
Türkiye	23.2	59.4	55.2	30.0	7.5	3.0	8.8	2.3	1.6	1.3	2.7	0.1	1.0	3.9
Turkmenistan	51.4	72.6	46.7	22.6	1.1	4.4	0.7	0.2	0.1	0.1	0.0	0.0	0.0	0.0
Uzbekistan	47.1	57.9	43.5	36.9	1.5	1.7	5.0	1.9	2.7	1.4	0.1	0.1	0.0	0.0
East Asia[a]	**57.3**	**55.3**	**13.2**	**15.7**	**9.2**	**9.5**	**8.4**	**8.0**	**3.9**	**5.6**	**2.8**	**3.0**	**5.1**	**2.9**
China, People's Republic of	50.3	46.5	15.0	18.8	9.1	9.2	6.6	8.1	5.7	8.3	4.2	4.5	9.2	4.6
Hong Kong, China	82.4	82.6	9.2	8.5	6.1	4.5	1.4	3.4	0.6	0.6	0.3	0.5	0.0	0.0
Korea, Republic of	52.9	54.1	12.9	13.0	11.2	13.9	18.9	14.1	2.7	3.0	1.2	1.8	0.0	0.1
Mongolia	35.9	47.6	32.5	29.7	4.3	2.9	0.1	0.2	0.3	0.2	0.2	0.1	26.8	19.3
Taipei,China	60.8	66.9	10.5	11.7	11.5	13.4	12.3	6.3	2.2	1.3	2.7	0.5	0.0	0.0
South Asia[a]	**37.5**	**44.1**	**19.1**	**20.4**	**6.2**	**7.1**	**25.5**	**20.0**	**3.3**	**3.2**	**7.5**	**5.2**	**1.0**	**0.1**
Bangladesh	68.4	69.4	9.4	6.9	3.9	5.4	8.4	8.3	2.5	5.3	1.1	4.1	6.4	0.5
Bhutan	92.9	98.6	5.4	0.7	0.5	0.1	0.8	0.2	0.0	0.1	0.1	0.0	0.4	0.3
India	33.4	40.1	20.2	22.2	6.5	7.5	27.6	21.6	3.4	3.1	8.4	5.5	0.6	0.0
Maldives	58.8	58.1	8.8	8.7	8.7	3.4	19.5	28.3	0.6	0.9	1.2	0.6	2.5	0.0
Nepal	85.4	84.8	4.5	6.1	1.7	1.9	5.0	3.9	1.9	1.1	0.1	0.4	1.5	1.9
Sri Lanka	64.9	69.5	15.8	11.5	4.2	3.0	13.4	12.1	0.9	0.5	0.4	0.6	0.4	2.7
Southeast Asia[a]	**67.3**	**71.9**	**12.3**	**9.6**	**9.8**	**8.8**	**7.6**	**5.5**	**1.7**	**2.2**	**0.8**	**1.6**	**0.5**	**0.3**
Brunei Darussalam	77.8	66.7	10.8	27.0	10.2	2.2	0.5	3.5	0.1	0.4	0.1	0.1	0.6	0.1
Cambodia	90.1	92.7	6.7	2.4	2.7	1.1	0.2	0.0	0.2	0.8	0.1	0.1	0.0	2.9
Indonesia	72.8	74.3	9.2	8.0	8.0	7.1	6.0	3.5	2.3	3.2	1.7	3.9	0.1	0.0
Lao People's Democratic Republic	98.0	92.8	1.4	2.8	0.5	4.1	0.0	0.1	0.0	0.1	0.0	0.1	0.0	0.0
Malaysia	68.8	69.5	11.4	9.5	12.2	10.6	3.8	5.8	1.8	2.1	1.5	2.5	0.6	0.0
Myanmar	93.6	92.0	2.0	3.1	0.8	1.0	2.6	2.5	0.2	0.3	0.1	0.2	0.7	0.9
Philippines	69.5	79.2	8.8	6.8	11.6	7.5	8.5	3.7	1.4	2.4	0.2	0.4	0.0	0.0
Singapore	60.0	62.0	15.5	14.7	12.6	13.9	9.6	6.5	1.4	1.7	0.3	1.1	0.5	0.0
Thailand	65.3	68.5	12.7	9.9	6.7	7.3	11.6	9.5	1.6	1.9	0.9	1.2	1.4	1.7
Timor-Leste	94.7	85.8	2.2	4.7	0.4	2.1	0.1	0.4	0.0	2.1	0.3	0.7	2.3	4.3
Viet Nam	80.2	82.7	10.5	5.8	5.0	4.6	1.8	3.4	2.1	2.6	0.4	0.9	0.0	0.0
The Pacific[a]	**80.3**	**86.3**	**11.2**	**7.0**	**5.5**	**2.4**	**0.1**	**0.8**	**0.1**	**1.1**	**0.6**	**0.5**	**2.2**	**1.9**
Cook Islands	91.8	94.6	0.0	0.5	2.8	2.9	0.0	0.0	0.0	0.0	0.0	0.0	5.4	2.0
Fiji	89.0	83.4	2.6	3.2	3.9	6.9	0.3	0.4	0.2	0.1	0.5	0.1	3.5	5.8
Kiribati	81.4	91.6	2.2	3.6	8.0	3.0	0.0	0.1	0.0	0.1	0.3	0.1	8.0	1.5
Marshall Islands	0.1	85.2	99.7	10.2	0.0	0.7	0.0	1.3	0.0	1.8	0.1	0.7	0.0	0.0
Micronesia, Federated States of	37.6	42.2	1.0	0.3	30.2	16.5	0.1	0.0	0.0	0.1	0.2	0.4	30.8	40.5
Nauru	80.2	97.9	3.7	0.6	16.1	1.4	0.0	0.0	0.0	0.1	0.0	0.0	0.0	0.0
Niue	...	...	...	...	...	...	...	...	...	...	...	...	...	...
Palau	47.1	39.2	0.4	11.9	25.9	17.8	0.0	0.1	0.0	0.1	0.2	0.2	26.4	30.7
Papua New Guinea	88.4	95.8	5.5	2.4	5.1	1.5	0.0	0.1	0.2	0.1	0.8	0.2	0.0	0.0
Samoa	88.2	89.2	0.0	0.0	11.6	9.0	0.0	0.0	0.0	0.0	0.0	0.0	0.2	1.9
Solomon Islands	97.2	95.9	1.1	1.7	1.6	2.4	0.0	0.0	0.0	0.1	0.1	0.0	0.0	0.0
Tonga	74.7	91.2	1.7	0.0	11.7	8.8	0.1	0.0	0.2	0.0	0.1	0.0	11.5	0.0
Tuvalu	93.4	97.4	0.1	0.6	4.1	1.6	0.4	0.1	0.0	0.0	1.1	0.1	0.8	0.1
Vanuatu	91.2	95.6	4.1	2.4	2.3	1.7	0.1	0.0	0.1	0.0	0.6	0.0	1.6	0.3
Developed ADB Member Economies[a]	**54.4**	**58.8**	**14.8**	**15.0**	**12.3**	**14.0**	**13.5**	**8.3**	**2.6**	**2.5**	**1.6**	**1.1**	**0.9**	**0.3**
Australia	59.0	64.3	19.7	17.7	12.7	14.0	2.3	1.3	1.1	0.7	1.4	1.0	3.8	1.0
Japan	52.6	56.1	13.2	13.7	12.2	14.2	17.1	11.6	3.2	3.3	1.6	1.2	0.0	0.0
New Zealand	63.2	67.2	16.5	18.1	12.3	12.1	6.2	1.0	0.7	1.1	0.8	0.4	0.2	0.0
DEVELOPING ADB MEMBER ECONOMIES[a]	**55.8**	**56.6**	**16.0**	**16.6**	**8.8**	**8.7**	**10.0**	**8.7**	**3.2**	**4.2**	**2.8**	**2.8**	**3.4**	**2.5**
ALL ADB REGIONAL MEMBERS[a]	**55.5**	**56.9**	**15.8**	**16.4**	**9.5**	**9.3**	**10.6**	**8.6**	**3.1**	**4.0**	**2.5**	**2.6**	**3.0**	**2.2**
WORLD[a]	**34.4**	**38.4**	**38.3**	**35.3**	**13.1**	**13.6**	**6.0**	**5.1**	**3.5**	**3.3**	**2.9**	**2.7**	**1.8**	**1.5**

... = data not available, 0.0 = magnitude is less than half of unit employed, ADB = Asian Development Bank.

a Aggregates include estimates derived from reports of partner economies for nonreporting and slow-reporting economies.

Sources: Asian Development Bank estimates using data from the International Monetary Fund's International Trade in Goods (by partner country/economy). https://data.imf.org/ (accessed 30 June 2025). For the Cook Islands: Economies' official sources; and for Taipei,China: Government of Taipei,China, Ministry of Finance.

Table 2.4.15: International Reserves and Ratio to Imports

ADB Regional Member	International Reserves[a] ($ million)				Ratio to Imports[b] (months)			
	2010	2015	2023	2024	2010	2015	2023	2024
Developing ADB Member Economies								
Central and West Asia	**163,865**	**203,969**	**264,104**	**299,827**	**7.1**	**7.5**	**...**	**...**
Afghanistan	5,147	6,990	...	...	12.9	11.6	...	...
Armenia	1,866	1,775	3,607	3,685	6.9	7.6	3.9	...
Azerbaijan	6,409	7,661	13,749	12,699	11.5	9.4	10.1	8.9
Georgia	2,264	2,521	5,002	4,447	5.4	4.3	4.2	3.5
Kazakhstan	28,275	27,871	35,965	45,824	10.3	9.9	7.1	9.0
Kyrgyz Republic	1,720	1,778	3,237	5,089	7.0	5.6	3.3	5.3
Pakistan	17,210	20,045	13,764	18,411	6.6	5.8	3.1	4.2
Tajikistan	403	494	3,607	...	1.7	2.1	8.4	...
Türkiye	85,971	110,527	140,867	155,142	5.8	6.5	5.0	5.9
Turkmenistan	...	...	...	...	...	...	...	...
Uzbekistan	14,600	24,307	34,565	41,182	17.5	25.2	12.0	14.9
East Asia	**3,825,703**	**4,564,136**	**4,874,417**	**4,882,868**	**20.0**	**19.7**	**14.3**	**...**
China, People's Republic of	2,875,894	3,405,385	3,449,546	3,456,141	27.8	26.1	16.0	15.7
Hong Kong, China	268,743	358,773	425,554	...	8.4	8.2	8.6	...
Korea, Republic of	291,571	367,944	418,799	414,252	8.4	10.4	8.3	8.3
Mongolia	2,288	1,323	4,922	5,510	8.9	4.1	6.3	5.7
Taipei,China	387,206	430,711	575,597	581,411	18.5	19.4	24.0	22.0
South Asia	**320,411**	**395,960**	**661,919**	**676,734**	**9.0**	**10.2**	**10.0**	**...**
Bangladesh	11,178	27,493	21,867	21,395	6.3	8.8	3.7	4.1
Bhutan	1,002	1,103	655	941	15.1	13.5	5.5	9.0
India	297,746	351,551	622,464	635,693	9.3	10.6	10.9	10.5
Maldives	350	564	591	674	3.3	3.6	2.2	2.4
Nepal	2,939	7,945	11,937	...	7.2	12.5	11.8	...
Sri Lanka	7,196	7,304	4,405	6,094	6.4	4.6	3.1	3.9
Southeast Asia	**688,196**	**731,611**	**1,068,385**	**1,109,398**	**9.3**	**8.5**	**...**	**...**
Brunei Darussalam	1,563	3,367	4,485	4,414	5.4	9.1	5.4	5.4
Cambodia	3,802	7,376	19,996	22,509	6.9	6.7	9.0	8.6
Indonesia	96,211	105,929	146,384	155,719	9.7	9.4	8.3	8.4
Lao People's Democratic Republic	817	1,072	1,770	...	4.8	2.3	2.8	...
Malaysia	106,525	95,287	113,474	116,220	8.6	7.8	6.8	6.3
Myanmar	5,729	4,599	9,339	...	16.0	4.0	...	...
Philippines	62,373	80,667	103,753	106,257	14.0	14.6	10.3	10.3
Singapore	225,715	247,746	351,019	371,448	8.7	9.8	10.5	10.2
Thailand	172,129	156,514	224,473	237,054	12.4	10.0	10.3	10.2
Timor-Leste	406	438	782	737	15.9	8.0	12.1	10.5
Viet Nam	12,926	28,616	92,909	83,931	2.0	2.2	3.6	2.8
The Pacific	**4,573**	**3,863**	**8,079**	**7,455**	**8.7**	**7.5**	**...**	**...**
Cook Islands	...	...	...	...	...	...	...	...
Fiji	721	919	1,548	1,599	5.6	5.9	6.5	6.7
Kiribati	...	...	...	...	...	...	...	...
Marshall Islands	...	...	...	...	...	...	...	...
Micronesia, Federated States of	56	135	...	...	4.2	9.7	...	...
Nauru	...	...	...	...	...	...	...	...
Niue	...	...	...	...	...	...	...	...
Palau	...	...	...	...	...	...	...	...
Papua New Guinea	3,092	1,738	3,858	...	10.5	7.3	8.6	...
Samoa	173	112	447	508	7.4	4.5	12.5	13.6
Solomon Islands	266	534	688	...	8.9	14.6	13.1	...
Tonga	105	156	397	377	6.0	6.8	7.5	6.8
Tuvalu	...	...	...	...	...	...	...	...
Vanuatu	161	269	644	615	8.1	10.5	19.3	18.9
Developed ADB Member Economies	**1,163,670**	**1,293,265**	**1,371,866**	**1,313,184**	**16.4**	**17.9**	**14.9**	**...**
Australia	42,268	45,412	61,742	60,403	2.6	2.7	2.5	2.5
Japan	1,104,680	1,233,153	1,294,636	1,230,715	21.2	23.5	20.4	20.6
New Zealand	16,723	14,700	15,487	22,065	6.5	5.1	3.8	...
DEVELOPING ADB MEMBER ECONOMIES	**5,002,749**	**5,899,539**	**6,876,904**	**6,976,281**	**15.4**	**15.4**	**...**	**...**
ALL ADB REGIONAL MEMBERS	**6,166,419**	**7,192,803**	**8,248,769**	**8,289,465**	**15.6**	**15.8**	**...**	**...**

... = data not available, $ = United States dollars, ADB = Asian Development Bank.

a Data refer to international reserves with gold at national valuation, unless otherwise specified, end of year. For Bhutan (2000–2018), Lao People's Democratic Republic (2020–2024), Samoa, Solomon Islands (2000–2011), Uzbekistan (2005–2012), and Vanuatu, data refer to international reserves without gold. For estimating regional aggregates, imputation was done for economies with missing data using available data from nearest years.

b Merchandise imports from the balance of payments were used in the calculations. The aggregate ratios were calculated using only reporting economies with data available for both reserves and imports in the years specified in the column headings.

Sources: For international reserves: International Monetary Fund (IMF). International Financial Statistics. http://data.imf.org/ (accessed 30 June 2025); and for Taipei,China: economy's official source. For the reserves-to-imports ratio: Asian Development Bank estimates using data from the IMF's International Financial Statistics; official communications from the IMF; and economies' official sources.

Table 2.4.16: Net Official Development Assistance from All Sources to Developing Economies
($ million)

ADB Regional Member	2010	2015	2019	2020	2021	2022	2023
Developing ADB Member Economies							
Central and West Asia[a]	**11,749**	**12,808**	**9,923**	**11,405**	**11,883**	**10,182**	**11,544**
Afghanistan	6,072	4,274	4,138	4,210	4,692	3,915	3,056
Armenia	297	347	418	128	163	301	205
Azerbaijan	121	70	120	124	11	48	123
Georgia	528	449	493	1,042	770	377	365
Kazakhstan	198	82	55	75	59	75	79
Kyrgyz Republic	327	775	444	475	454	735	440
Pakistan	2,658	3,764	2,010	2,593	2,924	1,734	3,962
Tajikistan	324	432	362	715	558	595	528
Türkiye	1,038	2,141	701	544	1,061	801	1,549
Turkmenistan	43	23	26	35	30	16	36
Uzbekistan	142	451	1,154	1,463	1,163	1,585	1,199
East Asia[a]	**1,213**	**-70**	**-296**	**133**	**-279**	**5**	**-8**
China, People's Republic of	958	-306	-607	-571	-562	-280	-268
Hong Kong, China	...	...	...	...	...	...	...
Korea, Republic of	...	...	...	...	...	...	...
Mongolia	256	236	311	703	283	286	260
Taipei,China	...	...	...	...	...	...	...
South Asia[a]	**5,031**	**7,558**	**8,712**	**9,667**	**10,224**	**9,549**	**10,418**
Bangladesh	1,220	2,593	4,383	5,376	5,091	5,205	5,684
Bhutan	87	97	180	204	128	195	157
India	2,561	3,174	2,551	1,796	3,137	2,818	2,376
Maldives	67	24	72	312	113	120	201
Nepal	636	1,224	1,334	1,760	1,600	1,199	1,173
Sri Lanka	459	445	193	219	155	12	827
Southeast Asia[a]	**5,307**	**6,243**	**4,796**	**9,065**	**6,649**	**6,214**	**7,417**
Brunei Darussalam	...	...	...	...	...	...	...
Cambodia	645	679	968	1,375	1,368	1,549	1,581
Indonesia	1,213	-28	-693	1,211	627	668	1,155
Lao People's Democratic Republic	350	471	623	531	577	547	515
Malaysia	-8	-1	-2	-4	15	6	7
Myanmar	355	1,169	2,045	2,871	1,508	1,001	1,141
Philippines	579	515	887	1,457	1,635	1,614	1,843
Singapore	...	...	...	...	...	...	...
Thailand	-21	59	-351	200	134	555	85
Timor-Leste	285	212	231	251	257	225	260
Viet Nam	1,909	3,167	1,089	1,173	528	50	831
The Pacific[a]	**1,395**	**1,576**	**1,747**	**2,520**	**2,888**	**2,393**	**2,035**
Cook Islands	14	26	29	...	...	...	...
Fiji	75	102	130	196	612	361	190
Kiribati	22	65	57	58	73	91	98
Marshall Islands	25	57	66	183	107	140	126
Micronesia, Federated States of	64	81	93	172	131	152	126
Nauru	28	31	54	28	34	35	38
Niue	15	20	19	22	28	24	28
Palau	28	14	25	66	49	56	29
Papua New Guinea	508	591	651	1,057	1,187	667	691
Samoa	101	94	125	168	86	128	117
Solomon Islands	333	190	224	214	265	254	244
Tonga	59	68	108	163	113	295	130
Tuvalu	13	50	36	43	36	64	68
Vanuatu	110	187	131	154	167	125	150
DEVELOPING ADB MEMBER ECONOMIES[a]	**24,696**	**28,115**	**24,882**	**32,243**	**30,265**	**28,344**	**31,406**
DEVELOPING ECONOMIES WORLDWIDE[b]	**120,088**	**146,743**	**163,609**	**194,793**	**204,519**	**245,823**	**258,712**

... = data not available, $ = United States dollars, ADB = Asian Development Bank.

Note: Net official development assistance (ODA) refers to concessional flows to developing economies and multilateral institutions provided by official agencies, including state and local governments, or by their executing agencies, administered with the objective of promoting the economic development and welfare of developing economies, and containing a grant element of at least 25%. Net flow takes into account principal repayments for loans, offsetting entries for forgiven debt, and recoveries made on grants. While rare, negative ODA can occur when an economy receives more aid repayments or remittances than what it received in official development assistance.

a For reporting economies only.
b Includes data for all developing economies as reported in the Organisation for Economic Co-operation and Development's OECD.Stat database.

Sources: Organisation for Economic Co-operation and Development. OECD.Stat Database. http://stats.oecd.org (accessed 30 June 2025). For Developing ADB Member Economies: Asian Development Bank staff estimates based on data from OECD.

Table 2.4.17: Net Other Official Flows from All Sources to Developing Economies
($ million)

ADB Regional Member	2010	2015	2019	2020	2021	2022	2023
Developing ADB Member Economies							
Central and West Asia[a]	**10,029.6**	**8,983.8**	**3,610.0**	**5,839.6**	**3,467.2**	**6,198.1**	**5,973.5**
Afghanistan	71.2	127.4	14.8	–1.5	1.7	2.8	–2.5
Armenia	288.3	111.1	225.3	81.8	96.8	164.1	17.0
Azerbaijan	179.9	801.8	343.6	–118.4	–559.7	–369.3	–193.6
Georgia	250.2	342.4	411.9	851.2	1,090.4	550.7	702.5
Kazakhstan	2,247.2	1,256.7	–53.5	568.7	401.3	349.1	34.4
Kyrgyz Republic	18.3	0.4	33.4	15.3	23.3	15.0	35.6
Pakistan	345.3	–343.9	755.9	1,536.3	868.0	1,080.8	–119.6
Tajikistan	6.4	68.1	75.4	62.4	89.1	62.7	68.3
Türkiye	5,959.5	3,732.7	581.7	1,205.3	1,162.0	1,872.4	2,919.0
Turkmenistan	647.4	2,356.6	–811.1	171.7	–657.7	–349.3	–261.9
Uzbekistan	16.0	530.5	2,032.6	1,466.7	951.9	2,819.2	2,774.4
East Asia[a]	**3,355.5**	**1,429.0**	**1,086.2**	**1,287.7**	**2,394.2**	**794.3**	**–512.5**
China, People's Republic of	3,196.3	1,215.8	664.0	931.2	1,911.4	666.1	–839.1
Hong Kong, China	...	...	...	...	...	...	...
Korea, Republic of	...	...	...	...	...	...	...
Mongolia	159.3	213.3	422.2	356.5	482.8	128.2	326.6
Taipei,China	...	...	...	...	...	...	...
South Asia[a]	**6,175.1**	**2,531.9**	**3,289.3**	**10,585.1**	**5,988.3**	**8,827.7**	**8,991.0**
Bangladesh	35.1	417.9	1,208.9	1,833.9	2,304.8	2,158.0	2,271.5
Bhutan	24.0	–2.8	6.4	4.2	3.9	8.2	3.4
India	5,967.5	1,811.5	1,899.4	8,224.4	2,606.7	5,530.9	6,147.8
Maldives	–33.9	–8.1	–6.6	–16.3	51.6	104.2	–52.7
Nepal	–6.9	–7.4	51.2	–2.8	53.9	61.8	19.9
Sri Lanka	189.3	320.8	130.0	541.7	967.5	964.5	601.2
Southeast Asia[a]	**3,916.6**	**8,205.9**	**5,858.8**	**7,684.6**	**6,795.5**	**1,955.9**	**5,189.4**
Brunei Darussalam	...	...	...	...	...	...	...
Cambodia	–5.0	84.6	86.5	15.7	–6.3	78.3	–39.8
Indonesia	1,783.7	3,775.4	1,804.8	2,164.1	1,714.5	–760.6	2,844.5
Lao People's Democratic Republic	–120.5	73.1	20.6	–27.7	–223.9	–8.9	97.0
Malaysia	159.2	–231.8	1,971.0	–475.3	–15.4	–127.7	66.3
Myanmar	30.9	427.5	130.4	417.7	–264.2	–901.0	–123.6
Philippines	–680.3	1,148.5	456.8	6,272.5	3,804.2	4,439.4	3,508.6
Singapore	...	...	...	...	...	...	...
Thailand	–71.5	138.7	718.6	211.7	915.6	27.8	–986.4
Timor-Leste	4.6	7.8	38.3	14.8	3.3	5.3	4.6
Viet Nam	2,815.4	2,782.1	631.8	–908.9	867.6	–796.6	–181.8
The Pacific[a]	**4,982.0**	**18.1**	**62.5**	**566.4**	**82.2**	**198.9**	**–97.9**
Cook Islands	9.7	–0.6	3.4	...	...	...	...
Fiji	14.2	–11.4	10.9	309.5	171.9	191.9	–12.0
Kiribati	0.5	0.2	0.3	...	...	...	...
Marshall Islands	–0.6	7.6	144.5	–38.6	–21.2	57.1	284.0
Micronesia, Federated States of	0.8	0.2	0.1	–0.3	–1.0	–0.4	–0.6
Nauru	0.3	...	0.1	...	...	...	...
Niue	...	...	0.1	...	...	...	...
Palau	6.4 (2011)	0.3	4.9	17.1	9.4	31.8	–8.1
Papua New Guinea	4,892.3	19.4	–181.4	281.5	–74.3	–80.1	–364.8
Samoa	4.1	–1.3	0.7	–2.0	–0.2	–0.2	–0.3
Solomon Islands	59.2	0.7	73.0	0.1	...	...	3.8
Tonga	0.3	2.1	2.0	–	...	...	...
Tuvalu	–0.1	0.2	0.2	–	...	...	...
Vanuatu	1.3	0.7	3.9	–0.9	–2.4	–1.2	–
DEVELOPING ADB MEMBER ECONOMIES[a]	**28,458.7**	**21,168.7**	**13,906.8**	**25,963.4**	**18,727.4**	**17,974.8**	**19,543.4**
DEVELOPING ECONOMIES WORLDWIDE[b]	**70,855.8**	**50,967.9**	**28,038.9**	**56,118.7**	**59,496.8**	**53,106.5**	**62,619.8**

... = data not available, 0.0 = magnitude is less than half of unit employed, $ = United States dollars, ADB = Asian Development Bank.

Note: Net other official flows refer to official sector transactions with economies on the Development Assistance Committee List of Official Development Assistance Recipients, which do not meet the conditions for eligibility as official development assistance, either because they are not primarily aimed at development or because they have a grant element of less than 25%. The Development Assistance Committee List of Official Development Assistance Recipients is available at http://www.oecd.org/dac/financing-sustainable-development/development-finance-standards/daclist.htm. Net other official flows also include net export credits. Net flow takes into account principal repayments for loans, offsetting entries for forgiven debt, and recoveries made on grants.

a For reporting economies only.
b Includes data for all developing economies as reported in the Organisation for Economic Co-operation and Development's OECD.Stat database.

Sources: Organisation for Economic Co-operation and Development. OECD.Stat Database. http://stats.oecd.org (accessed 30 June 2025).
For Developing ADB Member Economies: Asian Development Bank staff estimates based on data from OECD.

Capital Flows

Table 2.4.18: Net Private Flows from All Sources to Developing Economies
($ million)

ADB Regional Member	2010	2015	2019	2020	2021	2022	2023
Developing ADB Member Economies							
Central and West Asia[a]	**5,254**	**10,128**	**-1,240**	**6,859**	**6,739**	**6,526**	**4,224**
Afghanistan	-21	-6	2	-	1	-214	-348
Armenia	-69	34	107	4	50	99	-69
Azerbaijan	798	411	483	502	360	307	-272
Georgia	22	176	224	590	45	-118	247
Kazakhstan	-1,511	2,904	-1,020	2,718	3,783	668	10,345
Kyrgyz Republic	23	7	-1	-12	-20	-8	3
Pakistan	-75	75	93	107	239	675	-463
Tajikistan	18	-3	-18	41	-12	29	-0
Türkiye	6,076	6,510	-1,273	2,937	2,089	5,235	-5,644
Turkmenistan	-46	-21	-230	-316	-146	-21	122
Uzbekistan	39	41	394	287	349	-125	303
East Asia[a]	**46,322**	**14,203**	**42,949**	**20,081**	**26,255**	**36,230**	**29,193**
China, People's Republic of	46,301	14,105	42,360	21,275	27,098	33,430	20,954
Hong Kong, China	...	...	...	...	...	...	...
Korea, Republic of	...	...	...	...	...	...	...
Mongolia	22	98	589	-1,194	-843	2,799	8,239
Taipei,China	...	...	...	...	...	...	...
South Asia[a]	**20,237**	**5,273**	**20,318**	**5,985**	**11,911**	**11,674**	**16,772**
Bangladesh	-3	156	332	359	4	-621	351
Bhutan	18	0	0	1	-0	-0	3
India	19,976	4,804	19,550	5,959	12,035	12,164	16,538
Maldives	38	9	148	-33	41	100	-60
Nepal	-11	-2	30	26	16	27	46
Sri Lanka	218	304	259	-328	-185	5	-107
Southeast Asia[a]	**21,463**	**15,726**	**69,611**	**20,637**	**20,006**	**22,198**	**18,321**
Brunei Darussalam	...	...	...	...	...	...	...
Cambodia	256	321	644	1,033	744	493	392
Indonesia	3,348	9,355	13,843	6,214	8,870	2,532	7,045
Lao People's Democratic Republic	172	-17	97	9	64	266	-206
Malaysia	6,573	3,371	9,102	2,752	2,906	5,095	1,218
Myanmar	260	860	559	395	481	301	289
Philippines	2,424	1,503	31,544	2,215	-1,194	1,288	1,080
Singapore	...	...	...	...	...	...	...
Thailand	6,394	-2,361	7,476	2,657	3,436	6,401	1,652
Timor-Leste	-3	17	8	-0	40	22	-12
Viet Nam	2,038	2,677	6,337	5,362	4,659	5,800	6,863
The Pacific[a]	**978**	**-510**	**-1,091**	**40**	**-875**	**400**	**-195**
Cook Islands	-0	-2	-1	...	...	...	...
Fiji	-3	39	9	21	16	11	12
Kiribati	-0	3	5	...	0	-0	-1
Marshall Islands	974	1,574	30	-178	501	271	-114
Micronesia, Federated States of	3	798	-1,215	55	-790	58	-66
Nauru	-0 (2011)	-0 (2016)	-0	-12	...	...	...
Niue	-0 (2012)	-	0	2	9	17	-0
Palau	3	7	8	8	0	-1	1
Papua New Guinea	-40	-2,936	61	153	-687	-13	3
Samoa	17	3	-3	11	0	-6	6
Solomon Islands	3	11	3	1	2	3	-11
Tonga	-10	-1	4	0	-0	-	-
Tuvalu	1 (2011)	0	...	0	...	...	...
Vanuatu	31	-5	9	-22	73	60	-25
DEVELOPING ADB MEMBER ECONOMIES[a]	**94,254**	**44,819**	**130,546**	**53,602**	**64,036**	**77,028**	**68,316**
DEVELOPING ECONOMIES WORLDWIDE[b]	**324,145**	**92,502**	**216,925**	**-15,912**	**228,813**	**183,181**	**116,143**

... = data not available, – = magnitude equals zero, (-/+) 0 = magnitude is less than half of unit employed, $ = United States dollars, ADB = Asian Development Bank.

Note: Net private flows refer to the sum of direct investments and portfolio investments.

a For reporting economies only.
b Includes data for all developing economies as reported in the Organisation for Economic Co-operation and Development's OECD Data. http://data.oecd.org (accessed 30 June 2025).

Source: Organisation for Economic Co-operation and Development's OECD Data. http://data.oecd.org (accessed 30 June 2025).

Table 2.4.19: Aggregate Net Resource Flows from All Sources to Developing Economies
($ million)

ADB Regional Member	2010	2015	2019	2020	2021	2022	2023
Developing ADB Member Economies							
Central and West Asia[a]	**27,033**	**31,920**	**12,292**	**24,103**	**22,089**	**22,907**	**21,742**
Afghanistan	6,122	4,396	4,154	4,209	4,695	3,704	2,705
Armenia	516	493	751	213	310	565	153
Azerbaijan	1,099	1,282	947	507	−189	−14	−342
Georgia	800	967	1,129	2,483	1,905	809	1,315
Kazakhstan	935	4,243	−1,019	3,362	4,243	1,092	10,459
Kyrgyz Republic	369	782	476	479	457	743	479
Pakistan	2,928	3,495	2,860	4,236	4,031	3,490	3,380
Tajikistan	349	497	419	819	635	686	596
Türkiye	13,073	12,384	10	4,686	4,312	7,909	−1,176
Turkmenistan	645	2,358	−1,015	−109	−774	−354	−104
Uzbekistan	197	1,022	3,580	3,217	2,464	4,279	4,277
East Asia[a]	**50,891**	**15,562**	**43,739**	**21,502**	**28,370**	**37,029**	**28,673**
China, People's Republic of	50,455	15,015	42,417	21,636	28,448	33,816	19,847
Hong Kong, China	...	...	...	...	...	...	...
Korea, Republic of	...	...	...	...	...	...	...
Mongolia	437	547	1,322	−134	−77	3,213	8,826
Taipei,China	...	...	...	...	...	...	...
South Asia[a]	**31,443**	**15,362**	**32,319**	**26,237**	**28,124**	**30,051**	**36,181**
Bangladesh	1,253	3,167	5,923	7,569	7,399	6,742	8,306
Bhutan	130	95	186	209	132	203	163
India	28,504	9,790	24,000	15,979	17,778	20,513	25,062
Maldives	71	25	213	263	206	324	88
Nepal	618	1,216	1,414	1,783	1,670	1,287	1,239
Sri Lanka	867	1,070	582	433	938	981	1,322
Southeast Asia[a]	**30,686**	**30,175**	**80,266**	**37,387**	**33,450**	**30,368**	**30,928**
Brunei Darussalam	...	...	...	...	...	...	...
Cambodia	896	1,084	1,698	2,424	2,106	2,120	1,934
Indonesia	6,345	13,102	14,955	9,589	11,212	2,439	11,045
Lao People's Democratic Republic	401	528	740	512	417	805	405
Malaysia	6,724	3,139	11,072	2,273	2,906	4,973	1,290
Myanmar	646	2,456	2,734	3,684	1,724	400	1,306
Philippines	2,323	3,167	32,888	9,944	4,245	7,341	6,431
Singapore	...	...	...	...	...	...	...
Thailand	6,301	−2,163	7,843	3,068	4,485	6,985	751
Timor-Leste	287	238	277	266	300	252	253
Viet Nam	6,762	8,626	8,058	5,626	6,054	5,053	7,512
The Pacific[a]	**7,355**	**1,084**	**718**	**3,132**	**2,095**	**2,992**	**1,742**
Cook Islands	23	23	31	...	...	...	...
Fiji	87	130	150	527	801	564	190
Kiribati	23	68	62	58	73	91	97
Marshall Islands	998	1,639	240	−33	587	468	297
Micronesia, Federated States of	68	879	−1,122	226	−660	210	59
Nauru	28	31	54	17	34	35	38
Niue	15	20	19	24	37	41	28
Palau	31	21	37	91	59	86	22
Papua New Guinea	5,360	−2,325	530	1,492	426	574	329
Samoa	122	95	122	177	86	122	123
Solomon Islands	396	202	300	216	267	257	236
Tonga	50	70	114	163	113	295	130
Tuvalu	13	50	37	43	36	64	68
Vanuatu	142	182	143	131	238	184	125
DEVELOPING ADB MEMBER ECONOMIES[a]	**147,408**	**94,103**	**169,334**	**112,361**	**114,129**	**123,346**	**119,265**
DEVELOPING ECONOMIES WORLDWIDE[b]	**524,265**	**289,849**	**408,438**	**234,948**	**492,057**	**498,587**	**...**

... = data not available, $ = United States dollars, ADB = Asian Development Bank.

Note: Aggregate net resource flows refer to the sum of net official development assistance, net other official flows, and net private flows.

a For reporting economies only.
b Includes data for all developing economies as reported in the Organisation for Economic Co-operation and Development's OECD Data. http://data.oecd.org (accessed 30 June 2025).

Source: Organisation for Economic Co-operation and Development. OECD Data. http://data.oecd.org (accessed 30 June 2025).

External Indebtedness

Table 2.4.20: Total External Debt of Developing Economies—Dollar Amounts
($ million)

ADB Regional Member	Total External Debt			External Debt (Public and Publicly Guaranteed)		
	2010	2015	2023	2010	2015	2023
Developing ADB Member Economies						
Central and West Asia[a]	**541,452**	**694,853**	**932,201**	**162,073**	**213,570**	**337,856**
Afghanistan	2,436	2,597	3,428	1,976	1,990	1,857
Armenia	6,307	8,831	15,839	2,560	3,998	6,241
Azerbaijan	7,286	13,338	14,533	3,846	8,731	12,233
Georgia	8,790	14,875	24,468	3,274	5,721	10,264
Kazakhstan	119,151	153,470	163,155	3,845	20,404	25,231
Kyrgyz Republic	4,118	7,720	10,115	2,446	3,431	4,192
Pakistan	63,483	68,750	130,847	44,085	51,178	92,990
Tajikistan	3,561	5,144	6,873	1,806	2,093	3,091
Türkiye	316,657	399,739	499,842	93,299	103,610	149,369
Turkmenistan	1,682	7,004	3,918	1,513	6,869	3,502
Uzbekistan	7,981	13,385	59,184	3,423	5,546	28,887
East Asia[a]	**2,083,974**	**3,213,252**	**5,184,549**	**...**	**...**	**...**
China, People's Republic of	742,737	1,333,769	2,420,211	102,275	146,062	467,996
Hong Kong, China	879,034	1,300,348	1,910,101 (2024)	...	...	...
Korea, Republic of	354,693	396,064	672,903 (2024)	...	...	...
Mongolia	5,928	24,117	34,321	1,782	5,837	9,730
Taipei,China	101,581	158,954	219,947 (2024)	8,035	1,116	819 (2024)
South Asia[a]	**344,319**	**568,721**	**827,178**	**143,193**	**223,143**	**345,657**
Bangladesh	26,572	38,705	101,447	21,146	27,104	74,131
Bhutan	935	2,111	3,269	919	2,045	3,190
India	290,428	478,831	646,787	100,563	162,311	214,916
Maldives	914	1,004	4,000	628	685	3,418
Nepal	3,787	4,143	9,968	3,507	3,543	8,620
Sri Lanka	21,684	43,927	61,706	16,430	27,454	41,382
Southeast Asia[a]	**560,658 (2012)**	**620,399**	**918,286**	**212,613**	**292,453**	**412,385**
Brunei Darussalam	...	...	...	...	...	...
Cambodia	4,010	9,439	22,534	3,060	5,641	11,098
Indonesia	198,278	307,850	406,054	102,748	159,672	234,907
Lao People's Democratic Republic	6,554	11,694	20,350	3,751	6,742	11,034
Malaysia	...	...	...	...	...	...
Myanmar	9,990	10,220	12,162	8,433	9,714	10,036
Philippines	65,344	76,267	121,402	45,080	38,861	68,742
Singapore	...	...	...	...	...	...
Thailand	107,166	122,989	193,626	16,737	22,571	32,419
Timor-Leste	76 (2012)	117	307	0 (2012)	46	255
Viet Nam	45,022	81,825	141,850	32,805	49,207	43,894
The Pacific[a]	**8,368**	**23,361**	**24,484 (2022)**	**...**	**...**	**...**
Cook Islands	99	75	...	...	...	...
Fiji	1,107	1,492	3,348	426	678	1,595
Kiribati	14	33	28 (2024)	...	...	...
Marshall Islands	105	95	60	...	...	...
Micronesia, Federated States of	86	81	...	...	...	...
Nauru	...	...	...	...	...	...
Niue	...	...	...	...	...	...
Palau	66	64	212	...	...	...
Papua New Guinea	5,987	20,387	15,321	1,042	1,501	7,136
Samoa	325	466	432	299	408	296
Solomon Islands	231	207	528	125	81	198
Tonga	154	184	196	144	175	151
Tuvalu	15	19	2 (2022)	...	...	...
Vanuatu	178	257	471	103	172	362
DEVELOPING ADB MEMBER ECONOMIES[a]	**3,414,477**	**5,120,586**	**7,882,811**	**632,110**	**885,196**	**1,583,363**
DEVELOPING ECONOMIES WORLDWIDE[a,b]	**5,200,513**	**7,757,248**	**11,566,298**	**1,402,620**	**2,101,500**	**3,449,389**

... = data not available, 0 = magnitude is less than half of unit employed, $ = United States dollars, ADB = Asian Development Bank.

Note: Refers to the sum of public and publicly guaranteed long-term debt, private nonguaranteed long-term debt, use of International Monetary Fund credit, and estimated short-term debt.

a Regional aggregates include only reporting economies with data corresponding to the year heading.
b Refers to all low- and middle-income economies as classified by the World Bank. For developing member economies not covered by the World Bank, data are from the economies' official sources.

Sources: World Bank. International Debt Statistics. http://data.worldbank.org/data-catalog/international-debt-statistics (accessed 12 July 2025); and Asian Development Bank estimates using economies' official sources.

Table 2.4.21: Total External Debt of Developing ADB Member Economies—Proportion of Income
(% of GNI)

ADB Regional Member	Total External Debt			External Debt (Public and Publicly Guaranteed)		
	2010	2015	2023	2010	2015	2023
Developing ADB Member Economies						
Central and West Asia						
Afghanistan	15.3	13.5	19.8	12.4	10.3	10.8
Armenia	64.9	80.4	67.6	26.3	36.4	26.6
Azerbaijan	14.6	26.0	21.0	7.7	17.0	17.6
Georgia	72.0	100.0	86.2	26.8	38.4	36.2
Kazakhstan	92.6	88.8	69.0	3.0	11.8	10.7
Kyrgyz Republic	91.7	120.3	73.3	54.5	53.5	28.0
Pakistan	32.8	23.3	39.4	22.8	17.3	28.0
Tajikistan	51.1	52.5	45.4	25.9	21.4	20.2
Türkiye	41.1	46.8	45.2	12.1	12.1	13.5
Turkmenistan	8.1	20.8	6.5	7.3	20.4	5.8
Uzbekistan	15.8	15.3	58.7	6.8	6.3	27.9
East Asia						
China, People's Republic of	12.3	12.1	13.7	1.7	1.3	2.6
Hong Kong, China	376.8	412.6	426.4 (2024)	...	...	...
Korea, Republic of	29.7	25.7	35.5 (2024)	...	...	...
Mongolia	89.7	226.4	189.7	27.0	54.8	53.8
Taipei,China	22.2	29.0	26.7 (2024)	1.8	0.2	0.1 (2024)
South Asia						
Bangladesh	21.3	18.6	22.3	17.0	13.0	16.3
Bhutan	57.7	103.2	114.6	56.7	100.0	111.8
India	17.5	23.0	18.4	6.1	7.8	6.0
Maldives	40.1	26.4	68.7	27.6	18.0	58.6
Nepal	23.5	16.8	24.1	21.8	14.3	20.8
Sri Lanka	37.4	52.8	75.6	28.3	33.1	51.0
Southeast Asia						
Brunei Darussalam	...	...	...	...	...	...
Cambodia	29.9	40.7	54.5	22.8	24.3	26.8
Indonesia	27.0	37.0	30.4	14.0	19.2	17.6
Lao People's Democratic Republic	98.1	84.8	138.6	56.2	48.9	75.1
Malaysia	...	...	...	...	...	...
Myanmar	20.2	17.8	18.6	17.0	16.9	15.3
Philippines	28.2	22.3	25.0	19.5	11.4	14.2
Singapore	...	...	...	...	...	...
Thailand	32.8	32.3	38.5	5.1	5.9	6.4
Timor-Leste	1.8 (2012)	4.2	12.6	0.0 (2012)	1.6	10.5
Viet Nam	31.6	36.0	34.8	23.0	21.7	10.7
The Pacific						
Cook Islands[a]	41.0	24.8	...	...	...	...
Fiji	36.4	33.9	65.3	14.0	15.4	31.1
Kiribati[a]	8.5	20.0	9.0 (2024)	...	...	...
Marshall Islands[a]	65.5	51.5	23.0	...	...	...
Micronesia, Federated States of[a]	29.0	25.6	...	...	...	...
Nauru	...	...	...	...	...	...
Niue	...	...	...	...	...	...
Palau[a]	36.1	22.7	79.2	...	...	...
Papua New Guinea	45.4	100.4	53.2	7.9	7.4	25.0
Samoa	49.2	57.7	46.8	45.3	50.5	32.0
Solomon Islands	27.0	16.2	31.8	14.7	6.3	11.7
Tonga	40.6	41.7	38.6 (2022)	37.9	39.6	27.3
Tuvalu[a]	49.1	53.5	3.6 (2022)	...	...	...
Vanuatu	27.4	34.5	36.7	15.8	22.3	28.3

... = data not available, 0.0 = magnitude is less than half of unit employed, ADB = Asian Development Bank, GNI = gross national income.

a For total external debt as a percentage of GNI, gross domestic product is used in lieu of GNI.

Sources: For total external debt (% of GNI): World Bank. International Debt Statistics. http://data.worldbank.org/data-catalog/international-debt-statistics (accessed 14 July 2025); and economies' official sources. For public and publicly guaranteed external debt (% of GNI): Asian Development Bank estimates using the World Bank's International Debt Statistics and World Development Indicators; and economies' official sources.

External Indebtedness

Table 2.4.22: Total External Debt of Developing ADB Member Economies—Proportion of Exports
(% of exports of goods, services, and primary income)

ADB Regional Member	2010	2015	2019	2020	2021	2022	2023	2024
Developing ADB Member Economies								
Central and West Asia								
Afghanistan	88.7	152.4	142.4	177.1	...	...	...	...
Armenia	193.5	219.5	176.2	303.7	254.7	143.7	104.4	...
Azerbaijan	25.2	62.7	65.6	96.5	57.3	31.3	38.8	...
Georgia	191.5	213.9	171.8	291.6	241.4	162.9	143.4	...
Kazakhstan	171.4	306.4	228.2	314.6	218.2	165.4	172.1	...
Kyrgyz Republic	181.2	314.6	268.8	353.2	274.4	266.5	234.3	...
Pakistan	220.9	235.0	353.6	425.1	361.0	322.1	353.6	...
Tajikistan	158.4	200.6	230.0	234.0	156.2	121.1	125.9	...
Türkiye	194.7	180.6	159.4	201.1	148.4	129.1	135.6	...
Turkmenistan	...	...	...	...	...	...	...	...
Uzbekistan	60.5	96.5	114.9	204.6	213.8	193.7	194.9	...
East Asia								
China, People's Republic of	41.3	51.6	72.8	77.9	70.2	61.4	64.5	...
Hong Kong, China[a]	149.2	168.8	195.1	221.6	193.3	191.7	198.0	186.8
Korea, Republic of[a]	62.4	59.5	67.1	85.3	76.5	76.2	80.8	74.2
Mongolia	173.2	464.3	378.1	408.6	375.6	295.2	215.1	...
Taipei,China[a]	30.0	38.8	43.5	49.2	42.9	37.6	41.5	40.7
South Asia								
Bangladesh	122.1	110.2	138.4	190.1	184.3	160.4	170.9	...
Bhutan	154.0	282.2	344.1	396.6	429.2	387.4	384.0	...
India	81.1	108.0	98.5	111.4	91.8	77.4	79.7	...
Maldives	45.4	31.8	71.1	203.2	102.6	77.8	81.1	...
Nepal	212.7	154.5	190.1	347.0	296.2	275.2	253.2	...
Sri Lanka	189.8	257.3	285.4	428.2	389.3	357.3	346.8	...
Southeast Asia								
Brunei Darussalam	...	...	...	...	...	...	...	...
Cambodia	65.8	69.2	70.7	82.1	97.8	87.0	79.8	...
Indonesia	117.6	176.8	193.9	227.1	164.8	122.5	135.7	...
Lao People's Democratic Republic	284.0	252.9	271.4	324.6	245.7	219.9	207.2	...
Malaysia	...	...	...	...	...	...	...	...
Myanmar	127.2	70.2	59.2	86.8	111.1	93.1	93.3	...
Philippines	106.7	93.3	77.4	107.5	106.8	99.4	101.1	...
Singapore	...	...	...	...	...	...	...	...
Thailand	46.0	44.5	50.3	69.2	63.3	59.3	54.8	...
Timor-Leste	1.9 (2012)	8.3	12.3	11.8	9.1	13.3	25.2	...
Viet Nam	56.2	47.1	43.3	44.4	41.0	37.8	37.4	...
The Pacific								
Cook Islands[a]	118.0	29.7	22.0	...	...	...	...	...
Fiji	58.7	63.5	67.9	158.5	202.6	122.8	104.9	...
Kiribati[a]	13.7	11.9	11.8	15.1	15.3	13.6	9.4	...
Marshall Islands[a]	97.3	59.0	41.4	38.9	32.9	33.7	30.2	...
Micronesia, Federated States of	91.3	51.3	34.2 (2018)	...	...	...	...	...
Nauru	...	...	...	...	...	...	...	...
Niue	...	...	...	...	...	...	...	...
Palau[a]	66.8	37.7	66.2	167.3	448.8	278.2	240.1	...
Papua New Guinea	98.2	236.1	165.1	194.8	177.4	131.3	117.5	...
Samoa	154.0	194.7	126.5	378.7	459.5	245.7	114.4	...
Solomon Islands	68.9	35.9	47.6	66.4	95.8	99.7	86.2	...
Tonga	283.9	212.0	119.2	129.2	227.1	208.4	123.5	...
Tuvalu[a]	64.1	50.0	11.5	6.2	6.1	5.1	...	...
Vanuatu	48.9	73.5	86.0	165.4	164.9	128.1	100.9	...

... = data not available, ADB = Asian Development Bank.

a External debt as a percentage of exports of goods, services, and primary income was derived using balance-of-payments data.

Sources: World Bank. International Debt Statistics. http://data.worldbank.org/data-catalog/international-debt-statistics (accessed 21 July 2025); and Asian Development Bank estimates using economies' official sources.

Table 2.4.23: Total Debt Service Paid by Developing ADB Member Economies

ADB Regional Member	Debt Service Payment ($ million)					Debt Service Payment (% of exports of goods, services, and primary income)				
	2010	2015	2022	2023	2024	2010	2015	2022	2023	2024
Developing ADB Member Economies										
Central and West Asia[a]	**107,994**	**104,056**	**145,899**	**156,625**	**150,395**					
Afghanistan	10	56	27	44	142	0.4	3.3	2.7 (2020)	...	...
Armenia	969	1,546	1,991	2,773	2,530	29.7	38.4	18.0	18.3	...
Azerbaijan	415	1,908	1,623	1,841	3,699	1.4	9.0	3.3	4.9	...
Georgia	803	2,158	3,337	3,557	3,277	17.5	31.0	22.7	20.8	...
Kazakhstan	39,475	34,857	43,509	44,600	20,170	56.8	69.6	44.7	47.1	...
Kyrgyz Republic	525	442	610	1,180	1,748	23.1	18.0	16.7	27.3	...
Pakistan	4,351	4,236	16,660	16,009	26,154	15.1	14.5	42.0	43.3	...
Tajikistan	695	314	507	577	650	30.9	12.3	9.1	10.6	...
Türkiye	59,934	55,819	69,335	76,347	80,049	36.9	25.2	19.6	20.7	...
Turkmenistan	199	1,474	1,136	1,160	998	...	...	...	...	...
Uzbekistan	617	1,246	7,164	8,536	10,977	4.7	9.0	28.3	28.1	...
East Asia[a]	**55,962**	**134,632**	**440,378**	**407,611**	**242,011**					
China, People's Republic of	52,102	126,685	428,696	385,484	216,835	2.9	4.9	10.7	10.3	...
Hong Kong, China	...	...	...	...	...	...	...	...	...	...
Korea, Republic of	...	...	...	...	...	...	...	...	...	...
Mongolia	240	1,828	3,981	4,848	8,607	7.0	35.2	35.1	30.4	...
Taipei,China[b]	3,620	6,119	7,701	17,279	16,568	1.1	1.6	1.6	3.9	3.5
South Asia[a]	**27,276**	**55,469**	**77,006**	**93,690**	**96,943**					
Bangladesh	1,106	1,756	6,799	7,474	8,270	5.1	5.0	11.2	12.6	...
Bhutan	87	135	132	139	384	14.4	18.1	16.2	16.3	...
India	24,413	49,663	65,705	82,273	75,779	6.8	11.2	8.3	10.1	...
Maldives	73	138	695	499	693	3.6	4.4	13.5	10.1	...
Nepal	188	226	341	480	591	10.6	8.4	10.2	12.2	...
Sri Lanka	1,408	3,551	3,335	2,825	11,228	12.3	20.8	20.3	15.9	...
Southeast Asia[a]	**56,491**	**98,890**	**142,146**	**146,275**	**139,551**					
Brunei Darussalam	...	...	...	...	...	...	...	...	...	...
Cambodia	65	691	2,498	2,460	3,401	1.1	5.1	9.7	8.7	...
Indonesia	31,569	60,274	75,408	58,432	73,304	18.7	34.6	23.3	19.5	...
Lao People's Democratic Republic	302	421	1,104	1,228	4,646	13.1	9.1	12.7	12.5	...
Malaysia	...	...	...	...	...	...	...	...	...	...
Myanmar	242	502	946	912	1,337	3.1	3.4	7.0	7.0	...
Philippines	11,461	10,577	9,017	12,981	15,226	18.7	12.9	8.1	10.8	...
Singapore	...	...	...	...	...	...	...	...	...	...
Thailand	10,968	19,599	26,940	41,609	16,922	4.7	7.1	7.9	11.8	...
Timor-Leste	0 (2012)	1	15	25	31	0.0(2012)	0.1	0.7	2.1	...
Viet Nam	1,884	6,825	26,218	28,627	24,682	2.4	3.9	6.8	7.5	...
The Pacific[a]	**931**	**1,514**	**4,739**	**5,940**	**...**					
Cook Islands[b,c]	3	5	...	...	...	57.9	26.9	...	...	...
Fiji	59	345	193	219	374	3.1	14.7	7.9	6.9	...
Kiribati[b]	1	1	2	2	2	4.4	4.0	0.9	0.9	0.8
Marshall Islands	9	8	7	7	...	14.9	9.4	6.8	7.2	...
Micronesia, Federated States of[b]	5	7	...	...	...	13.5	7.4	...	...	...
Nauru	...	...	...	...	...	...	...	...	...	...
Niue	...	...	...	...	...	...	...	...	...	...
Palau	...	...	...	...	...	...	...	...	...	...
Papua New Guinea	812	1,098	4,453	5,600	2,075	13.3	12.7	29.8	42.9	...
Samoa	11	23	39	39	37	5.0	9.8	20.5	10.4	...
Solomon Islands	21	14	12	30	91	6.2	2.4	2.4	4.9	...
Tonga	5	6	11	18	22	9.3	7.4	11.0	11.0	...
Tuvalu	...	...	...	...	...	...	...	...	...	...
Vanuatu	6	7	22	25	21	1.6	2.0	6.1	5.5	...
DEVELOPING ADB MEMBER ECONOMIES[a]	**248,654**	**394,562**	**810,168**	**810,142**	**...**					

... = data not available, 0 or 0.0 = magnitude is less than half of unit employed, $ = United States dollars, ADB = Asian Development Bank.

a Aggregates include only reporting economies with data corresponding to the year heading.
b Refers to principal repayments on long-term debt plus interest on short-term and long-term debt.
c Refers to debt service as a percentage of total exports as reflected under "International Trade in Goods (by partner country/economy)" in the individual economy table available via the Key Indicators Database at https://kidb.adb.org.

Sources: World Bank. International Debt Statistics. http://data.worldbank.org/data-catalog/international-debt-statistics (accessed 21 July 2025); economies' official sources; and Asian Development Bank estimates using economies' official sources.

Tourism

Table 2.4.24: International Tourist Arrivals
('000)

ADB Regional Member	2010	2015	2019	2020	2021	2022	2023	2024
Developing ADB Member Economies								
Central and West Asia[a]	**40,652**	**51,936**	**81,127**	**21,972**	**40,434**	**70,894**	**80,945**	**...**
Afghanistan	...	...	...	...	...	...	...	...
Armenia	684	1,192	1,894	375	870	1,666	2,316	2,208*
Azerbaijan	1,280	1,922	2,864	519	462	1,058	1,403	...
Georgia	1,067	3,012	5,080	1,087	1,577	3,653	4,669	5,092*
Kazakhstan	2,991	...	...	...	...	...	...	...
Kyrgyz Republic	1,224	4,000	8,508	2,079	3,564	6,913	8,557	...
Pakistan	907	...	3,583	163	1,859	1,918	2,215	...
Tajikistan	160	414	1,257	351	296	...	...	...
Türkiye	31,364	39,478	51,192	15,894	29,925	50,453	55,159	60,576*
Turkmenistan	...	...	...	...	...	...	...	...
Uzbekistan	975	1,918	6,749	1,504	1,881	5,233	6,626	...
East Asia[a]	**90,570**	**107,630**	**119,396**	**13,282**	**6,891**	**...**	**...**	**...**
China, People's Republic of	55,664	56,886	65,700	7,967	5,662	...	...	...
Hong Kong, China	20,085	26,686	23,752	1,359	89	568	17,159	21,944*
Korea, Republic of	8,798	13,232	17,503	2,519	967	3,198	11,032	16,370*
Mongolia	456	386	577	59	33	286	594	727*
Taipei,China	5,567	10,440	11,864	1,378	140	896	6,487	7,858*
South Asia[a]	**8,005**	**17,136**	**23,367**	**7,796**	**8,791**	**17,360**	**23,280**	**...**
Bangladesh	139	126	323	182	135	...	...	...
Bhutan	41	155	316	30	–	21	...	...
India	5,776	13,284	17,914	6,337	7,010	14,330	18,899	20,569*
Maldives	792	1,234	1,703	555	1,322	1,675	1,879	...
Nepal	603	539	1,197	230	151	614	1,015	1,148*
Sri Lanka	654	1,798	1,914	508	194	720	1,487	2,053*
Southeast Asia[a]	**70,471**	**104,243**	**138,075**	**25,558**	**2,934**	**35,875**	**86,248**	**...**
Brunei Darussalam	214	218	333	62	4	36	134	...
Cambodia	2,508	4,775	6,611	1,306	196	2,277	5,453	6,700*
Indonesia[b]	7,003 |	9,963	15,455	3,915	1,546	...	...	...
Lao People's Democratic Republic	1,670	3,543	4,384	812	...	1,203	3,147	3,943*
Malaysia	24,577	25,721	26,101	4,333	135	10,071	20,142	25,017*
Myanmar	792	4,681	4,364	903	131	233	1,285	1,063*
Philippines	3,520	5,361	8,261	1,483	164	2,654	5,003	5,439*
Singapore	9,161	12,052	14,560	2,164	84	4,675	10,256	12,432*
Thailand	15,936	29,923	39,916	6,725	511	11,065	28,150	35,546*
Timor-Leste	40	62	81	18	6	...	76	...
Viet Nam	5,050	7,944	18,009	3,837	157	3,661	12,602	17,472*
The Pacific[a]	**1,310**	**1,570**	**1,762**	**292**	**84**	**939**	**1,459**	**...**
Cook Islands	104	125	172	25	26	114	144	170*
Fiji	632	755	894	147	32	636	930	983*
Kiribati	5	4	8	1	0	2	8	...
Marshall Islands	5	6	11	1	0	1	6	...
Micronesia, Federated States of	45	31	20	...	...	2	2	...
Nauru	...	...	...	...	...	...	...	...
Niue	6	8	11	1	0	...	...	...
Palau	85	162	94	18	5	12	41	56*
Papua New Guinea	140	183	160	39	17	67	...	...
Samoa	122	128	172	23	3	49	169	173*
Solomon Islands	21	22	29	4	1	7	26	25*
Tonga	47	54	67	9	0	18	56	...
Tuvalu	2	2	4	1	0	0	...	...
Vanuatu	97	90	121	22	...	30	77	...
Developed ADB Member Economies[a]	**16,836**	**30,225**	**45,050**	**6,892**	**697**	**8,915**	**32,253**	**45,141***
Australia	5,790	7,449	9,466	1,828	246	3,694	7,187	8,271*
Japan	8,611	19,737	31,882	4,116	246	3,832	25,066	36,870*
New Zealand	2,435	3,039	3,702	948	205	1,389	...	...
DEVELOPING ADB MEMBER ECONOMIES[a]	**211,008**	**282,515**	**363,727**	**68,900**	**59,134**	**...**	**...**	**...**
ALL ADB REGIONAL MEMBERS[a]	**227,844**	**312,740**	**408,777**	**75,791**	**59,831**	**...**	**...**	**...**
WORLD	**856,653**	**1,081,367**	**1,466,000**	**408,000**	**461,000**	**976,000**	**1,306,000**	**1,465,000***

... = data not available, | = marks break in series, – = magnitude equals zero, 0 = magnitude is less than half of unit employed, * = provisional or preliminary, ADB = Asian Development Bank.

Note: For Australia; Japan; the Republic of Korea; the Kyrgyz Republic; Taipei,China; Tajikistan; Uzbekistan; and Viet Nam: Data refer to international visitor arrivals at frontiers (including tourists and same-day visitors). For the rest of the economies and the world total: Data refer to international tourist arrivals at frontiers (overnight visitors only, i.e., excluding same-day visitors).

a Includes only reporting economies with data corresponding to the year heading.
b Prior to 2015, data refer to international tourist arrivals at frontiers (overnight visitors only, i.e., excluding same-day visitors). For 2015 onward, data refer to international visitor arrivals at frontiers (including tourists and same-day visitors).

Sources: United Nations World Tourism Organization. UNWTO.eLibrary. https://www.e-unwto.org (accessed 19 June 2025) and World Tourism Barometer and Statistical Annex, May 2025. https://www.e-unwto.org/toc/wtobarometereng/23/2.

Table 2.4.25: International Tourism Receipts
($ million)

ADB Regional Member	2010	2015	2019	2020	2021	2022	2023	2024
Developing ADB Member Economies								
Central and West Asia[a]	**26,379**	**35,410**	**46,087**	**17,104**	**32,456**	**57,048**	**65,015**	**71,770***
Afghanistan	75	79	72	65	...	...	...	...
Armenia	646	936	1,528	287	784	2,439	3,009	2,441*
Azerbaijan	657	2,309	1,792	304	313	823	1,492	2,047*
Georgia	659	1,868	3,269	542	1,245	3,517	4,125	4,425*
Kazakhstan	1,005	1,632	2,456	613	608	1,491	2,256	2,571*
Kyrgyz Republic	160	426	644	151	207	756	1,024	...
Pakistan	305	317	494	439	559	738	859	752*
Tajikistan	3	1	14	6	11	18	20	20*
Türkiye	22,585	27,315	34,305	14,347	28,133	45,829	50,063	56,311*
Turkmenistan	...	...	...	...	...	...	...	...
Uzbekistan	284	527	1,513	350	596	1,437	2,167	3,203*
East Asia[a]	**86,731**	**109,974**	**100,536**	**24,915**	**24,749**	**31,103**	**70,382**	**89,641***
China, People's Republic of	45,814	44,969	35,832	9,951	11,330	13,474	25,036	39,747*
Hong Kong, China	21,689	35,574	28,913	2,859	1,850	3,134	20,863	22,618*
Korea, Republic of	10,263	14,798	20,867	10,276	10,804	12,462	15,294	16,717*
Mongolia	244	246	513	29	21	251	531	635*
Taipei,China	8,721	14,387	14,411	1,800	744	1,782	8,658	9,924*
South Asia[a]	**17,244**	**27,290**	**38,697**	**15,611**	**13,083**	**27,794**	**39,611**	**39,462***
Bangladesh	81	150	388	217	273	421	453	440*
Bhutan	40	94	120	84	2	0	89	199*
India	14,490	21,013	30,720	13,036	8,650	21,360	32,209	35,023*
Maldives	1,713	2,569	3,157	1,398	3,508	4,498	4,230	...
Nepal	344	483	705	194	143	379	562	631*
Sri Lanka	576	2,981	3,607	682	507	1,136	2,068	3,169*
Southeast Asia[a]	**68,484**	**105,091**	**146,981**	**31,531**	**10,700**	**49,332**	**101,877**	**126,113***
Brunei Darussalam	...	147	217	38	2	14	71	...
Cambodia	1,519	3,137	4,769	1,015	184	1,418	3,083	...
Indonesia	6,958	10,761	16,911	3,382	521	6,781	14,001	16,706*
Lao People's Democratic Republic	382	724	935	214	1	265	1,043	...
Malaysia	18,152	17,666	19,829	2,974	78	6,520	14,918	20,904*
Myanmar	72	2,120	2,483	...	...	...	...	...
Philippines	2,645	5,272	9,781	1,791	600	4,174	9,118	9,709*
Singapore	14,178	16,617	20,346	5,456	4,019	11,402	20,768	23,849*
Thailand	20,104	41,246	59,810	13,403	5,134	14,874	29,665	42,691*
Timor-Leste	24	51	70	26	12	43	51	64*
Viet Nam	4,450	7,350	11,830	3,232	149	3,841	9,159	12,190*
The Pacific[a]	**1,256**	**1,620**	**1,855**	**368**	**...**	**...**	**...**	**...**
Cook Islands	111	173	228	37	43	...	...	...
Fiji	635	817	962	151	35	696	1,051	...
Kiribati	4	2	3	0	0	2	2	...
Marshall Islands	4	1	4	4	...	...	...	...
Micronesia, Federated States of	24	25	...	...	...	...	...	...
Nauru	1	2	...	...	...	...	...	...
Niue	...	...	...	...	...	...	...	...
Palau	73	149	83	41	4	15	...	...
Papua New Guinea	2	2	4	2	1	1	3	...
Samoa	123	142	207	24	...	59	220	231*
Solomon Islands	44	51	71	6	...	5	23	28*
Tonga	16	43	57	47	9	10	44	62*
Tuvalu	2	5	8	1	0	1	9	...
Vanuatu	217	208	229	55	2	39	...	...
Developed ADB Member Economies[a]	**48,219**	**68,701**	**102,109**	**41,950**	**24,796**	**37,802**	**93,109**	**116,045***
Australia	28,472	34,269	45,522	25,821	16,998	24,647	46,126	51,807*
Japan	13,224	24,968	46,054	10,700	4,861	9,238	38,587	54,673*
New Zealand	6,523	9,464	10,533	5,751	2,866	3,601	7,930	9,565*
DEVELOPING ADB MEMBER ECONOMIES[a]	**200,093**	**279,385**	**334,156**	**89,529**	**81,082**	**166,105**	**278,237**	**...**
ALL ADB REGIONAL MEMBERS[a]	**248,312**	**348,086**	**436,265**	**131,479**	**105,878**	**203,907**	**371,346**	**...**
WORLD	**940,236**	**1,203,092**	**1,487,000**	**558,000**	**655,000**	**1,142,000**	**1,536,000**	**1,746,000***

... = data not available, 0 = magnitude is less than half of unit employed, * = provisional or preliminary, $ = United States dollars, ADB = Asian Development Bank.

a Includes only reporting economies with data corresponding to the year heading.

Sources: United Nations World Tourism Organization. UNWTO.eLibrary. https://www.e-unwto.org (accessed 19 June 2025); and United Nations World Tourism Organization. 2025. World Tourism Barometer, Statistical Annex. Volume 23.

Data Issues and Comparability

Most of the data on international transactions presented in this section were taken from balance-of-payments statistics as reported by individual economies. International Monetary Fund (IMF) guidelines are followed by most governments in compiling these statistics. However, authorities have difficulty accurately recording nonofficial transactions such as migrant workers' remittances and private capital flows, which is one of the reasons that the IMF's Balance of Payments Manual (BPM) was updated to the sixth edition (BPM6) in 2009. All economies in the region have adopted BPM6 in recent years, except for two economies that still rely on the IMF's BPM5. However, there is not a single framework for an extended time series available for all economies. At present, there are 20 economies reporting a mix of BPM5 and BPM6, and three economies reporting a mix of BPM4 and BPM6. This therefore affects the comparability of data across economies.

The World Trade Organization and other international agencies closely monitor international trade statistics. Common definitions are used by all economies, with the larger economies throughout Asia and the Pacific using standard forms and procedures for data processing.

Data on official development assistance, other official flows, and private direct investment and other private capital are compiled by the Organisation for Economic Co-operation and Development's Development Assistance Committee. These data are standardized on a calendar-year basis for all donors, but may have discrepancies for some economies owing to the fiscal-year data available in budget documents. Commitments from donors do not necessarily translate to actual disbursements to recipient economies of official development assistance.

Table 2.5.1: Road Indicators—Total Network, Passenger Kilometers Travel, Freight Kilometers Travel

ADB Regional Member	Road Indicators Network, Total (km)			Road Passenger Travel[a] (p-km million)			Road Freight Kilometers Travel[b] (t-km million)		
	2010	2015	2023	2010	2015	2023	2010	2015	2023
Developing ADB Member Economies									
Central and West Asia									
Afghanistan	19,138 (2011)	37,090	...	...	...	...	6,796.0 (2011)	4,423.0	...
Armenia	9,125	10,368	11,190	2,344.3	2,395.9	2,028.5	235.8	479.4	1,149.6
Azerbaijan[c]	18,977	19,016	78,632	16,633.0	23,825.0	25,645.0	11,728.0	16,038.0	12,450.0
Georgia	...	...	41,098	...	...	...	619.7	664.3	737.7
Kazakhstan	96,018	96,529	94,352 (2024)	...	...	...	80,300.0	161,864.7	146,895.1 (2022)
Kyrgyz Republic	...	...	...	7,209.5	9,005.6	9,801.7 (2024)	1,281.5	1,401.7	1,531.2 (2024)
Pakistan	260,040	265,404	...	...	...	...	...	...	...
Tajikistan	...	...	...	...	7,137.2	9,514.8	...	5,672.3	11,815.7
Türkiye	367,263	238,899	261,156	...	...	...	190,365.0	244,329.0	335,126.0
Turkmenistan	...	...	13,773 (2021)	27,657.0	...	...	11,399.0	...	...
Uzbekistan	41,950	42,013	41,888 (2024)	78,400.0	109,100.0	134,504.7	9,076.3	12,752.6	22,290.7
East Asia									
China, People's Republic of	4,008,200	4,577,300	5,436,800	1,502,080.0	1,074,270.0	474,000.0	4,338,970.0	5,795,570.0	7,395,020.0
Hong Kong, China	2,076	2,101	2,241 (2024)	...	...	...	...	...	...
Korea, Republic of	...	99,024	107,149	104,671.0	385,018.1	385,788.2 (2022)	103,898.0	132,382.0	...
Mongolia	...	109,567 (2017)	111,917 (2024)	1,480.2	1,940.5	2,204.6 (2024)	1,834.0	2,374.0	12,746.1 (2024)
Taipei,China	40,335	41,952	42,992	...	...	...	29,631.6	37,805.3	33,171.0
South Asia									
Bangladesh	21,269	21,365	22,476 (2022)	...	...	...	...	...	...
Bhutan	4,661	11,177	18,343 (2022)	...	...	...	...	...	...
India	4,582,439	5,472,144	6,360,004 (2020)	8,409,000.0	15,428,000.0	...	1,287,300.0	2,027,400.0	...
Maldives	...	...	...	...	...	...	...	...	...
Nepal	23,209	28,308	35,809 (2022)	...	...	...	...	...	...
Sri Lanka	29,119	31,280	31,388 (2022)	...	...	...	...	...	...
Southeast Asia									
Brunei Darussalam	3,127 (2011)	3,355	3,820	...	...	...	...	...	...
Cambodia	44,919	58,000	67,715 (2022)	...	...	...	...	...	...
Indonesia	487,314	529,073	550,735	...	...	...	...	...	...
Lao People's Democratic Republic	47,491	56,332	59,101 (2020)	2,556.0	3,202.1	5,150.0 (2022)	513.0	434.7	628.7 (2022)
Malaysia	144,403	214,816	303,076 (2022)	...	...	...	...	...	...
Myanmar	...	...	136,464 (2021)	...	40,840.0	8,162.1 (2021)	507.9	419.4	243.8
Philippines	31,242	32,633	35,526 (2024)	...	...	...	...	...	...
Singapore	8,895	9,246	9,644	...	...	...	...	...	...
Thailand	...	...	706,345 (2024)	452,040.0	663,561.0	...	185,884.0	193,911.4	187,728.0 (2020)
Timor-Leste	...	8,701	...	...	...	...	...	...	...
Viet Nam	295,100	360,216	...	69,197.4	105,382.2	107,373.2 (2022)	36,179.0	51,514.9	94,155.3 (2022)
The Pacific									
Cook Islands	...	...	...	...	...	...	...	...	...
Fiji	...	...	...	...	...	...	...	...	...
Kiribati	...	...	...	...	...	...	...	...	...
Marshall Islands	...	...	...	...	...	...	...	...	...
Micronesia, Federated States of	...	...	...	...	...	...	...	...	...
Nauru	...	...	...	...	...	...	...	...	...
Niue	...	...	...	...	...	...	...	...	...
Palau	...	...	...	...	...	...	...	...	...
Papua New Guinea	...	30,000 (2016)	...	...	...	...	...	...	...
Samoa	1,152 (2012)	...	...	...	...	...	...	...	...
Solomon Islands	...	...	...	...	...	...	...	...	...
Tonga	...	...	...	...	...	...	...	...	...
Tuvalu	...	120 (2017)	...	...	...	...	...	...	...
Vanuatu	1,776 (2012)	2,241 (2014)	...	...	...	...	...	...	...
Developed ADB Member Economies									
Australia	872,292	874,143	...	281,717.1	300,758.2	293,414.7 (2024)	181,480.7	202,454.0	248,986.9 (2024)
Japan	1,210,000	1,221,000	1,228,100 (2020)	78,962.0	67,019.0	44,185.0 (2022)	286,538.0	240,195.0	226,886.0 (2022)
New Zealand	94,126	94,822	97,231	...	...	...	21,265.0	23,078.0	25,939.0

... = data not available; ADB = Asian Development Bank; p-km = passenger-kilometer; t-km = ton-kilometer.

a A passenger-kilometer, abbreviated as p-km, is a unit of measurement representing the transport of 1 passenger by a defined mode of transport over 1 kilometer.

b A ton-kilometer, abbreviated as t-km, is a unit of measurement representing the transport of 1 metric ton of goods (including packaging and tare weights of intermodal transport units) by a defined mode of transport over 1 kilometer. Only the distance on the national territory of the reporting economy is taken into account for national, international and transit transport.

c For 2010 and 2015, road network only covers republican and local importance roads.

Source: Asian Development Bank. Asian Transport Outlook (ATO) National Database. https://asiantransportobservatory.org/snd/ (access 23 June 2025).

Table 2.5.2: Road Indicators—Registered Vehicles

ADB Regional Member	2010	2015	2016	2017	2018	2019	2020	2021	2022	2023
Developing ADB Member Economies										
Central and West Asia										
Afghanistan	1,197,574(2011)	1,831,900	1,849,199	1,933,931	1,927,387	1,978,846	2,009,407	2,011,692	2,020,589	2,326,538
Armenia	...	...	...	...	...	...	...	...	...	...
Azerbaijan	982,553	1,322,610	1,333,841	1,345,401	1,373,780	1,422,473	1,473,563	1,566,743	1,645,253	1,738,940
Georgia	702,700	1,081,400	1,167,200	1,228,100	1,289,000	1,339,300	1,404,400	1,490,200	1,563,200	1,680,400
Kazakhstan	3,579,200	4,397,369	4,383,139	4,382,662	4,342,159	4,325,293	4,433,522	4,386,620	4,449,332	5,744,100(2024)
Kyrgyz Republic	...	...	...	...	...	...	...	...	...	...
Pakistan	7,853,002	18,502,109	21,067,850	23,812,676	26,566,167	29,137,562	30,757,539	...	...	...
Tajikistan	...	...	...	...	...	...	...	...	...	...
Türkiye	15,095,603	19,994,472	21,090,424	22,218,945	22,865,921	23,156,975	24,144,857	25,249,119	26,482,847	31,301,389(2024)
Turkmenistan	...	...	...	...	...	...	...	...	...	...
Uzbekistan	...	...	...	...	...	...	...	...	...	...
East Asia										
China, People's Republic of	78,018,100	162,844,400	185,745,400	209,066,700	232,312,300	253,763,900	273,409,200	294,185,900	311,844,300	329,115,500
Hong Kong, China	664,726	798,316	818,316	840,597	865,661	879,154	912,790	926,238	925,171	904,260(2024)
Korea, Republic of	...	23,151,659	23,984,039	24,724,770	25,410,979	25,914,261	26,654,988	27,124,938	27,700,841	28,540,156(2024)
Mongolia	608,274(2012)	789,720	841,552	900,145	970,880	1,043,028	1,136,734	1,234,701	1,264,892	1,339,005(2024)
Taipei,China	18,176,222	21,400,863	21,510,650	21,704,365	21,871,240	22,111,807	22,297,000	22,597,694	22,844,046	23,136,070
South Asia										
Bangladesh	1,509,028	2,441,829	2,818,752	3,238,702	3,690,000	4,075,411	4,451,671	4,927,601	5,463,420	...
Bhutan	43,581	60,651	68,149	75,490	81,160	88,264	92,167	99,194	102,236	...
India	129,499,241	209,284,140	229,557,955	253,310,000	272,586,500	295,771,514	326,299,000	335,551,000	354,018,000	...
Maldives	46,027	77,775	87,125	97,212	108,530	121,700	130,153	142,498	158,743	177,281
Nepal	1,178,911	2,339,169	2,783,428	3,221,042	3,539,519	...	...	...	...	...
Sri Lanka	3,954,311	6,302,141	6,795,469	7,247,122	7,727,921	8,095,224	8,297,852	8,331,702	8,352,213	8,380,103
Southeast Asia										
Brunei Darussalam	164,071(2009)	266,139	276,119	276,013	281,066	288,762	...	276,373	310,163	320,659
Cambodia	...	...	...	...	...	...	...	...	...	...
Indonesia	76,907,127	120,786,914	128,069,103	118,922,708	126,508,776	133,617,012	136,137,451	142,334,222	148,618,398	157,080,504
Lao People's Democratic Republic	1,008,788	1,717,144	1,850,020	1,979,054	2,104,655	2,233,133	2,342,844	2,997,485	3,044,568	3,157,832
Malaysia	19,695,114	25,164,473	27,052,231	26,350,246	29,277,453	30,497,054	31,642,275	...	...	...
Myanmar	2,084,819	4,969,096	5,444,045	6,216,988	6,721,124	7,278,431	7,482,330	7,633,963	...	...
Philippines	6,634,710	8,706,607	9,251,565	10,410,814	11,595,434	12,725,306	11,851,192	12,996,497	13,856,622	...
Singapore	945,829	957,246	956,430	961,842	957,006	973,101	973,990	988,755	995,746	1,007,094(2024)
Thailand	28,263,065	36,240,902	38,618,297	37,786,347	39,006,652	40,145,613	40,889,852	41,706,531	42,755,903	43,705,286
Timor-Leste	10,940	17,801	19,498	21,969	23,974	...	...	...	...	...
Viet Nam	32,362,000	46,137,400	49,646,700	56,850,000	61,317,400	65,572,500	...	...	...	...
The Pacific										
Cook Islands	...	...	...	...	...	...	...	...	...	...
Fiji	81,926	101,425	110,763	117,623	119,960	131,571	131,687	138,650	144,339	...
Kiribati	...	...	...	...	...	...	...	...	...	...
Marshall Islands	2,343(2008)	...	...	...	...	...	...	...	...	...
Micronesia, Federated States of	7,586	8,314	9,004	8,140	9,433	11,751	...	...	...	...
Nauru	1,737(2011)	...	...	...	...	...	...	...	...	...
Niue	846(2011)	1,392(2014)	...	...	...	...	...	...	...	...
Palau	5,643	4,120	7,413	6,656	7,592	8,140	7,575	7,761	7,891	7,225
Papua New Guinea	...	...	...	...	...	...	...	...	...	...
Samoa	16,349(2011)	17,397(2013)	...	22,045	...	...	...	...	...	...
Solomon Islands	...	...	...	...	...	...	...	...	...	...
Tonga	19,432	...	...	...	...	...	...	...	...	...
Tuvalu	...	...	...	...	...	...	...	...	...	...
Vanuatu	5,368(2009)	...	...	...	...	...	...	...	...	...
Developed ADB Member Economies										
Australia	16,061,100	18,007,767	18,387,136	18,781,204	19,173,279	19,505,241	19,805,331	20,267,832	20,678,174	21,736,966(2024)
Japan	78,653,371	80,892,607	81,256,449	81,541,204	81,764,583	81,849,782	82,077,752	82,174,944	82,451,350	82,568,673
New Zealand	3,415,714	3,812,556	3,972,677	4,137,889	4,267,140	4,375,437	4,426,339	4,526,928	4,621,519	4,689,672

... = data not available, ADB = Asian Development Bank.

Source: Asian Development Bank. Asian Transport Outlook (ATO) National Database. https://asiantransportobservatory.org/snd/ (access 23 June 2025).

Table 2.5.3: Road indicators—Safety

ADB Regional Member	Estimated Road Traffic Deaths, 2021		Road User Deaths, 2021[a] (%)				
	Total	Death Rate (per 100,000 people)	Four-Wheeled Vehicles	Two- and Three-Wheeled Vehicles	Cyclists	Pedestrians	Others
Developing ADB Member Economies							
Central and West Asia[b]	**47,592**	**13.3**					
Afghanistan	9,684	24.1	...	...	...	...	...
Armenia	379	13.6	68.0	–	–	32.0	–
Azerbaijan	1,769	17.2	52.0	1.0	1.0	42.0	4.0
Georgia	476	12.7	45.0	1.0	1.0	27.0	27.0
Kazakhstan	2,340	12.2	64.0	1.0	–	27.0	8.0
Kyrgyz Republic	869	13.3	28.0	2.0	–	40.0	30.0
Pakistan	27,568	11.9	16.0	39.0	–	41.0	4.0
Tajikistan	1,352	13.9	...	...	...	...	...
Türkiye	...	...	...	...	...	...	...
Turkmenistan	...	...	...	...	...	...	...
Uzbekistan	3,155	9.3	...	...	...	...	...
East Asia[b]	**252,083**	**17.0**					
China, People's Republic of	248,099	17.4	13.0	26.0	20.0	29.0	12.0
Hong Kong, China	...	...	...	...	...	...	...
Korea, Republic of	3,570	6.9	19.0	22.0	6.0	35.0	19.0
Mongolia	414	12.4	66.0	–	1.0	34.0	–
Taipei,China	...	...	...	...	...	...	...
South Asia	**259,290**	**15.9**					
Bangladesh	31,578	18.6	42.0	11.0	2.0	32.0	14.0
Bhutan	95	12.2	95.0	2.0	–	3.0	–
India	216,618	15.4	13.0	45.0	3.0	19.0	20.0
Maldives	7	1.3	–	75.0	–	25.0	–
Nepal	8,479	28.2	35.0	34.0	4.0	23.0	5.0
Sri Lanka	2,513	11.5	15.0	12.0	43.0	27.0	4.0
Southeast Asia[b]	**97,256**	**14.4**					
Brunei Darussalam	...	...	...	...	...	...	...
Cambodia	3,113	18.8	6.0	74.0	2.0	10.0	8.0
Indonesia	31,063	11.3	2.0	80.0	–	–	18.0
Lao People's Democratic Republic	1,217	16.4	19.0	67.0	3.0	10.0	2.0
Malaysia	4,680	13.9	20.0	63.0	1.0	6.0	11.0
Myanmar	10,405	19.3	11.0	47.0	3.0	12.0	27.0
Philippines	11,062	9.7	1.0	14.0	1.0	3.0	81.0
Singapore	110	1.9	18.0	47.0	10.0	22.0	4.0
Thailand	18,218	25.4	–	51.0	–	2.0	46.0
Timor-Leste	159	12.0	...	...	...	...	...
Viet Nam	17,229	17.7	35.0	57.0	7.0	–	...
The Pacific[b]	**...**	**...**					
Cook Islands	3	17.6	20.0	80.0	–	–	–
Fiji	...	...	...	...	...	...	...
Kiribati	8	6.2	40.0	20.0	–	40.0	–
Marshall Islands	...	...	...	...	...	...	...
Micronesia, Federated States of	...	...	...	...	...	...	...
Nauru	...	...	...	...	...	...	...
Niue	–	–	...	...	...	...	...
Palau	...	...	...	...	...	...	...
Papua New Guinea	...	...	...	...	...	...	...
Samoa	21	9.6	21.0	–	–	63.0	16.0
Solomon Islands	...	...	...	...	...	...	...
Tonga	...	...	...	...	...	...	...
Tuvalu	...	...	...	...	...	...	...
Vanuatu	...	...	...	...	...	...	...
Developed ADB Member Economies	**4,805**	**3.1**					
Australia	1,163	4.5	–	17.0	4.0	12.0	67.0
Japan	3,304	2.7	27.0	12.0	16.0	35.0	9.0
New Zealand	338	6.6	70.0	15.0	2.0	8.0	5.0
DEVELOPING ADB MEMBER ECONOMIES[b]	**656,253**	**15.8**					
ALL ADB REGIONAL MEMBERS[b]	**661,058**	**15.4**					

... = data not available, – = magnitude equals zero, ADB = Asian Development Bank.

a Nature of road user deaths might not add up to 100% due to rounding.
b Regional aggregates include reporting economies only.

Source: World Health Organization. 2023. Global Status Report on Road Safety 2023. Geneva. (accessed 23 June 2025).

Table 2.5.4: Rail Indicators—Total Route, Length per Land Area

ADB Regional Member	Rail Lines, Total Route (km)			Rail Network, Length per Land Area (km per km^2 '000)		
	2010	2015	2023	2010	2015	2023
Developing ADB Member Economies						
Central and West Asia						
Afghanistan	106.0 (2011)	106.0	...	0.2 (2011)	0.2	...
Armenia	871.1	823.6	809.3	30.6	28.9	28.4
Azerbaijan	2,079.0 (2011)	2,068.0 (2016)	2,180.0	25.2 (2011)	25.0 (2016)	26.4
Georgia	1,566.0	1,576.0	1,576.5	22.5	22.7	22.7
Kazakhstan	15,016.1	15,341.1	16,008.5 (2024)	5.6	5.7	5.9 (2024)
Kyrgyz Republic	...	...	...	...	...	...
Pakistan	7,791.0	7,791.0	7,791.0 (2020)	10.1	10.1	10.1 (2020)
Tajikistan	...	...	...	...	...	...
Türkiye	8,722.0	8,947.0	9,235.0	11.1	11.4	11.8
Turkmenistan	...	...	...	...	...	...
Uzbekistan	4,227.2	4,238.0	4,800.0	9.9	9.6	10.9
East Asia						
China, People's Republic of	91,200.0	121,000.0	158,700.0	9.7	12.8	16.8
Hong Kong, China	...	...	...	...	...	...
Korea, Republic of	3,557.3	3,873.5	4,131.2 (2022)	36.6	39.8	42.4 (2022)
Mongolia	...	1,810.0 (2016)	1,100.0 (2019)	...	1.2 (2016)	0.7 (2019)
Taipei,China	1,085.0	1,065.0	1,065.0	30.0	29.4	29.4
South Asia						
Bangladesh	2,460.0	2,877.0	3,100.6 (2022)	18.9	22.1	23.8 (2022)
Bhutan	...	...	...	...	...	...
India	64,460.0	66,252.0	69,181.0 (2024)	21.7	22.3	23.3 (2024)
Maldives	...	...	...	...	...	...
Nepal	...	...	...	...	...	...
Sri Lanka	1,263.0	1,568.0	1,611.0	20.1	25.3	26.0
Southeast Asia						
Brunei Darussalam	...	...	...	...	...	...
Cambodia[a]	604.0	257.0	652.0 (2019)	3.4	1.5	3.7 (2019)
Indonesia	4,816.4	5,286.0	6,466.2 (2021)	2.7	2.9	3.4 (2021)
Lao People's Democratic Republic	...	...	...	...	...	...
Malaysia	1,792.0	1,775.0	1,775.0 (2022)	5.5	5.4	5.4 (2022)
Myanmar	5,487.8	6,107.4	6,112.3	8.4	9.4	9.4
Philippines	452.0	452.0	452.0 (2020)	1.5	1.5	1.5 (2020)
Singapore	...	...	...	...	...	...
Thailand	4,507.9	4,507.9	4,801.3 (2020)	8.8	8.8	9.4 (2020)
Timor-Leste	...	...	...	...	...	...
Viet Nam	2,577.0	3,147.0	2,646.0 (2020)	8.3	10.1	8.5 (2020)
The Pacific						
Cook Islands	...	...	...	...	...	...
Fiji	...	590.0 (2014)	...	...	32.3 (2014)	...
Kiribati	...	...	...	...	...	...
Marshall Islands	...	...	...	...	...	...
Micronesia, Federated States of	...	...	...	...	...	...
Nauru	...	...	...	...	...	...
Niue	...	...	...	...	...	...
Palau	...	...	...	...	...	...
Papua New Guinea	...	...	...	...	...	...
Samoa	...	...	...	...	...	...
Solomon Islands	...	...	...	...	...	...
Tonga	...	...	...	...	...	...
Tuvalu	...	...	...	...	...	...
Vanuatu	...	...	...	...	...	...
Developed ADB Member Economies						
Australia	...	33,343.0	31,190.8 (2024)	...	4.3	4.1 (2024)
Japan	...	...	16,579.6 (2021)	...	...	45.5 (2021)
New Zealand	...	...	3,700.0 (2019)	...	...	14.1 (2019)

... = data not available, ADB = Asian Development Bank, km = kilometer, km^2 = square kilometer.

a Data refers to railways rehabilitated and constructed.

Sources: For rail lines, total route: Asian Development Bank. Asian Development Bank. Asian Transport Outlook (ATO) National Database. https://asiantransportobservatory.org/snd/ (access 23 June 2025). For rail network: Asian Development Bank estimates using land area data from World Bank. World Development Indicators. https://data.worldbank.org/indicator (accessed 23 June 2025).

Table 2.5.5: Railways—Passengers Carried and Goods Transported

ADB Regional Member	Passengers Carried[a] (p-km million)			Goods Transported[b] (t-km million)		
	2010	2015	2023	2010	2015	2023
Developing ADB Member Economies						
Central and West Asia						
Afghanistan	...	...	...	...	...	...
Armenia	125.6	104.3	164.0	743.2	640.3	907.1
Azerbaijan	834.0	439.0	314.0	8,331.0	6,269.0	7,097.0
Georgia	...	544.5 (2016)	687.3	6,227.5	4,261.3	4,193.2
Kazakhstan	16,056.0	17,011.6	16,459.5	213,200.0	267,400.0	307,558.3
Kyrgyz Republic	98.7	40.8	25.0 (2024)	737.7	917.8	1,013.8
Pakistan	20,619.0	21,201.0	20,485.0 (2020)	4,846.9	3,301.4	7,369.9 (2020)
Tajikistan	...	16.0	23.3	...	...	...
Türkiye	5,491.0	8,326.1	20,912.7	...	...	...
Turkmenistan	1,685.0	...	...	9,715.0	...	...
Uzbekistan	3,500.0	4,180.5	3,930.0	22,300.0	22,934.9	...
East Asia						
China, People's Republic of	876,220.0	1,196,060.0	1,472,940.0	2,764,410.0	2,375,430.0	3,594,570.0
Hong Kong, China	...	...	...	...	...	...
Korea, Republic of	58,381.8	68,371.0	82,899.5 (2022)	9,452.4	9,479.3	...
Mongolia	1,220.0	996.7	847.6 (2024)	10,286.7	11,462.6	14,948.8
Taipei,China	20,930.8	27,110.9	29,769.4	866.3	636.2	474.5
South Asia						
Bangladesh	8,052.3	8,711.0	8,663.4 (2021)	693.0	694.0	...
Bhutan	...	...	...	...	...	...
India	978,508.0	1,149,835.0 (2016)	1,064,700.0	625,723.0 (2011)	...	871,816.0
Maldives	...	...	...	...	...	...
Nepal	...	...	...	...	...	...
Sri Lanka	4,568.0	7,407.0	7,044.0	162.8	127.4	138.7
Southeast Asia						
Brunei Darussalam	...	...	...	...	...	...
Cambodia	...	...	...	...	...	...
Indonesia	20,340.0	22,296.0	24,974.0	6,559.0	10,057.0	18,568.0 (2023)
Lao People's Democratic Republic	...	130.0	45.0 (2022)	...	...	930.0
Malaysia	1,532.2	426.1	251.2	1,482.8	1,474.5	...
Myanmar	5,371.4	3,416.2	738.0	1,059.4	812.3	333.7 (2021)
Philippines	...	...	...	...	...	...
Singapore	7,880.0	9,391.0 (2014)	...	...	...	...
Thailand	8,246.0	6,133.4	2,876.6 (2022)	...	2,545.3	...
Timor-Leste	...	...	...	...	...	...
Viet Nam	4,377.9	4,149.6	1,598.4 (2022)	3,960.9	4,035.5	4,099.9 (2021)
The Pacific						
Cook Islands	...	...	...	...	...	...
Fiji	...	...	...	...	...	...
Kiribati	...	...	...	...	...	...
Marshall Islands	...	...	...	...	...	...
Micronesia, Federated States of	...	...	...	...	...	...
Nauru	...	...	...	...	...	...
Niue	...	...	...	...	...	...
Palau	...	...	...	...	...	...
Papua New Guinea	...	...	...	...	...	...
Samoa	...	...	...	...	...	...
Solomon Islands	...	...	...	...	...	...
Tonga	...	...	...	...	...	...
Tuvalu	...	...	...	...	...	...
Vanuatu	...	...	...	...	...	...
Developed ADB Member Economies						
Australia	14,553.6	15,473.8	15,205.9 (2024)	261,830.6	413,937.5	445,347.7
Japan	393,466.0	427,486.2	352,853.0 (2022)	20,398.0	21,519.0	18,042.0 (2021)
New Zealand	...	477.3	428.5 (2024)	4,768.0 (2012)	4,348.0	3,823.4 (2023)

... = data not available; ADB = Asian Development Bank; km = kilometer; t = metric ton.

a A passenger-kilometer, abbreviated as p-km, is a unit of measurement representing the transport of 1 passenger by a defined mode of transport over 1 kilometer.

b A ton-kilometer, abbreviated as t-km, is a unit of measurement representing the transport of 1 metric ton of goods (including packaging and tare weights of intermodal transport units) by a defined mode of transport over 1 kilometer. Only the distance on the national territory of the reporting economy is taken into account for national, international and transit transport.

Source: Asian Development Bank. Asian Transport Outlook (ATO) National Database. https://asiantransportobservatory.org/snd/ (access 23 June 2025).

Table 2.5.6: Air Transport

ADB Regional Member	Aviation Total Passenger Kilometers[a] (p-km million)			Aviation Freight Transport[b] (t-km million)		
	2010	2015	2023	2010	2015	2023
Developing ADB Member Economies						
Central and West Asia						
Afghanistan	…	…	…	…	…	…
Armenia	1,278.6	27.4 (2016)	3,090.9	9.7	– (2016)	17.7
Azerbaijan	1,613.0	3,338.0	5,280.0	139.0	582.0	3,017.0
Georgia	368.9	548.9	875.3	0.9	41.3	425.8
Kazakhstan	6,469.2	11,153.3	28,300.7 (2024)	88.6	115.4	141.3 (2022)
Kyrgyz Republic	814.2	1,966.1	2,126.7 (2024)	64.4	57.4	252.3 (2024)
Pakistan	16,209.0	13,751.0	14,938.0 (2019)	188.9	135.5	66.2 (2020)
Tajikistan	…	2,028.6	2,007.4	…	6.3	2.4
Türkiye	…	…	…	…	…	…
Turkmenistan	2,712.0	…	…	29.0	…	…
Uzbekistan	5,800.0	6,786.0	13,800.0	168.0	131.1	226.3
East Asia						
China, People's Republic of	403,899.6	951,303.6 (2017)	1,030,900.0	17,890.0	20,807.0	28,362.0
Hong Kong, China	…	…	…	…	…	…
Korea, Republic of	135,770.8	198,443.4	106,873.1 (2022)	145.0	112.0	…
Mongolia	907.2	1,993.5	4,893.7 (2024)	…	…	…
Taipei,China	60,051.2	80,054.8	20,938.5 (2020)	11,873.3	9,079.7	10,297.6 (2020)
South Asia						
Bangladesh	5,027.0	6,645.0	6,005.0 (2022)	123.0	199.0	786.0 (2022)
Bhutan	…	…	…	…	…	…
India	103,171.0	145,787.0	81,800.0 (2022)	…	…	…
Maldives	…	…	…	…	…	…
Nepal	…	…	…	67.4	68.0	85.6 (2021)
Sri Lanka	9,399.6	12,737.3	12,265.3	1,472.7	1,146.4	1,379.5
Southeast Asia						
Brunei Darussalam	…	…	…	…	…	…
Cambodia	…	…	…	–	…	…
Indonesia	59,435.9	65,171.7	65,950.3	11,591.5	5,940.6	5,038.2
Lao People's Democratic Republic	82.8	846.1	610.0 (2022)	1.2	0.4	0.6 (2022)
Malaysia	66,719.0	87,210.0	25,018.0 (2020)	…	…	…
Myanmar	566.1	1,452.2	14,699.3 (2021)	1.3	5.0	107.3 (2021)
Philippines	…	…	…	…	…	…
Singapore	…	…	…	…	…	…
Thailand	…	…	…	29,309.0	27,221.0	24,232.0 (2019)
Timor-Leste	…	…	…	…	…	…
Viet Nam	21,162.0	42,068.4	54,918.3 (2022)	426.8	599.5	…
The Pacific						
Cook Islands	…	…	…	…	…	…
Fiji	…	…	…	…	…	…
Kiribati	…	…	…	…	…	…
Marshall Islands	…	…	…	…	…	…
Micronesia, Federated States of	…	…	…	…	…	…
Nauru	…	…	…	…	…	…
Niue	…	…	…	…	…	…
Palau	…	…	…	…	…	…
Papua New Guinea	…	…	…	…	…	…
Samoa	…	…	…	…	…	…
Solomon Islands	…	…	…	…	…	…
Tonga	…	…	…	…	…	…
Tuvalu	…	…	…	…	…	…
Vanuatu	…	…	…	…	…	…
Developed ADB Member Economies						
Australia	60,223.3	70,162.1	74,274.7 (2024)	321.5	273.1	210.0 (2024)
Japan	133,649.0	172,984.0	143,407.0 (2022)	1,032.0	1,056.0	707.0 (2022)
New Zealand	…	…	…	…	…	…

… = data not available, – = magnitude equals zero, ADB = Asian Development Bank, p-km = passenger-kilometer, t-km = ton-kilometer.

a A passenger-kilometer, abbreviated as p-km, is a unit of measurement representing the transport of 1 passenger by a defined mode of transport over 1 kilometer. For air transport, it includes both domestic and international flights.

b A ton-kilometer, abbreviated as t-km, is a unit of measurement representing the transport of 1 metric ton of goods (including packaging and tare weights of intermodal transport units) by a defined mode of transport over 1 kilometer. For air transport, it includes both domestic and international flights.

Source: Asian Development Bank. Asian Transport Outlook (ATO) National Database. https://asiantransportobservatory.org/snd/ (access 23 June 2025).

Table 2.5.7: Logistics

ADB Regional Member	Container Port Traffic (teu '000)			Liner Shipping Connectivity Index[a]			Logistics Performance Index[b]		
	2010	2015	2022	2010	2015	2023	2012	2018	2023
Developing ADB Member Economies									
Central and West Asia									
Afghanistan	...	...	...	...	...	...	2.3	1.9	1.9
Armenia	...	...	...	...	...	...	2.6	2.6	2.5
Azerbaijan	...	...	...	...	...	...	2.5	...	...
Georgia	242	277	401 (2021)	22.6	19.2	26.8	...	2.4	2.7
Kazakhstan	...	...	...	...	...	...	2.7	2.8	2.7
Kyrgyz Republic	...	...	...	...	...	...	2.4	2.5	2.3
Pakistan	2,224	2,706	3,384	138.1	126.2	149.4	2.8	2.4	...
Tajikistan	...	...	...	...	...	...	2.3	2.3	2.5
Türkiye	5,743	8,144	12,366	180.5	217.0	284.5	3.5	3.1	3.4
Turkmenistan	...	...	...	...	...	...	...	2.4	...
Uzbekistan	...	...	...	...	...	...	2.5	2.6	2.6
East Asia									
China, People's Republic of	135,918	195,509	268,990	886.6	925.1	1,191.3	3.5	3.6	3.7
Hong Kong, China	23,699	20,114	16,573	572.3	485.0	387.8	4.1	3.9	4.0
Korea, Republic of	19,202	25,477	28,502	509.8	529.4	639.5	3.7	3.6	3.8
Mongolia	...	...	...	...	...	...	2.3	2.4	2.5
Taipei,China	12,737	14,492	14,689	339.9	355.9	341.0	3.7	3.6	3.9
South Asia									
Bangladesh	1,364	2,066	3,200	40.7	60.0	79.5	...	2.6	2.6
Bhutan	...	...	...	...	...	...	2.5	2.2	2.5
India	9,236	12,319	19,717	242.7	252.2	340.0	3.1	3.2	3.4
Maldives	...	...	...	18.7	19.4	18.9	2.5	2.7	...
Nepal	...	...	...	...	...	...	2.0	2.5	...
Sri Lanka	4,120	5,185	6,860	175.1	195.8	243.7	2.8	2.6	2.8
Southeast Asia									
Brunei Darussalam	...	...	...	26.8	24.3	25.0	...	2.7	...
Cambodia	223	392	732 (2021)	22.0	37.5	46.5	2.6	2.6	2.4
Indonesia	8,636	10,011	12,381	243.9	225.8	224.6	2.9	3.2	3.0
Lao People's Democratic Republic	...	...	...	...	...	...	2.5	2.7	2.4
Malaysia	18,133	24,013	27,294	460.1	478.0	504.1	3.5	3.2	3.6
Myanmar	335	827	846	23.8	51.7	46.0	2.4	2.3	...
Philippines	5,138	7,175	9,249	134.5	153.7	185.2	3.0	2.9	3.3
Singapore	28,431	30,922	37,290	578.8	559.2	600.5	4.1	4.0	4.3
Thailand	7,179	8,884	10,497	207.6	213.2	265.7	3.2	3.4	3.5
Timor-Leste	...	...	...	7.8	11.4	11.9	...	...	...
Viet Nam	6,431	10,615	20,519	226.9	266.6	414.6	3.0	3.3	3.3
The Pacific									
Cook Islands	...	...	...	6.8	10.7	8.2	...	...	...
Fiji	...	...	...	43.2	38.6	41.1	2.4	2.4	2.3
Kiribati	...	...	...	10.5	13.0	16.8	...	...	...
Marshall Islands	...	...	...	10.5	18.6	21.6	...	...	...
Micronesia, Federated States of	...	...	...	6.1	7.6	15.0	...	...	...
Nauru	...	...	...	4.2	6.9	–	...	...	...
Niue	...	...	...	4.3	–	5.8	...	...	...
Palau	...	...	...	11.8	–	6.9	...	...	...
Papua New Guinea	142	194	205 (2020)	30.3	45.5	49.4	...	2.2	2.7
Samoa	22	28	41 (2020)	22.5	23.4	30.3	...	...	...
Solomon Islands	...	...	...	20.3	34.1	30.7	...	2.6	2.8
Tonga	...	...	...	19.3	19.6	29.0	...	...	...
Tuvalu	...	...	...	6.8	8.8	5.1	...	...	...
Vanuatu	...	...	...	13.8	23.4	25.1	...	...	...
Developed ADB Member Economies									
Australia	6,452	7,732	9,376	160.2	155.9	145.0	3.7	3.8	3.7
Japan	20,015	21,095	22,516	474.4	424.3	415.0	3.9	4.0	3.9
New Zealand	2,318	2,931	3,426	83.1	90.8	106.6	3.4	3.9	3.6

... = data not available, ADB = Asian Development Bank, teu = twenty-foot equivalent unit.

a The Liner Shipping Connectivity Index captures how well economies are connected to global shipping networks. It is based on five components of the maritime transport sector: number of ships, their container-carrying capacity, maximum vessel size, number of services, and number of companies that deploy container ships in an economy's ports. The index generates a value of 100 for the economy with the highest average index in 2004.

b The index ranges from 1 to 5, with higher scores representing better performance.

Source: Asian Development Bank. Asian Transport Outlook (ATO) National Database. https://asiantransportobservatory.org/snd/ (access 23 June 2025).

Communications

Table 2.5.8: Access to Fixed Telephones, Mobile Phones, and Internet—Total Subscriptions
('000)

ADB Regional Member	Fixed Telephone Subscribers		Mobile Phone Subscribers		Fixed Broadband Subscribers	
	2010	2023	2010	2023	2010	2023
Developing ADB Member Economies						
Central and West Asia[a]	**16,633.0**	**15,274.7**	**181,113.8**	**324,179.3**	**2,558.4**	**21,754.2**
Afghanistan	16.6	182.0	10,215.8	23,027.1	1.5	33.2
Armenia	592.3	331.0	3,865.4	3,959.5	93.6	545.9
Azerbaijan	1,506.6	1,635.3	9,100.1	11,111.3	475.3	2,154.7
Georgia	1,111.9	278.0	3,978.2	5,911.1	182.4	1,115.9
Kazakhstan	4,057.6	2,686.9	19,402.6	25,842.6	869.6	2,916.5
Kyrgyz Republic	489.1	185.5	5,275.5	7,681.2	23.1	456.0
Pakistan	6,079.1	2,573.4	99,185.8	189,439.0	789.5	3,356.7
Tajikistan	367.7	520.0 (2022)	5,940.8	12,845.9 (2022)	4.7	6.2 (2022)
Türkiye	...	...	...	...	...	...
Turkmenistan	520.0	735.5 (2022)	3,197.6	6,254.7 (2021)	0.7	377.2 (2022)
Uzbekistan	1,892.2	6,147.1	20,952.0	38,106.9	118.0	10,791.9
East Asia	**343,914.6**	**217,578.8**	**953,913.9**	**1,966,920.8**	**151,087.1**	**670,711.3**
China, People's Republic of	294,383.0	179,414.0	859,003.0	1,824,420.0	126,336.8	636,304.4
Hong Kong, China	4,361.7	3,486.7	13,793.7	23,779.1	2,167.7	2,968.5
Korea, Republic of	28,543.2	22,155.0	50,767.2	83,891.8	17,194.3	24,098.1
Mongolia	193.2	481.7	2,510.5	4,841.9	76.8	499.4
Taipei,China	16,433.5	12,041.4	27,839.5	29,988.0	5,311.6	6,840.8
South Asia[a]	**40,845.6**	**33,711.6**	**847,557.4**	**1,428,413.8**	**11,717.3**	**56,571.4**
Bangladesh	1,280.8	296.3	67,923.9	196,081.0	414.6	13,533.0
Bhutan	26.3	18.4	394.3	752.0	8.7	10.4
India	35,090.0	30,933.2	752,190.0	1,158,550.0	10,990.0	39,480.1
Maldives	28.4	12.9	494.4	744.8	15.6	98.5
Nepal	841.7	744.1 (2022)	9,195.6	39,602.6 (2022)	60.2	1,435.9 (2022)
Sri Lanka	3,578.5	1,706.6	17,359.3	32,683.4	228.3	2,013.6
Southeast Asia[a]	**73,120.0**	**32,470.6**	**532,636.0**	**893,105.7**	**14,515.4**	**63,724.1**
Brunei Darussalam	79.9	121.8	435.1	582.9	21.7	92.8
Cambodia	358.9	32.7	8,150.8	21,049.6	35.7	634.5
Indonesia	40,931.1	9,160.1	211,290.0	352,157.0	2,280.3	13,543.9
Lao People's Democratic Republic	103.1	1,233.8	4,003.4	4,963.8	5.9	208.5
Malaysia	4,609.8	8,401.8	33,858.7	50,136.5	2,097.8	4,576.5
Myanmar	493.3	587.7	594.0	65,516.9	22.9	1,514.8
Philippines	3,335.4	4,627.1	83,150.1	134,739.0	1,791.0 (2011)	7,513.1
Singapore	1,996.1	1,900.5	7,384.6	10,026.7	1,338.4	1,588.2
Thailand	6,835.2	4,087.0	71,726.3	120,921.0	3,251.8	11,291.2
Timor-Leste	2.9	1.8	473.0	1,559.4	0.5	0.1
Viet Nam	14,374.4	2,316.3	111,570.0	131,453.0	3,669.3	22,760.5
The Pacific[a]	**338.8**	**256.7**	**3,105.0**	**5,704.7**	**38.6**	**74.0**
Cook Islands	7.2	7.0 (2022)	7.8	18.1 (2022)	1.7	3.1 (2022)
Fiji	129.8	41.3 (2022)	697.9	1,027.5 (2022)	23.3	23.3 (2022)
Kiribati	8.4	0.0	10.6	67.9	0.8	0.1
Marshall Islands	...	1.9 (2022)	...	15.9 (2022)	...	0.9(2022)
Micronesia, Federated States of	8.5	6.5 (2022)	27.5	22.4 (2022)	1.0	6.5 (2022)
Nauru	...	...	6.2	10.3 (2022)	0.9	1.2 (2022)
Niue	1.0	1.0 (2022)	...	...	...	...
Palau	7.0	6.2 (2022)	14.5	24.0	0.2	1.3
Papua New Guinea	121.2	172.7 (2022)	1,909.1	3,538.6	6.1	21.9 (2022)
Samoa	8.0	4.6 (2022)	90.0	134.3 (2022)	0.2	1.9 (2022)
Solomon Islands	8.4	7.0 (2022)	115.5	484.8 (2022)	2.5	0.8 (2022)
Tonga	31.0	3.3 (2022)	54.3	64.8 (2022)	1.1	8.6 (2022)
Tuvalu	1.2	2.1 (2022)	1.6	9.9 (2022)	0.2	0.5 (2022)
Vanuatu	7.1	3.2	169.9	286.1	0.5	4.0
Developed ADB Member Economies	**78,123.7**	**66,449.7**	**150,497.0**	**258,241.0**	**40,703.7**	**59,686.4**
Australia	10,625.0	6,458.0	22,500.0	29,761.0	5,510.0	9,682.3
Japan	65,618.7	59,326.7	123,287.0	221,918.0	34,101.7	48,046.0
New Zealand	1,880.0	665.0	4,710.0	6,562.0	1,092.0	1,958.1
DEVELOPING ADB MEMBER ECONOMIES[a]	**474,856.3**	**299,294.2**	**2,518,342.2**	**4,618,325.0**	**179,918.1**	**812,835.0**
ALL ADB REGIONAL MEMBERS[a]	**552,980.0**	**365,743.9**	**2,668,839.2**	**4,876,566.0**	**220,621.8**	**872,521.4**

... = data not available, 0.0 = magnitude is less than half of unit employed, ADB = Asian Development Bank.

a Regional aggregates are calculated as the sum of the reporting economies. Imputation was done for economies with missing data by substituting available data from the nearest years.

Source: International Telecommunication Union. World Telecommunication/ICT Indicators Database. https://datahub.itu.int/indicators/ (accessed 15 July 2025).

Table 2.5.9: Access to Fixed Telephones, Mobile Phones, and Internet—Subscriptions per 100 People

ADB Regional Member	Fixed Telephone			Mobile Cellular			Fixed Broadband			Internet Users		
	2010	2015	2023	2010	2015	2023	2010	2015	2023	2010	2015	2023
Developing ADB Member Economies												
Central and West Asia[a]	**5.4**	**4.6**	**3.8**	**58.9**	**70.4**	**82.7**	**0.8**	**2.7**	**5.8**	**11.3**	**20.2**	**40.2**
Afghanistan	0.1	0.3	0.4	36.1	58.3	55.5	0.0	0.0	0.1	4.0	8.3	17.7
Armenia	20.2	18.9	11.2	131.9	118.6	134.5	3.2	9.8	18.5	25.0	59.1	80.0
Azerbaijan	16.5	18.4	15.8	99.5	109.7	107.7	5.2	19.5	20.9	46.0	77.0	89.0
Georgia	28.5	25.1	7.3	102.1	146.4	155.3	4.7	16.8	29.3	26.9	47.6	81.9
Kazakhstan	24.1	22.9	13.2	115.2	145.5	127.1	5.2	12.7	14.3	31.6	70.8	92.9
Kyrgyz Republic	8.9	6.8	2.6	96.1	126.3	108.6	0.4	3.5	6.4	16.3	30.2	88.5
Pakistan	3.1	1.6	1.0	49.8	57.9	76.5	0.4	0.8	1.4	8.0	11.0	27.4
Tajikistan[b]	4.8	5.3	5.1	77.6	98.2	126.2	0.1	0.1	0.1	11.6	19.0	56.8
Türkiye	...	...	...	...	...	...	...	...	...	...	...	...
Turkmenistan[c]	9.3	10.4	10.2	57.5	126.2	88.2	0.0	0.5	5.2	3.0	15.0	...
Uzbekistan	6.7	9.2	17.2	73.8	70.8	106.9	0.4	5.8	30.3	15.9	42.8	89.0
East Asia[a]	**24.0**	**18.8**	**14.4**	**66.6**	**94.6**	**130.4**	**10.5**	**20.6**	**44.5**	**36.7**	**52.2**	**78.5**
China, People's Republic of	21.8	16.5	12.6	63.6	92.5	128.2	9.3	19.8	44.7	34.3	50.3	77.5
Hong Kong, China	61.4	58.8	46.8	194.2	227.0	319.5	30.5	31.9	39.9	72.0	84.9	96.0
Korea, Republic of	58.5	56.7	42.8	104.1	115.6	162.1	35.3	39.3	46.6	83.7	89.9	97.4
Mongolia	7.2	8.6	14.0	92.9	103.1	141.1	2.8	7.0	14.6	10.2	22.5	83.0
Taipei,China	70.8	59.1	51.6	119.9	126.1	128.6	22.9	24.0	29.3	71.5	78.0	93.1
South Asia[a,d]	**2.8**	**2.0**	**2.0**	**58.7**	**77.1**	**85.0**	**0.8**	**1.5**	**3.4**	**7.1**	**14.8**	**54.3**
Bangladesh	0.8	0.5	0.2	44.6	82.4	114.4	0.3	3.1	7.9	3.7	12.9	44.5
Bhutan	3.7	2.9	2.3	56.2	91.2	95.6	1.2	3.8	1.3	13.6	39.8	88.4
India[e]	2.8	1.9	2.2	60.5	75.4	80.6	0.9	1.3	2.7	7.5	14.9	55.9
Maldives	7.9	5.1	2.4	137.0	172.8	141.6	4.3	5.4	18.7	26.5	54.5	84.7
Nepal[b]	3.1	3.0	2.5	33.6	98.9	133.3	0.2	1.1	4.8	7.9	17.6	55.8
Sri Lanka	17.1	15.1	7.4	83.1	110.0	142.3	1.1	2.9	8.8	...	15.3	51.2
Southeast Asia[a,f]	**12.1**	**5.4**	**4.7**	**88.2**	**124.5**	**129.4**	**2.5**	**4.0**	**9.2**	**18.9**	**31.3**	**75.5**
Brunei Darussalam	20.4	18.0	26.5	110.9	109.8	127.0	5.5	8.2	20.2	53.0	71.2	99.0
Cambodia	2.5	1.6	0.2	56.2	133.5	120.8	0.2	0.5	3.6	1.3	6.4	60.7
Indonesia	16.6	4.0	3.3	85.8	129.5	125.2	0.9	1.5	4.8	10.9	22.1	69.2
Lao People's Democratic Republic	1.6	14.2	16.1	63.2	54.8	64.8	0.1	0.2	2.7	7.0	18.2	63.6
Malaysia	16.1	14.4	23.9	118.2	141.2	142.7	7.3	9.8	13.0	56.3	71.1	97.7
Myanmar	1.0	1.0	1.1	1.2	80.2	121.0	0.0	0.1	2.8	0.3	10.9	58.5
Philippines[g]	3.5	3.1	4.0	86.3	111.9	117.3	1.8	2.8	6.5	25.0	36.9	83.8
Singapore	39.3	36.5	32.8	145.5	149.0	173.2	26.4	26.9	27.4	71.0	79.0	94.3
Thailand	10.0	7.5	5.7	104.6	145.9	168.6	4.7	8.8	15.7	22.4	39.3	89.5
Timor-Leste	0.3	0.2	0.1	43.6	114.2	112.6	0.0	0.1	0.0	3.0	18.6	34.0
Viet Nam	16.4	7.9	2.3	127.6	129.6	131.0	4.2	8.2	22.7	30.7	45.0	78.1
The Pacific[a,h]	**3.4**	**2.5**	**2.0**	**31.4**	**48.6**	**36.1**	**0.4**	**0.4**	**0.6**	**4.0**	**12.3**	**31.4**
Cook Islands[i]	42.6	37.5	47.5	46.0	79.9	122.9	9.9	15.3	21.0	35.7	51.0	...
Fiji[b]	14.3	7.9	4.5	76.7	105.2	111.7	2.6	1.4	2.5	20.0	42.5	79.3
Kiribati[j]	7.7	1.3	0.0	9.7	35.1	51.3	0.8	0.1	0.0	9.1	14.9	88.0
Marshall Islands[k]	...	4.7	4.9	...	31.8	39.7	...	2.0	2.4	7.0	19.3	65.7
Micronesia, Federated States of[b]	7.9	6.3	5.8	25.6	20.7	20.0	0.9	3.0	5.8	20.0	31.5	39.4
Nauru[l]	19.0	...	...	61.7	85.8	87.2	9.5	...	10.0	54.0	62.4	81.7
Niue[m]	56.6	56.2	54.3	...	...	...	...	...	...	77.0	...	...
Palau[n]	37.9	40.5	34.7	78.9	133.6	135.4	1.3	6.9	7.3	...	...	...
Papua New Guinea[h,o]	1.6	1.7	1.7	25.0	40.7	34.1	0.1	0.2	0.2	1.3	7.9	24.1
Samoa[b]	4.1	5.7	2.1	46.6	59.7	62.4	0.1	1.0	0.9	7.0	25.4	58.1
Solomon Islands[b]	1.6	1.2	0.9	21.7	66.4	62.1	0.5	0.2	0.1	5.0	10.0	42.5
Tonga[b]	28.9	12.5	3.1	50.6	69.3	61.7	1.0	2.3	8.2	16.0	38.7	58.5
Tuvalu[b]	11.3	18.2	21.1	15.1	60.2	98.9	2.3	4.1	4.5	14.6	27.3	74.3
Vanuatu	3.0	1.8	1.0	71.3	65.7	89.3	0.2	1.6	1.2	8.0	22.4	45.7
Developed ADB Member Economies[a]	**50.5**	**47.5**	**42.6**	**97.3**	**123.2**	**165.5**	**26.3**	**30.3**	**38.3**	**78.0**	**89.9**	**89.0**
Australia	48.0	35.5	24.4	101.6	107.6	112.5	24.9	28.5	36.6	76.0	84.6	97.1
Japan	51.2	50.1	47.7	96.2	126.2	178.4	26.6	30.5	38.6	78.2	91.1	87.0
New Zealand	43.2	40.1	12.9	108.3	121.4	126.9	25.1	31.4	37.9	80.5	85.2	96.2
DEVELOPING ADB MEMBER ECONOMIES[a,f]	**12.5**	**9.0**	**7.0**	**66.3**	**90.5**	**106.9**	**4.7**	**9.0**	**19.0**	**20.4**	**31.7**	**46.2**
ALL ADB REGIONAL MEMBERS[a,f]	**14.0**	**10.4**	**8.2**	**67.5**	**91.7**	**109.0**	**5.5**	**9.8**	**19.7**	**22.7**	**33.9**	**47.7**

... = data not available, 0.0 = magnitude is less than half of unit employed, ADB = Asian Development Bank.

a Regional aggregates are derived from table 2.5.8 regional aggregate levels and population data from International Telecommunication Union.
b For fixed telephone, mobile cellular, and fixed broadband, data for 2023 refers to 2022.
c For fixed telephone and fixed broadband, data for 2023 refers to 2022. For mobile cellular, data for 2023 refers to 2021.
d For internet users, data for 2022 refers to 2020.
e For internet users, data for 2023 refers to 2022.
f Regional aggregates are calculated as the sum of the reporting economies. Imputation was done for economies with missing data by substituting available data from the nearest years.
g For fixed broadband, data for 2010 refers to 2011.
h For fixed telephone and fixed broadband, data for 2023 refers to 2022.
i For fixed telephone, data for 2015 refers to 2016, and data for 2023 refers to 2022. For mobile cellular, data for 2015 refers to 2016, and data for 2023 refers to 2022. For fixed broadband, data for 2015 refers to 2013, and data for 2023 refers to 2022.
j For fixed telephone, data for 2022 refers to 2020.
k For fixed telephone, data for 2015 refers to 2014, and data for 2023 refers to 2022. For mobile cellular and fixed broadband, data for 2023 refers to 2022.
l For fixed telephone, data for 2010 refers to 2009. For mobile cellular and fixed broadband, data for 2023 refers to 2022. For internet users, data for 2010 refers to 2011, data for 2015 refers to 2017, and data for 2023 refers to 2020.
m For fixed telephone, data for 2022 refers to 2021.
n For fixed telephone data for 2023 refers to 2022.
o For fixed telephone and mobile cellular, data for 2022 refers to 2021.

Source: International Telecommunication Union. World Telecommunication/ICT Indicators Database. https://datahub.itu.int/indicators/ (accessed 15 July 2025).

Data Issues and Comparability

Issues with data organization, collection, compilation, and dissemination affect the availability, quality, and timeliness of road statistics. Some regions, especially the Pacific, have incomplete or no data.

Most data on telephone and internet subscriptions came from questionnaires sent by the International Telecommunication Union to participating economies. Other information and reports were sourced from national ministries in charge of telecommunications and from staff estimates.

Table 2.6.1: Electricity Production and Sources

ADB Regional Member	Total Electricity Production (kWh billion)		Sources of Electricity (% of total): Combustible Fuels[a]		Hydropower		Solar		Others[b]	
	2010	2022	2010	2022	2010	2022	2010	2022	2010	2022
Developing ADB Member Economies										
Central and West Asia[c]	**521.3**	**765.8**	**70.1**	**65.2**	**28.0**	**21.6**	**0.0**	**2.7**	**1.9**	**10.5**
Afghanistan	0.9	1.4 (2023)	14.0	9.2 (2023)	86.0	86.2(2023)	...	4.6 (2023)	...	...
Armenia	6.5	9.2	22.2	42.2	39.4	21.1	...	5.7	38.5	31.0
Azerbaijan	18.7	29.0	81.6	94.0	18.4	5.5	...	0.2	0.0 (2009)	0.3
Georgia	10.1	14.2	6.8	23.8	93.2	75.6	...	...	...	0.6
Kazakhstan	82.7	128.1 (2023)	90.3	88.7 (2023)	9.7	6.9(2023)	0.0	1.5 (2023)	0.0 (2012)	3.0 (2023)
Kyrgyz Republic	12.1	13.8 (2023)	8.2	13.0 (2023)	91.8	87.0(2023)	...	...	...	...
Pakistan	94.4	127.9	62.6	49.7	33.7	27.6	...	0.9	3.7	21.9
Tajikistan	16.4	21.9 (2023)	0.2	5.6 (2023)	99.8	94.4(2023)	...	...	...	...
Türkiye	211.2	328.4	73.7	60.1	24.5	20.3	...	5.1	1.7	14.4
Turkmenistan	16.7	32.6	100.0	100.0	0.0 (2011)	0.0	...	...	...	...
Uzbekistan[d]	51.7	74.3	79.0	90.7	21.0	8.7	...	0.6	...	–
East Asia[c]	**4,971.9**	**9,795.0**	**78.2**	**66.5**	**15.4**	**14.3**	**0.0**	**4.8**	**6.4**	**14.4**
China, People's Republic of	4,207.2	8,848.7	79.2	66.5	17.2	15.3	...	4.8	3.6	13.3
Hong Kong, China	38.3	37.5 (2023)	100.0	100.0 (2023)	...	...	...	...	...	...
Korea, Republic of	475.1	613.9	67.0	64.2	1.4	1.2	0.2	4.7	31.5	29.9
Mongolia	4.4	8.5 (2023)	98.9	91.0 (2023)	0.8	0.6(2023)	0.2	2.2 (2023)	0.0	6.3 (2023)
Taipei,China	247.1	288.6 (2024)	...	...	...	...	...	...	...	...
South Asia[c]	**1,017.1**	**1,951.2**	**82.6**	**78.2**	**12.9**	**9.8**	**0.0**	**5.4**	**4.4**	**6.5**
Bangladesh	40.8	94.9	98.1	98.9	1.9	0.8	...	0.3	...	0.0
Bhutan	7.3	10.5 (2023)	0.0	0.0 (2023)	100.0	100.0(2023)	0.0	0.0 (2023)	...	0.0 (2023)
India	954.5	1,816.8	83.3	78.3	12.0	8.9	...	5.8	4.7	7.0
Maldives	0.4	1.3 (2023)	99.2	95.5 (2023)	...	...	0.1	4.3 (2023)	0.7	0.2 (2023)
Nepal	3.2	12.8 (2023)	0.1	0.0 (2021)	99.9	99.2(2023)	...	0.8 (2023)	...	0.0 (2021)
Sri Lanka	10.8	16.7	47.2	50.7	52.3	40.5	0.1	4.3	0.5	4.4
Southeast Asia[c]	**676.5**	**1,266.6**	**85.3**	**76.0**	**11.8**	**17.8**	**0.0**	**3.0**	**2.9**	**3.2**
Brunei Darussalam	3.8	5.6	100.0	99.9	...	...	0.1 (2011)	0.1	...	...
Cambodia	1.0	10.6	96.6	35.3	3.1	57.9	0.3	6.8	...	...
Indonesia	169.6	344.2	84.2	87.6	10.3	7.3	0.0	0.1	5.5	5.1
Lao People's Democratic Republic	8.4	51.2 (2023)	...	23.9 (2023)	100.0	75.9(2023)	0.0 (2012)	0.2 (2023)	...	...
Malaysia	116.8	187.4	94.6	82.2	5.4	16.6	0.0	1.2	...	...
Myanmar	8.6	20.9 (2023)	28.2	53.9 (2023)	71.8	44.3(2023)	...	1.8 (2023)	...	...
Philippines	67.8	111.5	73.7	79.0	11.5	9.1	0.0	1.6	14.7	10.3
Singapore[d]	45.4	57.4 (2023)	100.0	97.9	...	...	0.0	2.1	...	...
Thailand	159.5	218.9 (2023)	96.5	92.9 (2023)	3.5	3.1(2023)	0.0	2.3 (2023)	0.0	1.7 (2023)
Timor-Leste	0.1	0.5 (2023)	98.9	99.6 (2023)	1.1	0.3(2023)	...	0.1 (2023)	...	...
Viet Nam	95.4	276.4	70.5	51.7	29.4	35.4	...	9.6	0.1	3.3
The Pacific[c]	**5.1**	**6.6 (2023)**	**64.4**	**72.2 (2023)**	**28.1**	**25.0(2023)**	**0.0**	**1.2 (2023)**	**7.5**	**1.6 (2023)**
Cook Islands	0.0	0.0 (2023)	99.8	78.2 (2023)	...	...	0.2	21.8 (2023)	...	...
Fiji	0.9	1.1 (2023)	50.9	44.5 (2023)	48.4	54.4(2023)	0.1 (2012)	1.1 (2023)	0.8	0.0 (2023)
Kiribati	0.0	0.0 (2023)	97.1	86.6 (2023)	...	...	2.9	13.4 (2023)	...	...
Marshall Islands	0.1	0.1 (2023)	100.0	97.8 (2023)	...	...	0.3 (2012)	2.2 (2023)	...	...
Micronesia, Federated States of	0.1	0.1 (2023)	98.8	94.0 (2023)	...	1.4(2023)	1.2	3.4 (2023)	...	1.2 (2023)
Nauru	0.0	0.0 (2023)	99.8	92.7 (2023)	...	...	0.2	7.3 (2023)	...	...
Niue	0.0	0.0 (2023)	97.9	88.2 (2023)	...	...	2.1	11.8 (2023)	...	...
Palau	0.1	0.1 (2023)	100.0	95.9 (2023)	...	...	...	4.1 (2023)	...	...
Papua New Guinea	3.6	4.6 (2023)	62.9	76.2 (2023)	26.7	21.5(2023)	0.0	0.1 (2023)	10.3	2.2 (2023)
Samoa	0.1	0.2 (2023)	57.1	67.6 (2023)	42.9	22.5(2023)	0.0	9.8 (2023)	...	0.1 (2023)
Solomon Islands	0.1	0.1 (2023)	99.4	96.2 (2023)	0.6	0.9(2023)	1.4 (2011)	3.0 (2023)	...	...
Tonga	0.1	0.1 (2023)	100.0	90.6 (2023)	...	...	...	7.2 (2023)	...	2.3 (2023)
Tuvalu	0.0	0.0 (2023)	97.9	80.6 (2023)	...	...	2.1	19.4 (2023)	...	...
Vanuatu	0.1	0.1 (2023)	80.9	79.9 (2023)	11.6	11.0(2023)	0.1 (2011)	4.0 (2023)	7.5	5.0 (2023)
Developed ADB Member Economies[c]	**1,468.5**	**1,334.8**	**68.6**	**71.4**	**8.8**	**9.7**	**0.3**	**9.6**	**22.4**	**9.4**
Australia	252.7	271.5	92.5	70.2	5.4	6.3	0.2	12.8	2.0	10.7
Japan	1,170.9	1,018.6	65.0	74.2	7.7	8.4	0.3	9.1	27.0	8.3
New Zealand	45.0	44.7	28.2	15.0	54.9	58.8	0.0	0.6	16.9	25.6
DEVELOPING ADB MEMBER ECONOMIES[c]	**7,191.9**	**13,784.9**	**78.9**	**69.0**	**15.7**	**14.4**	**0.0**	**4.6**	**5.4**	**12.0**
ALL ADB REGIONAL MEMBERS[c]	**8,660.4**	**15,119.7**	**77.1**	**69.3**	**14.5**	**14.0**	**0.1**	**5.0**	**8.4**	**11.7**

... = data not available, 0.0 = magnitude is less than half of unit employed, ADB = Asian Development Bank, kWh = kilowatt-hour.

a Electricity from combustible fuels refers to the production of electricity from the combustion of fuels that are capable of igniting or burning, which would include coal, natural gas, oil, and other combustible fuels.
b Includes chemical heat, geothermal, nuclear, tide, other marine electricity, wind, wave, and other sources of energy.
c Includes only reporting economies with data corresponding to the year heading.
d Partial 2023 energy data are available from the United Nations' Energy Statistics Database. However, 2022 figures were reflected in this table to ensure comparability of data.

Sources: United Nations. Energy Statistics Database. http://data.un.org/Data.aspx?d=EDATA&f=cmID%3aEL (accessed 21 June 2021). For Taipei,China: Government of Taipei,China; Directorate-General of Budget, Accounting and Statistics; Official communication, 16 May 2025.

Electricity

Table 2.6.2: Electric Power Consumption
(kWh per capita)

ADB Regional Member	2010	2015	2018	2019	2020	2021	2022	2023
Developing ADB Member Economies								
Central and West Asia	**1,094.5**	**1,227.4**	**1,374.6**	**1,331.1**	**1,318.8**	**1,429.5**	**1,371.2**	**...**
Afghanistan	85.9	134.2	151.1	152.6	147.4	143.7	144.2	142.6
Armenia	1,592.2	1,839.0	1,856.6	2,010.8	2,037.6	2,209.7	2,334.4	...
Azerbaijan	1,467.1	2,109.5	2,072.2	2,141.2	2,160.5	2,288.2	2,252.6	...
Georgia	1,967.2	2,616.5	3,153.7	3,183.1	3,032.9	3,472.4	3,535.0	...
Kazakhstan	3,742.8	4,357.1	5,034.6	4,199.1	4,108.9	5,240.4	4,736.0	4,437.0
Kyrgyz Republic	1,296.7	1,776.6	1,886.7	1,915.9	1,840.0	1,912.8	1,902.7	...
Pakistan	387.0	416.2	482.3	492.0	488.0	495.7	436.4	...
Tajikistan	1,850.5	1,447.4	1,492.4	1,486.5	1,535.0	1,382.2	1,433.5	1,529.2
Türkiye[a]	2,345.7	2,715.9	3,059.0	3,014.1	3,051.4	3,307.2	3,291.8	...
Turkmenistan	1,951.5	2,371.1	2,492.6	2,327.2	2,338.5	2,356.4	2,488.5	...
Uzbekistan	1,560.0	1,539.9	1,653.0	1,643.4	1,546.8	1,688.6	1,672.3	...
East Asia	**3,052.6**	**3,965.3**	**4,740.3**	**4,933.2**	**5,097.2**	**5,598.6**	**5,810.4**	**...**
China, People's Republic of	2,681.9	3,623.2	4,413.0	4,624.7	4,803.3	5,308.4	5,530.3	...
Hong Kong, China	5,894.9	5,961.1	5,930.1	6,000.6	5,901.1	6,121.0	6,008.8	6,094.6
Korea, Republic of[a]	9,400.8	9,937.4	10,563.0	10,397.3	10,181.5	10,649.4	10,777.7	...
Mongolia	1,249.5	1,775.1	2,036.1	2,118.3	2,071.5	2,322.2	2,390.8	2,517.3
Taipei,China	10,638.1	10,971.1	11,646.1	11,582.0	11,832.6	12,353.7	12,305.1	12,430.6 (2024)
South Asia	**514.3**	**718.1**	**792.6**	**872.2**	**796.5**	**812.0**	**927.8**	**...**
Bangladesh	226.8	325.9	443.8	480.2	480.3	523.9	548.1	...
Bhutan	2,750.1	2,777.6	2,876.9	2,980.3	2,546.3	3,165.6	3,159.5	4,718.7
India	558.4	778.9	846.7	933.8	846.4	857.0	988.6	...
Maldives	939.6	1,332.7	1,491.2	1,556.8	1,345.0	2,122.6	2,139.5	2,184.1
Nepal	100.2	139.0	227.8	230.0	256.0	303.1	306.2	142.0
Sri Lanka	441.0	540.3	634.5	661.2	649.6	688.5	655.2	...
Southeast Asia	**1,002.1**	**1,252.9**	**1,439.7**	**1,488.4**	**1,471.1**	**1,504.6**	**1,597.3**	**...**
Brunei Darussalam	8,322.0	8,851.0	8,415.2	9,722.2	11,464.6	11,458.9	10,778.4	...
Cambodia	155.3	332.7	530.4	618.3	675.9	696.1	780.4	...
Indonesia	598.0	812.7	932.7	947.2	910.4	934.1	1,055.0	...
Lao People's Democratic Republic	385.3	623.2	759.9	911.3	1,108.5	1,299.8	1,464.2	1,450.5
Malaysia	3,868.4	4,232.7	4,644.8	4,746.0	4,489.0	4,532.9	4,733.4	...
Myanmar	128.8	262.2	342.8	354.9	362.1	323.5	318.6	307.0
Philippines	573.7	643.9	754.7	786.2	742.7	783.7	801.4	...
Singapore	8,322.2	8,599.3	8,955.9	9,124.2	9,035.3	9,643.1	9,714.3	9,567.5
Thailand	2,177.3	2,467.4	2,634.6	2,700.9	2,745.7	2,777.4	3,025.5	3,008.0
Timor-Leste	93.9	211.0	262.9	295.4	279.3	281.5	284.8	286.1
Viet Nam	979.6	1,547.9	2,002.4	2,130.7	2,199.7	2,259.3	2,261.7	...
The Pacific	**450.9**	**454.7**	**439.5**	**457.8**	**444.8**	**435.2**	**441.2**	**437.8**
Cook Islands	1,829.7	1,782.2	2,403.4	2,304.1	2,068.7	2,106.2	2,420.8	2,768.4
Fiji	839.5	899.2	1,008.5	1,038.4	955.2	904.5	1,045.5	1,052.9
Kiribati	183.2	193.5	240.0	254.2	262.5	246.2	251.4	247.5
Marshall Islands	1,306.6	1,536.9	1,722.4	1,772.4	1,803.0	1,670.4	1,971.2	2,034.7
Micronesia, Federated States of	488.9	437.6	430.7	478.8	540.9	585.9	600.3	602.0
Nauru	1,543.4	1,769.2	2,448.4	2,591.0	2,606.4	3,104.3	3,119.4	3,115.8
Niue	1,571.3	1,681.8	1,847.7	1,896.3	1,834.4	1,820.2	1,966.0	2,025.3
Palau	3,924.8	4,445.7	4,805.2	4,775.8	4,833.6	4,892.3	4,898.9	4,907.8
Papua New Guinea	415.7	420.6	388.8	409.0	401.9	396.7	390.7	385.0
Samoa	516.5	577.0	666.8	723.4	739.9	713.2	713.5	835.5
Solomon Islands	140.7	129.3	123.4	121.3	118.6	114.1	107.9	97.8
Tonga	396.9	463.4	548.5	594.3	616.8	634.2	661.6	683.6
Tuvalu	509.4	515.6	631.5	637.7	840.1	698.7	717.9	896.2
Vanuatu	256.3	230.5	263.1	257.8	230.0	221.8	243.4	228.8
Developed ADB Member Economies	**8,492.2**	**7,903.5**	**7,872.4**	**7,764.1**	**7,675.6**	**7,755.1**	**7,693.2**	**...**
Australia[a]	10,063.4	9,489.6	9,377.2	9,376.9	9,325.9	9,214.2	9,303.9	...
Japan	8,192.2	7,571.4	7,563.6	7,427.2	7,335.0	7,454.1	7,359.1	...
New Zealand[a]	9,333.3	8,831.1	8,155.2	8,080.9	7,779.5	7,746.7	7,607.2	...
DEVELOPING ADB MEMBER ECONOMIES	**1,586.7**	**2,029.1**	**2,366.0**	**2,461.3**	**2,478.9**	**2,669.8**	**2,786.3**	**...**
ALL ADB REGIONAL MEMBERS	**1,851.9**	**2,244.8**	**2,564.0**	**2,650.8**	**2,663.1**	**2,848.6**	**2,957.4**	**...**

... = data not available, ADB = Asian Development Bank, kWh = kilowatt-hour.

Note: All figures presented in this table are Asian Development Bank estimates using data from the United Nation's Energy Statistics Database, Government of Taipei,China; Directorate-General of Budget, Accounting and Statistics, and the United Nations' World Population Prospects 2024.

a Partial 2023 energy data are available from the United Nations' Energy Statistics Database. However, 2022 figures were reflected in this table to ensure comparability of data.

Sources: For electric power consumption: United Nations Energy Statistics Database. http://data.un.org/Data.aspx?d=EDATA&f=cmID%3aEL (accessed 22 June 2025).
For Taipei,China: Government of Taipei,China; Directorate-General of Budget, Accounting and Statistics; Official communication, 16 May 2025.
For total population: United Nations. World Population Prospects 2024. https://population.un.org/wpp/ (accessed 2 June 2025).

Table 2.6.3: Use of Energy

ADB Regional Member	Energy Use (PJ)			GDP per Unit Use of Energy (constant 2021 $ million PPP per PJ)		
	2010	2015	2022	2010	2015	2022
Developing ADB Member Economies						
Central and West Asia[a]	**14,740.3**	**15,753.7**	**18,799.2**	**224.6**	**276.1**	**307.0**
Afghanistan	140.6	167.5	180.8	573.0	599.5	444.8
Armenia	106.2	134.7	170.3	299.4	292.5	311.9
Azerbaijan	486.2	605.4	725.1	371.0	329.6	294.4
Georgia	139.8	197.4	239.4	306.0	281.8	325.2
Kazakhstan	3,363.4	3,180.4	2,901.2	132.0	175.7	231.4
Kyrgyz Republic	115.5	167.2	188.9	230.8	202.3	226.7
Pakistan	3,031.3	3,038.2	3,921.0	277.9	332.2	343.5
Tajikistan	143.4	166.6	221.3	130.7	157.8	193.9
Türkiye	4,441.9	5,389.9	6,530.2	322.2	373.6	426.2
Turkmenistan	951.4	971.5	1,706.0	51.7	83.5	72.6
Uzbekistan	1,820.6	1,734.8	2,015.1	89.8	133.5	166.6
East Asia[a]	**112,780.4**	**133,056.1**	**168,293.5**	**144.5**	**174.1**	**198.8**
China, People's Republic of	101,618.4	120,744.3	155,622.3	137.9	169.8	195.1
Hong Kong, China	544.0	575.9	469.2	727.7	794.8	1,002.7
Korea, Republic of	10,454.1	11,462.7	11,734.1	178.3	189.0	219.2
Mongolia	164.0	273.0	467.9	158.8	154.9	112.4
Taipei,China	...	...	...	...	...	...
South Asia	**29,766.1**	**38,000.5**	**47,528.1**	**242.6**	**259.7**	**295.5**
Bangladesh	1,496.5	1,853.4	2,260.5	419.6	460.3	591.1
Bhutan	63.0	70.6	83.2	111.2	130.0	132.0
India	27,421.7	35,155.3	44,075.8	229.4	245.1	277.9
Maldives	13.4	18.4	31.5	450.3	438.2	355.7
Nepal	432.6	493.9	676.9	195.0	211.0	209.1
Sri Lanka	338.8	408.9	400.2	605.9	683.6	734.3
Southeast Asia	**21,822.9**	**25,626.1**	**32,429.2**	**276.5**	**302.4**	**306.7**
Brunei Darussalam	135.7	113.8	180.1	256.1	303.9	193.0
Cambodia	130.6	186.0	303.8	412.1	417.3	365.7
Indonesia	8,072.8	8,708.7	12,519.2	270.0	327.5	297.0
Lao People's Democratic Republic	100.3	168.8	257.2	312.4	270.2	240.5
Malaysia	2,965.0	3,429.1	4,158.7	225.3	252.3	267.6
Myanmar	564.4	768.2	922.0	338.2	353.4	311.9
Philippines	1,700.8	2,135.9	2,578.0	355.3	379.2	418.1
Singapore	883.2	1,216.8	1,604.7	548.7	495.6	469.2
Thailand	4,931.9	5,685.2	5,634.2	232.6	233.4	264.4
Timor-Leste	4.5	7.1	9.4	966.5	762.6	775.0
Viet Nam	2,333.6	3,206.6	4,261.8	272.6	267.7	303.6
The Pacific[a]	**185.1**	**219.4**	**247.7**	**227.8**	**245.2**	**245.0**
Cook Islands	1.1	1.2	1.2	...	...	...
Fiji	19.9	28.3	26.5	465.5	393.6	442.3
Kiribati	1.4	1.4	1.6	167.3	214.5	251.5
Marshall Islands	2.0	2.0	2.0	111.1	114.0	137.2
Micronesia, Federated States of	1.5	2.1	2.2	267.4	193.6	196.4
Nauru	0.6	0.8	0.8	119.9	164.2	178.0
Niue	0.1	0.1	0.1	...	...	...
Palau	2.9	2.8	3.0	105.4	125.8	91.3
Papua New Guinea	139.0	163.6	192.2	196.6	222.0	219.0
Samoa	4.2	5.0	4.8	294.2	261.1	261.0
Solomon Islands	8.0	7.6	7.4	179.4	224.5	267.1
Tonga	1.7	1.6	2.1	339.3	417.3	339.4
Tuvalu	0.1	0.1	0.1	274.1	366.4	395.1
Vanuatu	2.7	2.8	3.6	301.0	317.5	282.3
Developed ADB Member Economies	**27,278.5**	**24,438.5**	**22,718.3**	**241.0**	**288.5**	**327.4**
Australia	5,426.8	5,333.8	5,370.5	213.5	248.7	290.1
Japan	21,014.9	18,141.9	16,452.9	249.1	304.1	342.0
New Zealand	836.8	962.7	894.9	214.6	215.3	283.7
DEVELOPING ADB MEMBER ECONOMIES[a]	**179,294.8**	**212,655.8**	**267,297.7**	**183.6**	**212.5**	**236.7**
ALL ADB REGIONAL MEMBERS[a]	**206,573.3**	**237,094.2**	**290,016.0**	**191.1**	**220.3**	**243.8**
WORLD[a]	**508,384.6**	**539,300.6**	**599,386.5**	**211.3**	**236.6**	**256.2**

... = data not available, $ = United States dollars, ADB = Asian Development Bank, GDP = gross domestic product, PJ = petajoule, PPP = purchasing power parity.

a Aggregates include only reporting economies with data corresponding to the year heading.

Sources: For Energy Use: United Nations. Energy Statistics Database. https://data.un.org/SdmxBrowser/start (accessed 2 July 2025). For GDP per Unit Use of Energy: Asian Development Bank estimates using data from World Bank's World Development Indicators Database. https://databank.worldbank.org/source/world-development-indicators# (accessed 2 July 2025); and United Nation's Energy Statistics Database. https://data.un.org/SdmxBrowser/start (accessed 2 July 2025).

Energy

Table 2.6.4: Energy Production and Imports

ADB Regional Member	Energy Production (PJ)			Energy Imports, Net (% of total energy use)		
	2010	2015	2022	2010	2015	2022
Developing ADB Member Economies						
Central and West Asia	**17,747.1**	**18,708.0**	**19,789.9**	**-20.4**	**-18.8**	**-5.3**
Afghanistan	41.4	61.0	85.1	70.5	63.6	53.0
Armenia	38.9	44.5	47.9	63.4	67.0	71.9
Azerbaijan	2,759.3	2,474.0	2,626.1	-467.5	-308.7	-262.2
Georgia	57.5	55.1	51.9	58.8	72.1	78.3
Kazakhstan	6,769.9	6,812.2	6,753.1	-101.3	-114.2	-132.8
Kyrgyz Republic	53.1	75.3	114.0	54.1	55.0	39.7
Pakistan	2,251.6	2,272.7	2,267.9	25.7	25.2	42.2
Tajikistan	114.7	131.3	167.9	20.0	21.2	24.1
Türkiye	1,355.1	1,317.0	2,113.1	69.5	75.6	67.6
Turkmenistan	1,982.0	3,407.3	3,579.9	-108.3	-250.7	-109.8
Uzbekistan	2,323.7	2,057.7	1,983.1	-27.6	-18.6	1.6
East Asia[a]	**91,160.2**	**104,160.4**	**131,093.4**	**18.8**	**21.4**	**21.9**
China, People's Republic of	88,642.0	101,382.4	127,765.1	12.8	16.0	17.9
Hong Kong, China	...	...	...	...	...	...
Korea, Republic of	1,863.1	2,123.0	2,381.4	82.2	81.5	79.7
Mongolia	655.0	655.1	946.9	-299.5	-139.9	-102.4
Taipei,China	...	...	...	...	...	...
South Asia	**23,029.6**	**24,063.7**	**29,710.7**	**22.6**	**36.7**	**37.5**
Bangladesh	1,306.7	1,508.0	1,486.5	12.7	18.6	34.2
Bhutan	72.9	76.8	92.9	-15.7	-8.7	-11.7
India	21,115.9	21,903.9	27,491.2	23.0	37.7	37.6
Maldives	0.2	0.2	0.3	98.9	99.0	99.0
Nepal	371.0	415.9	475.2	14.2	15.8	29.8
Sri Lanka	163.0	158.8	164.6	51.9	61.2	58.9
Southeast Asia	**28,898.2**	**30,706.4**	**36,298.6**	**-32.4**	**-19.8**	**-11.9**
Brunei Darussalam	775.2	672.8	504.7	-471.3	-491.2	-180.2
Cambodia	58.7	79.4	88.2	55.1	57.3	71.0
Indonesia	16,605.0	17,364.0	23,286.8	-105.7	-99.4	-86.0
Lao People's Democratic Republic	97.7	162.1	374.9	2.6	4.0	-45.8
Malaysia	3,450.0	3,748.6	4,042.4	-16.4	-9.3	2.8
Myanmar	871.2	1,098.0	1,173.2	-54.3	-42.9	-27.2
Philippines	998.9	1,091.9	1,246.6	41.3	48.9	51.6
Singapore	24.9	26.3	30.2	97.2	97.8	98.1
Thailand	2,951.4	3,147.9	2,733.5	40.2	44.6	51.5
Timor-Leste	318.0	280.7	94.4	-6,899.1	-3,874.5	-899.2
Viet Nam	2,747.2	3,034.7	2,723.7	-17.7	5.4	36.1
The Pacific[a]	**105.0**	**544.7**	**629.5**	**41.7**	**-150.6**	**-156.2**
Cook Islands	0.1	0.1	0.1	94.4	94.0	92.9
Fiji	5.2	7.4	6.7	74.0	73.8	74.6
Kiribati	0.5	0.6	0.6	60.6	59.2	62.8
Marshall Islands	–	–	–	100.0	100.0	100.0
Micronesia, Federated States of	0.0	0.0	0.0	98.4	98.4	97.9
Nauru	0.0	0.0	0.0	100.0	99.9	98.6
Niue	0.0	0.0	0.0	98.9	99.1	97.5
Palau	...	0.0	0.0	...	99.7	99.5
Papua New Guinea	93.5	530.7	616.4	32.7	-224.4	-220.6
Samoa	1.6	1.6	1.4	62.9	67.9	71.7
Solomon Islands	3.2	3.3	3.3	59.6	56.4	54.8
Tonga	0.0	0.0	0.0	98.9	98.0	97.9
Tuvalu	0.0	0.0	0.0	99.6	97.7	95.9
Vanuatu	0.9	0.9	0.9	66.7	67.5	75.3
Developed ADB Member Economies	**18,624.2**	**18,141.5**	**20,941.1**	**31.7**	**25.8**	**7.8**
Australia	13,646.0	16,032.9	18,186.1	-151.5	-200.6	-238.6
Japan	4,205.1	1,318.1	2,068.0	80.0	92.7	87.4
New Zealand	773.2	790.4	687.0	7.6	17.9	23.2
DEVELOPING ADB MEMBER ECONOMIES[a]	**160,940.0**	**178,183.2**	**217,522.1**	**10.0**	**16.0**	**18.5**
ALL ADB REGIONAL MEMBERS[a]	**179,564.3**	**196,324.7**	**238,463.2**	**12.8**	**17.0**	**17.6**
WORLD[a]	**525,933.1**	**566,277.3**	**626,813.6**	**-3.3**	**-4.8**	**-6.0**

... = data not available, 0.0 = magnitude is less than half of unit employed, – = magnitude equals zero, ADB = Asian Development Bank, PJ = petajoule.

a The aggregates for energy production include only economies with available data corresponding to the year heading. The aggregates for net energy imports include only economies with available data corresponding to the year heading for both energy use and energy production. Net energy imports are calculated as the difference between total energy use and total energy production divided by total energy use.

Sources: For Energy Production: United Nations. Energy Statistics Database. https://data.un.org/SdmxBrowser/start (accessed 2 July 2025). For Net Energy Imports: Asian Development Bank estimates using data from United Nations' Energy Statistics Database. https://data.un.org/SdmxBrowser/start (accessed 2 July 2025).

Table 2.6.5: Retail Prices of Fuel Energy
($/L)

ADB Regional Member	Gasoline (Premium)			Diesel		
	2010	2015	2024	2010	2015	2024
Developing ADB Member Economies						
Central and West Asia						
Afghanistan	...	...	...	...	...	...
Armenia	1.01	0.90	1.14 (2022)	0.92	0.89	1.36 (2022)
Azerbaijan	...	...	...	...	...	...
Georgia	1.03	0.82	1.14	1.00	0.82	1.21
Kazakhstan	0.58	0.56	0.44 (2023)	0.53	0.44	0.64 (2023)
Kyrgyz Republic	...	...	...	...	...	...
Pakistan	0.80	0.68	...	0.83	0.78	...
Tajikistan	...	...	...	...	...	...
Türkiye	...	...	...	...	...	...
Turkmenistan	...	...	...	...	...	...
Uzbekistan	...	...	...	...	...	...
East Asia						
China, People's Republic of	...	...	...	...	...	...
Hong Kong, China	1.75	1.77	2.67	1.25	1.41	3.08
Korea, Republic of	1.48	1.34	1.21	1.30	1.15	1.10
Mongolia	1.01	0.79	0.71	0.96	0.91	0.93
Taipei,China	0.94	0.75	0.91	0.82	0.68	0.85
South Asia						
Bangladesh	...	...	...	...	...	...
Bhutan	...	...	...	...	...	...
India	1.05	1.18 (2014)	...	0.83	0.91 (2014)	...
Maldives	...	...	...	...	...	...
Nepal	1.22	1.22	1.30	0.95	0.97	1.21
Sri Lanka	1.18	0.94	1.23	0.65	0.70	0.95
Southeast Asia						
Brunei Darussalam	...	...	...	...	...	...
Cambodia	...	...	...	...	...	...
Indonesia	0.50	0.66	0.79 (2023)	0.50	0.64	1.05 (2023)
Lao People's Democratic Republic	...	...	...	...	...	...
Malaysia	0.67	0.63	...	0.57	0.49	0.64
Myanmar	150.50	0.76	...	145.57	0.80	...
Philippines	0.96	0.90	1.14	0.76	0.60	1.02
Singapore	...	1.59	2.26	...	0.85	1.71
Thailand	1.02	0.81	1.06	0.91	0.72	0.90
Timor-Leste	...	...	...	...	...	...
Viet Nam	1.42 (2011)	1.12	1.53 (2023)	0.93 (2011)	0.68	0.86 (2023)
The Pacific						
Cook Islands	...	...	...	...	...	...
Fiji	...	...	...	...	...	...
Kiribati	...	...	...	...	...	...
Marshall Islands	...	...	...	...	...	...
Micronesia, Federated States of	...	...	...	...	...	...
Nauru	...	...	...	...	...	...
Niue	...	...	...	...	...	...
Palau	...	...	...	...	...	...
Papua New Guinea	...	...	...	...	...	...
Samoa	...	...	...	...	...	...
Solomon Islands	1.14	1.11	1.25	1.15	1.07	1.31
Tonga	...	...	...	...	...	...
Tuvalu	...	...	...	...	...	...
Vanuatu	1.50	1.36	1.47	...	...	...
Developed ADB Member Economies						
Australia	1.16	0.97	1.25	1.17	0.97	1.24
Japan	1.64	1.23	1.23	1.28	0.97	1.02
New Zealand	1.34	1.41	1.72	0.85	0.80	1.21

... = data not available, $ = United States dollars, ADB = Asian Development Bank, L = liter.

Source: Economies' official sources.

Data Issues and Comparability

Energy data are compiled by the United Nations Statistics Division (UNSD) using standard procedures that follow the definitions of the United Nations International Recommendations for Energy Statistics.[2] The UNSD Annual Questionnaire on Energy Statistics to the United Nations member economies is the primary source of information for the division's energy database. The UNSD sometimes prepares estimates where official data are incomplete or inconsistent. For the indicator on gross domestic product per unit use of energy, the energy statistics adopt the territory principle, while national accounts are being compiled on the residency principle, which could be a potential source of inconsistency, although in practice differences are not huge.[3]

For data on access to electricity, the Sustainable Energy for All (SE4ALL) database from the SE4ALL Global Tracking Framework—led jointly by the Energy Sector Management Assistance Program, the International Energy Agency, and the World Bank—provides data on the proportion of access for an entire economy, as well as in rural and urban areas. The data for this indicator are a combination of economy-reported data and modeled estimates by the World Bank.

2 The full definitions can be found at https://unstats.un.org/UNSD/energy/ires/.

3 More information can be found at https://unstats.un.org/unsd/energystats/methodology/documents/ESCM_2017850E.pdf.

Table 2.7.1: Agriculture Land Use
(% of total land area)

ADB Regional Member	Agricultural Land			Arable Land			Permanent Cropland		
	2010	2015	2023	2010	2015	2023	2010	2015	2023
Developing ADB Member Economies									
Central and West Asia[a]	**65.3**	**65.6**	**65.8**	**15.5**	**15.7**	**15.6**	**0.8**	**0.9**	**1.0**
Afghanistan	58.1	58.1	58.4	11.9	11.9	12.0	0.2	0.2	0.4
Armenia	60.9	58.9	58.6	15.8	15.7	15.7	1.9	2.0	2.2
Azerbaijan	57.7	57.7	57.8	22.8	23.4	25.3	2.8	2.9	3.3
Georgia	35.4	34.8	34.1	5.7	5.3	4.4	1.8	1.6	1.8
Kazakhstan	80.4	80.1	79.4	10.6	11.0	11.0	0.0	0.0	0.0
Kyrgyz Republic	55.3	55.0	54.0	6.7	6.7	6.7	0.4	0.4	0.4
Pakistan	45.7	47.0	46.7	38.1	39.4	39.3	1.1	1.0	1.0
Tajikistan	27.2	27.1	27.9	5.3	6.0	6.1	1.0	1.0	1.5
Türkiye	50.7	50.1	50.1	27.8	26.8	26.3	3.9	4.3	4.8
Turkmenistan	72.4	78.3	84.2	3.8	3.7	3.4	0.1	0.1	0.1
Uzbekistan	58.7	58.0	58.1	9.6	9.2	9.1	0.8	0.9	1.0
East Asia[a]	**58.2**	**57.8**	**56.9**	**11.1**	**10.7**	**10.1**	**1.3**	**1.5**	**1.8**
China, People's Republic of	56.2	55.8	55.4	12.8	12.2	11.5	1.5	1.7	2.0
Hong Kong, China	5.2	4.9	3.8	3.3	3.0	1.9	1.0	1.0	1.0
Korea, Republic of	18.2	17.8	16.1	15.5	15.0	14.9	2.1	2.2	2.1
Mongolia	73.3	73.0	69.0	0.8	0.9	0.7	0.0	0.0	0.0
Taipei,China	23.0	22.5	22.0	16.9	16.8	16.6	6.1	5.6	5.4
South Asia[a]	**58.6**	**58.6**	**58.3**	**50.3**	**50.1**	**49.3**	**4.2**	**4.5**	**5.0**
Bangladesh	71.0	70.4	72.3	61.3	59.6	60.6	5.1	6.1	7.1
Bhutan	13.6	13.8	13.8	2.6	2.6	2.6	0.3	0.3	0.4
India	60.4	60.4	60.1	52.8	52.6	51.8	4.1	4.4	4.9
Maldives	23.0	21.3	19.8	13.0	13.0	13.4	6.7	5.0	3.0
Nepal	28.8	28.0	26.1	15.2	14.2	12.6	1.1	1.3	1.0
Sri Lanka	41.8	44.3	48.6	19.1	21.0	22.2	15.6	16.2	19.3
Southeast Asia[a]	**28.0**	**29.3**	**30.0**	**14.6**	**14.7**	**14.3**	**9.5**	**10.8**	**11.9**
Brunei Darussalam	2.5	2.5	2.5	0.8	0.8	0.8	1.1	1.1	1.1
Cambodia	30.5	32.0	34.9	21.2	22.3	23.3	0.8	1.2	3.0
Indonesia	26.6	27.6	29.1	9.5	9.5	9.4	11.2	12.3	13.9
Lao People's Democratic Republic	9.5	10.5	9.9	6.1	6.5	5.3	0.4	1.0	1.7
Malaysia	22.5	26.1	26.1	2.6	2.5	2.4	19.0	22.7	22.7
Myanmar	19.2	19.5	19.9	16.5	16.7	16.9	2.2	2.3	2.3
Philippines	40.6	42.0	42.7	17.8	18.7	18.7	17.8	18.2	18.9
Singapore	1.1	0.9	0.9	0.9	0.8	0.8	0.1	0.1	0.1
Thailand	44.7	44.7	43.8	35.2	33.1	31.0	7.9	10.0	11.2
Timor-Leste	22.7	22.9	23.0	7.8	7.7	7.5	4.8	5.2	5.4
Viet Nam	34.3	38.8	39.2	20.5	22.3	21.5	11.7	14.4	15.7
The Pacific[a]	**3.9**	**4.0**	**4.2**	**0.8**	**1.0**	**0.9**	**2.2**	**2.3**	**2.4**
Cook Islands	8.3	7.9	7.9	2.5	2.1	2.1	5.8	5.8	5.8
Fiji	17.5	17.3	17.1	3.5	3.8	4.2	4.5	4.0	3.4
Kiribati	42.0	42.0	42.0	2.5	2.5	2.5	39.5	39.5	39.5
Marshall Islands	47.2	38.9	38.9	2.8	2.8	2.8	44.4	36.1	36.1
Micronesia, Federated States of	7.1	7.1	7.1	2.9	2.9	2.9	...	...	...
Nauru	20.0	20.0	20.0	...	...	...	20.0	20.0	20.0
Niue	18.5	18.5	18.5	3.8	3.8	3.8	10.8	10.8	10.8
Palau	9.3	9.3	9.3	0.7	0.7	0.7	4.3	4.3	4.3
Papua New Guinea	2.8	2.9	3.1	0.7	0.7	0.7	1.7	1.8	2.0
Samoa	14.7	26.7	17.6	4.2	11.5	3.9	8.3	11.0	11.4
Solomon Islands	3.4	3.6	3.9	0.7	0.8	0.8	2.4	2.5	2.8
Tonga	44.4	48.6	48.6	23.6	27.8	27.8	15.3	15.3	15.3
Tuvalu	60.0	60.0	60.0	...	...	...	60.0	60.0	60.0
Vanuatu	15.3	15.3	15.3	1.6	1.6	1.6	10.3	10.3	10.3
Developed ADB Member Economies[a]	**47.3**	**43.8**	**45.4**	**3.7**	**4.3**	**4.3**	**0.1**	**0.1**	**0.1**
Australia	49.0	45.3	47.2	3.3	4.0	4.0	0.0	0.0	0.1
Japan	13.6	13.3	12.6	11.7	11.5	11.1	0.9	0.8	0.7
New Zealand	43.3	40.7	36.9	1.9	1.8	2.0	0.3	0.3	0.3
DEVELOPING ADB MEMBER ECONOMIES[a]	**53.7**	**53.8**	**53.6**	**17.7**	**17.5**	**17.1**	**3.0**	**3.3**	**3.7**
ALL ADB REGIONAL MEMBERS[a]	**52.1**	**51.4**	**51.6**	**14.3**	**14.3**	**14.0**	**2.3**	**2.5**	**2.8**
WORLD	**36.8**	**36.8**	**36.9**	**10.5**	**10.6**	**10.6**	**1.2**	**1.3**	**1.5**

... = data not available, 0.0 = magnitude is less than half of unit employed, ADB = Asian Development Bank.

a Aggregates are weighted averages estimated using total land area for the respective year headings.

Source: Food and Agriculture Organization of the United Nations. FAOSTAT Database. http://www.fao.org/faostat/en/#data/RL (accessed 23 June 2025).

Pollution

Table 2.7.2: Deforestation and Pollution

ADB Regional Member	Deforestation Rate[a,b] (average % change)			Carbon Dioxide Emissions[c] (t '000 CO_2 equivalent)			Nitrous Oxide Emissions[c] (t '000 CO_2 equivalent)		
	2010	2015	2023	2010	2015	2023	2010	2015	2023
Developing ADB Member Economies									
Central and West Asia	**-0.23**	**-0.41**	**-0.45**	**969,586**	**998,771**	**1,174,415**	**104,354**	**114,255**	**140,761**
Afghanistan	–	–	–	7,789	8,347	8,707	3,650	3,842	3,557
Armenia	0.06	0.06	0.13	4,299	5,617	7,725	370	485	482
Azerbaijan	-0.44	-0.85	-1.00	26,636	34,522	42,766	1,863	2,092	2,221
Georgia	-0.22	–	–	6,292	10,646	12,864	1,463	1,521	1,636
Kazakhstan	0.24	-1.39	-0.83	249,892	205,386	239,867	12,569	12,850	15,300
Kyrgyz Republic	-0.40	-0.35	-1.35	6,605	10,316	10,464	1,456	1,556	1,955
Pakistan	1.01	0.81	1.13	155,627	178,255	200,510	43,231	44,753	59,817
Tajikistan	–	-0.56	-0.23	3,071	5,092	9,308	1,371	1,671	2,090
Türkiye	-0.45	-0.51	-0.69	312,146	367,804	438,316	24,534	27,765	34,195
Turkmenistan	–	–	–	61,652	65,534	65,988	4,733	5,968	5,809
Uzbekistan	-1.17	-1.14	-0.69	135,577	107,254	137,900	9,115	11,752	13,700
East Asia	**-1.06**	**-0.87**	**-0.76**	**9,789,333**	**11,757,739**	**13,895,965**	**413,522**	**438,436**	**437,749**
China, People's Republic of	-1.19	-0.93	-0.84	9,134,072	10,776,913	13,259,639	397,426	414,102	414,538
Hong Kong, China	...	...	...	42,228	44,245	34,673	539	536	480
Korea, Republic of	0.14	0.16	0.16	598,128	642,691	573,536	12,118	12,952	14,333
Mongolia	0.06	0.01	0.01	14,906	18,024	28,117	3,439	6,256	8,397
Taipei,China	–	-4.54	–	276,284 (2011)	275,867	283,160 (2021)	4,925 (2011)	4,591	5,412 (2021)
South Asia	**-0.26**	**-0.33**	**-0.31**	**1,824,699**	**2,375,485**	**3,123,290**	**242,442**	**264,255**	**304,406**
Bangladesh	0.17	0.05	–	60,755	85,431	124,793	21,756	22,914	26,505
Bhutan	-0.37	-0.07	-0.07	896	1,305	1,987	148	170	183
India	-0.27	-0.38	-0.37	1,743,693	2,260,131	2,955,182	214,138	233,651	270,031
Maldives	–	–	–	1,054	1,588	2,876	31	37	56
Nepal	-0.30	–	–	4,785	7,322	17,934	4,256	5,010	6,064
Sri Lanka	0.30	-0.24	0.15	13,517	19,708	20,518	2,113	2,472	1,568
Southeast Asia	**0.20**	**0.62**	**0.52**	**1,220,583**	**1,459,365**	**1,911,103**	**146,360**	**161,698**	**168,839**
Brunei Darussalam	0.45	–	–	7,379	7,365	9,716	120	122	481
Cambodia	0.18	3.79	2.01	5,158	8,514	17,970	3,103	3,190	3,097
Indonesia	0.16	0.97	0.67	443,706	512,407	674,536	66,863	73,076	78,867
Lao People's Democratic Republic	0.29	0.21	0.21	2,961	8,927	26,021	2,027	2,338	3,135
Malaysia	0.39	-0.53	0.26	215,575	252,929	283,324	10,603	10,780	10,371
Myanmar	1.08	0.96	1.04	8,629	19,735	33,368	12,897	15,428	11,867
Philippines	0.68	-0.50	-0.48	84,945	113,162	161,288	10,061	11,939	15,585
Singapore	-0.41	1.52	1.18	48,891	55,188	57,068	1,242	545	512
Thailand	-0.54	0.01	0.18	246,284	279,738	274,160	20,403	19,782	18,898
Timor-Leste	0.15	0.15	0.15	334	695	703	173	216	216
Viet Nam	-1.21	-0.97	-0.51	156,721	200,705	372,949	18,869	24,282	25,809
The Pacific	**0.01**	**0.06**	**0.07**	**9,002**	**9,803**	**11,094**	**1,040**	**1,047**	**985**
Cook Islands	-0.01	–	–	...	...	...	...	...	...
Fiji	-0.63	-0.61	-0.58	1,696	1,616	2,211	291	180	193
Kiribati	–	–	–	61	62	97	6	6	7
Marshall Islands	–	–	–	1	–	–	0	0	0
Micronesia, Federated States of	-0.04	-0.04	-0.05	–	–	–	10	11	12
Nauru	...	...	...	–	–	–	0	0	0
Niue	0.03	-0.05	-0.05	...	...	...	...	...	...
Palau	-0.24	-0.21	-0.19	2,111	1,195	1,440	35	23	28
Papua New Guinea	0.03	0.09	0.09	4,231	5,973	5,952	491	618	564
Samoa	0.29	0.29	0.30	263	329	468	43	50	41
Solomon Islands	0.03	0.03	0.03	358	334	419	31	31	34
Tonga	–	–	–	126	135	220	23	23	25
Tuvalu	–	–	–	–	–	–	1	1	1
Vanuatu	–	–	–	155	159	287	109	104	78
Developed ADB Member Economies	**0.13**	**-0.42**	**-0.01**	**1,669,095**	**1,671,278**	**1,354,170**	**69,356**	**72,378**	**73,699**
Australia	0.17	-0.54	–	415,273	400,542	373,616	39,610	43,826	47,436
Japan	-0.04	0.02	–	1,220,454	1,235,419	944,759	19,234	17,710	15,814
New Zealand	0.00	0.00	-0.19	33,368	35,317	35,795	10,512	10,842	10,449
DEVELOPING ADB MEMBER ECONOMIES	**-0.37**	**-0.18**	**-0.20**	**13,813,203**	**16,601,164**	**20,115,866**	**907,717**	**979,691**	**1,052,740**
ALL ADB REGIONAL MEMBERS	**-0.26**	**-0.23**	**-0.16**	**15,482,298**	**18,272,442**	**21,470,036**	**977,074**	**1,052,068**	**1,126,439**

continued on next page

Table 2.7.2: Deforestation and Pollution *(continued)*

ADB Regional Member	Methane Emissions[c] (t '000 CO_2 equivalent) 2010	2015	2023	Total Greenhouse Gas Emissions[c] (t '000 CO_2 equivalent) 2010	2015	2023
Developing ADB Member Economies						
Central and West Asia	**427,129**	**493,663**	**603,689**	**1,508,357**	**1,615,421**	**1,937,512**
Afghanistan	15,278	14,935	16,452	26,937	27,408	29,460
Armenia	2,174	2,538	2,305	7,004	8,824	10,836
Azerbaijan	15,584	15,746	15,951	44,945	53,363	62,550
Georgia	4,187	4,240	4,216	11,999	16,571	19,049
Kazakhstan	53,962	50,497	61,842	317,902	270,568	320,350
Kyrgyz Republic	6,142	7,842	9,446	14,107	19,574	21,698
Pakistan	175,398	205,858	262,836	377,482	433,006	532,375
Tajikistan	6,302	8,261	10,099	11,871	15,260	21,438
Türkiye	77,120	99,801	130,476	414,362	496,649	606,430
Turkmenistan	22,427	28,808	26,836	88,848	100,355	98,794
Uzbekistan	48,556	55,138	63,230	192,901	173,844	214,531
East Asia	**1,577,939**	**1,698,668**	**1,912,461**	**12,012,284**	**14,216,415**	**16,721,705**
China, People's Republic of	1,516,970	1,626,320	1,814,207	11,262,908	13,118,896	15,943,987
Hong Kong, China	4,497	4,704	5,121	47,120	49,357	40,168
Korea, Republic of	36,535	38,100	45,904	663,999	709,360	653,846
Mongolia	19,937	24,439	47,228	38,256	48,687	83,705
Taipei,China	6,226 (2011)	5,105	4,453 (2021)	292,607 (2011)	290,115	297,054 (2021)
South Asia	**938,552**	**944,099**	**1,027,352**	**3,021,905**	**3,617,085**	**4,516,513**
Bangladesh	117,354	119,801	128,459	200,128	228,565	281,381
Bhutan	1,029	1,116	1,096	2,066	2,583	3,255
India	773,624	775,678	848,535	2,747,618	3,302,488	4,133,554
Maldives	95	123	166	1,174	1,740	3,088
Nepal	30,883	31,016	32,978	39,799	43,216	56,831
Sri Lanka	15,567	16,364	16,118	31,120	38,494	38,404
Southeast Asia	**736,569**	**774,956**	**884,566**	**2,129,866**	**2,430,624**	**3,041,033**
Brunei Darussalam	2,424	2,212	1,712	10,027	9,823	12,158
Cambodia	24,269	25,027	27,243	32,666	36,910	48,775
Indonesia	267,497	316,701	433,485	781,990	907,315	1,200,200
Lao People's Democratic Republic	9,799	11,159	12,934	14,765	22,398	42,056
Malaysia	28,980	29,720	30,252	256,557	296,046	325,406
Myanmar	86,781	86,592	69,538	108,365	121,878	115,077
Philippines	65,324	68,331	73,265	162,365	196,066	256,147
Singapore	3,687	4,750	5,819	58,052	65,752	74,290
Thailand	129,609	112,903	112,797	408,581	428,128	440,783
Timor-Leste	1,634	1,339	1,095	2,136	2,244	2,007
Viet Nam	116,567	116,223	116,427	294,362	344,065	524,134
The Pacific	**3,920**	**4,822**	**4,907**	**13,977**	**15,697**	**17,110**
Cook Islands	…	…	…	…	…	…
Fiji	1,091	736	815	3,130	2,602	3,401
Kiribati	21	23	27	86	90	130
Marshall Islands	3	3	3	3	3	3
Micronesia, Federated States of	32	35	37	41	46	49
Nauru	1	1	1	1	1	1
Niue	…	…	…	…	…	…
Palau	60	36	34	2,205	1,254	1,502
Papua New Guinea	1,832	3,081	3,157	6,537	9,648	9,641
Samoa	165	189	138	469	566	646
Solomon Islands	204	238	282	584	591	721
Tonga	92	95	99	239	251	342
Tuvalu	3	3	3	4	4	4
Vanuatu	418	384	311	677	642	670
Developed ADB Member Economies	**251,043**	**248,645**	**233,727**	**2,013,538**	**2,021,672**	**1,697,062**
Australia	143,767	148,739	139,334	604,604	602,058	571,840
Japan	67,368	61,039	57,641	1,324,226	1,333,584	1,041,013
New Zealand	39,908	38,867	36,752	84,708	86,030	84,210
DEVELOPING ADB MEMBER ECONOMIES	**3,684,109**	**3,916,207**	**4,432,974**	**18,686,388**	**21,895,242**	**26,233,873**
ALL ADB REGIONAL MEMBERS	**3,935,152**	**4,164,852**	**4,666,701**	**20,699,926**	**23,916,914**	**27,930,935**

… = data not available, – = magnitude equals zero, 0 or 0.00 = magnitude is less than half of unit employed, ADB = Asian Development Bank, CO_2 = carbon dioxide, t = metric ton.

a Rate refers to percentage change over previous year. A negative value indicates that the deforestation rate is decreasing (i.e., reforestation).
b Aggregates are calculated as the percentage change of the sum of forest land area of the reporting economies.
c Regional aggregates include only reporting economies with data corresponding to the year heading.

Sources: Food and Agriculture Organization of the United Nations. FAOSTAT Database. http://www.fao.org/faostat/en/#data/RL (accessed 23 June 2025); and World Bank. World Development Indicators. https://databank.worldbank.org/source/world-development-indicators (accessed 30 June 2025). For Taipei,China: Government of Taipei,China, Directorate-General of Budget, Accounting and Statistics.

Freshwater

Table 2.7.3: Freshwater Resources

ADB Regional Member	Internal Renewable Freshwater Resources (m³ billion per year)	Internal Renewable Freshwater Resources (m³ per inhabitant per year)	Annual Freshwater Withdrawals (m³ billion)	Water Productivity[a] (constant 2015 $ per m³)
	2022[b]	2022[c]	2022[b]	2021[d]
Developing ADB Member Economies				
Central and West Asia	**597**	**1,299**	**394**	**5.2**
Afghanistan	47	1,162	20	0.8
Armenia	7	2,381	3	4.3
Azerbaijan	8	788	13	4.2
Georgia	58	15,318	1	11.9
Kazakhstan	64	3,212	25	8.7
Kyrgyz Republic	49	7,034	8	1.0
Pakistan	55	226	179	1.4
Tajikistan	63	6,232	11	1.2
Türkiye	227	2,607	64	19.4
Turkmenistan	1	194	26	2.0
Uzbekistan	16	468	43	2.8
East Asia[e]	**2,913**	**1,927**	**598**	**29.4**
China, People's Republic of	2,813	1,931	568	27.9
Hong Kong, China	...	...	...	...
Korea, Republic of	65	1,252	29	58.1
Mongolia	35	10,278	0	29.7
Taipei,China	...	...	...	...
South Asia	**1,880**	**1,140**	**706**	**4.5**
Bangladesh	105	620	36	8.0
Bhutan	78	99,883	0	7.4
India	1,446	1,014	648	4.3
Maldives	0	57	0	1,078.3
Nepal	198	6,670	9	3.3
Sri Lanka	53	2,312	13	7.5
Southeast Asia	**4,993**	**7,286**	**504**	**6.1**
Brunei Darussalam	9	18,666	0	143.6
Cambodia	121	7,011	2	15.1
Indonesia	2,019	7,240	223	4.8
Lao People's Democratic Republic	190	25,188	7	2.6
Malaysia	580	16,717	7	53.1
Myanmar	1,003	18,654	33	1.8
Philippines	479	4,203	91	4.3
Singapore	1	106	0	739.7
Thailand	225	3,130	57	7.7
Timor-Leste	8	5,999	1	2.3
Viet Nam	359	3,606	82	4.1
The Pacific[e]	**884**	**73,248**	**0**	**58.6**
Cook Islands	...	...	...	...
Fiji	29	31,052	0	48.5
Kiribati	...	...	...	...
Marshall Islands	...	...	...	...
Micronesia, Federated States of	...	...	...	...
Nauru	0	847	...	...
Niue	...	...	...	...
Palau	...	...	...	...
Papua New Guinea	801	78,505	0	60.7
Samoa	...	...	...	...
Solomon Islands	45	57,229	...	...
Tonga	...	...	...	...
Tuvalu	...	...	...	...
Vanuatu	10	31,944	...	...
Developed ADB Member Economies	**1,249**	**7,955**	**101**	**61.8**
Australia	492	18,778	12	133.1
Japan	430	3,440	80	57.2
New Zealand	327	63,721	10	21.3
DEVELOPING ADB MEMBER ECONOMIES[e]	**11,266**	**2,658**	**2,202**	**11.8**
ALL ADB REGIONAL MEMBERS[e]	**12,515**	**2,848**	**2,304**	**14.0**

... = data not available, 0 = magnitude is less than half of unit employed, $ = United States dollars, ADB = Asian Development Bank, m³ = cubic meter.

a Gross domestic product in 2015 United States dollars per cubic meter of total freshwater withdrawal.
b Regional aggregates are calculated as the sum of the economies.
c Regional aggregates are weighted averages estimated using population.
d Regional aggregates are computed from economies with data on both annual freshwater withdrawal and GDP in constant 2015 US dollar.
e For reporting economies only.

Sources: Food and Agriculture Organization of the United Nations. AQUASTAT Database. https://data.apps.fao.org/aquastat/?lang=en (accessed 10 June 2025); and World Bank. World Development Indicators. https://databank.worldbank.org/source/world-development-indicators (accessed 10 June 2025).

Table 2.7.4: Temperature and Climate-Related Disasters

ADB Regional Member	Temperature change with respect to a baseline climatology, corresponding to the period 1951–1980			Climate related disasters frequency: Total Number of Disasters[a,b]		
	2010	2015	2024	2010	2015	2024
Developing ADB Member Economies						
Central and West Asia				**18**	**18**	**22**
Afghanistan	1.7	1.1	2.2	4	5	8
Armenia	2.7	1.9	2.4	–	–	1
Azerbaijan	2.4	1.7	2.2	1	–	–
Georgia	2.4	1.7	2.4	–	1	–
Kazakhstan	1.3	1.6	2.1	2	1	1
Kyrgyz Republic	1.3	1.4	2.2	1	–	3
Pakistan	1.2	0.5	1.5	7	7	6
Tajikistan	1.3	1.2	2.0	2	3	1
Türkiye	...	...	...	1	1	2
Turkmenistan	2.0	1.5	2.4	–	–	–
Uzbekistan	1.8	1.4	2.1	–	–	–
East Asia				**25**	**35**	**22**
China, People's Republic of	1.0	1.3	2.3	21	31	16
Hong Kong, China	0.5	1.1	1.7	1	–	–
Korea, Republic of	0.5	1.0	2.5	1	–	3
Mongolia	0.3	2.2	2.6	–	1	–
Taipei,China	0.6	0.7	1.8	2	3	3
South Asia				**28**	**30**	**29**
Bangladesh	1.1	0.9	1.6	6	7	6
Bhutan	1.3	1.0	1.8	–	–	–
India	1.1	0.7	1.1	18	19	15
Maldives	0.8	0.9	1.2	–	–	–
Nepal	1.1	0.6	1.3	2	2	4
Sri Lanka	1.0	0.9	1.6	2	2	4
Southeast Asia				**34**	**45**	**47**
Brunei Darussalam	0.9	1.1	1.6	–	–	–
Cambodia	1.2	1.1	2.1	1	2	–
Indonesia	0.7	0.8	1.5	8	11	14
Lao People's Democratic Republic	1.2	1.2	2.0	–	2	2
Malaysia	0.9	1.1	1.6	–	1	–
Myanmar	1.2	1.1	2.0	3	6	2
Philippines	1.0	1.1	1.5	13	16	14
Singapore	0.6	1.1	1.6	...	...	...
Thailand	1.2	1.1	2.0	2	2	6
Timor-Leste	0.7	0.5	1.1	–	–	–
Viet Nam	1.2	1.3	2.0	7	5	9
The Pacific				**4**	**15**	**4**
Cook Islands	1.2	0.2	1.0	1	–	–
Fiji	0.7	0.5	1.0	1	1	–
Kiribati	0.5	1.1	2.1	–	1	–
Marshall Islands	0.5	0.6	1.0	–	1	2
Micronesia, Federated States of	0.6	0.7	1.2	–	1	–
Nauru	...	...	...	...	...	...
Niue	...	...	...	...	...	...
Palau	0.5	1.0	1.7	–	1	–
Papua New Guinea	0.9	0.1	1.3	–	3	2
Samoa	1.0	0.6	1.5	–	1	–
Solomon Islands	0.6	0.3	1.2	2	3	–
Tonga	1.0	0.7	1.6	–	1	–
Tuvalu	0.9	0.8	1.4	–	1	–
Vanuatu	0.8	0.5	1.2	–	1	–
Developed ADB Member Economies				**10**	**20**	**8**
Australia	0.6	1.0	1.4	8	8	2
Japan	0.9	0.8	2.2	2	10	5
New Zealand	0.6	0.5	0.6	–	2	1
DEVELOPING ADB MEMBER ECONOMIES				**109**	**143**	**124**
ALL ADB REGIONAL MEMBERS				**119**	**163**	**132**
WORLD	**1.3**	**1.4**	**2.1**	**364**	**356**	**360**

... = data not available, – = magnitude equals zero, ADB = Asian Development Bank.

a Regional aggregates include only reporting economies with data corresponding to the year heading.
b Disasters may include drought, extreme temperature, flood, landslide, storm, or wildfire.

Source: IMF. 2022. Climate Change Indicators Dashboard. Annual Surface Temperature Change and Climate-related Disasters Frequency, https://climatedata.imf.org/pages/access-data (accessed on 30 June 2025).

Data Issues and Comparability

Data on greenhouse gases (GHGs), particularly for carbon dioxide, methane, nitrous oxide, and total GHGs, were compiled from the Emissions Database for Global Atmospheric Research (EDGAR) Community GHG Database, a collaboration between the European Commission, Joint Research Centre, and the International Energy Agency. Data presented refer to emissions data excluding GHG fluxes caused by land use, land-use change, and forestry.

There may be substantial uncertainty in economy-level data due to the limited accuracy of international activity data and the emission factors selected for calculating emissions on an economy level. However, since the Intergovernmental Panel on Climate Change methodologies are consistently used, and data are based on international information sources, there is sound basis for comparability.[4]

The Food and Agriculture Organization of the United Nations (FAO) monitors land use and forestry data using its own expert sources, country or economy reports, satellite imagery, and official data reported on through questionnaires conducted by the organization. In addition, data on freshwater resources are compiled from the AQUASTAT Database, the FAO's global information system on water resources and agricultural water management.

Data gaps on water resources and uses still exist mainly due to incomplete national participation and inconsistent or outdated national data in some cases. It also heavily depends on the capacity and coordination of national agencies. Discrepancies in data quality require complex validation processes to ensure international comparability.[5]

Annual surface temperature change data compiled by the International Monetary Fund are sourced from FAO data based on the publicly available GISTEMP data, the Global Surface Temperature Change data distributed by the National Aeronautics and Space Administration Goddard Institute for Space Studies,[6] while data on climate-related disasters frequency are sourced from the Emergency Events Database, the Centre for Research on the Epidemiology of Disasters, and the Université catholique de Louvain in Brussels, Belgium.

4 For more information on the methodologies of the Emissions Database for Global Atmospheric Research, go to https://edgar.jrc.ec.europa. eu/methodology.

5 For more information on the AQUASTAT methodology, go to https://www.fao.org/aquastat/en/overview/methodology.

6 Refer to https://fenixservices.fao.org/faostat/static/documents/ET/ET_e.pdf to learn more about FAO's method to estimate annual economy level and global temperature change.

Table 2.8.1: Government Net Lending/Net Borrowing
(% of GDP)

ADB Regional Member	2010	2015	2019	2020	2021	2022	2023	2024
Developing ADB Member Economies								
Central and West Asia								
Afghanistan[a]	2.4	-1.4	-1.7	-4.4	...	...	...	...
Armenia	-5.0	-4.8	-0.8	-5.1	-4.6	-2.2	-1.9	-3.5*
Azerbaijan	15.4	-2.8	6.3	-5.3	4.8	10.2	...	...
Georgia	-4.3	-1.0	-1.6	-9.0	-5.9	-2.2	-2.2*	...
Kazakhstan	5.0	-2.2	-0.5	-7.1	-3.4	-0.7	0.2	0.4
Kyrgyz Republic[b]	-4.9	-1.4	-0.1	-3.1	-0.2	-1.0	1.0	2.4
Pakistan[c]	-5.3	-4.7	-7.8	-7.0	-6.0	-7.8	-7.7	-6.8
Tajikistan[d]	-9.2 |	-7.4	-7.6	-7.8	-7.9	-9.0	-10.8	-7.8*
Türkiye	-2.7	0.5	-4.4	-5.0	-1.3	-2.3	-4.9	...
Turkmenistan	2.0	-0.7	...	...	...	...	...	...
Uzbekistan	...	3.1	0.4	-1.3	-3.4	-3.5	-4.5	...
East Asia								
China, People's Republic of	-1.6	-3.4	-4.8	-6.1	-3.7	-4.6	-4.5	-4.8
Hong Kong, China[e]	4.1	1.4	1.9	-8.9	1.0	-10.1	...	...
Korea, Republic of	1.1 (2012)	1.1	0.8	-2.5	-0.3	0.0	-1.2	...
Mongolia	-3.2	-11.1	-8.9	-20.2	-13.9	-8.8	-5.9	-10.4*
Taipei,China	-2.6	0.2	0.5	-0.3	1.4	1.2	-2.3	...
South Asia								
Bangladesh[c]	-1.7	-2.2	-4.6	-4.3	-3.2	...	...	...
Bhutan[c]	1.4	1.4	-0.4	-2.0	-5.9	-4.9	-4.5	0.8
India[e]	-4.9	-3.9	-4.7	-9.2	-6.7	-6.5	-5.5*	-4.7*
Maldives	-8.7	-5.2	-3.3	-18.0	-10.9	-8.9	-10.6	-12.5
Nepal[f]	-1.4	0.9	-4.8	-4.9	-4.1	...	...	...
Sri Lanka	-6.1	-7.2	-6.5	-13.4	-11.6	-9.2	-9.3	-6.8
Southeast Asia								
Brunei Darussalam	15.1	-14.8	-5.6	-19.6	-5.4	1.1	-11.9	...
Cambodia	-3.6	-0.6	1.6	-2.8	-5.2	-0.8	-3.3	-2.5
Indonesia	-0.6	-2.7	-2.1	-6.1	-4.4	-2.3	-1.6	-2.2*
Lao People's Democratic Republic[g]	-0.9	-3.7	-2.9	-5.1	-0.6	0.2	...	...
Malaysia	-5.0	-3.1	-3.4	-6.1	-6.4	-5.5	-5.0	...
Myanmar[h]	-4.4 (2012)	-4.4 |	-4.0	...	...	...	...	...
Philippines	-3.2	-1.2	-3.3	-7.4	-8.3	-7.2	-6.1	-5.7
Singapore[i]	7.5	4.2	7.4	-7.4	1.7	1.5	1.9	...
Thailand[g]	-0.7	0.2	0.4	-4.5	-6.7	-4.5	-2.0	-1.3*
Timor-Leste	...	7.4	-4.9	-3.9	-5.8	2.9	...	...
Viet Nam	-2.2	-5.0	-0.3	-2.8	-1.4	-3.6	...	...
The Pacific								
Cook Islands[c]	2.9	-7.8	5.7	-6.8	-18.7	-10.8	...	...
Fiji[j]	-2.6	-2.2	-4.6 (2018)	...	...	...	...	...
Kiribati	-6.9 (2011)	56.1	19.0	30.8*	-3.3*	-13.1*	...	...
Marshall Islands[g]	3.5	2.8	-1.8	2.6	0.2	0.7	0.7	...
Micronesia, Federated States of[g]	0.5	10.5	19.5	7.9	8.1	20.4	...	...
Nauru[c]	0.1	10.5	29.9	35.7*	44.5 |	24.8	19.1*	13.6*
Niue	...	...	...	...	...	...	...	...
Palau[g]	-1.0	5.1	-0.4	-13.2	-15.2	-5.2* |	0.3*	...
Papua New Guinea	...	-4.2	-5.0	-8.9	-6.8	-5.3	-4.3	-3.2*
Samoa	-5.5	-3.8	2.4	4.3	1.7	5.0	2.7	9.3
Solomon Islands	5.7	0.8	-1.5	-2.4	-1.2	-2.9	-7.0	-5.2
Tonga[c]	...	1.5 (2016)	3.1	0.9	-1.7	-0.9	-1.7	...
Tuvalu	11.5 (2012)	40.0	-1.1	-4.6	-10.7	...	...	...
Vanuatu	-2.6	8.5	5.3	-2.8	0.2	-5.4	0.7	...
Developed ADB Member Economies								
Australia[c]	-5.5	-2.9	-1.2	-7.7	-9.2	-3.8	-0.9	-1.7
Japan[i]	-8.8	-3.6	-3.1	-10.0	-5.9	-3.6	-1.9	...
New Zealand[c]	-3.5	0.2	1.2	-6.2	-2.5	-4.4	-3.9	-3.2

... = data not available; | = marks break in series; * = preliminary, provisional, estimate; ADB = Asian Development Bank; GDP = gross domestic product.

Note: In general, economies follow the guidelines of the International Monetary Fund on Government Finance Statistics (GFS). Some economies still use the 1986 version of the GFS guidelines, while others have switched to the 2001 or 2014 guidelines. The comparability of the data in this table is limited by variations in the concepts and definitions used in different versions of the GFS framework. Data refer to government net lending/net borrowing as classified in the GFS 2001 or GFS 2014 framework, except for Bhutan; Brunei Darussalam; the People's Republic of China; India; the Kyrgyz Republic; Nauru; Pakistan; Taipei,China; Tajikistan; and Turkmenistan, where data refer to overall budgetary surplus/deficit as classified in the GFS 1986 framework. Data refer to general government, except for Armenia (2000–2009); Bangladesh; Bhutan; Brunei Darussalam; Cambodia; the People's Republic of China; Fiji; India; the Lao People's Democratic Republic; Malaysia; the Marshall Islands; the Federated States of Micronesia; Nauru; Nepal; Palau; the Philippines; Solomon Islands; Sri Lanka; Taipei,China; Timor-Leste; Turkmenistan (2000–2010); Tonga; Tuvalu; Vanuatu; and Viet Nam, where data refer to central government. For Azerbaijan: Data for 2000–2007 (featured in the Key Indicators Database) are based on the state budget. For Cambodia: Data refer to central government excluding extra budgetary central government. For Pakistan: Data refer to the consolidated government. For the People's Republic of China: Data refer to consolidated central and local governments.

a The longer time series featured in the Key Indicators Database refers to GFS data for 2005–2011 based on fiscal year beginning 21 March. For 2012, data cover 9 months from 21 March to 20 December. For 2013 onward, GFS data are based on fiscal year ending 20 December. For 2005–2015, national accounts data are based on fiscal year beginning 21 March. For 2016 onward, national accounts data are based on fiscal year ending 20 December.
b For 2007 onward, data are calculated excluding net lending.
c Data are based on fiscal year ending 30 June.
d National accounts data prior to 2015 are based on the 1993 System of National Accounts while figures for 2015 onward are based on the 2008 System of National Accounts.
e Data are based on fiscal year beginning 1 April.
f Data are based on fiscal year ending 15 July.
g Data are based on fiscal year ending 30 September.
h The longer time series featured in the Key Indicators Database refers to GFS data for 2012–2018 based on fiscal year beginning 1 April. Starting 2019, GFS data are based on fiscal year beginning 1 October.
i Data are based on fiscal year ending 31 March.
j The longer time series featured in the Key Indicators Database refers to GFS data for 2000–2014 based on fiscal year ending 31 December. For 2015 onward, GFS data are based on fiscal year ending 31 July.

Sources: Economies' official sources. For Timor-Leste: International Monetary Fund (IMF). Government Finance Statistics. https://data.imf.org/ (accessed 10 June 2025). For Nauru (2012–2014): IMF. Staff Country Reports. Republic of Nauru: 2017 Article IV. http://www.imf.org/en/Publications/CR/Issues/2017/04/03/Republic-of-Nauru-2017-Article-IV-Consultation-Press-Release-Staff-Report-and-Statement-by-44794 (accessed 9 May 2021). For Nauru (2015–2016): IMF. Staff Country Reports. Republic of Nauru: 2019 Article IV. https://www.imf.org/en/Publications/CR/Issues/2020/01/29/Republic-of-Nauru-2019-Article-IV-Consultation-Press-Release-Staff-Report-and-Statement-by-49001 (accessed 9 May 2021). For Nauru (2017–2020): IMF. Staff Country Reports. Republic of Nauru: 2021 Article IV. https://www.imf.org/en/Publications/CR/Issues/2022/02/07/Republic-of-Nauru-2021-Article-IV-Consultation-Press-Release-Staff-Report-and-Statement-by-512874 (accessed 28 May 2023). For Nauru (2021–2023): IMF. Staff Country Reports. Republic of Nauru: 2023 Article IV Consultation - Press Release; Staff Report; and Statement by the Executive Director for Republic of Nauru. https://www.imf.org/en/Publications/CR/Issues/2023/11/28/Republic-of-Nauru-2023-Article-IV-Consultation-Press-Release-Staff-Report-and-Statement-by-541784 (accessed 3 February 2025). For Republic of Palau: 2023 Article IV Consultation- Press Release; Staff Report; and Statement by the Executive Director for Republic of Palau. https://www.imf.org/en/Publications/CR/Issues/2023/12/21/Republic-of-Palau-2023-Article-IV-Consultation-Press-Release-Staff-Report-and-Statement-by-542638 (accessed 23 May 2024).

Government Finance

Table 2.8.2: Government Taxes
(% of GDP)

ADB Regional Member	2010	2015	2019	2020	2021	2022	2023	2024
Developing ADB Member Economies								
Central and West Asia								
Afghanistan[a]	8.8	7.1	8.4	7.5	...	...	...	...
Armenia	17.7	21.3	22.6	22.5	22.7	22.4	23.1	23.3*
Azerbaijan	12.3	15.7	14.3	15.4	13.6	15.6	...	...
Georgia	22.3	23.6	24.1	22.3	22.6	23.7	28.4	...
Kazakhstan	19.6	13.6	15.1	12.5	13.8	16.7	16.7	15.1
Kyrgyz Republic	17.9	19.7	18.6	16.7	19.3	22.4	22.1	22.9*
Pakistan[b]	8.9	9.9	9.7	9.3	9.4	10.1	9.3	9.5
Tajikistan[c]	18.0 |	20.8	19.9	18.3	19.5	18.5	19.4	19.0*
Türkiye	19.4	18.7	16.9	18.0	18.2	17.3	18.8	...
Turkmenistan	17.5 (2011)	15.6	...	...	...	...	...	...
Uzbekistan	...	19.3	16.6	17.0	16.9	16.1	15.4	...
East Asia								
China, People's Republic of	17.5	17.8	15.7	14.9	14.7	13.5	14.0	13.0
Hong Kong, China[d]	13.5	14.4	13.3	14.0	14.6	14.8	...	...
Korea, Republic of	17.2 (2012)	16.7	18.9	19.1	20.9	22.4	19.5	...
Mongolia	24.2	17.9	20.6	18.5	20.7	23.3	24.9	28.3*
Taipei,China	7.7	8.6	9.0	8.0	9.2	10.1	10.5	...
South Asia								
Bangladesh[b]	10.2	8.9	8.9	7.7	8.5	...	...	...
Bhutan[b]	12.6	13.3	14.1	12.5	10.1	11.3	12.3	13.2
India[d]	7.5	6.9	6.8	7.2	7.6	7.8	7.7*	7.7*
Maldives	8.7	18.5	17.8	18.6	17.6	19.7	22.8	22.6
Nepal[e]	13.4	14.7	19.8	15.8	17.8	...	...	...
Sri Lanka	10.9	11.7	10.9	7.8	7.4	7.3	9.9	12.4
Southeast Asia								
Brunei Darussalam	...	...	...	...	...	...	...	...
Cambodia	6.0	10.9	14.6	13.3	12.0	13.5	12.2	11.6
Indonesia	11.3	12.0	11.1	9.5	10.3	11.6	11.7	11.3*
Lao People's Democratic Republic[f]	13.8	13.5	11.5	9.3	10.3	12.2	...	...
Malaysia	13.3	14.1	11.9	10.9	11.2	11.6	12.6	...
Myanmar[g]	6.6 (2012)	7.5	7.0	...	...	...	...	...
Philippines	11.6	13.0	14.5	14.0	14.1	14.6	14.1	14.4
Singapore[d]	12.8	13.1	13.2	12.7	12.7	11.8	13.9	...
Thailand[f]	16.1	17.6	16.1	15.7	15.6	15.8	16.1	16.0*
Timor-Leste	...	7.9	7.6	7.6	8.1	11.6	...	...
Viet Nam	17.5	14.5	14.1	12.8	13.5	13.9	...	...
The Pacific								
Cook Islands[b]	27.0	23.5	29.5	34.0	18.9	23.7	...	...
Fiji	21.6	24.0	24.0	20.6	15.5	16.8	19.3	23.5
Kiribati[b]	18.3 (2011)	22.7	24.9	26.6*	27.8*	23.7*	...	...
Marshall Islands[f]	15.9	14.1	15.0	13.9	13.8	13.9	13.6	...
Micronesia, Federated States of[f]	12.2	12.5	26.9	14.8	15.8	26.8	...	...
Nauru[b]	8.1 | (2012)	21.7	36.1	48.4* |	36.7	37.3	29.7*	11.5*
Niue	...	...	...	...	...	...	...	...
Palau[f]	16.9	20.0	18.4	18.7	17.5	15.7*	20.9*	...
Papua New Guinea	...	14.6	13.0	11.9	12.1	14.8	15.9	15.2*
Samoa[b]	20.5	22.2	22.7	18.1	23.7	24.0	23.6	24.2
Solomon Islands	22.0	25.7	22.2	21.1	21.6	20.7	21.5	22.0
Tonga[b]	...	...	20.9	23.0	22.9	21.7	18.9	...
Tuvalu	28.5 (2012)	33.1	...	20.3	22.3	...	...	...
Vanuatu	16.2	16.9	17.6	14.0	15.9	16.2	18.1	...
Developed ADB Member Economies								
Australia[b]	25.5	27.3	28.8	27.8	28.4	29.3	29.4	30.0
Japan[d]	15.6	18.6	18.9	19.9	21.0	22.0	21.1	...
New Zealand[b]	29.1	30.7	31.7	30.5	32.5	33.7	31.4	32.6

... = data not available; | = marks break in series; * = provisional, preliminary, estimate; ADB = Asian Development Bank; GDP = gross domestic product.

Note: In general, economies follow the guidelines of the International Monetary Fund on Government Finance Statistics (GFS). Some economies still use the 1986 version of the GFS guidelines, while others have switched to the 2001 or 2014 guidelines. The comparability of the data in this table is limited by variations in the concepts and definitions used in different versions of the GFS framework. Data refer to government taxes as classified in the GFS 2001 or GFS 2014 framework, except for Bhutan; Brunei Darussalam; the People's Republic of China; India; the Kyrgyz Republic; Nauru; Pakistan; Taipei,China; Tajikistan; and Turkmenistan, where data refer to tax revenue as classified in the GFS 1986 framework. Data refer to general government, except for Armenia (2000–2009); Bangladesh; Bhutan; Brunei Darussalam; Cambodia; the People's Republic of China; Fiji; India; the Lao People's Democratic Republic; Malaysia; the Marshall Islands; the Federated States of Micronesia; Nauru; Nepal; Palau; the Philippines; Solomon Islands; Sri Lanka; Taipei,China; Timor-Leste; Turkmenistan (2000–2010); Tonga; Tuvalu; Vanuatu; and Viet Nam, where data refer to central government. For Azerbaijan: Data for 2000–2007 (featured in the Key Indicators Database) are based on the state budget. For Cambodia: Data refer to central government excluding extra budgetary central government. For Pakistan: Data refer to the consolidated government. For the People's Republic of China: Data refer to consolidated central and local governments.

a The longer time series featured in the Key Indicators Database refers to GFS data for 2005–2011 based on fiscal year beginning 21 March. For 2012, GFS data cover 9 months from 21 March to 20 December. For 2013 onward, GFS data are based on fiscal year ending 20 December. For 2005–2015, national accounts data are based on fiscal year beginning 21 March. For 2016 onward, national accounts data are based on fiscal year ending 20 December.
b Data are based on fiscal year ending 30 June.
c National accounts data prior to 2015 are based on the 1993 System of National Accounts while figures for 2015 onward are based on the 2008 System of National Accounts.
d Data are based on fiscal year beginning 1 April.
e Data are based on fiscal year ending 15 July.
f Data are based on fiscal year ending 30 September.
g For 2012–2018, GFS data are based on fiscal year beginning 1 April. For 2019, GFS data are based on fiscal year beginning 1 October. For 2012–2015, national accounts data are based on fiscal year beginning 1 April. For 2016 onward, national accounts data are based on fiscal year beginning 1 October.

Sources: Economies' official sources. For Timor-Leste: International Monetary Fund (IMF). Government Finance Statistics. https://data.imf.org/ (accessed 10 June 2025). For Nauru (2012–2014): IMF. Staff Country Reports. Republic of Nauru: 2017 Article IV. http://www.imf.org/en/Publications/CR/Issues/2017/04/03/Republic-of-Nauru-2017-Article-IV-Consultation-Press-Release-Staff-Report-and-Statement-by-44794 (accessed 9 May 2021). For Nauru (2015–2016): IMF. Staff Country Reports. Republic of Nauru: 2019 Article IV. https://www.imf.org/en/Publications/CR/Issues/2020/01/29/Republic-of-Nauru-2019-Article-IV-Consultation-Press-Release-Staff-Report-and-Statement-by-49001 (accessed 9 May 2021). For Nauru (2017–2020): IMF. Staff Country Reports. Republic of Nauru: 2021 Article IV. https://www.imf.org/en/Publications/CR/Issues/2022/02/07/Republic-of-Nauru-2021-Article-IV-Consultation-Press-Release-Staff-Report-and-Statement-by-512874 (accessed 28 May 2023). For Nauru (2021–2023): IMF. Staff Country Reports. Republic of Nauru: 2023 Article IV Consultation - Press Release; Staff Report; and Statement by the Executive Director for Republic of Nauru. https://www.imf.org/en/Publications/CR/Issues/2023/11/28/Republic-of-Nauru-2023-Article-IV-Consultation-Press-Release-Staff-Report-and-Statement-by-541784 (accessed 3 February 2025). For Republic of Palau: 2023 Article IV Consultation- Press Release; Staff Report; and Statement by the Executive Director for Republic of Palau. https://www.imf.org/en/Publications/CR/Issues/2023/12/21/Republic-of-Palau-2023-Article-IV-Consultation-Press-Release-Staff-Report-and-Statement-by-542638 (accessed 23 May 2024).

Table 2.8.3: Government Revenue
(% of GDP)

ADB Regional Member	2010	2015	2019	2020	2021	2022	2023	2024
Developing ADB Member Economies								
Central and West Asia								
Afghanistan[a]	23.0	23.9	26.9	24.1	...	...	...	...
Armenia	23.2	23.8	24.7	26.0	25.0	25.1	26.0	26.6*
Azerbaijan	47.0	34.4	43.1	35.3	36.7	37.8	...	...
Georgia	26.9	30.4	29.2	27.3	27.4	28.6	35.0	...
Kazakhstan	25.5	17.6	19.1	17.0	15.8	20.7	24.7	23.8
Kyrgyz Republic	23.1	27.7	23.5	21.9	25.1	27.6	28.2	29.5*
Pakistan[b]	12.6	12.9	11.2	13.2	12.4	12.1	11.5	12.5
Tajikistan[c]	19.3 |	23.7	22.5	20.6	21.0	20.5	21.2	21.4*
Türkiye	33.1	31.8	30.4	30.8	31.0	27.5	30.3	...
Turkmenistan[d]	15.8	16.6	...	...	...	...	...	...
Uzbekistan	...	26.2	24.0	23.5	23.7	26.7	25.9	...
East Asia								
China, People's Republic of	19.8	21.7	18.9	17.7	17.3	16.5	16.8	16.3
Hong Kong, China[e]	22.3	21.7	23.3	23.3	26.2	20.5	...	...
Korea, Republic of	31.9 (2012)	30.7	32.1	32.3	34.5	36.3	34.0	...
Mongolia	32.0	26.1	28.8	25.2	29.2	31.8	33.1	37.0*
Taipei,China	10.7	11.4	11.0	10.9	11.0	11.9	12.4	...
South Asia								
Bangladesh[b]	13.0	10.6	10.4	9.6	10.7	...	...	...
Bhutan[b]	26.0	19.0	16.4	21.0	21.9	17.9	18.0	21.1
India[e]	10.8	9.1	8.7	8.5	9.3	9.1	9.3*	9.5*
Maldives	22.8	27.1	26.4	26.7	26.4	30.5	33.4	31.3
Nepal[f]	18.1	18.6	23.2	20.1	21.1	...	...	...
Sri Lanka	12.6	12.6	11.9	8.8	8.3	8.4	11.2	13.7
Southeast Asia								
Brunei Darussalam	49.0	20.9	26.4	12.4	25.3	27.6	17.4	...
Cambodia	11.3	13.8	18.3	16.2	14.4	16.1	14.8	13.3
Indonesia	15.6	15.0	14.3	12.3	13.7	15.2	15.2	14.4*
Lao People's Democratic Republic[g]	21.7	20.3	15.6	12.6	14.6	14.9	...	...
Malaysia	19.4	18.6	17.5	15.9	15.1	16.4	17.3	...
Myanmar[h]	9.8 (2012)	11.8	10.2	...	...	...	...	...
Philippines	12.8	14.7	16.1	15.9	15.5	16.1	15.7	16.7
Singapore[i]	16.8	18.0	20.9	18.1	17.1	15.9	18.2	...
Thailand[g]	20.6	22.2	20.9	20.7	19.8	19.8	20.8	21.2*
Timor-Leste	...	91.3	78.1	79.9	100.1	111.1	...	...
Viet Nam	19.9	18.2	17.4	16.2	16.5	16.6	...	...
The Pacific								
Cook Islands[b]	38.3	39.7	43.0	51.2	44.5	39.7	...	...
Fiji[j]	25.5 |	28.5	27.1	25.5	23.6	21.7	23.2*	28.0
Kiribati[b]	64.4 (2011)	127.8	121.3	130.0*	106.7*	54.0*	...	...
Marshall Islands[g]	62.9	59.3	64.0	70.6	70.3	67.0	66.7	...
Micronesia, Federated States of[g]	68.9	66.9	76.8	67.0	71.0	93.8	...	...
Nauru[b]	39.2 |	74.5	136.0	151.4* |	103.9	138.5	119.5*	100.0
Niue	...	...	...	...	...	...	...	...
Palau[g]	46.5	40.6	42.4	44.6	48.5	54.5*	45.9*	...
Papua New Guinea	...	18.2	16.3	14.7	15.1	16.6	17.9	18.6
Samoa[b]	23.9	26.8	28.5	26.3	34.5	36.2	31.5	35.6
Solomon Islands	28.2	35.1	27.4	30.1	30.3	27.8	25.5	26.3
Tonga[b]	...	...	41.7	51.6	41.9	47.3	51.9	...
Tuvalu	105.3 (2012)	184.0	111.8	137.4	108.4	...	...	...
Vanuatu	25.7	33.7	41.8	37.7	43.7	31.8 |	35.7*	...
Developed ADB Member Economies								
Australia[b]	32.1	34.1	35.6	34.4	34.9	35.7	36.0	36.6
Japan[i]	29.9	35.0	35.4	36.7	37.8	39.2	38.1	...
New Zealand[b]	36.6	37.7	37.8	36.2	37.6	38.8	37.0	38.7

... = data not available; | = marks break in series; * = provisional, preliminary, estimate; ADB = Asian Development Bank; GDP = gross domestic product.

Note: In general, economies follow the guidelines of the International Monetary Fund on Government Finance Statistics (GFS). Some economies still use the 1986 version of the GFS guidelines, while others have switched to the 2001 or 2014 guidelines. The comparability of the data in this table is limited by variations in the concepts and definitions used in different versions of the GFS framework. Data refer to government revenue as classified in the GFS 2001 or GFS 2014 framework, except for Bhutan; Brunei Darussalam; the People's Republic of China; India; the Kyrgyz Republic; Nauru; Pakistan; Taipei,China; Tajikistan; and Turkmenistan, where data refer to total government revenue as classified in the GFS 1986 framework. Data refer to general government, except for Armenia (2000–2009); Bangladesh; Bhutan; Brunei Darussalam; Cambodia; the People's Republic of China; Fiji; India; the Lao People's Democratic Republic; Malaysia; the Marshall Islands; the Federated States of Micronesia; Nauru; Nepal; Palau; the Philippines; Solomon Islands; Sri Lanka; Taipei,China; Timor-Leste; Turkmenistan (2000–2010); Tonga; Tuvalu; Vanuatu; and Viet Nam, where data refer to central government. For Azerbaijan: Data for 2000–2007 (featured in the Key Indicators Database) are based on the state budget. For Cambodia: Data refer to central government excluding extra budgetary central government. For Pakistan: Data refer to the consolidated government. For the People's Republic of China: Data refer to consolidated central and local governments.

a The longer time series featured in the Key Indicators Database refers to GFS data for 2005–2011 based on fiscal year beginning 21 March. For 2012, GFS data cover 9 months from 21 March to 20 December. For 2013 onward, GFS data are based on fiscal year ending 20 December. For 2005–2015, national accounts data are based on fiscal year beginning 21 March. For 2016 onward, national accounts data are based on fiscal year ending 20 December.
b Data are based on fiscal year ending 30 June.
c National accounts data prior to 2015 are based on the 1993 System of National Accounts while figures for 2015 onward are based on the 2008 System of National Accounts.
d For 2010, data refer to central government revenue. For 2015 onward, data refer to general government revenue.
e Data are based on fiscal year beginning 1 April.
f Data are based on fiscal year ending 15 July.
g Data are based on fiscal year ending 30 September.
h For 2012–2018, GFS data are based on fiscal year beginning 1 April. For 2019, GFS data are based on fiscal year beginning 1 October. For 2012–2015, national accounts data are based on fiscal year beginning 1 April. For 2016 onward, national accounts data are based on fiscal year beginning 1 October.
i Data are based on fiscal year ending 31 March.
j The longer time series featured in the Key Indicators Database refers to GFS data for 2000–2014 based on fiscal year ending 31 December. For 2015 onward, GFS data are based on fiscal year ending 31 July. National accounts data are based on calendar year.

Sources: Economies' official sources. For Timor-Leste: International Monetary Fund (IMF). Government Finance Statistics. https://data.imf.org/ (accessed 10 June 2025). For Nauru (2012–2014): IMF. Staff Country Reports. Republic of Nauru: 2017 Article IV. http://www.imf.org/en/Publications/CR/Issues/2017/04/03/Republic-of-Nauru-2017-Article-IV-Consultation-Press-Release-Staff-Report-and-Statement-by-44794 (accessed 9 May 2021). For Nauru (2015–2016): IMF. Staff Country Reports. Republic of Nauru: 2019 Article IV. https://www.imf.org/en/Publications/CR/Issues/2020/01/29/Republic-of-Nauru-2019-Article-IV-Consultation-Press-Release-Staff-Report-and-Statement-by-49001 (accessed 9 May 2021). For Nauru (2017–2020): IMF. Staff Country Reports. Republic of Nauru: 2021 Article IV. https://www.imf.org/en/Publications/CR/Issues/2022/02/07/Republic-of-Nauru-2021-Article-IV-Consultation-Press-Release-Staff-Report-and-Statement-by-512874 (accessed 28 May 2023). For Nauru (2021–2023): IMF. Staff Country Reports. Republic of Nauru: 2023 Article IV Consultation - Press Release; Staff Report; and Statement by the Executive Director for Republic of Nauru. https://www.imf.org/en/Publications/CR/Issues/2023/11/28/Republic-of-Nauru-2023-Article-IV-Consultation-Press-Release-Staff-Report-and-Statement-by-541784 (accessed 3 February 2025). For Republic of Palau: 2023 Article IV Consultation-Press Release; Staff Report; and Statement by the Executive Director for Republic of Palau. https://www.imf.org/en/Publications/CR/Issues/2023/12/21/Republic-of-Palau-2023-Article-IV-Consultation-Press-Release-Staff-Report-and-Statement-by-542638 (accessed 23 May 2024).

Government Finance

Table 2.8.4: Government Expenditure
(% of GDP)

ADB Regional Member	2010	2015	2019	2020	2021	2022	2023	2024
Developing ADB Member Economies								
Central and West Asia								
Afghanistan[a]	20.6	25.2	28.6	28.5	...	...	...	...
Armenia	28.2	28.6	25.5	31.1	29.5	27.3	27.9	30.1*
Azerbaijan	31.6	37.2	36.8	40.6	31.9	27.6	...	...
Georgia	31.2	31.4	30.9	36.3	33.3	30.8	37.2*	...
Kazakhstan	20.4	19.8	19.5	23.8	19.1	20.7	23.7	23.3
Kyrgyz Republic	31.2	31.3	25.7	26.9	27.0	30.5	28.5	28.0*
Pakistan[b]	18.2	18.2	18.9	20.4	18.5	19.7	19.4	19.4
Tajikistan[c]	27.2 |	31.9	30.1	29.6	29.0	29.9	32.4	29.6
Türkiye	35.8	31.3	34.8	35.7	32.3	29.8	35.2	...
Turkmenistan	13.8 |	17.3	...	...	...	...	...	...
Uzbekistan	...	23.1	23.5	24.8	27.1	30.2	30.3	...
East Asia								
China, People's Republic of	21.4	25.0	23.7	23.7	20.9	21.1	21.2	21.1
Hong Kong, China[d]	18.1	20.3	21.4	32.2	25.2	30.5	...	...
Korea, Republic of	30.8 (2012)	29.6	31.3	34.9	34.7	36.2	35.2	...
Mongolia	35.2	37.2	37.7	45.3	43.1	40.6	39.0	47.4*
Taipei,China	13.4	11.2	10.6	11.2	9.7	10.7	14.7	...
South Asia								
Bangladesh[b]	14.8	12.7	15.0	13.9	13.9	...	...	...
Bhutan[b]	33.8	26.4	22.9	31.6	34.7	30.4	27.0	26.5
India[d]	15.7	13.0	13.4	17.7	16.0*	15.6*	14.8*	14.2
Maldives	31.5	32.3	29.6	44.7	37.3	39.4	44.0	43.8
Nepal[e]	19.5	17.6	28.0	25.0	25.1	...	...	...
Sri Lanka	18.7	19.8	18.4	22.1	19.9	17.6	20.5	20.5
Southeast Asia								
Brunei Darussalam[f]	34.0	35.7	32.0	31.5	30.7	26.5	29.3	...
Cambodia	14.9	14.5	16.7	19.0	19.6	16.9	18.1	15.8
Indonesia	16.2	17.7	16.4	18.5	18.1	17.5	16.8	16.6
Lao People's Democratic Republic[g]	22.7	24.1	18.5	17.8	15.2	14.7	...	...
Malaysia	24.4	21.7	20.8	22.0	21.5	21.9	22.3	...
Myanmar[h]	14.2 (2012)	16.2 |	14.2	...	...	...	...	...
Philippines	16.1	15.9	19.4	23.4	23.8	23.2	21.8	22.4
Singapore[d]	9.3	13.8	13.5	25.4	15.5	14.4	16.3	...
Thailand[g]	21.3	22.0	20.5	25.2	26.5	24.3	22.8*	22.5
Timor-Leste	...	84.0	83.0	83.8	105.9	108.2	...	...
Viet Nam[i]	22.1	23.2	17.8	19.1	17.9	20.2	...	...
The Pacific								
Cook Islands[b]	35.5	47.5	37.3	58.0	63.2	50.5	...	...
Fiji[j]	31.5 |	36.0	33.1	31.5	35.1	33.9	30.2	32.9
Kiribati[b]	71.3 (2011)	71.7	102.3	99.2*	110.0*	99.8*	...	...
Marshall Islands[g]	59.4	56.4	65.8	68.1	70.1	66.3*	66.0*	...
Micronesia, Federated States of[g]	68.4	56.4	57.3	59.1	62.9	73.4	...	...
Nauru[b]	83.6 |	83.1	118.9	134.5* |	93.0	133.5	116.2*	115.2
Niue	...	...	...	...	...	...	...	...
Palau[g]	25.7	25.9	30.8	45.0	48.1	43.9*	46.2*	...
Papua New Guinea	...	22.4	21.3	23.5	22.0	21.9	22.3*	21.8
Samoa[b]	29.4	30.6	26.1	22.0	32.9	31.2	28.8	26.3
Solomon Islands	22.6	34.3	29.0	32.6	31.6	30.8	26.8	35.4
Tonga[b]	...	...	38.6	50.7	43.6	48.1	53.5	...
Tuvalu	93.8 (2012)	144.0	...	142.0	119.1	...	...	...
Vanuatu	28.3	25.2	36.5	40.5	43.5	37.2	35.0	...
Developed ADB Member Economies								
Australia[b]	37.6	37.1	36.9	42.1	44.2	39.4	36.8	38.3
Japan[d]	38.7	38.6	38.5	46.6	43.7	42.8	39.9	...
New Zealand[b]	40.2	37.5	36.6	42.4	40.0	43.2	40.9	41.9

... = data not available; | = marks break in series; * = provisional, preliminary, estimate; ADB = Asian Development Bank; GDP = gross domestic product.

Note: In general, economies follow the guidelines of the International Monetary Fund on Government Finance Statistics (GFS). Some economies still use the 1986 version of the GFS guidelines, while others have switched to the 2001 or 2014 guidelines. The comparability of the data in this table is limited by variations in the concepts and definitions used in different versions of the GFS framework. Data refer to government expenditure as classified in the GFS 2001 or GFS 2014 framework, except for Bhutan; Brunei Darussalam; the People's Republic of China; India; the Kyrgyz Republic; Nauru; Pakistan; Taipei,China; Tajikistan; and Turkmenistan, where data refer to total government expenditure as classified in the GFS 1986 framework. Data refer to general government, except for Bangladesh; Bhutan; Brunei Darussalam; Cambodia; Fiji; India; the Lao People's Democratic Republic; Malaysia; the Marshall Islands; the Federated States of Micronesia; Nauru; Nepal; Palau; the Philippines; Solomon Islands; Sri Lanka; Taipei,China; Timor-Leste; Tonga; Tuvalu; Vanuatu; and Viet Nam, where data refer to central government. For Cambodia: Data refer to central government excluding extra budgetary central government. For Pakistan: Data refer to the consolidated federal and provincial governments. For the People's Republic of China: Data refer to consolidated central and local governments. For Turkmenistan: Data prior to 2011 refer to central government.

a The longer time series featured in the Key Indicators Database refers to GFS data for 2005–2011 based on fiscal year beginning 21 March. For 2012, GFS data cover 9 months from 21 March to 20 December. For 2013 onward, GFS data are based on fiscal year ending 20 December. For 2005–2015, national accounts data are based on fiscal year beginning 21 March. For 2016 onward, national accounts data are based on fiscal year ending 20 December.
b Data are based on fiscal year ending 30 June.
c Prior to 2015, national accounts data are based on the 1993 System of National Accounts; and, for 2015 onward, are based on the 2008 System of National Accounts.
d Data are based on fiscal year beginning 1 April.
e Data are based on fiscal year ending 15 July.
f The longer time series featured in the Key Indicators Database showing Brunei Darussalam's government expenditure for 2003 onward are based on fiscal year beginning 1 April.
g Data are based on fiscal year ending 30 September.
h For 2012–2018, GFS data are based on fiscal year beginning 1 April. For 2019, data are based on fiscal year beginning 1 October. For 2012–2015, national accounts data are based on fiscal year beginning 1 April. For 2016 onward, national accounts data are based on fiscal year beginning 1 October.
i Until the 53rd edition of the Key Indicators of Asia and the Pacific, Viet Nam's data on government finance from the Ministry of Finance (MOF) was presented using the GFS 1986 standard. Starting in the 54th edition of the Key Indicators of Asia and the Pacific, with the support of the World Bank and International Monetary Fund (IMF), the MOF submitted its 2003–2019 government finance data following GFS 2014 standard. The MOF is currently working with IMF to convert its 2020 onward government finance data.
j The longer time series featured in the Key Indicators Database refers to GFS data for 2000–2014 based on fiscal year ending 31 December. For 2015 onward, GFS data are based on fiscal year ending 31 July. National accounts data are based on calendar year.

Sources: Economies' official sources. For Nauru (2012–2014): IMF. IMF. Staff Country Reports. Republic of Nauru: 2017 Article IV. http://www.imf.org/en/Publications/CR/Issues/2017/04/03/Republic-of-Nauru-2017-Article-IV-Consultation-Press-Release-Staff-Report-and-Statement-by-44794 (accessed 9 May 2021). For Nauru (2015–2016): IMF. Staff Country Reports. Republic of Nauru: 2019 Article IV. https://www.imf.org/en/Publications/CR/Issues/2020/01/29/Republic-of-Nauru-2019-Article-IV-Consultation-Press-Release-Staff-Report-and-Statement-by-49001 (accessed 9 May 2021). For Nauru (2017–2020): IMF. Staff Country Reports. Republic of Nauru: 2021 Article IV. https://www.imf.org/en/Publications/CR/Issues/2022/02/07/Republic-of-Nauru-2021-Article-IV-Consultation-Press-Release-Staff-Report-and-Statement-by-512874 (accessed 28 May 2023). For Nauru (2021–2024): IMF. Republic of Nauru: 2023 Article IV Consultation - Press Release; Staff Report; and Statement by the Executive Director for Republic of Nauru. https://www.imf.org/en/Publications/CR/Issues/2023/11/28/Republic-of-Nauru-2023-Article-IV-Consultation-Press-Release-Staff-Report-and-Statement-by-541784 (accessed 3 February 2025); past issues. For Palau (2023): IMF. Staff Country Reports. Republic of Palau: 2023 Article IV Consultation- Press Release; Staff Report; and Statement by the Executive Director for Republic of Palau. https://www.imf.org/en/Publications/CR/Issues/2023/12/21/Republic-of-Palau-2023-Article-IV-Consultation-Press-Release-Staff-Report-and-Statement-by-542638 (accessed 23 May 2024). For Timor-Leste: International Monetary Fund (IMF). Government Finance Statistics. https://data.imf.org/ (accessed 10 June 2025).

Table 2.8.5: Government Expenditure by Economic Activity
(% of GDP)

ADB Regional Member	Health 2010	Health 2015	Health 2020	Health 2021	Health 2022	Health 2023	Health 2024	Education 2010	Education 2015	Education 2020	Education 2021	Education 2022	Education 2023	Education 2024
Developing ADB Member Economies														
Central and West Asia														
Afghanistan[a]	0.9	1.2	1.8	...	...	...	...	3.6	3.6	2.1	...	...	...	...
Armenia	1.6	1.7	2.4	2.3	1.7*	1.5	1.5	3.2	2.9	2.8	2.7	2.4*	2.5	2.8
Azerbaijan	1.0	1.3	2.3	1.5	1.1	...	...	2.9	3.1	4.0	3.4	2.9	...	...
Georgia	2.1	2.7	3.7	4.4	2.9*	2.6	...	2.8	4.4	4.4	4.2	3.8*	5.2	...
Kazakhstan	2.5	2.1	2.8	2.9	3.1	2.7	...	3.5	3.3	4.8	5.2	5.3	4.7	...
Kyrgyz Republic	2.9	3.0	2.7	2.7	2.4*	2.2	...	5.4	5.9	6.2	5.6	6.3*	5.6	4.8
Pakistan	...	...	...	...	...	...	2.2	...	...	...	...	...	...	...
Tajikistan[b]	1.4	2.0	3.1	2.8	2.2	2.5	2.4	4.0	5.0	5.1	5.2	5.3	5.4	5.7
Türkiye	6.4	5.2	5.9	5.2	4.4	5.2	...	3.8	3.7	3.3	2.8	2.6	3.0	...
Turkmenistan	...	...	...	...	...	...	...	...	...	...	...	...	...	...
Uzbekistan	...	2.4	2.9	2.8	2.9	2.8	...	...	5.7	5.5	5.8	6.5	7.0	...
East Asia														
China, People's Republic of	1.1	1.7	1.9	1.6	1.8	1.7	1.5	3.0	3.7	3.5	3.2	3.2	3.2	3.1
Hong Kong, China[c]	2.4	3.2	3.9	4.1	5.2	...	...	3.5	3.4	4.1	3.7	3.9	...	...
Korea, Republic of	0.2	0.3	0.4	0.8	1.0	0.4	...	2.7	2.9	3.4	3.5	4.1	3.6	...
Mongolia	2.5	2.5	4.5	5.7	5.8*	1.9	...	5.1	3.0	3.4	3.3	4.4*	6.1	...
Taipei,China	0.2	0.1	0.1	0.1	0.3	1.4	...	1.7	1.4	1.5	1.3	1.5	1.4	...
South Asia														
Bangladesh[d]	0.8	0.7	0.6	0.7	...	...	...	2.0	2.0	2.3	2.3	...	...	...
Bhutan[d]	2.8	2.5	3.5	3.2	3.2	3.1	3.1	6.4	5.3	7.0	5.6	4.7	5.6	5.0
India[c,e]	1.0 (2011)	1.2	1.5	1.6	1.3	1.4		4.4 (2011)	4.4	4.7	4.3	4.3	4.3	...
Maldives[f]	3.1	5.1	7.5	5.9	6.6*	7.4	7.3	4.9	4.7	5.8	4.6	4.4*	4.8	4.3
Nepal[g]	1.5	1.2	1.0	1.2	...	...	...	3.9	3.3	1.0	0.9	...	...	...
Sri Lanka	1.1	1.5	1.5 (2019)	2.2	1.3	1.5	...	1.6	1.9	1.8 (2019)	1.8	1.5	1.6	...
Southeast Asia														
Brunei Darussalam[h]	1.8	2.3	2.3	2.1	...	...	...	3.6	4.1	4.2	3.7	...	...	...
Cambodia	...	...	1.5	3.2	0.7*	1.0	...	...	...	2.3	2.1	2.0*	2.0	...
Indonesia	0.9	1.1	1.7	2.4	1.6	1.4	1.0	3.2	3.3	3.0	2.9	2.4	2.4	1.8
Lao People's Democratic Republic	...	...	...	...	...	...	...	...	...	...	...	...	...	...
Malaysia	2.0	2.0	2.2	2.3	2.0	2.0	...	6.1	4.8	4.5	4.2	4.0	4.2	...
Myanmar[i]	0.7 (2012)	1.0|	0.8 (2019)	...	...	...	...	1.5 (2012)	2.1|	2.0 (2019)	...	...	...	...
Philippines[j]	0.3	0.8	1.4	1.6	1.3	1.4	1.2	2.4	2.8	3.7	3.9	3.4	3.4	3.5
Singapore[c]	1.2	2.1	3.3	3.1	2.5	2.5	...	3.0	2.9	3.1	2.3	2.0	2.4	...
Thailand[k]	...	1.1	1.4	1.8	1.9*	1.7	1.7	...	3.8	3.1	3.1	2.7*	2.6	2.6
Timor-Leste	4.0	3.7	3.4 (2018)	...	...	...	...	7.8	6.5	4.8 (2018)	...	...	...	...
Viet Nam	...	...	...	...	...	...	...	...	...	...	...	...	...	...
The Pacific														
Cook Islands[d]	3.9	3.0	5.6	5.6	5.8	...	...	4.0	3.5	4.5	4.3	4.3	...	...
Fiji	...	...	...	...	...	...	...	...	...	...	...	...	...	...
Kiribati[d]	...	9.9	11.0*	11.3*	8.9*	...	...	...	9.9	12.2*	14.2*	12.5*	...	...
Marshall Islands[k]	8.2	7.6	9.1	...	...	...	...	20.6	16.6	12.9	...	...	...	...
Micronesia, Federated States of	...	...	...	...	...	...	...	...	...	...	...	...	...	...
Nauru	...	...	...	...	...	...	...	...	...	...	...	...	...	...
Niue	...	...	...	...	...	...	...	...	...	...	...	...	...	...
Palau	...	...	...	...	...	...	...	...	...	...	...	...	...	...
Papua New Guinea	...	...	...	...	...	...	...	...	...	...	...	...	...	...
Samoa[d]	3.6	5.2	3.7	5.6	5.6	5.1	4.9	4.2	4.3	3.5	5.6	5.7	4.6	4.5
Solomon Islands	...	...	...	...	...	...	...	...	...	...	...	...	...	...
Tonga	...	...	...	...	...	...	...	...	...	...	...	...	...	...
Tuvalu	8.5 (2012)	9.4	...	...	...	...	...	16.0 (2012)	23.2	...	...	...	...	...
Vanuatu	3.0 (2011)	2.5	2.7 (2018)	...	...	...	...	6.4 (2011)	5.6	6.7 (2018)	...	...	...	...
Developed ADB Member Economies														
Australia[d]	6.6	6.8	7.5	7.8	7.8	7.1	7.2	5.9	5.4	5.8	5.6	5.3	5.1	5.2
Japan[c]	6.8	7.3	7.7	8.2	8.5	7.7	...	2.8	2.6	2.7	2.6	2.6	2.4	...
New Zealand[d]	7.0	6.8	7.1	7.5	8.5	7.7	7.7	6.7	6.2	6.3	5.7	5.8	5.5	5.5

Governance

Table 2.8.5: Government Expenditure by Economic Activity *(continued)*
(% of GDP)

ADB Regional Member	Social Protection						
	2010	2015	2020	2021	2022	2023	2024
Developing ADB Member Economies							
Central and West Asia							
Afghanistan[a]	0.5	1.4	1.1	...	...	...	...
Armenia	7.1	7.7	8.9	8.9	7.2*	7.5	8.4
Azerbaijan	6.8	6.8	9.6	8.6	5.4	...	...
Georgia	6.5	7.3	9.6	7.8	6.7*	8.7	...
Kazakhstan	4.5	4.5	6.5	3.5	5.2	5.3	...
Kyrgyz Republic	5.0	5.8	5.4	4.7	4.7*	4.4	4.1
Pakistan	...	...	...	...	...	...	...
Tajikistan[b]	3.5	5.2	4.6	4.1	3.9	3.5	3.9
Türkiye	9.6	9.1	10.6	8.8	6.9	11.3	...
Turkmenistan	...	...	...	...	...	...	...
Uzbekistan	...	7.0	8.1	6.2	7.0	6.5	...
East Asia							
China, People's Republic of	2.2	2.7	3.1	2.9	3.0	3.1	3.1
Hong Kong, China[c]	2.4	2.9	4.2	3.9	4.2	...	...
Korea, Republic of	4.1	5.0	7.7	7.3	7.3	7.6	...
Mongolia	11.1	7.6	10.7	12.6	11.8*	4.3	...
Taipei,China	3.1	3.3	3.3	3.1	3.1	3.6	...
South Asia							
Bangladesh[d]	0.9	0.7	1.2	1.2	...	...	...
Bhutan[d]	3.0	2.8	3.2	2.8	2.7	2.4	2.3
India[c,e]	1.4 (2011)	1.8	2.1	1.8	1.7	1.9	...
Maldives[f]	2.8	2.7	6.2	5.0	2.4*	2.5	2.6
Nepal[g]	0.8	0.6	1.7	1.7	...	...	...
Sri Lanka	1.6	4.8	...	...	...	...	...
Southeast Asia							
Brunei Darussalam[h]	0.8	0.8	0.7	0.6	...	...	...
Cambodia	...	...	1.7	1.9	2.1*	2.3	
Indonesia	0.1	0.3	2.0	1.7	1.5	1.3	1.2
Lao People's Democratic Republic	...	...	...	...	...	...	...
Malaysia	...	...	...	...	...	...	...
Myanmar[i]	0.4 (2012)	0.8	0.9 (2019)	...	...	...	...
Philippines[j]	1.6	1.3	3.6	2.4	2.7	2.7	2.8
Singapore[c]	1.1	1.8	7.8	1.8	0.9	2.0	...
Thailand[k]	...	2.5	5.6	5.2	4.9*	4.1	4.3
Timor-Leste	16.3	11.8	8.7 (2018)	...	...	...	...
Viet Nam	...	...	...	...	...	...	...
The Pacific							
Cook Islands[d]	3.9	4.2	6.9	12.6	4.9	...	...
Fiji	...	...	...	...	...	...	...
Kiribati[d]	...	1.4	1.1*	3.8*	8.8*	...	...
Marshall Islands[k]	...	0.6 (2016)	2.4	...	...	...	...
Micronesia, Federated States of	...	...	...	...	...	...	...
Nauru	...	...	...	...	...	...	...
Niue	...	...	...	...	...	...	...
Palau	...	...	...	...	...	...	...
Papua New Guinea	...	...	...	...	...	...	...
Samoa[d]	0.3	1.8	0.8	1.6	2.3	2.6	3.3
Solomon Islands	...	...	...	...	...	...	...
Tonga	...	...	...	...	...	...	...
Tuvalu	6.1 (2012)	18.3	...	...	...	...	...
Vanuatu	0.0 (2011)	0.1	0.0 (2018)	...	...	...	...
Developed ADB Member Economies							
Australia[d]	9.8	10.4	11.0	11.7	10.6	9.7	10.6
Japan[c]	2.1	2.5	2.8	2.8	2.8	2.7	...
New Zealand[d]	12.4	11.5	11.1	11.8	12.6	12.3	12.5

... = data not available; | = marks break in series; * = provisional, preliminary, estimate; 0.0 = magnitude is less than half of unit employed; ADB = Asian Development Bank; GDP = gross domestic product.

Note: In general, economies follow the guidelines of the International Monetary Fund on Government Finance Statistics (GFS). Some economies still use the 1986 version of the GFS guidelines, while others have switched to the 2001 or 2014 guidelines. The comparability of the data in this table is limited by variations in the concepts and definitions used in different versions of the GFS framework. The table refers to government expenditure by economic activity as classified in the GFS 2001 or GFS 2014 framework, except for Bhutan; Brunei Darussalam; the People's Republic of China; India; the Kyrgyz Republic; and Taipei,China, where data refer to health, education, and social security and welfare, as classified in the GFS 1986 framework. For Maldives, data prior to 2017 are classified in the GFS 1986 framework, while data for 2017 onward follow the GFS 2014 framework. Data refer to general government, except for Bangladesh; Bhutan; Brunei Darussalam; Cambodia; India; Malaysia; Maldives; the Marshall Islands; Nepal; the Philippines; Samoa; Sri Lanka; Taipei,China; Timor-Leste; Tuvalu; and Vanuatu, where data refer to central government. For Cambodia: Data refer to central government excluding extra budgetary central government. For the People's Republic of China: Data refer to consolidated central and local governments.

a For 2010, data based on fiscal year beginning 21 March. For 2015 onward, GFS data are based on fiscal year ending 20 December. For 2010 and 2015, national accounts data are based on fiscal year beginning 21 March. For 2016 onward, national accounts data are based on fiscal year ending 20 December.
b National accounts data prior to 2015 are based on the 1993 System of National Accounts while data for 2015 onward are based on the 2008 System of National Accounts.
c Data are based on fiscal year beginning 1 April.
d Data are based on fiscal year ending 30 June.
e Data exclude local bodies.
f Prior to 2012, refers to total expenditure. For 2012 onward, refers to total budget. For 2020, GDP estimates used are projections available as of 15 March 2021, forecasted by the Government of Maldives' Ministry of Finance.
g Data are based on fiscal year ending 15 July.
h For 2003 onward, data are based on fiscal year beginning 1 April.
i For 2012–2018, GFS data are based on fiscal year beginning 1 April. For 2019, data are based on fiscal year beginning 1 October. National accounts data for 2012–2015 are based on fiscal year beginning 1 April, and for 2016 onward on fiscal year beginning 1 October.
j For 2010–2018, data refer to obligation basis. For 2019 onward, data refer to cash basis. For 2010, data on education include expenditure on recreation, culture, and religion.
k Data are based on fiscal year ending 30 September.

Sources: Economies' official sources. For Nepal and Hong Kong, China: Asian Development Bank estimates using data from the International Monetary Fund's Government Finance Statistics. https://data.imf.org/ (accessed April–June 2023).

Table 2.8.6: Corruption Perceptions Index

ADB Regional Member	Corruption Perceptions Index Scores							Corruption Perceptions Index Rank	
	2012	2015	2020	2021	2022	2023	2024	2023[a]	2024[a]
Developing ADB Member Economies									
Central and West Asia									
Afghanistan	8.0	11.0	19.0	16.0	24.0	20.0	17.0	162	165
Armenia	34.0	35.0	49.0	49.0	46.0	47.0	47.0	62	63
Azerbaijan	27.0	29.0	30.0	30.0	23.0	23.0	22.0	154	154
Georgia	52.0	52.0	56.0	55.0	56.0	53.0	53.0	49	53
Kazakhstan	28.0	28.0	38.0	37.0	36.0	39.0	40.0	93	88
Kyrgyz Republic	24.0	28.0	31.0	27.0	27.0	26.0	25.0	141	146
Pakistan	27.0	30.0	31.0	28.0	27.0	29.0	27.0	133	135
Tajikistan	22.0	26.0	25.0	25.0	24.0	20.0	19.0	162	164
Türkiye	49.0	42.0	40.0	38.0	36.0	34.0	34.0	115	107
Turkmenistan	17.0	18.0	19.0	19.0	19.0	18.0	17.0	170	165
Uzbekistan	17.0	19.0	26.0	28.0	31.0	33.0	32.0	121	121
East Asia									
China, People's Republic of	39.0	37.0	42.0	45.0	45.0	42.0	43.0	76	76
Hong Kong, China	77.0	75.0	77.0	76.0	76.0	75.0	74.0	14	17
Korea, Republic of	56.0	54.0	61.0	62.0	63.0	63.0	64.0	32	30
Mongolia	36.0	39.0	35.0	35.0	33.0	33.0	33.0	121	114
Taipei,China	61.0	62.0	65.0	68.0	68.0	67.0	67.0	28	25
South Asia									
Bangladesh	26.0	25.0	26.0	26.0	25.0	24.0	23.0	149	151
Bhutan	63.0	65.0	68.0	68.0	68.0	68.0	72.0	26	18
India	36.0	38.0	40.0	40.0	40.0	39.0	38.0	93	96
Maldives	...	...	43.0	40.0	40.0	39.0	38.0	93	96
Nepal	27.0	27.0	33.0	33.0	34.0	35.0	34.0	108	107
Sri Lanka	40.0	37.0	38.0	37.0	36.0	34.0	32.0	115	121
Southeast Asia									
Brunei Darussalam	55.0	...	60.0	...	...	...	...	...	...
Cambodia	22.0	21.0	21.0	23.0	24.0	22.0	21.0	158	158
Indonesia	32.0	36.0	37.0	38.0	34.0	34.0	37.0	115	99
Lao People's Democratic Republic	21.0	25.0	29.0	30.0	31.0	28.0	33.0	136	114
Malaysia	49.0	50.0	51.0	48.0	47.0	50.0	50.0	57	57
Myanmar	15.0	22.0	28.0	28.0	23.0	20.0	16.0	162	168
Philippines	34.0	35.0	34.0	33.0	33.0	34.0	33.0	115	114
Singapore	87.0	85.0	85.0	85.0	83.0	83.0	84.0	5	3
Thailand	37.0	38.0	36.0	35.0	36.0	35.0	34.0	108	107
Timor-Leste	33.0	28.0	40.0	41.0	42.0	43.0	44.0	70	73
Viet Nam	31.0	31.0	36.0	39.0	42.0	41.0	40.0	83	88
The Pacific									
Cook Islands	...	...	...	...	...	...	...	...	...
Fiji	...	...	...	55.0	53.0	52.0	55.0	53	50
Kiribati	...	...	...	...	...	...	...	...	...
Marshall Islands	...	...	...	...	...	...	...	...	...
Micronesia, Federated States of	...	...	...	...	...	...	...	...	...
Nauru	...	...	...	...	...	...	...	...	...
Niue	...	...	...	...	...	...	...	...	...
Palau	...	...	...	...	...	...	...	...	...
Papua New Guinea	25.0	25.0	27.0	31.0	30.0	29.0	31.0	133	127
Samoa	...	...	...	...	...	...	...	...	...
Solomon Islands	...	...	42.0	43.0	42.0	43.0	43.0	70	76
Tonga	...	...	...	...	...	...	...	...	...
Tuvalu	...	...	...	...	...	...	...	...	...
Vanuatu	...	...	43.0	45.0	48.0	48.0	50.0	61	57
Developed ADB Member Economies									
Australia	85.0	79.0	77.0	73.0	75.0	75.0	77.0	14	10
Japan	74.0	75.0	74.0	73.0	73.0	73.0	71.0	16	20
New Zealand	90.0	91.0	88.0	88.0	87.0	85.0	83.0	3	4

... = data not available, ADB = Asian Development Bank.

Note: The Key Indicators Database features a longer time series of scores on the Corruption Perceptions Index. This includes scores for 2000–2011, which refer to perceptions of the degree of corruption as seen by business people and analysts. Those scores range from 0 (highly corrupt) to 10 (very clean) and are not comparable over time. From 2012 onward, an updated methodology was used to calculate scores, and these are presented on a scale from 0 (highly corrupt) to 100 (very clean). Due to the differences in methodology, scores prior to 2012 should not be compared with scores for 2012 onward.

a Based on Transparency International's methodology, an economy's rank indicates its position relative to the Corruption Perceptions Index of other economies of the world; 2023 and 2024 rankings compare 180 economies.

Source: Transparency International. Corruption Perceptions Index. https://www.transparency.org/en/cpi/2024 (accessed 1 April 2025).

Table 2.8.7: Pillar III - Operational Efficiency of Business Entry

ADB Regional Member	3.1 Domestic Firms				3.2 Foreign Firms		
	Pillar III Overall[a]	Category 3.1 Overall[b]	Total Time to Register a New Domestic Firm[c]	Total Cost to Register a New Domestic Firm[d]	Category 3.2 Overall[b]	Total Time to Register a New Foreign Firm[c]	Total Cost to Register a New Foreign Firm[d]
	2024	2024	2024	2024	2024	2024	2024
Developing ADB Member Economies							
Central and West Asia							
Afghanistan	...	...	...	...	...	...	...
Armenia	...	...	...	...	...	...	...
Azerbaijan	...	...	...	...	...	...	...
Georgia	91.00	49.00	24.25	24.75	42.00	17.25	24.75
Kazakhstan	...	...	...	...	...	...	...
Kyrgyz Republic	63.00	28.25	22.25	6.00	34.75	22.75	12.00
Pakistan	97.50	49.75	25.00	24.75	47.75	23.00	24.75
Tajikistan	...	...	...	...	...	...	...
Türkiye	...	...	...	...	...	...	...
Turkmenistan	...	...	...	...	...	...	...
Uzbekistan	...	...	...	...	...	...	...
East Asia							
China, People's Republic of	...	...	...	...	...	...	...
Hong Kong, China	99.25	49.50	24.75	24.75	49.75	25.00	24.75
Korea, Republic of	...	...	...	...	...	...	...
Mongolia	...	...	...	...	...	...	...
Taipei,China	...	...	...	...	...	...	...
South Asia							
Bangladesh	85.75	43.25	20.00	23.25	42.50	18.50	24.00
Bhutan	...	...	...	...	...	...	...
India	...	...	...	...	...	...	...
Maldives	...	...	...	...	...	...	...
Nepal	70.75	47.25	24.50	22.75	23.50	23.25	0.25
Sri Lanka	...	...	...	...	...	...	...
Southeast Asia							
Brunei Darussalam	...	...	...	...	...	...	...
Cambodia	9.00	7.75	7.75	–	1.25	1.25	–
Indonesia	26.50	24.75	11.25	13.50	1.75	1.75	–
Lao People's Democratic Republic	...	...	...	...	...	...	...
Malaysia	...	...	...	...	...	...	...
Myanmar	...	...	...	...	...	...	...
Philippines	14.25	1.25	–	1.25	13.00	–	13.00
Singapore	99.00	49.50	24.50	25.00	49.50	24.50	25.00
Thailand	...	...	...	...	...	...	...
Timor-Leste	40.50	21.00	17.50	3.50	19.50	18.50	1.00
Viet Nam	66.00	45.75	21.00	24.75	20.25	1.50	18.75
The Pacific							
Cook Islands	...	...	...	...	...	...	...
Fiji	...	...	...	...	...	...	...
Kiribati	...	...	...	...	...	...	...
Marshall Islands	...	...	...	...	...	...	...
Micronesia, Federated States of	...	...	...	...	...	...	...
Nauru	...	...	...	...	...	...	...
Niue	...	...	...	...	...	...	...
Palau	...	...	...	...	...	...	...
Papua New Guinea	...	...	...	...	...	...	...
Samoa	97.25	48.50	24.25	24.25	48.75	24.25	24.50
Solomon Islands	...	...	...	...	...	...	...
Tonga	...	...	...	...	...	...	...
Tuvalu	...	...	...	...	...	...	...
Vanuatu	14.00	8.00	0.25	7.75	6.00	0.50	5.50
Developed ADB Member Economies							
Australia	...	...	...	...	...	...	...
Japan	...	...	...	...	...	...	...
New Zealand	99.00	49.50	24.75	24.75	49.50	24.75	24.75

... = data not available, – = magnitude equals zero, ADB = Asian Development Bank.

a Pillar III, Operational Efficiency of Business Entry analyzes the time and cost it takes in practice to incorporate a domestic firm and a foreign firm (operational efficiency). The scores are calculated using the Normal Cumulative Density Function (CDF) transformation method on a scale of 0 to 100, where 0 and 100 represent the lowest and highest possible scores.

b Data refer to the combined score for the time and cost to incorporate a domestic or foreign firm, with a maximum of 50 points.

c Refers to the total time required to register a new domestic or foreign firm—including pre-registration, registration, and post-registration processes—with a maximum score of 25 points.

d Refers to the total cost required to register a new domestic or foreign firm—including pre-registration, registration, and post-registration processes—with a maximum score of 25 points.

Source: World Bank. 2024. Business Ready 2024. Washington, DC: World Bank. doi:10.1596/978-1-4648-2021-2. License: Creative Commons Attribution CC BY 3.0 IGO (accessed 17 June 2025).

Data Issues and Comparability

Most economies generally follow the International Monetary Fund's Government Finance Statistics (GFS) guidelines: some still use the 1986 version, while others have switched to the 2001 or 2014 GFS releases. The comparability of the data is limited by variations in the concepts and definitions used in different versions of the GFS framework. Furthermore, there is no single framework for an extended time series available in most economies that are using the 2014 guidelines, with most economies recording their transactions on a cash basis (and a few on an accrual basis).

Data on government expenditures and revenue are derived from economy sources and are therefore not standard throughout Asia and the Pacific. Data refer to general government for some economies, and central government for other economies.

Statistics on perceived corruption are taken from nonofficial sources. Common procedures are used in all economies and the researchers producing these data have refined their procedures over several surveys. However, because of the subjective nature of many of the data, they can only be used to give a broad idea of trends, levels, and rankings, so small changes from one year to the next should be interpreted with caution.

Data on the operational efficiency of business entry are sourced from consultations with experts and firm-level surveys. When using these data for economic analysis, interpretation should be appropriately contextualized.

APPENDIX 1

Compiling the ADB Environmentally Extended Multiregional Input-Output Tables

Introduction

The environmentally extended multiregional input-output tables (EE-MRIOTs) are compiled by the Asian Development Bank (ADB), closely following the methodology of Genty et al. (2012). The EE-MRIOTs include adjustments based on alternative datasets and standard practices in other environmentally extended multiregional databases, primarily differing in data sources and allocation approaches. Guided by the System of Environmental Economic Accounting (SEEA) framework for compiling Air Emissions Accounts, the process adheres to the conceptual foundations and accounting principles of such accounts, which are harmonized with the System of National Accounts (SNA). The compilation integrates both inventory-first and energy-first approaches, and applies the general emissions model, to ensure a systematic and robust representation of emissions linked to economic activities.

The inventory-first approach, which starts from existing emissions inventories, leverages the detailed greenhouse gas (GHG) inventories from Crippa et al. (2024). Meanwhile, the energy-first approach, which uses energy statistics and/or balances as a starting point, utilizes energy balance data from the International Energy Agency (IEA) to identify the flow of energy products across various industries, serving as the basis for an allocation key using Tier 1[1] air emissions methodology. Emissions estimated by the Emissions Database for Global Atmospheric Research (EDGAR) are allocated to corresponding industries and economies adjusted to the MRIOT format.

These core datasets and approaches, supported by segment-specific data, ensure comprehensive allocation of emissions throughout the production processes and consistency with SNA and input-output principles, accounting for residence corrections, and industry classification across datasets.

---

1 Emissions can be estimated at varying levels of complexity. Following the Intergovernmental Panel on Climate Change Guidelines, these levels are categorized into three tiers, each representing increasing methodological sophistication. Tier 1 is the simplest method that relies on readily available statistical data (activity rates) and default emission factors. These factors assume a linear relationship between process intensity and emissions, based on average or typical conditions. Tier 2 is a more detailed method that builds on Tier 1 but uses economy-specific emission factors, accounting for local process conditions. Tier 3 is an advanced approach that includes a broad range of methodologies beyond Tier 2.

Accounting Principles Applied

One of the key challenges the EE-MRIOTs address is the incompatibility between the territorial and process-based nature of emissions reported in environmental inventories and the structure of economic accounts. To bridge this gap, data transformations were implemented to align emissions data with the SNA and the principles of the input-output framework. This process ensures the creation of an integrated emissions database that is coherently linked with economic accounts.

The accounting principles applied in the EE-MRIOT compilation methodology are outlined below.

Production-Based and Consumption-Based Recording

Production-based recording accounts for GHGs emitted during an economy's production activities, regardless of consumption location. These emissions are measured using either the "territory principle" (emissions within geographic boundaries, as in GHG inventories) or the "residence principle" (emissions from residents' activities, even abroad, as in Air Emissions Accounts), which is applied in the EE-MRIOTs. For instance, to produce a car, Economy A is responsible for the emissions generated during the manufacturing and assembly stages, as shown in Figure A1.1.

Figure A1.1: Accounting Principles Applied in the Environmentally Extended Multi-regional Input-Output Table Compilation

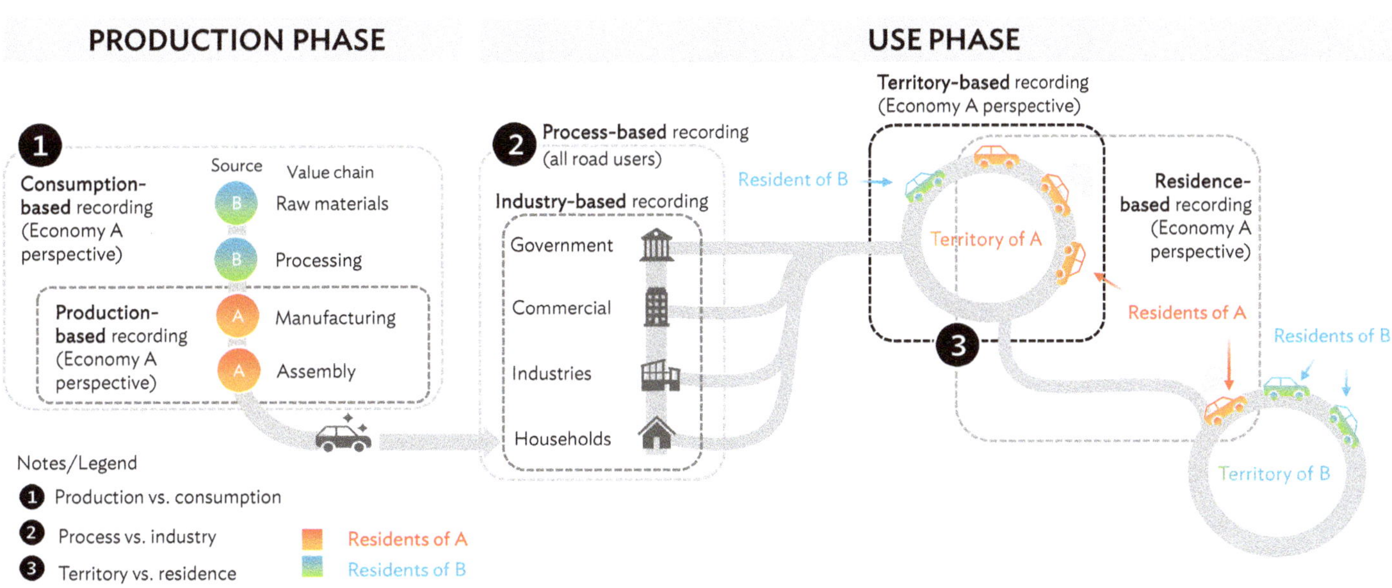

Source: Asian Development Bank compilation and visualization.

The EE-MRIOT framework also enables consumption-based recording, which captures GHGs along global production chains, measuring emissions linked to goods and services consumed by residents, including imports. Using the example in Figure A1.1, if the vehicle uses raw materials and processing from Economy B, those emissions are attributed to the purchase of car by Economy A. This gives a full picture of the emissions tied to the entire production chain of the vehicle. Both methods include direct household emissions, such as vehicle use.

Industry-Based Versus Process-Based Recording

The EE-MRIOT framework addresses the process-based nature of emissions in emissions inventories and assigns emissions to industries. It does so by mapping the concordance between the energy balance and emissions inventory items and the multiregional input-output industries/sectors, including households. In the EE-MRIOTs, industry-based recording is utilized, which attributes emissions to the economic unit causing the emissions, such as a business or household. For instance, emissions from road transport reported in inventory databases are aggregated emissions from on-road activities as seen in Figure A1.1. However, road vehicles are utilized by all economic industries, from agriculture to services and households. The EE-MRIOT breaks down the aggregated inventory data and allocates the emissions to all these units based on the level of their road fuel combustion.

Residence-Based Versus Territory-Based Recording

The EE-MRIOTs apply residence-based recording, such that emissions reported within national territories include emissions by residents in the rest of the world and exclude emissions by nonresidents in domestic territories. In this manner, emissions are directly comparable to a given economy's gross domestic product. Residence adjustment is mostly applied to transport industries such as road transportation, water-borne navigation, and aviation. This includes international maritime and aviation transport with fuel bunkering abroad (or fuel purchases not included in national statistics for resident ships and aircraft), fishing vessels operating abroad, and foreign vessels in national waters. In these cases, activities of residents operating abroad (e.g., international transport services provided by domestic residents) were added and activities of foreign residents operating within the national territory (e.g., tourists driving a car) were deducted.

Data Sources and Uses

The EDGAR emissions database serves as one of the core datasets in compiling the EE-MRIOTs. It offers an independent estimate of GHGs for each economy and utilizes a robust and consistent methodology derived from the latest Intergovernmental Panel on Climate Change (IPCC) guidelines and the most current activity data. The database covers anthropogenic emissions across five broad sectors and 37 major activities, capturing emissions from both market and nonmarket sources. These include emissions from agricultural activities (e.g., methane from enteric fermentation and manure management), biomass burning, waste disposal, and fugitive emissions (e.g., unintended leaks). Coverage spans carbon dioxide (CO_2), methane, nitrous oxide, and fluorinated gases, including their CO_2-equivalent values, as detailed in Table A1.1.

Table A1.1: Activities Covered by the Emissions Database for Global Atmospheric Research

Standard Report Name	IPCC Code	Broad Activity
Main Activity Electricity and Heat Production	1.A.1.a	Energy
Petroleum Refining - Manufacture of Solid Fuels and Other Energy Industries	1.A.1.bc	Energy
Manufacturing Industries and Construction	1.A.2	Energy
Civil Aviation	1.A.3.a	Energy
Road Transportation (no resuspension)	1.A.3.b_noRES	Energy
Railways	1.A.3.c	Energy
Water-Borne Navigation	1.A.3.d	Energy
Other Transportation	1.A.3.e	Energy
Residential and Other Sectors	1.A.4	Energy
Non-Specified	1.A.5	Energy
Solid Fuels	1.B.1	Energy
Oil and Natural Gas	1.B.2	Energy
Cement Production	2.A.1	IPPU
Lime Production	2.A.2	IPPU
Glass Production	2.A.3	IPPU
Other Process Uses of Carbonates	2.A.4	IPPU
Chemical Industry	2.B	IPPU
Metal Industry	2.C	IPPU
Non-Energy Products from Fuels and Solvent Use	2.D	IPPU
Electronics Industry	2.E	IPPU
Product Uses as Substitutes for Ozone Depleting Substances	2.F	IPPU
Other Product Manufacture and Use	2.G	IPPU
Enteric Fermentation	3.A.1	AFOLU
Manure Management	3.A.2	AFOLU
Emissions from Biomass Burning	3.C.1	AFOLU
Liming	3.C.2	AFOLU
Urea Application	3.C.3	AFOLU
Direct N_2O Emissions from Managed Soils	3.C.4	AFOLU
Indirect N_2O Emissions from Managed Soils	3.C.5	AFOLU
Indirect N_2O Emissions from manure management	3.C.6	AFOLU
Rice Cultivation	3.C.7	AFOLU
Solid Waste Disposal	4.A	Waste
Biological Treatment of Solid Waste	4.B	Waste

continued on next page

Standard Report Name	IPCC Code	Broad Activity
Incineration and Open Burning of Waste	4.C	Waste
Wastewater Treatment and Discharge	4.D	Waste
Indirect N_2O emissions from the atmospheric deposition of nitrogen in NOx and NH_3	5.A	Other
Fossil Fuel Fires	5.B	Other

IPCC = Intergovernmental Panel on Climate Change, N_2O = nitrous oxide, NH_3 = ammonia, NOx = nitric oxide and nitrogen dioxide.

Source: Emissions Database for Global Atmospheric Research. https://edgar.jrc.ec.europa.eu/ (accessed October 2024). Based on Intergovernmental Panel on Climate Change classification of activities.

The EDGAR database is chosen as the core source for GHG emissions data due to its independent estimates, strong focus on comparability and consistency, and extensive historical coverage with frequent updates. Recognized as the most comprehensive dataset, it is the choice of the IPCC's AR6 Working Group III for emissions analysis. Additionally, EDGAR offers relatively low uncertainty for CO_2 emissions, reinforcing its reliability in climate assessments. While it has some limitations—such as reliance on the simpler Tier 1 methodology and gaps in coverage for local pollutants and land-use change emissions—its broad coverage, regular updates, and standardized approach make it an essential source of GHG emissions data.

Table A1.2 provides a comparative overview of nine emissions datasets, highlighting key characteristics such as the use of IPCC emissions factors, inclusion of cement and other carbonates, treatment of nonfuel sources, and industrial and fuel-type reporting. This comparison illustrates EDGAR's strengths and weaknesses relative to other datasets, showing that it is the best alternative to Common Reporting Format submissions under the United Nations Framework Convention on Climate Change. Its key advantage lies in its broader coverage, as not all economies submit data to the framework, making EDGAR a crucial resource for comprehensive global emissions monitoring.

Meanwhile, the IEA energy balances provide detailed data on the flow of energy and energy products from their sources to their end uses for different economies. In total, there are 68 fuel products and 108 flows[2] for all the stages captured by the energy balances from production to final consumption, which are used to further disaggregate the inventory data.

Given the aggregated, territory-based, and non-standardized nature of EDGAR and IEA data, additional datasets are used to disaggregate, adjust for residence, and standardize the emissions. ADB's MRIOTs (at current prices) and detailed supply and use tables from reference economies are used for the industry and economy disaggregation.

2 A full breakdown of flows may be found in Appendix 3.

Table A1.2: Key Features and Comparisons of Global Emissions Datasets

Dataset	Primary Source	Uses IPCC Emissions Factors	Includes Venting and Flaring	Includes Cement	Includes Other Carbonates	Nonfuel Use Based On	Reports Bunkers Separately	By Fuel Type	By Sector	Includes Official Estimates
CDIAC	Yes	No	Yes	Yes	No	National data	Yes	Yes	No	No
BP	Yes	Yes	No	No	No	National data	No	No	No	No
IEA	Yes	Yes	No	No	No	National data	Yes	Yes	Yes	No
EDGAR	Yes	Yes	Yes	Yes	Yes	National data	Yes	No	Yes	No
EIA	Yes	No	Yes	No	No	US Data	No	Yes	No	No
GCP	Partial	No	Yes	Yes	Partial	National data	Yes	Yes	No	Yes
CEDS	Mostly	No	Yes	Yes	Yes	National data	Yes	Yes	Yes	Yes
PRIMAP-hist	No	No	Yes	Yes	Yes	National data	Yes	No	Yes	Yes
UNFCCC CRFs	Yes	Partial	Yes	Yes	Yes	National data	Yes	Yes	Yes	Yes

BP = BP Statistical Review of World Energy; CDIAC = Global, Regional, and National Fossil-Fuel CO_2 Emissions; CEDS = Community Emissions Data System; EDGAR = Emissions Database for Global Atmospheric Research; EIA = Energy Information Administration International Energy Statistics; GCP = Global Carbon Budget; IPCC = Intergovernmental Panel on Climate Change; PRIMAP-hist = Potsdam Real-time Integrated Model for probabilistic Assessment of emissions Paths; UNFCCC CRFs = United Nations Framework Convention on Climate Change Common Reporting Formats: Annex I Party Greenhouse Gas Inventory Submissions.

Source: Adopted from Dhakal, S., J.C.Minx, F.L.Toth, Reisinger, W.F. Lamb, N. Döbbeling, T. Wiedmann, K. Hubacek, R. M. Andrew, M. Crippa, P. M. Forster, J. Olivier, G. P. Peters, J. Pongratz, M. Rigby, M. Saunois, S. J. Smith, E. Solazzo, H. Tian, K. Blok, H. Clark, A. Cowie, J. S. Fuglestvedt, O. Geden, V. Ginzburg, C. Guivarch, J. I. House, R. Mrabet, G. J. Nabuurs, K. Riahi, A. H. Strømman, R. Schaeffer, D. P. van Vuuren, A. Al Khourdajie, and R. Slade, 2022: Emissions Trends and Drivers Supplementary Material. In P.R. Shukla, J. Skea, R. Slade, A. Al Khourdajie, R. van Diemen, D. McCollum, M. Pathak, S. Some, P. Vyas, R. Fradera, M. Belkacemi, A. Hasija, G. Lisboa, S. Luz, J. Malley, eds. *Climate Change 2022: Mitigation of Climate Change. Contribution of Working Group III to the Sixth Assessment Report of the Intergovernmental Panel on Climate Change.* https://www.ipcc.ch/report/ar6/wg3/; R. M. Andrew. 2020. A comparison of estimates of global carbon dioxide emissions from fossil carbon sources. *Earth Systems Science Data.* 12 (2). pp. 1437–1465. doi:10.5194/essd-12-1437-2020; Minx, J.C., W.F. Lamb, R.M. Andrew, J.G. Canadell, M. Crippa, N. Döbbeling, P.M. Forster, D. Guizzardi, J. Olivier, G.P. Peters, J. Pongratz, A. Reisinger, M. Rigby, M. Saunois, S.J. Smith, E. Solazzo, and H. Tian. 2021. *A comprehensive and synthetic dataset for global, regional, and national greenhouse gas emissions by sector 1970–2018 with an extension to 2019. Earth System Science Data* 13: 5213–5252. https://doi.org/10.5194/essd-13-5213-2021.

ADB's MRIOTs capture the interindustry flows of 72 economies plus "the rest of the world" and uses a 35-industry aggregation of International Standard Industrial Classification Rev. 4 categories. The MRIOTs draw from the supply and use tables and input-output tables of individual economies, which typically include both formal and informal activities in line with the 2008 SNA. As such, the MRIOTs implicitly capture a range of market and nonmarket transactions, to the extent they are reflected in national statistics.

Meanwhile, industry-specific datasets are employed to accurately allocate emissions to the emitter's economy of residence, particularly in the transportation sector. Reference datasets are also used to standardize energy and emissions units. The summary of the data sources utilized is presented in Figure A1.2.

Figure A1.2: Data Sources Used in the Environmentally Extended Compilation

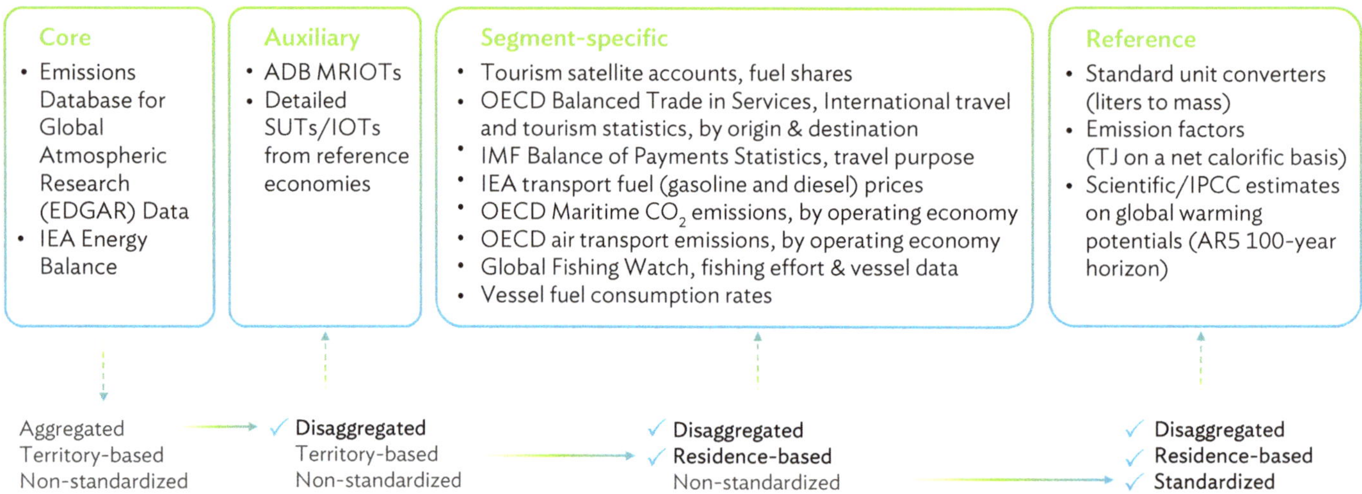

ADB = Asian Development Bank, AR5 = IPCC fifth assessment report; CO_2 = carbon dioxide, IEA = International Energy Agency, IMF = International Monetary Fund, IPCC = Intergovernmental Panel on Climate Change, IOT = input-output table, OECD = Organisation for Economic Co-operation and Development, SUT = supply and use table, TJ = terajoule.

Source: Asian Development Bank compilation and visualization.

Estimation Methodology

The EE-MRIOT compilation methodology follows a structured framework that integrates energy-first and inventory-first approaches, as seen in Figure A1.3. The energy-first approach, as seen on the left of Figure A1.3, begins with the IEA energy balance, which records energy production and consumption broken down by fuel type. The energy data include fuel products such as natural gas and diesel as well as specialized fuels that are unique to certain industries, such as blast furnace gas used in steelmaking. The energy-first approach is used to break down energy-related emissions in the inventory (EDGAR) such as emissions from electricity and heat generation, solid fuel production, manufacturing and construction, transportation, and others shown in Table A1.1.

Meanwhile, the inventory-first approach, as seen on the right of Figure A1.3, starts with the EDGAR inventory, which already details emissions from non-energy sources such as fugitive emissions from fuels, emissions from industrial processes and product use, emissions from agricultural activities, waste, and other human-related sources.

The integrated framework is organized around four key processes to allocate the emissions to the corresponding economy and industry:

(i) mapping and allocation key derivation,
(ii) residence adjustment,
(iii) emissions model, and
(iv) allocation key confrontation and final allocation.

Figure A1.3: Estimation Methodology of the Environmentally Extended Compilation

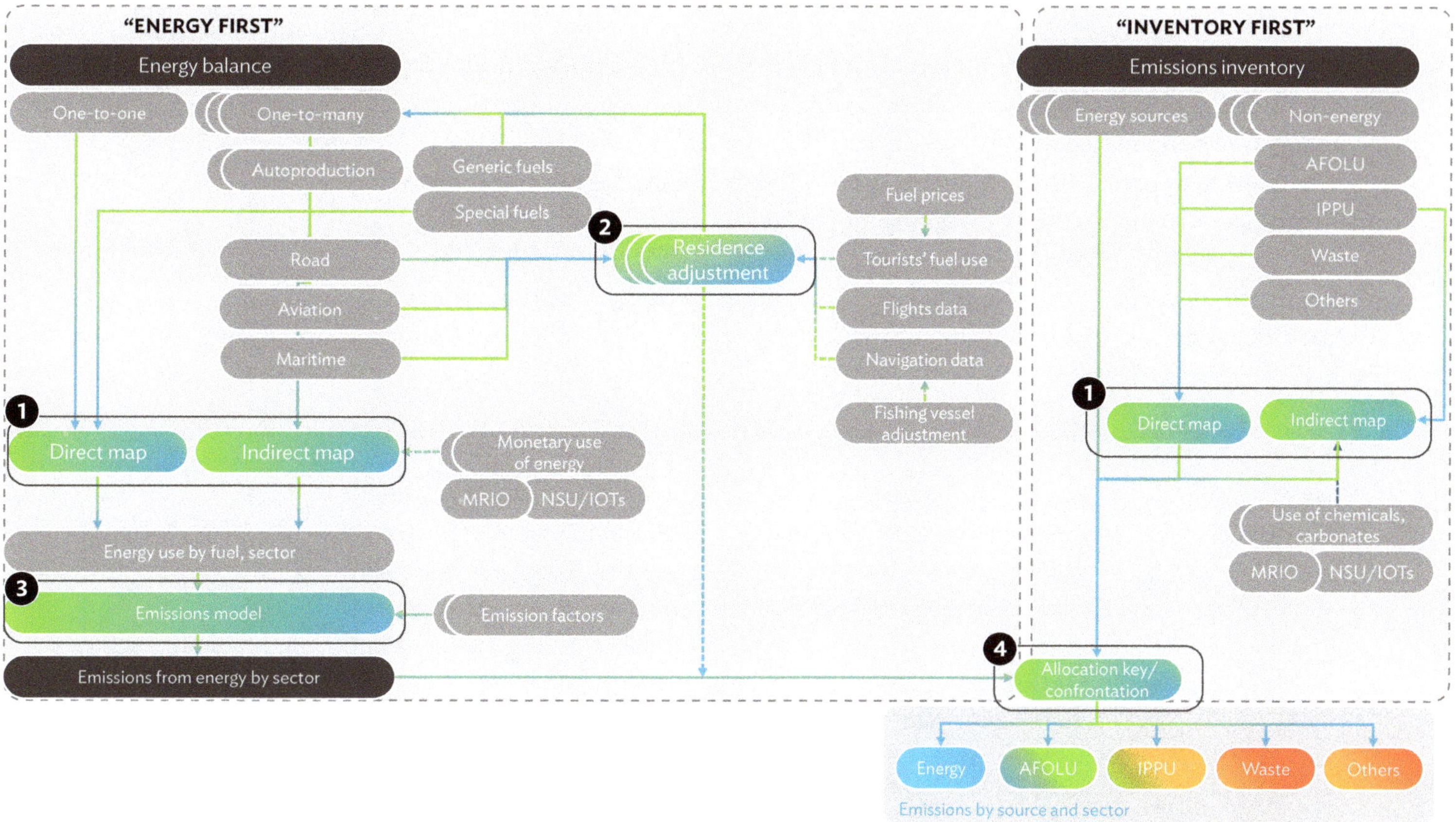

AFOLU = agriculture, forestry, and other land use; IOT = input-output tables; IPPU = industrial processes and product use; MRIO = multiregional input-output; NSU = national supply-use tables.

Source: Asian Development Bank compilation and visualization.

Key Process 1: Mapping and Allocation Key Derivation

The EDGAR database and IEA energy balances use process-based recording, tracking emissions and energy use at the industrial process level (e.g., electricity generation, cement production). However, these classifications, based on IPCC categories, differ from the International Standard Industrial Classification industries used in national accounts, which are defined by economic activities. This misalignment makes it challenging to directly link emissions data with economic industries for comprehensive analysis.

To address this, emissions and energy data from these core databases were mapped and aligned with the industry and regional structure of ADB's MRIOTs, enabling disaggregation and allocation consistent with the MRIOT framework.

For both energy-first and inventory-first approaches, the allocation of flows or emissions depends on the industry detail and concordance between EDGAR emission activities, IEA energy balance flows, and MRIOT industries. Direct allocation is possible when IEA energy flows and EDGAR emissions align with a single MRIOT industry classification, or a one-to-one mapping.

Direct Mapping and Allocation for Energy-First and Inventory-First Approaches

The energy-first approach allocates emissions and flows based on energy data from IEA energy balances. This approach requires identifying correspondences between IEA energy flows and MRIOT industries. Direct allocation is feasible when: (i) an IEA energy flow maps to a single MRIOT industry, and (ii) the mapping enables straightforward integration without requiring disaggregation or reallocation. For example, fuel used for power generation is clearly linked to the electricity industry. Table A1.3 presents a summary of the energy balance flows, directly correlating them with the MRIOT industries.

Table A1.3: Concordance Between Energy Balance Flows and Industries Under Direct Mapping

IEA Flow	Name	MRIOT Industry
MAINELEC	Main activity producer electricity plants	Electricity, gas, and water supply (c17)
MAINCHP	Main activity producer CHP plants	Electricity, gas, and water supply (c17)
MAINHEAT	Main activity producer heat plants	Electricity, gas, and water supply (c17)
THEAT	Heat pumps	Electricity, gas, and water supply (c17)
TBOILER	Electric boilers	Electricity, gas, and water supply (c17)
TELE	Chemical heat for electricity production	Electricity, gas, and water supply (c17)
EMINES	Coal mines	Mining and quarrying (c2)
ECOKEOVS	Coke ovens	Coke, refined petroleum, and nuclear fuel (c8)
EPOWERPLT	Own use in electricity, CHP, and heat plants	Electricity, gas, and water supply (c17)
EGASWKS	Gas works	Electricity, gas, and water supply (c17)
EREFINER	Oil refineries	Coke, refined petroleum, and nuclear fuel (c8)
ECOALLIQ	Coal liquefaction plants	Coke, refined petroleum, and nuclear fuel (c8)
EBKB	BKB/peat briquette plants	Coke, refined petroleum, and nuclear fuel (c8)
EBLASTFUR	Blast furnaces	Basic metals and fabricated metals (c12)
ECHARCOAL	Charcoal production plants	Chemicals and chemical products (c9)
EBIOGAS	Gasification plants for biogases	Coke, refined petroleum, and nuclear fuel (c8)
EOILGASEX	Oil and gas extraction	Mining and quarrying (c2)
ELNG	Liquefaction (LNG)/regasification plants	Electricity, gas, and water supply (c17)
EPATFUEL	Patent fuel plants	Coke, refined petroleum, and nuclear fuel (c8)
EPUMPST	Pumped storage plants	Electricity, gas, and water supply (c17)
ENUC	Nuclear industry	Coke, refined petroleum, and nuclear fuel (c8)
EGTL	Gas-to-liquids (GTL) plants	Coke, refined petroleum, and nuclear fuel (c8)
IRONSTL	Iron and steel	Basic metals and fabricated metals (c12)
CHEMICAL	Chemical and petrochemical	Chemicals and chemical products (c9)
NONFERR	Non-ferrous metals	Basic metals and fabricated metals (c12)
NONMET	Non-metallic metals	Other non-metallic mineral (c11)
TRANSEQ	Transport equipment	Transport equipment (c15)
MACHINE	Machinery	Machinery, nec (c13)
MINING	Mining and quarrying	Mining and quarrying (c2)
FOODPRO	Food and tobacco	Food, beverages, and tobacco (c3)
PAPERPRO	Paper, pulp and print	Pulp, paper, printing, and publishing (c7)

continued on next page

IEA Flow	Name	MRIOT Industry
WOODPRO	Wood and wood products	Wood and products of wood and cork (c6)
CONSTRUC	Construction	Construction (c18)
RESIDENT	Residential	Households (F1)
AGRICULT	Agriculture and forestry	Agriculture, hunting, forestry, and fishing (c1)
ONONSPEC	Final consumption not elsewhere specified	Renting of machinery & equipment and other business activities (c30)
RAIL	Rail	Inland transport (c23)
FISHING	Fishing	Agriculture, hunting, forestry, and fishing (c1)
DOMESNAV	Domestic navigation	Water transport (c24)
DOMESAIR	Domestic aviation	Air transport (c25)
PIPELINE	Pipeline transport	Inland transport (c23)
Non-Energy Use Flows with Direct Concordance with MRIOT Industry		
NECHEM	Memo: Non-energy use chemical/ petrochemical	Chemicals and chemical products (c9)
NEOTHER	Non-energy use in other	Construction (c18)
NENONFERR	Memo: Non-energy use in non-ferrous metals	Basic metals and fabricated metals (c12)
NENONMET	Memo: Non-energy use in non-metallic metals	Other non-metallic mineral (c11)
NECONSTRUC	Memo: Non-energy use in construction	Construction (c18)
NEIRONSTL	Memo: Non-energy use in iron and steel	Basic metals and fabricated metals (c12)
NEMACHINE	Memo: Non-energy use in machinery	Machinery, nec (c13)
NEMINING	Memo: Non-energy use in mining and quarrying	Mining and quarrying (c2)
NEFOODPRO	Memo: Non-energy use in food and tobacco	Food, beverages, and tobacco (c3)
NETRANSEQ	Memo: Non-energy use in transport equipment	Transport equipment (c15)
NEPAPERPRO	Memo: Non-energy use in paper/pulp and printing	Pulp, paper, printing, and publishing (c7)
NEWOODPRO	Memo: Non-energy use in wood and wood products	Wood and products of wood and cork (c6)
Manufacture of Secondary and Tertiary Energy Products		
TPATFUEL	Patent fuel plants	Coke, refined petroleum and nuclear fuel (c8)
TCOKEOVS	Coke ovens	Basic metals and fabricated metals (c12)
TBLASTFUR	Blast furnaces	Basic metals and fabricated metals (c12)
TNONSPEC	Non-specified (transformation)	Coke, refined petroleum and nuclear fuel (c8)
TGASWKS	Gas works	Electricity, gas, and water supply (c17)
TCOALLIQ	Coal liquefaction plants	Electricity, gas, and water supply (c17)
TBKB	BKB/peat briquette plants	Coke, refined petroleum, and nuclear fuel (c8)
TBLENDGAS	For blended natural gas	Electricity, gas, and water supply (c17)
TCHARCOAL	Charcoal production plants	Chemicals and chemical products (c9)
TGTL	Gas-to-liquid plants	Coke, refined petroleum, and nuclear fuel (c8)
TREFINER	Oil refineries	Coke, refined petroleum, and nuclear fuel (c8)
TPETCHEM	Petrochemical plants	Chemicals and chemical products (c9)

BKB = brown coal briquettes; CHP = combined heat and power; IEA = International Energy Agency, LNG = liquefied natural gas, MRIOT = multiregional input-output table.

Source: Asian Development Bank mapping and compilation.

Meanwhile, the inventory-first approach allocates emissions based on data from inventories such as EDGAR. This requires matching emissions from IPCC activity classifications to MRIOT industries. Similar to the energy-first approach, direct allocation is feasible when: (i) emissions from an IPCC activity align directly with a single MRIOT industry, and (ii) concordance tables ensure accurate mapping of emissions sources to industries. Table A1.4 summarizes the EDGAR activities that have direct concordance with the MRIOT industry, including IEA-linked activities from the energy-first approach mainly related to electricity and heat production, product uses as substitutes for ozone-depleting substances, and non-energy emissions.

Table A1.4: Concordance Between Inventory-Based Activities and Industries Under Direct Mapping

IPCC Code	Standard Report Name	MRIOT Industry
1.A.1.a	Main Activity Electricity and Heat Production From IEA flows: MAINELEC, MAINCHP, MAINHEAT, THEAT, TBOILER, TELE	Electricity, gas, and water supply (c17)
1.A.3.a	Civil Aviation	Air transport (c25)
1.A.3.d	Water-Borne Navigation	Water transport (c24)
1.A.3.c	Railways	Inland transport (c23)
1.B.1	Solid Fuels	Mining and quarrying (c2)
1.B.2	Oil and Natural Gas	Mining and quarrying (c2)
Non-Energy-Linked Activities		
2.A.3	Glass Production	Other nonmetallic mineral (c11)
3.C.1	Emissions from biomass Burning	Agriculture, hunting, forestry, and fishing (c1)
2.A.1	Cement Production	Other nonmetallic mineral (c11)
2.B	Chemical Industry	Chemicals and chemical products (c9)
2.C	Metal Industry	Basic metals and fabricated metals (c12)
3.C.2	Liming	Agriculture, hunting, forestry, and fishing (c1)
3.C.3	Urea Application	Agriculture, hunting, forestry, and fishing (c1)
2.A.2	Lime Production	Other nonmetallic mineral (c11)
4.C	Incineration and Open Burning of Waste	Other community, social, and personal services (c34)
5.B	Fossil Fuel Fires	Mining and quarrying (c2)
4.A	Solid Waste Disposal	Other community, social, and personal services (c34)
4.D	Wastewater Treatment and Discharge	Other community, social, and personal services (c34)
3.A.1	Enteric Fermentation	Agriculture, hunting, forestry, and fishing (c1)
3.A.2	Manure Management	Agriculture, hunting, forestry, and fishing (c1)
3.C.7	Rice Cultivation	Agriculture, hunting, forestry, and fishing (c1)
4.B	Biological Treatment of Solid Waste	c34
5.A	Indirect N_2O emissions from the atmospheric deposition of nitrogen in NOx and NH_3	Agriculture, hunting, forestry, and fishing (c1)
3.C.4	Direct N_2O Emissions from Managed Soils	Agriculture, hunting, forestry, and fishing (c1)
3.C.5	Indirect N_2O Emissions from Managed Soils	Agriculture, hunting, forestry, and fishing (c1)
3.C.6	Indirect N_2O Emissions from Manure Management	Agriculture, hunting, forestry, and fishing (c1)
2.E	Electronics Industry	Electrical and optical equipment (c14)
1.A.5	Non-Specified	Public administration and defence; compulsory social security (c31)

IEA = International Energy Agency, IPCC = Intergovernmental Panel on Climate Change, MRIOT = multiregional input-output table, N_2O = nitrous oxide, NH_3 = ammonia, NOx = nitric oxide and nitrogen dioxide.

Source: Asian Development Bank mapping and compilation.

Indirect Mapping and Allocation for Energy-First and Inventory-First Approaches

Indirect or one-to-many mapping is applied to aggregated IEA flows and emissions that correspond to multiple MRIOT industries.

Under the energy-first approach, this mapping and allocation technique is used for certain energy flows, including those related to textiles and leather, industries not elsewhere classified, commercial and public services, and transport not elsewhere classified. Additionally, this approach is applied to auto production, energy flows from various transportation activities, and non-energy flows with one-to-many correspondences within MRIOT industries. The energy flows requiring further disaggregation to align with the corresponding MRIOT industries are detailed in Table A1.5.

Table A1. 5: Concordance Between Energy Balance Flows and Industries Under Indirect Allocation

IEA Flow	Name	MRIOT Industries
AVBUNK	International aviation bunkers	To be allocated by economy
MARBUNK	International marine bunkers	To be allocated by economy
AUTOELEC	Autoproducer electricity plants	c1 - c35
AUTOCHP	Autoproducer CHP plants	c1 - c35
AUTOHEAT	Autoproducer heat plants	c1 - c35
ENONSPEC	Non-specified (energy)	Product-based
TEXTILES	Textiles and leather	c4 - c5
INONSPEC	Industry not elsewhere specified	c10, c14, c16
TRNONSPE	Transport not elsewhere classified	c23 - c26
COMMPUB	Commercial and public services	c19 – 22, c27, c35
ROAD	Road	c1 - c35
NETRANS	Non-energy use in transport	c1 - c35
NEIND	Memo: Non-energy use in industry	c2, c16, c18
NEINONSPEC	Memo: Non-energy use in non-specified industry	c10, c14, c16
NETEXTILES	Memo: Non-energy use in textile and leather	c4:c5

CHP = combined heat and power; IEA = International Energy Agency, MRIOT = multiregional input-output table.

Source: Asian Development Bank mapping and compilation.

The same method applies in the inventory-first approach for emissions from product uses as substitutes for ozone-depleting substances, other process uses of carbonates, other product manufacture and use, international bunkering, and IEA-linked emissions mapped to multiple MRIOT industries (Table A1.6).

Table A1.6: Concordance Between Inventory-Based Activities and Industries Under Indirect Allocation

IPCC Code	Standard Report Name	MRIOT Industries
1.A.1.bc	Petroleum Refining - Manufacture of Solid Fuels and Other Energy Industries	c8, c9
1.A.2	Manufacturing Industries and Construction	c3-c16, c18
1.A.3.b_noRES	Road Transportation no resuspension	c1-F1
1.A.3.e	Other Transportation	c23, c26
1.A.4	Residential and other sectors	c1,c19-c22,c26-c35,F1
2.A.4	Other Process Uses of Carbonates	c1,c3-c16,c18
2.D	Non-Energy Products from Fuels and Solvent Use	c1-F1
2.G	Other Product Manufacture and Use	c3, c13, c14, c30, c33
AIR	International Aviation	To be allocated by economy
SEA	International Shipping	To be allocated by economy

IPCC = Intergovernmental Panel on Climate Change, MRIOT = multiregional input-output table.

Source: Asian Development Bank mapping and compilation.

Disaggregating Flows and Emissions: Derivation of Allocation Keys

The primary objective of the mapping and allocation process is to align emissions data with the format and dimensions of the MRIOTs. This requires auxiliary datasets to disaggregate energy use (for IEA flows identified in Table A1.5) and emissions (for IPCC activities detailed in Table A1.6) by commodity and industry. This facilitates the derivation of allocation keys. These keys, also known as splitting keys, are ratios or indicators used to distribute aggregated data into more detailed categories.

Table A1.5: Energy Balance Flows by Stage

IEA Flow	Stage	IEA Flow Name
INDPROD	1_Supply	Production
IMPORTS	1_Supply	Imports
EXPORTS	1_Supply	Exports
STOCKCHA	1_Supply	Stock changes
TES	1_Supply	Total energy supply
STATDIFF	1_Supply	Statistical differences
TRANSFER	1_Supply	Transfers
AVBUNK	1_Supply	International aviation bunkers
MARBUNK	1_Supply	International marine bunkers
TOTTRANF	2_Transformation	Transformation processes
MAINELEC	2_Transformation	Main activity producer electricity plants
AUTOELEC	2_Transformation	Autoproducer electricity plants

continued on next page

IEA Flow	Stage	IEA Flow Name
MAINCHP	2_Transformation	Main activity producer CHP plants
AUTOCHP	2_Transformation	Autoproducer CHP plants
MAINHEAT	2_Transformation	Main activity producer heat plants
AUTOHEAT	2_Transformation	Autoproducer heat plants
TPATFUEL	2_Transformation	Patent fuel plants
TCOKEOVS	2_Transformation	Coke ovens
TBLASTFUR	2_Transformation	Blast furnaces
TNONSPEC	2_Transformation	Non-specified (transformation)
TGASWKS	2_Transformation	Gas works
TCOALLIQ	2_Transformation	Coal liquefaction plants
TBKB	2_Transformation	BKB/peat briquette plants
TBLENDGAS	2_Transformation	For blended natural gas
TCHARCOAL	2_Transformation	Charcoal production plants
TGTL	2_Transformation	Gas-to-liquid plants
TREFINER	2_Transformation	Oil refineries
TPETCHEM	2_Transformation	Petrochemical plants
THEAT	2_Transformation	Heat pumps
TBOILER	2_Transformation	Electric boilers
TELE	2_Transformation	Chemical heat for electricity production
DISTLOSS	3_Energy industry own use and losses	Losses
TOTENGY	3_Energy industry own use and losses	Energy industry own use
EMINES	3_Energy industry own use and losses	Coal mines
ECOKEOVS	3_Energy industry own use and losses	Coke ovens
EPOWERPLT	3_Energy industry own use and losses	Own use in electricity, CHP, and heat plants
EGASWKS	3_Energy industry own use and losses	Gas works
EREFINER	3_Energy industry own use and losses	Oil refineries
ECOALLIQ	3_Energy industry own use and losses	Coal liquefaction plants
ENONSPEC	3_Energy industry own use and losses	Non-specified (energy)
EBKB	3_Energy industry own use and losses	BKB/peat briquette plants
EBLASTFUR	3_Energy industry own use and losses	Blast furnaces
ECHARCOAL	3_Energy industry own use and losses	Charcoal production plants
EBIOGAS	3_Energy industry own use and losses	Gasification plants for biogases
EOILGASEX	3_Energy industry own use and losses	Oil and gas extraction
ELNG	3_Energy industry own use and losses	Liquefaction (LNG)/regasification plants
EPATFUEL	3_Energy industry own use and losses	Patent fuel plants
EPUMPST	3_Energy industry own use and losses	Pumped storage plants
ENUC	3_Energy industry own use and losses	Nuclear industry
EGTL	3_Energy industry own use and losses	Gas-to-liquids plants
TFC	4_Final consumption	Total final consumption
TOTIND	4_Final consumption	Industry
IRONSTL	4_Final consumption	Iron and steel
CHEMICAL	4_Final consumption	Chemical and petrochemical

continued on next page

IEA Flow	Stage	IEA Flow Name
NONFERR	4_Final consumption	Non-ferrous metals
NONMET	4_Final consumption	Non-metallic metals
TRANSEQ	4_Final consumption	Transport equipment
MACHINE	4_Final consumption	Machinery
MINING	4_Final consumption	Mining and quarrying
FOODPRO	4_Final consumption	Food and tobacco
PAPERPRO	4_Final consumption	Paper, pulp and print
WOODPRO	4_Final consumption	Wood and wood products
CONSTRUC	4_Final consumption	Construction
TEXTILES	4_Final consumption	Textiles and leather
INONSPEC	4_Final consumption	Industry not elsewhere specified
TOTTRANS	4_Final consumption	Transport
TRNONSPE	4_Final consumption	Transport not elsewhere classified
RESIDENT	4_Final consumption	Residential
COMMPUB	4_Final consumption	Commercial and public services
AGRICULT	4_Final consumption	Agriculture and forestry
ONONSPEC	4_Final consumption	Final consumption not elsewhere specified
NONENUSE	4_Final consumption	Non-energy use
NEINTREN	4_Final consumption	Non-energy use industry / transformation / energy
NECHEM	4_Final consumption	Memo: Non-energy use chemical/ petrochemical
MANUFACT	4_Final consumption	Manufacturing
RAIL	4_Final consumption	Rail
FISHING	4_Final consumption	Fishing
NEOTHER	4_Final consumption	Non-energy use in other
DOMESNAV	4_Final consumption	Domestic navigation
ROAD	4_Final consumption	Road
PIPELINE	4_Final consumption	Pipeline transport
WORLDMAR	4_Final consumption	World marine bunkers
WORLDAV	4_Final consumption	World aviation bunkers
DOMESAIR	4_Final consumption	Domestic aviation
NETRANS	4_Final consumption	Non-energy use in transport
NEIND	4_Final consumption	Memo: Non-energy use in industry
NENONFERR	4_Final consumption	Memo: Non-energy use in non-ferrous metals
NENONMET	4_Final consumption	Memo: Non-energy use in non-metallic metals
NECONSTRUC	4_Final consumption	Memo: Non-energy use in construction
NEIRONSTL	4_Final consumption	Memo: Non-energy use in iron and steel
NEMACHINE	4_Final consumption	Memo: Non-energy use in machinery
NEMINING	4_Final consumption	Memo: Non-energy use in mining and quarrying
NEFOODPRO	4_Final consumption	Memo: Non-energy use in food and tobacco
NEINONSPEC	4_Final consumption	Memo: Non-energy use in non-specified industry

continued on next page

IEA Flow	Stage	IEA Flow Name
NETRANSEQ	4_Final consumption	Memo: Non-energy use in transport equipment
NEPAPERPRO	4_Final consumption	Memo: Non-energy use in paper/pulp and printing
NEWOODPRO	4_Final consumption	Memo: Non-energy use in wood and wood products
NETEXTILES	4_Final consumption	Memo: Non-energy use in textile and leather
ELOUTPUT	5_Electricity output	Electricity output
ELMAINE	5_Electricity output	Electricity output (GWh) - main activity producer electricity plants
ELAUTOE	5_Electricity output	Electricity output (GWh) - autoproducer electricity plants
ELMAINC	5_Electricity output	Electricity output (GWh) - main activity producer CHP plants
ELAUTOC	5_Electricity output	Electricity output (GWh) - autoproducer CHP plants
HEMAINC	6_Heat output	Heat output - main activity producer CHP plants
HEAUTOC	6_Heat output	Heat output - autoproducer CHP plants
HEMAINH	6_Heat output	Heat output - main activity producer heat plants
HEAUTOH	6_Heat output	Heat output - autoproducer heat plants
HEATOUT	6_Heat output	Heat output

BKB = brown coal briquette, CHP = combined heat and power, IEA = International Energy Agency, GWh = gigawatt-hour, LNG = liquified natural gas.

Source: Asian Development Bank compilation.

Table A1.6: Concordance Between Energy Commodities and Input-Output Products Related to Energy Use

IEA Energy Commodity	IEA Description	MRIOT Sector
ANTCOAL	Anthracite	c2
COKCOAL	Coking coal	c2
BITCOAL	Other bituminous coal	c2
SUBCOAL	Sub-bituminous coal	c2
LIGNITE	Lignite	c2
PATFUEL	Patent fuel	c8
OVENCOKE	Coke oven coke	c8
GASCOKE	Gas coke	c8
COALTAR	Coal tar	c8
BKB	BKB/Peat briquette plants	c2
GASWKSGS	Gas works gas	c17
COKEOVGS	Coke oven gas	c8
BLFURGS	Blast furnace gas	c8
OGASES	Other recovered gases	c12
PEAT	Peat	c2
PEATPROD	Peat products	c2
OILSHALE	Oil shale	c2

continued on next page

IEA Energy Commodity	IEA Description	MRIOT Sector
INDWASTE	Industrial waste	c34
MUNWASTER	Municipal waste (renew)	c34
MUNWASTEN	Municipal waste (non-renew)	c34
PRIMSBIO	Primary solid fuels	c6
BIOGASES	Biogases	c8
BIOGASOL	Biogasoline	c8
BIODIESEL	Biodiesel	c8
OBIOLIQ	Other liquid biofuels	c8
CHARCOAL	Charcoal	c9
NATGAS	Natural gas	c17
CRUDEOIL	Crude oil	c2
NGL	Natural gas liquids	c2
REFFEEDS	Refinery feedstocks	c2
ADDITIVE	Additive/blending components	c2
NONCRUDE	Other hydrocarbons	c2
REFINGAS	Refinery gas	c8
ETHANE	Ethane	c8
LPG	Liquefied petroleum gases	c8
NONBIOGASO	Motor gasoline excl. bio	c8
AVGAS	Aviation gasoline	c8
JETGAS	Gasoline type jet fuel	c8
NONBIOJETK	Kerosene type jet fuel excl. bio	c8
OTHKERO	Other kerosene	c8
NONBIODIES	Gas/diesel excl. biofuels	c8
RESFUEL	Fuel oil	c8
NAPHTHA	Naphtha	c8
WHITESP	White spirit and SBP	c8
LUBRIC	Lubricants	c8
BITUMEN	Bitumen	c8
PARWAX	Paraffin waxes	c8
PETCOKE	Petroleum coke	c8
ONONSPEC	Non-specified oil products	c8
NUCLEAR	Nuclear	c8
HYDRO	Hydro	c17
GEOTHERM	Geothermal	c17
SOLARPV	Solar photovoltaics	c17
SOLARTH	Solar thermal	c17
TIDE	Tide, wave, and ocean	c17
WIND	Wind	c17
OTHER	Other sources	c17
ELECTR	Electricity	c17
HEAT	Heat	c17

BKB = brown coal briquette, IEA = International Energy Agency, MRIOT = multiregional input-output table, SBP = special boiling point.

Source: Asian Development Bank compilation.

The allocation key derivation process is organized into three distinct levels of disaggregation, each enhancing the refinement and precision of the data. The degree of disaggregation directly affects the complexity and specificity of the allocation keys used in the emissions data allocation process. As the disaggregation level increases, the allocation keys become more detailed and precise, thereby improving the accuracy of data allocation.

Level 1: Disaggregation by Industry

At this level, allocation keys are derived based on the intermediate use of energy commodities by industries in monetary terms from the MRIOTs. These broad keys assume relative price homogeneity across industries, i.e., that MRIOT industries under an aggregate IEA heading or EDGAR main activity (e.g., road transportation) pay the same price per energy unit and consume energy products in identical shares. For instance, road transport emissions from all MRIOT industries are assumed to be generated via proportional use of diesel and motor gasoline. This proportional allocation involves distributing the total energy consumption of a specific MRIOT industry based on the monetary values recorded in the use table.

Mathematically, the share of industry *j* in the use of product *i* within economy *r* is represented as:

$$s_{i,j,r} = \frac{U_{i,j,r}}{\sum_j U_{i,j,r}} \qquad (1)$$

where:
$s_{i,j,r}$ = share of industry *j* in the total use of product *i* in economy *r*
$U_{i,j,r}$ = use of product *i* by industry *j* in economy *r*
$\sum_j U_{i,j,r}$ = total use of product *i* across all industries *j* in economy *r*

Level 2: Disaggregation by Products

Level 2 adopts a more granular approach to product breakdown. In the MRIOTs, energy products such as diesel are often grouped with other petroleum products such as gasoline, kerosene, and heavy fuel oils (under industry c9). To allocate energy use specific to diesel within industries such as manufacturing, it becomes necessary to disaggregate diesel from the broader petroleum product group. Since product *i* is composed of *n* products i_1, i_2, *to* i_n, then total use of *i* by *j* in *r* is given by:

$$U_{i,j,r} = \sum_{p=1}^{n} U_{i_p,j,r} \qquad (2)$$

where:
$U_{i,j,r}$ = total use of product *i* by industry *j* in economy *r*
$\sum_{p=1}^{n} U_{i_p,j,r}$ = use of subproduct i_p by industry *j* in economy *r*
n = number of subproducts comprising product *i*

This disaggregation is facilitated through the use of detailed supply and use tables or input-output tables (IOTs). Specifically, IOTs from the Australian Bureau of Statistics (ABS) are employed to determine the specific shares of energy commodities within these aggregated industries. The preference for ABS data is due to its comprehensive availability and the assumption that there is significant variance in inputs across industries rather than between firms within the same industry. For instance, agricultural inputs are likely similar internationally, differing markedly from industries such as mining, supporting the use of model use tables for allocation, as justified in studies such as those by Genty et al (2012).

To facilitate this level of disaggregation, fuels in the IEA energy balance are mapped to the specified products in the IOTs from the ABS. For instance, to split the total energy use for road transportation across various industries and households, IEA road fuel products are mapped both to the ABS products (for the level 2 disaggregation) and the broader MRIOT industries (for the level 1 disaggregation), as seen in Table A1.7.

Table A1.7: Road Fuel Mapping with Statistical Product Groupings and Industries

Fuel Types Used in Road Transport (IEA)	ABS Product	ABS IOPC	MRIOT Industry
BIOGASOL	Other chemical products nec	18990090	c9
BIODIESEL	Other chemical products nec	18990090	c9
NATGAS	Natural gas (in the gaseous state)	07000030	c8
LPG	Liquefied petroleum gas produced at refineries	17010050	c8
NONBIOGASO	Automotive petrol; gasoline refining or blending; motor spirit (incl aviation spirit)	17010010	c8
NONBIODIES	Petrodiesel	17010031	c8
ELECTR	Other chemical products nec	18990090	c9
OBIOLIQ	Other chemical products nec	18990090	c9
BIOGASES	Other chemical products nec	18990090	c9
OTHKERO	Kerosene (incl kerosene type jet fuel)	17010020	c8
AVGAS	Automotive petrol; gasoline refining or blending; motor spirit (incl aviation spirit)	17010010	c8
RESFUEL	Gas oil or fuel oils nec (excl motor spirit and kerosene)	17010032	c8
WHITESP	Petroleum based solvents and chemical feedstocks	17090071	c8
LUBRIC	Pitch, tars, jellies, waxes and other lubricants manufactured from petroleum	17090041	c8
BITUMEN	Bituminous mixtures and other articles of asphalt	17090120	c8

ABS = Australian Bureau of Statistics, IEA = International Energy Agency, IOPC = industry of origin product classification, MRIOT = multiregional input-output table, nec = not elsewhere classified.

Source: Asian Development Bank mapping and compilation.

For example, MRIO product *c8* represents a broad fuel category that includes several products such as petrodiesel, gasoline, and others. Because this category is aggregated, it cannot be used directly to estimate the use of a specific fuel like diesel (or non-biodiesel in the IEA data). To isolate petrodiesel within *c8*, a disaggregation step is required. This is done using the more detailed ABS tables, which provide separate values for individual fuels. In this case, diesel corresponds to the ABS product labeled "petrodiesel." The share of petrodiesel in the total fuel group *c8* is calculated from the ABS data. This share is then applied to the MRIO total for product *c8* to estimate the portion attributable to petrodiesel.

Once the use of petrodiesel by industry is estimated, it is used as an allocation key for distributing IEA energy flow of non-biodiesel across industries upon conversion to physical units (liters) using fuel prices. For example, if industry *c1* accounts for a certain share of non-biodiesel use in the ABS data, that same share is applied to the petrodiesel portion of MRIO product *c9*. This approach ensures that each industry's share of total product usage accurately reflects its specific fuel allocation.

Level 3: Disaggregation by Purpose

At this level, the focus is on distinguishing how a product is used for different purposes. For example, diesel in industries is not limited to motor fuel use: it also powers generators, runs boilers, and supports other industrial processes. The goal is to break down product use by its specific end-use purpose.

This level of detail is largely aspirational as few economies can currently differentiate energy use by purpose with high accuracy. However, when product groups are narrowly defined, their uses can be reasonably approximated. For instance, wood products can be disaggregated into lumber, sawdust, and fuel wood, with fuel wood (sourced from datasets such as the IOTs from the ABS) primarily assumed for energy use. Similarly, jet kerosene is mostly used in aviation, while fuel oil is typical in shipping.

This approach improves energy accounting and supports more purpose-specific analysis in future assessments.

Key Process 2: Residence Adjustments

Corrections for the residence principle are mostly applied to the transportation sector given the multi-territorial nature of its activity. As mentioned earlier in this appendix, energy balances and existing GHG inventories record energy flows and emissions to territories irrespective of their residence. Residence adjustments ensure that emissions are attributed to the economy accountable for them, regardless of where they physically occur. Table A1.8 summarizes the adjustments made for the transportation sector.

Table A1.8: Residence Adjustments Applied to the Transportation Sector

<table>
<tr><th>Residence Adjustments</th><th>Covered Adjustments</th></tr>
<tr><td rowspan="3">Energy use on national territory
(+) Residents in the rest of the world including especially
• Road transport
• Air transport
• Water transport

(-) Non-residents on domestic territory including especially
• Road transport
• Air transport
• Water transport

= Energy use by resident units
(i.e., the national accounts definition)</td><td>ROAD:
• Foreign (tourist and company) cars driving and fueling in national territory
• National (tourist and company) cars driving and fueling abroad</td></tr>
<tr><td>AIR:
• Foreign plane's LTO and bunkering in national territory
• National plane's LTO and bunkering in foreign territory</td></tr>
<tr><td>WATER:
• Foreign vessels sailing and bunkering in national territory
• National vessels sailing and bunkering in foreign territory</td></tr>
</table>

LTO = landing and take-off.

Source: Asian Development Bank compilation.

Let E be the energy use from road, air, and maritime transportation for fuel f of economy r after allocation to the appropriate industry j. Further, let $\bar{E}$ be the residence-adjusted energy flow, which is given by:

$$\bar{E}(r,j,f) = E(r,j,f) * \alpha(r,h,f) \qquad (3)$$

where α is the adjustment factor for the fuel used for flow h where adjustments were applied to: road transport, aviation, and international maritime transport. Details of adjustments, data used, and adjustment factor calculations for road transport, aviation, and maritime are detailed in Table A1.9.

As shown in Table A1.9, the adjustment factor $\alpha(r, h_{road}, f)$ accounts for residence-based adjustments in road transport energy use by incorporating cross-border travel effects. It modifies the territory-based energy consumption by adding the energy used by residents traveling abroad and subtracting the energy consumed by nonresidents within the domestic territory. This ensures that energy use is attributed to the residents of a region rather than just the fuel sold within the region's borders. The adjustment factor is calculated as the ratio of this residence-adjusted energy use to the original territory-based energy flow.

The energy consumption adjustments for residents traveling abroad and nonresidents within the domestic territory are derived from fuel expenditures of inbound and outbound tourists, which are estimated using bilateral travel credits and debits from the Bilateral Trade in Services dataset maintained by the Organisation for Economic Co-operation and Development (OECD) and the World Trade Organization. Travel credits represent spending by inbound tourists (nonresidents) within the domestic economy, while travel debits reflect spending by outbound tourists (residents) abroad. The International Monetary Fund's travel credits data are further disaggregated into personal and business

Table A1.9: Adjustment Factor Calculations for the Transport Sector

Transport Industry	Details	Data Used	Adjustment Factor
Road	Adjusted based on diesel and gasoline purchases by tourists (nonresidents)	IMF's balance of payments data on travel credits OECD Balanced Trade in Services Tourism Satellite Accounts	$\alpha(r,h_{road},f) = \frac{E(r,j,f)+\sum_{d,w}\bar{V}(r,d,f,w)-\sum_{r,w}\bar{V}(r,d,f,w)}{E(r,j,f)}$
Aviation	Adjusted based on the Air Operator's Certificate, which indicates the economy in which the airline is registered and operates.	OECD Air transport CO_2 emissions (experimental) dataset	$\alpha(r,h_{air},f) = \frac{\sum_r\sum_s flight_o^{rs}}{\sum_o\sum_s flight_o^{rs}}$
Maritime	Adjusted based on vessel operator's residence	OECD Maritime transport CO_2 emissions (experimental) dataset	$\alpha(r,h_{sea},f) = = \frac{\varepsilon(r)}{\sum_r \varepsilon(r)}$

CO_2 = carbon dioxide, IMF = International Monetary Fund, OECD = Organisation for Economic Co-operation and Development.

Source: Asian Development Bank compilation.

travel, with personal travel assigned to households and business travel allocated across all economic industries. At the bilateral level, the tourist expenditure T on fuel f from visiting economy r to destination d for purpose w is given by:

$$T(r,d,f,w) = l(r,d,f,w)\frac{TSA(d,f,w)}{\sum_{i\epsilon f}TSA(d,i,w)} \quad (4)$$

where l is the bilateral travel credit for purpose w (w={*personal,business*}), TSA is the inbound tourism expenditure of destination d, f is the road fuel type used by inbound tourists, and i is the index for products purchased by tourists in the destination economy.

For economy r, which does not have published tourism satellite accounts, data from proxy economies r' are instead used, determined by similarities in economic characteristics and geographic proximity.

In detailed *TSAs*, a breakdown for each fuel type f is only available at most for diesel (IEA code: NONBIODIES) and gasoline (NONBIOGASO). As such, the use of biodiesel and biogasoline follow the same patterns as their fossil fuel counterparts.

Tourist expenditures T must then be converted from monetary values to physical volumes. To do this, average prices of diesel and gasoline for year t in the destination economy d are used, such that:

$$V(r,d,f,w) = \frac{T(r,d,f,w)}{\rho(d,f)} \quad (5)$$

V now refers to quantities (in liters) of fuel *f* used by tourists from *r* in destination *d*. The volume of fuel needs to be converted to the mass of carbon content and multiplied by the net calorific value of the fuel *f* to arrive the final energy use in joule units.

$$V(r,d,f,w) = V(r,s,f,w) * \lambda(f) * \kappa(f) \quad (6)$$

where $\bar{V}$ is the energy use in terajoules, λ is the standard converter of fuel *f* volume (liters) to mass (tons), and κ is the net calorific value per ton of fuel *f*. These last two parameters are taken from standard conversion tables and default calorific values in the United Nations Statistics Division's International Recommendations for Energy Statistics (2018).

For aviation, the adjustment factor $\alpha(r, h_{air}, f)$ accounts for jet fuel consumption by an operating economy, based on emissions from flights between origin and destination. It is calculated as the ratio of total emissions from flights operated by a specific economy to the total emissions from all flights across economies. This approach assumes a direct relationship between flight activity and energy use, which is reasonable in aviation since jet fuel loaded at airports is fully consumed during each trip (Yamano and Guilhoto 2020).

To convert territorial-based flows to residence-based estimates, the OECD's air transport emissions data are utilized. This dataset, compiled from the International Civil Aviation Organization's database and following Eurocontrol's methodology, provides detailed flight-level information. This includes the departure and arrival airports, the operating airline, and the aircraft type (covering more than 1,000 distinct aircraft models). Additionally, the database includes information on the economy that issued each airline's Air Operator's Certificate, allowing for the classification of flights by operating economy.

Since flights can be distinguished by the operating economy, the adjustment requires adding the following: (i) domestic flights outside of economy *r* operated by a resident airline of economy *r*, (ii) international flights arriving in economy *r* operated by a resident airline of economy *r*, and (iii) international flights outside of economy *r* operated by a resident airline of economy *r*. Conversely, the adjustment must subtract: (i) domestic flights within economy *r* operated by a nonresident airline and (ii) international flights departing from economy *r* operated by a nonresident airline. These additions and subtractions are inherently reflected in the adjustment ratio, ensuring a consistent and accurate allocation of aviation energy flows based on the residence principle.

For international maritime or shipping emissions, the OECD's maritime CO_2 emissions data are used to calculate each economy's share of total global shipping emissions, excluding emissions from fishing. Fishing emissions are excluded because they are categorized separately in the IPCC guidelines, even though they are included in the OECD's total global shipping emissions calculations. The OECD maritime CO_2 emissions dataset is used as the basis for this allocation since the data are already adjusted for the residence principle, as the OECD estimates CO_2 emissions for each voyage and assigns them to the economy of the ship operator, consistent with the residence principles of the international System of National Accounts and the System of Environmental-Economic Accounting. Each vessel in the global fleet is linked to a ship operator in the Automatic Identification System database, which includes information about the operator's economy of residence. After calculating each economy's share $\alpha(r, h_{sea}, f)$ of global shipping emissions, these shares can be directly used to allocate the EDGAR emissions from international maritime activities.

Key Process 3: Emissions Model

At this stage of compilation, energy and non-energy flows are used as auxiliary data for allocating the GHGs as reported in EDGAR. For each emission A at time t, EDGAR provides the following dimensions:

- r reporting economy
- h activity or flow
- g type of GHG

GHG emissions by energy commodity are calculated separately for energy and non-energy related emissions. An energy-first approach is applied for energy-related combustion. An inventory-first approach is applied for non-energy related emissions.

Given economy r and year t, the greenhouse emissions Ag for gas g can be expressed as:

$$A_g(r,j) = \sum_f A_g^E(r,j,f) + \sum_f A_g^{NE}(r,j,f) \quad (7)$$

where A_g^E and A_g^{NE} are the energy-related and non-energy related emissions of gas g, respectively.

In the case of energy-related greenhouse emissions, the method uses a simple emissions model with linear relationship between emissions and a given type of activity, such that:

$$Emissions(g) = Activity\ level\ x\ Emission\ factor(g) \quad (8)$$

where the activity level can be linked to the use of energy commodities and the emission factor is specific to the type of gas and fuel.

Applying the emissions model, the energy-related emissions A_g^E of gas g at time t is therefore calculated as:

$$A_g^E(r,j,h,f) = \bar{E}(r,j,h,f) * \varphi_g^E(r,f) * \omega_g(r,h) \quad (9)$$

where $\bar{E}$ is the residence-adjusted and emissions-relevant energy use of fuel commodity f by economy r and industry j from undertaking activity h, and φ_g^E is the emission factor from fuel combustion in economy r of fuel type f. Emission factors are obtained from the emission factors database of the IPCC. Default values are used for economies that are not available in the database. Lastly, ω_g is a scaling factor applied to ensure the total emissions match the aggregate emissions in the EDGAR database.

Given uncertainties in the emission factors, a scaling factor ω_g is applied to match the total emissions for any given aggregate in the EDGAR database. The scaling factor is calculated using:

$$\omega_g(r,h) = \frac{\sum_f A_g^*(r,h,f)}{\sum_{j,f} \bar{E}(r,j,h,f) * \varphi_g(r,f)} \qquad (10)$$

where A_g^* is the target total emission to match, which is also the residence-based total emissions for gas g in economy r due to use of fuel f in activity h.

Activities under this approach primarily include energy activities. However, emissions from non-energy products derived from fuel and solvent use, which encompass energy flows such as non-energy use in industry, transport, and other industries, also utilize the energy-first approach due to the availability of IEA flows for these activities. For emissions from use of non-energy products, calculations are as follows:

$$A_g^{NE}(r,j,h,f,t) = \bar{E}(r,j,h,f,t) * \varphi_g^{NE}(r,f,t) * \omega_g(r,h,t) \qquad (11)$$

A key difference from energy-related emissions lies in the calculation of the emission factor, which considers specific technical aspects of the non-energy product being used. For example, for f=lubricants, the emission factor is given by:

$$\varphi_g^{NE}(r,f,t) = CC(f) * ODU(f) * \pi(g) \qquad (12)$$

where:
CC is the specific carbon content of fuel f (metric ton of carbon per terajoule),
ODU is the fraction of fossil fuel carbon that is oxidized during use (e.g., the percentage that enters the combustion chamber of an engine in the case of lubricants),
$\pi(g)$ is the mass ratio of gas g (e.g., CO_2) to carbon. In calculations, the mass ratio of CO_2 to carbon is 44:12.

This method ensures that the emission factors reflect the specific characteristics of the non-energy products being used.

From the emissions derived using this model, allocation shares for each economy r, year t, gas g and activity h can be extrapolated. These allocation shares are then used to adjust EDGAR emissions accordingly and allocate the emissions to the corresponding MRIOT industry and economy.

Key Process 4: Allocation Key Harmonization and Final Steps

In both the energy-first and inventory-first approaches, emissions are allocated to the corresponding MRIOT industry using either direct or indirect allocation methods. Air emissions are then multiplied by their respective allocation keys and adjustment ratios to ensure accurate distribution. To standardize the impact assessment, all emissions are converted into CO_2 equivalents using 100-year global warming potentials. These conversions allow comparison of different GHGs based on their long-term climate effects. The values used in this process are sourced from the latest IPCC's Sixth Assessment Report (Masson-Delmotte et al. 2021), ensuring consistency with the most up-to-date scientific understanding of global warming potentials.

Therefore, industry GHG emissions are recalibrated to their global warming potentials:

$$\tilde{A}_g(r,j,h,f,t) = A_g(r,j,h,f,t) * GWP(g) \quad (13)$$

where GWP for each substance g is provided in Table A1.10.

The final emissions values give the final GHG emissions in gigagrams of CO_2 equivalent. These can then be aggregated at the economy r, sector j, flow h, and gas g for each year t.

Table A1.10: 100-Year Global Warming Potentials for 28 Greenhouse Gases

Substance	GWP100
Carbon Dioxide (CO_2)	1
Methane (CH_4)	27.9
Nitrous Oxide (N_2O)	273
Pentafluoroethane (HFC-125)	3740
1,1,1,2-Tetrafluoroethane (HFC-134a)	1530
1,1,1-Trifluoroethane (HFC-143a)	5810
1,1-Difluoroethane (HFC-152a)	164
1,1,1,2,3,3,3-Heptafluoropropane (HFC-227ea)	3600
1,1,1,3,3-Pentafluoropropane (HFC-245fa)	962
Difluoromethane (HFC-32)	771
1,1,1,3,3-Pentafluorobutane (HFC-365mfc)	914
1,1-Dichloro-1-fluoroethane (HCFC-141b)	860
1-Chloro-1,1-difluoroethane (HCFC-142b)	2300
Hexafluoroethane (C2F6)	12400
Tetrafluoromethane (CF4)	380
Sulfur Hexafluoride (SF6)	7380
Octafluoropropane (C3F8)	9290
Decafluorobutane (C4F10)	10000
Trifluoromethane (HFC-23)	14600
Octafluorocyclobutane (c-C4F8)	13900
1,1,2,2- Tetrafluoroethane (HFC-134)	1260
1,1,2-Trifluoroethane (HFC-143)	364
1,1,1,3,3,3Hexafluoropropane (HFC-236fa)	74.8
Fluoromethane (HFC-41)	135
1,1,1,2,3,4,4,5,5,5-Decafluoropentanes (HFC-43-10-mee)	1600
Nitrogen Trifluoride (NF3)	17400
Dodecafluoropentane (C5F12)	9220
Tetradecafluorohexane (C6F14)	8620

GWP100 = 100-year global warming potential.

Source: GWP-100 values obtained from V. Masson-Delmotte, P. Zhai, A. Pirani, S. L. Connors, C. Péan, S. Berger, N. Caud, Y. Chen, L. Goldfarb, M. I. Gomis, M. Huang, K. Leitzell, E. Lonnoy, J. B. R. Matthews, T. K. Maycock, T. Waterfield, O. Yelekçi, R. Yu, and B. Zhou, eds. 2021. *Climate Change 2021: The Physical Science Basis*. Contribution of Working Group I to the Sixth Assessment Report of the Intergovernmental Panel on Climate Change. Cambridge University Press, Cambridge, United Kingdom and New York, NY, USA. doi:10.1017/9781009157896.

References

Andrew, R. M. 2020. A Comparison of Estimates of Global Carbon Dioxide Emissions from Fossil Carbon Sources. *Earth Systems Science Data*. 12 (2). pp. 1437–1465. doi:10.5194/essd-12-1437-2020.

Crippa, M., D. Guizzardi, F. Pagani, M. Banja, M. Muntean, E. Schaaf, F. Monforti-Ferrario, et al. 2024. *GHG Emissions of all World Countries*. Publications Office of the European Union. https://publications.jrc.ec.europa.eu/repository/handle/JRC138862.

Dhakal, S., J.C.Minx, F.L.Toth, Reisinger, W.F. Lamb, N. Döbbeling, T. Wiedmann, et al. 2022. Emissions Trends and Drivers Supplementary Material. In: P.R. Shukla, J. Skea, R. Slade, A. Al Khourdajie, R. van Diemen, D. McCollum, M. Pathak, et al., eds. *Climate Change 2022: Mitigation of Climate Change. Contribution of Working Group III to the Sixth Assessment Report of the Intergovernmental Panel on Climate Change*. https://www.ipcc.ch/report/ar6/wg3/.

Genty, A., I. Arto, and F. Neuwahl. 2012. Final Database of Environmental Satellite Accounts: Technical Report on their Compilation. *World Input-Output Database Deliverable 4.6 Documentation*. https://www.rug.nl/ggdc/valuechain/wiod/wiod-2013-release?lang=en.

Masson-Delmotte, V., P. Zhai, A. Pirani, S. L. Connors, C. Péan, S. Berger, N. Caud, et al., eds. 2021. *Climate Change 2021: The Physical Science Basis*. Contribution of Working Group I to the Sixth Assessment Report of the Intergovernmental Panel on Climate Change. Cambridge University Press. doi:10.1017/9781009157896.

Minx, J.C., W.F. Lamb, R.M. Andrew, J.G. Canadell, M. Crippa, N. Döbbeling, P.M. Forster, et al. 2021. A Comprehensive and Synthetic Dataset for Global, Regional, and National Greenhouse Gas Emissions by Sector 1970–2018 with an Extension to 2019. *Earth System Science Data*. 13. pp. 5213–5252. https://doi.org/10.5194/essd-13-5213-2021.

United Nations Statistics Division. 2018. *International Recommendations for Energy Statistics*. https://unstats.un.org/unsd/energystats/methodology/documents/IRES-web.pdf

Yamano, N. and J. Guilhoto. 2020. CO2 Emissions Embodied in International Trade and Domestic Final Demand: Methodology and Results Using the OECD Inter-Country Input-Output Database. *OECD Science, Technology and Industry Working Papers*. No. 2020/11. https://dx.doi.org/10.1787/8f2963b8-en

APPENDIX 2

The Case for Input-Output Analysis as a Suitable Emissions Measurement Framework

In promoting climate resilience, decisionmakers and stakeholders worldwide need a deeper understanding of the mechanisms by which greenhouse gases (GHGs) are emitted, and diffused through economic activities. General literature distinguishes emissions based on where they occur along a value chain, categorized under either Scope 1, Scope 2, or Scope 3.

Scope 1 refers to emissions that an economic entity generates within its own production processes. For example, when considering a bread manufacturing company, Scope 1 covers GHGs emitted from the factories it operates as well as those emanating from its own vehicles that transport materials or are used for other business purposes. For activities falling outside the direct operational control of the enterprise, any consequent emissions are not covered in Scope 1.

Meanwhile, Scope 2 refers to the emissions embedded in purchased energy, such as emissions from entities that produce gas or electricity used by the bread manufacturer. Note that Scope 2 covers only the emissions directly induced by the manufacturer's demand for energy inputs needed to produce bread.

Lastly, Scope 3 emissions include all sources not within the Scope 1 and Scope 2 definitions (WBCSD and WRI 2004). It covers the emissions an economic entity is indirectly responsible for along the value chain it is participating in. Thus, from the bread manufacturer's perspective, Scope 3 will include not only emissions attributed to the suppliers of its non-energy intermediate inputs but also those coming from suppliers of raw materials to the producers of the gas or electricity it used. Ideally, it will also include any emissions borne out of the activities of its downstream consumers, such as GHG emissions from improper disposal (e.g., burning) of the packaging materials used for pastries.

While Scope 1 (direct emissions) and Scope 2 (indirect emissions from purchased energy) are relatively easy to quantify, Scope 3 emissions are more challenging to measure. Scope 1 emissions are wholly within an entity's control and ownership: the entity can directly monitor fuel consumption and maintain precise records of the operations that generate these emissions. The direct nature of these emissions provides straightforward data collection and measurement processes. Scope 2 emissions are based on energy consumption, which is typically well-documented through utility bills or energy meters. Conversely, companies have limited control over the activities and processes that generate Scope 3 emissions. Quantifying Scope 3 emissions often requires data from third parties such as suppliers, logistics providers, customers, and waste management companies. This, coupled with the fact that Scope 3 emissions account for the highest proportion of total emissions in any value chain (CDP 2022), prompts the need for viable measurement frameworks. Such frameworks need to trace interdependencies among productive sectors of the economy in meeting the demand of final consumers (e.g., households, nonprofit organizations, governments, and businesses). This is precisely where input-output analysis—a method employed long before climate resilience became a major concern—proves to be effective.

Researchers who initially sought to utilize input-output analysis found it difficult to implement the Leontief output model (Box A2.1) due to the inversion of large matrices, which typically included hundreds of industries. Thus, some adjustments to the methodology were applied to help reduce the computational burden, including aggregating the data into a smaller number of sectors. This relied on a partitioned matrix approach to derive the inverse of a larger matrix and generating an approximation to the Leontief inverse (Miller and Blair 2022). The third approach would eventually have an associated, useful economic interpretation that fits with the parameters for measuring climate accountabilities.

Given a considerably large number of sectors, the Leontief inverse L is approximated as follows:

$$\boldsymbol{L} = (\boldsymbol{I} - \boldsymbol{A})^{-1} = \boldsymbol{I} + \boldsymbol{A} + \boldsymbol{A}^2 + \boldsymbol{A}^3 + \cdots + \boldsymbol{A}^n$$

where A corresponds to the technical coefficients matrix that describes the direct input requirements among sectors[3], I is an identity matrix with the same dimension as A, $A^2 = A\,A$, , and so on. Since the total gross output needed to satisfy the final demand is given by $x = Ly$, a simple substitution of the power series approximation gives:

$$\boldsymbol{x} = \boldsymbol{Iy} + \boldsymbol{Ay} + \boldsymbol{A}^2\boldsymbol{y} + \boldsymbol{A}^3\boldsymbol{y} + \cdots + \boldsymbol{A}^n\boldsymbol{y}$$

In the body of literature that utilizes this approach to track environmental pressures arising from industrial activity, each term on the right-hand side of the equation is referred to as a "production layer". The initial production layer (often considered as the 0th layer), Iy, gives the total amount of gross outputs that each sector must produce to match their respective final demands. Since all industries depend on each other to provide inputs to production in an input-output economy, then gross outputs could not be equal to just the levels of respective final demand.

3 A typical element of the A matrix is a_{ij} which describes the monetary unit's worth of sector i output needed to produce one monetary unit worth of sector j output.

Returning to the featured example, the bread manufacturer directly purchases gas and electricity from other economic entities. It is reasonable to assume that these gas and electricity providers also cater to final consumers, thus making their output structure a combination of sales to enterprises that directly utilize their products and/or services for production purposes as well as sales to final consumers. This direct provision of inputs to meet final demand is captured in the first production layer, y.

Intuitively, to produce electricity or gas, certain amounts of output will also be required from the energy producer's associated economic entities. As mentioned in the example, an upstream supplier might sell raw materials to gas and electricity companies as essential inputs to their production processes. However, this supplier may also sell its products to final consumers either for household use or investment purposes. Thus, the structure of sales by the entities that sell raw materials will contain purchases by the entities that provide electricity and gas to meet the demand for inputs from the bread manufacturer. In this sense, the bread manufacturer is indirectly dependent on the entity that sells raw materials to electricity and gas companies. Since this chain of production becomes longer and more complex as additional interdependent actors are introduced, a reasonable framework that tracks these indirect transactions must consider all possible iterations, which are conveniently captured in the second, third, and all the way to the nth production layers, $A^2y + A^3y + \dots + A^ny$.

Given the sector-level emissions intensity coefficients vector, $f = (f_1 \quad f_2 \quad \cdots \quad f_n)$, emissions embodied in each production layer can be derived by simply pre-multiplying it to x resulting in:

$$\boldsymbol{fx = fIy + fAy + fA^2y + fA^3y + \cdots + fA^ny}$$

Here, the first term fIy can be treated as Scope 1 emissions since it measures emissions resulting from an industry's own production processes not involving any other industries. Since the second term fAy measures the emissions induced from direct dependencies among industries, it aptly measures Scope 2 emissions. All remaining terms capture Scope 3 emissions with the added convenience of allowing interested researchers to determine exactly which parts of a value chain account for considerable levels of emissions[4].

Beyond accounting for direct and indirect emissions, the input-output framework also serves as a tool for analyzing the drivers of changes to emissions over time. Structural decomposition analysis (SDA) builds on this by attributing shifts in environmental indicators to specific underlying drivers, such as emissions intensity, intermediate input composition, and final demand. SDA allows users to assess not just where emissions occur, but why they are rising or falling.

---

4 This is done by creating two diagonal matrices with the elements of the f and y vectors appearing on the main diagonals, respectively. Denoting the resulting matrices by $\hat{f}$ and $\hat{y}$, the following matrix operation is then performed: $\hat{f}L\hat{y}$. A typical element of this matrix will be $f_i l_{ij} y_j$, which represents the total GHG emissions of sector i induced by the final demand of sector j.

Box A2.1: Applying the Leontief Output Model

Input-output analysis has been recognized as one of the more useful ways to measure both the direct and indirect transactions among the productive sectors of an economy. The basic model popularized by Wassily Leontief in the 1930s depicts an economy as a collection of interlinked industries (or sectors) that produce output to meet exogenous final demand. Based on Miller and Blair (2022), this is represented by the system of equations below.

$$x_i = z_{i1} + z_{i2} + \cdots + z_{in} + y_i, \quad i = 1, 2, \ldots, n$$

We see from above that each industry i produces output, x_i, part of which goes to its counterparts to be used as intermediates in their respective production processes, $z_{ij}, j \neq i$. Each industry is comprised of several enterprises that fall under the same classification of economic activities based on established references such as the International Standard Classification of All Economic Activities. Since it is possible for these entities to sell products to each other for intermediate use, z_{ii} may be nonzero and is therefore included in the equation. Lastly, every industry also has sales to purchasers that are treated as exogenous to the industrial sectors. This is referred to as final demand and denoted by y_i. Expressing the preceding equation in matrix notation gives:

$$\begin{pmatrix} x_1 \\ x_2 \\ \vdots \\ x_n \end{pmatrix} = \begin{bmatrix} z_{11} & z_{12} & \cdots & z_{1n} \\ z_{21} & z_{22} & \cdots & z_{2n} \\ \vdots & \vdots & \ddots & \vdots \\ z_{n1} & z_{n2} & \cdots & z_{nn} \end{bmatrix} \begin{pmatrix} 1 \\ 1 \\ \vdots \\ 1 \end{pmatrix} + \begin{pmatrix} y_1 \\ y_2 \\ \vdots \\ y_n \end{pmatrix}$$

or:

$$\boldsymbol{x} = \boldsymbol{Zi} + \boldsymbol{y}$$

The basic model also makes use of technical coefficients, $a_{ij} = z_{ij}/x_j$, which are assumed to be fixed in a given time period. These represent the amount of an industry's output used by another in producing its output. Given this information, the gross output equation can be reexpressed as:

$$\boldsymbol{x} = \boldsymbol{Ax} + \boldsymbol{y}$$

With some rearranging and assuming that the matrix $I-A$ is nonsingular, we have the fundamental Leontief identity:

$$\boldsymbol{x} = (\boldsymbol{I} - \boldsymbol{A})^{-1}\boldsymbol{y}$$

The matrix $\boldsymbol{L} = (\boldsymbol{I} - \boldsymbol{A})^{-1}$ is often referred to as the Leontief inverse. Each element of this matrix, l_{ij}, is called a total output coefficient, which encapsulates the output needed from sector i needed to satisfy one unit's worth of j's final demand. The use of the word "total" is important because the solution to the basic input-output model shows that the final demand from exogenous sectors triggers back-and-forth transactions among economic sectors due to their interconnectedness.

Reference:

Miller, R. and Blair, P. 2022. Input-Output Analysis – Foundations and Extensions (3rd ed.). Cambridge University Press.

The simplest SDA decomposes changes in the emissions of an industry in an economy between two time periods into three effects: (i) intensity effect, which attributes changes in emissions due to changes in emissions released per unit of output; (ii) intermediate input composition effect, which attributes changes in emissions to changes in production structure captured by input coefficients and the Leontief inverse; and (ii) final demand effect, which captures changes due to the scale and composition of final demand.

Let F represent the total emissions and define it as:

$$F = f\,(I - A)^{-1}y$$

where:
f is the vector of emission intensities (i.e., emissions per unit of output),
A is the input-output coefficient matrix,
$(I-A)^{-1}$ is the Leontief inverse L, and
y is the vector of final demand.

Also, let F^0 be the value in base year and F^1 the value in another (typically more current) year. The change in emissions is given by:

$$\Delta F = F^1 - F^0$$

Change in emissions ΔF is decomposed into contributions from intensity Δf, production technology ΔL, and final demand Δy, such that:

$$\Delta F = \Delta f + \Delta L + \Delta y$$

A common decomposition approach uses the average of polar decomposition:

$$\Delta F \approx \frac{1}{2}[(f^1 - f^0)L^0y^0 + f^1(L^1 - L^0)y^0 + f^1L^1(y^1 - y^0)] +$$
$$\frac{1}{2}[(f^1 - f^0)L^1y^1 + f^0(L^1 - L^0)y^1 + f^0L^0(y^1 - y^0)]$$

where superscripts 1 and 0 denote the two time periods in comparison.

This yields three components.

Intensity effect is given by:

$$\Delta F_f = \frac{1}{2}[(f^1 - f^0)L^0y^0 + (f^1 - f^0)L^1y^1]$$

A negative intensity effect implies an improvement in emissions intensity, while a positive intensity effect implies a worsening of emissions intensity.

Intermediate input composition effect is given by:

$$\Delta F_L = \frac{1}{2}[f^1(L^1 - L^0)y^0 + f^0(L^1 - L^0)y^1]$$

A positive input composition effect indicates more demand for emissions-intensive sources of intermediate inputs, whereas a negative input composition effect indicates less demand for emissions-intensive inputs.

Final demand effect is given by:

$$\Delta F_y = \frac{1}{2}[f^1L^1(y^1 - y^0) + f^0L^0(y^1 - y^0)]$$

A positive final demand effect suggests increased consumption or investment in goods and services that are emissions-intensive to produce, whereas a negative final demand effect suggests a decline in consumption or investment in goods and services that cause emissions when produced.

Each term isolates one factor while holding others constant at either base (0) or current year (1) values. This decomposition is useful for pinpointing whether sustainability gains (or setbacks) stem from cleaner production, structural shifts, or changes in demand.

References

Carbon Disclosure Project (CDP). 2022. Relevance of Scope 3 Categories by Sector: CDP Corporate Questionnaire. *CDP Technical Note*. https://cdn.cdp.net/cdp-production/cms/guidance_docs/pdfs/000/003/504/original/CDP-technical-note-scope-3-relevance-by-sector.pdf.

Miller, R. and P. Blair. 2022. *Input-Output Analysis: Foundations and Extensions*. 3rd ed. Cambridge University Press.

World Business Council for Sustainable Development (WBCSD) and World Resources Institute (WRI). 2004. *The Greenhouse Gas Protocol: A Corporate Accounting and Reporting Standard*. Revised ed. https://ghgprotocol.org/sites/default/files/standards/ghg-protocol-revised.pdf.

APPENDIX 3

Measuring the Supply Chain for Green Goods

Based on a total of 14 studies and trade agreements, including four focused on trade negotiations and 10 centered on analytical and policy support, the Asian Development Bank (ADB) gathered information on "green" goods available across the world (Table A3.1).

From these references, ADB developed two distinct lists. The first is an overall list of all the green goods identified across all the references; a total of 1,062 goods. The second is a refined list that includes only the most recurring goods, referring to those that appeared in at least 10 of the 14 studies and agreements. This second list contains only 12 goods and constitutes the most conservative estimates of green goods.

This ADB study adapts the methodology presented in the United Nations Industrial Development Organization report *Measuring and Benchmarking the Green Industrial Performance of Countries and Economies: The GIP Index* by de Alba and Todorov (2022), while introducing key methodological refinements. Specifically, the study substitutes COMTRADE with BACI trade data for exports and utilizes the INDSTAT database for output data. Employment data were sourced from the International Labour Organization. To disaggregate green products within an industry, product-level export data were used as these are the most detailed available.

The methodology also uses data from ADB's multiregional input-output table (MRIOT) dataset, specifically the intermediate transactions matrix. It first derives the input and output shares. These shares represent the percentage distribution of each category, green and nongreen, within each sector. The intermediate transactions matrix is first disaggregated by columns using the diagonalized input shares. This step allocates the inputs consumed by green and nongreen firms across sectors. The resulting matrix is then further disaggregated by rows using the diagonalized output shares, which allocate the outputs supplied by green and nongreen firms. The result is an MRIOT that provides a clear separation of green and nongreen components within each MRIOT sector.
To estimate the contribution of green products, the methodology adopts the approach used in ADB's 2021 report *Capturing the Digital Economy: A Proposed Measurement Framework and Its Applications – A Special Supplement to Key Indicators for Asia and the Pacific 2021* in the context of measuring the digital economy.

Table A3.1: Studies and Agreements Relevant to Green and Environmental Goods

Title	Year Published
Trade Negotiations	
The APEC List of Environmental Goods	2012
Agreement on Climate Change, Trade and Sustainability (ACCTS)	2019
Trade and Environmental Sustainability Structured Discussions (TESSD)	2021
Singapore-Australia Green Economy Agreement (SAGEA)	2022
Analytic and Policy Support	
World Development Report 2010: Development and Climate Change	2007
Promoting the International Transfer of Low Carbon Technologies: Evidence and Policy Challenges	2013
OECD Combined List of Environmental Goods (CLEG)	2014
Eurostat Environmental Goods and Services Sector (EGSS)	2014
Critical Supply Chains: The Semiconductor Supply Chain	2021
IMF Climate Change Indicators Dashboard	2021
World Economic Forum Climate Trade Zero Initiative	2022
UNIDO Green Products List	2022
Decarbonization Technologies for a Net Zero Future	2024
Harmonized System and Schedule B Codes for the Environmental Technologies Industry	2024

APEC = Asia-Pacific Economic Cooperation, IMF = International Monetary Fund, OECD = Organisation for Economic Co-operation and Development, UNIDO = United Nations Industrial Development Organization.

Source: Asian Development Bank compilation.

References

de Alba, J. and V. Todorov. 2022. Measuring and Benchmarking the Green Industrial Performance of Countries and Economies: the GIP Index. *Inclusive and Sustainable Industrial Development Working Paper Series*. No. 1. United Nations Industrial Development Organization.

Asian Development Bank. 2024. *Capturing the Digital Economy: A Proposed Measurement Framework and its Applications*. https://data.adb.org/dataset/capturing-digital-economy-proposed-measurement-framework-and-its-applications.

Definitions

Sustainable Development Goals

Goals and Targets	Statistical Indicators	Definition
Goal 1. End poverty in all its forms everywhere		
Target 1.1: By 2030, eradicate extreme poverty (currently measured as people living on less than $2.15 a day) for all people everywhere.	1.1.1.a: Proportion of the population living below the international poverty line, by sex, age, employment status, and geographical location (urban or rural)	Proportion of the population living on less than $2.15 a day, measured at 2017 international prices, adjusted for purchasing power parity (PPP). Note: The PPP conversion factor for private consumption is the number of units of an economy's currency required to buy the same amount of goods and/or services in the domestic market as a United States (US) dollar would buy in the US.
	1.1.1.b: Proportion of the employed population living below the international poverty line, by sex	Proportion of the employed population living in households with per capita consumption or income below the international poverty line of $2.15 a day. Note: The proportion of working poor in total employment (also known as the working poverty rate) combines data on household income or consumption with labor force framework variables measured at the individual level, and sheds light on the relationship between household poverty and employment. The numbers are International Labour Organization modeled estimates. Employed persons refer to all persons of working age who, during a short reference period such as a day or a week, performed work for others in exchange for pay or profit.
Target 1.2: By 2030, reduce at least by half the proportion of men, women, and children of all ages living in poverty in all its dimensions, according to national definitions.	1.2.1: Proportion of the population living below the national poverty line, by sex, age, and geographical location (urban or rural)	Percentage of the total population living below the national poverty line. Note: National poverty rates are defined at economy-specific poverty lines in local currencies, which are different in real terms across economies and different from the international poverty line of $2.15 a day. Thus, national poverty rates cannot be compared across economies or with the poverty rate of $2.15 a day.
	1.2.2 Proportion of the population living in multidimensional poverty (%)	The proportion of the population living in poverty in all its dimensions according to national definitions. Note: Data collection methods used for calculating indicators differ from survey to survey in each country or economy.
Target 1.3: Implement nationally appropriate social protection systems and measures for all, including floors, and by 2030 achieve substantial coverage of the poor and the vulnerable	1.3.1: Proportion of the population covered by social protection floors/systems, by sex, distinguishing children, unemployed persons, older persons, persons with disabilities, pregnant women, newborns, work-injury victims and the poor and the vulnerable.	Percentage of the population effectively covered by a social protection system, including social protection floors, which provide old age pensions, social security, and health insurance benefits. Effective coverage of social protection is measured by the number of people who are either actively contributing to a social insurance scheme or receiving benefits (contributory or noncontributory). Coverage is expressed as a share of the respective population.

(continued on next page)

Goals and Targets	Statistical Indicators	Definition
		Population covered by at least one social protection cash benefit: proportion of the total population receiving at least one contributory or noncontributory cash benefit, or actively contributing to at least one social security scheme. (i) Older persons receiving a pension: ratio of persons above statutory retirement age receiving an old-age pension to the number of persons above statutory retirement age (including contributory and noncontributory). (ii) Poor persons receiving social assistance cash benefit: ratio of social assistance recipients to the population living below the national poverty line. (iii) Vulnerable persons receiving benefits: ratio of social assistance recipients to the total number of vulnerable persons (calculated by subtracting from total population all people of working age who are contributing to a social insurance scheme or receiving contributory benefits, and persons above retirement age receiving contributory benefits, i.e., pensions). (iv) Children covered by social protection benefits: ratio of children or households receiving child or family cash benefits to the total number of children or households with children.
Target 1.a: Ensure significant mobilization of resources from a variety of sources, including through enhanced development cooperation, in order to provide adequate and predictable means for developing countries (or economies), in particular least developed economies, to implement programmes and policies to end poverty un all its dimensions	1.a.1: Total official development assistance grants from all donors that focus on poverty reduction as a share of the recipient economy's gross national income	Total official development assistance (ODA) grants from all donors that focus on poverty reduction as a share of the recipient economy's gross national income. The OECD/Development Assistance Committee (DAC) defines ODA as "flows to countries and territories on the DAC List of ODA Recipients and to multilateral institutions which are i) provided by official agencies, including state and local governments, or by their executive agencies; and ii) each transaction is administered with the promotion of the economic development and welfare of developing countries as its main objective; and is concessional in character and conveys a grant element of at least 25 per cent (calculated at a rate of discount of 10 per cent). Poverty reduction items can be defined as ODA to basic social services (basic health, basic education, basic water and sanitation, population programs and reproductive health) and developmental food aid.
Goal 2. End hunger, achieve food security and improved nutrition, and promote sustainable agriculture		
Target 2.1: By 2030, end hunger and ensure access by all people, in particular the poor and people in vulnerable situations, including infants, to safe, nutritious, and sufficient food all year round.	2.1.1: Prevalence of undernourishment	Proportion of the population whose habitual food consumption is insufficient to provide the dietary energy levels that are required to maintain a normal active and healthy life. Note: Undernourishment is defined as the condition by which a person has access, on a regular basis, to the amount of food that are insufficient to provide the energy required for conducting a normal, healthy, and active life, given his or her own dietary energy requirements.
Target 2.2: By 2030, end all forms of malnutrition, including achieving, by 2025, the internationally agreed targets on stunting and wasting in children under 5 years of age, and address the nutritional needs of adolescent girls, pregnant and lactating women, and older persons.	2.2.1: Prevalence of stunting—height for age <-2 standard deviation from the median of the World Health Organization (WHO) Child Growth Standards—among children under 5 years of age	Prevalence of stunting—height-for-age <-2 standard deviation from the median of WHO Child Growth Standards—among children under 5 years of age. Note: Child stunting refers to a child who is too short for his or her age and is the result of chronic or recurrent malnutrition.

(continued on next page)

Goals and Targets	Statistical Indicators	Definition
	2.2.2.a: Prevalence of malnutrition—weight for height >+2 standard deviation from the median of the WHO Child Growth Standards—among children under 5 years of age (overweight)	Prevalence of overweight—weight for height >+2 standard deviation from the median of WHO Child Growth Standards—among children under 5 years of age. Note: Child overweight refers to a child who is too heavy for his or her height.
	2.2.2.b: Prevalence of malnutrition—weight for height <-2 standard deviation from the median of the WHO Child Growth Standards—among children under 5 years of age (wasting)	Prevalence of wasting—weight for height <-2 standard deviation from the median of WHO Child Growth Standards—among children under 5 years of age. Note: Child wasting refers to a child who is too thin for his or her height and is the result of recent rapid weight loss or the failure to gain weight.
Target 2.a: Increase investment, including through enhanced international cooperation, in rural infrastructure, agricultural research and extension services, technology development, and plant and livestock gene banks in order to enhance agricultural productive capacity in developing countries (or economies), particularly least developed countries (or economies).	2.a.1: The agriculture orientation index for government expenditures	The Agriculture Orientation Index for Government Expenditures is defined as agriculture's share of government expenditure, divided by agriculture's value-added share of gross domestic product (GDP), where "agriculture" refers to the agriculture, forestry, fishing, and hunting sector. The measure is a currency-free index calculated as the ratio of these two shares. National governments are requested to compile government expenditures according to the Government Finance Statistics system and the Classification of Functions of Government, and to calculate agriculture's value-added share of GDP according to the System of National Accounts. Note: "Government expenditures" are all expenses and acquisitions of nonfinancial assets associated with supporting a particular sector, as defined in the Government Finance Statistics Manual 2014 developed by the International Monetary Fund.
	2.a.2: Total official flows (official development assistance plus other official flows) to the agriculture sector	Gross disbursements of total official development assistance (ODA) and other official flows from all donors to the agriculture sector. Note: The Development Assistance Committee defines ODA as those flows to economies and territories on the committee's List of ODA Recipients and to multilateral institutions which are: (i) provided by official agencies, including state and local governments, or by their executive agencies; and (ii) each transaction is administered with the promotion of the economic development and welfare of developing economies as its main objective; and (iii) is concessional in character and conveys a grant element of at least 25% (calculated at a rate of discount of 10%). Other Official Flows are defined as transactions by the official sector which do not meet the conditions for eligibility as ODA, either because they are not primarily aimed at development, or because they are not sufficiently concessional. They also exclude officially supported export credits.

(continued on next page)

Goals and Targets	Statistical Indicators	Definition
Goal 3. Ensure healthy lives and promote well-being for all at all ages		
Target 3.1: By 2030, reduce the global maternal mortality ratio to less than 70 per 100,000 live births.	3.1.1: Maternal mortality ratio	Number of maternal deaths during a given time period per 100,000 live births during the same time period. It depicts the risk of maternal death relative to the number of live births and essentially captures the risk of death in a single pregnancy (proxied by a single live birth). Note: Maternal death refers to the death of a woman while pregnant or within 42 days of termination of pregnancy, irrespective of the duration and site of the pregnancy, from any cause related to or aggravated by the pregnancy or its management (from direct or indirect obstetric death), but not from unintentional or incidental causes.
	3.1.2: Proportion of births attended by skilled health personnel	Proportion of childbirths attended by skilled health personnel (generally doctors, nurses, or midwives, but can refer to other health professionals providing childbirth care). These are competent maternal and newborn health professionals educated, trained, and regulated to national and/or international standards. They are competent to: (i) provide and promote evidence-based, human-rights-based, quality, socioculturally sensitive, and dignified care to women and newborns; (ii) facilitate physiological processes during labor and delivery to ensure a clean and positive childbirth experience; and (iii) identify and manage or refer women and/or newborns with complications. Note: Having a skilled attendant at the time of childbirth is an important lifesaving intervention for both women and newborns. Not having access to this key assistance is detrimental to the health of women and newborns because lack of such access could cause adverse health outcomes such as the death of the woman and/or the newborn or long-lasting morbidity. Achieving universal coverage is therefore essential for reducing maternal and newborn mortality and morbidity.
Target 3.2: By 2030, end preventable deaths of newborns and children under 5 years of age, with all economies aiming to reduce neonatal mortality to at least as low as 12 per 1,000 live births and under-5 mortality to at least as low as 25 per 1,000 live births.	3.2.1: Under-5 mortality rate	The probability of a child born in a specific year or period dying before reaching the age of 5 years, if subject to age-specific mortality rates of that period, expressed as deaths per 1,000 live births. Note: The under-5 mortality rate as defined here is, strictly speaking, not a rate (i.e., the number of deaths divided by the number of population at risk during a certain period of time) but rather is a probability of death derived from a life table and expressed as a rate per 1,000 live births.
	3.2.2: Neonatal mortality rate	Probability that a child born in a specific year or period will die during the first 28 completed days of life, if subject to age-specific mortality rates of that period, expressed per 1,000 live births. Note: Neonatal deaths (deaths among live births during the first 28 completed days of life) may be subdivided into early neonatal deaths, occurring during the first 7 days of life, and late neonatal deaths, occurring after the seventh day but before the 28th completed day of life.

(continued on next page)

Goals and Targets	Statistical Indicators	Definition
Target 3.3: By 2030, end the epidemics of AIDS, tuberculosis, malaria, and neglected tropical diseases; and combat hepatitis, water-borne diseases, and other communicable diseases.	3.3.1: Number of new HIV infections per 1,000 uninfected population, by sex, age, and key populations	The number of new HIV infections per 1,000 persons among the uninfected population.
	3.3.2: Tuberculosis incidence per 100,000 population	Estimated number of new and relapse tuberculosis cases (all forms of tuberculosis, including cases in people living with HIV) arising in a given year, expressed as a rate per 100,000 population.
	3.3.3: Malaria incidence per 1,000 population	The number of new cases of malaria per 1,000 people at risk each year.
Target 3.4: By 2030, reduce by one third premature mortality from noncommunicable diseases through prevention and treatment, and promote mental health and well-being.	3.4.1: Mortality rate attributed to cardiovascular disease, cancer, diabetes, or chronic respiratory disease	Probability of dying between the ages of 30 and 70 years from cardiovascular diseases, cancer, diabetes, or chronic respiratory diseases, defined as the percent of 30-year-old people who would die before their 70th birthday from cardiovascular disease, cancer, diabetes, or chronic respiratory disease, assuming that s/he would experience current mortality rates at every age and s/he would not die from any other cause of death (e.g., injuries or HIV/AIDS). Note: Probability of dying refers to the likelihood that an individual would die between two ages given current mortality rates at each age, calculated using life table methods.
	3.4.2: Suicide mortality rate	The number of suicide deaths in a year, divided by the population and multiplied by 100,000.
Target 3.6: By 2020, halve the number of global deaths and injuries from road traffic accidents.	3.6.1: Death rate due to road traffic injuries	Number of road traffic fatal injury deaths per 100,000 population.
Target 3.7: By 2030, ensure universal access to sexual and reproductive health care services, including for family planning, information and education, and the integration of reproductive health into national strategies and programme	3.7.1: Proportion of women of reproductive age (15–49 years) who have their need for family planning satisfied by modern methods	The percentage of women of reproductive age (15-49 years) currently using a modern method of contraception among those who desire either to have no (additional) children or to postpone the next pregnancy. The indicator is also referred to as the demand for family planning satisfied with modern methods.
	3.7.2: Adolescent birth rate (15–19 years) per 1,000 women in that age group	Annual number of births to females aged 15–19 years per 1,000 females in the respective age group.
Target 3.8: Achieve universal health coverage, including financial risk protection, access to quality essential healthcare services and access to safe, effective, quality and affordable essential medicines and vaccines for all	3.8.1 Coverage of essential health services	Coverage of essential health services is defined as the average coverage of essential services based on tracer interventions that include reproductive, maternal, newborn and child health, infectious diseases, non-communicable diseases and service capacity and access, among the general and the most disadvantaged population. The indicator is an index reported on a unitless scale of 0 to 100, which is calculated as the geometric mean of 14 tracer indicators of health service coverage. Note: The index of health service coverage is calculated as the geometric means of tracer indicators. The tracer indicators are organized by four broad categories of service coverage: (i) reproductive, maternal, newborn, and child health; (ii) infectious diseases; (iii) noncommunicable diseases; and (iv) service capacity and access.

(continued on next page)

Goals and Targets	Statistical Indicators	Definition
Target 3.9: By 2030, substantially reduce the number of deaths and illnesses from hazardous chemicals and air, water, and soil pollution and contamination.	3.9.1: Mortality rate attributed to household and ambient air pollution	The mortality rate attributable to the joint effects of household and ambient air pollution can be expressed as: crude death rate or age-standardized death rate. Crude rates are calculated by dividing the brut number of deaths by the total population (or indicated if a different population group is used, e.g. children under 5 years), while the age-standardized rates adjust for differences in the age distribution of the population by applying the observed age-specific mortality rates for each population to a standard population. Note: Evidence from epidemiological studies has shown that exposure to air pollution is linked to, among others, the important diseases taken into account in this estimate: - acute respiratory infections (estimated in all age groups); - cerebrovascular diseases (stroke) in adults (estimated above 25 years); - ischemic heart diseases (IHD) in adults (estimated above 25 years of); - chronic obstructive pulmonary disease (COPD) in adults (estimated above 25 years); and - lung cancer in adults (estimated above 25 years).
	3.9.2: Mortality rate attributed to unsafe water, unsafe sanitation, and lack of hygiene—exposure to unsafe water, sanitation, and hygiene for all (WASH) services	Number of deaths from unsafe water, unsafe sanitation, and lack of hygiene —exposure to unsafe water, sanitation and hygiene for all (WASH) services—in a year, divided by the population, and multiplied by 100,000.
Target 3.c: Substantially increase health financing and the recruitment, development, training, and retention of the health workforce in developing economies, especially in least developed economies and small island developing States	3.c.1: Health worker density and distribution	Density of medical doctors: The density of medical doctors is defined as the number of medical doctors, including generalists and specialist medical practitioners, per 10,000 population in a given national and/or subnational area. The International Standard Classification of Occupations (ISCO) unit group codes included in this category are 221, 2211, and 2212 of ISCO-08. Density of nursing and midwifery personnel: The density of nursing and midwifery personnel is defined as the number of nursing and midwifery personnel per 10,000 population in a given national and/or subnational area. The ISCO-08 codes included in this category are 2221, 2222, 3221, and 3222.
Target 3.d: Strengthen the capacity of all economies, in particular developing economies, for early warning, risk reduction, and management of national and global health risks	3.d.1: International Health Regulations (IHR) capacity and health emergency preparedness	The revised International Health Regulations (IHR) were adopted in 2005 and entered into force in 2007. Under the IHR, States Parties are obliged to develop and maintain minimum core capacities for surveillance and response, including at points of entry, in order to early detect, assess, notify, and respond to any potential public health events of international concern. Article 54 of the IHR states that: States Parties and the Director-General shall report to the Health Assembly on the implementation of these Regulations as decided by the Health Assembly. The IHR States Parties Self-assessment Annual Reporting tool captures the level of self-assessed national capacities. They are essential public health capacities that States Parties are required to have in place throughout their territories pursuant to Articles 5 and 12, and Annex 1A of the IHR (2005) requirements.

(continued on next page)

Goals and Targets	Statistical Indicators	Definition
		Based on the lessons learned from the COVID-19 pandemic, the World Health Organization published the revised second edition of the IHR State Parties Self-assessment Annual Reporting Tool in 2021 with new indicators related to gender equality in health emergencies, advocacy for IHR implementation, and community engagement, to name a few. The revisions are intended to improve the assessment of the IHR core capacities and the preparedness of State Parties for health emergencies. The indicator SDG 3.d.1 reflects the capacities State Parties of the International Health Regulations (2005) (IHR) had agreed and committed to developing. Note: The second edition SPAR tool has been expanded from 13 to 15 capacities. The 15 core capacities are (1) Policy, legal and normative instruments to implement IHR; (2) IHR Coordination and National Focal Point Functions; (3) Financing; (4) Laboratory; (5) Surveillance; (6) Human resources; (7) Health emergency management (8) Health Service Provision; (9) Infection Prevention and Control; (10) Risk communication and community engagement; (11) Points of entry and border health; (12) Zoonotic diseases; (13) Food safety; (14) Chemical events; (15) Radiation emergencies.
Goal 4. Ensure inclusive and equitable quality education and promote lifelong learning opportunities for all		
Target 4.1: By 2030, ensure that all girls and boys complete free, equitable, and quality primary and secondary education leading to relevant and effective learning outcomes	4.1.1.b: Proportion of children and young people at the end of primary achieving at least a minimum proficiency level 4.1.1.c: Proportion of children and young people at the end of lower secondary achieving at least a minimum proficiency level	Percentage of children and young people achieving at least a minimum proficiency level in (i) reading and (ii) mathematics at the end of primary education and at the end of lower secondary education. The minimum proficiency level will be measured relative to new common reading and mathematics scales currently in development. Note: This indicator is expressed as proportion of children and/or young people at the relevant stage of education in a given year achieving or exceeding the pre-defined proficiency level in a given subject.
	4.1.2: Completion rate (primary education, lower secondary education, upper secondary education)	Percentage of a cohort of children or young people aged 3–5 years above the intended age for the last grade of each level of education who have completed that grade. Note: A completion rate at or near 100% indicates that all or most children and adolescents have completed a level of education by the time they are 3 to 5 years older than the official age of entry into the last grade of that level of education. A low completion rate indicates low or delayed entry into a given level of education, high drop-out, high repetition, late completion, or a combination of these factors.
Target 4.2: By 2030, ensure that all girls and boys have access to quality early childhood development, care, and preprimary education, so that they are ready for primary education.	4.2.2: Participation rate in organized learning (1 year before the official primary entry age), by sex	Percentage of children in the given age range who participate in one or more organized learning programs, including programs which offer a combination of education and care. Participation in early childhood and in primary education are both included. The age range will vary by economy depending on the official age for entry to primary education. Note: An organized learning program is one that consists of a coherent set or sequence of educational activities designed with the intention of achieving predetermined learning outcomes or the accomplishment of a specific set of educational tasks. Early childhood and primary education programs are examples of organized learning programs. The official primary entry age is the age at which children are obliged to start primary education, according to national legislation or policies.

(continued on next page)

Goals and Targets	Statistical Indicators	Definition
Target 4.c: By 2030, substantially increase the supply of qualified teachers, including through international cooperation for teacher training in developing economies, especially least developed economies and small island developing states.	4.c.1.a: Proportion of teachers in preprimary education who have received at least the minimum organized teacher training 4.c.1.b: Proportion of teachers in primary education who have received at least the minimum organized teacher training 4.c.1.c: Proportion of teachers in lower secondary education who have received at least the minimum organized teacher training 4.c.1.d: Proportion of teachers in upper secondary education who have received at least the minimum organized teacher training	Percentage of teachers by level of education taught (pre-primary, primary, lower secondary, and upper secondary education) who have received at least the minimum organized pedagogical teacher training pre-service and in-service required for teaching at the relevant level in a given economy. Note: Number of teachers in a given level of education who are trained is expressed as a percentage of all teachers in that level of education. A teacher is trained if they have received at least the minimum organized pedagogical teacher training pre-service and in-service required for teaching at the relevant level in each economy.
Goal 5. Achieve gender equality and empower all women and girls		
Target 5.3: Eliminate all harmful practices, such as child, early, and forced marriage, and female genital mutilation.	5.3.1: Proportion of women aged 20–24 years who were married or in a union before age 15 and before age 18	Proportion of women aged 20–24 years who were married or in a union before age 15 years and before age 18 years. Note: Both formal (i.e., marriages) and informal unions are covered under this indicator. Informal unions are generally defined as those in which a couple lives together (i.e., cohabits) for some time, intends to have a lasting relationship, but for which there has been no formal civil or religious ceremony.
Target 5.5: Ensure women's full and effective participation in, and equal opportunities for leadership at, all levels of decision-making in political, economic, and public life.	5.5.1: Proportion of seats held by women in national parliaments	The proportion of seats held by women in national parliaments, as of 1 January of reporting year, is currently measured as the number of seats held by women members in single or lower chambers of national parliaments, expressed as a percentage of all occupied seats. Note: National parliaments can be bicameral or unicameral. This indicator covers the single chamber in unicameral parliaments and the lower chamber in bicameral parliaments. It does not cover the upper chamber of bicameral parliaments. Seats are usually won by members in general parliamentary elections. Seats may also be filled by nomination, appointment, indirect election, rotation of members, and by-election. Seats refer to the number of parliamentary mandates, or the number of members of parliament.
	5.5.2: Proportion of women in managerial positions	Proportion of females in the total number of persons employed in senior and middle management. Senior and middle management correspond to major group 1 in International Standard Classification of Occupations (ISCO)-08 and ISCO-88, minus category 14 in ISCO-08 (hospitality, retail, and other services managers) and minus category 13 in ISCO-88 (general managers), since these comprise mainly managers of small enterprises.

(continued on next page)

Goals and Targets	Statistical Indicators	Definition
		Note: The indicator provides information on the proportion of women who are employed in decision-making and managerial roles in government, large enterprises, and institutions, thus providing some insight into women's power in decision-making and in the economy (especially compared to men's power in those areas).
Goal 6. Ensure availability and sustainable management of water and sanitation for all		
Target 6.1: By 2030, achieve universal and equitable access to safe and affordable drinking water for all.	6.1.1: Proportion of population using safely managed drinking water services	The proportion of the population using safely managed drinking water services is currently measured by the proportion of the population using an improved basic drinking water source that is located on premises, available when needed, and free from fecal and priority chemical contamination. Note: Improved drinking water sources include the following: piped water into a dwelling, yard, or plot; public taps or standpipes; boreholes or tubewells; protected dug wells; protected springs; packaged water; delivered water and rainwater. "Located on premises": a water source at the point of collection is within the dwelling, yard, or plot. "Available when needed": households are able to access sufficient quantities of water when needed. "Free from fecal and priority chemical contamination": water complies with relevant national or local standards. In the absence of such standards, reference is made to the WHO Guidelines for Drinking Water Quality https://www.who.int/teams/environment-climate-change-and-health/water-sanitation-and-health/water-safety-and-quality/drinking-water-quality-guidelines. E. coli or thermotolerant coliforms are the preferred indicator for microbiological quality, and arsenic and fluoride are the priority chemicals for global reporting. The WHO/UNICEF Joint Monitoring Programme (JMP) for Water Supply, Sanitation, and Hygiene estimates access to basic services for each economy, separately in urban and rural areas, by fitting a regression line to a series of data points from household surveys and censuses. This approach was used to report on use of 'improved water' sources for Millennium Development Goal monitoring. The JMP is evaluating the use of alternative statistical estimation methods as more data become available. The JMP 2017 update and SDG baselines report describes in more detail how data on availability and quality from different sources, can be combined with data on use of different types of supplies, as recorded in the current JMP database to compute the safely managed drinking water services indicator. https://washdata.org/report/jmp-methodology-2017-update https://washdata.org/report/jmp-2017-report-final

(continued on next page)

Goals and Targets	Statistical Indicators	Definition
Target 6.2: By 2030, achieve access to adequate and equitable sanitation and hygiene for all, and end open defecation, paying special attention to the needs of women and girls and those in vulnerable situations.	6.2.1.a: Proportion of population using safely managed sanitation services	The proportion of the population using a basic sanitation facility, including handwashing facility with soap and water, that is not shared with other households and where excreta is safely disposed in situ or treated off-site. Note: Improved sanitation facilities include flush or pour-flush toilets to sewer systems, septic tanks or pit latrines, ventilated improved pit latrines, pit latrines with a slab, and composting toilets. “Safely disposed in situ”: when pit latrines and septic tanks are not emptied, the excreta may still remain isolated from human contact and can be considered safely managed. For example, with the new SDG indicator, households that use twin pit latrines or safely abandon full pit latrines and dig new facilities, a common practice in rural areas, would be counted as using safely managed sanitation services. “Treated offsite”: not all excreta from toilet facilities conveyed in sewers (as wastewater) or emptied from pit latrines and septic tanks (as fecal sludge) reaches a treatment site. For instance, a portion may leak from the sewer itself or, due to broken pumping installations, be discharged directly to the environment. Similarly, a portion of the fecal sludge emptied from containers may be discharged into open drains, to open ground or water bodies, rather than being transported to a treatment plant. And finally, even once the excreta reach a treatment plant a portion may remain untreated, due to dysfunctional treatment equipment or inadequate treatment capacity, and be discharged to the environment. For the purposes of SDG monitoring, adequacy of treatment will initially be assessed based on the reported level of treatment. “A handwashing facility with soap and water”: a handwashing facility is a device to contain, transport or regulate the flow of water to facilitate handwashing.
Target 6.4: By 2030, substantially increase water-use efficiency across all sectors and ensure sustainable withdrawals and supply of freshwater to address water scarcity and substantially reduce the number of people suffering from water scarcity.	6.4.2: Level of water stress: freshwater withdrawal as a proportion of available freshwater resources	The level of water stress: freshwater withdrawal as a proportion of available freshwater resources is the ratio between total freshwater withdrawn by all major sectors and total renewable freshwater resources, after taking into account environmental water requirements. Note: Total freshwater withdrawal is the volume of freshwater extracted from its source (rivers, lakes, aquifers) for agriculture, industries, and municipalities. Freshwater withdrawal includes primary freshwater (not withdrawn before), secondary freshwater (previously withdrawn and returned to rivers and groundwater, such as discharged wastewater and agricultural drainage water) and fossil groundwater. Main sectors, as defined by International Standard Industrial Classification standards, include agriculture, forestry and fishing, manufacturing, electricity industry, and services. Environmental water requirements are the quantities of water required to sustain freshwater and estuarine ecosystems. This indicator is also known as water withdrawal intensity. Total renewable freshwater resources are expressed as the sum of internal and external renewable water resources.

(continued on next page)

Goals and Targets	Statistical Indicators	Definition
		Internal renewable water resources are defined as the long-term average annual flow of rivers and recharge of groundwater, generated from endogenous precipitation, for a given economy. External renewable water resources refer to the flows of water entering the economy, taking into consideration the quantity of flows reserved to upstream and downstream economies through agreements or treaties.
Target 6.a: By 2030, expand international cooperation and capacity-building support to developing countries (or economies) in water- and sanitation-related activities and programmes, including water harvesting, desalination, water efficiency, wastewater treatment, recycling, and reuse technologies.	6.a.1: Amount of water- and sanitation-related ODA that is part of a government-coordinated spending plan	Amount of water- and sanitation-related ODA that is part of a government-coordinated spending plan is defined as the proportion of total water- and sanitation-related ODA disbursements that are included in the government budget. Note: The amount of water- and sanitation-related ODA is a quantifiable measurement as a proxy for "international cooperation and capacity development support" in financial terms. A low value of this indicator (near 0%) would suggest that international donors are investing in water- and sanitation-related activities and programs in the economy, outside the purview of the national government. A high value (near 100%) would indicate that donors are aligned with the national government and national policies and plans for water and sanitation.
Goal 7. Ensure access to affordable, reliable, sustainable, and modern energy for all		
Target 7.1: By 2030, ensure universal access to affordable, reliable, and modern energy services.	7.1.1: Proportion of population with access to electricity	Percentage of the population with access to electricity. Note: Access to electricity addresses major critical issues in all the dimensions of sustainable development. The target has a wide range of social and economic impacts, including facilitating development of household-based income-generating activities and lightening the burden of household tasks.
	7.1.2: Proportion of population with primary reliance on clean fuels and technology	Number of people using clean fuels and technologies for cooking, heating and lighting divided by total population reporting that any cooking, heating or lighting, expressed as percentage. "Clean" is defined by the emission rate targets and specific fuel recommendations (i.e., against unprocessed coal and kerosene) included in the normative guidance WHO guidelines for indoor air quality: household fuel combustion.
Target 7.2: By 2030, increase substantially the share of renewable energy in the global energy mix.	7.2.1: Renewable energy share in total final energy consumption	Percentage of final consumption of energy that is derived from renewable resources. Note: Renewable energy consumption includes consumption of energy derived from hydro, solid biofuels, wind, solar, liquid biofuels, biogas, geothermal, marine sources, and waste. Total final energy consumption is calculated from national balances and statistics as total final consumption minus nonenergy use.
Target 7.3: By 2030, double the global rate of improvement in energy efficiency.	7.3.1: Energy intensity measured in terms of primary energy and GDP	Energy supplied to the economy per unit value of economic output. Note: Total energy supply, as defined by the International Recommendations for Energy Statistics, is made up of production, plus net imports, minus international marine and aviation bunkers plus-stock changes. GDP is the measure of economic output. For international comparison purposes, GDP is measured in constant terms at PPP.

(continued on next page)

Goals and Targets	Statistical Indicators	Definition
Goal 8. Promote sustained, inclusive, and sustainable economic growth, full and productive employment, and decent work for all		
Target 8.1: Sustain per-capita economic growth in accordance with national circumstances and, in particular, at least 7% GDP growth per annum in the least developed economies.	8.1.1: Annual growth rate of real GDP per capita	Percentage change in the real GDP per capita between 2 consecutive years. Note: Real GDP per capita is calculated by dividing GDP at constant prices by the population of an economy or area. The data for real GDP is measured in constant US dollars to facilitate the calculation of economy growth rates and aggregation of the economy data.
Target 8.2: Achieve higher levels of economic productivity through diversification, technological upgrading, and innovation, including through a focus on high-value-added and labor-intensive sectors.	8.2.1: Annual growth rate of real GDP per employed person	Annual percentage change in real GDP per employed person. Note: The real GDP per employed person being a measure of labor productivity, this indicator represents a measure of labor productivity growth, thus providing information on the evolution, efficiency, and quality of human capital in the production process.
Target 8.5: By 2030, achieve full and productive employment and decent work for all women and men, including for young people and persons with disabilities, and equal pay for work of equal value.	8.5.2: Unemployment rate, by sex, age, and persons with disabilities	Percentage of persons in the labor force who are unemployed. Note: Unemployed persons are defined as all those of working age (usually persons aged 15 and above) who were not in employment, carried out activities to seek employment during a specified recent period, and were currently available to take up employment given a job opportunity, where: (i) "not in employment" is assessed with respect to the short reference period for the measurement of employment; (ii) to "seek employment" refers to any activity when carried out, during a specified recent period comprising the past 4 weeks or 1 month, for the purpose of finding a job or setting up a business or agricultural undertaking; (iii) the point when the enterprise starts to exist should be used to distinguish between search activities aimed at setting up a business and the work activity itself, as evidenced by the enterprise's registration to operate or by when financial resources become available, the necessary infrastructure or materials are in place, or the first client or order is received, depending on the context; and (iv) "currently available" serves as a test of readiness to start a job in the present, assessed with respect to a short reference period comprising that used to measure employment (depending on national circumstances, the reference period may be extended to include a short subsequent period not exceeding 2 weeks in total, so as to ensure adequate coverage of unemployment situations among different population groups).
Target 8.6: By 2020, substantially reduce the proportion of youth not in employment, education, or training.	8.6.1: Proportion of youth (aged 15–24 years) not in education, employment, or training	Proportion of youth (aged 15–24 years) who are not in education, employment, or training, also known as "the youth NEET rate".

(continued on next page)

Goals and Targets	Statistical Indicators	Definition
Target 8.7: Take immediate and effective measures to eradicate forced labor, end modern slavery and human trafficking, and secure the prohibition and elimination of the worst forms of child labor, including recruitment and use of child soldiers, and, by 2025, end child labor in all its forms.	8.7.1: Proportion of children aged 5–17 years engaged in child labor, by sex and age	The number of children aged 5–17 years reported to be in child labor during the reference period (usually the week prior to the survey). The proportion of children in child labor is calculated as the number of children in child labor, divided by the total number of children in the population.
Target 8.10: Strengthen the capacity of domestic financial institutions to encourage and expand access to banking, insurance, and financial services for all.	8.10.1: Number of commercial bank branches and ATMs per 100,000 adults	The number of commercial bank branches per 100,000 adults refers to the number of commercial banks branches reported by the central bank or the main financial regulator of the economy every year. To make it comparable, this number is presented as a reference per 100,000 adults in the respective economy. The number of ATMs per 100,000 adults, refers to the number of ATMs in the economy for all types of institutions, such as commercial banks, non-deposit-taking microfinance institutions, deposit-taking microfinance institutions, credit unions, financial cooperatives, and others. This information is reported every year by the central bank or the main financial regulator of the economy. To make it comparable, this number is presented as a reference per 100,000 adults in the respective economy.
	8.10.2: Proportion of adults (aged 15 years and older) with an account at a bank or other financial institution or with a mobile-money service provider	Percentage of adults (aged 15+) who report having an account (of their own or held with someone else) at a bank or another type of financial institution or have personally used a mobile-money service in the past 12 months.
Target 8.a: Increase Aid for Trade support for developing economies, in particular least developed economies, including through the Enhanced Integrated Framework for Trade-related Technical Assistance to Least Developed Economies	8.a.1 Aid for Trade commitments and disbursements	Aid for Trade commitments and disbursements is the gross disbursements and commitments of total Official Development Assistance (ODA) from all donors for aid for trade.
Goal 9. Build resilient infrastructure, promote inclusive and sustainable industrialization, and foster innovation		
Target 9.1: Develop quality, reliable, sustainable, and resilient infrastructure, including regional and transborder infrastructure, to support economic development and human well-being, with a focus on affordable and equitable access for all.	9.1.a: Passenger volume by road transport, measured in millions of passenger-kilometers	Passenger and freight volumes are the sums of the passenger and freight volumes reported for the road and rail carriers in terms of number of people and metric tons of cargo, respectively. Note: The International Transport Forum collects data on transport (rail and road) statistics on annual basis from all its member economies. Data are collected from transport ministries, statistical offices, and other institutions designated as official data sources. Although there are clear definitions for all the terms used in this survey, economies might have different methodologies to calculate passenger-kilometers and ton-kilometers. Methods could be based on traffic or mobility surveys, using very different sampling methods and estimating techniques, which could affect the comparability of the statistics.

(continued on next page)

Goals and Targets	Statistical Indicators	Definition
	9.1.b: Freight volume by road transport, measured in millions of ton-kilometers	
	9.1.c: Passenger volume by rail transport, measured in millions of passenger-kilometers	
	9.1.d: Freight volume by rail transport, measured in millions of ton-kilometers	
Target 9.2: Promote inclusive and sustainable industrialization and, by 2030, significantly raise industry's share of employment and GDP, in line with national circumstances, and double its share in least developed economies.	9.2.1: Manufacturing value added as a proportion of GDP and per capita	Manufacturing value added (MVA) as a proportion of GDP is a ratio between MVA and GDP, both reported in constant 2015 US dollars. MVA per capita is calculated by dividing MVA in constant 2015 US dollars by the population of an economy or area.
	9.2.2: Manufacturing employment as a proportion of total employment	Share of manufacturing employment in total employment.
Target 9.4: By 2030, upgrade infrastructure and retrofit industries to make them sustainable, with increased resource-use efficiency and greater adoption of clean and environmentally sound technologies and industrial processes, with all economies taking action in accordance with their respective capabilities.	9.4.1: Carbon dioxide (CO_2) emissions per unit of value-added	CO_2 emissions per unit of value-added is an indicator calculated as ratio between CO_2 emissions from fuel combustion and the value added of associated economic activities. The indicator can be calculated for the whole economy (total CO_2 emissions/GDP) or for specific sectors, notably the manufacturing sector (CO_2 emissions from manufacturing industries per manufacturing value added (MVA)). CO_2 emissions per unit of GDP PPP are expressed in kilograms of CO_2 per constant 2021 US dollar PPP of GDP. CO_2 emissions from manufacturing industries per unit of MVA are measured in kilograms of CO_2 per constant 2015 US dollars.
Target 9.5: Enhance scientific research and upgrade the technological capabilities of industrial sectors in all economies, in particular developing economies, including, by 2030, encouraging innovation and substantially increasing the number of research and development workers per 1 million people and public and private research and development spending.	9.5.1: Research and development expenditure as a proportion of GDP	Amount of research and experimental development expenditure divided by the total output of the economy.
	9.5.2: Researchers (full-time equivalent) per million inhabitants	Number of research and experimental development workers per 1 million people.

(continued on next page)

Goals and Targets	Statistical Indicators	Definition
Target 9.a: Facilitate sustainable and resilient infrastructure development in developing economies through enhanced financial, technological, and technical support to African economies, least developed economies, landlocked developing economies, and small island developing States.	9.a.1: Total official international support (ODA plus other official flows) to infrastructure	Gross disbursements of total ODA and other official flows from all donors in support of infrastructure.
Target 9.b: Support domestic technology development, research, and innovation in developing economies, including by ensuring a conducive policy environment for, among other things, industrial diversification and value addition to commodities.	9.b.1: Proportion of medium- and high-tech industry value-added in total value-added	The proportion of medium-high and high-tech industry (MHT) value added in total value added of manufacturing (MVA hereafter) is a ratio value between the value added of MHT industry and MVA. Note: Industrial development generally entails a structural transition from resource-based and low technology activities to MHT manufacturing activities. A modern, highly complex production structure offers better opportunities for skills development and technological innovation. MHT activities generally correspond to the industries with higher value addition and labor productivity. Increasing the share of MHT sectors also reflects the impact of innovation.
Target 9.c: Significantly increase access to information and communications technology and strive to provide universal and affordable access to the Internet in least developed economies by 2020.	9.c.1.a: Proportion of population covered by narrowband (2G) mobile networks 9.c.1.b: Proportion of population covered by 3G mobile networks 9.c.1.c: Proportion of population covered by LTE mobile networks	Proportion of the population covered by a mobile network, broken down by technology, refers to the percentage of inhabitants living within range of a mobile-cellular signal, irrespective of whether or not they are mobile-phone subscribers or users. This is calculated by dividing the number of inhabitants within range of a mobile-cellular signal by the total population and multiplying by 100. Note: Coverage refers to Long-Term Evolution (LTE), broadband (3G), and narrowband (2G) mobile-cellular technologies: 2G mobile population coverage refers to the percentage of inhabitants within range of a mobile networks with access to data communications (e.g. Internet) at downstream speeds below 256 Kbit/s. This includes mobile-cellular technologies such as general packet radio service (GPRS), code division multiple access (CDMA) 2000 1x and most enhanced data for GSM (global system for mobile communications) evolution (EDGE) implementations. 3G population coverage refers to the percentage of inhabitants that are within range of at least a 3G mobile-cellular signal, irrespective of whether or not they are subscribers. Long-term evolution (LTE) population coverage refers to the percentage of inhabitants that live within range of LTE/LTE-Advanced, mobile WiMAX/WirelessMAN or other more advanced mobile-cellular networks, irrespective of whether or not they are subscribers.
Goal 10. Reduce inequality within and among economies		
Target 10.1: By 2030, progressively achieve and sustain income growth of the bottom 40% of the population at a rate higher than the national average.	10.1.1.a: Growth rates of household expenditure or income per capita among the bottom 40% of the population	The growth rate in the welfare aggregate of the bottom 40% of the population is calculated as the annualized average growth rate in per capita real consumption or income of the bottom 40% of the income distribution in an economy, using household surveys over a period of approximately 5 years.

(continued on next page)

Goals and Targets	Statistical Indicators	Definition
	10.1.1.b: Growth rates of household expenditure or income per capita	The national average growth rate in the welfare aggregate is calculated as the annualized average growth rate in per capita real consumption or income of the total population in an economy from household surveys over a roughly 5-year period.
Goal 11. Make cities and human settlements inclusive, safe, resilient, and sustainable		
Target 11.1: By 2030, ensure access for all to adequate, safe, and affordable housing and basic services, and upgrade slums.	11.1.1: Proportion of the urban population living in slums, informal settlements, or inadequate housing	The proportion of the urban population that lives in slums or informal settlements as well as those living in inadequate housing. Note: Most of the criteria for defining slums, informal settlements, and inadequate housing overlap. The criteria for informal settlements are essentially captured in the definition of slums, which combines both slums and informal settlements as one entity. Slums and informal settlements are therefore combined into one component of the indicator, providing some continuity with what was captured under Millennium Development Goal 7. At a later stage, a composite index will be developed that will incorporate all measures (combining slums, informal settlements, and inadequate housing) to provide one estimate.
Target 11.5: By 2030, significantly reduce the number of deaths and the number of people affected, and substantially decrease the direct economic losses relative to global GDP caused by disasters, including water-related disasters, with a focus on protecting the poor and people in vulnerable situations	11.5.2: Direct economic loss in relation to global GDP	The ratio of direct economic loss attributed to disasters in relation to GDP. Direct economic loss is the monetary value of total or partial destruction of physical assets existing in the affected area. Direct economic loss is nearly equivalent to physical damage.
Target 11.6: By 2030, reduce the adverse per capita environmental impact of cities, including by paying special attention to air quality and municipal and other waste management.	11.6.2: Annual mean levels of fine particulate matter (PM), e.g., PM2.5 and PM10, in cities (population weighted)	The mean annual concentration of fine suspended particles of less than 2.5 microns in diameters (PM2.5) is a common measure of air pollution. The mean is a population-weighted average for urban population in a economy, and is expressed in micrograms per cubic meter [$\mu g/m^3$].
Goal 12. Ensure sustainable consumption and production patterns		
Target 12.2: By 2030, achieve the sustainable management and efficient use of natural resources	12.2.1: Material footprint, material footprint per capita, and material footprint per GDP	Material footprint is the attribution of global material extraction to domestic final demand of an economy. The total material footprint is the sum of the material footprint for biomass, fossil fuels, metal ores, and nonmetal minerals. This indicator is calculated as domestic extraction of materials plus raw material equivalent of imports minus raw material equivalents of exports. For the attribution of the primary material needs of final demand, a global, multiregional input-output framework is employed.
	12.2.2: Domestic material consumption, domestic material consumption per capita, and domestic material consumption per GDP	Domestic material consumption (DMC) is a standard material flow accounting indicator and reports the apparent consumption of materials in a national economy. DMC measures the total amount of material (biomass, fossil fuels, metal ores and non-metallic minerals) directly used in an economy and based on accounts of direct material flows, i.e., domestic material extraction and physical imports and exports.

(continued on next page)

Goals and Targets	Statistical Indicators	Definition
		Note: DMC reports the amount of materials that are used in a national economy. It is a territorial (production side) indicator. DMC also presents the amount of material that needs to be handled within an economy, which is either added to material stocks of buildings and transport infrastructure or used to fuel the economy as material throughput. It describes the physical dimension of economic processes and interactions. It can also be interpreted as long-term waste equivalent. Per capita DMC describes the average level of material use in an economy – an environmental pressure indicator – and is also referred to as metabolic profile.
Target 12.c: Rationalize inefficient fossil-fuel subsidies that encourage wasteful consumption by removing market distortions, in accordance with national circumstances, including by restructuring taxation and phasing out those harmful subsidies, where they exist, to reflect their environmental impacts, taking fully into account the specific needs and conditions of developing countries (or economies) and minimizing the possible adverse impacts on their development in a manner that protects the poor and the affected communities.	Indicator 12.c.1: Amount of fossil-fuel subsidies (production and consumption) per unit of GDP	In order to measure fossil fuel subsidies at the national, regional and global level, three sub-indicators are recommended for reporting on this indicator: 1) direct transfer of government funds; 2) induced transfers (price support); and as an optional sub-indicator 3) tax expenditure, other revenue foregone, and under[1]pricing of goods and services. The definitions of the International Energy Agency (IEA) Statistical Manual (IEA, 2005) and the Agreement on Subsidies and Countervailing Measures (ASCM) under the World Trade Last updated: 2024-01-31 Organization (WTO) (WTO, 1994) are used to define fossil fuel subsidies. Standardized descriptions from the United Nations Statistical Office's Central Product Classification should be used to classify individual energy products. It is proposed to drop the wording "as a proportion of total national expenditure on fossil fuels" and thus this indicator is effectively "Amount of fossil fuel subsidies per unit of GDP (production and consumption)".
Goal 13. Take urgent action to combat climate change and its impacts		
Target 13.1: Strengthen resilience and adaptive capacity to climate-related hazards and natural disasters in all economies.	13.1.1.a: Number of people affected by disasters	The number of people who were directly affected by disasters, per 100,000 population. Note: People who are affected, either directly or indirectly, by a hazardous event. "Directly affected" are those who have suffered injury, illness, or other health effects. "Indirectly affected" are those who have suffered consequences, other than or in addition to direct effects.
	13.1.1.b: Number of deaths due to disasters	The number of people who died during, or directly after, a disaster as a direct result of the hazardous event, per 100,000 population.
	13.1.2: Number of economies that adopt and implement national disaster risk reduction (DRR) strategies in line with the Sendai Framework for Disaster Risk Reduction 2015–2030	The number of economies that adopt and implement national DRR strategies in line with the Sendai Framework for Disaster Risk Reduction 2015–2030, and the coverage score for the level of implementation that member states will report their status in the Sendai Framework Monitor. Note: Member states will assess the level of implementation for 10 key elements of their national DRR strategy, then enter those scores into the Sendai Framework Monitor. The national DRR strategy progress score E1 would be calculated as the arithmetic average across 10 national DRR strategy key elements (KE1).

(continued on next page)

Goals and Targets	Statistical Indicators	Definition
		The national DRR strategy progress score benchmarks strategies according to the following five categories: (i) Comprehensive implementation: E1 is higher than 0.75; (ii) Substantial implementation, additional progress required: E1 is higher than 0.5, but less than or equal to 0.75; (iii) Moderate implementation, neither comprehensive nor substantial: E1 is higher than 0.25, but less than or equal to 0.5; (iv) Limited implementation: E1 is higher than 0 but less than or equal to 0.25, (v) No national DRR strategy: If there is no implementation of national DRR strategy, or no existence of such plans, the score will be 0.
	13.1.3: Proportion of local governments that adopt and implement local DRR strategies in line with national DRR strategies	The percentage of local governments that adopt and implement local DRR strategies in line with national strategies. Note: Member states count the number of local governments that adopt and implement local DRR strategies in line with the national strategy and express it as a percentage of the total number of local governments in the economy. Local governments are determined by the economy reporting for this indicator, considering subnational public administrations with responsibility to develop local DRR strategies.
Goal 14. Conserve and sustainably use the oceans, seas, and marine resources for sustainable development		
Target 14.5: By 2020, conserve at least 10% of coastal and marine areas, consistent with national and international law and based on the best available scientific information.	14.5.1: Coverage of protected areas in relation to marine areas	The indicator shows trends over time in the mean percentage of each important site for marine biodiversity (i.e., those that contribute significantly to the global persistence of biodiversity) that is covered by designated protected areas and other effective area-based conservation measures. Note: The International Union for Conservation of Nature (IUCN) defines protected areas as clearly defined geographical spaces, recognized, dedicated, and managed through legal or other effective means, to achieve the long-term conservation of nature with associated ecosystem services and cultural values. Importantly, a variety of specific management objectives are recognized within this definition, spanning conservation, restoration, and sustainable use. The status "designated" is attributed to a protected area when the corresponding authority, according to national legislation or common practice (e.g., by means of an executive decree or the like), officially endorses a document of designation. The designation must be made for the purpose of biodiversity conservation, not de facto protection arising because of some other activity (e.g., military).
Goal 15. Protect, restore, and promote sustainable use of terrestrial ecosystems, sustainably manage forests, combat desertification, halt and reverse land degradation, and halt biodiversity loss		
Target 15.1: By 2020, ensure the conservation, restoration, and sustainable use of terrestrial and inland freshwater ecosystems and their services, in particular forests, wetlands, mountains, and drylands, in line with obligations under international agreements.	15.1.1: Forest area as a proportion of total land area	Size of forest cover in relation to land area. Note: Forest is defined as "land spanning more than 0.5 hectares with trees higher than 5 meters and a canopy cover of more than 10%, or trees able to reach these thresholds in situ. It does not include land that is predominantly under agricultural or urban land use". Land area is the area of an economy excluding area under inland waters and coastal waters.

(continued on next page)

Goals and Targets	Statistical Indicators	Definition
	15.1.2: Proportion of important sites for terrestrial and freshwater biodiversity that are covered by protected areas, by ecosystem type	Proportion of important sites for terrestrial and freshwater biodiversity that are covered by protected areas shows temporal trends in the mean percentage of each important site for terrestrial and freshwater biodiversity (i.e., those that contribute significantly to the global persistence of biodiversity) that is covered by designated protected areas and Other Effective Area-based Conservation Measures (OECMs). The status "designated" is attributed to a protected area when the corresponding authority, according to national legislation or common practice (e.g., by means of an executive decree or the like), officially endorses a document of designation. The designation must be made for the purpose of biodiversity conservation, not de facto protection arising because of some other activity (e.g., military). OECMs are defined by the Convention on Biological Diversity (CBD) as "A geographically defined area other than a Protected Area, which is governed and managed in ways that achieve positive and sustained long-term outcomes for the in-situ conservation of biodiversity, with associated ecosystem functions and services and where applicable, cultural, spiritual, socio-economic, and other locally relevant values."
Target 15.4: By 2030, ensure the conservation of mountain ecosystems, including their biodiversity, in order to enhance their capacity to provide benefits that are essential for sustainable development	15.4.1: Coverage by protected areas of important sites for mountain biodiversity	Coverage by protected areas of important sites for mountain biodiversity shows temporal trends in the mean percentage of each important site for mountain biodiversity (i.e., those that contribute significantly to the global persistence of biodiversity) that is covered by designated protected areas and Other Effective Area-based Conservation Measures (OECMs). The status "designated" is attributed to a protected area when the corresponding authority, according to national legislation or common practice (e.g., by means of an executive decree or the like), officially endorses a document of designation. The designation must be made for the purpose of biodiversity conservation, not de facto protection arising because of some other activity (e.g., military). OECMs are defined by the Convention on Biological Diversity (CBD) as "A geographically defined area other than a Protected Area, which is governed and managed in ways that achieve positive and sustained long-term outcomes for the in-situ conservation of biodiversity, with associated ecosystem functions and services and where applicable, cultural, spiritual, socio-economic, and other locally relevant values."
Target 15.5: Take urgent and significant action to reduce the degradation of natural habitats, halt the loss of biodiversity and, by 2020, protect and prevent the extinction of threatened species.	15.5.1: Red List Index	The Red List Index measures changes in aggregate extinction risk across groups of species. It is based on genuine changes in the number of species in each category of extinction risk on the IUCN Red List of Threatened Species (www.iucnredlist.org), which is expressed as changes in an index ranging from 0 to 1. Note: The Red List Index value ranges from 1 (all species are categorized as "Least Concern") to 0 (all species are categorized as "Extinct"), indicating how far the set of species has moved overall toward extinction. Threatened species are those listed on The IUCN Red List of Threatened Species in the categories Vulnerable, Endangered, or Critically Endangered (i.e., species that are facing a high, very high, or extremely high risk of extinction in the wild in the medium-term future).

(continued on next page)

Goals and Targets	Statistical Indicators	Definition
Goal 16. Promote peaceful and inclusive societies for sustainable development; provide access to justice for all; and build effective, accountable, and inclusive institutions at all levels		
Target 16.1: Significantly reduce all forms of violence and related death rates everywhere.	16.1.1: Number of victims of intentional homicide per 100,000 population	Total count of victims of intentional homicide divided by the total population, expressed per 100,000 population. Intentional homicide is defined as the unlawful death inflicted upon a person with the intent to cause death or serious injury (International Classification of Crime for Statistical Purposes, ICCS 2015). Population refers to total resident population in a given economy in a given year. Note: This indicator is widely used at national and international levels to measure the most extreme form of violent crime, providing a direct indication of lack of security.
Target 16.3: Promote the rule of law at the national and international levels and ensure equal access to justice for all.	16.3.2: Unsentenced detainees as a proportion of the overall prison population	Total number of persons held in detention who have not yet been sentenced, as a percentage of the total number of persons held in detention, on a specified date.
Target 16.5: Substantially reduce corruption and bribery in all their forms.	16.5.2: Proportion of businesses that had at least one contact with a public official and that paid a bribe to a public official, or were asked for a bribe by those public officials during the previous 12 months	Proportion of firms that were asked for a gift or informal payment when meeting with tax officials. Note: This indicator aims to ascertain whether or not firms have been solicited for gifts or informal payments (i.e., bribes) when meeting with tax officials. Paying taxes are required of formal forms in most economies, and the rationale for this indicator is to measure the incidence of corruption during this routine interaction.
Target 16.9: By 2030, provide legal identity for all, including birth registration.	16.9.1: Proportion of children under 5 years of age whose births have been registered with a civil authority, by age	Proportion of children under 5 years of age whose births have been registered with a civil authority.
Goal 17. Strengthen the means of implementation and revitalize the Global Partnership for Sustainable Development		
Target 17.4: Assist developing economies in attaining long-term debt sustainability through coordinated policies aimed at fostering debt financing, debt relief, and debt restructuring, as appropriate, and address the external debt of highly indebted poor economies to reduce debt distress	17.4.1: Debt service as a proportion of exports of goods and services	Percentage of debt services (principle and interest payments) to the exports of goods and services. Debt services covered in this indicator refer only to public and publicly guaranteed debt. Note: Concepts of public and publicly guaranteed external debt and exports of goods and services data are in accordance with the sixth edition of the Balance of Payments and International Investment Position Manual (BPM6) methodology

(continued on next page)

Goals and Targets	Statistical Indicators	Definition
Target 17.9: Enhance international support for implementing effective and targeted capacity-building in developing economies to support national plans to implement all the Sustainable Development Goals, including through North-South, South-South, and triangular cooperation.	17.9.1: Dollar value of financial and technical assistance (including through North-South, South-South, and triangular cooperation) committed to developing economies	Gross disbursements of total ODA and other official flows from all donors for capacity-building and national planning. Note: ODA refers to "those flows to economies and territories on the Development Assistance Committee List of ODA Recipients and to multilateral institutions which are (i) provided by official agencies, including state and local governments, or by their executive agencies; and (ii) each transaction is administered with the promotion of the economic development and welfare of developing economies as its main objective; and is concessional in character and conveys a grant element of at least 25% (calculated at a rate of discount of 10%). Other official flows (excluding officially supported export credits) are defined as transactions by the official sector that do not meet the conditions for eligibility as ODA, either because they are not primarily aimed at development or because they are not sufficiently concessional.
Target 17.18: By 2020, enhance capacity-building support to developing economies, including for least developed economies and small island developing states, to increase significantly the availability of high-quality, timely, and reliable data disaggregated by income, gender, age, race, ethnicity, migratory status, disability, geographic location, and other characteristics relevant in national contexts.	17.18.3: Number of economies with a national statistical plan that is fully funded and under implementation, by source of funding	Count of economies that are either (i) implementing a strategy, (ii) designing a strategy, or (iii) awaiting adoption of a strategy in the current year. Note: The indicator is based on the annual Status Report on National Strategies for the Development of Statistics. In collaboration with its partners, PARIS21 reports on economy progress in designing and implementing national statistical plans. This indicator can be disaggregated by geographical area. Regional-level aggregates are based on the total count of national strategies.
Target 17.19: By 2030, build on existing initiatives to develop measurements of progress on sustainable development that complement GDP, and support statistical capacity-building in developing economies.	17.19.1: Dollar value of all resources made available to strengthen statistical capacity in developing economies	US dollar value of ongoing statistical support in developing economies. Note: The indictor is based on the Partner Report on Support to Statistics, which is designed and administered by PARIS21 to provide a snapshot of the US dollar value of ongoing statistical support in developing economies.
	17.19.2: Number of economies that have conducted at least one population and housing census in the past 10 years	Economies that have conducted at least one population and housing census in the past 10 years. This includes economies that compile their detailed population and housing statistics from population registers, administrative records, sample surveys, other sources, or a combination of those sources.

(continued on next page)

Regional Trends and Tables

Indicator	Definition
PEOPLE	
Population	
Midyear Population	Estimates of the midyear de facto population. De facto population includes all persons physically present in the economy during the census day, including foreign, military, and diplomatic personnel and their accompanying household members; and transient foreign visitors in the economy or in harbors. Note: Some economies have population data referenced to different period end points (e.g., 1 January for the Kyrgyz Republic, 31 December for the People's Republic of China, and 1 October for India).
Growth Rates in Population	Number of people added to (or subtracted from) a population over a given period of time because of natural increase and net migration, expressed as a percentage of the population at the given period of time.
Net International Migration Rate	Number of immigrants minus the number of emigrants over a period, divided by the person-years lived by the population of the receiving economy over that period. It is expressed as net number of migrants per 1,000 population.
Urban Population (as % of total population)	Population living in urban areas, defined in accordance with the national definition or as used in the most recent population census. Because of national differences in the characteristics that distinguish urban from rural areas, the distinction between urban and rural populations is not amenable to a single definition that would be applicable to all economies. National definitions are most commonly based on size of locality. Population that is not urban is considered rural. The estimated population living in urban areas at midyear as a percentage of the total midyear population in an economy.
Age Dependency Ratio	Ratio of the nonworking-age population to the working-age population. Since economies define working age differently, a straightforward application of the definition will lead to noncomparable data. The Asian Development Bank therefore uses the following United Nations definition that can be calculated directly from an age distribution: $\frac{\text{Population aged (0–14) + (65 and over) years}}{\text{Population aged (15–64) years}} \times 100$
Labor Force and Employment	
Labor Force Participation Rate	Percentage of the labor force to the working-age population. The labor force is the sum of those employed and unemployed but seeking work. The labor force participation rate measures the extent of the economically active working-age population in an economy. It provides an indication of the relative size of the supply of labor available for the production of goods and services in the economy. It must be noted that the definition of working-age population varies across economies. Note: Recommendations from the 19th International Conference of Labour Statisticians have been adopted by some economies, and hence these economies may not have comparable data across years. The conference provides the statistical concept of work for reference purposes; and the operational concepts, definitions, and guidelines for (i) three distinct subsets of work activities, referred to as forms of work, which include own-use production work, employment work, and volunteer work; (ii) related classifications of the population according to their labor force status and main work status; and (iii) measures of labor underutilization. The concept of employment has also been refined to refer to work for pay or profit.

Indicator	Definition
Employment in Agriculture	Employment in agriculture, including forestry and fishing, that corresponds to division 1 (International Standard of Industrial Classification [ISIC] revision 2), tabulation categories A and B (ISIC revision 3), and category A of ISIC revision 4.
Employment in Industry	Employment in industry includes mining and quarrying; manufacturing; electricity, gas, steam, and air-conditioning supply; water supply; sewage, waste management, and remediation activities; and construction.
Employment in Mining and Quarrying	Employment in mining and quarrying that corresponds to division 2 (ISIC revision 2), tabulation category C (ISIC revision 3), and category B of ISIC revision 4.
Employment in Manufacturing	Employment in manufacturing that corresponds to division 3 (ISIC revision 2), tabulation category D (ISIC revision 3), and category C of ISIC revision 4.
Employment in Electricity, Gas, Steam, and Air-Conditioning Supply; Water Supply; Sewerage, Waste Management and Remediation Activities	Employment in electricity, gas, steam, and air-conditioning supply; water supply; sewerage, waste management, and remediation activities that corresponds to division 4 (ISIC revision 2), tabulation category E (ISIC revision 3), and categories D and E of ISIC revision 4.
Employment in Construction	Employment in construction that corresponds to division 5 (ISIC revision 2), tabulation category F (ISIC revisions 3), and category F of ISIC revision 4.
Employment in Services	Employment in service includes wholesale and retail trade; repair of motor vehicles and motorcycles; accommodation and food service activities; transportation and storage; information and communication; financial and insurance activities; real estate activities; and other services.
Employment in Wholesale and Retail Trade; Repair of Motor Vehicles and Motorcycles	Employment in wholesale and retail trade; repair of motor vehicles and motorcycles that corresponds to division 6 (subdivisions 61 and 62, ISIC revision 2); tabulation category G (ISIC revision 3); and category G of ISIC revision 4.
Employment in Transportation and Storage	Employment in transport and storage that corresponds to division 7 (subdivision 71, ISIC revision 2); tabulation category I (subcategories 60–63, ISIC revision 3); and category H of ISIC revision 4.
Employment in Accommodation and Food Service Activities	Employment in accommodation and food service activities that corresponds to division 6 (subdivision 63, ISIC revision 2); tabulation category H (ISIC revision 3); and category I of ISIC revision 4.
Employment in Information and Communication	Employment in information and communication that corresponds to division 7 (subdivision 72, ISIC revision 2); tabulation category I (subcategory 64, ISIC revision 3); and category J of ISIC revision 4.
Employment in Financial and Insurance Activities	Employment in financial and insurance activities that corresponds to division 8 (subdivisions 81–82, ISIC revision 2), tabulation category J (ISIC revision 3), and category K of ISIC revision 4.
Employment in Real Estate Activities	Employment in real estate activities that corresponds to division 8 (subdivision 83, ISIC revision 2); tabulation category K (subcategory 70, ISIC revision 3); and category L of ISIC revision 4.
Employment in Other Services	Employment in other services that corresponds to divisions 9 and 0 (ISIC revision 2), tabulation categories L to Q (ISIC revision 3), and categories M to U of ISIC revision 4.

(continued on next page)

Indicator	Definition
Underemployment	Persons in time-related underemployment comprise all persons in employment who satisfy the following three criteria during the reference period: a) are willing to work additional hours; b) are available to work additional hours i.e., are ready, within a specified subsequent period, to work additional hours given opportunities for additional work; and c) worked less than a threshold relating to working time (i.e., persons whose hours actually worked in all jobs during the reference period were below a threshold, to be chosen according to national circumstances). The time-related underemployment rate is calculated as follows: $TRU\ (\%) = \frac{\text{Persons in time-related underemployment}}{\text{Persons employed}} \times 100$
Poverty Indicators	
Proportion of Population below $3.00 a Day (2021 PPP)	Percentage of the population living on less than $3.00 a day at 2021 purchasing power parity (PPP).
Proportion of Population below $4.20 a Day (2021 PPP)	Percentage of the population living on less than $4.20 a day at 2021 PPP.
Income Ratio of Highest 20% to Lowest 20%	Income or consumption share that accrues to the richest 20% of the population, divided by the income or consumption share of the lowest 20% of the population.
Gini Coefficient or Index	Measure of the degree to which an economy's income distribution diverges from perfect equal distribution. A value of zero (0) implies perfect equality while a value of one (1) implies perfect inequality.
Human Development Index	Composite index of long and healthy life (measured by life expectancy at birth), knowledge (measured by expected years of schooling and mean years of schooling), and decent standard of living (measured by gross national income per capita in United States [US] PPP dollars).
Multidimensional Poverty Index	Proportion of the population that is multidimensionally poor, adjusted by the intensity of the deprivations.
Social Indicators	
Life Expectancy at Birth	Number of years that a newborn is expected to live if prevailing patterns of mortality at the time of his or her birth are to stay the same throughout his or her life.
Crude Birth Rate	Ratio of the total number of live births in a given period to the midyear total population of the same period, expressed per 1,000 people.
Crude Death Rate	Ratio of the number of deaths occurring within a given period to the midyear total population of the same period, expressed per 1,000 people.
Total Fertility Rate	Number of children that would be born to a woman if she were to live to the end of her childbearing years and bear children in accordance with current age-specific fertility rates.
Adult Literacy Rate	The percentage of the population aged 15 years and older who can both read and write (with understanding) a short simple statement on his or her everyday life. Generally, literacy also encompasses numeracy, i.e., the ability to make simple arithmetic calculations.
Expected Years of Schooling, Primary to Tertiary	Number of years a person of school entrance age can expect to spend within the specified level of education (from primary to tertiary level).
Mean Years of Schooling	Average number of completed years of education of an economy's population aged 25 years and older, excluding years spent repeating individual grades.

(continued on next page)

Indicator	Definition
Pupil to Qualified Teacher Ratio	The total number of pupils and students in the relevant level in a given academic year expressed as a percentage of the number of qualified teachers in the same level in that academic year. A qualified teacher has the minimum academic qualifications necessary to teach at a specific level of education in a given economy. This is usually related to the subject(s) they teach. The higher the pupil to qualified teacher ratio, the lower the relative access of pupils to qualified teachers.
Pupil to Trained Teacher Ratio	The total number of pupils and students in the relevant level in a given academic year expressed as a percentage of the number of trained teachers in the same level in that academic year. A trained teacher has fulfilled at least the minimum organized pedagogical teacher-training requirements (pre-service or in-service) to teach a specific level of education according to the relevant national policy or law. The higher the pupil to trained teacher ratio, the lower the relative access of pupils to trained teachers. Results can be compared with established national norms on the number of pupils per trained teacher for each level of education.
Physicians	Physicians, including general and specialist medical practitioners, expressed in terms of the number per 1,000 people.
Hospital Beds	In-patient beds for both acute and chronic care available in public, private, general, and specialized hospitals and rehabilitation centers expressed in terms of the number per 1,000 people.
Number of Adults Living with HIV	All adults, defined as men and women aged 15 years and older, with HIV infection, whether or not they have developed symptoms of AIDS, estimated to be alive at the end of a specific year.
ECONOMY AND OUTPUT	
National Accounts	
Gross Domestic Product	Unduplicated market value of the total production activity of all resident producer units within the economic territory of an economy during a given period. It is calculated without making deductions for depreciation of fabricated assets or for depletion and degradation of natural resources. Transfer payments are excluded from the calculation of gross domestic product (GDP). GDP can be calculated using the production, expenditure, and income approaches. Production-based GDP is the sum of the gross value added by all resident producers in the economy, plus any taxes and minus any subsidies not included in the value of the products. Gross value-added is the net output of an industry after adding up all outputs and subtracting intermediate inputs. Income-based GDP is the sum of the compensation of employees, mixed income, operating surplus, consumption of fixed capital, and taxes, less subsidies on production and imports. Expenditure-based GDP is the sum of final consumption expenditure of households, nonprofit institutions serving households, and the government; gross capital formation; and exports minus imports of goods and services. GDP can be measured at current prices (the prices of the current reporting period), and constant prices (obtained by expressing values in terms of a base period and chain volume measure).
GDP at PPP	Measures obtained by using PPP to convert the GDP into a common currency, and by valuing them at a uniform price level. They are the spatial equivalent of a time series of GDP for a single economy expressed at constant prices. At the level of GDP, they are used to compare the economic size of economies.

(continued on next page)

Indicator	Definition
GDP at Current US Dollar	GDP in USD sourced from economies' official sources; or GDP at local currency units obtained from economy sources and converted to US dollars using the official exchange rates from the International Monetary Fund (IMF) or using exchange rates from the economies' official sources. The exchange rates used are expressed as the average rate for a period of time (average of period), calculated as annual averages based on the monthly averages (local currency units relative to the US dollar).
GDP per Capita at PPP	GDP at PPP, divided by the midyear population.
GNI per Capita, Atlas Method	The gross national income (GNI) converted to US dollars using the World Bank Atlas method, divided by the midyear population. GNI is the sum of value added by all resident producers, plus any product taxes (less subsidies) not included in the valuation of output, plus net receipts of primary income (compensation of employees and property income) from abroad. GNI, calculated in national currency, is usually converted to US dollars at official exchange rates for comparisons across economies, although an alternative rate is used when the official exchange rate is judged to diverge by an exceptionally large margin from the rate actually applied in international transactions. To smooth fluctuations in prices and exchange rates, a special Atlas method of conversion is used by the World Bank. This applies a conversion factor that averages the exchange rate for a given year and the 2 preceding years, adjusted for differences in rates of inflation between the economy, and through 2000, the G-5 economies (France, Germany, Japan, the United Kingdom, and the US). From 2001, these economies include the Euro area, Japan, the United Kingdom, and the US.
GDP per Capita at Current US Dollar	GDP at current US dollar value, divided by the midyear population.
Agriculture Value Added	The gross output of the agriculture sector, less the corresponding value of intermediate consumption. The industrial origin of value-added is determined by ISIC revision 4, where agriculture corresponds to ISIC Section A and includes agriculture, forestry, and fishing.
Industry Value Added	The gross output of industry sectors, less the corresponding value of intermediate consumption. The industrial origin of value-added is determined by ISIC revision 4, where industry corresponds to ISIC Sections B-F and includes mining and quarrying (B); manufacturing (C); electricity, gas, steam, and air-conditioning supply (D); water supply; sewerage, waste management, and remediation activities (E); and construction (F).
Services Value Added	The gross output of services sectors, less the corresponding value of intermediate consumption. The industrial origin of value-added is determined by ISIC revision 4, where services corresponds to ISIC Sections G-U and includes wholesale and retail trade; repair of motor vehicles and motorcycles (G); transport and storage (H); accommodation and food service activities (I); information and communication (J); financial and insurance activities (K); real estate activities (L); professional, scientific, and technical activities (M); administrative and support service activities (N); public administration and defense; compulsory social security (O); education (P); human health and social work activities (Q); arts, entertainment, and recreation (R); other service activities (S); activities of households as employers; undifferentiated goods- and services-producing activities of households for own use (T); and activities of extraterritorial organizations and bodies (U).
Household Consumption Expenditure	Market value of all goods and services, including durable products (such as cars, washing machines, and home computers), purchased or received as income in kind by households. It excludes purchases of dwellings but includes imputed rent for owner-occupied dwellings. It also includes payments and fees to governments to obtain permits and licenses. The expenditure of nonprofit institutions serving households is generally included for most economies.
Government Consumption Expenditure	Includes all current outlays on purchases of goods and services (including wages and salaries of government employees). It also includes most expenditure on national defense and security but excludes government military expenditures that are part of public investment.

(continued on next page)

Indicator	Definition
Gross Capital Formation	Total value of gross fixed capital formation, changes in inventories, and acquisitions less disposals of valuables. Gross fixed capital formation is the total value of a producer's acquisitions, less disposals, of tangible goods (such as buildings) and intangible goods (such as computer software) that are intended for use in production during several accounting periods, plus certain specified expenditure on services that adds to the value of non-produced assets. Changes in inventories are changes in stocks of produced goods and goods for intermediate consumption, and the net increase in the value of work in progress. Valuables are goods (such as precious metals and works of art) that are not used up in production but are acquired as stores of value in the expectation that they will retain or increase their value over time.
Exports of Goods and Services	Consist of sales, bartering, or gifts or grants of goods and services from residents to nonresidents. The treatment of exports in the System of National Accounts is generally identical with that in the balance of payments accounts as described in the IMF's Balance of Payments Manual.
Imports of Goods and Services	Consist of purchases, bartering, or receipts of gifts or grants of goods and services by residents from nonresidents. The treatment of imports in the System of National Accounts is generally identical to that in the balance of payments accounts as described in the IMF's Balance of Payments Manual.
Gross Domestic Saving	Difference between GDP and final consumption expenditure, where final consumption expenditure is the sum of the final consumption of household, nonprofit institutions serving households, and the government.
Production	
Agriculture Production Index	Relative level of the aggregate volume of agricultural production for each year in comparison with the base period. It is based on the sum of price-weighted quantities of different agricultural commodities produced.
Manufacturing Production Index	An index covering production in manufacturing. The exact coverage, the weighting system, and the methods of calculation vary from economy to economy, but the divergences are less important than, for example, in the case of price and wage indexes.
MONEY, FINANCE, AND PRICES	
Prices	
Consumer Price Index	An index that measures changes in prices against a reference period of a basket of goods and services purchased by households. Based on the purpose of the consumer price index, different baskets of goods and services can be selected. For macroeconomic purposes, a broad-based basket is used to represent the relative price movement of household final consumption expenditure.
Food and Nonalcoholic Beverages Price Index	An index that covers food and nonalcoholic beverages purchased by the household mainly for consumption or preparation at home including services for food processing for own consumption. The index corresponds to Classification of Individual Consumption by Purpose (COICOP) Version 1999 and 2018 division 01. Excluded are food and nonalcoholic beverages that are provided as part of a food-serving service under COICOP division 11: restaurants and hotels (COICOP Version 1999) or restaurants and accommodation services (COICOP Version 2018).
Alcoholic Beverages, Tobacco, and Narcotics Price Index	An index that covers the purchase of alcoholic beverages, tobacco, and narcotics, regardless of where these are consumed, but not provided as part of a food-and-beverage-serving service under hotels and restaurants. Services for the production of alcohol for own consumption are also included. The index corresponds to COICOP division 02. Excluded are alcoholic beverages purchased for immediate consumption in hotels, restaurants, cafes, bars, kiosks, street vendors, automatic vending machines, etc. classified under restaurants, cafes, and the like (COICOP Group 11.1.1).

(continued on next page)

Indicator	Definition
Clothing and Footwear Price Index	An index that covers all clothing materials, garments, articles and accessories, footwear and related services, including cleaning, repair, and hire of clothing and footwear, and the purchase of secondhand clothing and footwear. The index corresponds to COICOP division 03.
Housing, Water, Electricity, Gas, and Other Fuels Price Index	An index that covers goods and services for the use of the house or dwelling and its maintenance and repair; the supply of water and miscellaneous services related to the dwelling; and energy used for heating or cooling. The index corresponds to COICOP division 04.
Furnishings, Household Equipment, and Routine Household Maintenance Price Index	An index that covers a wide range of products to equip the house or dwelling and the household durables, semidurables, and nondurables as well as some household services. Includes all kinds of furniture (including lightning equipment, household textiles, glassware, tableware, and household utensils), major and smaller electric household appliances, tools and equipment for house and garden, and goods for routine household maintenance. The index also includes the repair, installation, and rental services of the goods. Domestic services by paid staff in private service, supplied by enterprises or self-employed persons, window-cleaning and disinfecting services, as well as dry-cleaning and laundering of household textiles and carpets, are also included. The index corresponds to COICOP division 05.
Health Price Index	An index that covers health services provided during an overnight stay, services that do not require an overnight stay, diagnostic imaging services, medical laboratory services, patient emergency transportation, and emergency rescue services. The index also includes medicines and health products, covering all products that are separately invoiced from health services, except when administered under the direct supervision of a health care professional during an overnight stay. The index corresponds to COICOP division 06.
Transport Price Index	An index that covers four main categories of goods and services for transportation: (i) purchase of vehicles covers motor cars, motor cycles, bicycles, and animal-drawn vehicles; (ii) goods and services for the operation of the personal transport equipment cover parts and accessories for personal transport equipment, fuels and lubricants, and the repair and maintenance of personal transport equipment including expenditures for parking spaces in garages or in public places, expenditures for tolls, and expenditures to acquire a driving certificate; (iii) transport services provided by the market, structured by the mode of transport; and (iv) transport services of goods covers postal and courier services, removal and storage services, and the delivery of any kinds of goods when charged separately. The index corresponds to COICOP division 07. It excludes purchases of recreational vehicles such as camper vans, caravans, trailers, aeroplanes, and boats that are classified under the Recreation and Culture Price Index (COICOP Version 1999) or Recreation, Sport, and Culture (COICOP Version 2018).
Communication Price Index/Information and Communication Price Index	The index corresponds to division 08 in COICOP versions 1999 and 2018. In COICOP Version 1999, this index covers three main groups of goods and services: (i) information and communication equipment, including equipment for the capture, recording, and reproduction of sound and vision; software; and information and communication services; (ii) information and communication services, including telephones and other communication services; internet access services; television and radio licenses; fee and subscription services, including streaming services of films and music; and (iii) repair, maintenance, and rental of information and communication equipment. In COICOP Version 2018, this index covers three main groups and services: (i) information and communication equipment, including equipment for the reception, recording, and reproduction of sound and vision; (ii) software; and (iii) information and communication services, which include telephone and other communication services, internet access services, television and radio licences, fee and subscription services (including streaming services of films and music); and repair, maintenance, and hire of information and communication equipment.

(continued on next page)

Indicator	Definition
Recreation and Culture Price Index/ Recreation, Sport, and Culture Price Index	An index that covers a wide range of goods and services for recreation, sport, and culture and is structured into eight groups: (i) recreation durables such as photographic equipment, other major durables for recreation, such as camper vans, boats, yachts, aeroplanes, and the like; (ii) nonmajor durable recreational goods such as games and toys, including video game computers, celebration articles, equipment for sport, camping, and open-air recreation; (iii) garden products and plants and flowers and purchases of pets and expenditures for pets, excluding veterinary services; (iv) recreational services cover rental, maintenance, and repair of goods, veterinary and other services for pets, recreational and leisure services, such as amusement parks, games of chance and expenditures for sporting services, both expenditures for practicing sports as well as expenditures for attendance of sport events; (v) cultural goods such as musical instruments and audio-visual media; (vi) cultural services such as cinemas, theatres, concerts, museums, and other cultural sites, and photographic services; (vii) newspapers, all kinds of books, stationery and drawing materials; and (viii) package holidays that include transportation, accommodation, food provision, or tour guide. The index corresponds to COICOP division 09.
Education Price Index/Education Services Price Index	An index that covers educational services only. It includes: (i) education by radio or television broadcasting as well as e-learning and correspondence courses; (ii) admission and registration fees as well as tuition fees; and (iii) other education-related fees such as camps and/or field trips, course fees, diploma fees, examination fees, graduation fees, laboratory fees, physical education fees, etc. The index corresponds to COICOP division 10. It excludes expenditures on other education-related goods and services such as school uniforms, education support services, such as health-care services, transport services (except in the case of excursions that are part of the normal school program), text books and academic journals, stationery, catering services, and accommodation services.
Restaurants and Hotels Price Index/Restaurants and Accommodation Service Price Index	An index that covers food and beverage services provided by restaurants, cafes, and similar facilities, either with full or limited- or self-service, or by canteens, cafeterias, or refectories at work or at school and other educational establishment's premises. It also includes catering services and accommodation services. Services for visitors and other travelers away from their principal or secondary residence are included. If not separately invoiced, it also includes food and beverage services and other serving services, such as housekeeping, parking, laundry, swimming pools and exercise rooms, recreational facilities, and conference and convention facilities. The index corresponds to COICOP division 11.
Insurance and Financial Services Price Index	An index that covers insurance and financial services. Insurance and financial services are provided by financial corporations. Insurance services are subdivided by type of insurance. Financial services are subdivided by financial intermediation services indirectly measured and by other forms of actual and indirect charges and remittance fees for financial services. For the definition and measurement of insurance and financial services, specific national accounts concepts (under the 2008 System of National Accounts) do apply. The index corresponds to COICOP Version 2018 division 12.
Miscellaneous Goods and Services Price Index	An index that covers insurance and financial services. It also includes personal care, prostitution, personal effects not elsewhere classified, social protection, financial services not elsewhere classified, and other services not elsewhere classified. The index corresponds to COICOP Version 1999 division 12.

(continued on next page)

Indicator	Definition
Personal Care, Social Protection, and Miscellaneous Goods and Services Price Index	An index that covers goods and services for personal care, jewelry and watches, services of social protection, and all other services for households, which are not elsewhere classified. Goods and services for personal care cover electric and nonelectric appliances for personal care as well as hairdressing services. Goods of personal effects cover jewelry and watches, celebratorial and devotional items, and travel goods and items. Social protection services cover childcare, nonmedical retirement homes for elderly persons and disabled persons, and services to maintain persons in their private homes and related services. This index also covers all the other services for households, which are not elsewhere classified, such as fees for legal and administrative services, fees for real estate agencies, charges for undertaking, and payments for various personal services. This index also includes religious services. The index corresponds to COICOP Version 2018 division 13.
Wholesale Price Index	A measure that reflects changes in the prices paid for goods at various stages of distribution up to the point of retail. It can include prices of raw materials for intermediate and final consumption, prices of intermediate or unfinished goods, and prices of finished goods. The goods are usually valued at purchasers' prices.
Producer Price Index	A measure of the change in the prices of goods and services, either as they leave their place of production or as they enter the production process. A measure of the change in the prices received by domestic producers for their outputs or of the change in the prices paid by domestic producers for their intermediate inputs.
GDP Deflator	A measure of the annual rate of price change in the economy as a whole for the period shown, obtained by dividing GDP at current prices by GDP at constant prices.
Money and Finance	
Money Supply	Refers to the total amount of money in circulation in a specific economy. Money supply can be measured in different ways: M1 (Narrow Money) is a measure of money supply that includes all coins and notes (M0) as well as personal money in current accounts. M2 (Intermediate Money) is the sum of M1 and personal money in deposit accounts. M3 (Broad Money) is the sum of M2 and government and other deposits. According to the Organization for Economic Co-operation and Development, M3 includes currency, deposits with an agreed maturity of up to 2 years, deposits redeemable at notice of up to 3 months and repurchase agreements, money market fund shares or units, and debt securities up to 2 years. Not all economies publish the same types of aggregates, and even when aggregates are the same name (e.g., M1, M2, M3, etc.), their asset composition often differs significantly. Cross-economy differences in national definitions of lowered-ordered aggregates also arise from differences in the maturity categories of nontransferable deposits included in a particular money aggregate. For example, the definition of M2 in one economy may include time deposits with maturities of 1 year or less, whereas another economy's M2 definition may include time deposits with maturities of 2 years or less. When the monetary policy strategy consists of monetary aggregate targeting, the choice of the definition of the targeted aggregate is guided mainly by two considerations. The aggregate should be sufficiently sensitive to interest rate changes for the central bank to be able to control it and display a stable relationship over time to the movement of the overall price level. Liabilities excluded from broad money are the sum of all exclusions from broad money. They may include deposits; debt securities; loans; insurance, pension, and standardized guarantee schemes; financial derivatives and employee stock options; trade credit and advances; equity; or other items.
Interest Rate on Savings Deposits	Rate paid by commercial and similar banks for savings deposits.

(continued on next page)

Indicator	Definition
Interest Rate on Time Deposits	Rate paid by commercial and similar banks for time deposits.
Lending Interest Rate	Bank rate that usually meets the short- and medium-term financing needs of the private sector. This rate is normally differentiated according to creditworthiness of borrowers and objectives of financing.
Yield on Short-Term Treasury Bills	Rate at which short-term securities are issued or traded in the market.
Domestic Credit Provided by the Financial Sector	Includes all credits to various sectors on a gross basis, with the exception of credit to the central government, which is net. The financial sector includes monetary authorities and deposit money banks as well as other financial corporations where data are available (including corporations that do not accept transferable deposits but do incur such liabilities as time deposits and savings deposits). Examples of "other financial corporations" are finance and leasing companies, money lenders, insurance corporations, pension funds, and foreign exchange companies.
Ratio of Bank Nonperforming Loans to Total Gross Loans	Value of nonperforming loans divided by the total value of the loan portfolio (including nonperforming loans before the deduction of loan loss provisions). The amount recorded as nonperforming should be the gross value of the loan as recorded in the balance sheet, not just the amount that is overdue.
Stock Market Price Index	Index that measures changes in the prices of stocks traded in the stock exchange. The price changes of the stocks are usually weighted by their market capitalization.
Stock Market Capitalization	The share price times the number of shares outstanding (including their several classes) for listed domestic companies. Investment funds, unit trusts, and companies whose only business goal is to hold shares of other listed companies are excluded. Data are end of year values converted to US dollars using corresponding year-end foreign exchange rates. Also known as market value.
Exchange Rates	
Official Exchange Rate	The exchange rate determined by national authorities or the rate determined in the legally sanctioned exchange market. It is calculated as an annual average based on the monthly averages (local currency units relative to the US dollar).
Purchasing Power Parity Conversion Factor	Number of units of economy B's currency that are needed in economy B to purchase the same quantity of an individual good or service, which one unit of economy A's currency can purchase in economy A.
Price Level Index	Ratio of the relevant PPP to the exchange rate. It is expressed as an index on a base of 100. A price level index (PLI) greater than 100 means that, when the national average prices are converted at exchange rates, the resulting prices tend to be higher on average than prices in the base economy (or economies) of the region (and vice versa). At the level of GDP, PLIs provide a measure of the differences in the general price levels of economies. PLIs are also referred to as comparative price levels.
GLOBALIZATION	
Balance of Payments	
Trade in Goods Balance	Difference between exports and imports of goods.
Trade in Services Balance	Difference between exports and imports of services.
Current Account Balance	Sum of net exports of goods, services, net income, and net current transfers.
Total Remittances	Sum of personal remittances and social benefits. Personal remittances include personal transfers (part of current transfers); compensation of employees less taxes, social contributions, transport, and travel; and capital transfers between households. Social benefits include benefits payable under social security funds and pension funds: they may be in cash or in kind. Includes income from individuals working abroad for short periods, income from individuals residing abroad, and social benefits from abroad.

(continued on next page)

Indicator	Definition
Foreign Direct Investment	Refers to net inflows of investment to acquire a lasting management interest (10% or more of voting stock) in an enterprise operating in an economy other than that of the investor. It is the sum of equity capital, reinvestment of earnings, other long-term capital, and short-term capital as shown in the balance of payments.
External Trade	
Merchandise Exports and Imports	Covering all movable goods, with a few specified exceptions, the ownership of which changes between a resident and a foreigner. For merchandise exports, it represents the value of the goods and related distributive services at the customs frontier of the exporting economy, i.e., the free on board (FOB) value. Merchandise imports, on the other hand, are reported in cost, insurance, and freight (CIF) values.
Trade in Goods	Sum of merchandise exports and merchandise imports.
International Trade in Goods (by partner country/economy)	
International Trade in Goods (by partner country/economy): Merchandise Exports and Imports	International Trade in Goods (by partner country/economy), formerly known as Direction of Trade Statistics, includes goods (merchandise) export and import statistics disaggregated according to an economy's trading partners. Imports are reported on a CIF basis and exports are reported on an FOB basis, with the exception of a few economies for which imports are also available in FOB. Time-series data include estimates derived from reports of partner economies for nonreporting and slow-reporting economies.
International Liquidity	
International Reserves	External assets that are readily available to, and controlled by, monetary authorities for meeting balance-of-payments financing needs, for intervention in exchange markets to affect the currency exchange rate, and for other related purposes (such as maintaining confidence in the currency and the economy and serving as a basis for foreign borrowing). Consist of monetary gold, special drawing rights holdings, reserve position in the IMF, currency and deposits, securities (including debt and equity securities), financial derivatives, and other claims (loans and other financial instruments).
Ratio of International Reserves to Imports	International reserves outstanding at the end of the year as a proportion of imports of goods from the balance of payments during the year, where imports of goods are expressed in terms of a monthly average. It is a useful measure for reserves needs of economies with limited access to capital markets.
Capital Flows	
Net Official Development Assistance	Concessional flows to developing economies and multilateral institutions provided by official agencies, including state and local governments, or by their executing agencies, administered with the objective of promoting the economic development and welfare of developing economies, and containing a grant element of at least 25%. Net flow takes into account principal repayments for loans, offsetting entries for forgiven debt, and recoveries made on grants.
Net Other Official Flows	Official sector transactions with economies on the Development Assistance Committee List of Official Development Assistance Recipients, which do not meet the conditions for eligibility as official development assistance, either because they are not primarily aimed at development, or because they have a grant element of less than 25%. The Development Assistance Committee list of recipients of official development assistance is available at https://www.oecd.org/dac/financing-sustainable-development/development-finance-standards/daclist.htm. Net flow takes into account principal repayments for loans, offsetting entries for forgiven debt, and recoveries made on grants.

(continued on next page)

Indicator	Definition
Net Private Flows	Sum of direct investment and portfolio investment. Direct investment is a category of international investment made by a resident entity in one economy (direct investor) with the objective of establishing a lasting interest in an enterprise that is resident in an economy other than that of the investor (direct investment enterprise). "Lasting interest" implies the existence of a long-term relationship between the direct investor and the enterprise and a significant degree of influence by the direct investor on the management of the direct investment enterprise. Direct investment involves both the initial transaction between the two entities and all subsequent capital transactions between them and among affiliated enterprises, both incorporated and unincorporated. Portfolio investment is the category of international investment that covers investment in equity and debt securities, excluding any such instruments that are classified as direct investment or reserve assets.
Aggregate Net Resource Flows	Sum of net official development assistance, net other official flows, and net private flows.
External Indebtedness	
Total External Debt	Debt owed to nonresidents repayable in currency, goods, or services. It is the sum of public, publicly guaranteed, and private nonguaranteed long-term debt, use of IMF credit, and short-term debt. Short-term debt includes all debt having an original maturity of 1 year or less and interest in arrears on long-term debt. Use of IMF credit includes special drawing rights allocations.
Public and Publicly Guaranteed Debt	Comprises long-term external obligations of public debtors, including the national government, political subdivisions (or an agency of either), and autonomous public bodies, and external obligations of private debtors that are guaranteed for repayment by a public entity.
External Debt as a Percentage of Gross National Income (GNI)	Total external debt as a percentage of GNI. GNI is the sum of value added by all resident producers plus any product taxes (less subsidies) not included in the valuation of output, plus net receipts of primary income (compensation of employees and property income) from abroad.
External Debt as a Percentage of Exports of Goods and Services and Primary Income	Total external debt as a percentage of exports of goods, services, and primary income. Exports of goods, services, and primary income constitute the total value of exports of goods and services, receipts of compensation of nonresident workers, and investment income from abroad.
Total Debt Service Paid	The sum of principal repayments and interest actually paid in currency, goods, or services on long-term debt, interest paid on short-term debt, and repayments (repurchases and charges) to the IMF.
Total Debt Service Paid as a Percentage of Exports of Goods and Services and Primary Income	Total debt service paid as a percentage of exports of goods, services, and primary income.
Tourism	
International Tourist Arrivals	The number of tourists (overnight visitors) who travel to an economy other than that in which they usually reside, and outside their usual environment, for a period not exceeding 12 months, and whose main purpose of visit is other than the activity remunerated from within the economy visited. In some cases, data may also include same-day visitors when data on overnight visitors are not available separately. Data refer to the number of arrivals and not to the number of people.

(continued on next page)

Indicator	Definition
International Tourism, Receipts	The receipts earned by a destination economy from inbound tourism and covering all tourism receipts resulting from expenditures made by visitors from abroad. These include lodging, food and drinks, fuel, transport in the economy, entertainment, shopping, etc. This concept includes receipts generated by overnight visits as well as by same-day trips. It does, however, exclude the receipts related to international transport by contracted residents of the other economies (for instance ticket receipts from foreigners travelling with a national company).
TRANSPORT AND COMMUNICATIONS	
Transport	
Road Network	This includes both paved and unpaved roads. Paved roads are roads surfaced with crushed stone (macadam) with hydrocarbon binder or bituminized agents, with concrete, or with cobblestones. Unpaved roads are roads surfaced with a stabilized base, but not surfaced with crushed stone, hydrocarbon binder or bituminized agents, concrete, or cobblestones.
Passenger Kilometers Traveled	A passenger-kilometer is a unit of measurement representing the transport of 1 passenger by a defined mode of transport, e.g., road, over 1 kilometer.
Freight Kilometers Traveled	A ton-kilometer is a unit of measurement representing the transport of 1 metric ton of goods (including packaging and tare weights of intermodal transport units) by a defined mode of transport, e.g., road, over a distance of 1 kilometer. Only the distance on the national territory of the reporting economy is taken into account for national, international, and transit transport.
Registered Vehicles	Mode-specific vehicle registrations refer to the number of newly (first-time) registered vehicles recorded by the authorities. This publication reports cumulative number of vehicle registrations.
Road Traffic Deaths	Death caused by a road traffic crash and occurring within 24 hours (Kiribati, the Federated States of Micronesia, Solomon Islands, Timor-Leste, Tonga); 7 days (Azerbaijan, Bhutan, the People's Republic of China, Tajikistan, Turkmenistan, Viet Nam); 30 days (Armenia, Australia, Cambodia, Fiji, India, Indonesia, Japan, Kazakhstan, the Republic of Korea, Lao People's Democratic Republic, Malaysia, Mongolia, Myanmar, Nepal, New Zealand, Papua New Guinea, Singapore, Sri Lanka, Uzbekistan); unlimited time period (Afghanistan, the Cook Islands, Georgia, Maldives, the Philippines, Samoa, Thailand); within a year (the Kyrgyz Republic); no definition for other economies.
Rail Lines	Rail lines are the length of railway route available for train service, irrespective of the number of parallel tracks.
Rail Network	Length of rail lines divided by the land area.
Railways, Passengers Carried	Passengers carried by railway are the number of passengers transported by rail multiplied by kilometers traveled.
Railways, Goods Transported	Goods transported by railway are the volume of goods transported by railway, measured in metric tons multiplied by kilometers traveled.
Aviation Total Passenger Kilometers	The number of aviation passengers carried, including both domestic and international aircraft passengers of air carriers registered in a given economy, multiplied by kilometers traveled.
Aviation Freight Transport	The volume of aviation freight, express, and diplomatic bags carried on each flight stage (operation of an aircraft from takeoff to its next landing), measured in metric tons, multiplied by kilometers traveled.

(continued on next page)

Indicator	Definition
Container Port Traffic	Measures the flow of containers from land to sea transport modes, and vice versa, in twenty-foot equivalent units (TEU), a standard-size container. Data refer to coastal shipping as well as international journeys. Transshipment traffic is counted as two lifts at the intermediate port (once to offload and again as an outbound lift) and includes empty units.
Liner Shipping Connectivity Index (LSCI)	The current version of the LSCI is generated from the following six components: (i) the number of scheduled ship calls per week in the economy; (ii) deployed annual capacity in TEU: total deployed capacity offered at the economy; (iii) the number of regular liner shipping services from and to the economy; (iv) the number of liner shipping companies that provide services from and to the economy; (v) the average size in TEU of the ships deployed by the scheduled service with the largest average vessel size; and (vi) the number of other economies that are connected to the economy through direct liner shipping services.
Logistics Performance Index	An interactive benchmarking tool created by the World Bank to help economies identify the challenges and opportunities they face in their performance on trade logistics and what they can do to improve their performance.
Communications	
Telephone Subscribers	Fixed-telephone subscriptions refer to the sum of active number of analogue fixed telephone lines, voice-over-IP subscriptions, fixed wireless local loop subscriptions, ISDN voice-channel equivalents, and fixed public payphones.
Mobile Phone Subscribers	The proportion of individuals who used a mobile telephone in the 3 months prior to data collection. A mobile (cellular) telephone refers to a portable telephone subscribing to a public mobile telephone service using cellular technology, which provides access to the PSTN. This includes analogue and digital cellular systems and technologies such as IMT-2000 (3G) and IMT- Advanced. Users of both postpaid subscriptions and prepaid accounts are included.
Fixed-Broadband Subscribers	Fixed-broadband subscriptions refer to fixed subscriptions to high-speed access to the public internet (a TCP/IP connection), at downstream speeds equal to, or greater than, 256 kilobits per second. This includes cable modem, DSL, fiber-to-the-home/building, other fixed (wired)- broadband subscriptions, satellite broadband and terrestrial fixed wireless broadband. This total is measured irrespective of the method of payment. It excludes subscriptions that have access to data communications (including the Internet) via mobile-cellular networks. It should include fixed WiMAX and any other fixed wireless technologies. It includes both residential subscriptions and subscriptions for organizations.
Internet Users	The frequency of internet use by individuals who used the internet from any location in the 3 months prior to data collection. Internet can be used via a computer, mobile, phone, personal digital assistant, games machine, digital TV etc.
ENERGY AND ELECTRICITY	
Energy	
GDP per Unit of Energy Use	The ratio of GDP to total energy use (measured per petajoule) with GDP converted to 2021 constant international dollars using PPP rates. An international dollar has the same purchasing power over GDP as a US dollar has in the US.

(continued on next page)

Indicator	Definition
Energy Production	Primary energy production that is the capture or extraction of fuels or energy from natural energy flows, the biosphere, and natural reserves of fossil fuels within the national territory in a form suitable for use. Inert matter removed from the extracted fuels and quantities reinjected, flared, or vented are not included. The resulting products are referred to as primary products.
Energy Use	Energy production plus imports minus exports, minus international marine bunkers, minus international aviation bunkers, minus stock changes. Also referred to as energy supply.
Energy Imports, Net	Energy imports, net estimated as energy use less production, both measured in petajoules.
Electricity	
Electricity Production	Gross production, which is the sum of the electrical energy production by all the generating units and/or installations concerned (including pumped storage), measured at the output terminals of the main generators. Also referred to as electricity generation.
Sources of Electricity	Refers to the different types of technology and/or processes for the generation or production of electricity, including: (i) electricity from combustible fuels, which refers to the production of electricity from the combustion of fuels that are capable of igniting or burning, i.e., reacting with oxygen to produce a significant rise in temperature; (ii) hydroelectricity, which refers to electricity produced from devices driven by flowing, or falling fresh water; (iii) nuclear electricity, which refers to electricity generated by nuclear plants; and (iv) other electricity, which includes solar, wind, wave, tidal, other marine electricity, geothermal, electricity generated from chemical heat, and electricity from other sources not elsewhere specified.
Electric Power Consumption Per Capita	Total electricity consumption divided by midyear population, where consumption refers to energy-industries-own-use and final consumption. Energy-industries-own-use refers to the consumption of electricity for the direct support of the production and preparation for use of fuels and energy. Final consumption refers to the consumption of electricity by manufacturing, construction and nonfuel mining, transport, and households and other consumers (nonenergy use being irrelevant for electricity).
ENVIRONMENT	
Land	
Agricultural Land or Area	Land area that is arable, under permanent crops, and/or under permanent meadows and pastures.
Arable Land	Land under temporary agricultural crops (double-cropped areas are counted only once), temporary meadows for mowing or pasture, land under market, and kitchen gardens and land temporarily fallow (less than 5 years). The abandoned land resulting from shifting cultivation is not included. Data for arable land are not meant to indicate the amount of land that are potentially cultivable.
Permanent Cropland	Land cultivated with long-term crops that do not have to be replanted for several years (such as cocoa and coffee); land under trees and shrubs producing flowers, such as roses and jasmine; and nurseries (except those for forest trees, which should be classified under "forestry"). Permanent meadows and pastures are excluded from land under permanent crops.
Deforestation Rate	Rate of permanent conversion of natural forest area into other uses, including shifting cultivation, permanent agriculture, ranching, settlements, and infrastructure development. Deforested areas do not include areas logged but intended for regeneration or areas degraded by fuelwood gathering, acid precipitation, or forest fires. A negative rate indicates reforestation or increase in forest area.

(continued on next page)

Indicator	Definition
Pollution	
Carbon Dioxide Emissions	A measure of annual emissions of carbon dioxide (CO_2)—one of the six Kyoto greenhouse gases (GHGs)—from the agriculture, energy, waste, and industrial sectors, excluding land use, land-use change, and forestry (LULUCF). The measure is standardized to CO_2-equivalent values using the Global Warming Potential (GWP) factors identified in the 5th Assessment Report (AR5) by the Intergovernmental Panel on Climate Change (IPCC).
Nitrous Oxide Emissions	A measure of annual emissions of nitrous oxide (N_2O)—one of the six Kyoto GHGs—from the agriculture, energy, waste, and industrial sectors, excluding LULUCF. The measure is standardized to CO_2-equivalent values using the GWP factors identified in the AR5 by the IPCC.
Methane Emissions	A measure of annual emissions of methane (CH_4)—one of the six Kyoto GHGs—from the agriculture, energy, waste, and industrial sectors, excluding LULUCF. The measure is standardized to CO_2-equivalent values using the GWP factors identified in the AR5 by the IPCC.
Total Greenhouse Gas Emissions	A measure of annual emissions of the six GHGs covered by the Kyoto Protocol—CO_2, N_2O, CH_4, hydrofluorocarbons, perfluorocarbons, and sulphurhexafluoride (SF_6)—from the energy, industry, waste, and agriculture sectors, standardized to CO_2-equivalent values. This measure excludes GHG fluxes caused by LULUCF, as these fluxes have larger uncertainties. The measure is standardized to CO_2-equivalent values using the GWP factors identified in the AR5 by the IPCC.
Freshwater	
Internal Renewable Water Resources	Internal renewable water resources (IRWR) refer to the long-term average annual flow of rivers and recharge of aquifers generated from endogenous precipitation. Double-counting of surface water and groundwater resources is avoided by deducting the overlap from the sum of the surface water and groundwater resources. IRWR in billion cubic meters per year refers to surface water produced internally, plus groundwater produced internally deducted by the overlap between surface water and groundwater. IRWR in cubic meters per inhabitant per year is calculated as total annual IRWR divided by total population.
Annual Freshwater Withdrawals	Sum of surface water withdrawal and groundwater withdrawal. Total water withdrawal summed by sector deducted by desalinated water produced, direct use of treated wastewater, and direct use of agricultural drainage water.
Water Productivity	Water productivity is the ratio of the net benefits from crop, forestry, fishery, livestock, and mixed agricultural systems to the amount of water used to produce those benefits. It is calculated as GDP in constant US dollar prices, divided by annual total water withdrawal.
Temperature and Climate-related Disasters	
Temperature Change with Respect to a Baseline Climatology, Corresponding to the Period 1951-1980	Annual estimates of mean surface temperature change measured with respect to a baseline climatology, corresponding to the period 1951-1980. According to NASA, the global mean surface air temperature for that period was 14°C (57°F), with an uncertainty of several tenths of a degree (https://earthobservatory.nasa.gov/world-of-change/decadaltemp.php). The time series temperature change at a point is calculated as a weighted average of the GISTEMP data over all stations within a given radius, with the closest stations weighted most heavily. GISTEMP or the GISS Surface Temperature Analysis provides estimates of global surface temperature change. Estimates of changes in the mean surface temperature are presented in Degree Celsius.

(continued on next page)

Indicator	Definition
Total Number of Climate Related Disasters	Global climate related disasters are stacked to show the trends in climate related physical risk factors. Data is based on the Emergency Events Database (EM-DAT) maintained by the Centre for Research on the Epidemiology of Disasters (CRED)/ Université catholique de Louvain (UCLouvain), Brussels, Belgium. Only climate related disasters (wildfire, storm, landslide, flood, extreme temperature, drought, fog, wave action and glacial lake outburst) are covered. EM-DAT covers disasters that (i) killed ten (10) or more people; (ii) affected hundred (100) or more people; (iii) led to declaration of a state of emergency; and (iv) led to call for international assistance.
GOVERNMENT AND GOVERNANCE	
Government Finance	
Government Net lending/Net borrowing	Net lending (+)/net borrowing (–) is a summary measure indicating the extent to which government is either putting financial resources at the disposal of other sectors in the economy or abroad, or utilizing the financial resources generated by other sectors in the economy or from abroad. It may be viewed as an indicator of the financial impact of government activity on the rest of the economy and the rest of the world. Net lending (+)/net borrowing (–) is a balancing item calculated as the net operating balance (revenue minus expense) minus the net investment in nonfinancial assets. Net lending/net borrowing is also equal to the net acquisition of all financial assets minus the net incurrence of all liabilities from transactions. For economies following the IMF's Government Finance Statistics 1986 framework, the indicator refers to the overall budgetary surplus/deficit measured as the difference between total revenue (including grants) and total expenditure (including net lending).
Government Taxes	Taxes are compulsory, unrequited amounts receivable by government units from institutional units. Certain compulsory receivables, such as fines, penalties, and most social security contributions are not considered taxes. For economies following the IMF's Government Finance Statistics 1986 framework, tax revenue are compulsory transfers to the central government for public purposes, which includes social security contributions.
Government Revenue	Government revenue is an increase in net worth resulting from a transaction. Revenue transactions have counterpart entries either in an increase in assets or in a decrease in liabilities - thereby increasing net worth. General government units have four types of revenue: (i) compulsory levies in the form of taxes and certain types of social contributions; (ii) property income derived from the ownership of assets; (iii) sales of goods and services; and (iv) other transfers receivable from other units. For economies following the IMF's Government Finance Statistics 1986 framework, the total revenue (including grants) consists of current and capital revenues. Current revenue is the revenue accruing from taxes as well as all current nontax revenues, except transfers received from foreign governments and international institutions. Capital revenue constitutes the proceeds from the sale of nonfinancial capital assets.

(continued on next page)

Indicator	Definition
Government Expenditure	Government expenditure is the sum of expense and the net investment in nonfinancial assets. Expense is a decrease in net worth resulting from a transaction. The major types of expense are compensation of employees, use of goods and services subsidies, grants, social benefits, and other expense. The acquisition of a nonfinancial asset by purchase or barter is not an expense because it has no effect on net worth. Similarly, amounts payable on loans extended and repayments on loans incurred are not classified as expense. Nonfinancial assets are economic assets other than financial assets. Nonfinancial assets are stores of value and provide benefits either through their use in the production of goods and services or in the form of property income and holding gains. These assets are classified as fixed assets, inventories, valuables, and nonproduced assets. For economies following the IMF's Government Finance Statistics 1986 framework, total expenditure (including net lending) consists of current and capital expenditures. Current expenditure comprises purchases of goods and services by the central government, transfers to noncentral government units and to households, subsidies to producers, and interest on public debt. Capital expenditure covers outlays for the acquisition or construction of capital assets and for the purchase of intangible assets, as well as capital transfers to domestic and foreign recipients. Loans and advances for capital purposes are also included.
Government Expenditure on Education	Government expenditure on education includes expenditure on services provided to individual pupils and students and expenditure on services provided on a collective basis. Expenditure on education is allocated to pre-primary and primary education, secondary education, post-secondary nontertiary education, tertiary education, subsidiary services to education, education not definable by level, and research and development (R&D) education. For economies following the IMF's Government Finance Statistics 1986 framework, the indicator refers to government expenditure on education affairs and services.
Government Expenditure on Health	Government expenditure on health includes expenditure on services provided to individual persons and services provided on a collective basis. Expenditure on health is allocated to medical products, appliances, and equipment; outpatient services; hospital services; public health services; R&D health; and health not elsewhere classified. For economies following the IMF's Government Finance Statistics 1986 framework, the indicator refers to government expenditure on health affairs and services.
Government Expenditure on Social Protection	Government expenditure on social protection includes expenditure on services and transfers provided to individual persons and households and expenditure on services provided on a collective basis. Expenditure on social protection is allocated to sickness and disability, old age, survivors, family and children, unemployment, housing, social exclusion not elsewhere classified, and R&D social protection. For economies following the IMF's Government Finance Statistics 1986 framework, the indicator refers to government expenditure on social security and welfare affairs and services.

(continued on next page)

Indicator	Definition
Governance	
Corruption Perceptions Index	Scores and ranks economies and territories based on how corrupt their public sector is perceived to be by experts and business executives. It is a composite index, a combination of surveys and assessments of corruption, collected by a variety of reputable institutions. The CPI draws on 13 data sources from 12 independent institutions specializing in governance and business climate analysis. From 2000 to 2011, scores ranged from 10 (highly clean) to 0 (highly corrupt). From 2012 onward, calculation of the score has used an updated methodology and is now presented on a 100 (very clean) to 0 (highly corrupt) scale. Due to this difference in methodology, scores from years prior to and including 2011 should not be compared with scores from 2012 onward. An economy's rank indicates its position relative to the other economies or territories included in the index. It is important to keep in mind that an economy's rank can change simply because new economies enter the index or others drop out.
Pillar III - Operational Efficiency of Business Entry	The time and cost required to register new domestic and foreign firms in a given economy. The data are collected in number of days for time indicators and in local currency units for cost indicators. Cost is then recorded as a percentage of the economy's gross national income per capita. The scores for Pillar III indicators are calculated using the Normal Cumulative Density Function transformation method on a scale of 0 to 100, where 0 and 100 represent the lowest and highest possible scores, respectively. The higher the score, the better performance.

www.ingramcontent.com/pod-product-compliance
Lightning Source LLC
Chambersburg PA
CBHW041751220926
51847CB00014B/166
* 9 7 8 9 2 9 2 7 7 4 0 3 5 *